The Ultimate Guide to Fishing Skills, Tactics, and Techniques

The Ultimate Guide
to Fishing Skills,
Tactics, and Techniques

Edited by **Jay Cassell**

Skyhorse Publishing

Skyhorse Publishing books may be purchased in bulk at special discounts
for sales promotion, corporate gifts, fund-raising, or educational purposes.
Special editions can also be created to specifications. For details, contact
the Special Sales Department, Skyhorse Publishing,
307 West 36th Street, 11th Floor, New York, NY 10018 or
info@skyhorsepublishing.com.

Skyhorse® and Skyhorse Publishing® are registered trademarks of
Skyhorse Publishing, Inc.®, a Delaware corporation.

www.skyhorsepublishing.com

10 9 8 7 6 5 4 3 2 1

Library of Congress Cataloging-in-Publication Data is available on file.
ISBN: 978-1-61608-561-2

Printed in Canada

"I fish because I love to. Because I love the environs where trout are found, which are invariably beautiful, and hate the environs where crowds of people are found, which are invariably ugly. Because of all the television commercials, cocktail parties, and assorted social posturing I thus escape. Because in a world where most men seem to spend their lives doing what they hate, my fishing is at once an endless source of delight and an act of small rebellion. Because trout do not lie or cheat and cannot be bought or bribed, or impressed by power, but respond only to quietude and humility, and endless patience. Because I suspect that men are going this way for the last time and I for one don't want to waste the trip. Because mercifully there are no telephones on trout waters. Because in the woods I can find solitude without loneliness. ... And finally, not because I regard fishing as being so terribly important, but because I suspect that so many of the other concerns of men are equally unimportant and not nearly so much fun."

—Robert Traver

Contents

Introduction

JAY CASSELL

When Tony Lyons, the publisher of Skyhorse Publishing, asked me if I could put together a massive book of fishing tips, I had to pause. I know a fair amount about trout fishing, sure, and probably a thing or two about bass, panfish, and a couple of saltwater species, but I sure am not a walking encyclopedia on all things fishing. But the more I thought about this project, the more I realized that I would have to get other people involved if I wanted to assemble an all-encompassing tactics book that would be of use to fishermen anywhere. My plan? Simple: I would gather as many good fishing books as I could find, contact the various authors for permission to use some of their stuff, and then put together a compendium. There's no way I can speak knowledgeably about largemouths the way Bill Dance and Roland Martin can; nor can I talk the saltwater talk like Capt. Al Ristori or Conway Bowman; nor can I rival Tom Rosenbauer of Orvis on the many aspects of flyfishing for trout.

What you have in your hands is the result of my poring over innumerable books on fishing (not a bad way to spend your time, I have to admit). In these pages you'll see many well-known names in the world of fishing; of more importance, you'll see hundreds and hundreds of proven tips on the fish that you like to catch. They're all here: bass, trout, walleyes, panfish, pike, pickerel, muskellunge, salmon, catfish, shad, saltwater species such as stripers, bluefish, tarpon, and tuna . . . and more. There's a section on ice fishing, one on boating safety, one on gear for all types of angling. Cooking? Got that covered. Good stories to read at the end of the day? Got that covered as well.

So wade into these pages, and be prepared to learn some valuable tips on fishing. You'll become a better fisherman in the process, guaranteed!

Jay Cassell
Katonah, New York
October 27, 2011

Part 1
Gamefish

Largemouth and
Smallmouth Bass

A. Introduction

WADE BOURNE

Fish are some of the most interesting creatures on earth! They come in an amazing variety of species and sizes. They live in virtually all waters where their life basics are available to them. Some are predators; they feed on other fish and aquatic creatures. Others are prey species, spending their lives in danger of being gobbled by larger fish that share their waters.

The first step in learning to catch fish is learning about fish: which species are available, where they can be found, and what they eat. The more you know about your target species' life habits, the more likely you are to catch them. Many expert anglers learn even the smallest details about the daily patterns of the fish they're after. This helps them locate the fish and select just the right bait and technique to make them bite.

Following is a brief look at the freshwater fish species that are most popular with North American anglers. As your fishing skills grow and you become more specialized, you should add to this knowledge until you have a broad understanding of where to find individual species and what to do to catch them under varying conditions.

Black Bass

Many authorities consider black bass to be the most important fish in North America. Actually, this group (genus *Micropterus*) includes three popular species: largemouth bass, smallmouth bass and spotted bass. These fish are closely related genetically, but they differ in the waters they prefer, favorite foods, spawning habits and other life basics.

The largemouth is the most abundant bass, and it grows larger than smallmouth or spotted bass. Largemouth live in natural lakes, reservoirs, rivers, streams and ponds from Mexico to Canada and from the East Coast to the West Coast. These fish normally feed and rest in quiet, relatively shallow water, and they like to hold around such cover as vegetation, rocks, logs, stumps, brush, etc.

Largemouth Bass

Smallmouth Bass

As with many species, largemouth bass grow bigger in southern states where warmer weather provides a longer growing season. In Florida, Georgia, Texas, southern California, Mexico and other southern climes, largemouths over 15 pounds are occasionally boated. On the other hand, in northern states and Canadian provinces, largemouths over 7 pounds are rare. The world-record largemouth bass was caught in south Georgia in 1932. It weighed 22 pounds 4 ounces.

Largemouth bass are predators that eat a wide range of foods. Their primary diet consists of baitfish, crawfish, frogs and insects, but they will also strike baby ducks, mice, snakes and virtually any other living creature that it can swallow.

Smallmouth bass prefer clearer, cooler waters than largemouth. They like a rocky or sandy environment, and they adapt well to medium-strength currents. Because of these preferences, they thrive in streams, lakes and reservoirs of the Northeast, Midwest and southern Canadian provinces. Also, the Great Lakes support huge smallmouth populations. Smallmouth bass occur naturally as far south as north Alabama and Georgia, and they have been successfully stocked into lakes and rivers west of the Rockies. The world-record smallmouth was caught in Tennessee in 1969. It weighed 10 pounds 14 ounces.

Smallmouth bass are also feeding opportunists. Their favorite prey are minnows and crawfish, but they will also eat a wide variety of other foods when available.

Spotted bass (also called "Kentucky bass") are the third common member of the black bass family. For years this fish was confused with both largemouth and smallmouth bass, but it was recognized as a distinct species in 1927.

The spotted bass is something of an intermediate species between the largemouth and smallmouth both in appearance and habits. Its name comes from rows of small, dark spots running from head to tail below a lateral band of dark-green, diamond-shaped blotches. Spotted bass occur naturally from Texas to Georgia and north up the Mississippi, Ohio and Missouri River drainages. These fish have also been stocked in several western states. In fact, the current world-record spotted bass (10 pounds 4 ounces) was caught in California in 2001.

Spotted bass like some current, but not too much. They like deep water, but not as deep as smallmouth prefer. They collect in large schools and chase baitfish in open water. They feed primarily on baitfish, crawfish and insects.

Some lakes contain all three of these black bass species. Largemouth will be back in the quiet coves.

Smallmouth will hold along deep shorelines and main lake reefs; and spotted bass will roam through the open lake in search of prey. Sometimes these three bass species will mix to feed on the same food source. However, more often each species stays in areas where it feels most comfortable.

Spawning habits of black bass species are similar. When water temperature approaches the mid-50° F range, these fish all go on feeding binges to build up energy for the approaching egg-laying, and hatching process. Smallmouth and spotted bass begin nesting when the water temperature approaches 60°. These fish usually establish their nests on main-lake shorelines or flats, frequently next to a stump, rock, log, etc. that offers some shelter. Largemouth prefer 65° water before spawning, and they will fan their nests in wind-protected areas along the sides or back of lake embayments. Largemouth typically nest in shallower water (2–5 feet on average) than smallmouth or spotted bass.

—Wade Bourne

B. Nine Behavioral Reasons Why Black Bass Strike

ROLAND MARTIN

1 Feeding

W e'd fished Florida's Lake Okeechobee hard that November day, and the bass didn't hit well at all. We were trying to do a film segment for my TV fishing show, but the largemouths gave us very little cooperation. We'd thrown Johnson Spoons and plastic worms to the edges of the grass as well as back in the thick vegetation, and turned half a dozen fish. I was fishing

Feeding bass will strike just about anything.

with John Petre, who was my cameraman back then. His duties were to film, and if the fish were hitting and the sun was out bright, he didn't have time to fish.

John really enjoyed fishing, and he didn't say much about not getting to cast, but when the sun finally started dipping down below the horizon, he let out a little warwhoop and said it was his turn to fish. He was a light-tackle enthusiast, and he picked up his favorite little spinning rod and started throwing a small Rapala to the edge of the grass. What he was trying seemed a little ridiculous to me, because I thought his tackle was too light for Florida bass.

We came up to a main lake point leading back into a cove, and John flipped out and let the Rapala lie there for several seconds. A slight sucking sound was audible, and he set the hook and a bass bored down and headed out deep, With his light tackle, I took it for granted that he'd hooked nothing more than a 2-pounder. Suddenly a 5-pounder blew out of the water. He battled it and finally landed it. That was the biggest one we'd caught all day.

Five or six casts later he repeated this episode and got another one about the same size. That one also hit at the edge of the grass. We continued back in the cove, and I was still throwing Johnson Spoons and worms to the thick grass. John spotted a patch of submerged milfoil, and he threw in there and on three consecutive casts he got sucking strikes. He hooked and landed the bass, all of which were in the 2-to-6-pound range. He had five bass and I hadn't had a strike since he'd started fishing, and he'd got ten, all of 'em in less than ten minutes.

He was using a No. 11 gold Rapala on 8-pound line and a spinning rod. I happened to have an identical rig in my rod-storage locker, so I got it out and tied it on. We stayed in the back of that cove and for the next forty-five minutes we really slaughtered the bass. Richard Stunkard was in my backup boat. This was his first filming trip with us, and we were using him as a bird dog. He was the world's worst, most horrible fisherman, and he'd never caught any bass. All week long he was using a rod and reel I'd lent him, and I'd send him over to different points and tell him to cast a worm or a Johnson Spoon around, and if he got any sort of a strike he was to come back and report it. If he got one strike, it meant we could go to that spot and get probably thirty. Richard is a cousin to Jim Stunkard, my executive producer.

Anyhow, Richard put on a Rapala just before I did, and quickly he caught three bass. When I tried a Rapala I too started catching bass. I was getting them on an average of every other cast. I got to noticing there wasn't any wind that night, and Okeechobee was mirror-calm. This was very unusual, because the lake is forty miles wide.

We ended up catching twenty-five bass from 2 to 8 pounds. John caught the eight-pounder, and I ended up catching one about 6½. I know bass sometimes go on heavy feeds during the evening, but this was twenty-five bass in an hour. We had another fifteen strikes we didn't get. What we'd experienced was a feeding frenzy

Most fishermen think that most bass strike because they're hungry. Actually I find that hunger accounts for maybe no more than a third of my strikes—but that third is a very important part of the bass I catch. Maybe 35 percent of the time early in the morning or late in the evening the bass are on the feed.

In major slow periods the bass will feed for a short period of time. Another condition that causes bass to feed quite often is a weather change, such as a barometric drop or an approaching storm or possibly some cloud cover which has moved in—all of which affect atmospheric pressure and temperature. Another thing that could influence bass to feed would be a warming trend after a cold front.

There are several reasons bass feed. Feeding bass are the easiest to catch. You can catch them on almost

A productive way to work the shallow feeding flats is quietly wading and using spinning tackle and a Rapala. Wading provides a low silhouette that is less likely to spook fish in shallow water.

any lure in your tackle box, because basically all lures at one time or other will catch feeding fish.

My favorite, most basic pattern for catching feeding fish would be a dawn-and-dusk surface-plug pattern. I call this pattern—remember, I'm using the word "pattern" to mean the sum total of all the variables in the fishing situation—my topwater treat. It involves getting out before the sun rises or in the twilight hours of the morning or after the sun is setting in the evening and that magical hour begins, because there's no direct sun on the water

It's the time of day when generally the convection currents are low and there is very little sun to move the air around, producing almost a slick or mirror-calm surface. Another condition that is very important to this type of surface action is water temperature. You need warm water, in the 70-degree zone: 70 and up for your best surface-bait fishing.

The best depth would be the shallow depths less than 5 feet. The best cover would be any kind of an ambush point in the form of a stump or a rock or any type of a grass point. The best structure is a point—basically a main-lake point.

2 Reflex Action

Reflex action is the second most important reason fish strike, particularly why bass strike, and it accounts for 20 to 25 percent of the bass I catch in a year's time. A bass's reflex action is like the behavior of any predator—like a cat pouncing on a mouse.

A lurking bass is seeking two things. He's seeking shade for his non-eyelidded eyes. He can't stand direct sunlight, at least not for very long, so he's going to try to shade his eyes in the shadow of a boulder or a bush or a boat dock. Second, and probably more important, is that, being a predator, he is seeking concealment to hide or camouflage his body from the wary eyes of small baitfish of some description. So the bass is in the shadows of an object, in this case an ambush point.

Reflex action brought a strike from this 7-pounder, lurking in the shade of an old dock piling.

To get a reflex strike you need one of two types of lures; either a crank bait or a spinnerbait. They are fast-moving lures which come whipping through there. The concept of reflex-action fishing is to try to throw the lure right on the fish instead of just throwing past the bush, past the stump, or past the ambush point and quickly cranking the spinnerbait or crank bait right down to where you think he is. I think about which way the sun's shining so I can fish on the shady side. I think about which way the wind is blowing, because the wind will automatically position the fish on these shallow cover areas. If the wind is blowing from the north, the fish will be facing the wind because of the current it creates. They can't swim backward, and they face the current. I conjure up a mental image of exactly where that bass is positioned. Then I theoretically try

A fast moving spinnerbait or a crank bait is the best lure to coax a reflex strike.

to snag the fish—I'm trying to get right to his eyes. And really the lure is coming right at the fish, right at his eyes, and at the last second he can do one of two things. He can either move out of the way or he can strike it in self-defense, and quite often, since bass are fairly bold and pugnacious, they will strike at that lure simply out of reflex action. Taking advantage of the reflex action requires a very experienced fisherman with an eye or feel for the right kind of spot, and a little bit of analytical thought concerning the sun and which way the wind is blowing.

Another condition which is better for reflex-action fishing is a cool water temperature, because that means the lure can get just a little bit closer to the bass before he knows it's there. This is kind of an advantage. Water between 45 and 65 degrees is probably best for the spinnerbait and crank bait, because the fish does not detect the presence of the lure until it is pretty much right on top of him. Then he can see it and strike it.

When the water is muddy, it is the hotter water temperatures that are better for reflex-action strikes. When the water is below 50 degrees and muddy, you hardly ever get strikes on these kinds of lures. If the water temperature is from 60 to 90, and the water is real muddy, you'll get a lot of good reflex strikes. Here the fish doesn't see the lure well, but his lateral sensitivity is such that he detects its presence at the last second and he strikes it.

The pattern most representative of reflex-action strikes is bumping the stump with a crank bait. This is simply a great pattern because that's just a natural feeding spot. The best cover might be a stump on an exposed point, where the wave action has eroded under the roots so that there are some areas beneath that stump which the fish can use as his lair.

The best depth probably is less than 6 feet, because, remember, you need to make visual contact with these ambush points. You need to be able to identify where they are, and the best way is to spot them with Polaroid sunglasses. So look for stumps in about two to six feet of water.

3 Anger

The third most important reason bass strike is out of anger. Quite often the first cast you make to a spot produces a reflex strike or a hunger strike. But if you just keep throwing into the same spot and the fish isn't hungry, or the fish wasn't quite close enough to the lure, maybe after six, eight, or even ten casts he just gets thoroughly upset at that lure swimming through there. Any lure can invoke an anger strike if it is fished persistently enough.

There is a story I like to tell about when I really got onto the concept of anger fishing and started using it as a regular way to catch fish. This was in 1967 at Santee-Cooper Reservoir. I had just fished the evening before along this one grass point and had caught a couple of pretty good bass there, so early the next morning I told my guide party, a Mr. Smith, that

This 10-pound, 2-ounce largemouth is a prime example of what can happen when you aggravate a bass into striking out of anger. It took 20 casts to anger this Santee-Cooper bass into striking back.

I'd been catching a lot of fish on a Johnson Spoon by sweeping it across these grass points, particularly early in the morning.

So on the very first cast Mr. Smith made on this point in the grass, a tremendous bass makes a big wave and sucks up that spoon. He halfway sets the hook and the fish wiggles and right away is gone. The fish really didn't get a chance to feel the hook, so I said, "Throw back! Mr. Smith, he might hit again!"

Well, Mr. Smith threw back about three or four times, and I'm holding the boat with the trolling motor trying to keep him in good casting range. After six or seven casts he said, "Boy! That's the biggest fish I've ever had strike in my life. I bet that fish went 8 to 10 pounds."

I told him not to give up and that he might be able to catch him yet. He said, "No, after six or eight casts, he's not hitting now."

I suggested we anchor, and said I'd bet we could catch that fish if we just kept at it. He suggested we both cast. So I picked up my spoon. We had heavy 20-pound line and heavy casting rods. We made alternate casts to the grasspoint.

Finally, after about thirty casts, Mr. Smith began looking down the lake and he said, "What about those other grass points down there?" I said we'd go hit 'em— they were good spots and I was confident we could catch a fish or two off them—but I knew that there was a monster right here. He reminded me we'd made forty casts, and he said the big one was not going to hit. So he actually started throwing the other way. He acted kind of disgusted waiting for me to get tired of fishing this part of the lake, because he wanted to go try to get another one.

When I started fishing, I started counting. On the seventy-sixth cast, a 9-pound, 6-ounce largemouth bass launched himself through the canopy of the thick grass and skyrocketed right through my Johnson Spoon, actually clearing the water.

I've had bass hit on repeated casts, but undoubtedly this one hit with the most vengeance, the most anger, and the most power that I've ever seen. This was undoubtedly the angriest fish in the whole lake.

Since then on many occasions when I've located a bass I've made repeated casts. Quite often I will pull up to a spot which looks good and has all the depth, all the cover, and all the structure that is perfect for fish, and I'll tell my partner I know there's got to be bass here. Quite often I'll bet five dollars on it.

And sometimes the guy will say he'd bet a dollar against it. In a normal situation when I'm real positive, I'll just stop and anchor and cast from ten to fifteen times. Maybe on the first cast he'll hit, but after ten to fifteen casts in the same spot, I'll make him mad.

Probably the best lure for this is a crank bait or a buzz bait, which enables you to make a lot of casts. It's not the lure that's important, but recognizing a situation that demands repeated casts.

4 Protective Instinct

Protective instinct involves the spawning season. Largemouth bass spawn when the water temperature reaches 62 degrees, and smallmouth bass spawn when it reaches 59 degrees. No matter where you live, this is true. Generally the majority of bass spawn at or near a full moon. So in the southern United States—say in Florida, Alabama, and Georgia—quite often that first full moon in February or even late January might be a good spawning moon. In North Carolina and Virginia quite often they will spawn on the full moon in March and April. Up in Pennsylvania and Ohio, they spawn in May, and in the southern part of Canada and in the northern part of the U.S., they spawn as late as June. Theoretically, if you travel the country as I do, you have a six-month spawning season.

Another characteristic of spawning fish is that they never all spawn at the same time. Maybe 60 percent of the bass will spawn on the first good moon. On Santee-Cooper I learned my ABC's of bass fishing during seven years as guide, and every spring I would utilize my spawning patterns. Santee is a 171,000-acre reservoir,and you hit a lot of different water temperatures around the lake. In the warmer parts they spawn earlier than they do in the colder areas of Santee.

Bass often spawn for a six-week period on a large reservoir.

The best pattern and the best way to catch a spawning bass involves crawling a plastic worm through the spawning bed. People who catch spawning bass often are unaware that the fish are spawning. They're throwing plastic worms by bushes and little stick-ups and in the backs of the coves. They're not watching, and they don't have Polaroid glasses. They're not looking to see if there's a spawning bed there. They just feel a strike, set the hook, and catch a bass.

I look for the north or northwest coves, and there's a reason for this. On most lakes in the northern hemisphere, the cold winds come from the north. When the cold fronts come down from the north, they push cold water to the south side of the lake, so they are often 10 degrees colder in the spring than the north shores. Also, when a warm front hits, it blows generally from the south, and these are warm winds. Again, the warm winds push the water, so when they push

from the south, warm water is piled up against the north bank.

There's another reason I like to look for north banks. That is because of the southern sun exposure. The sun is still in the southern quadrant, and there's less shade created on the northern bank. The southern banks have the tall pine trees and a lot of shade. Bass seek sunny places for spawning areas. Bass also seek a hard bottom—they'll spawn on a mud bottom, too, but when they can find it, they will look for a sand bar. So quite often the pattern you are looking for involves finding a firm bottom on a north bank.

When they spawn they have a protective instinct. They hit not because of hunger or anger but merely because they're trying to guard the bed. They try to kill the intruder.

The male is the more aggressive fish. He builds the nest and goes out and rounds up the female. She is on the bed usually for only seventy-two hours, and then stays around for another two or three days. So she's

This 11-pounder bass was taken off of a spawning bed on Lake Okeechobee in 1987. But, realizing the importance of releasing such big spawners, it was quickly releasing unharmed.

there only for four or five days. The male guards the nest for an additional two to three weeks. He is there nearly a month. You're going to catch a lot more bass at spawning time, since the female is there a much shorter period.

When a male bass is caught, the biggest mistake many bass fishermen make is to move off the area and try somewhere else. Sure enough, they catch another male bass, but they don't catch any female bass—the trophies—because they're not fishing for them. They're just fishing for the males that hit first. To catch the females, you have to stop and make repeated casts to the spot. Possibly you're making them mad or angry. So maybe the big female doesn't hit the first couple of casts. Maybe she gets mad as well as having the protective instinct.

While the fish are spawning they are also hungry in the early-morning hours, so your best time to catch a spawner would be at dawn with your very first cast, which might cause a reflex strike or provoke a protective instinct. If that doesn't work, make a lot of repeated casts and provoke the anger.

5 Curiosity

A minor reason bass strike is out of curiosity. This amounts to only about 2 percent of the time, but it's still worth considering. Occasionally you see fish cruising around in clear water, such as in a gravel pit or a small pond. I've caught these fish because they were curious. They're not hungry. It's the middle of the day and they're out sunning themselves or just cruising around.

One of the best ways to catch them is by twitching a small surface plug. I take a small topwater bait and sneak up on them where the fish can't see me. I don't cast right on the top of the fish because that might scare them. I throw within 8 to 10 feet of them so I know they'll see the lure floating there. When the bait splats down, instantly you'll see the fins raise on the fish, and next you see him turn and look at the plug. Most of the time the fish is not going to do anything.

When he starts to turn away, I barely twitch that lure, and the little bit of movement gets him interested

The largemouth is just crusing, not actively feeding—but don't ignore it; maybe you can make it curious.

I spotted this bass crusing in clear water behind the reeds in Lake Okeechobee and coaxed it into hitting a small Rapala.

again. Invariably he moves in just a little bit closer. He'll look at it and maybe half-circle it.

The plug lies there for ten to fifteen seconds, and again the fish turns to move away slightly. Then I twitch it again, and the bass circles right up beneath it. Again the plug is still, and he starts to sink or turn. I twitch it once more, and he'll suck it in.

Many of these kinds of strikes are merely gentle sucking strikes with no more ripple than a popping bug makes when it's taken by a bluegill. A plastic worm fished on the bottom can produce the same type of strike: it's the same concept.

6 Competition

When you're structure fishing in deep water, you're fishing for bass schooled up in numbers. When they're schooled up like this and one fish hits, other bass hit out of competition. When this creates a frenzy, quite often you'll catch a limit in one spot. This is a condition which exists mostly in deep water structure on the creek channels and dropoffs. Occasionally the competition is so severe and so fierce you'll see the fish breaking and surfacing as a school.

A lot of anglers have caught "doubles"—two at once—on a lure. Most of them think two bass just zoomed in and tried to get the lure, but that very seldom is the case. Those fish really got caught out of competition. What almost always happens is you throw out, and one of the fish is a little more eager and grabs the bait first. Fish are so competitive that they try to pull the lure out of the other fish's mouth. Often bass actually tear a plastic worm like two dogs pulling on a towel or rug.

Often with a large topwater plug 4 to 6 inches long, enough of the lure is hanging out of the fish's mouth that the second fish tries to grab it and gets caught. I've caught a tremendous number of doubles because I do a lot of structure fishing on points where there are concentrations of fish. I'll throw most any type

of lure and when I get a strike and hook the fish, many, many times on these structural places I'll see other fish following the one I have on.

You have to capitalize quickly on this pattern, because they're only going to stay in a frenzy a very short time. You need to have a second rod rigged up and just drop the rod and reel and fish that you've caught and then pick up a heavy, compact lure such as a spoon, Little George, or a grub and throw it. I also like a crank bait in this situation. In a tournament I've had many rods rigged up at the same time.

In 1970 I was at Toledo Bend in my very first bass tournament, and I was fishing with Joe Palermo on the first day. He said he knew I fished a lot of spoons, but why did I have five rods and five spoons? And I answered that in case we got into a big school, I wanted to be able to catch a lot of them real quick. He said he had a spoon on and could catch them real quick, too. We pulled up to the first point and we caught one apiece. There wasn't much to it, because there wasn't a big school there. At the second or third point we each caught a single. About nine o'clock we pulled up on the edge of a river bend and threw into about 20 feet of water right over the channel. Joe threw in first, and right away one thumped his spoon. As he was pulling the fish up to the boat, I saw a couple more bass following it. I made a cast and one hit me, and as I got mine up to the boat, a couple of bass were following it, and I told him we were into a school.

I dropped my spoon and bass in the bottom of the boat and picked up my second rod and threw it and caught a fish. Without taking time to unhook the bass, I picked up my third rod and threw it and caught another one. I repeated this with the fourth and fifth rods, and I finally looked around and saw I had five rods and five fish thumping around in the boat. One of the spoons had come out of a bass, and I picked it up and caught a sixth one.

Joe was still there with his first bass and a pair of pliers, because that fish had sucked in his spoon pretty

A school of largemouths breaking the surface over a creek channel on Lake Bixoma, Okla.

good. It was halfway down his throat, and he was trying to pull the hook out.

Here I had six bass and he had one. To make a long story short, I didn't win that tournament, but I came in second, and I sure had beaten my partners. One reason was I had multiple lures rigged up and ready. I was in a school situation, and when I caught one fish, I would get another one. We always found at least one school a day, and I'd catch a limit or close to a limit out of it. This is competitive fishing for competitive fish.

7 Territorial Instinct

Occasionally I catch a bass that strikes out of territorial instinct, and this is a trophy-fish situation. Bass guard their territory just the way a big bear in the woods does; when other bears come around, he chases them off.

I kept an 11-pounder for a time at Santee-Cooper in a big tank. When any bass came his way, the 11-pounder would dart out and chase the other fish away. We'd sneak up to the tank and have a little popping bug on the line or a little minnow on a hook, and we'd throw in the tank and catch those bass. That 11-pounder I caught about fifteen times. But the other fish would hit the bug a lot quicker: the 3-and 4-pounders would eat it up right away. The 11-pounder was smart. He'd seen a lot more lures in his lifetime. It's kind of the same way on a lake.

What does the territorial area look like?

As I stress in this book, the most important thing in bass fishing is to establish a pattern. That is, locate the depth, cover, and structure and couple it up with whatever water temperatures are productive and the water currents and wind conditions present. Then you know what to look for, and you've got plenty of places to try.

Suppose you establish a pattern, such as a point with big stickups, and you've hit the last three points with big stickups and have caught some fish on every one of them, and you come to the fourth point with big stickups and it looks even better. It has bigger stickups than the rest of them, and there's deep water close by. The wind is just right, and there's some bait there. Everything looks absolutely perfect on that spot. And yet you don't catch fish there.

I've hit places such as that fourth point, and I used to leave and run on down the lake. Then I got to thinking maybe the reason I didn't catch one was that there was a smart old trophy bass lying on that point where he had everything he needed. He'd seen bass boats and he knew all about lures, and I'd probably made too much noise. The fact is there should have been some fish there, but maybe since I didn't catch one, there were no *small* bass present.

Then I'll go back and try for that big trophy fish. Often I will start with a different lure, such as a large plastic worm instead of the 6-inch worm which catches

A lone cypress tree is a likely place to hook a really big one—but there won't be any smaller ones around, as the big one owns that tree.

This 8-inch bass was just trying to kill that 6-inch lure, since he could never have swallowed it.

most of your bass I throw a 9-inch worm rigged up on heavy line with a big hook and put it right against the biggest stickup on the point and twitch it ever so slowly in that spot in hopes that the big trophy bass will be there.

8 Killer Instinct

This instinct has put a lot of fish in the boat for me. It also creates a lot of enjoyment. Always interesting to me is the fact that you can have a giant lure like a Musky Jitterbug or a huge propeller plug and consistently it will be the little tiny bass no longer than the plug itself that actually try to kill the big lure. That's killer instinct. The bass has a mouth not much bigger than the plug. He can't possibly be trying to eat it: all he can be doing is trying to kill it. Quite often you throw a large plug out and small bluegills will hit it.

Something else that intrigues me is that when I'm fishing a surface plug at a distance, some of the bigger

fish will suck the plug in and look like a bluegill hitting it. I don't know how many times I've been in an area working a surface plug really slow while hoping a big fish might be tricked any second, and out of killer instinct a little bluegill pops that plug. Since it might be a bass, occasionally I'll pull back so hard I've fallen down with a pair of waders on or tripped backward over a stump while anticipating a 10-pounder.

9 Ignorance

When I think of ignorant fish, I think of the bass in some of the Canadian lakes I've fished. One time I flew in a float plane to this little body of water a few hundred acres in size. The pilot cut the engine and started drifting back over where he had first touched down. I asked where we would fish, and he said to just throw out there anywhere. And he said any lure in my tackle box was just perfect. I sat there on the right float of that airplane and in the first ten casts I had ten fish on. On my second cast over to a little boulder, there was this funny sucking strike. It sounded like a toilet flushing, and it was a 2-to-3-pound smallmouth inhaling my plug.

Those bass were eager, and they really were ignorant fish. They never had seen a man or a lure before. Over the past ten years I have occasionally found small farm ponds which were unfished and had many of these eager, stupid fish. Places in Mexico are almost the same too.

In Mexico I had the same bass strike six times in a row. I actually caught him three times. I was doing a film with Dino Economos and my wife, Mary Ann, and we were in the courtyard of Padilla City, which is now covered by Lake Guerrero. I had asked Dino to film me fishing a plastic worm, and on my first cast a 2-pounder swam over and grabbed the worm, and Dino got it on film. I released the bass, and we could see him swim right back over to a little corner. It wasn't spawning season; the fish definitely wasn't spawning. I didn't think he would hit again, so Dino didn't film it, but I threw back a second time and the same bass grabbed the worm and I caught him again.

Dino said he didn't believe it. We were over a concrete patio and the water was only 2½ feet deep, and that was the only bass in sight. We could see the entire bottom. I released the bass again, and he went right back to the same corner. I asked Dino to film it in case he struck a third time. Sure enough, I caught that bass a third time and released him again.

Three more times that same bass struck the worm, but I didn't set the hook. I was afraid I'd kill him if I kept hooking him. I just threw back and he grabbed the worm and shook it, and I kept pulling and finally was able to case it away from him. Each time he followed the lure all the way to the boat.

That fish would have to be classified as either mentally disturbed or else the dumbest, most ignorant,

stupid fish that ever lived. I'm not saying this is not good; in fact, I would like to see a lot more of those fish, because that's my kind of fish! The problem is that in heavily fished waters, we've caught out those stupid fish. They're the first ones to hit a lure.

In hard-fished lakes, the ones that hit best are the ones that get caught, and the ones we keep are the big ones. What ends up in those lakes are small, smart fish, and a lot of them.

Dr. George Bennett, a leading biologist of the Illinois Natural History Survey, wrote a book on pond management back in the 1950s. He's recognized as one of the leading ichthyologists in the country on pond management. Bennett conducted a survey years ago on a lake which was initially stocked with 500 bass. They opened it to fishing three or four years after it was stocked. It was controlled experimental fishing: everybody who caught a fish had to fill out a report which was monitored. All who went in or out had to check with a warden, and a complete tally of how many fish had been caught was carefully made.

At the end of three years of experimenting, they decided to drain the lake to see how many fish were left. The first year they had caught several hundred fish. About half as many were caught the second year, and the third year only forty or so were caught. But when they drained the lake, they found approximately 1,400 bass! No more bass had been added to the lake, and five or six years had passed since they had initially stocked it. Many bass had reproduced, and many of them were small.

Lots of fish biologists have concluded that the initial few hundred bass which were caught were the dummies. The ones that were left to reproduce passed on to their offspring the genetic capabilities they possessed—in this case, wariness, stealth, and caution. The 1,400 which were left in the lake were basically cautious, wary fish.

Probably some fishermen will question whether ignorance is truly a behavioral reason why a bass may strike. After all, if the smartest bass in the water may

This one is not is as ignorant as he was a moment ago. I release about 98 percent of the fish I catch.

strike for any of the eight other behavioral reasons I've already listed, isn't it obvious that an ignorant bass will strike for those same reasons? Sure, but the point is that a dumb one doesn't hesitate, even under conditions that make a cautious bass refuse your bait. Where the fishing pressure is heavy, of course, the ignorant ones don't last long, and a lake that's supposed to be "fished out" may hold plenty of cautious bass but very few dummies. But this doesn't mean our waters can't be overfished. On the contrary, that happens all too often.

I want to see bass fishing around for my son, Scott, to enjoy when he gets to be twenty-four years old, and that's another twenty years from now. But the way it's going—a daily limit of fifteen bass in some states, and hundreds of thousands of bass anglers in virtually every state—I wonder what the future of the sport will be. We have created more water by building 10 million acres of line reservoirs in the past thirty years, and this has created more habitat for bass. However, in building 10 million acres of water, we have created an additional 10 million fishermen we didn't have thirty years ago. So we are overfishing our lakes.

Basically we have a good standard of living, and we don't have to live off nature. Our 10 million acres of water can't support all the fishermen if they want to eat all their bass. Lets have a comprehensive catch-and-release program. We don't need to kill these fish, particularly those eager ignorant ones and those bigger ones we all prize as trophies. I would like to see quality fishing reinstated in the average reservoir and lake in the U.S. The only way it's going to be done is to persuade the sportsmen—collectively and in clubs—to release their trophy fish.

It's hard to understand why more bass aren't released instead of killed. Maybe there's nothing wrong with a bass dinner once in a while, but I've eaten a lot of fish that taste better. Probably the most tasty fish I've eaten is a walleye. Another tasty fish is snook. I've tasted probably seventy-five species of fish, because I've lived in Brazil and have traveled in Europe and Africa, and most of these fish are tastier than bass.

Our waters contain plenty of other sources of protein which aren't being harvested. Ninety percent of the fishermen are harvesting the bass to eat, and 99 percent of the fish population is left unmolested. The latter could be utilized as a form of protein as well as delicious food. We just don't have an excuse to keep many bass.

C. Basic Bassing

MONTE BURCH

Basic Casting Techniques

Like many other activities, casting is fairly easy to learn, it just takes practice. Denny Brauer, one of the top pro anglers in the country, learned his famous pitching and flipping tactic during the winter months several years ago.

"I placed a coffee cup under some houseplants overhanging a table near the television set," he recalled impishly. "I'd stand in front of the couch, watch television and flip a lure at the cup. By the end of the winter I hit the coffee cup every time, but my wife's houseplants were goners!"

Each type of equipment requires somewhat different tactics. In addition to the standard overhead casting techniques there are some more unusual methods that can be used to reach into those hard-to-get-to spots, or to use other muscles during long days.

When first learning to cast, use a casting weight, or old plug or lure without hooks. Find a place without overhead lines or obstacles and plenty of casting distance behind and in front of you. Make sure your line is wound on the reel properly, and let out enough line so the casting weight dangles about four inches below the rod tip.

Spincasting, Over-Rod Style

1. Hold the rod tip at about 2:00, pointing at the target.

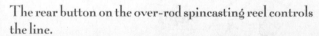

The rear button on the over-rod spincasting reel controls the line.

2. Press the button on the back of the reel spool and hold.
3. Bring the rod straight up and back over your shoulder to about 10:00.
4. Then with a smooth motion move the rod forward with a quick snap, releasing the button at about 2:00.
5. You can stop the line by pressing again on the button, however, in this case the line and lure are not feathered but stopped abruptly and lure entry is usually fairly loud. Quite often the lure will also hit the end of the line so abruptly it will be jerked backward causing you to miss the target. It's best to cast directly to the target without stopping the line and lure.
6. Turning the reel handle forward re-engages the spool and begins the retrieve.

The most common problem is letting the line go too soon. In this case the lure will shoot upward, just behind or close to you and drop straight back down. Or the opposite happens, you don't let the line go soon enough and the lure plops into the water at your feet. This is all solved with a little practice and remembering to release line at about 2:00.

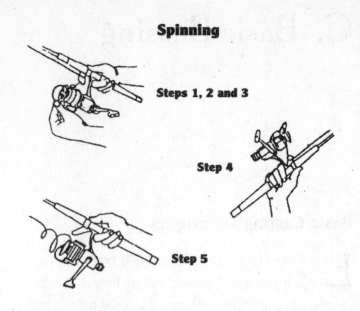

Spinning

Steps 1, 2 and 3

Step 4

Step 5

Spincasting, Under-Rod Style

The same basic casting technique is used with under-rod spinning reels, except they have a finger lever in front that is used to release and stop the line.

1. Depress and hold the line lever, disengaging the line.
2. While holding the line lever up, point the tip of the rod at the target, then swing it back over your head in a straight arc to about 10:00.
3. Still holding the line lever up, swing the rod back forward with a fast snap, releasing the lever at approximately 2:00.
4. To retrieve, turn crank handle forward.

Spinning

1. Turn the reel handle until the line roller on the bail is at top center position, just below the rod and with the lure hanging just a few inches below the rod tip.
2. Grasp the line with the first joint of your first finger and pinch the line up against the rod handle.
3. Then use your other hand to pull the bail open until it locks in position. You're now ready to make your cast.

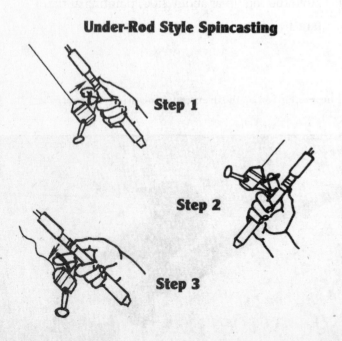

Under-Rod Style Spincasting

Step 1

Step 2

Step 3

4. Still holding the line in position, raise the rod to approximately 10:00.

5. Bring the rod forward and with a fast snapping action release the line from your finger at approximately 2:00.

6. Tapping or holding your finger lightly against the spool feathers the line or slows it down, providing a great deal of control. Some models also have a lever that can be used to open the bail as well as hold the line during the cast.

7. Turning the handle forward automatically closes the bail and begins the retrieve.

Baitcasting

For your first few casts start with the magnetic braking knob set at maximum anti-backlash control. After you've become proficient at this setting you can lower the magnetic setting and achieve longer casts.

1. Press the freespool button down, or push the thumb bar down, holding the spool in place with your thumb at the same time.

2. Most people hold a baitcasting reel incorrectly when they make a cast, holding it in an upright

The baitcasting cast begins with the reel handles pointing up.

At the end of your cast, the reel handles should be pointing down.

position. Turn the rod sideways so the reel's handle faces upward. The reel should stay this way throughout your cast.

3. Point the rod tip above the target.

4. Bring the rod backward over your shoulder to about 10:00, then swing it smoothly forward to about 2:00. The forward motion should be a quick accelerated forward motion with a snap of the wrist and forearm. Begin releasing thumb pressure about halfway through your forward casting motion to let line out. To prevent backlashes in the line, you must apply just enough pressure on the spool with your thumb as the lure flies through the air so that the rotating speed of the spool never exceeds the speed of the line coming off of it. The ability to apply the

Use your forefinger to feather the line and slow down the lure as needed for precise line control and a soft entry of the lure.

Casting motion should be straight back then straight forward.

right amount of thumb pressure is primarily a matter of practice, but you can also reduce backlashes if the reel's braking system is set properly.

Special Casting Tactics

Several special tactics can produce results when normal casting and retrieving just doesn't work. These include flipping, pitching, skipping, side-casting, backhand casting, slingshotting and skittering. Several specific lures are also best used for some of these special tactics.

Flipping

When bass move tight into cover such as standing timber, submerged trees, even under boat docks, flipping is a very popular and productive tactic. Professional anglers like Denny Brauer have made their reputation on their flipping expertise.

Flipping is best done with a rod specifically designed for the purpose. They are typically telescoping, 7-½ to 8 feet, fairly stiff-backed rods that have straight handles. Some rods utilize a combination of graphite and fiberglass to provide both sensitivity and strength. A baitcasting reel is most commonly mated to the rod, and many of these are also designed with a "flipping switch" that keeps the reel engaged except when the thumb bar is held down. This allows for an instant hookset when a big old bass inhales your lure as it drops down through the cover. The heavy cover dictates heavy line, and most pros fish with 25 to 30 pound test. Braided lines have become extremely popular due to their low stretch factor and strength.

Most common flipping lures are ⅜ to ½ ounce jig. Plastic of pork dressings are added to slow the fall of

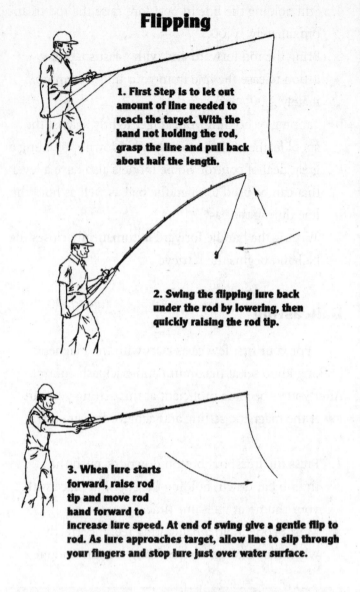

Flipping

1. First Step is to let out amount of line needed to reach the target. With the hand not holding the rod, grasp the line and pull back about half the length.

2. Swing the flipping lure back under the rod by lowering, then quickly raising the rod tip.

3. When lure starts forward, raise rod tip and move rod hand forward to increase lure speed. At end of swing give a gentle flip to rod. As lure approaches target, allow line to slip through your fingers and stop lure just over water surface.

the jig and provide a "taste/smell" sensation as well as enticing movement. At times a plastic crawdad trailer on jigs is also hard to beat.

Pitching

Basically an underhanded type of flip, pitching is a more versatile method and can be used when more distance is required than can be achieved with flipping.

Pitching rod-and-reel combinations are similar to flipping, except they may be somewhat lighter and shorter, usually 6 to 7 foot rod and from 15 to 20 pound test line.

Pitching lures are basically the same as for flipping, except sometimes lighter in weight because the weight of the lure pulls the line from the reel, rather than using a set-line distance as in flipping. ¼ to ⅜ ounce jigs combined with plastic trailers are extremely popular pitching lures. Another good choice is a plastic lizard with a small split shot about four inches above the lizard. Traditional plastic worms, rigged Texas style with the weight pegged in place to prevent hang-ups are also popular.

Over the years Denny Brauer has become so good at both flipping and pitching that he invented a tactic called "loop pitching" that adds even more momentum to the lure and increases the distance a lure can be pitched.

The decision of when to flip and when to pitch depends on water, weather and cover conditions. When fishing vertical cover, such as standing trees and stump beds, flipping is best. When fishing horizontal cover, such as laydowns, or under overhanging limbs, weeds

Loop Pitch

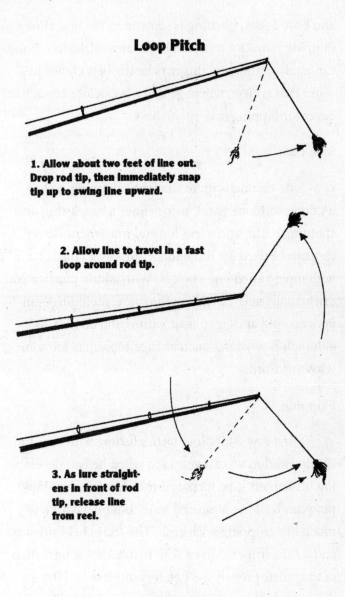

1. Allow about two feet of line out. Drop rod tip, then immediately snap tip up to swing line upward.

2. Allow line to travel in a fast loop around rod tip.

3. As lure straightens in front of rod tip, release line from reel.

Pitching

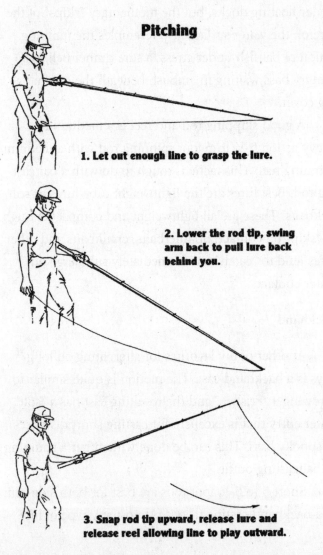

1. Let out enough line to grasp the lure.

2. Lower the rod tip, swing arm back to pull lure back behind you.

3. Snap rod tip upward, release lure and release reel allowing line to play outward.

Side-Cast

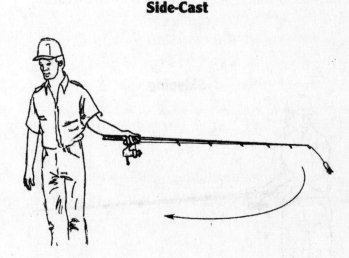

1. Side-cast is made by bringing the rod back sideways. Then swing it forward, stopping almost in front of you and releasing line at the same time.

and boat docks, pitching is sometimes the best choice. Flipping range for most anglers is around 16 feet. You can pitch further and this may be the best choice in water that is clear, where getting a boat close enough to cover for flipping may spook bass.

Side-Cast

Side-casting is quite similar to skipping except it's done with one hand, using either a baitcasting or spinning outfit, and a less forceful movement. This cast can be used for those longer-distance targets, and with more varied lure choices. With a little practice you can actually side-cast almost any lure, including spinnerbaits, pig-and-jig, plastic worms and crankbaits, although heavy lures such as large topwaters are somewhat awkward.

Skipping

I first saw "skipping" tactics fishing with bass pro Guido Hibdon several years ago when he was developing his famous tube lures and tube lure tactics. Skipping can be done in several ways, but my favorite is much like skipping a flat rock. The rod is held sideways and a side-arm cast given with two hands. A final snap of the wrists propels the lure forward low and flat on the water surface. Skipping is not only an excellent

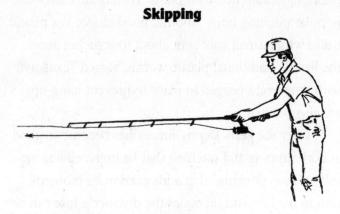

Skipping

2. Both hands are used to snap the rod forward sideways in a short, fast swing.

way to present a lure back under overhanging trees and under floating docks, but the momentary "skips" of the lure on the water surface also resembles the jumping action of baitfish under stress, a sure dinner bell to a hungry bass waiting in ambush beneath the overhanging cover.

A good skipping rod and reel is a medium to heavy action 5-½ to 6 foot spinning rod with a medium spinning reel. This tactic is tough to do with a baitcasting rod. Best lures are the lightweight tube lures or soft jerkbaits. These are all lightweight and compact enough to "skip" on contact. Spinnerbaits, crankbaits and other lures tend to "catch" and immediately submerge on water contact.

Backhand

Another of my favorites for alternating on long days is a backhand cast. The motion is quite similar to throwing a "Frisbee" and the resulting cast has a "soft" water entry that is excellent for casting short distances to spooky bass. This can be done with either a spinning or baitcasting outfit.

Short 5 to 5-½ foot rods are best for both side-arm and backhand casting tactics. Almost any type of lure

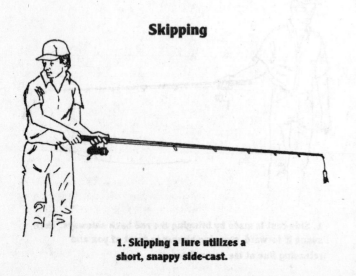

Skipping

1. Skipping a lure utilizes a short, snappy side-cast.

Backhand

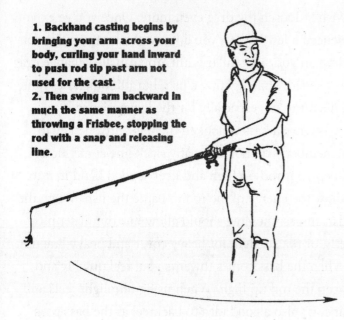

1. Backhand casting begins by bringing your arm across your body, curling your hand inward to push rod tip past arm not used for the cast.
2. Then swing arm backward in much the same manner as throwing a Frisbee, stopping the rod with a snap and releasing line.

can be used from spinnerbaits to crankbaits, jigs, even topwater.

Slingshotting

When you simply can't reach back in under an object, such as a long boathouse, pier, bridge or dock with other tactics, slingshotting can be used. It's a great way to reach a long distance under an obstacle. Spinning tackle is the best choice. I've used the tactic in desperation with a baitcasting outfit, but it's a bit awk-

ward because you have to turn your hand outward so the reel faces out. Almost any type of lure can be used, but compact lures work best because the gravity on the horizontal position of the line drops the lures fairly fast, and long, floppy type of lures, such as long worms or big spinnerbaits, tend to tangle on the cast.

Skittering

Also called "doodling," "doodle-socking," and a wide variety of other local names, this specialized technique is as old as bass fishing is popular. Invented in the cane-pole days, it still consists of a long pole, 12 foot or longer, however, these days it's more often fiberglass than cane. Add a short, 2- to 3-foot length of heavy, 20- to 30-pound line dangling from the end and then fasten a lure to the end of the line. I've quite often used my flipping rod for the tactic. The lure choice is usually a noisy topwater lure with propellers fore and aft. In practice the long rod is used to poke the lure back into places you can't reach with other types of casts. Allow the lure to settle on the water surface then "work in place" using sideways action with the rod tip to move the lure back and forth, yet hold it in the pocket under the cover. This is also an excellent tactic for fishing open pockets in weeds, lily pads and moss beds.

Slingshotting

1. Slingshotting is also sometimes called bow and arrow casting. Release about 3 feet of line, grasp the lure with one hand and pull it back toward your body, pulling the rod in a deep bow.
2. Release the lure and as the rod straightens in front of you, release line with your finger.

Skittering

1. Skittering is done with a long pole or rod and a short piece of heavy fishing line tied to the end. A heavy-duty flipping rod could also be used. A topwater lure is tied to the line and dropped into pockets and worked with the end of the rod.

A similar tactic is "dunking" using a sinking lure such as a Texas-rigged plastic worm or lizard, or even pig-and-jig, dropping it in the open spots in cover, allowing it to drop slowly and jigging it up and down, but still keeping it fairly shallow. You can literally fish in, around and through an almost impenetrable brushpile with this tactic, or reach back behind a dock to an open water spot you can't reach otherwise. When you get a big bass on the end of a 12-foot rod, however, the fun is just beginning.

Playing and Landing Bass

Make it a practice to always check and set your drag before you fish. To do so properly, pull the line from the reel against a small hand scale such as a fish deliar. Adjust the drag tension, according to your reel manufacturer's instructions to one-third to one-half the rated tensile strength of the line. This should be done when you install line on your reel. Once on the water you'll probably need to readjust the drag according to conditions. When flipping and pitching into heavy cover or buzzbaiting heavy weeds and cover using fairly stout line, you will probably want to crank your drag down tight so there is no give of the line in order to

Lipping is a very common way of landing bass. Grasping the point of the lower jaw with the thumb inside the mouth and the fingers outside temporarily paralyzes the fish. Be extremely careful of plugs with numerous sharp hooks.

horse fish out of the cover. If you're fishing light line and finesse lures with spinning gear, however, you may wish to loosen the drag even more. Once you've experienced a few battles, you'll know the best position for drag on your particular outfit. You can also change drag as needed while fighting a fish, but it's sometimes quite difficult to do, especially for the inexperienced.

Once a bass is hooked there is only one key to remember – do not allow any slack line at any time. Keep your rod tip high and keep a good bend in it to allow the energy of the rod to battle the fish. When the fish surges, the drag should allow line out, if properly, or not set tight for heavy cover and heavy line use. When the bass comes towards you, reel quickly and keep the rod tip high. When using ultralight reels and line, it's also a good idea to backreel as the bass goes away from you, then reel forward as it moves toward you. This method works if there is no cover or obstacle for the bass to tangle in. Believe me, a bass can find a tangled hidey hole and wrap your line up tight quicker than you can bat an eyelash. Backcranking takes a bit of practice. You want to allow line out, but above all else follow with the rod and not allow any slack in the line.

Pumping the fish it also a good tactic. Lift the rod to pull the fish toward you, then reel quickly at the same time dropping the rod tip slightly. Repeat reeling between pumps. This technology prevents overusing your reel, cushions line against shock and uses your equipment to the best advantage. Once the bass is at boatside or near the bank, let it fight a little longer to assure there will be no sudden last-minute runs that can break your line.

Bass can be netted or lipped once worn out from the battle. If it's a big bass, or you're positioned too high over the water to reach, netting may be the best tactic. To net, place the net in the water and lower it below the bass, then lead the fish into the net and lift the net once the fish is in place. Too many folks made the mistake of swinging the net at the fish, which immediately causes them to dash away and often results in lost fish.

Bass can also be lipped if you can reach them easily. This takes a bit of practice and you can easily lose a fish, or abrade your fingers if not done correctly. Make sure the bass is played out, then holding the rod top high to keep pressure on the line, grasp the fish at the tip of the jaw with your thumb inside and your fingers outside. Lifting bass in this manner will slightly paralyze them.

If you're releasing the fish, don't touch it in any other place. Carefully remove the lure and gently slide the fish back into the water mouth first. If placing in a livewell for tournament fishing, carefully measure, then release gently into the livewell.

Basic Bassing Knowledge

For many years bass anglers pounded the shores and shallows, quite successfully in fact. Then came Buck Perry and his structure tactics, followed by tournament angling, sonars and other technological gear such as pH monitors, color monitors and temperature

Understanding how bass relate to structure and cover as well as what techniques and lures to use in the various structures and cover is an important factor in consistent bass fishing success.

gauges. Shallow water, pound-the-bank bassing is still successful in small waters and in some instances of larger waters. Consistently successful anglers these days, however, must be more versatile. To compete not only in tournaments but against the numbers of weekend anglers pounding the more popular bassing waters, versatility and adaptability is a must. This often means going "offshore" and looking for bass honey holes away from the crowds. These tactics require the use of electronic gear such as sonars, along with a basic understanding of structure, cover and other factors.

Understanding Structure

Structure is simply a change in elevation of a lake bottom. Structure may be natural such as a submerged ditch, creek or river channel, or consist of points, flats, humps, underwater islands, ledges, boulder fields and rock piles. Structure may be man-made such as the rip-rap lining dam faces and bridge causeways, or the piers supporting bridges, old roadbeds and their ditches, or remains of underwater bridges and structures submerged when lakes are filled.

Bass relate to structure in different ways, depending on season, water temperature, clarity and other factors. Bass migrate between deep water structures

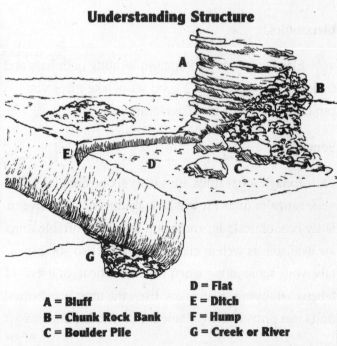

Understanding Structure

A = Bluff
B = Chunk Rock Bank
C = Boulder Pile
D = Flat
E = Ditch
F = Hump
G = Creek or River

and shallow water structures, according to the seasons, water temperature and clarity and water conditions, as well as the subspecies. They use specific migration routes. For instance bass may utilize ditches and underwater creek channels to move from deep water up onto flats. Bass along bluffs migrate more vertically in the water column, but still use definite migration routes. Remember bass like "edge," a term more often equated with hunting deer and birds. Edge consists of a place where one or more different types of structure, often combined with cover, merge together. For instance this might mean a transition zone where a bluff or chunk rock meets a gravel bank. Learning when and how bass use these various structures on your favorite bass lake is important.

Maps

Good topographical or contour maps are an invaluable source of information for a lake. Before putting a boat into a lake, study the map, pick out possible areas according to the time of the season, water and weather conditions. Don't be afraid to mark up your maps and keep a diary with indications of best fishing locations according to your map. You'll be mighty surprised at how effective years of information can be with a map and diary in hand.

Electronics

Electronics are important in locating both bass and structure. Coupled with a good set of lake maps you can easily pinpoint best bass locations.

Sonars

Today's sonar units are a marvel of technology. A wide range of units are available from very expensive to fairly economical, depending on features. Portable units are available as well as clamp-on brackets so you can take your sonar along when you rent a boat, or even when cartopping small lakes. Even the most economical units can provide a great amount of detailed informa-

tion. Choosing the type used, as well as transducer type and location is important for your particular bass fishing situation.

I run a Charger bass boat with three sonars to provide information when and how I need it. These include an in-dash digital, used only while running to constantly monitor water depth, a bow mounted LCD with transducer mounted on the trolling motor bottom for detailed information while fishing from the bow seat and a fairly sophisticated sonar located on the console for detailed "mapping" of structure areas. The latter is also coupled with Lowrance GPS enabling me to not only relocate prime fishing sorts away from the banks without having to refer to landmarks, but also provides for safer navigation in foggy and bad weather. Using these sonar units, I've often spent hours running back and forth over promising areas, locating underwater humps, bends in creek and river channels and many other "hotspots" to add details to my lake map.

Temperature Gauge

Above all else bass relate to temperature. Knowing the temperature in a given area can indicate whether the area will or will not hold bass and, if it does, at what depth or location. Largemouth bass are most active at an ideal temperature of 65 to 75 degrees. This naturally doesn't mean bass will not tolerate water warmer or colder, but will seek this temperature if it is available to them.

A temperature gauge can be one of your most valuable fishing tools in establishing seasonal locations of bass as well as lure choices. Any number of temperature gauges are available. I use two specific gauges on my bass boat, an Eagle in-dash digital temperature gauge that provides instant readings even while running from one location to another and a Combo-C-Lector which utilizes a probe on a reel and can provide water temperature at any depth. I also carry a small hand-held unit called Deptherm in my tacklebox which can be hand held for surface temperature or lowered on a string for depth readings.

Understanding Cover

Bass are also "cover" or object oriented. Unlike other fish that roam open waters chasing their prey, bass prefer to hide and ambush their food. They're skulkers and anything that provides them an opportunity to hide will be utilized including stand timber, submerged timber and brush, overhanging trees, laydowns, log jams, stump beds, weeds, moss, bulrushes, even floating debris and man-made docks. Unfortunately bass anglers often look for cover first. Former pro bass fisherman Jimmy Crisp once gave me a great piece of advice. "Look for structure first, then if it has cover, all the better. Structure with cover can be a deadly combination." A good example of this would be a long main point with underwater brush as opposed to a barren point, or a barren flat as opposed to one with a stump bed.

Once you've located good structure with your sonar, look for cover to pinpoint honey holes. This applies primarily to big waters, lake and reservoirs, but also to smaller lakes and to some degree ponds and rivers.

Tremendous amounts of cover may also exist in some areas and then you have to define the most important cover and this can get a little tricky. I've discovered lakes where bass would prefer one particular species and standing timber over another. Also certain types of cover are better at different seasons or under different water and weather conditions. An example is shallow water grass is a prime spot on rising water conditions, but bass leave these flats quicker than you can believe with the first drop in water levels. Heavy brush and laydowns are best choices on cold-front days.

Aquatic vegetation is also bass cover and different types are best at certain times of the year. The different types also require different lures to be successful. For instance crankbaits are excellent for submerged weeds, especially early in the year before the weedbeds reach the water surface, but you couldn't crank a crankbait through filamentous algae with a truck winch. Floating rat baits are best for those conditions. Laydowns and log jams are best with plastic worms, spinnerbaits and jigs.

Understanding Woody Cover

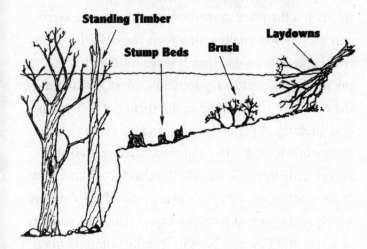

Understanding Aquatic Vegetation

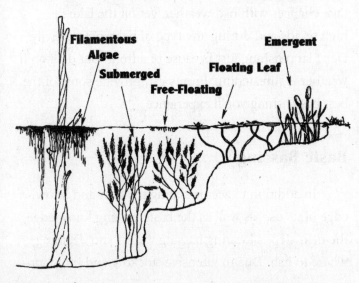

Understanding Weather

We all like to fish during the warm, sunny days of spring, but unfortunately we often have to go bass fishing when we get the opportunity. I've had the opportunity and also misfortune to fish from one end of this country to the other. It seems like a front moves in as soon as I travel to a new spot. I've found, like the pro bass angler, when that happens you have to adjust to the changing conditions.

I've discovered that in addition to the major fronts announced by the weather forecasters, many "minor" fronts also pass through a fishing day. These are announced only by the slight rise and fall of air pressure and temperature. In a day of fishing these fronts produce some stressful bass fishing as well as some frustration.

As a major front moves across the country, a low pressure cell precedes it, barometric and water pressure rise and bass go on a feeding binge. Be on the water from 24 to 36 hours preceding a major front and you can literally load a boat with bass. Not only is the rising pressure a factor in the sudden bass activity, but also the temperature. Usually air temperature rises in the period preceding a front, and during some times of the year, especially in the spring, this warming trend can be extremely productive. Bass will usually move shallow during this period. The best tactic is to cover a lot of water fast with buzzbaits, topwater, spinnerbaits and crankbaits.

Then the storm moves in and with it varying amounts and types of precipitation depending on the time of the year and air temperature. During a warm spring rain is one of my favorite times to fish. My largest bass stringer occurred during such weather. During periods of warm air temperatures creating a warm rain, the inflowing water brings fresh food into the lake or floods new areas for foraging, the wind stirs up the bait fish and the rain brings fresh oxygen into the lake. On lakes with flats and old fields, the single best tactic is to crank spinnerbaits or buzzbaits through the grass and flooded weeds. On steep bank highland lakes, a pig-and-jig bounced down the trickle run-off spots of bluffs will produce.

If on the other hand the air temperature is cold, bass have a tendency to go deeper or suspend and move less during the storm, although they are still more active than they will be when the storm moves on. Prospecting with spinnerbaits and crankbaits is the best bet.

Then the storm front moves through and things really get tough. The pressure as well as temperature drops and so do the bass. This is often the time many of us are on a strange lake for our much valued vacation.

Bass may go to deep water haunts, they may suspend on extremely deep lakes and in shallow lakes they go to "ground" or tuck tight into the thickest cover they can find. Best tactics depend on the type of lake and the time of year. Forget about fast-working exploring lures. You're going to have to dig bass up or out.

Deep water lake fishing requires a good sonar. Look for bass on the points, breaklines of creek channels, or any other deep water migratory structure. Then it's a matter of sitting over them and fishing vertically with a jig, spoon or small grub or worm. Bass in this situation are fairly dormant and don't move around much. They have a tendency to school or group up during this period and when you find one you'll usually find a bunch.

On the other hand, shallow water bass are scattered on a flat prior to the front and during the storm, and move horizontally rather than vertically. Look for them tight into cover. They'll move into the brushpiles, log jams and heavy shoreline cover and about the only way you're going to dig them out is flipping and pitching. A pig-and-jig, jig-and-worm or weedless grub worked in, around and through the tough stuff is your only hope for success. It's slow going and a lot of patience is needed. Work every bit of thick cover as slowly and thoroughly as you can. Again, bass won't be as active and you may have to literally bump them on the head to get a strike.

Fronts can also create dangerous moments. Don't take chances with bad weather, get off the lake in high winds and during any type of lightening activity. Don't stop fishing just because of a front, but do stop if weather is threatening. Fronts can provide some of the best bass fishing you'll experience.

Basic Bassing

In addition to accumulating the gear and knowledge of its use, as well as the basic bassing knowledge, the next step is locating bassing waters and deciding where to fish. Due to intensive stocking and the popu-

Big waters often mean big bass—if you can find them.

larity of black bass, bass fishing waters are available to bass anglers all over the country. Big lakes and reservoirs, small community lakes, strip pits, farm ponds, creeks and rivers can all offer good bass fishing.

Big Water Bassing

You've read about, and drooled over, the fabled bass catches from a famous lake or reservoir and decide this year you're going to spend your vacation traveling to the lake and get in on some of the hot action. In big waters, as opposed to smaller waters, the key to success is finding the fish. The single best tactic when visiting a lake for the first time is to hire a guide for a day or two. It's money well spent and will give you a basis for fishing the lake. Otherwise you may fish for a week before you discover the bass locations, patterns, best lure choices, etc.

If you're set on doing it yourself, first eliminate unproductive water and narrow down your fishing area. Otherwise, you'll spend your entire vacation aimlessly prowling the lake hoping to luck into a bass. The simplest method is to talk to the locals, especially the folks running the marinas and resorts. They want anglers to be happy and will usually give good advice. Local anglers can also be a help. Several years ago a local bass club president was kind enough to reveal a "hot" pattern while I was visiting Lake Chickamauga in Tennessee. I caught bass my entire three days on the lake, instead of looking for bass.

One technique used by the pros fishing a lake for the first time is concentrating on one major creek arm or tributary. This may yet result in several thousand possible fishing acres and the map work is still invaluable to locate best spots. Young Oklahoma pro Gene Pearcy likes to fish the bridge piers on a lake he's unfamiliar with. "Simply start at the shallowest and work to the deepest until you find bass," he states. "There's always fish around them on any lake."

The next step in locating bass is determining depth. Texas bass expert John Hope does radio tracking studies of bass and has come to the conclusion there are three distinct largemouth bass populations in most reservoirs – shallow water, deep water and mid-depth bass. Although the three may intermingle at specific times of the year, such as during spawning, they usually inhabit their preferred ranges the majority of the time. Sub-species also offer this same "stacking" of depths so it's important to know what type of bass inhabit a lake. For instance largemouth will normally be found the most shallow, smallmouth shallow to deep while Kentuckies are often found the deepest.

Depth will also vary according to the lake and geography. As I discovered in the crystal clear water of Lake Mead in Nevada, bass can be extremely deep any time of the year, while the bass in the relatively shallow, turbid water of Truman Reservoir in Missouri are normally more shallow throughout the year.

Most anglers have the best success when the majority of the bass are relatively shallow. Two seasons offer the best opportunities for the optimum shallow water bass, early spring to spawn and mid to late fall. Actually, spawning bass can be difficult to catch and, if you hit the tail end of the spawn or the post-spawn period, you'll have a tough time. The best bet is to fish for pre-spawn fish. These bass are moving, looking for places to spawn, feeding heavily before the spawn and are probably the single most "catchable" bass of the year. Timing of this period will vary from early March through May, and even into June, depending on the geographical location. Incidentally, if you're looking for a real trophy bass, the single best time is late winter through the pre-spawn period when the old sows are feeing heavily and holding eggs. Some states don't allow fishing during spawning season for spawning bass. It's extremely important for anglers fishing that time of the year or specifically for spawning bass to practice catch-and-release.

The fall, when bass leave their lethargic summer pattern and begin to forage for the coming winter, also provides some extremely good shallow water action, often with a lot less competition from other anglers. I've fished the popular bass lake Bull Shoals in Arkansas during the deer season without seeing a handful of anglers. Early in the fall is a short spurt with the first cooling down weather, then a period of less activity as the reservoir or lake begins to turn over. Once the turn-over period is complete a strong pattern begins again. For this reason a fall fishing vacation should be relegated to mid to late fall to add to your chances for hitting the best action. A call to marinas and tackle shops can reveal the best time to plan your vacation around either of these periods.

Don't let the massive size of large lakes and reservoirs scare you off of some of the best bass fishing in the country. Narrow down your search, choose the most promising fishing spots, the best possible bait for the time and you'll find you can catch big bass from big waters, even if you've never fished them before!

Small Water Bassing

In these days of big reservoirs and fancy bass boats some of the best bass fishing in the world is overlooked. Farm ponds, small community lakes, backwater river sloughs and bayous, creeks, small rivers and strip pits can all offer excellent bass fishing with a small boat, float tube or even from the bank.

I grew up fishing the farm ponds and strip pits near my home and still like to fish small waters. Over the years I've settled on two important facts. First, the lures should be smaller than those commonly used for bigger waters and, second, match the lure to the forage. The forage type and color will usually be different than silver for shad, the main forage in many bigger waters. Good color choices, regardless of the lure, include black, brown, gold and naturalistic forage patterns such as perch, bass, crawfish and frog.

Once the water begins to warm in early spring many aquatic creatures hatch and rise from the bottom of a pond or small lake. The most productive lures for this very early period are dark and those that can be moved slowly in the cold water, yet still create fish-attracting action. My first choice is a Mepps No. 3 Black Fury in-line spinner. Because this can be a line twister, tie it on with a snap swivel. Other early top producers includes a ¼ ounce Johnson Fishing Beetle Spin in black with yellow strip, or ¼ ounce Blakemore Road Runner in black or crawdad brown.

If you're fishing an area with rocks, such as a riprap pond dam, anything resembling crawfish can

For small waters, a quiet approach is often best.

wading or float tubing offers the best of both worlds to bank fishermen. Wading if the weather is warm and the water shallow and float tubing even with waders and cold weather gear in cooler and deeper water. There are several advantages to wading for bass. First, it's quite often the only way to get to them. Big bass love cover, especially weeds and moss beds, during the hot summer months. Often the only way you can wangle them out of these shallow-water hidey-holes is to crawl in with them. Even if you fish the edges of such cover with a boat, you won't be able to fish all the area. If you hook a big fish in a tangled patch of vegetation you won't be able to pull him to you. Quite often you simply can't get a boat to the fish.

Wear an approved flotation device for this type of fishing. A good PFD that fits properly and has pockets can not only be comfortable to fish in, but is handy for holding fishing lures and other goodies. If night wading, you should take along a small penlight to hold in your teeth when tying on lures. About the only other equipment needed is a stringer to loop to your belt and a small tacklebox to clip to a belt loop as well.

Another method quite popular with many anglers is "belly boating." You can float and wade in areas you can't reach with a boat and the float tube fits easily in or on your automobile. I'll never forget one float tube experience several years ago with Toby Bridges, then Public Relations Director for Bass Pro Shops. We were fishing a strip-pit in late spring and the bass were jumping all over the plastic worms. Setting the hook with a plastic worm while in a float tube turned out to be a lesson in physics. I almost turned over backwards several times attempting a hard hookset on the big bass I saw below me in the clear water. It was wet, but a fun, exciting and most productive bass fishing experience.

Basic Bassing Calendar

Bass can be patterned to some degree based on annual seasonal habits. The exact dates will vary across the country, but the biological and seasonal patterns will remain the same. By the same token the difference in water clarity from lake to lake as well as forage base and structure can have a great deal of influence. The same general patterns still exist; however, it's a matter

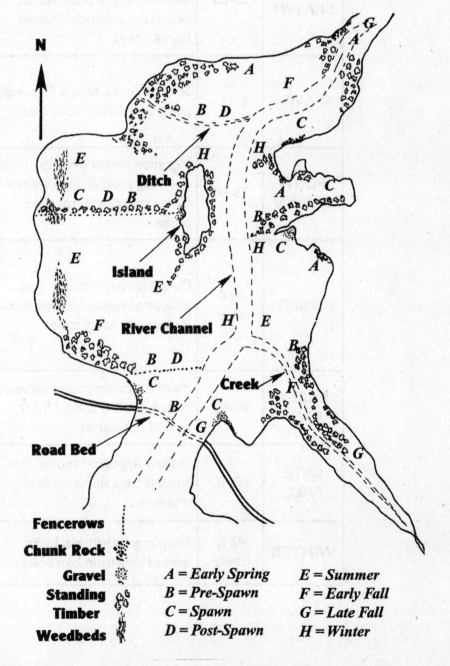

Fencerows
Chunk Rock
Gravel
Standing Timber
Weedbeds

A = Early Spring
B = Pre-Spawn
C = Spawn
D = Post-Spawn

E = Summer
F = Early Fall
G = Late Fall
H = Winter

PERIOD	SURF. TEMP.	LOCATION	LURE
EARLY SPRING	45-54	South facing banks & coves. Upper ends reservoir tributaries. Areas with material in water including turbidity & wood. Bolders, broken rock banks.	Pig'n Jig, black or brown; Weighted spinnerbaits; Deep running cranks, crawdad colors; Tiny crappie jigs.
PRE-SPAWN	55-65	Shallow water. Migration routes between deep water & spawning areas. Shallow flats near creek channels. Shallow bays & coves.	Spinnerbaits, cranks, jerkbaits, topwater, buzzbaits, lipless rattling cranks.
SPAWN	67-75	Shallow coves, bays & flats with pea gravel. Chunk rock banks.	Plastic worms, topwater lures, spinnerbaits, buzzbaits, tube lures, plastic salamanders.
POST-SPAWN	75-80	Migration routes between spawning areas & deep water. Creek channels & main lake points.	Plastic worms, tube lures, grubs, cranks, lipless rattling cranks, spinnerbaits.
SUMMER	80 & Over	Deep-Humps, islands & deep structure.Shallow-Weeds, moss, laydowns & heavy cover.	Deep-Plastic worms, grubs, tube lures, deep-running cranks. Shallow-Spinnerbaits, shallow-running cranks, buzzbaits, topwater.
EARLY FALL	80-60	Major migration routes between deep & shallow areas. Upper ends of tributaries.	Buzzbaits, spinnerbaits, cranks, lipless rattling cranks.
LATE FALL	60-45	Shallow-migration routes, flats, coves & bays, upper ends of tributaries.	Buzzbaits, cranks, spinnerbaits, lipless rattling cranks.
WINTER	42 & Lower	Deep creek channels, bluffs, ends of long main lake points.	Pig'n jig, grubs, jerkbaits, jigging spoons.

of adapting them to the situation. Local lakes may also have "mini" patterns with specific lures that are hot on that particular lake, again due to forage base and structure possibilities.

The bass fishing year is broken down into eight specific seasonal classifications: early spring, pre-spawn, spawn, post-spawn, summer, early fall, late fall and winter. Again there will be a great deal of variance in the time frame of these patterns across the country. For instance some of these time frames may stretch for months in the warmer southern regions while being compressed into weeks in the northern largemouth range.

The illustration on shows a seasonal look at a typical "good" bass fishing lake found in the Midwest. Southern lakes will have more shallow water and usually less clarity. Highland lakes and many western reservoirs will be deeper and have more clarity. Not all features shown will be found in all lakes, but those shown indicate the best locations for bass throughout the various seasons. If you can get a topographical map of a lake you intend to fish, mark the location of some of these prime areas on your own map by season and you'll be way ahead of the bass finding game this year.

D. 24 Basic Bassing Tips

BILL DANCE

1

Always match your hook size to the head diameter of the soft plastic bait you're using. Example: On an 8-inch plastic worm use either a size 4/0 or 5/0 hook: On a 4-inch worm a size 1/0 to 2/0 hook.

Match hook size to bait.

2

When fishing summertime bass in a small body of water such as farm ponds or soil conservation and natural lakes, remember that in the heat of summer most mini-waters lack enough oxygen down below. Bass rely on the shallows where there is a small, narrow, oxygen-rich band of water. Most anglers fish below the bass in low-oxygen areas, mistakenly thinking summertime bass ought to always be deep.

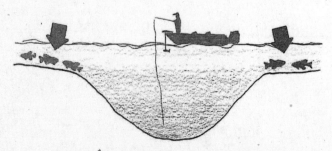

Go shallow for summertime bass.

3

When fishing muddy or off-colored water, fish shallow, fish objects, fish slow, and make repeated casts.

Vibrating lures for murky conditions

4

During the cold winter months the key to success is to fish *clear* water with *slow* presentation-type lures, especially when water temps are in the mid-to-low 40 degree range.

Brush near dropoffs holds promise.

5

When fishing murky or muddy conditions, use lures that vibrate. Dark-colored, bulky, shallowrunning crankbaits or single, Colorado-blade spinnerbaits are good choices.

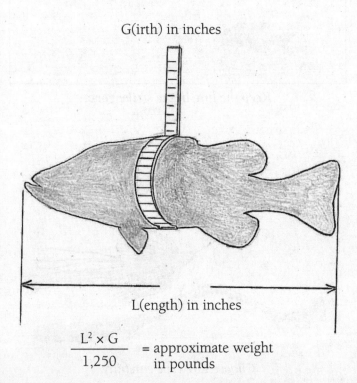

Crawfish create big bass.

6

Research has shown that mature bass show a decided preference for crawfish and, contrary to popular belief, the lowly crawfish is the most prevalent forage in our lakes, ponds, sloughs, creeks, and rivers. There are good reasons for the preference. Bass feeding on crawfish grow much faster than those who live where crawfish are not abundant. Crawfish also are much easier to catch, therefore bass expend less energy to gain the high protein nourishment that crawfish provide.

G(irth) in inches

L(ength) in inches

$$\frac{L^2 \times G}{1,250} = \text{approximate weight in pounds}$$

7

When shoreline fishing gets tough, make an about face. Why? Lakes change, fish change, and anglers must change as well. From the bass's point of view the advantages of open water are strong and numerous: less pressure, more forage, better habitat as a rule, and there's more comfort in the way of oxygen, safety, and temperature.

Don't neglect open water.

8

It's important to remember that fish feed heavily by sight in clear water, but in stained water, vision begins to lose its primary importance and fish use a mixture of sight, smell, and sound to locate their prey. In muddy water fish rely mostly on sound and smell.

Parallel casts keep lure in the strike zone.

9

A stump or a treetop, by itself, might hold a fish or two and so can a submerged point extending out toward deeper water. But a stump or treetop sitting right smack in the middle of this same point can really be a smokehouse! This is what we call multiple structure—a good fish holding spot located right on top of another.

Stay alert for multiple structures.

10

Taking springtime water surface temperatures is important because it gives you a starting point to consider, but bottom and mid-range temps are much more important, especially in shallow depths.

11

Never pass up fishing a boat-launch ramp. Most are made of concrete, stretch way out into the lake, and slope downward, thereby making a clear pathway from deeper to shallower water. Normally on a ramp you'll find rip-rap rock stretching out along the edge of the concrete into deeper water. Algae will grow on these hard rough surfaces during the late spring, summer, and early fall months. This attracts some of the bass' favorite food—shad, minnows and small bluegill—to feed on the algae. Bass then follow to feed on these baitfish.

12

Two of the most important controls a fisherman has at his disposal are depth control and speed control. This is especially true with crankbaits. If the lure is not worked at the fish's depth level, he may not hit it unless he's extremely active, so getting the lure down to his depth level is just as important as making an accurate cast to him. Once the lure is down, always remember that your retrieve—whether fast or slow—should be erratic. The key word here is "control."

Keep the lure in the strike zone.

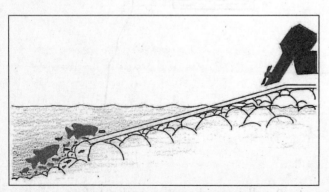

Look for fish at launch ramps.

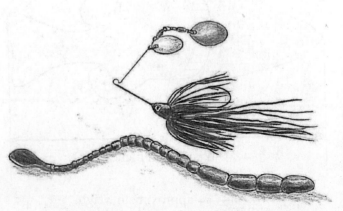

Choose lure type carefully.

13

When you're trying to catch bass in the wind, a few changes in tactics can make all the difference. First, cut back on the size of your line and increase the size of your weight. This will serve several purposes. It will allow you to gain depth quicker when you're using lures like a jig-n-trailer, a slip sinker worm, a grub, or a Carolina rig. The longer you must wait for your lure to sink, the more your boat will drift under poor control. Seconds can make the difference in success or failure. The smaller diameter line and heavier weight will also help eliminate those dreaded backlashes, which can be much more prevalent on windy days.

Minimal shade can hold bass.

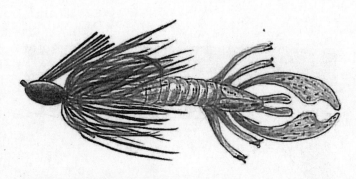

Light line and big baits beat windy days.

14

Rising water doesn't present nearly the bass fishing challenge to me as falling water. When lake levels drop, bass begin to lose their habitat—when lake levels rise, their habitat is expanded. This is a time to look for new, rich areas where fish will move to feed. I usually begin by finding water about a foot or two deep that has flooded a very large area. Large schools of shad will often move into these areas searching for plankton—one of their favorite foods. And naturally, the bass will follow the shad to feed on them. Watch carefully for baitfish activity on the surface. During the warmer months, when water temperatures are above 70 degrees, a buzzbait can be fantastic in such situations. If the water is murky, a spinnerbait might be the best offering.

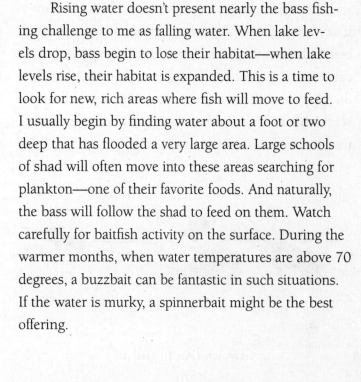

Electronics pinpoint suspended bass.

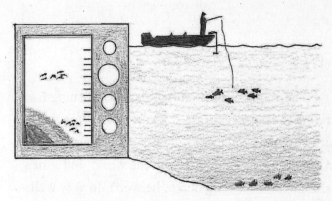

Rising water levels expands habitat.

15

One of the biggest mistakes topwater fisherman make is to fail to let the fish get a good hold on the lure before they set the hook. This is understandable, because nothing is more exciting than seeing bass explode on a topwater offering. Train yourself to wait before you set the hook. A good rule is to set the hook only after the lure has vanished from sight and you "feel" the fish.

Give 'em time to grab it!

16

The single most important factor in fishing is finding the correct depth. If you're not fishing the correct depth, you're wasting time. The finest angler around can fish the best bait in the world, but if he's fishing it at the wrong depth, he won't do very well. Fishing at the correct depth, almost anyone can catch a few fish.

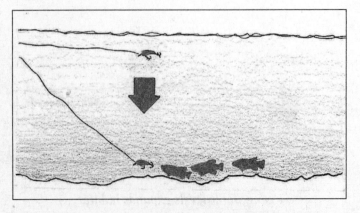

Correct depth is key to success.

17

Long, tapering points with bottoms of clay and gravel are great smallmouth spawning grounds. Some bigger females prefer points over other areas because they provide quicker access to deeper water. Look for isolated patches of weeds or stumps. You'll probably find nests a few feet from these, instead of right next to them.

Points provide prime spawning for smallmouths.

18

When night fishing, look for shallow shoals adjacent to where you usually find bass during the day and try breaks that lead to deeper water. At first, try dark colored lures like topwaters or shallow runners that create a lot of vibration or noise to attract the attention of the most active feeders. Next, switch to deeper runners or big plastic worms and fish even deeper.

Use noise and vibration at night.

19

Generally speaking, the best largemouth streams will have slow to moderate current and warm water. The best streams for smallmouth will have cooler, clearer water. Excellent holding spots for both species include eddies, deeper pools, undercut banks and gravel bars.

Gravel bars and points offer cover in moving water.

20

A rapid rise or fall in water level has a much greater impact on fish movement than a gradual change and it takes longer for water levels to change in lakes or reservoirs than it does in rivers and streams. When possible, plan your fishing trips accordingly.

21

Barometric pressure affects all living creatures. When the pressure changes rapidly, whether it's rising or falling, fishing also changes, and sometimes drastically. Bass can start feeding in a frenzy when a storm front approaches and this is usually indicated by fast-falling pressure. The exact opposite usually occurs when the pressure starts back up—it's almost impossible to get fish to hit until the barometer gets back to normal. When the mercury is on the rise, I usually direct my attention to bass in deeper water, or at least to fish that have quick access to deeper water. They simply aren't affected as much by pressure changes as bass in shallow water.

22

When bass are not in a chasing mood, slow down and offer them a slow presentation-type lure like a plastic worm, lizard, tube, grub, or light weight jig-and-plastic combination.

23

Cold water is denser than warm water, therefore it's reasonable to assume that your bait can achieve greater depths in 80 degree water than it can in 60 degree water. This 20 degrees of difference may allow your bait to reach another foot or so of depth, and at times, this can determine whether or not you catch fish!

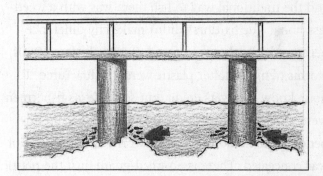

Bridge pilings and crappie are a natural combination.

24

Some good places to look for bass in reservoirs during the summer months are: Points long the main channel; deeper sections of submerged creek channels; bends along the main river channels; riprap on an embankment; along stair-stepped bluffs; and in feeding areas such as brushy flats.

Hunt the drops and depths in summer and winter.

E. 30 Bass Fishing Tips

1. The Texas Rig

Probably the most successful bass lure currently known to fishermen is The Texan worm rig—a weighted soft plastic worm with the hook point imbedded. Until about 1964, most worms had hard bodies, and the traditional way to fish them was with a weedless hook. The hardness didn't make any difference because the hook was exposed. But by the late 1960s, worms of much softer plastic were manufactured. I don't know who gets credit, but some Texas fishermen were taking plain 5/0 and 6/0 Sproat hooks and imbedding the hook into the soft worm so that the point was concealed. There is no weed-guard, just the plastic itself; when the hook is set, the point and barb come through the soft plastic and hook the fish. At that time, this was a popular lure in lakes around the Dallas and San Antonio area.

The first time I tried the Texas rig was at Santee-Cooper. S.C, in about 1968. I'd heard about it from a guy I fished with named Mark Workman. Mark was a tremendously tall man—he had been an All-American basketball player—and his favorite way of bass fishing was wading. He'd had special waders made and could wade in 5 feet of water, where I'd be up to my nose. Two of our big tricks at Santee in the spring were wading the blackwater ponds for spawning bass and wading around the cypress trees. Wading, as you probably know, should be a very quiet approach.

Mark brought out some plain hooks and commented that he knew I'd heard of the Texas rig. I said I'd heard of it, but down here it didn't work too well

Back then I was pouring my own worms. I'd take used plastic worms fishermen would leave in the boat and melt them down, ending up with a glob of plastic which was sort of a brown-black-greenish-red, and I'd pour it into the molds. These worms were about 9 inches long, and they were stiff. I'd use them with a big weedless hook

Mark gave me one of his plain hooks and suggested I try the Texas rig because the boys in Texas were killing the bass with it. At that time I was fishing for trophy bass and was using 30-pound-test line with heavy 7/0 hook. The hook he gave me was a little ol' 5/0 made of lighter wire. I buried it in one of my 9-inch worms and threw over near a spawning bed, and a 7- or 8-pound bass swirled up and grabbed the worm. I set the hook, but the fish got off. I reeled in and looked at my worm; the hook never had gotten through the plastic. Then I decided to work a hole in the plastic, so I wiggled the hook around until there was a little channel through the worm.

A few casts later, that bass hit again, and this time I set the hook real hard. The water was about to come in over the top of my waders as I was sloshing around after the fish, which was going through the lily pads. I was up to my chin in water, but Mark was only to his waist, so he said he'd go after the fish. He headed toward the lilies, but when he got there the bass made a sudden hinge and straightened out my hook.

Right then I told Mark the Texas worm was foolish. Worms were too stiff and you wouldn't get the fish hooked, and anyway the hook was too light.

Obviously I hadn't perfected my worm fishing. Now there are many plastic worm manufacturers who use softer plastics and also many hook manufacturers who make good plastic-worm hooks. (Plus it makes lots of difference if you sharpen the hooks and use a good stout line and a good stout worm rod and a good hook set.) Also, now we have graphite rods. They have much more impact, so you can set the hook pretty well through that plastic.

There are some advantages to the Texas worm rig over the old weedless-hook style of worm fishing. The biggest advantage is it's more compact and streamlined. We're using cone-shaped bullet worm weights instead of split shot or the old egg sinkers. The cone-shaped weights swim their way through grass and other cover much better. Also, the hook is less exposed. There's more hook in the worm, and less body of hook exposed. With the weedless hook, you have one or two wires and the entire bend of the hook hanging out. There is more exposed metal to pick up trash.

Another advantage to the Texas rig is there's no "sprong." With the old weedguard hook, the weedguard is under tension, and quite often in the fish's mouth, the weedguard will flip up and "sprong" 'em. Many times this scares the fish, and it spits out the worm. This is particularly true on light strikes or with Kentucky bass, which normally are spookier than largemouths. When I fished worms on weedless hooks, I had a lot of fish drop the rig.

Another factor is that the Texas rig is a lot cheaper to fish. Standard worm hooks are two to three cents apiece, whereas the weedless hooks are fifteen to twenty-five cents apiece. The way we fish today, worms are expendable. We're constantly throwing 'em into heavy cover and constantly getting hung up. And we're breaking them off. It's cheaper to break off a twelve-cent lure than a thirty-five-cent lure.

The real advantage, though, with the Texas rig is the fact that it can be snaked, crawled, and jigged across almost any bottom surface. With plastic worms, you're constantly looking for heavy cover. To me,

worm fishing is mostly reserved for the ultra-thick cover, such as brush, stumps, and rocks. I very seldom throw plastic worms to a bare shoreline.

The Texas rig has a lot of different variations, starting with the weightless varieties and ending with ones for jigging on structure in deep water with as much as ½ ounce of lead ahead of the lure. They vary from 5-inch to 10-inch rigs. Some fishermen even rig with double hooks on the Texas rig. (Another advantage to the rig is that during spawning season, when bass often strike shorter, you can move the hook point farther down the worm to catch those short-strikers.)

The 6-inch dark-grape or purple worm rigged Texas-style is the most popular of all these rigs. A poll of plastic worm manufacturers revealed that of all their worms sold, nearly 40 percent are 6-inch purple or dark grape. The second choice is 6-inch black. Black is an extremely popular color during the spawning season. Third most popular size and color is the 6-inch blue worm. Blue seems to be a particularly good hot-weather color after the fish have spawned and moved to deeper water. Red and green colors also sell pretty well, as do multiple and spotted colors.

The standard way I fish the Texas worm rig is to try to find heavy cover in the form of brush. My first choice is a submerged brushpile, a tree, or some other type of wood cover. My second pick is some type of weedy cover, such as lily pads or grass, and my third favorite is boulders and rocks. One problem with the last is that worms do get caught in the crevices. Worms are not entirely snagless. When that slip weight lodges between two boulders or in rip-rap, you're going to lose a lot of worms. You'll also lose a lot of worms when you snake them through brush, because sometimes that weight catches and hangs in forks of limbs and the hook gets caught.

But worms are expendable. The average worm fisherman carries at least twenty-five different worms in the same color. He'll likely have six different colors in the 6-inch size, six different colors in the 7-inch length, and so on. In all he has 200 to 300 worms with him. At ten to twelve cents apiece, counting hook and weight, plastic worms aren't an extravagance. Probably he'll lose a dozen or so worms a day, but compare that cost to the price of the gasoline and the meals on the trip. The trip might have cost him $20, and he's lost $1.50 worth of worms.

The plastic worm is cheap and efficient, and it can be fished at all depths and during almost all seasons of the year. There are some criteria for worm fishing, particularly the Texas-style. Most important of these is water temperature. It's been my experience and that of most bass fishermen I know that very few bass are caught on plastic worms in water cooler than 55 degrees. You'll catch a few; in fact, I've caught a few when ice was forming around the edges of the lake.

Plastic worm fishing starts early in the year when the water temperature reaches 55, but better worm fishing comes when the water reaches 60 to 65 degrees. Probably the best time to fish a plastic worm is when smallmouth and largemouth bass are spawning. Water temperature then is 59 degrees for smallmouth spawning activity and 62 degrees for largemouth spawning. At this time, bass really are hitting the plastic worm because the worm is a snaky-looking creature. When it comes crawling through a spawning bed, it rouses the fish's protective instinct; and he's going to carry it out

of there and try to kill it because he thinks it's after the eggs.

What size of plastic worm is right? I'm asked that virtually everywhere I talk with fishermen. I've often said the size doesn't make any difference as long as it's 6 inches, because then it'll work. But that's really an oversimplification. In tournament competition or if I'm merely trying to catch a limit of bass, I prefer the 5-to-6-inch worms for catching small to medium-sized bass. I've caught a lot more bass—not the big ones, but just good keepers—on the 6-inch worm. However, if I'm after trophy fish, I go to 8, 9, and even 10 inches.

One of my favorite stories about big worms concerns a trip my wife, Mary Ann, and I made to Florida back in 1973. We were bass fishing at Lake Eloise at Cypress Gardens. At the time the 13-inch J&W Hawg Hunter worm was new on the market. It has two giant weedless hooks attached to about a 50-pound-test braided line buried inside it, and the thing looks like a tractor-tire retread. A stiff casting rod and both hands are needed to cast it. It's the most horrible-looking worm you'll ever see. However, some anglers reportedly had caught some big bass on it.

Mary Ann was after a trophy. I'd caught several big bass, including a few over 10, but she'd never got a 10-pounder, and she said her whole trip was devoted to

How to make a Texas rig in three sizes.

Bullet-shaped slip sinker   3/0 Hook   6" Texas rig

Bullet-shaped slip sinker   1/0 Hook   4" Texas rig

*Eye of hook left exposed for clarity - normally it's imbedded in the worm.

4/0 Hook   7¼"-9" Texas lunker rig

Bullet-shaped slip sinker

catching a trophy bass. I agreed to try merely to catch a lot of bass, so I stayed with 6-inch worms. We fished mostly cypress trees and grass beds but also some 10-to-15-foot-deep potholes . . . all of this for five days.

She stayed with the 13-inch Hawg Hunter and in five days she caught only nine bass. Out of those nine, her smallest was 6 pounds and the largest was a little over 9 pounds. She had a 7-pound average for her nine fish. If we'd been in tournament competition, my total weight would have beaten her solidly. During those five days I averaged six to fifteen bass per day and totaled about fifty bass. But my fish were smaller. Most of them were 1 ½ to 2 ½ pounds, and maybe one out of ten was a 6-pounder.

So whether or not to use a large plastic worm, in my opinion, depends on whether you're after a trophy largemouth or several bass. When I'm tournament fishing, I'll start with the small, short worms in my quest for a limit. As soon as I catch that limit, I purposely go to a big worm. That was how I won the Bass Anglers Sportsman Society's New York Invitational in June 1978.

People who have never attended a tournament may not realize that these contests are basically catch-and-release events, not wasteful affairs that can reduce our bass populations. A tournament fisherman takes pains to keep his catch alive. He earns extra points for bringing in live fish and he's penalized for dead ones. When you compete in a tournament, it makes sense to try for a limit and then start culling—releasing a smaller fish from the live well each time you catch a bigger one so that the total weight increases while the number stays the same.

In the 1978 Invitational just mentioned, I caught a lot of small bass during the first round, although I had four pretty good ones in the 3-to-4-pound range. So I went to a 9-inch worm, and the first bass I caught on it weighed 5 ½ pounds.

I ran out of 9-inch worms, so I went to 8-inch worms. These are a lot bigger than a 6-inch worm; they have thicker bodies and weigh probably twice as much. I continued to catch some more 4-pound bass. I do think the huge worms discourage smaller bass from hitting them.

One thing about plastic worms which I think generally is overrated is the type of tail. I have seen few instances where the swimming type of tail, such as the beaver tail, twisted tail, and minnow-action tail, seemed to work better. Those occasions mostly have been when we were moving fast, such as on structure when we were working the worm fast or even trolling the worm. But 98 percent of the time you're working the worm very slow, and the worm basically is crawling through the branches and over the rocks.

I don't think the brand or shape of worm is particularly important as long as it's a good soft plastic. When I poured worms years ago I combined the worms of a dozen different manufacturers and poured them all in the same mold, and I caught bass on them just as good as with any brand-name worm. But soft plastic is one of the keys. I believe bass will hold the softer plastic longer than a harder plastic. My experience has been that hard plastic worms aren't nearly as effective.

Today you can buy both different worm weights and six basic worm-hook sizes. In *Fishing Facts* magazine, a hook chart I formulated was printed with one of my stories on plastic worm fishing. That chart basically stated that I prefer a 3/0 hook with a 6-inch plastic worm, a 4/0 for a 7-inch worm, a 5/0 for an 8-inch worm, and a 6/0 for a 9-inch worm. For worm weights, I like a ¹⁄₁₆-ounce lead for 8-to-10-pound-test line. However, with light line in ultra-clear water, I might go up to a ⅜-ounce slip sinker if I'm fishing 30 feet deep. With heavier lines, you need heavier worm weights.

I use a ⅛-ounce weight for worm fishing at 4-to-5-foot depths. Out on structure 25 feet deep, I might use a ½-ounce lead. Wind plays a big factor in choosing a suitable worm weight. If the wind's blowing ten to fifteen miles per hour, you might have to increase the weight one size. If it's blowing twenty to twenty-five miles per hour, you might have to go two sizes. If the

A 10-pound, 8-ounce bass that I caught on a Texas rig on Lake Okeechobee in January.

wind is blowing thirty-five miles per hour, you ought to get the hell out of there!

One of the first tournament pros ever to use the Texas worm rig was Bill Dance of Memphis. Bill started his tournament career before I did, and this likable guy has a super track record with the worm. He even wrote a book on plastic worm fishing, called *There He Is!*

I was late getting started using the Texas rig because, as I've said, for several years I was hung up using worms on weedless hooks. The old weedless hook is fairly effective, and even today several guys still use them. One pro who does is Johnny Morris of Bass Pro Shops. This is merely an idiosyncrasy of his. I don't consider the weedless-hook worm rig as good as the Texas rig.

I sometimes use a 4-inch worm Texas-style for light-line fishing in clear water. The 4-inch rig is merely a stepping down in worm length and line size. It's good for very clear water where you can see rocks on the bottom 20 feet deep. Lakes like this usually contain good populations of smallmouth bass as well as largemouths.

and smallmouth generally prefer smaller baits. Kentucky or spotted bass also likely are present.

In Alabama's Lake Martin, which I fished frequently in 1971 when I lived in Montgomery, Ala., you get far more strikes with a 4-inch worm than you can with a 6-inch worm on Kentucky bass. The smaller worm simply is what they prefer in that lake. A typical productive worm pattern in lakes like this is large, shaded boulders. Boulders, ledges, and cliffs usually are numerous in smallmouth bass and Kentucky bass lakes where I use the 4-inch worm mostly.

Boulders 2 to 6 feet in diameter in 5 to 15 feet of water and close to deep water tend to hold good smallmouth and spotted bass. When fishing this type of pattern I usually stand up in the boat and utilize the Polaroid sunglasses to see the obstructions. I'm conscious of the sun angle and am trying to spot the shady nooks and crevices in the boulders, rocks, and cliffs. I throw the 4-inch worm 5 to 10 feet beyond these ambush points and allow it to settle, then slowly hop it into the shadows of the rocks and boulders. In this type of fishing I hold the rod a little lower than normal, at approximately a 40-degree angle, so that I'm ready for the quick strike of a smallmouth or a spotted bass. I also try to set the hook very quickly, because they're apt to drop the worm very quickly. I try to set the hook within two seconds of the strike. Spotted bass often will rattle the worm. There are two ways to set the hook on a rattling strike. Sometimes the initial set will do it, but usually when you feel the rattle, the spotted bass has the tail or lower portion of the worm loosely in his lips and he's shaking it. At times I put a little bit of pressure on the fish. The worm partly slips out of his mouth, and he thinks it's getting away and he'll grab it better. Then I let him pull down before I set the hook. Sometimes this latter trick is about the only way to catch a spot on a worm.

Also, for this method I prefer a 5-foot graphite spinning rod and a medium-sized spinning reel. I don't like the ultralight spinning reels; I like a fairly good-sized reel, because when it's loaded with 6-or-8 longer cast, it has a larger spool diameter and I can make a longer cast. Also, the slightly larger reels have smoother, more efficient drag. I set the drag for a pound or two less pressure than my line test. With 6-pound line, I set the drag for about 4 pounds. How the hook is set is important, and I want the drag to be able to slip. With 6-pound line, it is very, very difficult to set a worm hook, because you have to drive the hook point through the worm as well as through the fish's mouth. With the drag just below the breaking point, I pretend I'm using 20-pound line when I set the hook. Every time I overset the hook—which is constantly—the drag slips and the line doesn't break. I also use the multiple hook set—I just repeat setting the hook five to ten times as the fish is running away.

One factor which is important in worm fishing, particularly with the Texas rig, is to avoid if possible setting the hook when the bass is running directly toward you. This is especially important during the spawning season because the spawners so often have the worm only in the lips. If the fish is facing you and headed right at you, you're apt to pull the worm out of his lips when you set the hook. If he's turned the other way, the hook sort of catches him in the corner of his mouth even if he had it only in his lips.

When they run directly at me, I try to put just a little pressure and hope they'll turn. I don't mind setting the hook when he's straight under the boat because I'm pulling straight up on him.

A lot of people ask me, "When do you set the hook with a worm?" Three of four variables determine this. For example, if I'm stickup fishing in Toledo Bend Reservoir or Ross Barnett Reservoir—some place like that with a lot of stickups—and throw in next to a shady stickup and a fish sucks it up instantly as they often do, I'm going to set the hook within a second or two. If he heads toward the obstruction, I don't want him to go in there, so I'm going to set almost instantly.

But suppose I throw in by that same stickup and the bass hits and starts moving away from the stickup. I might wait an additional two or three seconds. I

want him to move away from it, because this is to my advantage, especially if I'm using fairly light line. Again, if this is the spawning season, I'll strike back within three seconds, but if it's early summer and he's just trying to eat the worm as they often do, then with the Texas rig, I'll let him go a few feet as long as he's moving away from the heavy cover.

If the water's fairly clear and I see an exceptionally big bass hit the worm or see the boil of a lunker grabbing the worm, I try to give her a little more time if she's away from the cover. I've found that some of the larger bass don't always suck the worm into their mouths when they first hit. Quite often that first tap is the fish grabbing the worm with his lips, and that second tug you feel is the worm being sucked in. I've watched this happen in my 7,000-gallon aquarium and also while diving with outdoor photographer Glen Lau in Salt Springs and Silver Springs, Fla. When they've finally got the worm inside their mouths is the perfect time to set the hook. As a general rule when the water temperature is over 75 degrees, most bass inhale the worm on the initial strike as they hit it. When the water's cooler, such as during the spawning season, they often grab it with their lips and you've got to wait a little bit until they get it inside their mouths.

An experience I had several years ago really taught me to set the hook hard with a worm. I didn't realize a big bass has such tremendous jaw pressure until an incident in 1967. I had caught an 11-pound, 2-ounce largemouth one day at Santee-Cooper. I was guiding at Bill Jones' Landing on Santee's Diversion Canal. The shiner and herring season was over, and I put the bass in one of Bill's live-bait tanks. Of course, every time a new prospective customer came around and asked about fishing, I'd take him down to the tank and show him the 11-pounder along with some four-to-eight-pounders I had in there too. Naturally, this always whetted his enthusiasm for going fishing and hiring me as a guide. It helped his confidence.

Quickly I noticed that this 11-pounder took up a territory in the tank. He stayed in one corner and acted like he owned it. But he was shy and wouldn't eat for a long time. I'd throw in a handfull of minnows, and the smaller bass would feed on them right away. So I started holding minnows in front of the big one's face. When he'd look half interested, I'd let the minnows go and he'd suck them up as they swam by him.

Finally he grew a little bolder, and when I'd hold the minnows down in the water, he'd come up within a couple inches of them. After a couple weeks of this, he'd come up to my hand and actually suck the minnow out of my fingers. He'd simply flare his gills and open his mouth, and this created a suction which pulled the minnow 3 or 4 inches. This is much like the way they hit a plastic worm in the summertime. I've watched them, and a big one can be 4 or 5 inches away from the worm and suck it into his mouth.

Anyhow, one day my 11-pounder was just a little too hungry. He came up to the minnow, and instead of sucking it in as he'd been doing, he just crunched down on my hand. Believe it or not, the pain was excruciating! I estimated that he put at least 150 pounds of pressure per square inch on my fingers, and he almost broke them! Instead of letting go, he held on for three or four seconds and crunched and ground his jaws on my fingers, and I couldn't pull loose. Finally he let go and swam away.

I got to thinking about that. After all, it was the first time I had ever had a trophy bass actually bite me. This led me to realize, that with the tackle we use for bass, if a big fish is crunching down on a crank bait, worm, or spinner bait with all that jaw pressure, there is no way to move the hook into any flesh. It would stay right where it was in his grasp. You'd be trying to set the hook, but actually you wouldn't be moving it at all! After a couple seconds, the fish would release the pressure and spit the whole lure out.

Quite often during those early years at Santee, I had that very thing happen. I used up to a 40-pound-test line and would set the hook like a madman, but nothing would happen and the bass would spit

the worm out. Some giant bass—10-pounders and bigger—did that after I'd set the hook awfully hard.

I figured the secret would be to set the hook when the fish isn't exerting that tremendous jaw pressure. So I started setting the hook with a plastic worm after two or three seconds. After that hard first set, I don't know how much jaw pressure he's exerting, so I quickly reel in all the slack and set the hook again two seconds later. I keep the pressure on, and set it a third time two seconds after that. Then after that, I keep on setting the hook every two or three seconds, and I know that at some point, he's released the jaw pressure and the hook is penetrating his mouth. When I started using the multiple hook set, immediately I started hooking a much higher percentage of my strikes with a plastic worm.

That 11-pounder which bit the hand that fed him turned out to be a blessing for me, since from that experience I learned about the great jaw pressure and developed my practice of multiple hook setting. This has helped me boat many more bass and undoubtedly has helped my tournament success. I believe lots of bass fishermen lose many trophy bass on plastic worms because they don't use the multiple hook set and therefore don't get the hook to penetrate the bass's jaws. However, I don't think 1 ½-pound bass exert this kind of jaw pressure. I think the smaller ones hit the worm and can be hooked usually with the initial hard hook set.

Another important thing about worm fishing—something we discovered about twenty years ago—is to have a suitable rod to set the hook. We learned that ideal rods, which today the manufacturers call worm rods, are heavy-butted rods with a lot of backbone in the lower half of the rod. They have fairly light tips for good casting, but you're driving the hook with that butt section.

Regardless of the kind of worm rig I'm using, I like to position the rod at a 45-degree angle or higher. The main reason for this is I have far more feel of the bottom. The rod is about 90 degrees from the bass, and

I have the maximum feel of the tip of the rod. The maximum sensitivity with a worm rod comes with the tip high in the air, and I'm working the worm from a 45-degree to a 90-degree or greater angle. Then the second I feel the strike or detect line movement and determine I have a fish, I drop the rod tip and reel up all the slack line except for the last 2 or 3 inches, and then I set the hook on a slack line. Before I set it, I'm watching that little bit of slack line to see what way he's moving. When I finally set the hook, my arms are extended and I'm pulling the reel and the butt of the rod back toward me instead of merely jerking the tip upward. I'm actually setting the hook with my arms and wrist. My arms are in close to my body, and I bring my wrists up toward my face. Instantly I start reeling as fast as I can, and again I set the hook, reel fast, and repeat this procedure.

At seminars, I'm often asked how I work the worm. I fish it about three different ways. With the Texas rig, most of my fishing is done in fairly shallow water. Since the worm is a great ambush-point lure, I'm seeking out some type of cover. When I'm fishing heavy cover, I'm thinking to myself that the bass is right there by the stump or bush. So I'm either going to throw right to the obstruction or a couple feet past it. As I crawl the worm past the cover, I prefer for it to be falling straight down off

Usually with a plastic worm I set the hook quickly, before the bass drops it. But sometimes, especially in cooler water, that first tap, which I'm feeling in the first photo, just means the fish has grabbed the worm with its lips; if you strike then you won't hook it. I give the fish slack, with the rod low, for a few seconds, then set the hook hard—and more than once.

of things such as off a root. About 90 percent of my strikes on a worm come as the worm is coming off of something, such as off a boulder, stump, grass, or creek channel ledge. At this time, the worm usually is sinking or falling. Very seldom does the strike occur when I'm pulling the worm up on something.

After I've crawled and jigged the worm off all the obstructions and am free of all them, if I haven't had a strike I quickly reel in, because I'm not going to fish it all the way to the boat. This is what I do especially in shallow-water situations when I'm throwing directly into cover. Then I'll throw to the next ambush point.

As I've written many times and others have written about me, I'm a line watcher. I use Stren fluorescent line, and in shallow water I identify probably 75 percent of my worm strikes by seeing the line move before I ever feel the fish. When my worm's falling straight down—and I give it slack line so it'll fall straight down rather than glide off of something at an angle—I'll detect that little twitch in the line. To make sure it's a fish, I'll put on just a little pressure, and then I can determine which way he's moving. I'm watching the line not only to detect the strike, but also to see what the bass is doing after he's struck. I do check them a lot after the initial strike, but I'm doing it only on about half a pound of pressure—just enough to know he's there.

I don't always fish the worm as I've described above; sometimes I do work it all the way back to the boat, and I do this particulary on structure. When I'm out on a big point or a submerged bar, I'm not fishing an ambush point. I'm fishing open-water structure. In this situation, I don't know exactly where the obstructions are; I merely know that there should be some objects down there. So I throw the worm out there and crawl it along fairly quickly. But when I feel something, such as a stump, I think that might be where one is hiding. Then I slow the worm down and fish it more carefully, and I do this every time I hit some piece of cover.

When I'm fishing heavy brush or cover—shallow or deep—often I peg the slip sinker to make the weight part of the worm. I take a round toothpick and jab it in the hole next to the line and break the toothpick off so it's flush with the weight. I peg the pointed end of the bullet weight, but the toothpick can be inserted in either end of the weight. After a cast or two, water will cause the toothpick end to swell up and this makes it snug.

The reason for pegging the weight is if I'm fishing heavy cover, I don't want to pull the worm up on an obstruction and get it caught in a limb. If that happens, the weight will slip down the line when you give it some slack, and you'll think the worm is sinking, when really it isn't sinking at all. Also, when you've separated the weight from the worm, you'll get hung up more. By pegging the weight, the worm becomes more snagless because it isn't separated from the sinker.

2. The Carolina Rig

One of my second choices in plastic worm fishing is entirely different from the Texas rig. It's the Carolina rig. It doesn't have a slip weight down against the hook, and about half the time it doesn't have a self-weedless hook. It features a rather heavy egg sinker with a swivel, and 18 to 30 or more inches behind the weight and swivel is the worm, which usually is floating free. The worm has either a bare exposed hook or the Texas-style imbedded hook. The latter is used if this rig is fished in brushy areas.

This rig is important because it's great for fishing deep-water structure. Quite often on deep points, structures, bars, and channels the bass are down on the bottom, but they really can see a floating worm better. Remember the weight—the egg sinker, which often weighs from ½ ounce to 1 ounce—is plummeting the whole rig to the bottom, but the worm is floating up. I often use a plastic worm which has been injected with a lot of air bubbles, such as the Sportsman Catch-Em-Quick Super Floater, or some of the other styles of worms that float even with the hook inside.

This floating worm is more visible to bass 6 to 8 feet away. Also, the worm has a lot better action being away from the weight. It drifts, darts, and oscillates from any currents and wave action present under the water.

When a bass grabs the worm, he feels virtually no weight or resistance. When he starts to run with it, the line slips through the hole in the weight and you need to give him some line for the first couple of seconds. This method is an especially great way to get a worm deep in a hurry. You can take a small, delicate worm which floats and get it down 30 to 50 feet in a hurry with a ¾ ounce sinker. It's excellent in deep, rocky lakes like Bull Shoals in Arkansas, Clark Hill Reservoir on the Georgia-South Carolina border, Sidney Lanier in Georgia, and Lake Murray in South Carolina. These are all deep, relatively clear lakes, and they're perfect for the Carolina rig.

You can get the worm very deep in a few seconds. You have a lot of contact with the weight, but you need a good, sensitive rod and you need to hold it high to be able to give the fish line for a couple of seconds before you strike back at him.

In the hot summer when the water temperature is above 70 degrees, a lot of bass seek the thermocline. They get down in the depths, especially in clear water where the light penetration is pretty deep. I like to use a ½-ounce lead sinker with a small swivel and run it about 25 inches back. I usually use a spinning rod for this work, because this entire rig bolos when you cast it. It's sort of hard to throw and you get a lot of backlashes with a casting rod. I prefer 14-pound-test line. The leader—the monofilament which goes to the worm—can be a little bit lighter if the water's very clear. In fact, then you might want to use an 8- or 10-pound line to fool more bass. Another advantage of the lighter leader is that when you get hung up, you break your worm off but not the swivel and weight.

Hook size is extremely important. My favorite worm is the 6-inch DeLong Super Floater. It floats very well for its size, but this is true only if you use a hook no larger than a 1/0. Even a No. 1 hook works well. If you use a 2/0 or 3/0 hook, the rig won't float; the worm sinks to the bottom. If the water isn't obstructed with brush, I'll use the hook exposed most of the time. With the hook point out, I can set faster and better. I can troll or jig this rig along at a pretty good speed through quite a few stumps, boulders and rocks. It's fairly snagless because it's floating up.

3. The Weightless Spawning Rig

One of my super patterns in worm fishing is the weightless spawning rig. This is nothing but a plastic worm, a hook, and zero weight, rigged Texas-style with the hook embedded in the middle of the worm. I use this rig strictly in the spawning season, because, as I pointed out before, spawning bass aren't hungry and

In the Carolina rig the sinker is some distance from the plastic worm, so the worm, which often contains Styrofoam or air bubbles, drifts above the bottom. The hook is usually exposed but can be imbedded as in the Texas rig for fishing in brushy areas.

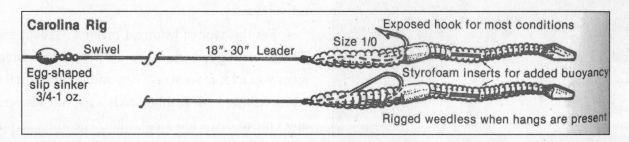

don't hit out of reflex action. Instead, they're hitting out of protective instinct; they're merely trying to move that worm which is threatening their nest and get it away from the spawning bed. They'll swim with it for three to five seconds and carry it a few feet from the nest and then spit it out.

Keep in mind that spawning bass usually pick up a worm near the middle. You need your hook back down the worm toward the tail, and you need to set the hook pretty quickly. I don't use particularly heavy tackle, because lots of times spawning bass are in clear, shallow water without much turbulence. Therefore, you need to go to fairly light line. I like to use at least 10-pound line because it's hard to set the hook through that plastic with 6-pound line. It can be done, but it's more difficult, and you'll miss a lot more bass on 6 than you will on 10, even though you'll get more strikes on 6-pound line. Most of the spawning bass I've found are around some type of cover, such as weeds. Even in

This Florida largemouth, over 10 pounds, wasn't going to let my weightless rig stay in her nest.

natural lakes in Minnesota and Wisconsin, the weeds and bullrushes so often found in spawning areas are enough to break a 6-pound line when a bass tangles around them. In the swamps of Lake Seminole or in Florida and in lakes in Oklahoma, where I live, bass spawn usually in the north coves around heavy brush or vegetation, and they easily can break a 6-pound line.

Another thing I do during the spawning season is continually use a new worm. I do this so that if I miss a strike, I can examine the worm and determine from the teeth marks where it was bitten. My favorite color and size of worm at this time of year is the 7- or 7 ¼ inch black worm. For some reason, whether you're fishing in Maine or Arizona, they seem to hit black the best when they're spawning.

Worm fishing really comes into its own when the spawning season arrives. Before that, the water is on the cold side for plastic-worm fishing, and bass don't hit worms good in cold water. But when the water reaches at least 62 degrees during the full-moon period in the spring, spawning activity begins and so does good worming. I stand up in my boat and wear Polaroid sunglasses to spot the beds and to determine the type of cover they're bedding near.

When you spot a spawning bed, cast 10 feet past it and swim the worm slowly up to it. Let the lure settle for fifteen to thirty seconds in the bed. When the bass picks up the worm, strike him within three seconds. If you wait too long, the fish is apt to drop the worm. If you catch the smaller male bass, keep casting to the bed and you might catch that trophy female. If you don't catch her, wait at least thirty minutes and then return to the area again. For particularly large bass, the period just before dusk is the best time to catch them.

For this type of fishing, I prefer a 5½-foot graphite bait-casting rod and 14-to-20-pound line. Graphite gives you a lot more sensitivity, and for almost all my worm fishing I use graphite rods. Graphite also enables me to cast a few feet farther. The line size varies with the amount of cover near the beds, but most spawning strikes are lip strikes, and the hardest spots to hook them. It's much easier to hook bass in the summertime when they're actually trying to eat the worm and have it back inside their mouths, where the flesh is softer. Extremely sharp hooks naturally are especially important.

One time before a B.A.S.S. tournament in January on the St. Johns River in Florida, my friend Paul Chamblee of Raleigh, N.C., and I practiced together during the pre-tourney warmup. We located a tremendous bunch of spawning bass, but they were shallow and the water was super clear. We had to drop down to 6-pound lines to get them to strike, but during the tournament the sun was bright, and we had trouble keeping from spooking them even with 6-pound line. This tough condition is much the same as smallmouth fishing on bright, sunny days in clear water, as Billy Westmorland often points out, and you really have to go to very light line to have any success. However, if there's a lot of cloud cover, you can step up your line size a bit.

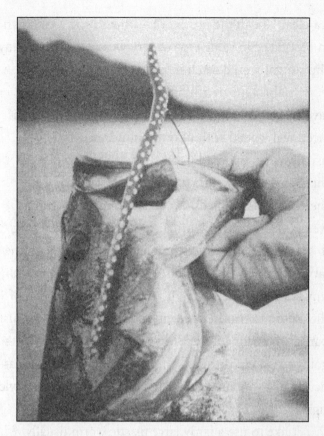

I fished this floating worm by twitching it like any surface lure, and the bass fell for it.

4. The Surface-Floating Worm

The surface-floating worm sometimes is confused with the Carolina rig, but the two are entirely different. This worm really floats, and that's the difference. A lot of anglers use a weightless worm and think it's the same thing, but a weightless worm and a floating worm are two different rigs.

In South Carolina the floating worm rig has a tail planted with Styrofoam so that it lies evenly on the surface in spite of having a hook attached. I first came across this particular type of rig in Salt Springs, Fla., where the local boys were catching huge strings of bass with it. This rig is best used in the spring in weed-infested warmer waters around spawning beds. The worm floats on the surface, and gentle twitches often provoke sucking strikes and huge swirls. The floating worm is fished about the same way as you would fish a small surface plug like the Rapala.

The surface-floating worm is really for an exceptional condition. Use it only in extremely clear, weedy water. The best examples of where to use it are in an ul-

You can make a floating worm rig by cutting strips from a Styrofoam cup and inserting them in the worm (I use a ballpoint-pen refill to make the holes and stuff in the foam). Note position of the exposed hook.

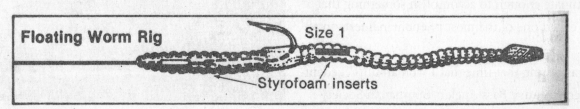

tra-clear lake in the north or in some spring area down in Florida or in some type of very weedy bay where any slip weight would catch moss or algae.

In this type of fishing I use spinning tackle. My favorite outfit is a light-action spinning rod and open-faced reel loaded with 6- or 8-pound line. The hook usually is left exposed in most weedy areas where there aren't many surface weeds. If surface weed is there, such as lily pads or coontail moss or a stringy weed, then I rig the worm Texas-style. But when I rig it Texas-style, instead of running the hook through the fat part of the worm, I'll just barely hook it through a tiny section of the worm. It has only about 1/16 inch of the plastic to tear loose from, and the hook point is just barely in, making it weedless. When I set the hook, it's going to pop loose quickly from that small slice of plastic. In all of my light-line fishing, I hook my Texas-style rigs this way.

I like to use a fairly large plastic worm usually one 7 ¼ to 7 ½ inches long for this type of fishing. You can't use a very large hook because you would sink the worm. I like a No-1 or a Style 84. A Style 84 is not really a worm hook. It's got a good open throat, and when I use a No. 1 or 1/0, I keep the hook exposed. It's a good, solid small hook with a lot of body that can hold a big bass.

Big spawners suck it in when it comes over the bed. You see them rise up as if for a surface plug, and then as the summer progresses in these same weedy areas, it's a good surface lure to use in the early morning and late evening or on cloudy days. It is a surface lure.

5. Jigs: Big Bass Lure for All Seasons

It was during a five-month period in 1980-81 that I was fortunate enough to accomplish something that has been called one of the most phenomenal feats in all of sports.

It was during that time that I won an unprecedented three consecutive Bass Anglers Sportsman Society

tournaments, an accomplishment that the outdoor press has ranked with Joe DiMaggio's 56-game hitting streak and the Miami Dolphins' perfect 17-0 season in 1971. I don't know about that, but I believe it is a record that won't soon be equaled.

The thought of being able to outdistance the nation's top pros in three consecutive contests was unimaginable to many—until it occurred. The streak started with 48 pounds of Lake Okeechobee bass. I followed that with a whopping 84 pounds of Toledo Bend largemouths and 43 pounds from Lake Eufaula.

I was definitely on a roll and extremely efficient during that stretch. But if you ask me to cite a common denominator between the three victories, I would single out my skill as a jig fisherman.

Jigs are my favorite bait for most lakes in this country and I'll tell you why. I've probably had more success with that lure as anything I've ever fished. It played a significant role in my three straight wins. The last four tournaments I've won came on a combination of baits and the jig-and-pig played a big role in each.

That's quite a statement of confidence in a specific lure, particularly considering that I have collected almost $300,000 in B.A.S.S. winnings and won sixteen tournaments and nine Angler of the Year awards in the process.

Jigs can be effective at any time of year.

From my experience with the rubber-skirted lead-headed lures in lakes and rivers all over America, I have come to consider the jig— particularly the jig-and-pig combination—to be the best big-bass bait of all in a wide variety of conditions. I believe the ability of the jig to produce large bass can be attributed to the fact that it resembles one of the bass' favorite food sources—crawfish. And a major reason why jigs are effective in radically different waters in all parts of the country stems from the fact that crawfish are a prevalent food source throughout America.

It is such a great big-bass lure because it simulates a crawfish better than any lure known to man. There's no question that the basic size and shape of a jig and the way it moves and hops emulates a crawfish more than anything else. The addition of a pork chunk makes it look even more like a crawfish.

Crawfish are a big source of protein for bass everywhere. Some southern lakes, particularly the rocky lakes, like Truman Reservoir and Lake of the Ozarks, and others like Toledo Bend have a lot of crawfish and, therefore, they are better jig lakes than others. For example, Florida has some lakes that aren't as good for jigs as they are for plastic worms because the basic make-up of the lakes are different from the rocky southern reservoirs and they have fewer crawfish. But Okeechobee sure fooled me.

Despite living on massive Lake Okeechobee in southern Florida for the past six years, I rarely tied on a jig. That all changed when Kentuckian Corbin Dyer used a jig-and-pig to catch 31 pounds (one of the largest seven-fish stringers in B.A.S.S. history) on the final round of the 1985 BASS Master Florida Invitational to come from nowhere to finish third. That opened the minds of many Floridians and others to the productivity of the lure in these shallow, weed-laden lakes.

I should have realized the power of a jig on Okeechobee bass long before Dyer's heroics. Years earlier, Californian Dave Gliebe introduced Floridians to the art of flipping by winning a national tournament on Okeechobee with an amazing 96 pounds—on a jig-and-worm combination. The second-place finisher had more than 60 pounds, a guy named Roland Martin.

The value of fishing a jig on Okeechobee doesn't escape me anymore. I've come to the conclusion that if you want to catch a big fish, use a big jig—anywhere.

In the last few years jig-makers have gone wild with colors, manufacturing every hue and color-combination under the rainbow (or Color C-Lector). As a result, the average jig angler is faced with deciding between as many skirt colors as a spinnerbait fisherman. But I have a simple system for selecting jig color.

The simplest way to choose color is to match the hatch. I use color combinations involving only four colors—brown, black, red and blue. All are colors that are found on crawfish during different times of the year in different parts of the country. There are probably more than 100 different species of crawfish and I think almost every lake has a slightly different coloration to its crawfish, so take the time to examine the crawfish and try to match your jig color to it.

The most productive color combination for me over the years has been brown and black. I team either a black jig with a brown pork chunk or vice versa.

Jig fishermen have adapted a variety of trailers for their use, including pork eels, plastic worms of various types, grubs and frogleg-like plastic extensions. For 90 percent of my jig fishing though, I rely solely on a jig teamed with a No. 11 Uncle Josh pork chunk, the combination that best resembles a crawfish.

But don't rule out a jig-and-worm combination. I still use a jig-and-worm or a jig with a Mr. Twister Twin Tail as a trailer sometimes when flipping isn't my main pattern that day.

Let me explain that. If you're fishing a hot day or you're running down the lake, the pork chunk can dry out very easily if flipping isn't your primary pattern. What I mean by that is you may stop first at a crankbait point. Then you might run to a surface-plug spot. Finally, five miles down the lake, you might see a tree that's fallen over in the water, which you decide to flip. By that time, your pork chunk has dried into nothing but a hard mass. So if you're just casually flipping, it might be best to have something like a worm or Twin Tail tied on as a trailer. Then, when you pull up to that tree, you're ready to go.

Jig fishing is most effective in water temperatures less than 60 degrees. Over the year, most of my big bass hit a jig in water between 45 and 35 degrees. Generally speaking, that makes a jig most effective in the winter and early spring for catching sheer numbers of bass, while a plastic worm is a better choice for late spring, summer and fall. But don't abandon the jig in the hot portions of the year if you're after big bass.

For many years, I thought jigs were just not a good summer bait, so I would automatically use worms once the water got over 60 degrees. But I conducted a pretty extensive experiment in 1980 that convinced me that jigs are a good big-bass lure in the summer, too.

I knew that Dave Gliebe and (fellow Californian and flipping pioneer) Dee Thomas had really done well flipping jigs most of the year, so rather than switch to worms when the weather got warm, I decided to stick with a jig-and-pork rind combination to see what would happen. That summer, I fished jigs in water with 90- and 95-degree temperatures all through Oklahoma and Texas and the tournament stops on the east coast. I fished it in every kind of condition.

I carefully documented everything and I found that I caught a lot fewer fish than I had on a worm. I had probably caught twice as many bass, on a plastic worm. But the fish I caught that summer on a jig-and-pig maintained a 4-pound average. A 4-pound average is fantastic. That proved to me that the jig is an excellent big-bass bait throughout the year.

Although my favorite size is a ¾-ounce jig, I advise anglers to match the lure size with the type of cover (and, to a lesser degree, water depth) they are fishing. The ¾-ounce jig is ideal for shallow-water situations like fishing a tree top or stump field because it falls at a tantalizingly slow speed. But thick cover like bulrushes, milfoil, hyacinths and hydrilla usually form an impenetrable barrier for jigs of that size. So I will usually switch to a ⅝-or 1-ounce jig—whatever size it takes to puncture such cover.

And I concentrate my jig attacks in some of the toughest cover imaginable, while avoiding open-water situations.

I never throw a jig in something that it can't bump through. When I'm fishing a jig, basically, I'm throwing it over things and through things.

Unless I can feel it pull up over a limb or pull up on a rock—actually be in contact with the cover—I don't feel like I'm fishing the jig in the manner that would be most productive. I've found a jig is most effective when you bump it into the cover or slowly pull it over a tree limb and, at the last moment, shake it over the top and let it flutter down the other side. As soon as I see it sink, I really concentrate hard because that's when bass will often hit it. So it's important to be a line-watcher when fishing jigs.

It was during my winning streak in 1980-81 that I developed a three-pronged attack for jig fishing that involves three distinctly different methods of getting the lure to the fish.

My most common method was the conventional California-born flipping technique that allows you to quietly and accurately present the lure to bass in heavy cover. The technique involves stripping off line from reel with one hand and using a pendulum motion to propel the jig just above the surface of the water before dropping it into the desired location.

It was during my tournament victory on famed Toledo Bend in 1980 that I developed my "flip-cast," a method of flipping long-distance that has paid major dividends for me since its invention.

It was a spring tournament and I was fishing water so clear that I could actually see the fish spook every time I got close enough to flip a big stump or tree.

I tried to flip these places the conventional way from a farther distance away, but the best I could get was a flip of 25 or 26 feet. Even at that distance, I was scaring the fish.

I couldn't cast to it because there was no way that a regular casting rod could handle these big fish in this heavy, heavy cover. So I had to use my flipping stick and that's when I developed my flip cast. The flip cast is a very simple cast. You simply let out enough line to match the length of your 7 ½-foot rod. You then grasp the jig in your left hand (assuming you are right-handed). Now, as I make an underhanded motion by swinging the rod upward sharply, I take the jig and both aim and propel it with my left hand like I was bowling. By using your left hand, you can get another 10 or 15 feet more than conventional flipping. That gives you a cast of 35 to 40 feet that is very accurate and still has a quiet lure presentation.

But even with the ability to flip-cast 40 feet, I found there were times when a fish would break the surface off in the distance and I had no way to present

As the lure arrives at the target, bring your left hand back to the reel and you are immediately on point in case a fish nails the lure as it hits the water.

my jig to it. Or I was unable to fish a solitary piece of timber away from the line of stick-ups I was flipping without taking the time to motor over to it.

It was then that I realized the potential value of being able to cast jigs on heavy tackle like flipping sticks.

It takes practice to develop a feel for using the big rods to make long casts, but the versatility this particular skill provides is well worth the effort to learn it. Not only can you make a long cast and cover more water, but you will also have the good hook-setting ability that a stout flipping stick gives you.

6. The Big Bass Willow-Leaf Spinnerbait

In 1985, the willow-leaf spinnerbait craze hit this country with a force never before seen in the fishing industry.

When *Bassmaster Magazine* unveiled the so-called Secret Bait of the Pros, it captured the imagination of America's bass fishermen. Here was an unusual big-bass lure that was dominating the national tournament scene, a bait that the pros guarded zealously, but finally the secret was out.

Bass anglers stormed their tackle stores in search of this magic lure, while the nation's manufacturers scrambled to respond to this sudden upsurge in interest. Only a few manufacturers, like Blue Fox, were ready when the flood-gates of enthusiasm broke loose.

The flip cast is a very simple cast. You simply let out enough line to match the length of your 7½-foot rod. You then grasp the jig in your left hand (assuming you are right-handed).

Now, as I make an underhanded motion by swinging the rod upward sharply, I take the jig and both aim and propel it with my left hand like I was bowling. By using your left hand, you can get another 10 or 15 feet more than conventional flipping.

This 8-pounder hit a No. 5-bladed willow-leaf spinnerbait as it fluttered down into a 6-foot deep hole in the hydrilla on Lake Okeechobee.

I'm a big believer in flash points. And with all of the experimenting I've done with the willow-leaf, Colorado and Indiana-style blades, I've carefully examined the flash points of each. And the willow-leaf blades just have a larger and brighter flash point than the more oval-shaped blades. Just look at the size of a No. 5 willow-leaf blade compared to a No. 5 Colorado. The surface area of the blade that gives off the sun's reflection is a heck of a lot bigger.

And with the big willow-leaf blades, like a No. 7, it would take the biggest Colorado blade in the world to match it.

Besides the size, the shape creates a different flash point. A Colorado-style blade condenses the flash of the blade to a smaller area because it is a wider piece of metal than a willow-leaf blade. But a willow-leaf blade spreads the flash out more because it is longer. And that's important.

What that longer flash creates as the blade is shining and rotating through the water is a hologram that more resembles the natural body shape of baitfish. And that is important. For the first time, a spinnerbait—the one lure that doesn't resemble anything a bass would eat upon close inspection—has a long shape that a fish could mistake for a shad.

Besides the superior vibration that a willow-leaf bladed spinnerbait emits as it's pulled through the water, that hologram effect is the secret to its fish-catching power. My good friend Cliff Shelby, an executive with Ranger Boats and an excellent bass fisherman from Arkansas, believes in the value of adjusting the size of that hologram by adjusting the size of the willow-leaf used as the shad grow bigger and bigger throughout the year.

With Blue Fox's Roland Martin Big Bass Spinnerbait series, I have developed three sizes of willow-leaf bladed lures to handle all fishing situations: No. 7 blade on a ½-ounce lead head; No. 5 blade on a ⅜-ounce body; and a No. 3 blade on a ¼-ounce body.

By understanding the applications for each size, you can greatly improve your catch rate. You will have much greater success than you will if you stick with throwing the biggest willow-leaf bladed spinnerbait available.

The No. 7 bladed spinnerbait has a definite, but limited application. It is not a real pleasant bait to fish. You have to use heavy tackle and it doesn't cast or retrieve very easily. People are really going to be dismayed by the performance of the No. 7 bladed spinnerbait if that's all they use throughout the year.

The No. 7 blade is effective in parts of the South where you can slow-roll it through milfoil and other grasses. On Lake Okeechobee, I put it on 30-pound line and it produces some big bass from the thick vegetation. It's a good grass bait for big bass, but you will not catch very many fish with it, because its size automatically eliminates some bass.

But the No. 7 bladed willow-leaf spinnerbait has some excellent applications for musky and pike in the North. I think it is of more value to the musky and pike fishermen than it is to bass anglers. Although I have caught 5-pound smallmouths in Canada on it, I was amazed at its ability to produce big pike and musky. And it is one of the few spinnerbaits with the body strength capable of handling big pike and musky.

This lure could prove to be the pike and musky enthusiast's ace in the hole.

But I use the No. 7 bladed spinnerbait selectively and seldom these days for bass.

The spinnerbait I use the most is the No. 5 Roland Martin Big Bass Spinnerbait, which is the best and most versatile all-around size.

The No. 5 casts and performs better than any size I've used. And it produces more big bass—4 pounds and up—than any other size of willow-leaf blade. And believe me, you may not be hearing about it, but quite a few national tournaments have been won recently on that No. 5 blade.

It casts like a bullet and is so much easier to fish than that big No. 7. The willow-leaf bladed spinnerbait seems to be most effective when it is slowly rolled over logs and through grass and the No. 5 bladed lure is the easiest to control in all types of cover. It is extremely weedless.

I haven't found a type of cover or structure that is immune to the No. 5 bladed spinnerbait. I will fish it in open water in a clear-water western lake like Lake Mead. I will bounce it off of boulders and standing timber. I will buzz the top of submerged grassbeds and then run it through the vegetation. It's a great lure for working boat docks. I often work it as a drop bait in cover like lily pad fields.

The No. 5 bladed spinnerbait has a good feel to it, which is important with spinnerbait fishing. You need to keep in good contact with your lure so that you know when you have bumped a log or have been bumped by a half-interested fish. That No. 5 blade resists your pull enough so that you can retrieve it with a tight line and still drop it deep. You have more control over it, which allows you to fish it more effectively. You can feel it as you pull it over a submerged tree limb and know exactly when to let it sink.

With so many spinnerbaits, once you cast it out, you just don't feel anything. With this No. 5 blade, you can really feel just how deep it is and how it's working. You can tell whether it's got grass on the blade, whether the blade is rotating properly. With a blade with good vibration, if you feel it missing a beat, you know that you have either hit a piece of grass or a bass has kind of half-struck at it.

This is one of the most responsive spinnerbaits you'll ever use.

If you're interested in numbers more than size, No. 3 Roland Martin big bass spinnerbait is the lure for you. If the sheer fun of catching fish more important than fishing all day for a single trophy bass, you'll really enjoy the No. 3 blade spinnerbait.

The No. 3 willow leaf spinnerbait is geared more for catching a lot of small fish. I've caught big bass on it—including a 3 pounder while filming a television show in 1987—but in general, that is the size lure that a 1½-pound bass will hit. If you run that No. 3 blade spinnerbait in front of a 1½-pound bass, he will go nuts over it. If you run a No. 5 spinnerbait by a 1½-pound bass and he's really hungry, he might hit it. Otherwise you would probably scare him off.

You will catch more bass on that No. 3 bladed spinnerbait than any size willow-leaf blade made. There's no question in my mind about that.

And it is a very versatile bait. I enjoy fishing it in clear-water situations on 12- to 14-pound line in relatively open water. It's an excellent bait for skimming it across the top of deep-water grass and then allowing it to sink as it reaches the edge of the grass. Or you can run it through thick grass.

It is a tremendous smallmouth bass lure as well.

In the spring of 1986, on Lake Ontario, we found that smallmouths go crazy over this little spinnerbait. We were catching 3- and 4-pound smallmouths consistently on it. It is as good a smallmouth bass bait as I've ever used.

When choosing the color of skirt and blade to use, I use a single criteria—water clarity.

As far as I'm concerned, there are only two skirt colors—white and chartreuse. I've fished every color known to man, but my consistent success has always come on those two colors. That doesn't mean that other colors won't produce fish, however. I probably should be more open-minded about spinnerbait colors, but success tends to make you a little complacent.

In clear water, I use mainly a white skirt and a nickel blade. That is a visible combination that a fish can often see from 35 feet away.

In the dark, off-colored water, I've had good success with chartreuse skirts and a copper or gold blade. In muddy water, I like a chartreuse skirt and copper blade combination.

The willow-leaf bladed spinnerbait has received more publicity than any other lure in recent years. It is not a magic lure. But if you will learn to fish all different sizes of the blades in a variety of situations, you will become a much more productive fisherman.

7. Slow-Rolling the Stickups

Stickups are one of my most productive patterns, and one reason is that most new lakes have stickups. I try to travel the country and fish as many of the new, productive lakes as I can—lakes which are five or six years old. I'm talking about hundreds and hundreds of different reservoirs in the south, the midwest, and even in the north. If you hit them after five to seven years, you'll find there are still a lot of stickups. This is secondary growth. After the timber was cleared, a lot of stickups grew during the first couple of years before the impoundment finally filled up. Quite often these stickups hold a lot of bass, and the spinnerbait is one of the fastest ways to catch 'em. You cover a lot of water making thousands of casts. Look for stickups along the shorelines.

This sounds really crazy, but a good, solid pattern is slow-rolling the stickups. What I do is throw past the stickup and then bump the stickup with the spinnerbait. As soon as it comes over the top of it, I drop it down with just a little bit of tension to the shady side of the stickup and just roll it over the limbs. Most of the time this gets their attention—the fact that it's bumping the stickups and limbs. As it rolls down to them in the

shadows, that's when they hit it. Bass have no eyelids, so most of the time they seek deep water in most reservoirs. But because of the heavy stickups that provide a lot of cover, even in the summertime the fish will be in 2 to 4 feet of water and often hiding beneath the dense, shadiest part of the stickup. Particularly in a new lake where there are simply a lot of bass, these fish are right in the shade. You've got to drop the lure right on top of them. And the strike is a reflex action. The lure's coming right into their territory—right into the space they're occupying. It doesn't work to cast by the stickup and retrieve it past the bass; you have to really bump through the limbs and drop it on top of the fish. That's the kind of retrieve which pays off.

All my deeper-water spinnerbait fishing is done with a single blade, because I can feel the blade rotate—particularly a No. 4 or 5 blade—if I'm using a good sensitive line like Stren. I put just enough back pressure on that spinnerbait with a No. 4 or 5 blade to feel the little thump, thump, thump as it's sinking. If you use two blades, you won't feel that thump because the two blades counteract each other. Anytime I'm dropping a spinnerbait deep, such as with the slow-roll stickup technique, I'm fishing the single blade on a long wire. I like the long arm for the weedless effect, and also the long wire gives me a flash point well back by the jig, so when they attack the jig or the flash point, they've got the hook.

There are a couple of patterns which are very important about slow-rolling. A bass can position himself in the shade of even a 1-inch-diameter stickup. It's not much cover, but he can angle himself so that the inch of shade falls over both his eyes. It's all the shade the fish needs on a hot summer day. Some of the best structure to look for during the feeding season in summer is the deepwater points on the main lake. During the hotter weather, the more extreme or more exposed points are best. Again, in the spring or pre-spawn season, the highly protected coves are usually best. Water temperatures which work best for this are in the 55-degree range. The water is fairly clear, and they start hitting spinnerbaits. If the water is a little dingier, they start hitting best in the 60-degree range. I continually monitor the water temperature; I leave a surface temp gauge turned on all day, and I also have a hand thermometer that I check at least five or six times during the day just to see if my surface temp gauge is working properly. I'm looking for the sections with the warmest water—usually the north pockets—in the spring, and in the summer it's usually the other way around. Then I'm looking for cooler water. The coves are usually warmer than the main lake. The optimum temperature is 72 degrees. When bass are at 72 degrees, they're at the maximum peak period of their feeding. They're going to leave 80-degree water to go to 72, and they're going to leave 65-degree water to go to 72, so you get 'em both ways.

One factor about spinnerbait fishing is the sun, and the reason stickups are so good is that sunny days concentrate the bass. They might have been roaming around in shallow water which has only one stickup every 50 feet, but when the sun comes out strong, they're going to go to areas with shade. With cloud cover, bass are going to spread out all over; you might catch a lot of fish then, but you're not going to catch them particularly in the stickups.

Wind also is an important factor. Bass cannot swim backward, and they're going to face the wind. Regardless if it's a stump, a rock, or a stickup, a bass will be in the shade facing the wind, because the wind creates a slight current. It's important to remember they're going to be facing the wind as well as being in that shade. To get the typical reflex strike, throw into the wind and retrieve downwind downsun, and as soon as you reach the stickup, he's going to be right behind it in the shade facing the current. Drop the bait right on top of the fish as close as you can to where you think his eyes are.

I like to play a little game by conjuring up an image of at least an 8-pound bass. Thinking big is fun, and it really is effective. Be optimistic and look at that stickup; there might be a hundred of 'em, but look at the one you're going to throw to and conjure up an image of a truly big fish—something you want to catch. It really instills confidence and keeps your enthusiasm going. Much of the enjoyment and pleasure of fishing is nothing more than to anticipate what's going to happen on the very next cast. Figure all the factors and drop that spinnerbait right on his eyeball and you'll catch him. He might not be 8 pounds; in reality he's probably 2, but the point is you've figured out where he is and had fun doing this anticipation bit with that fish.

What I use for most stickups is a ¼-ounce bait. I don't want it to drop very fast, and it makes a softer splash than a heavier spinnerbait would make. I'm throwing past the stickup, but when I come over the top of it and let the bait roll through the limbs, the ¼-ounce spinner bounces through there pretty good. I usually use all kinds of tails. I might use a plastic minnow body, a skirt, a worm trailer, or a piece of pork rind. There are all kinds of possible different combinations and variations you can experiment with. I have usually at least a No. 4 blade and sometimes a No. 5. Nickel and gold are my standard colors, but in very muddy water I might go to red, chartreuse, or bright orange.

I always throw either crosswind or slightly upwind with heavy tackle. The strike is nothing more than a tick when it's dropping through there; it's just a small tick, and in hot weather sometimes you don't even feel the tick. They sometimes overtake it, and all you see is the line moving to the right or left or toward you. And at other times in hot weather you'll feel the strike. The shady side is the key to stickup fishing, but I use Stren fluorescent line, and I can see what's going on even if the water's dingy. I watch for any side movement, because sometimes half the fish which hit you will hardly feel. You'll just see that line start to move maybe 3 to 6 inches to the side. If that happens just the slightest bit, the lure might be falling down a limb, but go ahead and set the hook anyhow. You'll get hung up a few times, but it'll be worth the effort. If the bass grabs the spinnerbait for more than four or five seconds and chews on it much, he's going to spit it out unless you set the hook quickly. By keeping a little back pressure on the lure you can tell what's happening.

You need heavy tackle unless you're in ultra-clear water which is fairly open except for a few isolated stickups. For the latter you can get by with light tackle and can throw 6-, 8-, or 10-pound line as long as you drop the spinnerbait on the close side of the stickup and there are no other stickups between you and the lure. In a lake like Santee-Cooper (which actually is two lakes—Marion and Moultrie) or Lake Seminole or some weedy lake in Texas, there are likely ten more stickups between you and where you dropped the bait, and you might not see any of them. In waters like this I favor at least 17-pound line. Sometimes under these conditions I've gone to 20-pound or 25-pound line with a 5½-foot stiff casting rod.

I do almost 99 percent of my heavy spinnerbait fishing with heavy casting tackle. I usually have my drag adjusted pretty tight in this kind of cover, because the object is to pull 'em upward and get 'em up to the top of the water if you're fishing 4 or 5 feet deep. I might have 30 feet of line out, so I can have a tight drag and yet the line will stretch. When I get one on top and he starts jumping or splashing, that's good because he's now away from the deep limbs and won't

snag the line. As soon as I get him right up to the boat, I loosen the drag. I constantly back my drag off a little bit on a real hot fish, because it's been only seconds since he was hooked, and he's lively and fighting every which direction. If you try to horse him into the boat, this is where you're apt to lose your fish. When you have a hot green bass, even though there might be stickups underneath the boat, you've almost invariably got to back off on your drag and give him some line if he's over 5 pounds.

Don't stop him at the boat, because it's too much of a shock even with 20-pound line. A 5-pound bass can break 20-pound line if you try to horse him into the boat within three or four seconds after he struck. Play him around the boat a little bit and keep him on top, but give him enough line if he wants to run. Let him run on top, and generally he'll tire after 10 to 15 seconds. Slide him into the net. If you want to play with him, play with him when he's in the boat.

8. Prodding the Weedlines

One of my favorite patterns is prodding the weedlines. These aren't weeds that you see; they're weedlines which often are out of sight.

Most newer lakes have stickups, and getting right in there where you can drop a spinnerbait on the fish is one good way to work such a pattern.

Back in 1971 when I was doing promotional work for Lowrance Electronics, Carl Lowrance told me to go out to Virginia because we wanted to sell a bunch of locators out there and it's a good section of the country. Mary Ann and I went to Smith Mountain Lake in Central Virginia. We got there on Sunday, and we met Bob Mayes, who was a Lowrance representative at the time and is a good fisherman from Roanoke. He had a trip lined up for us at Smith Mountain, and Roanoke newspaper outdoor writer Bill Cochran, and Tom Sutton, who is a draftsman and makes lake maps throughout the southeast, went along too. The five of us went out in two different boats. We caught about ten bass, including a 4-pounder, that day.

Sutton, Mayes, and I went back there early Monday morning, and we had a time limit. We had a store promotion that night, and a local TV station had called and said that if I could meet them at the store at noon, they would interview me and have the interview on the evening sports.

We got started fishing at eight a.m., and an idea hit me. I suggested we try a "nothing bank" and explained that sometimes in tournaments I pick the crummiest, worst-looking spot I can find, with my thinking being that every other fisherman thinks the same way and consequently the place never gets fished. There was a crummy-looking spot across from the boat ramp. It was adjacent to a farmer's field, sloping grass with nothing but solid grass coming into the water.

We went over there and worked back into a pocket and never got a strike. I started the big engine and looked at the locator. It showed a big line of weeds almost to the surface, although the water was about 5 feet deep. I shut the motor off and we drifted out to where the solid weeds quit and the water was 6 to 7 feet deep with a bare clay bottom on out. I threw back over the boat wake with a chartreuse Zorro spinnerbait and let it tick along the grass until I didn't feel anything, and I let it drop down. A good bass of about 3 ½ pounds stopped it. We were about 50 yards off the bank, and I grabbed a marker buoy and threw it to the edge of

the weedline. I circled around with the trolling motor and located the edge of the weeds again and threw out another marker.

Bob Mayes caught the next bass—about a 6-pounder—by throwing his spinnerbait right on top of the weeds and pulling it to the edge and then letting it settle to the bottom. Then he pumped the bait upward. The bass were right on the lip of the weeds about 3 feet deep, and they weren't difficult to catch. With the aid of the locator, we found a 100-to-150-yard stretch of weeds. They were the only weeds on this nothing bank and probably the only ones within five miles of where we were. We were right across from the ramp, and we hadn't burned a half gallon of gas.

We started nailing the bass. Sutton caught a couple around 5 pounds, and Bob caught his biggest bass ever in Virginia—an 8 ¼-pounder. I caught a few in the 5-to-7-pound range. We kept seventeen largemouths and put them in the live well. We hurried back to Roanoke and got there just in time for the television interview. They filmed our fish. We weighed the biggest ten and they totaled 55 pounds.

The film ran on the sports show following the six-o'clock news, and we had the biggest ten in a 40-gallon tub full of ice and water. Most of the bass had died, but a few still had their gills moving. Shortly after the news, we started hearing tires screeching in the parking lot, and a couple of red-faced fishermen rushed in and started questioning us. We convinced the first fifty people who came in the store that we actually had caught those bass that morning and what they had seen on TV was an interview conducted as soon as we got back to town.

There was a gross of Zorro spinnerbaits in the store, and they were all sold by seven-thirty p.m. They had about twenty-five fish locators, and we sold them and took orders for eleven more by the time the evening was over. Sutton sold several of his maps on Smith Mountain, and he marked all the areas we'd fished.

Every year I go to probably thirty different store promotions, but never have I seen a more enthusiastic crowd than those 500 to 600 people who came in the store that evening following the TV interview. Smith Mountain is not known for its big largemouths, and 5-to-8-pounders make news in Roanoke.

I had merely found a good shallow weedline, and we had worked the edge.

I grew up in Maryland near a few lakes with weeds, but this was before I fished spinnerbaits. During the past ten years, I've fished a lot in Minnesota, Michigan, Wisconsin, and all through the northern-tier states. In many of the natural lakes there, you'll find a lot of weedlines. With Al Lindner one time in Wisconsin, we hit a lake in late April, and the bass were on the weedlines. Toledo Bend has a lot of weeds, but often the weeds aren't visible, and early in the spring to find bass in the pre-spawn season you have to rely on your "underwater eyes"—a fish locator. Santee has some deep weedlines, and they're hard to see in the early spring before they really start to grow up good. Some sections of the upper lake in the Jack's Creek area have deep underwater weeds. Right on the weedline is the first area where the bass move into from deep water, and they hold on this structure until it's really warm enough for them to go in to spawn. The most productive depth depends on water clarity. In real clear waters of the north, the weedlines might be 15 feet deep. At Minnetonka in Minnesota in the spring we caught a lot of bass on both spinnerbaits and plastic worms in Jason Lucas' favorite lake, so it was a memorable experience for me.

If you go to a shallow, dingy lake such as Lake Seminole in Georgia, the weedlines might grow out to 6 feet deep. At Toledo Bend you're apt to find the weedlines growing no more than 7 feet deep. The type of lure I use here is a ⅜-ounce spinnerbait. It's kind of an intermediate depth, and since I'm working the edge of the weeds, I'm not concerned with the shallow water, only 2 to 3 feet deep. I really want to fish that part right on the edge, dropping the bait down. Some TVA lakes, mainly Pickwick and Guntersville, have a lot of milfoil, and milfoil is common in lakes even in Texas and Oklahoma. But in the spring when the water temperature

A bass caught in shallow water over a weedline can have lots of energy—always a thrill.

is still cold, it's recessed and is not growing right to the top. These milfoil weedlines are extremely productive with ½-ounce spinnerbaits.

The long-wire spinnerbait is needed to keep the lure from getting snagged up. Often in the weeds you can put on a trailer hook. This works good because you don't have much to hang up. If the trailer snatches some of the milfoil or elodea, snatch the bait just as hard as you can and often you will break the weed off the trailer hook. But you need at least 14-pound line. Actually, 17-pound is excellent for this because it doesn't stretch much.

The kind of structure I fish is adjacent to the spawning coves during pre-spawn conditions in the spring when the water is a little dingy. The irony of it is that most lakes with weeds normally are very clear. Many clear lakes aren't good spinnerbait lakes, but in the early spring before it really gets warm, a lot of rain and wind might give the water more color. The weeds have not grown up and they're still deep. Then you can get by with heavier lines. Figure the weedlines as a ledge, and if the sun is shining, it's forming a shadow on the ledge.

In the spring I like to find small, irregular features in the weedline; it isn't always straight and might have a little point or pocket. If the wind is blowing in, the bass are facing that wind, and they'll be on the current side of the grass. If there's a pocket, the pocket has two points—one on each side of the weedline. The point facing the wind usually is the best pocket. Pockets and points produce fish particularly when the wind blows.

The technique of retrieving the spinnerbait is important, but determining just how far out the weedline is is something you need to do before you even fish. Start zigzagging the weedline with your boat running if you're looking for a weedline in 7 to 10 or more feet of water. You might be able to approximate how far out it is from what you can see, but marker buoys and your electronic locator are the best way. I take four markers and try to cover 50 to 60 yards at a time. When I line all my markers up, I now have a reference point, and then I idle along the edge of those markers with the big motor or the trolling motor. Sometimes I can see the irregular parts of it, such as a point I didn't know was there.

For weedlines in 1 to 4 feet of water in the shallower lakes, you need to drift over them or perhaps use your trolling motor. Once you've got a couple of markers out or at least some reference where you can throw, the technique is to parallel-cast into the wind on the shady side and try to tick the weedline as I mentioned doing at Smith Mountain. When you quit feeling the tick, drop the spinnerbait and watch your line and keep a slight bit of back pressure on the lure. It's just as you do in stickup fishing. The strikes are not vicious, particularly from pre-spawners; they'll just stop it. Some of the biggest bass in the lake are on the edges of the grass line.

Florida is a perfect place for spinnerbait fishing in the spring. When the water's 55 degrees, you can catch a 12-pound or 13-pound largemouth in Florida in the eel-grass areas of Lake George, all through Rodman Reservoir and in Lake Kissimmee. The possibilities here are fantastic. There are not only exposed weeds, but some waters have underwater weeds. Lake Jackson has a lot of clear water, and a lot of weeds are 10 to 11 feet deep before they form the weedline. Weedlines are the key

to some trophy bass just before they spawn, and this is true from California to Connecticut. Any weeds will do.

9. Ticking the Logs

When I think of the lying-log pattern, I immediately think of Jeff Green, a former guide at Toledo Bend. He now lives in central Texas; he used to be from Tulsa. When I'd go down there for tournaments in the early 1970s, I'd look up Jeff and ask him what the fish were doing. He'd invariably tell me it didn't make any difference where I fished in the early spring, the pattern to look for was a log lying out in the water. It could be in 2 feet or 20 feet, but it offered shade, and he'd say just cast a spinnerbait out there and run it down the shady side of that log.

Since Jeff told me about that pattern, I've tried it, and it really does work. Another good friend of mine from Oklahoma is Jimmy Houston, and lying logs are one of his favorite patterns. Jimmy's one of the finest spinnerbait fishermen in the country. He designed the Red Man spinnerbait, and he won the B.A.S.S. tournament at Santee-Cooper in 1976 by fishing stickups and lying logs—always the shady sides. He and Jeff Green used to fish a lot together in Oklahoma.

Fishing the shady sides of lying logs sounds easy, but there's more to it than meets the eye. Lots of fishermen don't consider boat position, and this is critical. You need to cast your spinnerbait within 2 or 3 inches of the log and retrieve it from 1 to 4 inches deep along the entire length of the log. You simply must have perfect boat position to fish the entire length of a 60-foot log. Remember, too, with the reflex strike you get with a spinnerbait, the first cast is the most important cast. When you see a log, don't just cast at it, because if the lure doesn't come right past the bass, he doesn't get a chance to hit it out of reflex action. Then he's alerted; he's heard that spinnerbait go by; he's going to be leery and hard to catch. The average fisherman who comes up to a log—and it's apt to be lying in most any direction—simply throws at the log and bounces his bait over it. That's not the way to fish a lying log. That first cast has to be right down the log. If it takes you 20 seconds to get lined up properly on the log, then it does. But don't make that first cast until you're positioned right.

Bass get beneath these lying logs because they're some of the only horizontal cover they have. Logs frequently lodge against the shoreline, and as they stick out in the lake, the opposite end might be in over 10 or 15 feet of water. Along such a log bass can travel from a foot of water next to the bank to 15 feet of water in the shade as they search for baitfish. The logs offer horizontal movement to the fish, and this horizontal movement is not found in standing trees. The little bit of shade behind the standing timber is only in that one spot, and the same applies to a stickup. But with a lying log they might have from 40 to 60 feet of running room, and with all this latitude, a lying log in timber is better than the timber itself. A lying log on a regular shoreline with no timber is better than a lying log in timber. The more isolated the log, the better its potential.

Jimmy Houston placed high in a tournament at Ross Barnett Reservoir in Mississippi, and he did this by running to every lying log on the west side of the lake and fishing only the shady sides. That west side of Barnett must have only twenty to thirty lying logs, but he'd run from log to log, and most of those logs had one bass apiece beneath them. Lying logs are not school-bass situations, but it's a fast pattern where you can run up to the log, drop your trolling motor, get into position, and make one to three casts and leave and look for the next log. This is pattern fishing supreme!

The larger logs are better because they obviously provide more shade. Logs are enhanced if they're near a point, a creek channel, or any deep water. The best lying-log pattern usually is in the spring when the water tends to be a little dingy and on the

cool side, such as in the 50s. But if the lake's very muddy, spinnerbaits are productive in 80-to-90-degree water temperatures, and lying logs are apt to pay off good then, too. A light spinnerbait with a fairly small blade is good for lying logs because the bait moves fairly slowly, and also a heavier spinnerbait, such as a ⅜-ounce with a No. 4 to 6 blade, is good because the resistance slows it down and permits it to travel 2 to 4 inches deep.

Most of the time with the lying-log pattern, you can watch your lure and never lose eye contact with it, because it's traveling barely beneath the surface. Always use a trailer hook, because there are virtually no limbs to hang on, and if you make an accurate cast, you'll seldom get hung up. Sunny days are good on the lying logs because the sun concentrates the fish. On cloudy, overcast days they don't need to go beneath the logs for shade.

A maze of logs lying in many different directions is not good for this type of pattern because the bass could be beneath any of the logs and that first cast likely will spook them. The spinnerbait is good for fishing single logs at a time. The best logs almost always are lodged into timber or against the shoreline. Free-floating logs

A lying log is a great pattern in early spring. The tricky part is positioning your boat so that you retrieve your bait along the entire length of the shady side of the log.

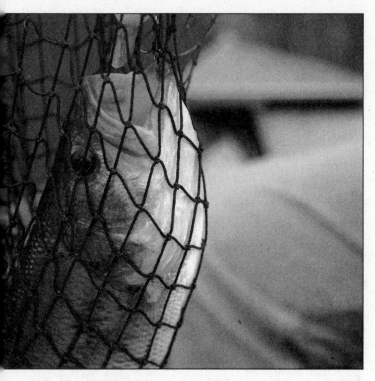

This bass hit a crankbait fished along a sunken log.

out in the lake do not pay off well. The logs need to be stationary, just as floating hyacinths do. I catch bass on hyacinths which are stationary but not on the ones drifting free in the lake.

Even in a lake which has been cleared of timber, a lying-log situation can develop because of high water in the spring. The high water might move logs off the shore. Not too long ago I was fishing for smallmouths on Rainy Lake across into Canada from Minnesota, and I was amazed at the logs in the lake. Masses of cut timber headed for paper mills are floated down the lake. I guess that in periods of rough water, these logs had drifted away from the logging operation. In the backs of a lot of pockets were logs. Some of them had sunk, but others were floating and sticking out along the rocky shoreline, and smallmouths would smack spinnerbaits and crank baits when the lures came past them. The fish were beneath the logs.

Most all lakes have fallen trees, and the pattern for fishing them is similar to the lying-log pattern. Position your boat so that the branches and forks in the limbs point toward you. Cast toward the base of the tree and retrieve toward the end of it. If the branches and forks are pointing toward you you'll have less risk of getting the lure snagged up. If there are a lot of branches and forks on the tree, you might be better off to remove the trailer hook on your spinnerbait to reduce hanging up. If there are several big limbs coming out from the tree, you need to make repeated casts to each of the limb areas. Also, you might need to move your boat around to the other side of the tree to get good shots at limbs on that side. Take it easy and slow. I use 17-to-25-pound line for this fishing, reserving the heavier line for dingy water. Particularly in fallen trees you have to get the fish to the top of the water and keep him on top to prevent him from tangling in the deeper limbs.

10. Bumping the Stumps

Regardless of where you are, today you're probably within a two- hour drive at the most from some decent bass fishing. The U.S. has 15 million acres of good bass water in reservoirs, natural lakes, and farm ponds. The natural lakes don't have many stumps, but many farm ponds, impoundments, and flowages have plenty. A plain simple truth in bass fishing is that you can catch a bass on a stump with a spinnerbait.

In the big southern impoundments, such as the TVA and the Army Corps of Engineers lakes, there are millions of stumps, particularly on the edges of the river channels. Bass will lie on these edges, but more specifically they lie on the stumps. At Pickwick Lake in Tennessee, they night-fish with spinnerbaits and catch smallmouths around stumps in 3 to 5 feet of water. At Santee-Cooper, they fish spinnerbaits in the stumps in the Pinopolis and Russellville areas. At Sidney Lanier, a deep, clear lake at the outskirts of metropolitan Atlanta, points might have two, three, or five stumps, but that's where the bass are in early spring. A knowledgeable bass fisherman who knows where the stumps are and can see stumps with Polaroid sunglasses really catches bass on spinnerbaits in the dingy waters in the spring and in the windswept waters in the fall when the current caused by the wind moves shad into these stumpy banks.

Bumping the stump is an excellent way to catch a bass. This is strictly a reflex-action strike. The fish is lying right next to the stump; it's his only cover and shade and protection perhaps within a 100-foot area. He's so close to the stump that his body likely is in contact with the lower section where the roots start to spread out. That stump is probably 18 inches to 3 feet high, and it gives him just enough depth to have shade.

That's the time to play the old game again and conjure up an 8-pounder image and picture him in the shade. Throw past the stump, make a wake with the spinnerbait, and when it gets to the stump, drop it and bump the stump and fall right on the bass. It really works!

At Santee I had a lot of experience with spinnerbaits in the stumps in the fall months when the water level was lower. In the spring the twin lakes were high, and there would be so much good shallow cover, such as button bushes, weeds, and lily pads, that I fished this cover and didn't mess much with the stumps. But when the lakes were pulled 3 feet in the fall and the best remaining cover in the 171,000 acres of water were stumps, that's where I put my spinnerbaits to good use.

The trick is first knowing exactly where the stumps are. You can fan-cast stumpy areas and bump the stump and catch 'em that way, but the best way is to spot the stump and keep visual contact with it. Most of the time when I fish I'm standing up. I seldom sit down, particularly in tournaments. This high location plus keeping the sun at my back when I'm looking for underwater cover helps me find the stumps. If you're looking in the water and the sun's back over your shoulder, you can see a little deeper and you can spot the stumps a little better.

You don't always have to bump the stump. You can buzz the spinnerbait over it as long as you get really close to the bass. You'll get the same kind of reflex strike. I like to make contact with the stump, but don't always drop the bait down. Sometimes I bump

the stump and keep running my bait, and they grab it. The long-arm spinnerbait is good for this kind of fishing, and I like a ¼-ounce bait because heavier ones get lodged more easily in the cracks at the top of the stump. You don't have to use extra-heavy line; I usually use 14 or 17.

Especially with autumn fishing, it really pays to study the wind. Often in southern reservoirs shad are blown into bays. In the fall, shad populations reach their peak, as many of them are winter-killed. Part of the fall pattern is to learn the direction of the prevailing winds. Study them for the previous week. If the wind's been blowing out of the south, it's been pushing a lot of shad slowly to the north coves. Then find north coves which have stumps, and fish them. If there's any deepwater structure, such as a good point with ten to fifteen stumps on it, imagine how many schools of shad are moved through there. It's a perfect ambush point for not only one bass, but a big school of them. Where the wind's blowing and pushing water in a shallow lake in the fall is the only condition I've seen fish break the surface to any extent.

I'm not talking about a big school of bass, but maybe two or three running two or three shad. This doesn't seem like much, but an alert fisherman will watch for this. At this time of the year the shad are 2 to 4 inches long and are mostly threadfin shad with a few gizzard shad mixed in. Anytime you see a couple of shad skipping on the top or a good boil on the surface, throw your spinnerbait at least 6 feet past the spot. Don't drop your lure on the boil, because you'll scare the bass, but throw it past where he was and run it 4 to 6 inches deep right through the spot. If he doesn't strike, let the bait fall to the bottom and bounce it a few times. Intermittent twitches and pauses have about the same effect as bumping the stump, because you're interrupting the rotation of the blade, and this gives the bass following it all the more reason to nail it right then.

A crank bait is good in deep stumps. If you're on a point in a fairly clear lake and you can see stumps 4 to 6 feet deep, this is a good place to throw a crank bait.

A spinnerbait, however, is much more shallow-running and snagless.

I won two major tournaments at Watts Bar Lake in Tennessee on spinnerbaits. One of the tourneys was in the spring, and I was fishing stumps and duck blinds in the upper end of the lake. The water wasn't more than 2 ½ feet deep, and I was buzzing the lure. I would move along for 100 yards and not see anything, but occasionally spot a dark stump. The water was very dingy, and the dark spots usually turned out to be stumps. I did the same basic thing as at Santee; I'd go into shallow bays and look for the dark spots. Then I'd drag the bait up to the stump and try to bump it. I moved the bait faster in the fall when the water was warmer and slower in the spring when it was cooler. In the fall when the water isn't quite as dingy, you can make a wake with the bait right under the surface. This is particularly good if the bass are busting shad, because the wake makes the bait look like a minnow skittering along on top.

A buzzing situation like that is a good time to use a tandem-bladed spinnerbait, but when I'm dropping the bait I like the single blade so I can feel it better. In 2 to 3 feet of water with stumps, a double blade is good because it has extra flash and might look more like a shad.

Stumps in deep water are excellent, but the problem is in finding them. They're extremely difficult to find. Some contour maps show you where the trees used to be and where the fields once were. If you can find where the trees used to be, you can expect to find the stumps.

On Kentucky Lake and Lake Barkley in Kentucky and Tennessee, a pattern exists which is similar in many man-made farm ponds. Shallow bays will have small creek channels which are only 3 or 4 feet deeper, but there'll be three to five times more stumps and trees along those creek channels than anywhere else. It's the same in man-made farm ponds, especially where a creek was dammed up to impound the water. The creek channel might be only 5 feet wide, but that's where the majority of the stumps will be. Since these creek channels often twist and turn, it really helps to watch your locator. You can, with the aid of the locator, stay directly over the creek channel and fan-cast around and feel the stumps and work your way all along the creek. On Lake Barkley, this is the best way to execute this pattern. When you find the stumps on the edge of the creek channel, you've done a double deal; you've got the structure, cover, deep water—the whole ball game.

I'm frequently asked by beginners and novices how to get a spinnerbait to run right. A combination of things make a spinnerbait run right. The wire with the spinners on it—the arm—needs to be directly over the wire leading to the jig head, and the angle of the wire is important. Generally if the wire leading to the jig head comes off at a 30-degree angle and then makes another 45-degree angle to the wire attached to the spinner, this latter angle balances it out. The line pull is now above the jig, and the torque of the blade and weight of the jig are counteracted. It's a triangle situation with the line pull in the middle, the torque of the blade (or blades) pulling on top, and the weight of the jig on the bottom. This way the bait will run true and will not roll over or run with the blades off to the side.

Houston, Ricky Green, and Jerry Rhyne are three of the best spinnerbait fishermen I know, and Cliff Craft is another excellent spinnerbait man. I'm not as good with the spinnerbait as those guys are and I seldom rely on it as much as they do, but I do know their tricks. I fish it on six to eight different patterns in almost every tournament. In 1976 Jerry Rhyne qualified for his first BASS Masters Classic, and he said he used spinnerbaits to catch 90 percent of his bass. That's really relying heavily on a spinnerbait.

One advantage to spinnerbait fishing is that the pattern is usually fast, especially in the case of stumps. In a shallow bay at a lake such as Santee-Cooper, there might be as many as 3,000 stumps in the cove. There all you need to do is flip your trolling-motor switch on high and get as many casts to as many stumps as you can. Stand up high, stay alert, and make a bunch of casts. The cast has to be accurate, because the first cast

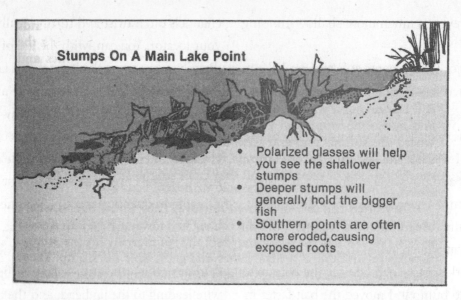

Stumps On A Main Lake Point

- Polarized glasses will help you see the shallower stumps
- Deeper stumps will generally hold the bigger fish
- Southern points are often more eroded, causing exposed roots

Lake points are as important in stump-bumping as in other patterns. However, a spinnerbait may not get you down to the deeper stumps; you'll need a crank bait.

almost always is the one that gets him. Throw 6 feet past the stump, bump the stump, and hold on! With a good, sharp hook and a good stiff rod, you'll get 'em.

Speaking of sharp hooks—and now's as good a time as any to mention this subject—it's super important to have extra-sharp hooks, I use a Weber stone about 3 inches long and an inch wide. It costs about 75 cents. I sharpen each single hook about twenty seconds and put a needle point on it. Another thing I do is angle the point of the hook out just a few degrees. This increases the hook size about one size.

A spinnerbait is a deadly night bait for smallmouths, Kentucky bass, and largemouths in several deep, clear TVA and Corps of Engineers lakes in Tennessee and Alabama. This fishing's still a bump-the-stump deal. In lakes such as Pickwick, Guntersville, Wilson, Center Hill, Watts Bar, Dale Hollow, and several others, guys like Stan Sloan, who manufactured the Zorro Aggravator, bump the stumps on the edge of the river channel. Smallmouths from 6 to even 9 pounds come up out of that river channel and get in the stumps lining the channels. Those channels have solid rows of stumps for miles and miles. Where they find a little feeder creek coming in to the main creek or a little bar that splits or drops off deep, guys like Sloan and Bill Dance and a whole bunch of those Tennessee boys

get out there and bump the stumps at night with their spinnerbaits. They know where the stumps are, and with a single blade and a slow retrieve, they feel the lure hit the stumps. At night, of course, they don't get much of a view of their line and they can't see the strike; they have to feel it.

They often use sort of a yo-yo retrieve. They throw out to where they think the stump is and keep raising and lowering the bait almost as you'd fish a worm. When they feel the spinnerbait hit the stump, they keep twitching it a little faster and get it over the stump. These stumps aren't merely stumps alone; with their root systems, they're like pedestals, because the dirt beneath them is eroded away and each stump has ten to fifteen roots which make contact with the bottom. Smallmouths often are in the maze of roots, and they really bust that spinnerbait as it falls down on 'em.

One night back in 1974 I was fishing Pickwick Lake, right on the exact spot of the intersection of Mississippi, Tennessee, and Alabama, with Bill Dance, and he said to remember one thing about smallmouths: When you feel the spinnerbait bump over a stump and then you feel a little teeny tick, set the hook. I kept my rod sort of low and was really concentrating on this little tick. I threw over this stump in 6 feet of water, and there wasn't a tick. Something hit my bait on the run and seemingly at twenty miles per hour. I was using 17-pound line, and the drag zoomed and about 30 feet of line went out. A super-acrobatic smallmouth blew through the surface and went airborne. That fish jumped and thrashed four or five more times. I landed him finally, and he weighed 4 ½ pounds. We caught several other nice ones that night, but all of 'em really crashed the spinnerbaits rather than ticking them. Looking back, I sort of think Bill was kidding me about waiting for a tick.

11. Pumping the Timber

Deepwater spinnerbait fishing is something I very seldom used to do before being paired with a good ol' Georgia boy named Cliff Craft in the B.A.S.S. tournament at Toledo Bend in 1976. I wasn't very familiar with the pattern one might call "pumping the timber" with a spinnerbait until I fished with this young pro who lives near Lake Lanier. Cliff is quite a spinnerbait fisherman, and Lanier is a deep lake, and he likes to fish deep with the spinner.

I'd gone out in practice at Toledo Bend with a good friend, Paul Chamblee from Raleigh, N.C. Paul's a regular fishing partner of that Columbia, S.C., fisherman Billy Goff, who, as I've mentioned, first showed me what I'd been missing at Santee-Cooper by not using the spinnerbait. Anyway, Paul and I fished that warmup period when it was cloudy and the bass were real active and eager. We'd thrown a lot of small red crank baits and a few jigs, and we'd caught some really nice bass. One day we caught sixteen from 4 pounds on up. We figured we really had found the best spot in the whole 190,000 acres of Toledo Bend. We were fishing the upper end of the lake along some ridges and timbered areas. We weren't worried, and we just knew we'd take the first two places in the tournament.

Well, I got paired with Craft in the first round, and he had several spinnerbaits tied on his rods, and he mentioned he'd been catching bass 10 to 15 feet deep with the spinners. We got out to my jig-and-eel hole

and I told him the bass were 10 to 15 feet deep but they weren't hitting spinnerbaits—they were hitting the jigs and eels. My first cast through the hole produced a bass slightly over 5 pounds. Then I threw back and caught another 5-pounder. Cliff believed me and said he was going to try the jig too, if that's what they were hitting.

We threw jigs, and even threw some worms, but after those two bass the action slowed down. That's all we caught, and finally after about half an hour on that spot, Cliff said he'd fished too many spinnerbaits deep in this kind of heavy timber not to believe the bass in this spot wouldn't hit 'em. He tied on a white spinnerbait with a ½-ounce head and a No. 4 nickel blade, and he cast out there to where we'd been fishing the jigs and eels. He let the spinnerbait sink to the bottom, and then he just pumped it up about a foot or so and let it sink back down as if he were fishing a worm.

On his first cast, he was holding the rod high, and as the bait was fluttering down, he said, "Oh! There's a strike!"

He didn't set the hook instantly; he just lowered his rod and reeled in the slack and about three seconds later he set the hook and caught a 6-pounder. I asked him about not setting the hook when he felt the fish. He said that in deep water they'll hold the bait a few seconds and he just reels down so he'll get a good hook set. He was using a standard spinnerbait with no plastic or pork trailer! I couldn't half believe what I saw!

I missed a couple of bass on the jig and eel, and I figured I'd stay with it. But Cliff repeated his procedure. He said he had a strike, and then he reeled down and set the hook and got another one. He started catching 4-to-6-pounders. Every five to ten minutes he'd nail a big bass, and I wasn't getting any strikes.

The area we were fishing was a flooded forest with limbs everywhere in the timber. Cliff simply pulled his spinnerbait up into the limbs and shook it through them. When he got it 3 or 4 feet off the bottom, he'd let it flutter back down. Many of his strikes came near the bigger trees. As his lure fell, he watched his line and would detect a little twitch. Then he'd reel down and set the hook two to three seconds later. He had eleven strikes and put ten of 'em in the boat and those ten totaled 44 pounds. I ended up with only five fish weighing 19 pounds. Cliff led the tournament after the first day. I finally put on a spinnerbait, and on my first strike I set the hook too quickly and missed him. Then on another fish I set too hard and broke my line.

The second day Cliff tried some different water, and he caught only a couple of fish, but they were 5-to-6-pounders. In the meantime Paul Chamblee had been fishing spinnerbaits early in the shallower pockets and shallower ridges, and later in the day he worked out deeper with his red crank baits (he was using a Mud Bug). Paul finished second in the tournament, and Cliff Craft was third as the result of having a good third round. Cliff also caught the largest bass. Spinnerbaits helped account for second and third places in that tournament, and it was the pumping technique which really worked for Chamblee and Craft. I just didn't catch on to it.

Paul and Cliff were both using spinnerbaits with ½-ounce heads. They were using the long-wire models with the wire coming all the way back to the hook.

This bass fell for a spinnerbait that was allowed to sink all the way to the bottom.

This made the bait very snagless, and both of them were using No. 4 and No. 5 blades. Paul was using a white blade, and Cliff used a nickel blade. Neither was using a trailer hook, because it was so brushy you couldn't get a trailer hook through the limbs and timber without hanging up. They were using single blades because they wanted to feel the thump as the bait settled. Paul was fishing a little shallower than Cliff, but he also was pumping the timber. Paul was setting the hook a little faster than Cliff was, and he missed a few fish.

This was early spring, and the water temperatures were in the low- to middle-50s. It was a pre-spawn condition, and the pre-spawners were in schools and were slow and lethargic. When the water's cloudy and warming up fast, these fish will come up a little shallower and will hit crank baits better. But when it's bright and sunny, they'll lie under the brush and they're quite hard to catch. You really have to aggravate them.

While pumping seems to work best in big timber, don't be afraid to try the smaller trees.

That's exactly what the spinnerbait was doing when it fluttered down on 'em. I think they were hitting it somewhat out of reflex action and out of anger.

The jig and eel is a good bait for some of this type of fishing, but I think they strike it more out of hunger when they're more active. At times the spinnerbait with it's slow, fluttering action in heavy timber will outproduce virtually any other bait.

The south has twenty-five to thirty good timbered reservoirs where this pumping technique will catch a lot of bass. These reservoirs range from Table Rock in Missouri to Santee-Cooper in the southeast, Seminole in Georgia and Toledo Bend and Rayburn in the southwest. This type of bassing is best in pre-spawn conditions when the water is 50 to 60 degrees, and the basic depths are 5 to 15 feet. Almost all water clarities pay off, but in a very clear lake such as Table Rock, the bass will be a little deeper—maybe 20 feet down. In the dingier lakes, they might be only 5 feet deep.

I prefer the ½-ounce and ⅛-ounce spinnerbaits for pumping the timber. When you're fishing deeper, such as in Table Rock, the slightly heavier spinnerbait flutters down a little faster and gets to the bottom of the cedar trees better. Table Rock has a lot of cedar trees 15 to 25 feet deep, and you almost can jig the spinnerbait in some of these trees and catch bass. With this pattern, wind doesn't seem to make any difference, but the sun puts them a little deeper. I like a stiff-action casting rod—almost a worm type of rod—and look for heavy matted timber and throw well past the big trees. I cast and leave the button pushed on my reel until the lure settles to the bottom. I also use 20-pound line.

When the bait's on the bottom, the retrieve is similar to deepwater worm fishing. Pull up the bait until you hit a few limbs. If there aren't any limbs, pump it up a foot or so and let it flutter back to the bottom. Hold a little bit of back pressure on the lure so you can feel the strike. In deep water, 90 percent of the strikes occur as the bait is falling. This is true with plastic worms, spoons, and grubs as well as with spinnerbaits. If there's a lot of heavy brush, your spinnerbait actually has to ride up 5 or 6 feet to clear a lot of those limbs when you're retrieving it. The bait will get hung temporarily in the limbs, and you have to lower it a foot or so and sort of jerk it a little to get it to roll over the limb. Occasionally you'll get hung up and lose your bait. Also, you need to be a line watcher for this fishing.

I've never been one to let a bass run with a spinnerbait, but Cliff Craft says when they strike in cool water, he likes to let them take it and get the slack out of his line and lower his rod to get a good hook set. Cliff pumps the spinnerbait in Lake Lanier where there's very little timber. He just calls it pumping the structure. He's fishing rocks, boulders, and structure. This same basic pumping technique could be applied to pumping weedlines and rock shoals in northern lakes during this pre-spawn period—provided, of course, that the state fishing season is open.

12. Rapala Types for Spawners

There is an interesting history behind the Rapala Plug since it initially was introduced in this country in 1959. (Many anglers call it the "Ra-PAL-uh," but if you want to pronounce it as the inventor, Laurie Rapala, pronounces his last name, say "RAP-ul-uh.") For the past four years I've worked with the Normark Corporation, which imports and distributes the Rapala, and so I know Ray Ostrom and Ron Weber. They're the two guys who discovered the plug over in Finland and brought it to the U.S. to check it and test it out. They and their friends caught so many fish on it that they finally got the U.S. distributorship on it. They tell some exciting stories about the first year it came on the market.

No balsawood types of minnows were on the U.S. market back then, and the old floating/shallow-running plugs of that era were like the Heddon floating River Runt in that they floated at rest and wiggled slowly on the retrieve. The Flatfish and the Lazy Ike were similar. But this small, thin swimming balsa minnow was great for twitching on the top. It had a lifelike, quick little wobble underwater and would pop back to the top real quick on slack line. The high flotation caused an exciting wiggle which bass and other sportfish had never seen before.

Ray Ostrom said that in several of the natural lakes in the Minneapolis area, guys used the Rapala and started catching bass immediately and caught fifty to a hundred in a day. These were taken on the initial dozen or so Rapalas Ray and Ron brought back to this country. There was such a demand for the plugs that Ray and Ron, who had a small tackle shop, started renting out the baits for fifteen to twenty dollars per day. Whoever rented a Rapala had to put up a deposit, and if the guy lost the lure, he forfeited his deposit. This was also done in Florida with the first Rapalas in that state.

Finally in 1959 Ostrom and Weber acquired the distributorship for Rapalas in this country. The plugs cost two to three dollars apiece, but because of the demand and quite often in the tackle shop itself, the plugs were marked up to four, five, and six dollars. The Rapala for a long time was an "under-the-counter" bait. You had to ask for one, because you wouldn't see it on the shelf. Many tackle-store operators reserved Rapalas for themselves and their friends.

One thing that added greatly to the demand for Rapalas was a feature story in *Life* magazine about 1960 on Laurie Rapala and his lure. Billy Westmorland, a pro and friend of mine from Celina, Tenn., remembers well when the Rapala craze hit Dale Hollow Reservoir, his home lake. He was guiding back then, about 1960, and boat-dock operators wanting newspaper publicity on the fishing out of their docks supplied him with one Rapala at a time. Westmorland says his customers wanted to buy the lures but couldn't because there just weren't any for sale.

The fishing-tackle industry credited the Rapala's introduction into American waters for bringing back the "hard bait" market, which had sagged in the late 1950s after the plastic-worm craze struck.

Ostrom and Weber tell me that to get shipments of Rapalas in from Finland takes almost a year because of the procedure involved. They first have to negotiate the price and figure in the current exchange rate. Then they have to contract for X number of plugs. Then the Rapalas are slowly built by hand. Each one is hand-carved and hand-tested, and it is a very laborious process. After months and months have passed, the plugs are ready for shipment. Then comes the delay in exporting the baits. They have to go through customs, and then they're held in U.S. ports until they're finally cleared and counted and finally distributed up to Normark. From there the baits are shipped to the distributors and then to the tackle shops.

At first, Normark was a small company, and they didn't have enough front money to order a million Rapalas. They had to pay cash for a year in advance, and it was hard for the small company to come up with from $200,000 to $500,000 against sales which would occur the next year. This is why for the first couple of years there was a continual shortage. Normark just couldn't get the financing to order enough plugs.

This shortage of Rapalas really helped create a demand for American-made plugs which are similar to the plug from Finland. The original Rapala was more in demand than the American baits, but the fact that it was so unavailable led to millions of dollars in sales for other companies. Two of the early American long minnow-type baits on the market were the Rebel Minnow (made by Plastics Research and Development at Ft. Smith, Ark.) and Jim Bagley's Bang-O-Lure (manufactured by the Bagley Bait Co. at Winter Haven, Fla.). The Rebel and the Bang-O-Lure got hot not only because they caught fish, but because fishermen had to settle for them when they couldn't get Rapalas. Bagley was able to carve out Bang-O-Lures quickly and sell and distribute them in a month or so. With plastic injection molding, Rebel was able to mass-produce their lures in a hurry, too.

My first experience with the Rapala was on the Eastern Shore of Maryland on the Chicamacomico River in 1961. I was fishing with Lynn Torbett. Lynn, who died a few years ago, was a casting expert. He machined his own casting reels. He'd take his Pflueger Supreme reels and lap the gears with toothpaste to get them to run faster and smoother, and he even drilled holes in the reel handles to make them lighter. He used very light parabolic rods and light lines, 8-to-12- pound-test. His bag was long-distance casting accuracy, and he was probably the finest caster I've ever met. Torbett machined out a Pflueger Supreme for me several years ago, and we could take a No. 11 Rapala, which weighs only ¼ ounce, and throw it with a casting rod. You can't do this today with even our modern casting gear, even with a lightweight Ambassador reel, though you can throw a No. 13 Rapala fairly well. Lots of bait casters today use the No. 13 Magnum Rapala, which is 5 ½ inches long and fatter than the regular model, or the No. 18, which is about 7 inches long.

The small No. 11s were relegated mainly to spinning and spin-casting tackle, and this is another reason the Rapala became so popular. In the late 1950s, American fishermen were being swept up with the spinning-tackle craze. The little ⅕-ounce and ¼-ounce Rapalas were just perfect for novice and veteran fishermen alike with their spinning or pushbutton (spin-casting) outfits, and the lures were universally used. Virtually everybody could catch bass, trout, northern pike, or some type of gamefish on these little floating-diving-swimming plugs from Finland.

My first bass over 10 pounds in Florida ironically was caught on a No. 11 Rapala out of a small lake in the Ocala National Forest in 1976. That fish weighed 10½ pounds. I had a four-wheel-drive Suburban, and we found a 200-acre lake with no launching facilities. With that Suburban, we launched my bass boat. I'd taken light spinning tackle—8-pound line and a 6½-foot rod—and started twitching Rapalas along the north shore where there were some spawning areas. That's how I caught that bass.

The biggest bass I ever heard of on a Rapala was an 18-pounder caught from Wall Lake, about twenty miles out of Palatka. Larry Mayer did a newspaper story on Lonnie Petty, the man who caught the monster. Petty, who used to operate a country bar near his

In clear, shallow water where bass typically spawn, light spinning or spincasting tackle makes a good match with a Rapala.

Putnam Hall, Fla., residence, was fishing with a No. 11 Rapala, Zebco pushbutton reel, and 8-pound line back in January of 1964 when he caught that fish. Petty said the bass headed out to deep water and the line got caught on one springy strand of bullrush, and the rush kept giving and caused the fish to tire out. I hope I'm that fortunate if I ever hook one that big on 8-pound line—or even on 30-pound line, for that matter.

The pattern which produced that 10½-pounder for me on the Rapala is a dandy one involving spawning bass. A spawning bass hits quite often, and this is particularly true with surface plugs. He's not hungry; he hits the plugs out of protective reasons, and he's trying to kill the bait. The best day I ever had with a surface bait at Santee was with a large propeller-type plug, the Diamond Rattler. The bass were rolling on the bait that day and were hitting it with their mouths closed. I finally changed the hooks and put real sharp trebles on the bait and actually foul-hooked the four largest ones I landed that day—two 9s and two 8s. One of them was hooked in the tail, two were hooked in the side, and one was hooked on the side of the gill plate. These fish weren't trying to eat the bait, although they were striking it hard.

The same thing happens when you fish a Rapala or a plug similar to it for spawners. When the plug is thrown right over the bed, it intimidates the bass. It's barely twitching for seconds right over the bed, and finally the bass comes up and sort of rolls on it to push it away. Maybe half the time he's eating the plug, but quite often his mouth isn't even open. A Rapala has three fine-wire Aberdeen treble hooks, which are extremely sharp. If the angler's quick on his reflexes when the bass rolls on the plug, lots of times he can drive the hooks into the area of the mouth. He might hook the fish on the side of its jaw, its face, or even on the side of its body and still land it.

The pattern for fishing the Rapala for spawners means going out and finding the spawning areas first. A good fish thermometer will work. When you find a spawning bed, go slow with your trolling motor or get out and wade. If you find several bass in a little pocket, you really need to work slowly and cautiously. Fish the Rapala early in the morning or late in the evening or during cloudy weather. The technique is to throw 2 to 3 feet past the spawning bed. When you're in shallow water and are looking toward the bed, it often appears to be a little closer to you than it actually is. This is because of the reflection angle of the water. When I'm casting to the bed, I purposely throw a couple of feet past the actual outline of the bed.

This type of fishing needs to be done on a completely calm day. Wind messes up this pattern because it drifts the plug away, and if the bass is there on the bed, he doesn't have to be concerned with the lure because it drifts away by itself. But if it's completely calm, the plug hits a foot or so from his bed and lies there motionless. Keep sufficient slack line in the water and don't put any pressure on the lure, because any tension would cause it to move. Let the plug lie there for ten to even thirty seconds. The bass really gets nervous at this point, and usually it's the small male bass that gets the most nervous. He's normally more aggressive than the female, and he'll often be the first to rise up and slap at the bait.

After ten to thirty seconds, give it that first small twitch. Don't even make the bait go beneath the surface. Finally after about three twitches, make it dart under for the first time. If he didn't hit it during those twitches, he's apt to be looking at it. Now the bait is probably a few feet from the bed. Run it 2 or 3 feet beneath the water and let it float back up to the top. Then run it down for 2 or 3 more feet and let it float up to the top again. Usually if a bass is following it that first couple times it dives, he often will nail it when it floats up that second time. At this time the plug is still halfway between you and the bed, so you can reel it back in. Occasionally you'll be reeling it in a foot or so beneath the surface, and you'll come over another bass or another spawner you didn't see, and you might get that one to hit. This swimming action back to the boat accounts for 10 to 15 percent of my strikes with this pattern, even though these can be considered somewhat accidental.

This is one reason the Rapala and similar plugs are more effective than the old surface plug which floats all the time. With the strictly floating plug, when you've fished the ambush point (in this case, the spawning area), you finally reel in the plug and it skits along the top, and you get very few strikes on a regular surface plug during that last part of the retrieve. With the Rapala, you get those bonus strikes on the last part of the retrieve.

Sometimes the topwater twitching technique doesn't work. After a couple of casts where I've worked the lure in those small twitches and didn't get the fish to hit, I might try a faster retrieve. I know the fish is there, and I'm trying to provoke him. I cast repeatedly and run the lure faster right over the bed. Sometimes after six to ten casts, each time swimming the lure over the bed, the bass blows his cool and hits out of anger in addition to his protective instinct. I don't really give up on a spawning bass.

As I've explained previously, the male not only is more aggressive and less cautious than the female, but he spends three weeks guarding the nest, so chances are you'll catch a lot more males. Sometimes you'll still see a big female bass, but she won't strike. After I catch the male, I release him and usually return later, because with topwater fishing, the first cast is probably the most important cast. If the female doesn't hit after eight or nine casts, I figure she's a real trophy and I'll return and try again for her later. I like to go back about thirty minutes later. Bass don't have a long memory; when they spook, they normally get over their wariness in fifteen to twenty minutes. In thirty minutes I sneak back there and try to make that first long cast perfect.

Generally you need light spinning tackle for the long cast, because most of the spawning waters are in clear, shallow areas. If there's any wind blowing, you probably won't be able to cast properly. A small Rapala floats in the wind. On that first cast, give the lure another ten-to-thirty-second pause and then the series of slight twitches. This is most effective for a big female, and after you've caught the male, she usually hits on that very first cast when you return.

Another thing about spawning bass is that you definitely need to be ready for a tiny strike. For some reason—I've never been able to figure out why—lots of times when a big female hits a topwater plug of any description, she sucks the bait in so delicately that it looks like a bluegill has barely pulled the plug under. What she does is flare her gills and create a suction or vacuum which pulls the plug under and into her mouth with no wake, boil, or swirl on the surface. The plug sort of just disappears, and that's exactly what happened when I got that 10 ½-pounder on the Rapala.

13. Prop Plugs for Feeders

When I was a kid, I fished Heddon's Tiny Torpedo for smallmouths in the Potomac River, but I had never caught any lunker bass on a propeller-type surface plug. My first serious experience with these prop plugs was in 1967, when I met Jim Strader out of Florida. Jim had come to Santee-Cooper for me to guide him. He had heard about my success with Santee's big largemouths, and he had designed a new plug, the Diamond Rattler. The plug is a cigar-shaped propeller plug about 4 inches long, and it has little glass diamond-like eyes with two very sharp English-type treble hooks with round-ground points like the old Mepps Spinner hooks of several years ago.

When Jim met me that morning, he said he was promoting a new bait which he really wanted to fish at Santee. He wanted me to fish the plug, too, and he was confident we'd catch a lot of bass on 'em. I reminded him the time was July, the water was 85 to 88 degrees, and the weather was clear, and that we'd catch ten times more bass on worms than on his propellered topwater plug.

Billy Goff and I had a theory called "big bass, high noon." We'd go to the heavy stickups and thick cypress trees and catch bass on plastic worms on the hottest days of summer at high noon. Writers like Earl Shelsby, who was with a Baltimore newspaper back then, had done stories on us catching big bass in the middle of the day. But the whole thing had been with plastic worms, and none of us really had ever tried surface plugs then. The bass were in about 5 feet of water which was fairly clear, and they were way down in the shade beneath those heavy branches.

Anyhow, Jim Strader said he still thought he could catch a few bass on his Diamond Rattler. He had a blue one, and he said blue was the best color. We started out first thing in the morning and went to some grass beds and lily pads. Sure enough, he caught a couple, including a 6-pounder, on his new plug. I explained—sort of dismissed it—that he'd caught those bass because the sun hadn't gotten up yet on the water. Jim was working the plug pretty fast, and one thing about hot weather is that you often can work a surface plug quick over a lot of weeds, whereas in the early spring you have to slow it down. Bass have high metabolism rates when the water's warmer, and they'll hit a plug pretty fast.

About nine o'clock the bass quit hitting in the shallow water, and I told him that for us to catch any really trophy bass, we'd have to go to the heavy, deep willows and fish about 5 feet deep in the center of the lake and the center of the bays. He still was confident he could catch a few of 'em on his topwater plug, but I thought his optimism was completely ridiculous. No bass would come out of 5 or 6 feet of water to hit a dumb ol' topwater plug in the middle of the day. About an hour later we were fishing in these heavy willows, and Jim gets a strike. The bass was about 8 pounds, and he smashed the plug pretty hard. The fish was already on the top, and with 20-pound line and a fairly stiff rod, Strader rolled him right on out past the last couple of limbs and into open water. The bass jumped five or six times. I really was amazed at a topwater strike like that in clear weather in hot July.

Of course, I'd been worm fishing, and I thought the bass I'd been catching were on the bottom, but I figured out that many of the fish weren't always on the bottom. Some were probably only a couple of feet deep in the shade of the bigger limbs. Jim, who is a very accurate caster, was putting his plug right in next to the logs and limbs.

Next we came to some cypress trees, and again he could cast his heavy plug beneath the overhanging limbs to the shady side of the trees right next to the trunk. That's what I was doing with plastic worms. You needed to have your lure right against the trunk on the shady side beneath the limbs. There was almost no wind, and his Diamond Rattler lay there for fifteen to twenty seconds, and the very first time he twitched it, a 6-pounder blew all over it. I couldn't say much at this point; I knew the bass were in the shade, but the fact they were hitting topwater plugs really freaked me out! I had caught several bass on surface baits in the spring around the shallow weeds and the spawning areas, but certainly not in the middle of the summer. We were

fishing deepcover, 5 and 6 feet of water, in the middle of the lake, and he was catching big bass.

Finally about noon I told him I just had to try one of those plugs. I caught one almost 8 pounds, and we ended the day with four big bass. I had caught a few on the worms, but the largest bass were the ones we got on topwater plugs. We took some fine photos of those big bass, and Jim Strader subsequently used some of the pictures in his advertising.

I've been throwing topwater plugs for a long time, and I recognize their limitations, but a propeller plug for feeding bass is a super- strong pattern. You need fairly clear water, and the pattern usually works from 2 feet to 6 feet deep. If the water's clear enough, they'll hit a surface plug in 6 feet of water. This is a very old pattern which old-timers used in the summertime. They'd go out on the water at the crack of dawn and be back in by the time the rest of the people were getting up around the resort, and they'd get three or four big bass on a good morning. All a lot of 'em used back twenty-five years ago were prop plugs like the South Bend Nip-I-Dee-Dee, the Heddon S.O.S. or the Wounded Spook, and the Creek Chub Injured Minnow. Those were big ol' fat plugs with propellers on both ends, and they were heavy enough to cast good with 25-pound braided nylon line and the level-wind casting reels of that era.

The best and probably the major feeding time of the whole day is the first two hours of the morning. That's when the old guys went out—when it was just light enough to see, and somewhere about eight or eight-thirty a.m., the sun got on the water and the activity quit. Many times you'll not see any fish breaking on the lakes. Part of the pattern is the fact that no matter what I'm fishing, if I see any surface activity, I know the prop plugs will catch those fish. These are feeders in that area actually feeding. A prop plug excites them and makes a lot of noise. It draws fish from a long distance away. Those short twitches which make the propellers churn the water are really effective on feeding fish.

I basically look for shallow points, shallow brush, or shallow weed beds during the first two hours of dawn. I move the prop plug fairly quickly. Throw it out and let it sit four or five seconds, give it a short twitch, and then repeat this procedure. With the ambush points, I use a different system. I throw to a single tree, bush, or stump, and once I twitch the plug 4 or 5 feet past the ambush point, I don't think he'll hit if he hasn't done so already, and I retrieve the lure back quickly and throw to another ambush point. Along shallow weedlines or shallow points I retrieve the lure all along the area, because the bass could be anywhere along the point or weeds.

One spring I was in Tyler, Texas, for a store promotion. It was May, and the bass had finished spawning. We went up to Lake Palestine, which is a timbered reservoir characteristic of many of the Corps of Engineers lakes in Texas. Texas has 179 major reservoirs with a total of over 2 million acres of water. The guide took me into a big cove where he said the bass had spawned a week or two before, but now the water was 75 degrees. I had my 18-foot Ranger bass boat. He said we needed to get in behind a bunch of logs, and right away the boat got hung up in the logs. I made a few casts with a spinnerbait and a worm and caught a couple of small ones, but way back in there where we couldn't reach with the boat, I saw some bass chasing shad. We didn't have any waders, but I suggested we jump out of the boat anyhow and go wading back into there. So we did that. I had some plastic worms in my pocket and also a Devils Horse wrapped up in a piece of paper. (The Devils Horse is one of the modern favorites in the propeller-plug family, and it's been that for probably twenty years.)

A lot of logs were lying under the surface. I tied on the Devils Horse and threw it back where the shad were jumping. I was twitching it along in little short spurts when about a 4-pounder blew over it. I wasn't ready for him and I didn't have heavy enough line, and the bass dived down in the heavy brush and hung the plug on the log. That's the problem with logs and brush

fishing when you're not using heavy line. Much of the lure usually is on the outside of the fish's mouth, and when he goes beneath the brush, the plug gets snagged on something. This is true with a crank bait as well as a surface bait.

The bass was hung on the log and was thrashing around, and he put so much pressure on the hooks that he straightened them out and got off. That's what usually happens with a good-sized bass when he gets hung up like that. I got my plug back and bent back the hooks and proceeded to catch another one of almost 5 pounds. This was early in the morning, and for the next two hours those bass continued to feed. I went back to town for the store promotion with my limit, and they weighed a little more than 30 pounds. We had a pair of 6-pounders and some 4- and 5-pounders. My companion said he had a small pond which he'd like to put those bass in, so we put them in my giant live well in the boat and that afternoon took them out to his pond and released them. They all survived, and they're in his small pond to be caught again another day.

Topwater patterns really can pay off if you observe the conditions and particularly if you see any fish breaking early in the morning. Put on a good prop plug and cover some water and work it fast, and you're liable to hit some of the most explosive fishing you've ever had. It might not last long—maybe only twenty or thirty minutes—but it certainly might be memorable.

14. Burning the Spot

Two of the most popular lures for this pattern are the Cordell Spot and the Heddon Sonic. I like the small ⅓-ounce Sonic in a yellow finish, and I use the ½-ounce Spot. These are similar plugs in that they're sinking and also are fast vibrators. I throw them with both spinning and casting tackle, but with high-speed reels.

This is mainly a springtime pattern to use when the water is 50 to 60 degrees and the bass first come up on the dingy clay banks and points. You can burn these

Burning the Spot is a water–covering technique, and it's hard work: long casts and quick retrieves of the heavy swimming plug, hour after hour. But it's rewarding.

plugs down these crummy-looking flat banks and catch a lot of bass. Guys like James Thomas of Birmingham, Ala., and Junior Collis of Decatur, Ga., do especially well in spring tournaments with this pattern. In lakes like Gaston in North Carolina, all Thomas does is throw a small yellow Sonic on these flat-looking banks. Junior uses spinning tackle and about 12-pound line, and he fishes the dingier waters of Lake Lanier, Hartwell, and Clark Hill with a ½-ounce Spot. He looks for clay banks, puts his trolling motor on high, and makes a cast every 15 to 20 feet, and his trolling motor's running three to four miles an hour. He fishes all day like that, and sometimes he catches thirty to fifty bass a day.

There's really not much skill involved in "burning the Spot," but there's a lot of thought and hard work involved. First, it's like using a crank bait, but you're making more casts and retrieving a bit faster than you

would with a crank bait. If you burn one of these baits all day long, you'll cover more water than with any other method of fishing I've ever seen. There's no other method where your lure travels through more feet of water than when you're burning the Spot. You need to be in excellent physical condition to do this. A lot of fishermen aren't able to make these long casts and fast retrieves all day long for eight to ten hours. These lures have a lot of lead in them, and they cast a long way, and this is good because you're fishing flat water and you need to cover a lot of it. You're not fishing dropoffs, and you're not really fishing targets all that much. You'll occasionally see a stump or a stick coming out of the water, and you'll want to throw near that, but these lures aren't like crank baits; they won't bounce over obstructions or through heavy cover. You don't want to try to bump the stump as you would do with a crank bait or a spinnerbait, because the Sonic or Spot will get hung up.

This type of fishing usually is for pre-spawners when the water is about 55 degrees. The banks usually are sloping, and you should stay a cast-length out from the bank in water less than 10 feet deep. Good places to fish this way are in the backs of major creek channels where the channel itself is pretty silted over and is no longer very defined. The last mile of that creek might be a massive flat and often has a few stumps around. Junior Collis will stop half a mile from the end of the cove and with his trolling will work around the sides of the cove. Again, he'll get out on the main lake and find clay points without much definition or deep water nearby, and he fires that Spot up to the bank and hums it all the way back.

When you're humming that Spot, it has a very definite throb, and this throb is one of the most important parts in working the lure. You really need to identify the feel of the throb, because you seldom identify the feel of the strike. What often happens is in that 55-degree water, the bass hears the plug or feels the vibrations from it, or both, and he is apt to follow it and hit it from behind. Probably 75 percent of the time when you get a strike, the only thing you detect is the stopping of the plug's vibrations. When the bass hits, the plug quits vibrating. With the small Sonic when the wind's blowing, at times the only thing I notice is my line moving off to the side. I'm using a graphite rod and am really watching, but this line movement is the only indication of the strike. Sometimes the fish moves toward you, and you don't see the line move. But if you're paying close attention, you'll quit feeling the vibration. I like graphite rods for this fishing because you can feel the throb better. Graphite is more sensitive. Set the hook at even the slightest interruption in the throb. It also pays to watch your line, and set the hook when the line makes the slightest deviation in the arc it's making as you're retrieving the bait while your trolling motor is moving the boat.

A lot of fishermen miss a lot of bass when they're burning the Spot. A big reason for this is that they don't sharpen their hooks enough. Super-sharp hooks are especially important in this type of fishing.

There's another situation which arises that is almost the reverse. In Louisiana there's a bait made which is called the Rattletrap. The manufacturers advertise that with the Rattletrap, you'll get the most jarring, vicious, startling strike you've ever experienced with a crank bait. It's a good late-spring and early-summer bait on the flats in lakes such as Toledo Bend where there's timber and stickups and where you're fishing for suspended bass around the trees and in deeper stump fields and creek channels. The Rattletrap looks like the Spot. It weighs about the same and burns through the water with about the same vibrations.

But for some strange reason—and I figure it's just a quirk of the bass—when the water temperature's 65 to 70 degrees, instead of hitting it from behind, the bass sort of angle in from the side and really smash it. The strikes are very vicious and hard, and the bait is moving fast anyhow. Mary Ann and I agree with the advertising on the lure box. We fished the Rattletrap at Percy Priest in Tennessee, and we had super-vicious strikes. We fished it again at Toledo Bend in the spring before her

Bass'n Gals tournament, and the bass really nailed it. They just stopped it cold!

The same basic principles apply to the Sonic, the Spot, and the Rattletrap. All three are high-speed, underwater-swimming, fast- vibrating lures. They're not crank baits because they don't float, and the way to fish 'em is not so much at ambush points as with crank baits and spinnerbaits, but rather along shallow banks and flats and the ends of coves. These are useful tournament lures because during practice or even in the actual competition, if you want to know if there are fish in a certain area, you can find out in a relatively short time with them. If you spent one hour burning the Spot in a big flat, you would have made over 200 casts, and you'd get some indication if there were any bass there.

One other consideration is that when you burn these plugs, you probably catch bass which are feeding and hungry more than any others. It's not particularly a reflex-action bait because you're not primarily throwing at ambush points. You're mainly catching bass which are roaming and feeding. That's why they chase down these fast-swimming baits. Early morning and late evening are prime times to look for feeding fish, and then you want to cover a lot of water. You might also check the Solunar Tables and fish these lures during a major period. When you find them feeding good on a flat or a point, you can limit out in an hour with these vibrators.

15. Counting Down

A totally different pattern exists with a slow-sinking plug such as the Countdown Rapala or that slow-sinking River Runt which the late Lynn Torbett used. Counting down is a relatively new pattern in my repertoire. It's not something I've been doing long. They have made a Countdown Rapala for years, and it looks just like the floating models, but it's an entirely different lure for entirely different uses.

The Countdown is a lead-filled Rapala which sinks fairly fast and swims and wobbles along. It also has a good wobble while it's sinking. Don't throw it into 2 or

3 feet of water as you do with the floating models, but instead fish it on relatively shallow structure, such as on a rocky point. One of the best places to fish it is in the shade of a weedline. One of my favorite places to fish it is on a point. I try to estimate in my mind how deep the water is by judging from the slope of the point out of the water. Doing this takes a bit of mental geometry. If I think the fish should be about 10 feet deep, and from the slope of the point I judge that I'll find 10-foot water 100 yards out, that's where I'll start fishing the Countdown.

On my first cast, I'm counting to myself . . . one . . . two . . . three . . . as the plug is sinking. (This is why the name "Countdown"; you can actually count it down to the desired depth.) If it hits the bottom on a count of ten and takes about ten seconds to sink, I'll figure the water is close to 10 feet deep. I also might check my locator to see exactly how deep it is. I don't want the lure to run 10 feet deep because it would get hung on everything on the bottom. On the next cast—if I can get that first one in without hanging up—I'll count it down to eight or nine and start my retrieve with the plug about a foot or two off the bottom. You have good depth control with this plug.

This is a technique I learned as a teenager years ago from Jason Lucas, my favorite fishing writer back then, in his book *Lucas on Bass*. He didn't use a depthfinder, and he didn't care much for plastic worms, but he made some amazing discoveries in fishing. The most important thing he ever wrote about, I think, was counting down a sinking lure. I count down every sinking lure I use, whether it's a Countdown Rapala, plastic worm, grub, jig and eel, or whatever. Every single cast I make with a worm (other than a floating worm), I'm counting as it sinks. I even do this in stickups; stickups are in different depths of water. If I'm catching bass on plastic worms 3 ½ feet deep in stickups, and I throw to a 5-foot-deep stickup and don't get a strike and then I throw to a stickup 2 feet deep and don't get a strike, this makes me aware that nearly all the bass—if not all of 'em—in the area I'm fishing are hitting at 3 ½ feet

deep. When you're throwing 40 feet away from you, lots of times you don't know if there's a ditch or depression there or if the bottom's flat or there's a hump in that spot. But you can learn what's out there by counting. I count *every time* I make a cast with any lure that sinks.

One thing about a Countdown Rapala is that it'll hang up on everything it bumps. You can't bump anything with this plug and not get it hung up. And other than wasting time trying to get your lure free and blowing that cast and that shallow spot, keep in mind that Countdown Rapalas aren't exactly as inexpensive as plastic worms! A Countdown Rapala is an open-water

When in open water, a countdown Rapala can be deadly.

lure, but it can be used in areas with cover as long as you count it down properly and get your depth control worked out. Another thing to keep in mind about depth control is that when you make a long cast with a sinking plug, you're pulling the lure at a horizontal angle during the first part of your retrieve and it swims at that depth pretty good. But as you keep retrieving, you're building up line on your reel and you're pulling at a sharper upward angle on your lure. For example, if you make a 50-foot cast and count the plug down to about 6 feet, it might be running right at that depth for the first 10 or so feet. But if you're turning your reel handle two revolutions per second, by the time you get the plug back to 20 feet from you, you've got a bigger line buildup on your reel and you're moving the bait faster when you crank your reel handle two revolutions per second, and you're also pulling the bait upward and shallower instead of horizontally. So to keep that 5-to-6-foot depth, the closer you get to the boat, the slower you need to retrieve. It's not easy to keep this consistent depth control; doing so takes quite a bit of practice. Lots of little tricks like this you can learn, but don't be disappointed if you don't master them overnight. I certainly didn't, and neither did Bill Dance, Homer Circle, Tom Mann, Rick Clunn, or any of the experts I know.

One way to learn to maintain this consistent depth control is to use your locator and find a big flat where the bottom is almost as level as your living-room floor. If the water's, say, 9 feet deep everywhere out there, make a long cast and count the lure to the bottom. If it took you nine counts, the next time cast out long again and count to eight. When you get the lure about halfway back to you, let it free-fall to the bottom. If you were retrieving it 8 feet deep, it should reach the bottom on a one-count. If it hit the lake floor on a three-count, you were bringing it in only 6 feet deep at the moment you let it fall. This is a good way to practice and learn depth control. Remember, too, the size of your line affects the speed at which the lure will sink. A Countdown Rapala will sink slower with a 14-pound-test line than it will with 8-pound-test. Different reels

affect this, too, because they have different speeds. By practicing and working out the system, you can learn to maintain an almost totally horizontal retrieve. It's all a matter of timing, and once you get it down pat, you can get this lure to run at any depth you want it to run.

Some fishermen stick their rods straight down in the water almost to the handle and maintain depth control that way. It works, but I don't like to do this because I'm all out of position for the strike. I prefer to work out the system and occasionally check by letting the lure free-fall halfway through the retrieve, as described above.

This counting down is very popular at Watts Bar, Dale Hollow, and Percy Priest in Tennessee. The boys up there take No. 7 Countdown Rapalas and run 'em on 6- or 8-pound line with spinning tackle. Most of the lakes up there are gravelly, with a few stickups and stumps and chunky rocks. They like to fish particularly on points with the wind blowing in, because that little No. 7 Countdown closely resembles a small threadfin shad. They throw it across the point and count it down to whatever depth they want it to run, and they retrieve it at a slow speed.

You really need to run the Countdown slower than you would a crank bait such as a Bomber or a Fat Rap. The difference between a Countdown and a conventional crank bait coming across the same point, even if they're similar in size and color, is that you have to run the crank bait much faster to get a desired depth. There are times when bass won't hit a fast-moving lure, but they'll hit the slow-swimming bait. I do like to use crank baits, but there are times when the fish might be deeper than the crank bait will go. If the bass are down 15 feet, there's not a small crank bait in your tackle box that will reach them. Even if you have a crank bait that will run 11 feet deep, you can't get it down there immediately, and it might be moving too fast for the fish.

But you can fish a Countdown deep and bring it slowly across a point. Most of the strikes are discernible; you don't have much difficulty with this factor because you're usually fishing the bait slow and the plug does not wobble with a violent action as a crank bait does. You're not putting much pressure on your lure. The line isn't slack, but it does have a slight bow in it. When they hit it, they usually knock the bow out, and you feel the strike. The hooks are extremely sharp, and you don't miss many fish with it. Often you're fishing it slow and in clear water, and they zero in on it and engulf it. Sometimes they take the small Countdowns way down in their throats, and you need a pair of needle-nose pliers to extract the hooks.

16. Cranking The Creek Channels

This is a pattern I reserve for early spring. In many of the shad lakes in the flatlands—reservoirs like Toledo Bend, Sam Rayburn, and Santee-Cooper—there are creek channels back through big flats. When you get back in the cove, it might be big, half a mile wide, but the water is pretty shallow. The entire flat might be only

Big females come back in the creeks in early spring before they spawn and lie up on top of the creek ledges.

4 to 8 feet deep, but the creek channel is another 5 to 10 feet deeper. Most of the time I crank the creek channel, which is a little bit dingy in the back of a major cove.

Big female bass come back in the creeks in early spring. Just before they spawn they lie up on top of the creek ledge, and the depth ranges from 3 to about 8 feet. I work my boat down the center of the creek. In timbered reservoirs it's a little easier to stay in the creek channel, because you can look at the trees and tell where the channel is. In an open reservoir the creek channel ledges are lined with stumps, and it's more difficult to follow the creek. In the latter you need to put out buoys to mark the channel. There are apt to be just as many fish in an open cove as in a timbered cove, but it is easier to fish in a timbered cove.

One February I was fishing Sam Rayburn with Jim Walker. February isn't considered a top bass month for Rayburn, but an extreme warming trend was in progress when we got there. The water was pretty dingy, and nobody had been catching any bass anywhere. The shallow water had really warmed up, and I told Jim I thought there might be some bass working in the creek channels and we might get them to hit crank baits. We went to the back end of Ash Bayou and found 55-degree water instead of the 45-degree water in the main lake. It was just a perfect temperature for crank baits. There were a lot of old oak trees on the edge of a small creek channel we went into. The channel was hard to follow because it was less than 10 feet wide and it twisted and turned.

Jim and I went down the center of the creek as best we could and cast to the sides of the trees. Because the big females were looking for the warmest water they could find, they were on the sunny side of the trees. They were only 3 feet deep in about 5 feet of water, and sometimes we'd see the swirl of a fish after the plug. The trick was to bump the edge of the tree, and that often produced strikes. I caught mine on an old brown Bomber, that had been in my box for years. Jim and I had ten bass over 5 pounds that day. We had

Often in the summer I turn the trolling motor on high and go up the creek channel, casting at every tree.

some smaller ones, too. Later that day we talked to several guides and other fishermen who had spent the day mostly on the main lake. They caught some bass, but nobody had big ones like ours. What I think happened is we found the best available water temperature for those big pre-spawners, and that's why they were there. That pattern lasted all week, and that also is one of the first patterns to develop in the early spring. Jim Walker died as a young man. He was my age, but a couple of years ago he had a heart attack which was fatal.

Since most lakes are not timbered, most creek channels are in open water in the coves. The way I approach this fishing is to run back into the cove until I hit a bottom depth of about 8 feet. This is about as deep as I can crank a crank bait effectively. I put out a marker buoy there. If I have a contour map of the lake, I'll look on it for a major bend in the creek I'm on. A creek bend usually has a better dropoff, and the structure aspects of fishing creek channels are important. Chances are, this major bend is undercut, and any stumps which might have been there probably have exposed roots which stick out over the water. This is a good suspending place for bass, and the severity of the dropoff often indicates that the bend will hold bigger bass and more of 'em. I keep working back toward the end of the cove to shallower water until I get shallow enough that I can see the stumps. With Polaroid glasses, they'll appear as dark spots in the water. This is as shallow as I'll fish with a crank bait, although occasionally the bass will be shallower. If they're in a foot of water, this isn't a crank-bait depth, and in that case I'll probably go to a spinnerbait or a plastic worm or something else.

Five-foot depths on the bends of the creek channel are usually very good places to fish. Sometimes you need to mark these spots with a marker buoy or two. It's important to stay in the deeper water in the creek and throw the crank bait on the flats. I like to throw it 10 feet past the edge of the creekbank and make it bump bottom. With luck, the plug will hit a stump. This is the key to this fishing, as often the stumps are right on the edge of the channel. Even if before the lake was impounded the area you're fishing was a farmer's field, the farmer probably left the trees on the edge of the creek through his land. Look at any farm and you'll almost never see the trees cleared along a creek which runs through the land.

While you want to bump those stumps, you don't want to get hung up, so you need to use a crank bait with a big lip which will deflect off the stump. Sometimes I cut the lead hook off the front set of treble hooks on the plug, but I prefer not to do this. I'd rather use heavier line if I'm getting hung up a lot and try to rip the lure loose. With 25-pound line I usually can rip the lure free by half straightening the hooks out. The Bomber is an excellent lure for this because it's relatively snagless. The deep-diving Bagley B baits also are good. I helped design the Fat Rap series, and the No. 7 size is good for this creek channel pattern. The No. 7 has a large lip and bounces off stumps real well. Almost

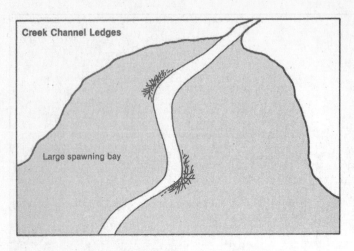

Pre-spawn bass will often hold on brushy ledges of a creek channel, usually at 5 to 10 feet in clear water or 3 to 6 feet in dingy water.

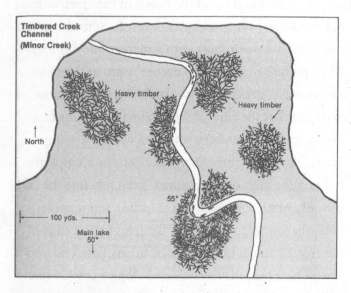

Minor creek channels in flat or gradually tapered coves located on the north side of the lake can hold concentrations of pre-spawners. The timber can be either permanently submerged or just temporarily flooded.

any crank bait with a large, extended lip is relatively snagless.

I mentioned this pattern relating to pre-spawn fish, but there's another time cranking the creek channels pays dividends. In Oklahoma there are some 800,000 acres of reservoirs, including timbered reservoirs like Kerr in southern Oklahoma and 102,000-acre Eufaula.

These are super crank-bait waters, but for some reason Oklahoma's often so muddy, cold, and windy in the spring that you don't often have good creek-channel fishing in the spring. Some of Oklahoma's best crank-bait fishing occurs during the hot summer, because it might be the only time of the year when the water clears up. The bass are there the whole time, but they really start feeding good only when the water starts clearing up, even though the water temperature might be 80 degrees.

We pretty much fish exclusively on the creek channel edges during the entire summer. Probably 90 percent of our summer fishing is done there on Kerr, Eufaula, and Lake Oolagah. These are large lakes with a lot of timber, dingy water, and shallow creek channels. I fish these channel edges with crank baits, spinnerbaits, and worms, but when I really think they're feeding and I want to cover a lot of water, I use a crank bait. I can find the bass with it better, too. Often in the summer I turn my trolling motor on high and go up a creek channel and cast at every tree. In the summer they're usually in the shade of the trees. I throw to the shady side and bump the tree and retrieve back. I make one cast per tree and keep on going up the channel.

Bass in the summer often are concentrated, just as pre-spawn fish get bunched up. You're apt to find an area where every tree has a bass. Maybe all thirty trees around one bend have a bass. You might not get all of 'em to strike, but they're apt to be there just the same. You're likely to get several strikes and maybe catch five or six of 'em, and they easily could be 5-pound or better fish. We usually get several 5-pounders on crank baits in the summer in Oklahoma, and I've heard of 40- and 50-pound strings getting caught on crank baits. My experience has been I don't catch 'em all on crank baits. When I catch two or three on crank baits, I've located the school. Then I might go to a worm or a flipping jig and pull up to those trees and flip a jig or a worm in there on the shady side, or I'll slow-roll a spinnerbait through that same spot. Changing lures sometimes helps, but the bait certainly is a fast way to find 'em.

17. Bump More Stumps

If we were to add up all the stumps in all the lakes, rivers, and ponds in this country, we might come up with something like 8.2 billion trillion stumps. And there probably is no stump in less than 10 feet of water in any southern reservoir which hasn't at some time or other had at least one bass on it.

When I speak of bumping the stumps, I'm thinking mainly about the stumps on the points and on the creek channels. Sometimes I find stumps on an underwater ridge or a submerged island on a shallow lake. On the exposed areas—the points and shoals—wave action usually causes erosion, and the dirt, sand, or gravel bases of these stumps are washed away. Then instead of being merely a stump flush with the bottom, it is almost suspended, with roots coming out in all directions, looking like an octopus. The more the stump is eroded, the better the ambush point it makes for bass. It becomes a dynamite spot for a bass in spring, summer, and fall.

To fish these eroded stumps, I have to prepare for heavy fishing, because I know I'm going to get hung up. Since I'm usually fishing dingy water, I'm using a large crank bait with a big lip to bounce off the wood and very heavy line. The big line is not necessarily for the size of the bass, but because I'm getting hung up a lot and I want to be able to pull the plug loose as many times as possible. With 12- or 14-pound line, I'd lose a lot of lures, but you can rip most of 'em loose with 20- or 25-pound mono. Another reason for the heavy line is it prevents the plug from going as deep as it would travel on lighter line. I might be fishing a point and want to hit only the tops of the stumps and not run too deep. With 12-pound line, the crank bait would go considerably deeper, and when it hung up, I might not be able to reach it with my rod tip to poke it loose. It's human nature to get exasperated when you start hanging up a lot, and you tend to pull too hard. If you're using lighter line, you'll break off some plugs. And lots of these crank baits today cost four and five bucks apiece.

This young angler caught the bass of his life near an eroded stump.

When I think of bumping the stumps with a crank bait, I think back to the B.A.S.S. tournament at Ross Barnett Reservoir in Mississippi in 1973. The craze in crank-bait fishing which was spawned by Fred Young's hand-carved balsawood Big-O was getting into full swing. I'd located some bass in front of Pine Island, which is in the midsection of the lake, and they were on the south bank. The wind was blowing hard from the north. I had only one bait they'd hit—a hand-carved balsa plug made by Mike Estep of Oak Ridge, Tenn. It had a black back and chartreuse sides. Since it was the only thing they were hitting, I decided to run it on 25-pound line so I wouldn't lose it. I got back into 7 or 8 feet of water to throw up on those 2-to-4-foot flats with stumps along the edge of the drops.

My game plan was going good except that during the first day of the tournament, the wind blew thirty miles an hour! When I got to my area, the wind was whitecapping the water across that bar. Four or five others had found those same bass. Tom Mann had found 'em, and Bobby Murray knew the bass were there, and so did Billy Westmorland. A lot of us had planned to go fish that area, but the wind was nearly impossible to deal with. I was determined to fish it anyhow. I threw my anchor out and tried to hold the boat that way. This didn't work, so I ended up running my big engine in reverse and running the bilge pump to pump out the water which was sloshing in over the stern. I also ran my trolling motor as fast as it would go against the wind. Fishing that place was almost impossible, and I was continually getting hung up. I didn't want to run up to the ridge where the shallow water was, so I had to pull the plug loose and hope like heck my line wouldn't break. Two or three times my line did break, but my plug floated up and was out there bobbing in the waves. I'd wait for it to drift away from those bass, and then I'd circle around in the rough water and go net my plug.

I fished for three days in that rough water and ended up catching a little over 72 pounds of bass to win the tournament, simply because I got out there and stuck it out. I had only that one lure they were hitting. The last morning I caught nine bass which were good ones. One of 'em was over 6 and another was over 5. About one o'clock that afternoon I was trying for my tenth bass, and I hung the plug up and broke the line and it didn't float up. I had several other similar plugs, and I tried them, but they didn't work. I even had some other Estep plugs almost the same size and color, but they didn't produce either. Finally I managed to catch one more bass, which made my limit. But the point is I had the secret lure the fish wanted.

Bumping the stumps with a crank bait is saturation fishing; you just keep fan-casting around until you bump something. You might want to make three or four casts to the same stump, because lots of times they won't hit on the first couple of casts and you have to anger them a little. But often they strike out of reflex action on the first cast. Sometimes on my crank baits I use in the stumps, I replace heavier hooks with lighter wire hooks. I don't want to use hooks which won't straighten out partly when I pull the bait off a stump with 20- or 25-pound line. I have had bass hit when the plug pulls loose from the stump. It zings off and I start the retrieve, and that bass has been watching it wiggling there on the stump and all of a sudden it shoots off the stump and then wobbles away, and he pounces on it.

18. Throwing into a Crowd

When I speak of throwing into a crowd, I mean throwing into a whole bunch of bass. Lots of times I'll be fishing a variety of lures when I run into this situation. I've gotten strikes on other lures, and when I'm bringing that bass up to the boat and the water's at least reasonably clear, I'll see another fish following the one I've got on or my partner has on. Then I'll pick up a crank bait and throw in there.

One time when this happened, I really capitalized on this little trick. I was fishing with Pete Churchwell of Tulsa, who at the time worked for Lowrance Electronics, and we were using worms at Grand Lake. I needed to catch a couple of big bass for some publicity photos for Lowrance. We'd fished all day and hadn't had any luck at all with big fish. Pete made a long cast to a willow bush leaning over the water, and he had a strike and set the hook. His rod bowed over, and the fish took some drag and boiled at the top. When it boiled, I saw a second boil right by it. When his bass came past the boat, I thought I saw another bass with it. He said, "Get the net!" and I said, "Wait a minute—another big bass is following your fish." I had a crank bait on another rod I hadn't been throwing, and I picked it up and threw out right next to his fish, which was about a 5½-pounder. I cranked the plug down about 3 feet and paused it for a second, and *wham*! Another big bass had hit my plug, and we managed to get both of 'em.

Pete started to rig up another worm, and I said there was a school of 'em there, and the fastest way to catch 'em would be with a crank bait. I threw out and caught a second bass and then a third one. Pete got a crank bait tied on, and we were making double casts. As soon as one of us got one on, the other guy would throw right in near the hooked fish, and he'd get one. The ten to fifteen bass that were there would be chasing after the bass which was hooked. We sat there and caught ten bass, and seven of them were 5 pounds and over. This happened in about ten minutes.

The average fisherman would have made a mistake here. He would have caught the first one near the willow bush on the worm, and then he would have put it in the live well after looking it over leisurely and guessing how much it weighed. He probably would have taken his De-Liar out of his tacklebox and weighed the bass, and likely measured its length, too. Maybe his wife or buddy in the boat would have dug out the camera and taken a picture right then. Then he would have rerigged his worm and three or four minutes later he would be ready to make another cast. He might have even moved on down the bank to another willow bush. By this time, those bass would have lost their frenzy and would have calmed back to normal. Quite possibly he wouldn't have gotten another strike.

The point is to keep in mind the possibility of a school of fish, and sometimes it really pays off to have a crank bait ready for such an occasion. When my partner hooks a fish, if I have even the slightest idea there's another bass or several more right there, I pick up a crank bait and throw in there. That's the quickest way to find out. Throwing into a crowd really means throwing into a school of bass. When bass get worked up and are super-excited, you don't want to give them any time to cool off, and with a crank bait, you can keep them excited by making several quick casts and whipping the plug through them. Even if they're not hitting every cast, you're creating more excitement that you would by throwing a plastic worm repeatedly to that spot. Even if you catch a fish on a plastic worm, it certainly doesn't hurt anything to throw back to that spot two or three times with a crank bait. Sometimes this will add four or five bass to your stringer in a hurry. Even if you're worm fishing, have a crank ready on another rod for such situations.

I like to keep a rod rigged with a crank bait handy, so if I suspect the one I just hooked has some excited friends, I'm ready to take advantage.

19. Running the Points

Back in the early 1970s, I drew Ricky Green for a partner in an old Project: Sports Incorporated tournament at Lake Ouachita in Arkansas. He's a fine pro who is noted as a spinnerbait fisherman. He's a super caster and a good crank-bait fisherman as well. We flipped a coin to decide whose boat we would take, and I won, so we went in my boat. He asked what patterns I wanted to fish, and I said I had five or six points, and he said he had five or six more. We compared notes and discovered we were on the same pattern. We were doing about the same thing with similar lures in similar depths of water and in about the same areas.

I pointed out that if we were finding bass on these ten or twelve points, there were another hundred spots on the lake that were identical to those, and I suggested we hit as many of those points as we could after we fished the ones we'd tried. He agreed, and we worked out a game plan where we'd alternate running the boat. For one point he'd run the boat and I'd be up front, and then we'd switch around. We'd come in fast straight at the point, and 100 feet from it we'd shut off the big engine. The bass we'd found in practice were in 6 to 8 feet of water out off the points, and we were keying in to what we figured would be 6 to 8 feet of water. The forward momentum of the boat would carry us on in, and about 40 feet away from the point, we'd turn the steering wheel to broadside the boat. The guy up front got the first cast, but we'd both fire long casts across the point, and we'd crank our crank baits down. The pattern was to crank all the way down until we hit the bottom and then we'd pause and let the bait float up about a foot and then we'd crank it back down to the bottom and pause it again. Somewhere between the time it hit the bottom and floated up a foot or so, the bass would nail it.

The fishing wasn't red-hot that day, and we didn't catch 'em on every point, but on every three or four points, one of us would catch a bass. We'd make three casts apiece on the point and then hit the starter and take off like the proverbial bat for the next point. We never even took time to unzip our life vests, and we didn't waste any time. Usually we didn't even put the trolling motor down. We added up the points we fished, and the tally ran to seventy-five points that day. On two or three points we caught three or four bass per point. 1 caught twenty-two bass that day, and Ricky had twenty-three. We were within a bass of each other, and our weights were almost identical. We each weighed in ten bass which totaled slightly over 20 pounds. Right near the end of the day I had caught about a 5-pounder and ended up with a pound or so more than he had.

Some points have hidden structure, such as a dropoff, patch of stumps, or boulders. A locator helps you figure out the best route for your crank bait.

This was in May right during the spawning season, and some bass were spawning whereas others either had finished nesting or hadn't started spawning yet. Not all the bass spawn at the same time. The points were excellent places because of all three of these conditions being present, and Ouachita is well known for its point fishing. The water had been a little dingy, and there was a little bit of wind and overcast weather. One of the major considerations for point fishing, I think, is the wind, and what I like to find are points with the wind blowing in—not any super amount of wind, but a ten-to-fifteen-mile-per-hour breeze. I don't want it whitecapping, although I have caught 'em on points when it was whitecapping.

When you're fishing a point, those initial three or four casts usually are the most important. They need to be well placed. First I try to establish just how deep the bass are on the points. I keep marker buoys handy and throw them to the shallow and the deeper parts of the point, and I'll try all different depths on that point. Finally when I get a strike, before I even get the fish in, I reach down and throw a marker out to where I think the fish hit. After I catch one, I'll cast back five or six times to that same spot. Even if I don't catch one, I still want to establish the exact depth and the structure that's there. Some points have hidden structure and cover you might not be aware of, such as a dropoff, a patch of stumps, or a big boulder or two. I get out on the point and use a locator and probe around to find exactly what's there. I want to find out if the bottom is rock, gravel, or mud, and sometimes poke around with my rod tip or a push pole to find out these things. Knowing what's there could be an extremely important part of the pattern. For example, on a gravel bottom, it could be they were in there feeding on crawfish. On a mud bottom, they might be feeding on shad. If they were feeding on crawfish, I'd want to use a crawfish-colored crank bait; if they were hitting shad, I'd want to use a shad color.

Running the points is a matter of efficiency. It's one of the reasons I run a big, fast boat. It's not that I merely want to go sixty miles an hour down the lake. If points are the pattern, then I want to be able to fish seventy-five of 'em in a day, if that's what it takes. If I think the bass might be on the points, then I'll check it out. This is one of the fastest patterns to check out that I know of. In one hour of running points, I can hit perhaps ten points—one every six or seven minutes. I'll try different types of points, including some which the wind is blowing in on, some which are rocky, some with gravel and some with mud bottoms. I'm trying to establish a pattern, and when I find a bass or two on a point, there's usually a definite pattern. It might be a rocky point, whereas the others I tried weren't rocky, and the bass also are apt to be at a certain depth on a certain type of dropoff. Ricky Green and I were looking for a certain depth on a certain kind of bank, and by near the end of the day when we pulled in on a point, we could pretty well tell if we were or weren't going to catch a bass. We had hit so many points that day that we really knew the pattern.

In general, the windswept points have been the most successful for me. I have seen times when I didn't catch 'em on points where the wind was blowing away from the point, but I could go across the lake to points where the wind was blowing in to the point and catch 'em there. The wind needs to be at least pushing the water in front of the point.

One thing I've noticed when scuba diving is that I can be still underwater on a point and stuff will come drifting by in front of my face mask. There might be a one mile-per-hour current moving suspended particles along. The wind will be blowing, and it pushes and circulates the water. I don't know whether bass simply are inclined to feed better in the wind or if the baitfish look like they're distressed and more vulnerable then, but I've always done better with crank baits on overcast, windy days than on bright, calm days. Bright, calm days are usually the worst there are for crank baits.

20. Working the Weedlines

Working the weedlines with a crank bait really takes some skill. It's not simply a toss-and-retrieve type of fishing. I'm talking of weeds such as coontail moss, elodea, water cabbage, moss, and other aquatic vegetation which is only partly visible if at all visible. Often the weeds cranked are completely invisible, and the only way I know they're there is by using the locator.

When your crank bait runs into a bunch of weeds, they're a total nemesis. You can't crank into a bunch of coontail moss or milfoil without getting your crank bait trashed up, and with a glob of vegetation hanging on it, you're not going to get anything to hit it. An extremely sensitive feel is needed here. When I crank down and hit the vegetation for the first time, I stop cranking instantly. Maybe the plug will float free. If it's still caught, I give it a hard yank and sometimes it will tear free, and then I let it float up again to clear the weeds before I start cranking it. Sometimes you'll get a strike as it's floating up. Again, if you feel a tick when you start cranking, then let it float up again, but the problem here is sometimes the ticks are light strikes. You've blown the opportunity to catch that bass if the tick was a light strike and you let the plug float up.

In most instances I'm not really cranking over the top of the weeds. I'm throwing to the weed edge where it quits growing and drops off to a bare bottom. That's the dropoff and the structure for the bass. Parallel casting is how I usually work the weedline, but this is difficult because you don't always know where the weedline might bend. If I cast and don't feel any grass, I throw nearer to where I think the grass line might be, and I keep doing this until I tick the moss. I'm very carefully feeling for the weeds so I'll know where the line is. A graphite rod is helpful for this fishing, although at other times when I'm throwing crank baits, I don't normally use a graphite rod because I get hung up so much. But in moss and weeds you don't get hung up that often and it's good to have the extra sensitivity of graphite.

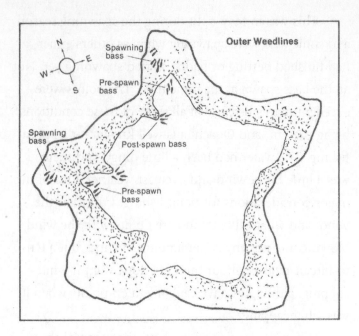

Except for the closed in spawners, bass like the coves and projections along the outer weedline. You have to probe with your lure to locate these irregularities.

One thing very important about cranking the weedlines is to keep in mind that this is structure. And the irregularities of structure are what pay off. Therefore, a straight weedline is not nearly as good as a broken weedline. Where that weedline changes, for example where there's a nook or a little point, is usually where most of the bass are. If you're really watching closely, you might come to a spot on the weedline where a 100-foot nook goes back, and in the back of that nook is where you're apt to find a concentration of bass. A little point of grass which strikes out 20 feet farther than the other grass also is apt to be where the bass are. It takes careful observation to detect those kinds of places. If suddenly you bump into some grass, then you know the grass extends out on a little point, and you might have to use marker buoys to figure out where the grass point extends out to. Two places they'll usually be on a grass line are at the end of a grass point and in back of a nook.

Sometimes you'll find a grass line which runs straight and then maybe 20 feet on out in the lake there'll be another small rise again and another patch of grass along it. Those are really hard to find because you're casting the grass line and you don't know that little grassy island is out there isolated. Again it relates back to structure in that some of the best structure is isolated structure. Sometimes about the only way to find these isolated spots is by running and watching your depthfinder and being observant. It doesn't help here to look at a contour map, because it won't tell you where the weeds actually grow.

In working the weedlines, you don't need to use the deepest-running crank bait in your tacklebox. Often the bass are suspended along the weed edges, and they might be only 4 to 6 feet deep. Shallower crank baits often are excellent. If you find a big moss bed or grass patch all 5 feet deep, it wouldn't hurt to stay out in deeper water and throw in on top of the moss or weeds and retrieve out to the edge. They will be on top of the moss or weeds in the flats, but the bigger concentrations will be on the edges of the vegetation.

This is a clear-water pattern. You're not going to find deep moss or deep vegetation in a muddy lake. The best time to fish this clear water is when there are low light conditions, and again if the water is clear, the cooler water temperatures pay off better. A light wind or breeze will help somewhat because it breaks up the light penetration into the water. There is much more light penetration from the sun down through slick water. That added light helps them detect your line and see the lure too well. With some riffles or chop on the surface, they don't get that good a look at the lure as it comes past. In ultra-clear water a very fast retrieve sometimes works best because they don't see the bait as well and it can fool them.

In clear, weedy waters, the best crank-bait colors seem to be the chromes, shads, and the other light colors. But in a muddy lake where you're cranking stumps or creek channels, the best colors are the crawfish colors, reds and chartreuse colors—the bright colors. In very clear water is one occasion when you can benefit from using light lines. At times then I use spinning tackle with 8- or 10-pound line. This will enable you to get your crank bait considerably deeper.

Also, that lighter line will pay off better in super-clear water.

Weedline crank-bait fishing is an entirely different type of crank-bait fishing. When you're cranking the weedlines, you really need to pay close attention and keep thinking structure.

21. Tweaking the Grub

The grub lure has been around in saltwater fishing for a long time—probably twenty-five years or more. They used the old Salty Dog grub for seatrout and channel bass off the coast. It's been a standard. Never had it been used much in freshwater bass fishing until late 1970 or early 1971. This type of lure has a jig head with the hook protruding upward through a soft or semi-soft molded plastic body. Usually the body mimics a grub but it can be an imitation of some other live and tasty morsel.

The guys most responsible for the freshwater application of the grub were the Murray brothers—Bobby and Billy—from Hot Springs, Ark. Bobby Murray used the grub in the spring of 1972 when he won the B.A.S.S. tournament at Ouachita. I came in second; he beat me by a pound.

After the tournament was over, he gave me a couple of grubs and told me how to use 'em. I'd heard rumors about grubs, but I wasn't crazy about light spinning tackle and I wasn't too excited about them. Finally a month later I was back in Oklahoma and I went up to Grand Lake. It's similar to Ouachita in that it's clear and has a lot of rock shoals and very little cover. It has a lot of spotted bass and largemouths and a variety of panfish and other gamefish. I put the grub on and started jigging around some of the bluffs. My first fish was a white bass, and then a crappie, and finally I started catching some Kentuckies. I was fishing the grub much as I would work a regular jig. I was just swimming it along rather than "tweaking" it.

Eventually I learned how to "tweak" or jig it properly as a structure lure. A guy named Jack Perry

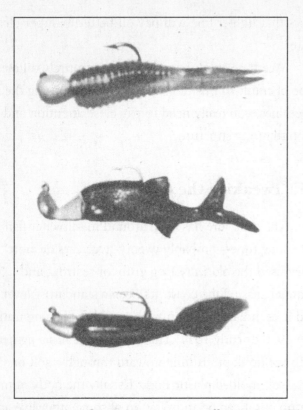

Three basic styles of grub. These are very effective deep-water lures for jigging on structure.

was doing an article for *Field & Stream*, and I took him fishing and told him I had a brand-new bass lure which just had been developed and wasn't really on the market yet. I also told him how I'd been catching a lot of fish on it. That day we caught 300 pounds of assorted fish. We had only seven bass, and they ranged up to 5 pounds, but what was so amazing is we had thirty-seven drum, and these ran to more than 5 pounds. I caught a 29-pound buffalo (it's similar to a carp) and had a couple of 2-pound channel catfish as well as some crappies and white bass. All of them were caught on the grub.

I don't know of any other lure in my tackle box I've experimented with and caught so many different species of fish on as the grub. Through the years I've caught just about as many other species of fish on the grub as bass. The grub is a very effective deep-water lure for jigging on structure.

That summer on Grand Lake, through experimenting I came up with a way to tweak the grub. How I do this is either make a short cast or merely open my bail and let the lure go to the bottom and then jig it. Instead of simply pulling the lure up off the bottom as I would a worm or a jig and eel, I actually bounce it off the bottom. I use a 5 ½- or 6-foot stiff graphite rod and 6- or 8-pound line. I want the grub to jump violently off the bottom much as a crawfish does. A grub is the size, color, and shape of a crawfish. A crawfish jumps off the bottom and then falls back down, moving in little short motions or spurts. This must be what the grub imitates.

But by tweaking it, you have one other advantage, and this is that lots of times bass will soft-mouth a lure as it's sinking back down. You're keeping the slightest amount of back pressure on the lure and you're watching your line closely, so you'd think you'd feel the strike, but lots of times you don't! The strike almost always comes as the lure is sinking. By tweaking it—ripping it upward—you set the hook in bass which hit it undetected, ones you didn't know were there. You're setting the hook blindly without even knowing there's a fish around. This tweaking also enhances the action of the grub; I get more strikes when I tweak it off a foot or two and then let it flutter back down. I keep a slight bit of back pressure on it and watch the line as it sinks, and again, as with all jigging lures, 98 percent of the strikes occur on the fall.

My biggest day with the grub came that autumn when I qualified for the Project: Sports Tournament of Champions. It was held on Lake Amistad on the Texas-Mexico border. Bobby Murray and I were the only two grub fishermen there. I went way up the lake on the Mexican side and found an old vertical ledge in a cove. On the top of the ledge was 10 to 15 feet of water, but it dropped straight down into 100 feet of water, and there were mesquite bushes on the edge of it. Rather than casting, I just dropped the grub down through the bushes to the top of the ledge. The advantage here of jigging it vertically is that if you jig it directly straight down, it frequently dislodges itself if it hits a bush or any other cover. If you jig it around carefully through the cover, you probably won't lose more than a few a day, and grubs are cheap. If you're vertical, you actually can tweak pretty heavy brush and cover.

My partner that first day asked me what I was going to do and I told him I was going to grub the ledge. He said he sure as heck didn't know what that was, and he added that he was going to use plastic worms. I put out two marker buoys about 20 feet apart and fished right between them where the ledge was. All I did was open the bail on my spinning reel, and the grub dropped to the top of the ledge. I was watching my locator, and in addition to the mesquite, I thought I saw a school of fish. As it turned out, I pulled up right on top of a school of largemouths, and the first eleven times I opened my bail and let the grub sink, I caught ten largemouths and missed one. My partner had made a long cast off the ledge, and instantly I hooked one and asked him to get the net. He put his rod down and netted my first bass.

Then I dropped back down and he picked up his rod and I was yelling for the net again. He put his rod back down and netted the second one. I finally had five or six bass in the boat which he had netted, and he still hadn't retrieved his first cast. After that, he says, "Now, wait a minute! You net your own damn fish and let me fish awhile."

I had a limit in the boat, and those bass totaled 23 or 24 pounds. Finally he asked me if I had a grub that he could borrow. I said I did, but really I was planning to leave the spot immediately. He said he didn't have his limit yet, and I reminded him this was the Tournament of Champions and that I'd found this spot and I couldn't afford to let him sit there and catch the bass I'd found. He got a little upset, and I said I'd make a deal with him. I'd give him a grub and show him how to use it and let him catch one or two bass on that spot, but then we were going to leave that hole. He went along with that idea and dropped his grub down there and followed my instructions, but he didn't react quick enough to his first couple of strikes and missed them. I'd seen his line move, and he didn't notice it or

feel anything. Finally he caught two, and I said, "Okay. We're gone!"

Well, the next day, it was exactly the same deal on that spot. I caught my ten and left again. On the third and last day of the tournament it was real windy and I couldn't get on the ledge and couldn't anchor because I didn't have a long enough rope. All I could do was make a few wild casts, and I managed to catch a couple of bass in those 3-foot waves. I had to go back into a cove and tie up to some trees and fish plastic worms, but I did manage to win the tournament by 5 or 6 pounds. Tweaking the grub enabled me to win.

Lots of fishermen ask me when to use the grub. I consider it a summer structure type of lure. I usually fish it in water over 10 feet deep and down to 40 feet deep, and normally I fish it on points and ledges and in creek channels. I generally reserve a grub for more open areas, whereas I reserve the other jigging lures (the heavy spoons, tailspin lures such as the Little George, and plastic worms) for heavy cover. The grub is a clear-water lure, whereas the spoons and worms sometimes don't pay off as well in crystal-clear water. On a lake

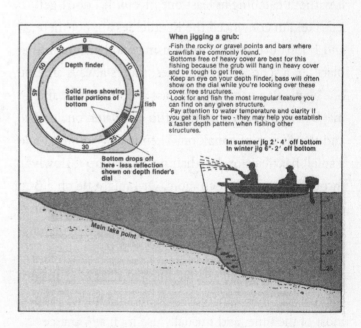

You really need a depth finder to pinpoint the structure for a vertical method like jigging. I often use two, one on the transom and the other on the bow, to give me a kind of stereo effect when I'm scouting structure.

like Mead in Nevada or Powell in Utah, I'd likely fish the grub because the spoon might be too gaudy and flashy. An advantage to the grub is that you can fish it with as light as 4-pound line, although I prefer 6- and 8-pound. With light lines you should use a jig head with a sharp Aberdeen hook. This makes for easy penetration when you set the hook.

I mainly fish the grub in the structure months—June through October—when the water temperature is 70 degrees or higher. It's more of a summer and fall lure than a springtime lure, but I have seen it work right around spawning season on deeper points adjacent to the spawning areas in clear lakes like Bull Shoals. An advantage of the grub over the plain jig is that the grub is a much faster lure. The grub is a school-bass lure, especially with Kentucky bass. I think it's the most effective lure ever devised for a school of medium-sized Kentucky or spotted bass. Spots eat many crawfish, and the grub is a very quick way to check if they're there. You can drop a grub down into a school of spots, and you might catch only one or two before you spook 'em, but I've never gotten over a school of them and dropped the grub down and jigged it without catching at least one of 'em. If I don't get a strike, I'm convinced the Kentuckies are not there, and I don't even think about using another lure in that place. In a school of Kentuckies, there's always at least one aggressive fish. Spotted bass are smart fish, and maybe I'll find 'em with the grub and catch one or two, and they'll sort of spook off. Then is when I might take a small bear-hair or deer-hair jig and pump it slowly through there and catch more. Or I might tie on a 3- or 4-inch plastic worm and crawl it along through that area, and I might even try to catch a couple by jigging a spoon.

Today there are several different sizes of grubs on the market. I use a medium size about 3 inches long most of the time, and I usually use it on a ¼-ounce jig head. Sometimes I go to a slightly smaller head—about ⅕-ounce—and if the wind's strong, I might go to a ⅜-ounce. A grub head is different from a regular jig

head in that the grub head has a tiny spur on it. When you run the grub on the hook, you continue with it up on the lead, and that spur helps hold it in place. With just a plain jig head, the grub will slide back down the hook and bunch up at the bend, or it will twist on the hook. When I rig the 3-inch grub, I always have the tail flat rather than up and down. (One of my favorite grubs is the little Vibortail, which has a little fin near the tail and looks like a minnow. There's only one way for it to be attached.) On the Bagley and Mann grubs, the tails are flat and should be run on the hook so that when they're sinking or being jigged, the tails are flat with the surface of the water. This gives it a better flutter and makes it sink slower.

I don't know if the grub is as good for small-mouths as the hair jig and pork rind, but I'm convinced the grub is a better Kentucky bass lure, and it's also an excellent lure for largemouths in clear lakes and particularly on rocky points. I like to fish it on rock ledges and rocky, gravelly points without much cover. It's a very fast way to learn if there's a school of fish present.

22. Jigging with Spoons, Worms, and Tailspins

About the time I started guiding at Santee-Cooper in 1963, a guy about my age from Summerville, S.C., named Tommy Salisbury became serious about his bass fishing. We got acquainted and really hit it off, and for nearly fifteen years now we've been very good friends. Tommy had fished three or four bass tournaments, and he asked me when I was going to enter a tournament. I told him that when I entered one, I really was going to be prepared! Well, I decided to go to Toledo Bend with him for a Bass Anglers Sportsman Society tournament in January of 1970. It was my first tournament, and I especially wanted to do well.

Tommy and I sent off and got a bunch of topographical maps, and we really did our homework long before we left South Carolina and drove to Texas. We marked creek channels and high spots and everything that looked good on the topo maps, and we went out there ten days early. We got out there about three o'clock one morning, and there was ice on the trailer steps at Pendleton Bridge Marina. It was really cold. Tommy had his boat and I had mine, and the best day either one of us had was three bass the first three days we were there. We fished mostly jigs and eels. And we'd heard about jigging those Texas spoons, so we jigged them in the creek channels.

We ran into Billy and Bobby Murray, and they were catching bass, and they showed us how they were jigging their spoons. Toledo Bend was only three years old then, and the trees had all the branches on 'em. The Murrays were pulling their boat through the branches and dropping their jigging lures right down alongside the tree trunks, and they were catching bass. We started doing what they were doing, and we started catching some fish.

The weather started warming up, and about three days before the tournament it got up to 80 degrees. Tommy and I agreed to meet one day about lunchtime at the Texas Bluff area. Tommy was headed there, and he came across a cove and smelled some fish. He thought maybe they were bass, so he suggested we go back there. The cove was almost solid trees in 60 feet of water. I had a spinnerbait on and started throwing it, and every little alley I could get the bait through, we'd see ten to twenty bass coming out of the trees after it. And the water was 50 to 60 feet deep below them! We finally measured the water temperature, and for the first three feet, the water was 55 to 58 degrees. Below that it dropped about 10 degrees. Those bass were up near the surface sunning themselves. That afternoon we caught about seventy-five bass. The next day we split up, and each of us looked for similar coves where the water was slick. Where we found slick water, we could run the spinnerbaits and catch 'em close to the top.

The morning of the first round of the tournament, we got out on the water with the rest of the boats. It was just getting daylight, and we saw this big, black cloud coming. It was what the Texans call a blue norther. The wind blew, and it rained and stormed, and man, did it turn cold! This all hit within five minutes after Ray Scott shot the gun. Tommy fished with Glenn Carver, who now owns Mr. Twister lures, and they jigged spoons about 20 feet deep in Slaughter Creek, and Tommy was in eighteenth or nineteenth place after the first day. I'd drawn Joe Palermo. (I told earlier about having five rods rigged up with five spoons and catching six bass in a row while he was catching one and trying to get the hooks out of it.) I culled bass—releasing the smaller ones—after about nine a.m., and I soon got into the top twenty-five.

There were two different jigging patterns on Toledo Bend during that tournament. There were school bass suspended 20 feet deep over 50 feet of water on the river channel. These were mostly 1 ¼-to-1 ½-pounders, and they were what I caught the first day. The second day I drew J. B. Warren from Arkansas. He and Jack Price had found five or six super holes full of big bass in the creek channels. J.B. was confident about his chances of winning because he and Price had all these big bass located. The first day he'd caught only five or six, but they were in the 4-pound range. He took me into a creek. He was fishing a jig and eel, but I'd been fishing spoons for a couple of weeks, and I knew they were hitting spoons. He caught the first one, about a 4-pounder, on the jig and eel.

I told him I was going to try a spoon. The water temperature was about 50 degrees, because another cold front had hit, and the way to fish the spoon was to raise it up about 2 feet off the bottom in this heavy tree-and-brush cover and almost lower it down by keeping slight back pressure on the lure as it fell. These were cold-water bass, and cold-water bass don't strike hard; they just sort of stop the lure. I use fluorescent line and watch for the slightest twitch when I'm fishing this way in cold water. If the bait doesn't sink back all the way, usually it's a fish and you need to set the hook. That day they were halfway hitting at the spoon and missing it, and the lure would fall on their backs. I'd feel the hesitation and set the hook, and two or three of the bass I caught with J.B. were foul-hooked in the side of their gills. The bass I caught were mostly 3-to-5-pounders, and I weighed in 39 pounds that second day. It put me way up in the standings with one day left. J.B. had a slow day, and that evening he told me he didn't stand a chance to win, but I did, and he said he wanted me to go back to that creek channel he knew about and stay there and win the tournament on that hole. I told him I didn't want to do that and that I wanted to honor his hot spot.

The third day I didn't go to J.B.'s hot spot. I went to another creek with my partner, Jim Saxton from Texas, and we jigged spoons around different high spots. I caught 26 pounds and finished second. But the odd part about it was that when I came back to the weigh-in, J. B. Warren asked me if I'd gone back to that creek he and I had fished, and I told him I hadn't. Well, as it turned out, he hadn't gone back there either! It was the hottest place on the lake, and neither of us had fished it! I figured he should fish it, and he figured I should fish it. Nobody fished it!

Here again, I count down the spoon as I do my other underwater lures, and this is important. Lots of times when you're drifting and jigging, you'll find a little mound or a dropoff much easier and quicker if you're counting the spoon down. In the winter and cold water, I don't lift the spoon more than 2 feet off the bottom, but in the summer you can jig it much faster and lift it higher.

The biggest tournament I ever won with a jigging spoon was at Santee-Cooper in the 1975 South Carolina Invitational B.A.S.S. event. I fished the lower lake (Moultrie) and jigged with a Hopkins Spoon. The water temperature was 75 degrees during the first week of June when the event was held, and there was a lot of wind. The bass were active, and I lifted the spoon much higher, and they hit much harder. I was using a large popping type of rod, and I'd lift the spoon 4 to 8 feet off the bottom. With a 6-foot rod, you can lift a spoon 15 feet off the bottom when you put the rod tip

almost to the water and then bring it back over your head and finally your shoulder. We learned this jigging the spoons for striped bass at Santee, and we found the rockfish like a much higher lift and much more violent jigging motion.

Jigging fish are structure fish whether they're stripers or black bass. In the summer a good jigging spot could be a submerged hill, a point, or the edge of a creek channel. But in the winter, creek channels generally pay off better. Bass generally like high spots in the summer and creek channels in the winter. I prefer jigging heavy spoons rather than casting lures because jigging is more direct. The only time I cast is when I'm looking for fish, but I miss a lot of fish casting because I don't have the direct control of the lure. The best way to catch 'em is to get vertical and drop the lure right down on the fish and jig it on the structure. I don't fish the spoon shallower than 15 feet because deep-structure fish are 15 feet or deeper. Most of the deep-structure lakes where you can catch bass good by jigging spoons are clear-water lakes, and particularly in the summer those bass on structure are at a minimum of 15 feet deep and often 20 to 30 feet deep. I have caught 'em deeper. I came in second in the B.A.S.S. tournament at Sam Rayburn in 1971, and the best string I caught there, about 30 pounds, was by jigging a spoon 46 feet deep. Those were the deepest bass I've ever caught in a tournament.

I get asked by fishermen when I use the spoon and when I vertical-jig the plastic worm. The spoon is for both warm and cold water, whereas the worm is strictly a hot-weather bait. In the summer the bass on deep structure will be at the thermocline levels in water 60 to 80 degrees, and this is a good time to jig the worm. Jigging a spoon really gets 'em excited. But I do a lot of changing up. I might be jigging a spoon and catch two or three bass and then they quit hitting the spoon. Then I drop a worm or a grub down there, and often I'll catch more after changing lures. I have seen times when they would hit the worm and not the spoon, but usually when you run into a school of bass, you catch a

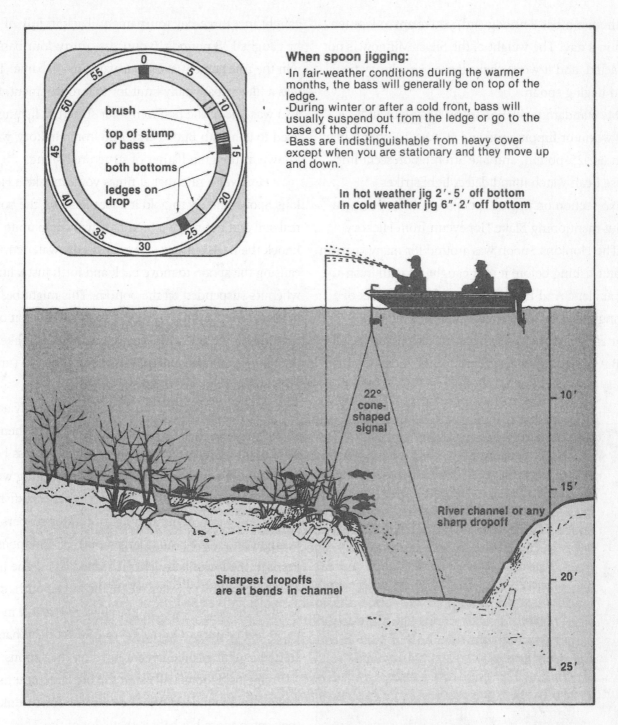

When spoon jigging:
-In fair-weather conditions during the warmer months, the bass will generally be on top of the ledge.
-During winter or after a cold front, bass will usually suspend out from the ledge or go to the base of the dropoff.
-Bass are indistinguishable from heavy cover except when you are stationary and they move up and down.

In hot weather jig 2'- 5' off bottom
In cold weather jig 6"- 2' off bottom

brush
top of stump or bass
both bottoms
ledges on drop

22° cone-shaped signal

River channel or any sharp dropoff

Sharpest dropoffs are at bends in channel

10'

15'

20'

25'

Once you've located structure like this, you can fish it very effectively with a spoon; unlike a grub, a spoon will usually come free when hung up.

couple right quick on whatever you're using. The spoon is simply the fastest way to find them. Nothing sinks as fast as a spoon. When I jig a worm, I use 6-to-8-inch worms rigged regular Texas-style, but I usually use a ⅜- or ½-ounce lead.

Four of the popular jigging spoons on the market today are the Hopkins, Bomber Slab, Salty Dog by Bagley, and Mann-O-Lure. One thing about these heavy spoons with their heavy treble hooks is that you might jig one of 'em all day without losing it. When it hangs in heavy cover, you can keep jiggling it and the weight of it often will cause it to knock loose. You might not believe it, but you can jig the same cover all day with a single-hook Johnson Spoon (the Silver Minnow), and even though it has a weedguard, you're apt to lose ten of 'em in a day! The weight of the Silver Minnow is not compacted, and it won't shake loose like a heavy metal-bodied jigging spoon.

My standard tackle for spoon jigging includes a heavy worm or flipping rod and at least 20-pound line. I often use 25-pound, and like Stren Fluorescent line because I can watch it and detect light strikes.

No section on jigging spoons would be complete without mentioning Blake Honeycutt from Hickory, N.C. The Hopkins Spoon was around for many years in saltwater fishing before it ever caught on with fresh-water anglers. And Blake was one of the pioneers of adapting the Hopkins to freshwater bassing. He's a master at jigging the spoons, and he also holds the all-time B.A.S.S. tournament record for the most pounds caught in a three-day tournament. Back in July of 1969 he caught 138 pounds, 6 ounces—thirty-four bass—to win the tournament at Lake Eufaula in Alabama. There was a fifteen-bass daily limit for that tournament. Blake also was one of the first to master structure fishing. He used to fish with Buck Perry, also from Hickory, who is known as the grandfather of structure fishing.

Honeycutt says that at times you can take a Hopkins Spoon and try to hold it a foot or so off the bottom real still and not move it, and bass will come up to it and knock the heck out of it. He believes the water current is causing the spoon to move back and forth just a little bit when it's suspended off the bottom. This might be, but I believe, too, that from using the spoon, a little bit of line twist develops, and when you're holding it still like that, the line straightens out and causes the spoon to turn a little bit, and this is what attracts the bass.

We got onto using the jigging spoons early at Santee-Cooper, as far back as 1963, but back then we used them exclusively for stripers. The first bass I ever caught on one was one time when I was fishing with another guide, Bob George. He's an expert rockfish guide, and we were out fishing for fun for stripers, and I caught about a 4-pound largemouth off Pinopolis Point in the lower lake. Then I started trying the jigging spoon in shallower water where the largemouths stayed. Most of the stripers we caught jigging were out in 40 to 50 feet of water. On the 20-to-25-foot-deep bars, I started catching some largemouths on the spoons.

Jigging spoons will catch the big largemouths which are down deep, but the reason I don't think they catch more big bass is that a lot of the 7-to-10-pounders are in shallower cover rather than down 20 to 30 feet deep. At Santee during the seven years I fished regularly there, I caught twenty-four bass over 10 pounds, but only two of them ever came off deep structure. However, the jigging spoons are super for catching bass from 2 to 4 or 5 pounds, and that size I'm sure after when I'm in a tournament.

The most popular of a few tailspin lures on the market is the Little George. Tom Mann, the manufac-

A heavy-weighted worm designed for deep-water structure produced this 9-pound bass on Georgia's West Point Lake way back in 1987. Note the antique depthfinder!

turer, named it after the Alabama governor, George Wallace, and Tom says Wallace got quite a kick out of the name. It has an oval-shaped lead body and a spinner which revolves on a wire behind the body. The spinner revolves as the lure sinks as well as when it's pulled upward. Tom's sold probably a zillion of 'em, and one of the reasons is it's not like a Hula Popper that you can fish for fourteen years without losing it. Having one Little George is like having one potato chip; it's not enough. You're going to leave some Little Georges hanging on stumps and lodged between rock crevices in deep water.

I like the Little George more for casting than for vertical jigging. If I'm fishing a bar, shoal, or dropoff, I make casts with it. These tail-spinners can be vertical-jigged, and they're great lures, but they don't get to the bottom as fast as the spoons do.

23. Grazing the Grass

This pattern brings back some very fond memories of the late 1960s when I was at Santee-Cooper. I did some experimenting by taking a black Johnson Spoon (the Silver Minnow) and attaching a 4- or 5-inch tail section of a black plastic worm. The first good bass catch I made on it was in the spring of 1967 in the lower lake near the mouth of the Diversion Canal. Two weeks later I was guiding a Mr. Smith, and I was telling him all about catching several 8- and 9-pounders on the black Johnson Spoon with the worm trailer.

I rigged one up for him, and he threw out by this grass bed, and he hooked a 6 ½-pounder which really ate up his spoon. He fought the fish to the boat and I netted him, but he didn't say a word. I'm all excited and telling him about this brand-new technique and how great it is. I'll never forget what he then said.

"Son," he said slowly, "I'm seventy-six years old, and the Johnson Spoon was my father's favorite bait."

I was catching those bass in May of 1967, and by May the next year, I'd figured out something most of us didn't realize. We thought that after April, Santee's bass were through spawning. We didn't realize that during May and even early June, we could look around and actually find a few spawners. In May of 1968 about the middle of the month my customers and I caught two or three bass from 8 to 10 pounds per day, and this lasted for a week. We got them on the black Johnson Spoons, around the full moon. The full moon in June also produced well in the grass. At that time, however, the grass beds were dying, and the next year there'd be only two-thirds as much grass as the year before. From one standpoint this was good, because it tended to concentrate the bass more.

Finally by May 1969 I'd gone to big, heavy popping rods, 30-pound line, and hooks that I'd bent out on the spoons to make them a little bigger. I also switched to Bagley's Hardhead plastic worms, which were a harder plastic. And I'd figured out to throw into the wind so the grass I was pulling the spoon over was bent toward me and the lure would slide over it better. When fishing clear water, you often want the sun at your back because your visibility is then good, and fish don't like to look into the sun. But when you're grazing the grass, you won't see much anyway and the fish are more likely to see your shadow than to see you. So I also learned to throw into the sun as much as I could in order to keep my shadow down.

That year was a super year, and in that month of May was when I set all my personal bass records at Santee. My customers and I caught forty-two bass over 8 pounds that month. On May 14, I caught ten largemouths which totaled 87 pounds, and they all were caught on that ½-ounce No. 2 Johnson Spoon with the black worm trailer. Five days later I caught ten on the spoon that totaled 79 pounds, and three of them were each over 10 pounds. Both days were cloudy days.

A couple of things Tommy Salisbury and I discovered about our "grazing the grass" pattern with the Johnson Spoons was, first of all, unless it was a cloudy day, we had to catch our bass before nine o'clock in the morning or at dusk when the sun got off the water. Between nine a.m. and dusk, the pattern was dead if the weather was clear. We had one good hole, and we got to wondering if those bass would hit at night. I was guiding two college students one day, and I talked them into getting up at three a.m. and going to that hole. We fished for an hour and a half without a strike. We waded all along those grass beds and threw everywhere, and finally the sun started showing through the trees.

I saw a boil and threw over there and caught a 1 ½-pound white bass on the Johnson Spoon, my first and last white bass ever caught on the spoon. I told the guys we'd messed up and that there weren't going to be any bass coming in there. Finally it was full daylight, and just before the sun broke completely over the trees I caught a 2-pounder. When the first rays of the sun finally hit the grass bed, a herring about 10 inches long went skipping across the surface, and I threw in there and caught an 8 ½-pounder. One of the college boys caught one about 8 pounds. Then we got a 7-pounder. This continued until about nine o'clock, and then they quit. But in an hour and a half we caught a bunch, and our ten biggest weighed 70 pounds. And we'd fished there for an hour and a half before we got the first strike.

The best fishing always came during the first couple weeks of May when the green grass grew up and laid a mantle on the surface. Before that we caught some bass on the Johnson Spoons around the brown grass. I run my spoons on the surface or just an inch or two under, but Tommy Salisbury likes to skip his spoon across the top and use it strictly as a topwater lure.

Tiny Lund, the racecar driver who owned a fish camp on the lower lake, used to fish for bass only with a black Johnson Spoon and a worm behind it as I did.

Despite the fact that a Johnson Spoon has a single hook and a weedguard, I don't lose many bass on it. When I first started fishing it, I was using a 6-foot rod and an Ambassadeur and 20-pound line, and I lost several fish. The 20-pound line is marginal; 25 and 30 is better. That's what I want. The other problem is that with that heavy spoon, you have a tendency to make a long cast. When I was on a big grass bed, I'd find myself making 100-foot casts, and when they hit way out there, I couldn't get the hook set good enough on 'em. To set the hook properly, I went to a popping rod and a casting rod with a big saltwater handle. I wanted something I could hold in my stomach for leverage.

Probably the most important aspect of grass-bed fishing is to point the rod at the spoon. If you hold the rod high, then you don't have any way to strike back good. Also the low rod position enables you to work the spoon better.

This pattern works very well in Florida. A Johnson Spoon probably catches more bass over 8 pounds in Lake Okeechobee today than anything other than a live shiner. In fact, it probably catches more than the shiners, because shiners aren't all that popular down there. It's a great springtime lure for spawning bass, and down there January and February are big spawning months. The spoon also works good in Wisconsin and Minnesota in the lily pads and weeds, and in Canada for northern pike as well as bass. I like the black spoon for a dark day and the gold one for a sunny day.

Even in Oklahoma and Texas, you don't think of having grass beds in lakes like the grass and milfoil in North Carolina's Currituck Sound, for example. But the Lone Star State and the Sooner country has grass called pond weed. It grows usually in 2 to 4 feet of water, sometimes a little deeper, and it has oblong leaves about 1 ½ inches long. Snaking the spoon right on top of the grass really pays off, and the heavier the grass, the slower you can work it. Work it slow in that heavy cover, because there's so much stuff for them to get through to hit the spoon.

I've experimented with all sorts of trailer hooks on the Johnson Spoon, but none of 'em performs well. You're fishing so much heavy vegetation that a trailer hook just doesn't work good. I advise you to forget about even trying a trailer hook.

Some guys thread their plastic worm on the weedguard of the Johnson Spoon and then run it up to the bend of the hook. This gives the lure a different action, but I don't rig it this way very often. I guess it's just that I've seen so many bass from 8 to over 11 pounds blow up on it the way I rig it that I've never seen any reason to change. My biggest on the spoon weighed 11 pounds, 3 ounces.

Some guys really like the Weed Wing Spoon which Johnny O'Neill designed. It's a very fast spoon, and it's great in hot weather, but one thing I've found out is that when the water's in the 50s to low 60s in the spring, the big bass don't move real fast for the spoon, and a slower retrieve catches lots more of 'em. The hotter the water, the faster they move for a spoon. Another good spoon on the market is the Timber King, which Charles Spence of Memphis, Tenn., manufactures. It's similar to the old Rex Spoon made years ago by the old Weetzel Bait Company in Cincinnati.

Tommy Salisbury and I thought our grazing-the-grass pattern was strictly a springtime deal, but we later found it would work to some degree in June, July, and even August. We caught some bass then in the grass.

One thing to remember is that in different lakes in different regions, the aquatic vegetation changes. At Santee we fished Johnson grass. Lake Kissimmee in Florida has the same type of grass, but in Okeechobee, it's pepper grass. At Currituck Sound, which is probably the finest Johnson Spoon water on the continent, it's Eurasian milfoil. Toledo Bend has milfoil and some pond weed. And if you fish the Johnson Spoon in your uncle's farm pond in Illinois, you might be fishing lily pads. Regardless of the type of vegetation, the spoon approach still works, even if you're using it in reeds.

Think *big* bass when you're grazing the grass.

24. Drifting and Trolling Shiners

I used to look down on live-bait fishing at one time in my career. Back then I didn't realize its potential or what a fine way it is to catch trophy fish. My first experience with big river shiners—and I'm talking about the 10-to-12-inch wild shiners which weigh up to a pound—was in Florida with a guy named Chuck Mooney. He's formerly from Ohio and is a guide down in central Florida, and he's caught some 200 bass over 10 pounds, with his biggest 16 ¼ pounds. I met him during a Bass Anglers Sportsman Society tournament in 1970, and aside from any tourney fishing he does, he's strictly a shiner fisherman. All his really giant bass are caught on these large shiners.

My first bass over 10 pounds on a shiner was caught at Watermelon Pond in Florida in 1970 in August while fishing with Chuck.

This was back when Watermelon Pond was a full 7,000 acres. Now it's only about 3,000 acres. Back then it was probably the best lunker hole in Florida. What we did essentially was anchor out in the center near small potholes 10 to 15 feet deep. We also drifted across some potholes with a float and a shiner on about 6 feet of line. We'd get only a couple of fish a day, but very seldom would we ever get a bass under 6 pounds. Normally what we caught would be from 7 to 10 pounds or a little bigger.

I was all keyed up. I'd been fishing at Cape Hatteras and was using a surf rod and had 40-pound line on the reel and my drag set real tight. I got a strike, and he really pulled that float down, and Chuck said to let him take it for a while. When I hit him, I struck back so hard that I sloshed the bass right up to the top. I had to pull him through some lily pads with stems as thick as my thumb. That fish weighed 10 ½ pounds, and he probably would have wrapped up and broken 20-pound-test line. But my 40-pound cut through the lily pads and I finally landed him.

One thing about shiners I found out is that you just can't buy those big river shiners anywhere for the kind of bass fishing Chuck talks about. Basically you have to go out and catch your own shiners. A few guides and commercial outfits go out and trap them. When you can buy them, they normally cost from four to six dollars per dozen. A 12-inch shiner is probably a five-year-old fish, and in a pond it would take so long to raise them that size that it wouldn't be profitable. Of course, you can buy lots of 3-inch shiners, and that's what lots of fishermen use.

Trolling live bait on big lakes is a great way to get into big bass.

About half the fun of shiner fishing is catching your bait. First you have to go out and put the bread out and bait up the spot. You also can use oatmeal or meal cake or something like that to attract the shiners. In most of the Florida lakes shiners are found around coontail moss and underwater grass out from lily pads in the backs of bays and coves. After you put the shiner bait out, you have to wait anywhere from a couple of hours until even the next day, and then you come sneaking back and anchor real quietly on the spot. You catch them with a hook and line, and they're hard to catch. I like to use a 12- to-16-foot cane pole with 8- or 10-pound line and about a No. 12 trout hook with a small shank and an itsy bitsy split shot a couple of inches above the hook. Normally you fish from 3 to 10 feet deep for shiners, and I use a tiny float which is very sensitive to the slightest nibble. I use either a very tiny piece of wadded-up bread or biscuit dough about the size of a medium-sized garden pea. Some guys even use tiny gobs of peanut butter. Fish right over your chum spot, and watch your float real close. Even though these shiners are ½ pound or bigger, they'll suck in that bread or dough much the same as a carp would do. Lots of times the float will just quiver a couple of times, and they'll steal your bait easily. Shiners fight, jump, and thrash around about like a trout. They just go crazy, and they're a lot of sport to catch.

You need a big live well to put three or four dozen shiners in. I usually use a bass-boat live well with a pump which circulates lake water to keep them fresh and alive. Don't put your hands on the shiners any more than you have to, because their scales will fall off and you'll kill 'em. If you can, swing the shiner into your live well and flip him off the hook without touching him. You have to be careful when you open the lid on your live well because shiners will jump clear out of your boat. You need a real lively shiner if you want to catch a super-big trophy bass.

When you've got several dozen shiners and you're ready to go bass fishing, you need to rig up your heavy tackle. What I mean by heavy tackle is line that's at least 20-pound-test, and really 20-pound is rather light. I prefer 25-to-40-pound. In creek channels and deeper areas of the lake, you probably can fish deeper with lighter line if there's not too much trash. But quite often when you're trolling or drifting the weed edges, which are the shallower edges where the lily pads start, you really need to use heavier line because the bass are hunkered up in heavy cover. When they hit and go back into that grass you can set the hook and still pull 'em out of places like that with 40-pound line.

The trick is to put a giant live shiner on about an 8/0 hook. I like to use two hooks when I can, such as a 5/0 or 6/0 hook in the front and maybe an 8/0 hook in the tail. Sometimes in open water where there are no weeds I use a treble hook in the shiner's anal fin and run a 40-pound leader up to my front hook and then extend the leader up to the float. Even if I'm drifting, I like to use the float to see when I'm getting a strike. The float helps tell you where the shiner is, such as a couple of feet out from a weed edge. The float really is your reference point concerning which direction the shiner is moving.

If your shiner is real lively, he gets scared and nervous when a bass comes toward him. The shiner starts quivering, and the float twitches and jumps. Lots of times the shiner comes to the top just before the bass grabs him, and the shiner actually jumps out of the water three or four times. A really big bass often misses the shiner on two or three surges before he catches him, and this adds to your excitement and anticipation. The shiner keeps jumping and the bass keeps charging, and after three to five big swirls the bass gets him and the float goes under. If you've got a treble hook on and you're in a lot of cover, I set the hook quickly, as with a plastic worm. I just drop the rod tip and reel up the slack and bust him hard to try to move him out of the cover. When he first hits the shiner, he might get it crossways in his mouth and both hooks could be hanging on the outside. If it's open water and I can let him run for ten seconds, I'll do that. After he moves off 5 or 6 feet he'll usually stop and turn the shiner in his mouth and engulf it. Then you've got twice as good a chance of hooking the fish. There's a lot of visual contact in shiner fishing when you're using a lively shiner and you get that explosive strike on the surface and the bobber goes under.

When you set the hook, one thing a big Florida bass likes to do is jump right away. He usually doesn't run to deep water when he's around the weed lines. In Florida when you hook one which tries to jump but doesn't clear the water, a standard rule of thumb is that you've got one on over 10 pounds. I have seen 12-pound and even 14-pound bass clear the water, but that's an exception. Huge fish usually slosh around on the top, with the shiner in their mouths.

I think most of the trophy-bass hunters in America prefer to fish shiners in central Florida over any other place in the United States. For some reason southern Florida doesn't seem to have the strain of really big bass. They catch fewer bass over 10 pounds from Orlando on south than they do from Orlando on north. The biggest trophy bass come from Orlando to Jacksonville between Lake Kissimmee and Lake Jackson at Tallahassee. This seems to be the area where the genetically largest bass are. I've caught my biggest ones in the smaller lakes. In Lake George I've never caught many giant bass, but all around Lake George in the Ocala National Forest there are some 200 smaller lakes from an acre in size up to about 7,000 acres. I prefer those 500-to-1,000-acre lakes where I can get my bass boat in and out. I winch my way in and out of those lakes. One main reason I prefer those smaller lakes is they don't get the fishing pressure many other lakes get.

One of my favorite tricks when I can afford it is to fly a day over these lakes, and I'll especially look for one which doesn't look as if it's had any travel. The road to it looks overgrown and there's no trash around the shoreline, and it doesn't look as if anyone's been in there for quite a while. On the average I spend two weeks a year fishing for trophy bass. I fish with my wife, one of my cameramen, and possibly with one of the trophy-bass guides such as Dennis Rahn. In the average two weeks we land three to six bass over 10 pounds. Even though I've caught a couple a day, you don't catch them every day. A good average is one every two or three days.

The time of year which seems the most productive with shiners in those smaller lakes is the colder winter months when the water temperature's in the 50s. From 50 to 60 degrees seems to be the ideal water temperature. The good fishing starts as early as December, but January usually is a better month. February is an excellent month, and March usually is the best month. I'd say February and March are the two months when trophy-bass fishing with shiners is best. Generally the biggest ones you catch are pre-spawners. Of course, in

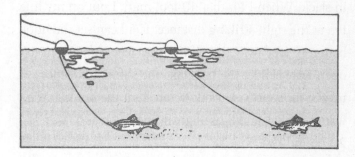

For open water I like to use two treble hooks—a 5/0 or 6/0 in the front and an 8/0 in the tail. When fishing around or through cover, a single weedless hook is better.

some of the bays and warmer springs they'll spawn in January and February, but the majority of the central-Florida bass spawn in March. Just before they spawn and the water's 50 to 55 degrees the big female bass aren't taking artificial lures well at all.

Many fishermen know that until the water gets over 60 degrees, Florida bass don't hit plastic worms good. They hit surface lures some, and they'll hit crank baits some, but Florida bass basically like to hit lures in hot weather. I don't like to use artificial lures in Florida except during the summer months.

Trolling shiners is generally the same as drifting them, except in some lakes with structure such as Rodman Reservoir and Lake Eloise near Cypress Gardens. In these latter the structure might be trenches or potholes, and in them I like to take marker buoys and put them on the dropoffs where the depth drops from 10 to maybe 20 feet. With three or four markers I'll outline that hole, channel, or point. Then with my trolling motor I'll fish a shiner real deep. I don't need to use a float for this type of fishing because I'm in open water with very few obstructions to get hung on. Sometimes I mark my line 40 feet from the hook with a black felt-tip marker. Then I let about 70 feet of line out and use a small weight to slowly bump that shiner along the dropoffs as I circle the structures. When something shakes my bait and I can tell something heavy is pulling on my shiner, I open my bail (on a spinning reel) or push the button (on a free-spool bait-casting reel) and let the bass take out line. Then I reverse the trolling motor and run toward where I think the fish is and reel in slack. When I hit that 40-foot mark I put on my line, I'm at the right striking distance; feel I can set the hook better 40 feet away than if I was 90 feet away. If I'm in open water I'll let the bass take the shiner in deeper, maybe for twenty seconds before I set the hook. If the water's real clear, I'll use lighter line, such as 17- or 20-pound-test.

One time I troll is if it's a calm day when I'm not getting much minnow action. When you hook a shiner through the lips and troll him, he'll live a lot longer, because he's getting lots of oxygen. The problem with a single-hook system like that is you really have to let the bass swallow the bait. But you can do that by going back to your 40-foot mark on your line and getting all the slack out.

One of my favorite hooks for big shiners is the Kahle hook, which is made in Minnesota. Throughout Florida, where they do a lot of shiner fishing, you can find Kahle hooks in most any tackle shop. The Kahle is a real big offset hook with a huge bend in it. Even though the shiner's head takes up part of the bend, there's still enough throat left in the bend to set the hook point properly. Some of the biggest bass I've ever caught were taken while trolling shiners rather than just drifting them along the weed edges.

I usually use a muskie rod—a Fenwick 5 ½- or 6-footer—which is big and stout and has a straight handle with a saltwater reel seat. It has power; you'll never break a muskie rod on a bass. The rod also has a long butt which you can stick into your stomach to get a better hook set. Some worm rods such as Fenwick's and Lou Childre's are No. 6 actions. Based on a number system, a shiner rod would have to be a No. 10. It has to be about twice as stiff as the heaviest, stiffest worm rods. You not only have to drive a very large-diameter hook through a bass' mouth, but you also just cannot afford to miss a single strike when you're shiner fishing. You might get only one or two strikes all day, and you have to have it all together—complete efficiency.

Every year when we go to Florida in February, we try to do a film on shiner fishing. For the past four years I've fished with Dennis Rahn, and for four years in a row we've caught a bass over 10 pounds on film. This is quite an accomplishment considering we had only a few days. We've had two over 12 on film. One day I was fishing with my wife, Mary Ann, and it was raining and we couldn't film. Dennis said we'd try the old Ocklawaha River because lots of times in real cold weather some big fish move up into the warmer waters of the Ocklawaha. It's fed by Silver Springs and has a little bit warmer water following major cold fronts, and fish migrate up that river at these times. We looked for the sharpest, deepest bends in the river, and in some of those the water is 40 feet deep.

We had anchored out in the river, with the sharp, deep dropoff bend about 30 feet away. We were fishing in a circle around the bend, and there were a lot of logs and trees jutting out into the water. We had saltwater rods and reels with 40-pound line and double trailer hooks, because there are so many trees and logs there that the second a fish hits, you have to set the hook. If you get one, he'll be over 10 pounds, but if you let him go three seconds he'll be underneath a log and you'll lose him. Actually you let the shiner swim up real close to the log so that he's just about 4 inches from the log. The bait's right up on top, and you have to keep him from going beneath the log. You let the shiner swim back into crevices and holes in the cover, and then you pull him back out. He keeps cruising up and down the bank and makes a 100-foot circle while staying up against the bank.

Finally after a few minutes a great big bass hit Mary Ann's shiner right by this big log. She set the hook just right and caught a 10 ½- pounder. It was her first 10-pounder in her life. A tornado warning was out, and the wind was howling about forty miles per hour, but we were fairly well protected by the big trees around the shore. Well, one hit me, and I waited too long before setting the hook, and he got under the log on me and wrapped up my line and I finally had to break him off. I rerigged and threw my shiner in again and about that time this big limb came crashing down out of the tree and fell on my line. At the same time I had a bass taking my shiner, and I set the hook with the big limb over my line. I reeled this bass, which was about 10 pounds, up into the limb and he got all tangled up in it and I ended up losing him too.

Mary Ann threw out a shiner away from the cover out in the middle of the river. The shiner was the biggest one we had in the live box, and this tremendous bass crashed it about three times. I could see the bass

My wife, Mary Ann, used shiners to catch these "little fellows" — 9 ½, 10 ½ and 12 ½ pounds!

and I guessed it at 12 pounds. Well, she set the hook and rolled it up on top and finally got it into the net. It weighed almost 12 ½ pounds. She had two big ones and I hadn't caught anything.

A little later she had a shiner out and a bass about 9 ½ pounds crashed her shiner by a log, but by this time it was raining hard and she was cold and miserable. Anyway, she caught the 9 ½ and that one gave her three big ones, and I've still not caught my first one. It was about noon and I took her back to the motor home, and she told me to go back out and fish because I was still after a trophy; she was going to get warm and take a nap.

I went back out and did some trolling and did manage to catch two bass. One was almost 10 and the other was about 9 pounds. We ended up with five fish that day, and the five of 'em weighed almost 50 pounds.

The most exciting shiner fishing I ever saw was back in the early 1970s when they first impounded Rodman Reservoir. There weren't any boat docks on Rodman and not many people were fishing it. There were many trees in the water, and probably this discouraged people. It was a navigational hazard to fish it unless you ran your boat slowly and were extra-careful. It also was hard to get into. You had to go through the locks if you came from Welaka, and there were just a few little ramps along the Ocala Forest. For the first five or six years thousands of bass grew big in this 14,000-acre lake, and they were pretty much unmolested.

Back about 1973 or 1974 I started fishing Rodman, and I saw right away that it was the best big-bass hole in Florida. Rodman was better than Jackson was when it was hot, and also better than Watermelon Pond was when it was hot. From 1972 through 1974 it was the best lake in the country for bass over 10 pounds. I was doing a film in 1974 with Glen Lau for Lowrance Electronics. There was a lot of underwater camera work involved, and we'd been out filming all day. Dennis Rahn was on the lake that day and had caught a 12-pounder. I knew the bass were biting, and I'd brought along thirteen shiners in hopes I'd have a little time to fish that day. It was sundown when we finished our film work, and Glen commented that I hadn't had a chance to fish that day. I told Glen to go on in and that I had thirteen shiners along and planned to fish until dark and then I'd meet him at his house.

Glen leisurely went back to the boat dock, and on his way home he stopped to get gas. I had only thirty or forty minutes to fish before black dark. I think he also stopped to get a sandwich at a convenience store. Anyhow, when he was turning into his driveway I had caught up with him and was right behind him.

What I'd done in those forty-five minutes or so was pull up to a spot near the canal they'd dug through Rodman. I put down my anchor and put out four rods with shiners, and almost instantly all four bobbers went

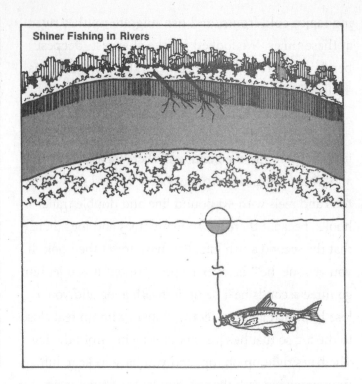

When shiner fishing in rivers, look for the bigger fish in the deeper water around the outside bends or turns, especially where there are fallen trees, brush piles, or other debris. The double treble hook is appropriate for fishing next to this cover.

under. I landed three of those four fish. One of 'em was about 10, another was about 9, and the third one was about 7. The fourth bass broke my line. The next time I baited up with two rods and threw them out, and I got strikes on them. In just 20 minutes I used up my thirteen shiners and ended up with ten bass.

Glen asked me if I'd gotten a strike, and I said that as a matter of fact I had. I said I'd gotten a limit, and he didn't believe me. He said I hadn't been out there long enough to have gotten a limit. I had 'em on a rope, and Glen was saving a lot of bass at that time for underwater work on the movie *Bigmouth* and films for The Fisherman series we did with Homer Circle, and he needed big bass to put in his big aquarium. I'd kept 'em alive in my live well, and we put the rope full of 'em on his big scales and they weighed 73 pounds.

That was the fastest action I've ever seen. Back then at Rodman there were actually schools of these big bass, and I'd gotten into one. They often roamed the middle of the lake, and when you caught one, five or six or eight bass would follow the one you'd hooked right up to the boat. Quite often you could just anchor at that point and cast all around and doggone near catch your limit right from that one spot. There's still a lot of big bass in Rodman, but it's nothing like it was back in 1974. At the hole I had where I'd caught those ten, in a month's time I caught a total of sixty bass 6 pounds and over. I really didn't catch all that many bass over 10 pounds from that hole; I probably averaged one every two or three days.

On one of my best days at Rodman I had an 11¾, an 11¼, a 10½, and a 10¼. I also had two bass right at 9 pounds.

But my best day was with Glen Lau's eleven-year-old son, Davie. We fished one day in April of 1975 when I was finishing up some film work. When I took Davie with me, Glen told me not to spoil him by letting him catch too many fish because he'd think bass fishing was too easy. But I really did spoil him. I let him set the hook, and he caught an 11 ¾-pounder that day as well as a 10 ½ and a 10 ¼. Imagine that! An eleven-year-old with three over 10 in one day! I also caught a 10-pounder, and we weighed our top eight bass and they hit 68 pounds.

25. Running Shiners

"Running" the shiners is a completely different pattern from drifting or still-fishing with shiners. When you run shiners, you're seeking out heavy cover and remaining stationary while the shiner does the moving. You let him go beneath the cover. The hyacinth beds in Florida are where running shiners really pays off. Some of the central-Florida lakes in particular have huge shelves of hyacinths which stick out from the bank. Typical lakes with these masses of hyacinths are any lakes along the St. Johns River system. Probably half the lakes in the Ocala National Forest—and these are public lakes—all have big patches of hyacinths.

The wind blows the hyacinths around, and they move from day to day. When you find hyacinths which

have blown against a good edge with deep water beneath them, let your boat drift up to the edge or anchor about 10 feet out. Put a single hook near the tail of the shiner above the anal (bottom) fin of the baitfish and don't use any weight. The weight of the hook holds him upright. Cast him to the edge of the hyacinths, and by pulling him backward a little bit, you get him to run away from you. Cast him softly, because you want to keep him as lively as possible. Keep fiddling with him and give him slack so that he runs away from you and goes beneath the hyacinths. The bass almost always lie in the shade beneath the hyacinths, and sometimes they're 10 to 20 feet back beneath the hyacinths.

If the shiner is running high in the water, he'll get wrapped in the hyacinths, so you need to keep him running as low as possible. The roots of the hyacinths hang down about 2 feet, and if you keep him running low, he'll get back beneath them without hanging up. Maybe out of a dozen shiners, only three or four will make good runs beneath the hyacinths. Many of them will circle out to open water, and others will run beneath the hyacinths a few feet and see a bass and then they'll head out toward open water. They're not dumb; they don't want to become lunch for the largemouth.

When you get a shiner back there 15 or 20 feet, he might wrap up slightly around the hair roots of the hyacinths. Just let him sit there. When a bass hits him, he blows the shiner upward. Lots of times you'll see the hyacinths rise up in a huge bulge. That's the bass boiling up and engulfing the shiner.

Quite often it's hard to tell if you've got a bass on or if the shiner is doing the moving. It takes some practice to tell the difference. When you pull back, if you all of a sudden feel a surge on your line, you've got a bass on. But often when a bass hits, you'll see the line jump and take off at a fairly steady rate. The shiner moves along in short twitches or spurts.

Even though the shiner is way back beneath the hyacinths, when a bass hits, I like to let him run 10 to 20 seconds before I set the hook. Before you set the hook, the best thing to do is get as far forward in the boat as you can and try to get all of your slack line reeled in. Stretch out forward toward where you think the bass is, reel in the line fast until it's tight, and then set the hook with a big sweeping motion with the long rod. Then back up three or four steps and set the hook again, and back up some more and set again. Finally after all that hook setting, you've straightened your line out and you've got the bass hooked.

For this type of fishing I like to use extremely heavy line; I prefer 40-pound-test. The bass that hits way back in the hyacinths still is apt to get wrapped up and tangled in all the vegetation. Getting him out of there is not very glamorous, but he's apt to be a trophy fish.

Occasionally you can run shiners in lily pads, but in the lilies, the shiner is going to get hung up a lot worse. Pull up to the edge of the pads and let the shiner out and let him run up into them. Quite often you don't ever get the shiner back, because he will wrap up in them. When you pull him back, you tear him off the hook. When you run shiners, you use a lot of shiners. Sometimes I'll use six to eight dozen in a day. You're constantly losing your bait because it gets wrapped up in vegetation. You also get a lot of strikes which pull the bait off the hook. Chain pickerel or "jackfish" are bad about doing this or killing your shiners.

When I'm running shiners, I frequently use the smaller shiners instead of the larger ones. I like the 6-to-7-inch shiners because they run good. The 12-inch ones have power, but they don't have as much stamina as the smaller ones. A good, lively 7-inch shiner will do more swimming around and will last longer than a big one.

My father-in-law, Paul Colbert, thinks there's no greater fishing in the world than running shiners. He'd rather anchor 10 feet out from a hyacinth patch and sit there and run shiners back in under the hyacinths all day than do any other kind of fishing. Every winter when he and his wife, Mary, accompany Mary Ann and me on our annual migration to Florida, Paul makes sure we've got Dennis Rahn booked up for a few days of

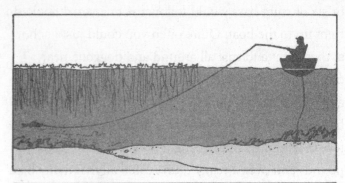

A large, lively golden shiner which is allowed to swim unweighted beneath a blanket of floating vegetation will often bring out a trophy bass. A single weedless hook will help avoid hangups.

guide work so we can run shiners and catch some big ones.

One of the best places in the world to run shiners has been a big hyacinth patch Dennis found three years ago in Rodman Pool. He and his customers caught more than 1,600 bass of all sizes from that two-acre area back in 1976. He's taken Paul and me in there, and at times the action was so fast that we'd all three have bass on at the same time. Sometimes when the bass are super-active, they chase the shiners out from beneath the hyacinths, and we've seen them run the shiners right up close to the boat and blow and swirl and grab them right in front of our eyes a few feet away.

One time J.D. Skinner of Birmingham, Ala., and I were in the Welaka, Fla., area waiting for the start of the three official practice days for a B.A.S.S. tournament on the St. Johns River. The St. Johns, and any water connected to it, was off limits to all the tournament fishermen before the practice round, so I suggested to J.D. that he and I fish a little lake not connected to the river system. I had fished a 200-acre lake called Silver Lake and suggested we go over there and fish shiners and try to catch a trophy bass. J.D. was all for this, so I got four dozen shiners and we took his bass boat and my four-wheel-drive vehicle.

We'd caught a 7-pounder drifting, but not much else was happening. Finally we found a patch of dead hyacinths, which were about the only ones in the lake. We anchored about 15 feet away and started running shiners. I had three or four strikes and caught a 4-pounder, but J.D. hadn't had a strike. Then I pulled a shiner out to the edge of the hyacinth patch, and a huge bass rolled up and crashed my bait. I gave him a few seconds and then set the hook real hard, but I didn't get him hooked. J.D. started reeling in and said real excitedly, "Boy, I'm going to catch him!"

"You want to bet?" I asked as I reached into the shiner box and grabbed one and got it on my hook as fast as I could and threw back. There was a big race to see who could get in there first, and my bait hit half a second before his did. Instantly that bass grabbed him. I won't recount what J.D. said. I let the bass run for twenty seconds before driving the hook home. That bass weighed 12 pounds, 13 ounces. When I rolled him up to the boat, I yelled for J.D. to net him. We didn't know how big he was, but when the bass came sloshing up out of the water, it scared J.D. so bad that he froze. I was yelling, "Net him! Net him!" and finally he overcame the shock and did.

26. Leeching Smallmouths

I'd never heard of catching a bass on a leech until I got to talking with Spence Petros of *Fishing Facts* magazine. He'd run a few articles in the magazine about guys catching smallmouths on leeches. I was wanting to do some filming three years ago in Minnesota, and I called Al Lindner, Al said he had a good buddy, Grant Hughes, up on Lake Vermilion who had a lodge called Muskego Point. Al told me Grant caught a world of 5- and 6-pound smallmouths all summer long.

I reminded Al that I'd fished for smallmouths a long time and pointed out that nobody catches a world of 5- and 6-pound smallmouths just all summer long, especially during August. Al countered by saying August was the best month and that Grant Hughes just murders 'em then and catches dozens of 'em over 5 pounds in August. I said *nobody*. . . . Al wouldn't argue. He just said call Grant.

Well, I called Grant at Cook, Minn., which is on the banks of Lake Vermilion and about a hundred miles south of the Canadian border. Vermilion has about 50,000 acres, and for years it's been known for walleye and northern pike fishing, and I'd never heard anybody talk about how good Vermilion's smallmouth fishing was. Grant tells me on the phone he's about the only one up there who fishes for smallmouths. He said that during the seven or eight years he had been there, he'd fished for smallmouths about every day during the season but there weren't more than three or four other guys on the entire 50,000-acre lake who fished strictly for smallmouths. He said walleye and northern pike fishermen caught smallmouths but almost by accident because the lake had so many of 'em.

Grant also pointed out that during the previous twenty to thirty years, Vermilion's smallmouths had been virtually unmolested, and if a guy knew structure and how to fish a leech, he could catch nearly a limit of 5-pound smallmouths every day! Within three hours I was all packed up and was driving my Chevy Suburban about seventy-five miles an hour headed north.

This was the third week of August, and Grant had some walleyes and some northerns located. When I first saw the lake, I wasn't very impressed with it. There were a lot of cottages on the shoreline. Grant stretched out a contour map of the lake, and it showed a bunch of rockpiles way out in the lake, which is not a deep lake. Every couple of miles was a major rock shoal which stuck up 5 to 10 feet off the sand bottom.

I didn't know how to fish a leech, and I was a bit reluctant to even pick one up. I thought they'd bite and suck blood, but I watched Grant stick his hand down in a bucket of 'em and pull out about twenty which were clinging all over his hand. He simply picked 'em off one by one and went ahead and baited up. These leeches, when curled up, are only about an inch long and ½ inch wide. When they're stretched out, they are from

2 to 3 inches long. Grant used 4-pound line and a tiny Size 8 or 10 Style 84 hook, and about 6 inches above the hook he put on a tiny split shot. Leeches have both a tail sucker and a mouth sucker. Grant ran the hook through the mouth sucker and back again through it and then through the body. His hook was exposed. He almost vertical-jigs the bait. He fishes the rockpiles, and if you make a long cast to them, your split shot and bait frequently get caught in the rock crevices, and then you spend more time tying on hooks than fishing. You need to use a front locator on your boat and get right over the fish, then open the bail on your reel and drop the leech to the bottom. Then with your trolling motor work very carefully all around that rockpile. Our pattern depth during the week we were there was about 20 feet deep. Jig the leech up 3 or 4 feet and drop it back to the bottom. When you get hung up, you're directly over the bait and all you have to do is twitch your rod tip a little and you usually get loose.

Don't set the hook the instant a smallmouth hits the leech. Open your bail and let him run with it for four to five seconds. With 4- or 6-pound line—and I prefer the 6-pound—you don't set the hook hard when you close the bail. Just set it firm and keep a tight line. The smallmouth exerts a slow, steady pressure, and with a big one you won't feel any tail movement. The bigger the fish, the steadier the pressure he exerts.

Grant Hughes made a believer out of me real quick. The first bass he stuck was about 5 pounds. He had found some schools of 2-to-3-pound smallmouths, but he didn't want to fish for them. He had some lunker holes—some rockpiles which produced strictly 4-and 5-pounders. We'd catch only one or two big ones on a spot like that, but during our first full day of leeching, we caught ten smallmouths over 4 pounds, and three were over 5. My biggest weighed 5 ½.

Leeches made my day on a trip this past spring with Tommy Salisbury, my old buddy from South Carolina, and Mike Vierzba of the Stearns Company. We went to Lac LaCroix in Canada with my film crew, and for the first few days we caught several 1-to-3-pound small-

This leech-caught 5-plus-pounder helped Grant Hughes make a believer out of me.

mouths, but we weren't getting the big ones. They were spawning, and we located five or six beds, but all we could catch were the small males. The big females—some we saw were 5 to 6 pounds—would follow our plugs and sometimes roll up at them, but they wouldn't strike.

Bill Zupp, who operates the camp where we stayed on the lake, said he just had received a shipment of leeches from the U.S. I got to wondering if they'd work on those bedding females. We took some leeches with us, and we got the cameras all ready and I threw a leech on a bed. We saw this big smallmouth moving off, and my line moved off, too. I set the hook, and she boiled up on the surface and gave me a real battle. We were yelling, and the cameras were going, and everybody was excited. I finally worked the fish up to the boat, and 3 feet away from the boat, she tore off the hook.

We went on and did some more filming, but I got to thinking about that one bass being on the bed and how she might hit again. So we went back to that spot again. I made two casts in there without a strike, and the camera was on when I threw in a third time. My line started moving off, and I set the hook into that same big bass. We got the cast, the strike, and six or seven jumps from this big bass all on film, and I landed her. She weighed 5 pounds, 9 ounces. That bass on the bed hit twice within an hour. For the previous two days, we'd thrown at that fish with lures and hadn't got her to hit. But the leech did the trick.

There are times, such as during the spawning season and also during hot weather when the smallmouths are on structure, that lures just don't produce well. But at these times if you drop a leech in there, you're likely to get your line stretched!

I'm convinced leeches would work on small-mouths even in places where they don't use leeches. I told Billy Westmorland about my experience with this live bait and asked him if they ever used 'em at Dale Hollow Reservoir where he lives in Tennessee. He said he didn't know of anyone who ever used leeches for smallmouths. The largest smallmouths in the world probably are in Dale Hollow, and I'm curious about how effective leeches might be for them.

27. Muddy-Water Spinnerbaiting

In some areas, particularly many parts of states such as Oklahoma, the water is muddy at spawning time. For some reason, when it's very muddy, the spinnerbait is the king spawning bait. Spawning bass normally will hit the worm anywhere, but the spinnerbait gives you the advantage of being able to cover a lot more water in a day. If you're in an area with a lot of brush, cover, and muddy water, you can work a spinnerbait through a lot of water. Even though they'll hit the worm, it's much slower to use.

Since muddy-water spawners are very, very shallow, such as a foot to 18 inches deep, you need a light spinnerbait with a fairly large blade. The large blade slows the bait down. The larger the blade, the slower

it runs, and the lighter the body weight, the shallower it runs. I prefer a No. 5 or 6 gold blade if the water's muddy, but if it's super-muddy I like a red or bright-orange blade. I use copper if the water is semi-muddy. I'll take a ¾-ounce head and with a knife shave off quite a bit of the lead to lighten the lure. The torque of that big blade on a little spinnerbait would roll the bait in the water, but since you're running it slow, it doesn't roll. Hold your rod high and this allows it to run slower, and the blade almost creates a wake.

Since the timbered reservoirs in Kansas, Oklahoma, and Texas are flood-control lakes, by spawning time there is almost automatically high water which gets up in the grass and bushes. Often even in reservoirs without the timber you're fishing in flooded fields. Since you don't spot many fish in muddy water, you need to look for movement more than anything else. I try to avoid the wind and find a calm cove so I can detect fish move-

A muddy-water spawner.

ment. Spawning bass are always moving around. You'll see carp moving, too, but throw to them anyway.

One of the best strings of bass I ever caught was when I thought I was throwing to carp, and they turned out to be half carp and half bass. Mary Ann and I caught ten bass totaling 45 pounds at Oolegah Reservoir in Oklahoma by throwing to where we saw a lot of carp working. We threw spinnerbaits and caught 4-, 5-, and 6-pound spawning largemouths. They were right up where the carp were rolling. Usually carp spawn at the same water temperatures and in the same areas bass spawn in. You can tell the movements of carp from bass because when you spook them, carp take off straight as an arrow, but bass move out for 10 feet or so and then make an arc and slow down. Bass end up about 10 feet from their beds after they make that loop. Then they ease back to the bed.

Spawning bass are notorious for hitting a spinnerbait with their mouths closed. All they're trying to do is bump it out of the way. I almost always use a trailer hook, and if the area is a little bit open, I sometimes put a treble hook on the regular trailer hook. You can use the short-arm spinnerbait for spawners because you're running it so shallow and are coming over the logs and submerged bushes. Two good short-arm models on the market are the Scorpion by Bass Buster and the Red Man which Jimmy Houston designed and sold to Norman. You can go to a No. 3 or 4 blade if you shave the head down to about ⅛ ounce. You definitely don't want a fast-moving spinnerbait, however.

Sometimes if the water's a little deeper and I think I know exactly where the bed is, I'll buzz the spinnerbait right over the bed and at the last instant drop it right on her. If it falls right on her, out of instinct she's apt to inhale it.

When you're wading for spawning bass, you want to avoid stepping in a nest and messing up the eggs. The bed is usually 2 to 6 inches deeper than the regular bottom. Balance your weight on your rear foot, and slide the foot you're going to step with as if you're trying to find your way in the dark in a motel room. Slide

your foot and plant it and then shift your weight to it. Also, this helps keep you from tripping over stumps and logs. If you feel the edge of a depression, that's likely the bed, so then you can wade around without disturbing it.

28. Deer Hair for the Quiet Approach

Deer-hair bugs are very popular with smallmouth fishermen, particularly the old-timers such as the late John Alden Knight. When I go to good lakes in Minnesota and Canada, such as Lac LaCroix, in June, a dynamite pattern for me is the deer-hair bug for the quiet approach. Most of this fishing is for smallmouths, although deer-hair bugs work equally well for largemouths. I probably have no greater fun than catching smallmouths in those northern waters on a flyrod and deer-hair bug. I use a small bug because a big deer-hair bug is hard to cast. It's compact and doesn't have hair legs, which are too wind-resistant. It's tied on a No. 2 hook and looks like a miniature mouse with its small leather tail. Another one I like has a little tuft of hair coming back by the hook. This hair makes it almost weedless.

When these bugs are dry, they land softly on the water. For some reason smallmouths in those clear northern lakes like a quiet bug. They probably see it coming through the air, and they don't like the noisy splat of cork or plastic-headed bugs; I've found I can catch more on the deer-hair bugs. These smallmouths are seldom in shallow water except around spawning time, and then they're cautious, wary fish. Early in the morning and late in the evening and on a cloudy day they've got their eyes tuned to the surface. When they're spawning, this could be the best flyrod bass bugging you'll ever find.

I'm looking for spawners, and again I'm looking in the northern coves in the lake. In these coves I look for large individual boulders and small submerged grass patches. These are key areas. I throw the bug in there and let it sit motionless for a long time. With Polaroid glasses, often I can see the smallmouth rise up to

Here are a few of my deer-hair favorites for northern smallmouths.

within a foot of the bug and sit there and watch it. If you twitch it too hard, you'll spook him. But when you twitch it gently, he usually charges right into it. Smallmouths usually rush the bug rather than suck it in as largemouths normally do. Occasionally when they're really active, they'll shoot up into the air and come down on the bug and take it on the way down. These are the most exciting strikes you'll ever get. In fact, I've been trying for five seasons to get this aerial-bombardment type of strike on film because it's just so dramatic.

Deer-hair bugs don't make nearly the popping sound on the water that a regular popping bug makes. They're quiet and resemble a moth on the surface. They're designed to be worked slowly and quietly. With the weedless type of deer-hair bug I mentioned, you can pull it and skitter it along over the grass and catch bass that way.

Some of the greatest smallmouth fishing I've ever enjoyed was a couple of summers ago with Spence Petros at Lac LaCroix on the Canada-Minnesota border. We found a shallow bar out on the main lake, and the bass were on this structure. We'd caught bass around the edge of that bar on crank baits during the day, but that evening the fish moved up on the bar and started chasing minnows on the surface. I suggested we try a bug, and we got into a school of 4-to-5-pounders. Spence caught a 5 ½-pounder—his biggest ever—on a bug,

and I landed a 5-pounder. We caught approximately forty bass in a couple of hours until it was pitch black, and our top ten averaged 4 pounds apiece. Five or six times we each had good ones on. Those were the most smallmouths over 4 pounds I've ever caught in any two-hour period, and we got them on flyrods and bugs.

Nothing is any stronger in fresh water, and nothing tests flyrod tackle any better, than a big northern smallmouth bass. Four-pound smallmouths on flyrods and bugs are the ultimate.

29. Poppers: Attention Getters

Popping bugs are one of my favorite patterns for catching largemouths. While the Peck's Popper with a No. 2 hook and a concave mouth has been my old standby, this past year I found an excellent bug made in Norfork, Va. It looks like the Peck's bug, but it has epoxy rather than paint and it's the strongest, finest bug I've ever seen. I bounced it off numerous cypress trees along the North River near Currituck Sound, N.C., and I caught twenty to thirty bass per day on it, and yet it still looks brand new. Most popping bugs are fragile; the paint gets knocked off the head and the hook works loose from the cork. But this bug is super-strong.

One advantage with a popping bug is that even with 6- or 8-pound leader, when you set the hook with that limber rod you hardly ever lose a bass. The bug hook is light wire and sharp, and I sharpen them even more. Once you hook a fish, you very seldom lose it. Lots of times a largemouth will inhale that bug and you'll hook him in his tongue area. This is really a super place to hook one. About the only way you'll lose a bass on a bug is if he breaks your leader. When he jumps, he doesn't get the leverage from the light bug to throw the hook that he does if you hook him on a ⅝-ounce topwater plug.

All you have to do is nurse him along. Hold your rod high in the air and put some pressure on him—not too much—by holding the line. In lakes with lots of cover, they easily can dive into the brush or pads and break your leader. This is a problem at Okeechobee and Kissimmee and on the east shore of Lake George in Florida. But in an open lake like Lac LaCroix, you never have to worry about even a 5-pounder wrapping up and breaking your leader.

It's an advantage to have a flyrod and popping bug rigged up in your boat when you're out fishing for fun. If the bass simply aren't hitting much and the action is slow, you can tie on a tiny popper with a Size 8 or 10 hook and probably catch some nice bluegills. This can make the day when the bass don't cooperate. Bluegills will knock a bass bug, but they very seldom get the hook; you need a smaller bug with a smaller hook to catch them. In Oklahoma and some states there's a species of panfish called the green sunfish. They have bigger mouths than bluegills, and you can hook them on small to medium-sized bass bugs. I've frequently caught them on my bass bugs. They're fun, too, because they really blast into a bug.

Many old-timers insist that bass bugs are among the most effective lures you can throw in the summer when the sun's up bright and the bass are in weeds and pads, because the bugs offer a much quieter approach. Something I experimented with at Currituck turned out to work good, and that was making my bugs weedless. I took some 60-pound steel leader and pushed a 2-inch length of it through the eye of the bug and then right into the cork head so that it came out the top of the head. Then with needlenose pliers I bent the wire and made a weedguard. I could drag the bug over the milfoil without the hook snagging. I missed a few more strikes because of the weedguard, but not enough to offset the advantage of the weedguard.

Thinking of popping bugs and Currituck Sound reminds me of a funny incident I experienced there seven or eight years ago. I was fishing with a variety of lures, and saw a flyrodder wading near an island. Every few minutes I'd see him hook a bass which would jump and thrash around. He was stringing them, and with the North Carolina daily limit being eight bass, he was already culling fish. I could tell he had a bunch of 'em 3 pounds and better. I'd been fishing all morning and had caught some bass, too, but mine weren't running as large as his fish. Finally I eased up to him and asked him how he was doing. He said casually he'd caught a few, and I tried to be real nonchalant and said I'd caught a few, too. I didn't want to make it obvious I really wanted to know what he was on to. I mentioned that I'd seen him catch a couple of nice ones, and he held up his stringer which had eight all over 3 pounds. His biggest was about 5 ½. His fish made my mouth water, and he was catching and releasing them right and left.

I really was trying to figure out his pattern, and he sensed this. He was an older gentleman, and finally he

This largemouth fell for a popper fished near weedy cover.

says, "Well, I'll tell you what, son. It really doesn't make much difference what color or size these bugs are as long as they're these one-inch bugs in a frog color with green feathers."

I've found out since then at Currituck that he's right. That frog color with greenish-yellow feathers in that certain size he was talking about is far the best bug in that water. I'll catch three bass on that size and color to one on something else.

I have noticed too that in certain lakes, a certain-sized popper in a certain color will be far superior. I can't find any rule of thumb to this, such as saying in clear water use a light-colored bug. I do know it pays to go into a tackle shop around a good popping-bug lake and ask what their best-selling popper is. The color and size makes a lot of difference in some areas.

30. Delicate Worming

I hate to have to worm fish with anything less than 10-pound line. With the Texas rig, I've always maintained that with any line smaller than 10-pound, it's very difficult to get the hook through the plastic and still have enough power to hook the fish solidly.

When I do use less than 10-pound line, such as in this delicate worming pattern, I modify my worm rigs drastically. If you're in open, clear water, you can fish the worm on 6-pound line with an exposed Aberdeen hook. Instead of using a large-diameter 1/0 or 2/0 hook, I'm apt to go to a No. 2 Aberdeen hook, which is nothing more than a crappie hook.

Sometimes it's necessary to rig the worm weedless for cover. Then I rig it Texas-style, but instead of going through the middle of the worm, I'll put the hook point at the side of it and make the slightest little indention into the plastic. Only a tiny slither of plastic is holding the hook point. This isn't quite as weedless as the standard Texas rig, but I'm not working this rig in heavy, heavy cover.

Charlie Brewer from Lawrenceburg, Tenn., invented what he calls the Slider and a technique called Slider fishing. He put an Aberdeen-type hook on a small, flat-bottomed jig head. The flat bottom makes the jig head slither down rather than fall straight. On the back of the head he uses a small-diameter 3-to-4-inch plastic worm. For years I've fished similarly by using an ⅛-ounce or even smaller slip sinker and a No. 1 or 2 hook with 6-pound line and a short worm with an exposed hook for Kentucky bass on Smith Lake and Lake Martin in Alabama. I swim the worm along the bluffs, and I was doing this back in 1965 when I was in the army stationed at Ft. Benning, Ga.

Charlie calls this method a "do-nothing" method. I'd get parallel to the rock bluff and throw out and let the worm sink about ten seconds and slowly wind it back. The two techniques are basically the same. In clear water the fish have so much vertical and horizontal visibility that this small lure attracts them from long distances.

One helpful thing which Charlie Brewer pointed out about his "do-nothing" retrieve with Sliders was the delay in setting the hook. I used to set the hook the instant I got a strike when swimming the small worm, but missed a lot of fish. When Charlie feels the pressure from the strike, he keeps reeling. Pressure from his tight line keeps the bass from being able to spit out the lure. The hook is against some part of his mouth. Finally after a few seconds the fish usually turns and goes the other way, and then is when Charlie sets the hook. The fish's mouth is away from him. When I was setting the hook with the fish facing me, it would be easy to pull the bait out of his mouth, and I'm sure that at times I did exactly that. The principle is virtually the same as described in the section on weedless lures when I talked about fishing the plastic frogs. Let them take the lure and hit them when they turn their heads and go away from you. Charlie has told me that sometimes out of ten strikes, he gets all ten fish.

F. 25 Bass Fishing Tips

JIMMY HOUSTON

1. The Big Four

I'm always talking about the four things to take into account whenever you're making your game plan for a day of fishing. I say it so often that my daughter Sherri could recite it in her sleep by the time she was five (just kidding – but certainly by the time she was seven!).

First, there's the time of year. Fish behavior revolves around the seasons, whether it's spawning in the spring, trying to keep cool during the summer, or feeding up during the fall in preparation for winter.

Second is the type of water. By that I mean whether you're fishing a lake, a river, a stream, a pond, or another body of water.

Third is water conditions. Is the water temperature rising or falling? Is the level rising or falling? Is the water clear or stained or murky? What's its pH level?

Fourth is the matter of weather. Fish react to air temperature, wind, cloudy or clear sky, and especially to rising or falling barometric pressure. If I had to pick the one factor that most people consider over all the others, I'd choose weather.

You're going to hear a great deal about these four factors throughout this section. They're so important that when I lecture at fishing seminars around the country, I tell the audience to write them on the top of their tackle boxes. You should do that too. That way, you'll have the list in front of you as a visual aid, so if your original game plan isn't working out, you won't waste time wracking your brain about what you need to know for making revisions.

2. Game Plans

The key thing about game plans is they can always be refined or reworked. Fishing is kind of like shooting at a moving target, and conditions change all the time. When conditions change, so should your strategy.

For example, suppose it's a real clear morning when you start out. You use a light-colored plastic worm and you're catching lots of big 'uns, but then a cloud cover rolls in and the fish stop biting. That's a signal to change your game plan. The first three factors – season, type of water, and water conditions – haven't changed, but the weather has. The arrival of those big ol' clouds may call for a switch to a topwater bait, and when you do change over, you start catching fish again.

That's called refinement.

3. Spring for Spawning

Remember Jimmy Houston's #1 Rule? (Okay, repeat after me, class – "If it's important to a bass, I make it important to me.") Well, bass reproduce only once a year, so you can bet that spawning is mighty important to them.

Most fishermen divide the spawning season into three parts: prespawn, spawn, and postspawn. However, I see it as four.

There's also a pre-prespawn period, when bass first move toward the water where they'll lay their eggs. Generally speaking, these are points of coves and pockets. I consider the pre-prespawn area covers as the first 50 percent of the coves and pockets, about halfway

Any fish caught on their spawning beds should be released immediately.

in from the main point or body of water. North banks are best because the surface water warms up quicker, thanks to getting more sunshine than south banks do. Spinner baits, topwater baits, and jigs seem to work best, while deep-diving crawdads, and colored crankbaits on light line are often a productive alternative.

The prespawn stage marks when bass arrive into the spawning area (the magic water temperature that marks when they come with spawning on their mind is fifty-eight degrees). The smaller males move onto the banks, while the females stay in four to seven feet of water. Because the ladies have major appetites before they spawn, you'll want to attract them with maximum-size baits like a magnum spinnerbait with a long trailer or a crankbait.

Once the bass are on their spawning beds along the banks, try a "Gitzit" or a lizard or minnow type of bait. No matter what you use, however, any fish caught on their spawning bed should always be released. If you don't, pretty soon that lake of yours won't have any fish to catch at any time.

Of all four periods, the postspawn period is the hardest to catch fish. After bass spawn, they move to where they suspend between five and ten feet over deeper water. They often do their suspending amid standing timber, and that's the first place I look. Edges

of creek channels are other likely places, and so are the pre-prespawn points of coves and pockets, the same points where you caught them ten or twelve weeks earlier.

4. Summertime Concentration

Forget about coves and pockets during summertime, and concentrate on the main body of a lake especially those points that are close to main channels and creek channels.

Still, if you want to work a spinnerbait or plastic worm shallow, avoid inlets and covers where the water temperature and the pH are likely to be higher than on the main part of the lake.

5. Fall is for Feeding

Fall is when bass are feeding up big-time before winter sets in. They follow the schools of shad and other baitfish. So should you.

You'll find bass in the pockets and coves where they were during the spring, generally in the prespawn areas. As the temperature drops, bass will move to the tail ends of the pockets (again, the magic water temperature is fifty-eight degrees).

6. Slow Down for Winter

Wintertime's cold water and low pH means that fish become inactive. A study at the University of Oklahoma's biology lab revealed that big bass didn't eat but every eight or ten days during winter. Take that to its logical conclusion you have a one-in-eight or one-in-ten chance of being out on the lake the day that Mr. Bass decides to head to the dinner table (but also remember that, at any given time, some bass are eating).

Because fish don't eat much during winter, you'll need to fish slowly and work your spots thoroughly. Stick to main river and creek channels, especially around structures that include steep drops.

7. Barometers and Bass

It's real easy to use circumstances as excuses, isn't it?

Sometimes the prettiest day is the worst day for fishing. And sometimes the worst days for fishing are the best days for catching.

Bass react strongly to changes in barometric pressure. A rapid drop in pressure invariably causes them to bite. That's because of an increase in the size of the strike zone, a term I coined a few years ago to describe the area that a bait must be in before a fish will strike.

A strike zone can be small (like it seems to be whenever I go fishing!) or it can be big. And when a strike zone is really big, a bass will move eight or even a dozen feet to get to your bait.

A storm front coming in brings with it a rapid drop from high to low pressure. That's when strike zones are at their largest, when fish move out from cover.

After a front goes through, the barometric pressure starts climbing and the strike zone shrinks. It's that rising stable pressure that causes bass to retreat. They go back into the deepest, most inaccessible part of the structure, and you're faced with a really small strike zone and very difficult conditions.

Lots of folks think that bass move to deeper water and suspend there when the barometer is rising. Not so – bass simply hide deeper wherever they are.

8. Some Light on the Subject

Bright days are the hardest to fish because, just like with humans, sunlight hurts a bass's eyes. Lighter colored lures work best for me, especially clear topwater bait that has a little bit of blue. All the fish see are the silvery hooks, which look to them like itty-bitty shad.

Bright days may also mean fishing deeper. Look for heavy structures and drop-off places, shallow or deep, where the wind blows into a bank. The wind breaks up the water surface, and the bass feel safer in the low-light conditions (the wind also blows baitfish into the area). It's also an area where oxygen and pH are mixing up (you'll learn about the role of pH later in the book). Remember that fishing deeper means fishing slower, and you'll want to switch to lighter line that sinks deeper and faster than thick heavy line does.

On the other hand, dark cloudy days are the best days for fishing. Fish are active, and they don't stay tight to cover like they do on sunshiny days.

My number one choice under these conditions is a spinnerbait with a single highly visible gold or copper blade. Fish it shallow. In fact, you can't work it too shallow, even if you're throwing it into just inches of water.

Polaroid sunglasses are essential. They filter out rays that interfere with making out fish and other underwater objects on dark days. As a matter of fact, I wear Polaroid glasses whenever I fish, whether it's sunny or cloudy.

9. Windows on the Water

We measure water clarity as muddy, stained, or clear. In muddy water, a white probe disappears from sight within two feet from the surface. According to studies, bass can distinguish colors in muddy water up to six or eight feet.

In stained water, the probe disappears at a depth of two to four feet. The same studies show that bass can recognize colors at thirty feet.

Clear water means the probe can be seen deeper than four feet. As for a bass's vision under those conditions, a fish tank at the University of Oklahoma's biology lab is thirty feet long, and tests prove that bass are able to distinguish colors from one end to the other, or at least thirty feet.

10. Casting Tips

Throwing a bait works better if the line comes off a baitcasting reel horizontally instead of vertically, so right-handed people should cast a bait reel with the crank handles up (handles down for you lefties).

Always keep your thumb on the spool. That's where it belongs throughout the cast, resting light enough so that the spool can roll, but with enough pressure to avoid overspinning into a backlash. How much pressure is "enough"? That's for you to determine. Just make sure your thumb keeps constant contact with the spool.

Good baitcasting reels have adjustable magnetic drag systems or balanced weights that let the spool spin faster or slower. Too fast leads to backlashes, so adjust the system kind of tight until you get the hang of how the reel casts.

Throwing a baitcasting lure comes from the wrist, not from the forearm like in fly-fishing or the shoulder like in surf-casting. Keep your elbow in close to your body, not straight out like you're signaling for a left turn.

The quickest way to throw your bait a grand total of five feet smack into the water (and end up with the granddaddy of all backlashes too) is by casting it out in a straight line ahead of you. Instead, throw it up and out at about a forty-five-degree angle. And don't try and heave it as far as you can. If you've got to cast seventy-five feet to reach your target, you're better off moving your boat closer . . . or finding a closer target.

Most people who fish with spinning tackle use either an overhand or a sidearm cast. But before you throw, you've got to release the pickup bail. You can do it either manually or with the reel's trigger if it has one, and then catch the line with your index finger.

Here's an important deal to know about rewinding a spinning reel. The pickup bail automatically engages when you crank the handle, but it also automatically puts a one-quarter twist in the line. Although that may not seem like much, over the course of a day's fishing when you make hundreds and hundreds of casts, the twisting ends up bad enough to really cause you some major problems. The simple remedy is to flip the bail yourself by hand. Believe me, you're going to love me for this tip.

11. Underhanded Gives Me the Upper Hand

When it comes to casting, I'm underhanded. No, I'm not sneaky (although some people might disagree!), I cast with a snap-of-the-wrist underhand motion. That's because of my belief that the longer you keep your bait in the strike zone, the more fish you'll catch.

Sidearm and overhand casting require a lot of effort from your arm and shoulder muscles. When those muscles get tired, you can't keep up your casting speed. That means your bait isn't in the water as much of the time it could be. The result: fewer chances to catch fish.

Nor can you cast with consistent accuracy when your arm and shoulder muscles are complaining. And there are other benefits to underhanded casting too. A cast that's low to the water gets to fish that are under low branches and other overhead obstructions. I can throw into the wind more effectively. My bait lands softly, and I spook fewer fish.

And I end up in an ideal hook-setting position. The rod tip is low when the bait hits the water, and my hands are low and tight to my chest, ready to set the hook.

Getting back to the matter of time, an underhand snap shoots the bait straight forward, low to the water. That's more efficient than an overhand or a sidearm throw, where the bait sails through the air in a wide arc.

Since I prefer bass to flying fish, I'm not big on wasting precious time that my bait could be in the water.

And a lot of precious time too. An overhand cast takes four to six seconds before the bait hits the water. I figure my underhand snap takes about two or three seconds less. That's a savings of between 33 percent and 50 percent. So if you cast the conventional way, you and I can be out on the lake for the same amount of time, but I'll fish almost twice as long as you do.

So you might say that underhand gives me the upper hand.

12. Spinnerbaits

Of all the baits I use, spinnerbaits are my favorite. And they're my favorite because I catch more fish on them than on anything else. Maybe 55 percent to 60 percent, which is a pretty good percentage.

That's kind of funny because nothing in nature looks like a metal arm with a spinner blade on one side and a rubber or plastic skirt on the other. Maybe when bass see a spinnerbait, they think to themselves, "Golly, if those things get started in this lake, they'll ruin the neighborhood – we'd better get rid of them fast."

Vibration is the name of the spinnerbait game, vibration that you can feel through your rod tip. That's why I never fish a spinnerbait the way it comes out of the package. Instead, I bend the wire arm to open the angle between the arm and the hook. The greater the angle, the more vibration.

Gold or copper blades are easier for a fish to see than silver or nickel, which work best only in the clear water.

One blade or two? A single blade, which will catch more fish in the sheer numbers, gives off greater vibration than tandem blades do, plus single blades cast more accurately. However, two blades produce greater flash, which is important in low-light conditions, so the choice boils down to whether you want more audible or more visual appeal.

A willowleaf-shape blade, long and slender, gives off lots of flash but not much vibration. That shape moves most easily through thick grass and other heavy cover.

On the other hand, magnum-sized heavyweight blades produce lots of vibration. I like using them in muddy water and when fishing for big fish. I'll attach a worm as a trailer to create a big ugly bait that little eight- or ten-inch fish won't bother with. (Bother with them? Those little 'uns will jump up on the bank and run away!) But when it comes to big grown-up bass looking for a big grown-up meal, especially in the spring or the fall of the year, this is the ticket. I'll chunk it out and slow-roll it back five to eight feet deep.

Talk about being loaded for bear: A big magnum tandem willowleaf on a five-eighths-ounce magnum head looks like a school of shad coming through the water. These things give off so much vibration that after twenty-five hours or so, the vibration breaks the arm off the spinnerbait. But after twenty-five hours of fishing it, your arm breaks off too, so it doesn't matter!

It's a smart idea to match your spinnerbait to the size of the baitfish in the area. If you haven't a clue, a smallish – maybe one with quarter-ounce blades – is a good size to start with. That's especially true in tournaments, where you first want to catch your limit. Then when you do, you can always change to a larger blade size to attract bigger bass.

I haven't said much about spinnerbait skirts because they're less important than blades. As far as their colors go, I like chartreuse-and-white or chartreuse-and-blue.

Spinnerbaits work best in the spring of the year, during the prespawning and the spawning periods when fish are in shallow water. But they also work great in summer, fall, and winter. Like I once told someone, the only time not to use a spinnerbait is if you have a weak heart – you're liable to ruin your fishing partner's day (as in "stop the boat, step over Harry!").

13. A Seminar on Structure

Bass fishermen talk an awful lot about "structure." It's a key concept, but it's also one that many fishermen misunderstand.

"Structure" means nothing more than something found under the water that fish like to hang around. It might be a weed bed or a dock or pier piling or even a single log in the water, but to a fish it's home. And like a den or rec room at home where there are bowls of chips and dip next to a comfortable easy chair and a good football game on the TV, there's no place on earth a critter would rather be.

Weed beds are one of the most prevalent – and one of the best – structures for holding bass. Sure, we've all dragged in tons of grass, but fishing weeds is more than worth any inconvenience. There's always a little space between the bottom of the weed bed and the lake bottom. That's where bass like to hold, and if you can get a lure down under the grass, you stand a good chance of catching a big 'un.

One way to penetrate this thick cover is with a Texas-rigged worm and a heavy – half- or three-quarter-ounce – slip-sinker. Flippin' the worm will get it where you want it. Otherwise, heavy jigs down under or weedless spoons over the top are other good methods.

Rocks are always prime structure. The way to analyze big boulders at a water's edge is to check out the part that's out of the water. Cracks and crevices on top usually continue down into the lake, so if you work the water below where they enter the water, the breaks in the rock are likely to lead you right to fish.

I always equate rocks with crawdads. When you see rocks, start thinking about crawdad-colored crankbait.

Fishing around rocks really increases the chance that your line will become nicked and frayed. Check your line frequently, even the "superbraid" type, and retie your bait if you spot any weakness. It can mean the difference between landing that big lunker and just talking about it.

Logs are an example of what I call "junction areas." That's where any two different objects meet; for example, where two logs run together or a limb comes off a log or where one log meets a boulder or the end of the log meets the water. In such a case, the junction is the spot to work your bait – don't even bother anywhere else along the log.

"Junction" also applies to where two different substances meet, like where sand and gravel come together on the bottom of a lake (swimming beaches are prime examples). If you come across one with another structure like logs or a weed bed, you've actually got yourself a dynamite structure.

When it comes to stumps, the root system is the most important part. Work slowly and systematically around the roots. Spinnerbaits work especially well, and when you throw one, aim so it bumps the stump during your throw.

When you find stumps and logs together, the deal is to fish the least populous structure. That's where bass try to avoid the competition of other feeding fish. If there are, say, twenty logs and ten stumps, bass will tend to hold around the stumps. On the other hand, ten logs and twenty stumps means focusing your attention on the logs. Why? Because bass just seem to hang around on the most isolated cover. Kind of like having your house in a big old field instead of in a neighborhood.

Pier and dock pilings fit in the "stumps" category. Each piling qualifies as a separate structure, so fish all of them and not just the one or two closest to you. Then when you catch a fish, pay attention to whether you caught it deep or shallow. That way, when you move on to the next pier, you'll know the right depth right off and you can eliminate the rest.

One of the best places to fish on a lake is around boat docks, especially those that have rod holders or boats with fishing rigs or any other clue that the owner is a fisherman. Those docks are more likely to hold fish than other docks will, and usually within one cast length away from the dock.

You see, if the fisherman who owns the place is smart, he's set out good brush piles no further than one cast away so he won't have to work very hard. He probably sinks the family Christmas tree there every January, or tosses out tree branches and limbs – anything that will hold fish.

That's why I always keep an eye out for old ratty docks that look like a redneck's fishing hole. They're much more promising places than beautifully painted docks with their waterski platforms or swimming ladders (that's not to say, though, that ladders around boat docks aren't worth trying too). You might be a redneck if your boat dock looks like the community fishing hole. Lights on the dock almost guarantee fish – I'll fish that ol' boy's dock anytime!

Another type of structure you'll find on man-made lakes and reservoirs is what I call a deepwater structure. It's usually a roadbed that got submerged when the land was flooded to make the lake. Using your boat's depth locator, mark the path of the road with buoys. Then go back to the start and work your way down that road, looking for breaks, brush piles, or a creek along the way.

14. Crankbaits

I call crankbaits "idiot baits" because they're the easiest lures to catch fish on. Just throw them out and reel them in, and if that sounds like too much work, you can troll them behind your boat around the lake.

One of the ways to choose your crankbait is by color. Red-pink or brown crawdad works best early in the season, and shad color is most effective during summer and fall months.

If you're planning on working a crawdad color, walk down the lake shoreline and turn over rocks until you come across a crawdad. Then match your bait color to the color of the critter.

If you're fishing a shad-colored bait, match it to the size of the baitfish the bass are feeding on. Count the bill on the front of the lure as part of the length only if it's colored. Clear bills don't count because the fish can't see them.

The longer its bill, the deeper a crankbait will dive. You can also control depth by the line you're using. The lighter and thinner the line, the deeper a bait will run. And speaking of line, make sure what's on your reel is appropriate. A tiny crankbait towed around on a big thick line won't catch many fish. It sure won't run very deep, and the action will be "dead."

A "pull bait" like a Hot Spot or a Rattle Spot can't be fished too fast, no matter how hard you try. Use a stiff rod, one with heavy action. It's harder to cast, but you sure won't lose many fish.

Crankbait can become more effective with an attractor tail. A strip of dry rind fluttering behind is like a combo sandwich to a bass.

No matter what color or size crankbait you use or whatever modifications you make, work the bait with a stop-and-go action, never a steady rewind. Vary your rewind between "slow-and-stop, slow-and-stop . . ." with "burn and stop, burn and stop . . ." Mix up the patterns, because variety produces more fish.

If you think you feel your crankbait hit a log or stump but the bump doesn't feel like a strike, pause for a few beats before continuing your rewind. A fish may be studying your lure before he decides to hop on.

Some people who are put off by all the hooks on crankbaits avoid using them in heavy cover. Boy, is that wrong! The possibility of snagging is nothing compared to the chance to hook into some big 'uns lurking in tall grass or tall timber. In the heavy stuff, you might want to remove the front hook – the modified bait will still catch fish, but it'll hang up less.

Crankbaits should be one of every bass fisherman's primary lures. In fact, they're so effective maybe they should be called "idiot baits" only by those idiots who don't use 'em.

15. Get Set to Set that Hook

Lots of people ask me, "Jimmy, what's the one single biggest mistake that recreational fishermen make." My answer is the same every time: You don't set the hook hard or fast enough.

Now, I'm not saying that each and every time you think there's a fish near your bait, you've got to pull hard enough to rip his lips off. And as I point out elsewhere in this book, there are times to wait till you're sure the fish really does have the hook in his mouth.

But when you are sure, or you're even halfway sure, then set the hook. Don't stop and think, or freeze like somebody's ol' bird dog on point. Set the hook fast and hard, and set it once. Here's how to do it:

A good hookset comes from rod speed, which has absolutely nothing to do with strength. My wife, Chris, isn't a big strong woman, yet she sets a hook as well as anybody. So do lots of other women, and youngsters too. The trick is to move the rod tip quickly, so fast that it's a blur. If you move it quickly, the rod speed will drive the hook. That's why you want to keep your hands and your reel close to your body, in a position to work your wrists and elbows as fast as you can.

Setting a hook is easier when your hook has a razor-sharp point to it. A sharp point makes a nice clean hole that will hold a fish better than a ragged hole will.

I'm not a big fan of multiple hooksets. If you're fishing with a sharp hook, one good tug is all you need. More than one tug creates a break in the line tension and it's a steady tension that prevents a fish from spitting out or shaking off a hook.

Five or six isn't too young to start a kid fishing.

Work on your hookset technique at every opportunity until it becomes second nature. Even if you think you've lost a fish, set the hook anyway. You've nothing to lose. Besides, the fish may still have the hook in his mouth or is striking again just as you pull. There's no excuse for losing a fish because of a poor hookset or, even worse, no set at all. As a friend of mine puts it, every hookset involves a jerk. If you remember to set the hook, the jerk is at the hook end of the line. And if you forget to, the jerk is at the other end – holding the rod.

16. Young 'Uns and Big 'Uns

Taking a youngster fishing is a wonderful experience at any time, one of the greatest gifts that is in your power to give.

The best age for a child's first lesson depends on his or her attention span and coordination skills. Five or six isn't too early for most kids to hold a short pole or drop a line and pay attention to the bobber at the end of the line. Baiting the hook and casting the line, however, is better left to an adult.

When youngsters are able to handle a rod and reel and cast their lures on their own, they should be encouraged to do as much for themselves as they can safely manage. Putting worms, leeches, or other live bait on the hook is also a neat way for kids to get over any reluctance to handle "yucky" creatures. Backlashes and snagged hooks are all part of the game (and at any age, I might add). To the extent your young fishing buddies are able, encourage them to try their best at fixing the problem before going to you for help.

If you and I get antsy and cranky when the fish aren't biting, imagine how a youngster will feel. The name of the game is catching fish, so work the part of the pond or creek or lake where you know perch, bluegills, or other easy-to-attract species can be caught. Use surefire panfish bait like worms, doughballs, or crickets. The size of the fish or the fight it puts up doesn't matter. What's important is the number of times the bobber jiggles and goes under.

How long to stay out should be based on your young 'un's attention span. Call it a day at the first sign of restlessness, before real boredom sets in, even if going home early means passing up that big bass you've been close to hooking into. Some kids may want to stop fishing for a while and do some other fun thing – like exploring an anthill or going to the john – before going back to their rods and reels. They'll want room to walk around, which is why a dock or a shore is often a better idea than a confining space like a boat. But, like I say, it all depends on the individual, and you're the best judge of that.

The first time a child goes fishing sets a pattern. As the adult role model, it's not only what you say, but it's what you demonstrate by example. The qualities that you'd like to see your young 'un grow up with – patience, courtesy, safety, respect for nature and the rules and laws – are learned by watching and by copying how grown-ups act.

I'll never forget the first times I took Sherri and Jamie fishing, and when I took my grandboys too. Sure, I had to untangle lots of backlashes and dodge lots of flying baits. But I number those images – like the glow of wonderment and pride in Sherri's eyes when she caught her first really big bass all by herself – among my most cherished memories.

17. Patterns

You hear a lot of talk about patterns. Folks make it sound as complicated as doing your income tax, but like most other things in fishing, it really isn't. A pattern is nothing more than a method of catching fish the same way more than once. Put even more simply, it's how and when you caught the bass that you caught.

Every time you catch a fish, try and figure out where and how it happened. Was it in five feet of water? On a point? Was a cold front coming in? Did the critter jump on a spinnerbait after you switched from a topwater bait? Whatever the combination of factors involved, the bottom line is it makes up a pattern. And if that pattern worked once, chances are real good it'll work again.

Since patterns are based on repetition, whenever you go fishing, and especially when you're done for the day, make notes on what worked and what didn't. Write them down, factoring in the four basic considerations of time of year, weather, type of water, and water conditions. You'll want that information for the next time you fish so you can start figuring out patterns even before you put your boat in the water.

We pros do it all the time, except we call it doing our homework.

18. Topwater Baits

If spinnerbaits and buzzbaits look like nothing that's found in nature, topwater baits are the exact opposite. They're made to resemble minnows or shad or other baitfish, and they're primarily warm-weather baits, most effective whenever the water temperature is eighty degrees or above.

Topwaters come in four basic types. I'd guess the most popular are the "cigar" shapes, like the Zara Spook. These baits really do look like baitfish, so if I had to pick one color as my favorite, it would be silver shad. You work them by making them "walk" across the surface, fluttering along like a panicky or injured baitfish. Keep your rod tip low and coordinate your wrist movement with cranking the reel to twitch the bait along, zigzagging maybe six or eight inches at a time. You can start feeling proud when you're able to work a topwater around a stump or log.

Although Zara Spooks can be used on both calm and windy days, they're really excellent when there's some chop on the water. It's a big bait that creates a lot of commotion, especially when you fish it fast. The calmer the water is, however, the slower you need to fish a Spook.

"Chugger" baits have concave faces that scoop through water to make their distinctive chugging action. Raise your rod tip while retrieving in a sideways motion that emphasizes the "spit" and varies the bait's sound. If you don't think the one you're using is creating enough spit, take a file, sandpaper, or sharp knife and scoop away more of the face.

Long thin stickbaits look like minnows. They work best under quiet, calm conditions, especially when you retrieve them slowly.

Propbaits have little metal propellers on their front or their back ends and sometimes on both. Like spinnerbaits and buzzbaits, they're designed to make lots of noise. The deal is to retrieve them in steady, smooth cadences, cranking in "one-two-pause, then repeat" or "one-two-three-pause, then repeat" patterns.

Any of these topwaters can be modified by attaching one or more strips of Mylar or another shiny material to the rear hooks. The extra bit of flash often attracts fish when plain baits don't.

The rule about topwaters is, after you've thrown one, to let it sit on the surface until all the splash and ripples disappear. Then wait a few seconds longer before starting to work the bait. Sure, waiting isn't easy, especially for hard-charging (some might say impatient) guys like me. But that's the right way to catch fish on topwaters.

Actually, you might not have to work the bait at all. I've thrown a topwater when I knew a big bass was lurking and let it sit long after the ripples died away. That bass stared at the bait, and stared some more, wondering what it was that fell out of the sky and if it's dead. The longer I did nothing, the more tension built up in the bass until when I finally did twitch the topwater or even take up slack line . . . wham! That's known as the stare syndrome. Scientists still haven't explained why bass do it, but waiting on a largemouth that way is a proven tactic.

Here's something else that requires patience: Don't set the hook on a topwater until you're sure you feel the fish. A bass may hit or bump these lures two or three times before settling it. Setting the hook prematurely at the "boil" or the "blowup" usually jerks the bait right out of the fish's mouth.

If you retrieve a topwater until it gets back to two or three feet from your boat without a hit, quit cranking and let it float for a few seconds more before you lift it out of the water. That way, any bass that has been following has a chance to hit before the topwater gets out of reach.

Even with all the patience in the world, you're going to miss fish on topwaters. When that happens, don't cast the bait right back. Instead, reach for your other rod and throw a plastic worm. You see, usually that ol' bass is wondering what in the world just happened – dinner was there and then it wasn't. He wants to eat – you know that, and throwing the same bait back just might catch him, but he also might be real leery about striking it again. A worm or jig that's presented gently won't spook him.

Some folks call stickbaits "jerkbaits" because of the action they're worked with. I stick to "stickbaits," because I've heard folks use the word "jerkbaits" to refer to the jerks at the reel end of the line.

19. Strange Lakes

Nothing is more intimidating to more fishermen than an unfamiliar lake. You show up at the lake, take a long look, and get all weak-kneed. There's so much water, maybe a few thousand or more acres, but even if it's just a little bitty lake, you take a deep breath and ask yourself, "What do I do first?"

You're not alone. That's a question we tournament guys ask ourselves all the time. And over the years I've come up with a few answers that seem to work.

First of all, as I've said, you should put the idea of fishing deep out of your mind. There are two reasons not to. First, most of the bass are in shallow water along the lake's edges. Second, by ruling out anything deeper than seven feet, you've eliminated most of the water. That makes the prospect of fishing a big lake suddenly much more psychologically manageable.

The only times Chris and I fish deep – more than seven feet – is when we're on a lake we know *extremely* well. Like our home lake, Lake Tenkiller, or another place that we're certain has lots of fish, such as Lake Guntersville in Alabama. Otherwise, we fish shallow.

The next step is to look for points, places where pieces of land jut out into the water. They needn't be long thin strips of land to qualify as points. Any projection of land will do.

Starting at the shallowest water of the point, throw a crankbait, crawdad-colored in spring and shad in summer and fall. Work your way around the point, and chances are pretty good you'll find fish.

Using that technique, move from point to point until you work your way around the lake. If you're catching 'em on the crankbait, fine, but you might need to switch to a spinnerbait or a plastic worm.

Another technique involves your electronic fish finder. From the time you set out from the boat dock, look for schools of shad and other baitfish. They're probably down six or seven feet or wherever the pH breakline is for that part of the lake. Once you've sighted in on the baitfish, look for the heaviest brush piles,

Bass become especially active right after sundown.

the steepest drop-offs, or any other important structure or cover at that depth.

It's hard to believe the first time you look at a monster lake, but with experience, a strange lake or river becomes less of a horror show waiting to happen than a neat challenge to be figured out and defeated. All it takes is experience fishing with game plans to turn anxiety and doubt into ancient history.

20. Night Fishing

Bass become especially active after sundown, starting to move about an hour after the sun sets and continuing to feed for a couple of hours afterwards and sometimes all night. Like the predators they are, they like to prowl under cover of darkness the way muggers prefer dark streets. Also, they're not as spooky at night.

Night fishing is a good teacher. You can't see your line so you have to depend on your other senses, like feeling the line with your fingertips and listening for the sound of bass, baitfish and other critters.

The best nights to fish are when the moon is full. Bass become hyperactive hunters then, the way that a full moon seems to bring about the worst behavior in all critters. (It's a fact: police records show the greatest

If there is a moon overhead, chances are the bass will be feeding.

amount of domestic violence and speeding accidents happen during full moons.)

Solunar tables tell if major and minor feeding is predicted for a particular night. If you don't happen to have a table handy, a food rule of thumb is that a moon overhead usually indicates a high-volume feeding period. If no moon is visible, you'll have to rely on your eyesight. Watch the water surface: As a feeding period approaches, the calm surface is broken by little circles, then bigger ones, and finally the great sight and sound of a big 'un crashing after a frog or a mouthful of shad – or hopefully your black Jitterbug.

The unique feature of night fishing comes from bass being forced to rely on their sense of sound. They pick up vibrations through the sound-sensitive lateral lines along their bodies, "zoning" into the source of the sound just like sonar detectors on boats. That's why

you'll want to use baits that attract a bass's attention more through sound than sight: big poppers, crank-baits, buzzbaits, spinnerbaits, rattles in jigs and worms – all the noisier the better.

Erratic retrieves that work so well during daylight aren't the best way to work a bait at night. Because bass can't always "lock" onto the bait's location during those one-two-stop, one-two-three-four-stop retrieves, you're better off using a steady rhythm so the fish can figure out exactly where the lure is.

Moonlight coming from above makes the water surface appear kind of silvery from below. Black, dark purple, or dark red are the most effective bait colors because they stand out as a good silhouette target.

Often at night, a big female largemouth will slap a lure with her tail in an attempt to stun or kill it. When that happens, you know you're working your bait right because Big Mama has been fooled into thinking it's alive. When that happens, stop your retrieve and wait for her to come back for her "stunned" dinner. However, if she doesn't return, grab another rod and throw a spinnerbait or plastic worm well past the slapped bait and then work it to where that bait is sitting. You'll get a bite, I can almost guarantee you, since Big Mama will think another bass is coming to get what's rightly hers.

Bass seem to splash louder, hit harder, and pull stronger under cover of darkness. Every strike feels like a giant grabbed your bait, and that's what brings me out when the sun goes down.

21. Buzzbaits in the Dark

If the thrill that comes from a sudden explosive strike of a largemouth isn't enough during daylight hours, try night fishing with a buzzbait at the end of your line.

When buzzbaits came into the picture a little more than twenty years ago, old-timers called them gimmicks and said they'd never last. Well, the old-timers were wrong. Buzzbaits continue to be the hot-ticket items because when they're used correctly, they produce big bass. Now we even have buzzbaits with clackers that really make noise.

My favorite conditions for night buzzing is on a lake with huge weed beds, especially weed beds along a creek or in deeper water. Another ideal situation is shallows with weeds about three feet under the surface. That's where big bass settle down into the tops of the weeds and wait for their supper to swim by.

Like spinnerbaits, loud and fast-moving buzzbaits resemble nothing found in the natural food supply. That's when a bass's reflexes take over. And do they ever! When I run a buzzbait over the top of a grass bed and the bait blows up right at the side of my Ranger boat, and right under the buzzbait is the huge yawning mouth of an eight-pounder, and the bass crashes back

into the water under the buzzbait that's falling on top of the foaming water, and the rod tip dives down, and I set the hook and hang on for all I'm worth while the reel is stripped of line . . . let me tell you, folks, that's why my tackle box always has a bushel of buzzbaits!!

22. The Heat is On

Changes in water temperature can lead you into making tactical mistakes. As I pointed out earlier, fifty-eight degrees seems to be something of a "magic" number. When the water temperature in the spring hits fifty-eight degrees, fish move into prespawning staging areas, pockets that range in depth from about four to seven feet, before they spawn in more shallow water.

Let's suppose it's the spring of the year and you're in a tournament. The afternoon of the day before the tournament starts, you're out practicing, and you come upon a bunch of bass in one of these staging areas. They're good 'uns, so you make a note to race back first thing the next morning. You fish that pocket for an hour or so, but you can't believe you haven't gotten even a bite.

What happened was that the water temperature, which was fifty-eight degrees the previous afternoon, fell three, four or five degrees during the night, which is not an unusual change during spring conditions. When you get around to checking the thermometer on your fish-finder, you see that's where it is, at fifty-three or fifty-five degrees.

That means you've wasted an hour or so of fishing time, and you know how critical time is during a tournament. So you and your partner, who's gotten grumpy over not catching anything, move to another spot. Later you learn that some ol' boy who moved into where you had been started catching lots of big 'uns. How come? Because by the time he got to that pocket, the water temperature had risen back up to fifty eight and the fish moved back.

Don't feel so bad when this happens to you – it's happened to me lots of times (well, at least once or twice).

23. Jigs

Jigs are a real basic bait, consisting of nothing more than a lead head and something hanging off it. That can be a rubber or plastic skirt or a trailer like a dry rind or a Salt Craw.

Because jigs are so simple, people have come up with all kinds of variations. There's the "Gitzit," where the jig head goes all the way inside the bait, with only the hook sticking out. Another, a jig and plastic worm combination of a little one-eighth-ounce head and four-inch worm, often produces fish where larger baits don't. A "creepy crawler" has a jig head inserted into a two-piece twister tail with a weed guard. This bait is excellent around rocks.

Jig skirts that are made of stiff fiberguards scrunch up inside the package they come in. The trick is to flare the skirts open after you put them on the jig head. It not only allows better hooking, but it makes them easier to work through weeds.

When you remove a jig head from its package, adjust the hook with your pliers so that instead of pointing straight ahead, it angles out a couple of degrees. The result will be better hooksets.

The best way to throw jigs is using a flippin' technique. Bass often jump on a jig as soon as it goes below the surface, and flippin' puts you in a position to immediately set the hook. The right way to hookset here is by using both hands in a pivot motion. As soon as you've flipped the jig using your right hand (assuming you're a rightie), your left hand should grab the rod up close to the reel. Then to set the hook, push down with your right hand at the butt end of the rod as you jerk up toward your chest with your left hand. That's the pivot, and that's the hookset.

24. The Care and Feeding of Lakes and Ponds

No matter where a pond or lake is or whether it's natural or man-made, it takes time and effort to turn it into a first-class fishing environment.

(As a matter of definition, the line between "pond" and "lake" varies from place to place, and probably from person to person. To my mind, anything over thirty acres qualifies as a lake. Although the suggestions here apply to ponds – or "tanks," as they're called in Texas – too, I'll refer to lakes just to keep things simple.)

Most nonbiologist types can handle a lake that's anywhere under 150 acres without too much risk of failure. Anything larger, and the effectiveness of your efforts would be greatly reduced. Besides, you want to spend most of your time catching fish, not nursemaiding them.

First, you'll want fish to catch. You need to select a strain of largemouth bass that will survive and reproduce in whatever part of the country you live in. The Florida strain, great big tough fighting fish that I introduced into my Otter Creek lake, can't handle locations that are too far north. However, a decent lake maintenance program will let native largemouths found throughout the South grow into as good a trophy-class fish as the Florida variety, and they'll tolerate some colder climates too. If you have any questions in that regard, get in touch with your state's fish and game commission or county extension agent for the name of an expert you can consult with.

Two competitive species, such as largemouth and striped, Kentucky, or white bass, in the same lake isn't a good idea; they'll spend more time competing against each other than jumping on your spinnerbait. As you might imagine by now, my advice is stick to largemouths – they're the most fun.

To grow into big 'uns, fish need to eat well and eat regularly. The steak and taters of their menu should be bluegill and bream. You'll want lots, so these baitfish should be stocked and managed to produce an annual spawn that guarantees a plentiful population. Our Otter Creek property has eight brood ponds, and we transfer the new bluegill and bream into the lake on a regular basis.

Check your thermometer before you start fishing. It will tell you where fish are likely to be.

A fish biologist or another expert who's familiar with your area can recommend other forage. (The owner of any Federal Soil Conservation lake needs to check with the appropriate state agency, since forage is often covered in the lake construction agreement.) Shad, tilapia, and crawfish are all excellent, and they're readily available from commercial sources.

Hauling shad over long distances can be kind of tricky. They're a fragile species, and peculiar too: You need round containers because they like to swim in circles, plus you'll need to add a chemical to keep them alive.

Tilapia need to be replenished on an annual basis, because they don't survive when the water temperature drops below fifty-eight degrees. But since they reproduce in large hatches about every thirty days, they'll provide a tremendous amount of food.

As to vegetation, cattails and bulrushes along the banks provides excellent cover for the bass and their forage to spawn (as well as making a natural protective barrier against poachers). The trick is to keep it under control. That's especially important with coontail, hydrilla, and other surface plants. Lily pads, in particular, are beautiful and provide great cover, but they can literally take over a lake if they're overplanted or left unchecked.

That leads to something I hear all the time. "Help, Jimmy," folks say, "the vegetation is taking over my lake!"

There are two solutions. One is to stock your lake with grass carp. The species thrives on plants of all kinds, routinely growing up to thirty or forty pounds. Once grass carp get all the vegetation out of a lake, they're supposed to starve to death and die. Trouble is, they don't. They'll switch to a diet of baitfish, insects, and anything else they can find, and then they get to be nuisances. They muddy the shallow water, and they're real hard to catch and remove.

A chemical alternative is copper sulfate added to the water. By removing the oxygen, it prevents vegetation from growing (but without strangling fish in the process). Because copper sulfate can be tricky, in the sense that it can be easily misused, either apply it in small areas or else hire a lake management company to do the job correctly.

Another common complaint is muddy water. The answer is another chemical, lime, which is both inexpensive and effective. When we built dikes and little islands that significantly increased Otter Creek's shoreline by creating lots of bays, covers, and points, the bulldozers really churned up the water into a muddy mess. Lime cleared up the problem – literally – and did it pronto.

Nothing turns a lake into a prime fishing hole better than lots of varied cover. Brush piles, old Christmas trees and other timber, logs, boulders, and pilings . . . use your ingenuity to recycle natural objects that will attract and hold bass.

Although your bass fishing should be limited to catch-and-release (and with barbless hooks too, please remember), you'll need to cull your baitfish population to keep them under control. Eating-sized crappies and bluegills can be removed regularly, and, on a more limited basis because they don't reproduce as quickly, catfish. Funny thing, but no matter how hard you try to keep carp, drum, and other rough fish out of your pond, like uninvited drop-in guests, they'll find a way there, so you can be aggressive about removing them whenever you have the chance.

Stay in touch with the state or county fish biologist or extension agent. At least once a year, the expert should inspect your lake in terms of fish population, health (including the presence of any parasites), forage consumption, and pH control. The expert will then submit a list of recommendations that, if you follow them, will make the fishing even better.

Actually, your lake may be so good all the time that your biggest problem will be unwanted visitors of the human variety, including poachers. If you don't live on the lake and you can't afford full-time maintenance, and if fencing and locked gates aren't practical or possible, consider inviting a family to move their house or mobile home onto the property. Their presence all year long will go a long way to keeping the lake off-limits to anyone you'd rather not have fish there.

25. Catch-and-Release

I'm a strong supporter of "catch-and-release" fishing.

Until about twenty years ago, tournaments or not, people used to keep almost every fish they caught. There were always lots more in the lake, and even if you didn't plan to eat your catch or give it away, waving a big stringer full of bass was the macho way to end a day. So was hanging a stuffed and mounted hawg on your office or den wall – after all, that's where the expression "trophy bass" came from.

After a while, spectators at tournament weigh-ins couldn't help noticing how many pounds of fish were taken out of the same lakes they fished. They complained to tournament officials, which didn't exactly make for positive public relations for the tournament or its sponsors.

In response to the complaints, Ray Scott passed a rule in 1972 that all competitors in B.A.S.S. tournaments had to use boats that had livewells. To make sure the livewells were used, any fisherman whose string included a dead fish had pounds deducted from his

Catch and release: Try it—it'll grow on you.

score. Finally, after all the fish were weighed, they were released back into the lake or river.

The idea caught on, big-time. When weekend fishermen saw what us pros were doing, they bought boats with livewells and started releasing their fish too.

Catch-and-release makes good sense from a purely practical standpoint. If tournament fishermen cut into lake's bass population on one day, we're not going to do real well the rest of the week. Or at the next year's tournament there either.

But there's deeper reasons too. Ruining other folks' fishing breaks the Golden Rule, just the way needlessly slaughtering fish shows no respect for the Good Lord's bounty. Unless we protect and preserve our natural resources, there won't be any fish around for the next generation to catch. And their kids too.

I really like the slogan: "Catch-and-release: Try it – it'll grow on you." It means we're giving the fish we caught a chance to grow bigger. And we all want big 'uns to catch again and again.

G. 175 Bass Tactics

LAMAR UNDERWOOD

This good-sized largemouth was taken on a spinnerbait retrieved across the surface.

1. It's All About FINDING the Bass

"The great professional anglers are great because they find bass. Almost anyone can catch them if he or she knows where they're hiding. Finding them is the trick, not catching them."

—"Charley Hartley's Bass Wars," Feb. 9, 2009, on the BASS site at www.sports.espn. go.com/outdoors/bassmaster/index

2. An Essential Truth About Bass Fishing

"When I'm casting toward the shoreline, I know 90 percent of the bass in the lake are behind me."

—Remark attributed to Bill Dance, legendary angler and luremaker

3. The Pattern Tells You What to Do

"Just go about experimenting in a systematic manner, and be aware of what you're trying at all times. When you catch a fish . . . you'll know the reasons . . . Then, most

importantly, you can duplicate the technique and catch another."

—Grits Gresham, *Complete Book of Bass Fishing*, Outdoor Life/Harper & Row, 1966

4. My Most Important Bass Fishing Lesson

It took a lot of casts, and a lot of years, and a lot of wasted time before I finally grasped the most important lesson in largemouth bass fishing: You *must* fish weedless lures and baits. You will occasionally catch bass

alongside cover with lures using exposed hooks, but the majority of your strikes will come when you fish your lure right among the stumps, limbs, lily pads, and weedy holes. Sure, open-water fishing is more visual and less work, but do you want to catch bass or do you just want to mess around?

5. Top-Water Patience Can Pay

You're probably familiar with the surface lure tactic of letting your lure lie motionless on the water after it splashes down—at least until the ripples spread out and die away. There's another method—requiring infinitely more patience—that sometimes pays big dividends: Let your lure lie still for about three minutes, then jiggle it every so slightly. Then jiggle it some more, and eventually start it moving very, very slowly. You might be surprised by what happens.

6. Where'd They Go?

People who tell you that bass don't school don't know what they're talking about, as Grits Gresham points out in his *Complete Book of Bass Fishing* (1966): "The truth is bass *do* school. It follows then that there must be a great part of every lake which is virtually devoid of bass."

7. Those Important Scatter Points

The areas along bass migration routes where the fish break away from their schools and begin fanning out individually along the shoreline are called scatter points. Think of them as exits off the turnpikes. Grits Gresham points out in his *Complete Book of Bass Fish-ing* (1966): "Big bass school in tighter groups than do the yearlings, and they are especially reluctant to move past the scatter point. They seldom do so, in fact, in any numbers." That's exactly why you seldom find the real lunkers along the shoreline, and why big catches can be made if the school can be located in deeper water.

8. They're Not Hitting Because They're Not There!

As pointed out elsewhere in this book, when a stretch of shoreline that has been producing good fishing suddenly goes cold, the usual angling lament is, "They've stopped biting." Other stretches of shoreline are deemed to be poor because they seldom or never produce fish. The key thing to remember about the "good" stretches of shoreline is that when the fish "aren't biting," they probably have moved out along their migration routes to deeper water. Turning your back on the shoreline and exploring outside water, using charts, electronics, and local knowledge (if it is available), should lead to better catches when they're "not biting" along your favorite, dependable shorelines.

10. Here Today, Gone Tomorrow

The pros have a great way of describing a honey hole that suddenly goes dry. They lament, "I lost my fish!"

11. How to Fish Points

Points are favorite bass holding spots. Here's how the noted angler and luremaker, Tom Mann Jr., fished them, as related in the book *Structure Basics: A Complete Guide to Bass Hideouts*, B.A.S.S. Publications, (1999), by Wade L. Bourne: "Mann positions his boat off the end of a promising point. 'I think the jig works better coming downhill, and the important thing is to work it slow and keep bottom contact. Don't swim it.' Mann often makes multiple casts to a point to interest or tease sluggish fish."

12. Deep-Water Bass Bonanza

When you hook a deep-water bass, by trolling or casting, keep working the area and the same depths—hard!

13. Wolf Pack Bass

"The only way deep-water bass can effectively feed is in a pack, slashing into schools of baitfish together, so where there is one, there are usually more nearby."

—Rick Clunn's *World Championship Bass Fishing,*
Cordovan (1978) by Steve Price and Rick Clunn

14. A Bass Fishing Revolution Begins

It happened in the 1950s and '60s. Two great events came along that changed bass fishing forever. ("Ruined it!" some disenchanted stalwarts proclaim.) First, Carl Lowrance's "fish finder" underwater tracking device was invented, and then Buck Perry began preaching the gospel of bass following migration routes from shoreline shallows into deeper water away from the banks at varying distances.

15. When Bass Seem to Disappear

Bass migrate, just like ducks and geese, leaving for the winter. THERE ARE SELDOM ANY BASS ALONG THE BANKS WHERE YOU'VE BEEN FISHING. That was the amazing sermon preached by revolutionary luremaker Buck Perry back in the 1950s and '60s. " . . . might just as well have been fishing in your bathtub," Perry is reported as saying in Grits Gresham's classic *Complete Book of Bass Fishing* (1966). Perry believed (and was probably right) that bass were along the shorelines only during brief periods every day, mostly early and late. Anglers who thought the bass weren't hitting were mistaken, Perry believed. They weren't hitting because, in Perry's words, "they weren't there."

16. Finding Those Disappearing Bass

Fish finders, GPS units, and other devices, coupled with sophisticated boats and motors and a new knowledge of fishing honey holes in the vast waters of lakes and reservoirs, has lead not only to tournaments and halcyon days for cashing in on exploding tackle demands, but to the notion that would have made our grandfathers faint: "Turn your back on the shore . . . get out in the lake . . . that's where the fish are."

17. Buck Perry and His Magic Plug

A North Carolinian (1915–2006) and World War II veteran, Buck Perry is regarded as the father of structure fishing and a pioneer in pointing out bass migration routes and deep-water holding spots away from shorelines. He invented the Spoonplug, which is still sold today, as well as the first diving and deep-running lures to exploit structure fishing. The Spoonplug burst into national headlines in 1957 when Tom McNally, writing in the *Chicago Tribune*, told of Perry catching

of the first major books published on bass fishing in the modern era. Grits, a good friend, pointed out the discoveries of Buck Perry and went on to add, "Bass spend most of their time in deep water, in schools, and in a very restricted area—their sanctuary. That sanctuary is most often found in the deepest water of a lake or immediately adjacent to it."

19. Sanctuaries: Where Peak Action Awaits

In his *Complete Book of Bass Fishing* (1966), Grits Gresham said he looks for bass sanctuaries on bars, ridges, or reefs, or even clean spots in the lake bottom, and that bass would be moving along a regular underwater highway toward those spots twice a day. Expect to find the migration route along a ridge, with the sanctuary occurring at a break in the ridge—a fairly level spot somewhere along the ridge, "below 20 feet if the water is that deep."

20. Smart Bass Versus Naïve Bass

An incredible experiment on bass striking habits was reported by Grits Gresham in his *Complete Book of Bass Fishing* (1966). It seems that Missouri fisheries biologists placed tagged bass from heavily fished waters into a pond. They also placed tagged bass that came from waters that had never been fished into the same pond. They fished this pond with artificial lures in the spring and fall, and caught *twice as many* bass that had come from the unfished waters.

enormous strings of bass in heavily fished local lakes. Perry published *Spoonplugging: Your Guide to Lunker Fishing* in 1973. For more information go to www. BuckPerry.com.

18. Bass Travel Lanes: You've Got to Find Them!

Like it or not, the big reservoir and lake dilemma of bass moving away from the shoreline at various times of the day is very real. Buck Perry was perhaps the first—or certainly one of the first—anglers to focus on catching these wandering fish, but others soon followed. Grits Gresham, destined to become a television personality as well as top writer, discussed migrating bass in his *Complete Book of Bass Fishing* (1966), one

21. B.A.S.S. Pro Analyzes Moon Phases

Check out pro Richie White on the *Insider BASSlog Blog* at the B.A.S.S. site www.sports.espn. go.com/outdoors/bassmaster/index. White has done some amazing work on studies of the moon phases. The site also has many good articles on best lures and tactics.

22. A Creature of Habits

A bass caught in Texas or Georgia has virtually the same habits as one caught in Ohio or Pennsylvania. Their individual traits and preferences don't make a dime's bit of difference in terms of their needs in differing parts of the country. They all need food, cover, oxygen, and bottom cover they can relate to while feeding, moving, or hiding. The timing of their various activities may differ from place to place, but the way they go about their lives is virtually the same.

23. She—Not He—Is the Big One That Got Away

Anglers invariably call fish "he," but in the world of bass, the females are the biggest fish. When an angler says, "He got away!" he probably should have said, "*She* got away!"

24. For Dedicated Bass Anglers

(And "Bassmaster" Wannabes)

Operated by the ESPN sports channel, the Internet's most intense and rewarding site for bass anglers is the B.A.S.S. organization site: www.sports.espn.go.com/outdoors/bassmaster/index. Here you can join B.A.S.S. and the B.A.S.S. INSIDER groups, for which you receive the *Bassmaster* magazine and all sorts of benefits. Tournament news and information, a vast array of how-to from the pros, blogs of the tournament pros, videos, the works—B.A.S.S. has it all. There are free trial memberships and introductory memberships.

25. Suspended Bass—They're Tough to Catch

When bass are holding, suspended at mid-water levels, with no baitfish near them, they sometimes can seem to be locked in those positions all day. You see them on your depth finder, but they seem to have little interest in your deep-running lures. As a last-ditch effort, try jigging for them, straight down.

26. Stay in the Strike Zone for Suspended Bass

On the www.lurenet.com site, a tip from bass expert Bill Dance dealt with the suspended bass dilemma: "Suspended bass can be some of the most difficult fish to catch—simply because when they're suspended they're usually in an inactive mood and don't want to chase a lure. But if you can keep something appealing in the strike zone long enough, they're much more apt to bite. Two of the most effective lures I've found for this situation are the Smithwick 4 ½-inch Rogue and the Bomber Long A. [The Rogue indicated is the one that works below 4 feet.] The reasons these baits work so well is that they have the

ability to deliver an enticing darting action and they suspend well in between twitches on or just above the bass's depth level."

27. If You're a Bass Fan . . .

The bass-fishing site www.bassfan.com is one of the best sites I've visited for tips, articles, news, and videos. It's a keeper.

28. Gimmicks and Gadgets

"An angler without the gadgets is *fishing* for bass, whereas one with all the modern equipment is *hunting* for bass. Indeed, some of the new breed of bassmen enjoy the hunt more than the catch. It's a separate sport, really."

—A.D. Livingston, *Fishing for Bass: Modern Tactics and Tackle*, Lippincott, 1974

29. Go Early for Spring Bass

"Bass stage sooner than many people realize as they typically can spawn in cooler water, often going through the spawn weeks before the big waves

of smaller fish move up. It's also surprising to many anglers how active these early fish can be."

—Pro guide Troy Jens, Lake Guntersville, Alabama, in the article "A Great Spot for Spring," on the Web site www.lurenet.com

30. Finding and Fishing Bass Highways

In his column in *Bassin'* magazine back in May/ June 1992, veteran pro Hank Parker revealed a deadly system for finding bass after they've left shoreline cover once spring is over. Parker looks for points leading from shoreline areas where he usually finds and catches bass in the spring. In particular, he searches for "a long tapering flat that eventually plunges into a channel." In summertime, he drops a buoy at the spot the point drops into the channel, then starts working along the point back toward the shore. He uses deep and shallow crankbaits and Carolina-rigged worms, and lizards. He also keeps a rod handy with a topwater plug.

31. Let Don Wirth Help You Catch More Bass

One of the most prolific, informative, and entertaining writers in the "Bassmaster" lineup is Don Wirth. His columns and articles are packed with the kind of information that really counts when it comes to finding and catching bass. Check him out at the Bassmaster site www.sports. espn.go.com/outdoors/bassmaster/.

32. A Pro's Favorite Wintertime Lures

Pro Richie White, who fishes 200-plus days a year at Lake Fork in Texas, writes from his *Insider BASSlog Blog* at the B.A.S.S. site www.sports.espn.go.com/ outdoors/bassmaster/index. White's articles on moon phases and lures and tactics offer solid advice on a variety of subjects. On wintertime bass fishing, White says he catches more bass with lipless crankbaits than any others. "As a guide on perhaps the best big bass lake in the country [Lake Fork, Texas], I've caught giants on quite a variety of baits. But I get more on the lipless crankbait than all other baits combined in the winter." White described how, in February, he caught a 10-pounder next to the ramp with the wind blowing about 30 mph. "She hit a ¾-ounce Xcalibur crankbait in the Rayburn red color." Almost every crankbait White uses in winter has red or orange in it.

33. Rigging Up for Winter Bass

Pro Richie White's complete rig for winter bass: "So be sure to have a lipless crankbait with some red or orange in it, a good casting reel, a long rod that has some flex, and the right line for long casts." He uses a 7-foot Kistler Helium rod, medium for lighter lures and medium-heavy for ½- to ¾-ounce lures. His reels are Citica by Shimano and Revo by Ambassadeur. His line is 15-pound Berkley Big Game.

34. Florida Bass with Larry Larsen

Veteran Florida outdoor writer Larry Larsen is an expert on many kinds of fishing, with books and magazine articles galore, but he is perhaps best known for his prowess on largemouth bass. In that regard—but with assorted side dishes of bluegills, redbreasts, and catfish—Larry serves up superb fishing guides to Florida bass-fishing lakes and streams in his books, *Larry Larsen's Guide to Florida Bass Waters*, Larsen's Outdoor Publishing, with separate books covering North Florida, Central Florida, and South Florida. Larry gives Florida rivers their full due, showing you where to put into and float classic black-water streams through swamps of cypress, mossdraped oaks, and tall pines on the hillsides. Available at www.amazon.com.

35. Florida's Beautiful, Natural Spring Creeks

Florida has so many good bass lakes that it's easy to overlook the great river fishing. Florida is blessed with twenty-seven spring creeks, with clear 72-degree water gushing up from the earth all day, all year—just like the famed spring creeks in Pennsylvania and out West, where trout thrive. Many of Florida's spring creeks are famous, like Silver Springs and Rainbow Springs, but there are others tucked away that you may not have heard of. Consider Alexander Springs Run, in the Ocala National Forest, a 1½-hour drive from Ocala. It has campgrounds and canoe rentals, but, of course, you can launch your own. This is a great river-fishing float, with scenic natural beauty that somehow seems even better than your dreams of Tarzan Country.

36. Let It Blow, Let It Blow!

"I actually like the wind! It does three things for me: 1) It moves the boat so I don't have to stay on that trolling motor all day; 2) It allows us to cover a LOT of water; and 3) It puts chop on the water to greatly reduce light penetration. That means the fish will stay shallow rather than hiding down deep in the grass to get away from the bright light."

—Jim Porter's *Guide to Bass Fishing*, at www.stickmarsh.com

37. Cracking the Code of Huge Impoundments

Impoundments with largemouth bass are mostly huge, and vast portions of the water on any impoundment hold no bass at all. Without a guide or insider information, how can we find the fish in all that water without spending weeks doing it? In his excellent book, *Rick Clunn's World Championship Bass Fishing* (1978), written with Steve Price, veteran tournament pro Rick Clunn describes the process as a systematic approach that eliminates alternatives, one by one, until a pattern is found. Random casting won't work. Going from spot to spot only eliminates spots, not water types. "At least when you eliminate types of water," says Clunn, "you can consider yourself getting closer each time to where the bass will be found. This is one of the hardest lessons to learn in big impoundment bass fishing."

38. Finding Those Early-Spring Bass

In the same book, *Rick Clunn's World Championship Bass Fishing* (1978), written with Steve Price, veteran tournament pro Rick Clunn describes a tournament at Tennessee's Percy Priest Lake, with all insider information forbidden. Arriving at the lake in early spring, he was given a topo map and immediately started studying the potential spawning areas to fish—points, flats, coves. On the morning of practice day, he fished many types of water before locating most of the fish he caught at the mouths of coves. There were no fish inside the coves. As the sun rose over Percy's clear water, the fish seemed to prefer brush piles, planted by crappie fishermen. Clunn spent the afternoon looking for brush piles at the mouths of coves. In the tournament he fished these with a buzzbait, backed up by a plastic worm. He won the tournament.

39. Why Bass Change Depths

"The various depths bass will descend to are never determined by existing water temperatures at those levels. Instead, the depths bass will go to are determined by a combination of other conditions such as existing light penetration, water stratification (when in evidence), and water oxygen."

—John Weiss, *Advanced Bass Fishing*,
Stoeger Publishing, 1978

40. Oxygen Monitoring to Find Preferred Bass Depths

Early in 1974, when I was editing *Sports Afield* magazine, a young writer named John Weiss shook up the bass-fishing world with an article on the development of oxygen-monitoring equipment by Dr. Martin Venneman—the Sentry Oxygen Monitor. Dr. Venneman had discovered that an amazing 50 to 80 percent of the water in any lake does not contain enough oxygen to support fish life. Calling for the use of the Oxygen Monitor as just one more device to help find the fish, John Weiss pointed out that the monitors should always be kept in mind as the advanced angler commences his search for bass. "Oxygen monitoring equipment does not guarantee you will consistently be able to find or catch fish. It does guarantee you will not waste one minute of time fishing where no fish can possibly survive." In his book, *Advanced Bass Fishing* (1976), Weiss goes on to say, "It should also be mentioned that bass found in rivers and streams are not likely to be influenced by changing oxygen levels. . . . The greatest applications of oxygen evaluation are on the larger lakes and reservoirs." [Check out today's modern oxygen monitors at Bass Pro Shops and Cabela's.]

41. Best Oxygen Levels for Bass

"For the bass species, optimum oxygen levels are found in the range of 5 to 13 parts per million (PPM) though they highly prefer and will seek out the 9 to 12 PPM level."

—John Weiss, *Advanced Bass Strategies* (1976)

42. When River Bass Turn On

In an excellent article I published as editor in the 1972 *Sports Afield Fishing Annual*, Charles W. Edghill reminded our readers that smallmouth fly fishers often overlook using their trout dry flies and nymphs for

This Susquehanna River smallmouth hit a small crankbait, fished below a riffle.

© Jay Cassell

river smallmouths in high summer. You won't catch the big bronzebacks, but you'll get plenty of action from the fish in the 10- to 15-inch class.

43. Smallmouth Floats on the Upper Delaware

If you're hankering for some great action with small smallmouths (a 14-incher is big up there), book a guided float on the Upper Delaware and be ready to use light spinning gear with jigs and soft-plastic grubs. You could easily get a fifty-fish day. If you insist on using your fly rod, you'll catch fish, but far fewer than you can spinning. These floats should be made in summer, not in the early season trout and mayfly times.

44. Summer's Smallmouth Dividends

Tired of getting skunked on your favorite trout waters during high summer? Then turn your fly and light spinning rods toward the smallmouth rivers. You'll find plenty of action from battling fish that are as strong and jump as much as any trout you ever saw.

45. Best in the West

In the western United States, among the blue-ribbon trout waters that get the attention of most anglers, are bass lakes and reservoirs that deliver solid, consistent action and lots of fish. If you're bored with the trout treadmill and live in the West, turn your attention to bass to put more fun back in your fishing.

46. Bass Fishing in the West

The site www.westernbass.com is loaded with information, tips, and observations of anglers from all over the western states. The site covers California, Washington, Oregon, Idaho, Montana, Wyoming, Arizona, Nevada, Utah, and New Mexico.

47. What to Expect on Post-Spawn Bass

"In some lakes the post-spawn bass do move off and suspend and an angler can't catch many of them for two months or so. Those waters during the post-spawn months are notoriously tough fishing."

—Larry Larsen, *Bass Fishing Facts* (1989)

48. Taking More Bass in Streams and Creeks

"Streams are typically not as wide, have swifter current and are clearer, so more natural colored baits work best. Rivers are usually deeper, wider and have more color, meaning brighter baits work best, but this isn't always true."

—Elite Series pro Brian Snowden, in a www. Bassmaster.com archive article by David Hunter Jones. Snowden grew up fishing small waters and continues to wade and float small streams near his home in Reeds Spring, Missouri

49. Smallmouth Tackle: Heavy Vs. Light

In his blog for smallmouth bass lovers, Bassmaster smallmouth guru Stephen Headrick takes on critical, interesting subjects with no-nonsense advice, such as: "Heavy tackle is great when you can get away with it—like in dirty water or really heavy cover. But heavy tackle will adversely affect how you fish deep water for smallmouth bass. It takes longer for heavy lines to get pulled to the bottom. Heavy lines are more visible to the bass. Heavy lines dull the action of your lures. And by heavy I'm talking about anything over 10-pound test. I use a lot of 4-, 6-, and 8-pound line for my smallmouth fishing here at Dale Hollow Lake and elsewhere." Check out Hedrick's great articles at: www. sports.espn.go.com/outdoors/bassmaster/index.

50. Jump the Gun for Fall Smallmouths

Anglers waiting for hot weather to subside and fall action with smallmouths to kick in can miss the boat, literally, according to smallmouth Bassmaster guru Stephen Headrick, who writes a blog for the popular Bassmaster and Bass site, www.sports.espn .go.com/outdoors/bassmaster/index. Headrick says he starts checking on creeks in highland reservoirs before the heat breaks—just checking for lunkers, not spending the day there yet. "My favorite bait at this time is a ³/₁₆-ounce shaky head jig with a 4-inch Go To Bait Co. worm in pumpkin pepper. I throw it on a spinning outfit and 8-pound line. It's not a fast way of fishing, but it'll catch bass of all sizes, and I have a lot of confidence in it. If I'm out at night (and you can

catch smallmouths at night all year long), I like to fish a ¾-ounce black and blue Punisher spinnerbait with a big blue blade."

51. Fishing Flooded Timber: Rule One

All flooded timber looks inviting to the bass angler. All that cover, all those shadows for bass to hide in and wait for prey. But when you're looking at hundreds—or thousands—of acres of flooded timber, you soon realize the fish aren't scattered throughout. They are not lying in wait behind every tree. Instead, as in other lakes, they relate to bottom contours. The timber near the right bottom contours and channels will be the timber that holds the fish. Think *bottom contours and conditions* first. *Timber*, second.

52. Targeting Docks and Bridge Pilings

Those shadowy docks and bridge pilings always look like great cover for fish. And they are! Bass, all kinds of panfish, pickerel, pike, even walleyes are

probably lurking there. You'll catch more fish at docks or pilings by getting your boat into position and making your first casts parallel to the target. Cast in toward the bank and run your lure alongside the dock—as close to the boards as you can get it—back to the boat. Next, if there's room under the dock, try skipping side-arm casts to get your lure under the boards into the shadows.

53. Fish Rip-Raps for Early Spring Bass

Cold-water early spring bass can be tough to catch, but one way to cut the odds, says pro Timmy Horton, is to fish rip-raps—those rocky barriers supporting roads across lakes and reservoirs and dams along ponds. The rocks heat up with the warming spring sun, and the fish move into the adjacent waters. They can be on the rocks or as far as 30 feet outside. Especially good are the breaks in the rip-rap where boats can slide through. Horton likes jerkbaits for this fishing, and goes deep with the longer-bill models. Vary your retrieve from sudden jerks, to smooth pulls, to slow twitches. You'll catch bass, Horton says, on his "The Bass Pro" feature on the Versus Country Internet site.

54. How to Fish Early-Spring Bass

In another section of this book, I touched on the strategy of fishing river and creek inlets at the heads of lakes and reservoirs. These waters warm up first in early spring. Here's a tip on fishing them. It's from *Advanced Bass Strategies*, The Hunting and Fishing Library (1995), by Dick Sternberg: "In early spring, before spawning begins, look for clean Vs (shoreline breaks) in the back ends of creek arms. The weedlines of these Vs holds fish through the day, but the action is fastest in late afternoon because of the warming water." The Carolina rig is especially effective for fishing these spots.

55. How to Fish Jigs for Spring Bass on Points

Bass expert and luremaker Tom Mann, Jr., explained his favorite way to fish points in early spring: "If I'm fishing 15 to 25 feet of water, I use a $\frac{6}{7}$-ounce lead-headed jig. If I'm fishing shallower than this, I use a $\frac{5}{16}$-ounce jig. In clear water I like a brown jig with a black twin-tail grub. In stained water, I reverse the colors, going with a black jig and a brown grub."

—*Structure Basics: A Complete Guide to Bass Hideouts*, Wade L. Bourne, Publications, 1999

56. Where'd They Go? (Part One)

Ohio writer John Weiss was one of my regular contributors in the years I was editing *Sports Afield*. He was a reader favorite, and with good reason. His observations were backed up by real field experiences and research. In March 1973, John did a remarkable article on finding bass in big lakes. Called "Reading Substructure: The Pro Method of Fishing Big-Lake Bass," the article likened finding bass to finding coveys of quail on a big farm. The quail aren't everywhere; they are bunched up in certain locations. So are the bass. John's basic idea game plan calls for the following:

1. Fishing the midday hours, because that's when the bass have moved from scattering along the shorelines back to their sanctuaries, which are always on substructure.
2. Find the depth in the lake where the ideal temperature of 72 degrees shows consistently. (Be aware that 72 degrees is used as the optimum in John's Ohio area. Yours may be different. John uses the example of 72 degrees occurring mostly at 20 feet.)
3. Study your charts to find the areas where substructure is located in the 20-foot, 72-degree zone depths.

4. Eliminate poor habitat over muddy or murky bottoms. You want gravel, hard-packed sand, weeds, etc. In John's words: "Simply locating structure is not the key to success. You must locate substructure. If a treeline is considered structure, a gap in that treeline is considered substructure. If a creek channel is structure at the 20-foot level, substructure may be a sharp bend in the channel or a patch of brush along the edge of the channel. Bass will use the entire structure as a migration route to other places in the lake, but it is the substructure that will draw and hold the school for long periods of time. Locate the substructure and you've located a bass sanctuary."

57. Where'd They Go? (Part Two)

Continuing with the expertise John Weiss shared with readers of *Sports Afield* when I was editor there, he presented another landmark article in May 1973 called "The Best Bass Fishing Starts Where Light Stops." In it, John cited several scientific studies suggesting that light penetration—even more than desired temperatures—is what sends bass deeper in the water. Bass will go to whatever depth is necessary to escape light penetration. So how deep are the fish? Well, the answer is whatever depth it takes to get out of the light. For more of John Weiss' great bass-fishing tips, see his *Bass Angler's Almanac: More Than 650 Tips and Tactics*, The Lyons Press (2002), at www.amazon.com, www.finefishing.com, and other outlets.

58. Field & Stream's Largemouth "Ultimate Lure" Survey Winners

In what it called the "Ultimate Lure Survey," published in March 2008, *Field & Stream* magazine asked 1,000 of its hard-core readers to name their favorite lures. The winners for the Largemouth Bass category were:

Soft-Plastic, 30%, Yamamoto Senko, with Zoom Finesse Worm second

Top Water, 16%, Arbogast Jitterbug, with Zara Spook second

In-Line Spinners, 16%, Mepps Aglia, with Worden's Rooster Tail second

Spinnerbaits, 11%, Generic Double Colorado Blades, with Booyah Pond Magic second

Crankbaits, 11%, Bomber A with Rapala Shad Rap second

Minnow-Type Lures, 8%, Original Rapala, with Rebel second

Jigs, 6%, Jig with Mister Twister, Strike King Skirted Jig and Trailer second

Spoons, 1%, Little Cleo, with Dardevle second

59. *Field & Stream's* Smallmouth "Ultimate Lure" Survey Winners

In what it called the "Ultimate Lure Survey," published in March, 2008, *Field & Stream* magazine asked 1,000 of its hard-core readers to name their favorite lures. The winners for the Smallmouth Bass category were:

In-Line Spinners, 27%, Mepps Aglia

Soft-Plastics, 23%, Yamamoto Senko, with Zoom Finesse Worm second

Crankbaits, 13%, Bomber A

Minnow-Type Lures, 12%, Original Rapala

Jigs, 10%, Jig with Mister Twister

Top Water, 8%, Heddon Tiny Torpedo

Spinnerbaits, 6%, Booyah Pond Magic

Spoons, 2%, Dardevle

A deep-diving crankbait fooled this smallmouth.

60. Bass Fishing's Super-Rig: It's Famous Because It Works

If you seriously want to catch bass—and not simply enjoy a nice day on the water—then sooner or later you're going to have to fish plastic worms or other soft-plastic baits. Yes, worm fishing makes some anglers yawn. Yes, it's tough to get the hang of, requiring patience and the development of all-important feel and touch. But the tactic catches bass, lots of them, big ones and little ones. Sometimes it catches them on days when nothing else works.

61. Rick Clunn's Most Deadly Lure Advice

Tournament bass pro Rick Clunn, writing with Steve Price in *Rick Clunn's World Championship Bass Fishing* (1978), says, "Plastic worms are probably the most deadly lures . . . but for many anglers they are the most disliked. The usual complaints include, 'It's too slow,' and 'I can't tell if I've got a bass or a stump.' The plain truth about worm fishing is that it takes practice, practice, and more practice to become efficient."

62. Smart and Easy Plastic Worm Fishing

In *Rick Clunn's World Championship Bass Fishing* (1978), pro Rick Clunn recommends fishing small ponds or slow-moving, clear creeks to get the hang of working plastic worms in the obvious holes and structure where bass are likely to be holding.

63. Plastic Worm Action: Are You Missing Out?

What pro Rick Clunn called the "most deadly" back in 1978 has not lost its appeal today. Plastic worms and soft-plastic baits are catching bass everywhere these fish swim, and if you want to snub the technique, you do so at the risk of having a lot of those slow, "nice days" on the water.

64. The Mother of All Plastic Worm Rigs

Today there are many, many methods and variations on fishing plastic worms and soft-plastic baits, but one stands alone as the mother of all plastic worm rigs. It's the famous Texas rig; once you learn to fish it, you'll catch more bass and bigger bass.

65. How to Set Up the Texas Rig

The rig starts with your favorite worm or soft-plastic bait, a worm hook, and a bullet-type sinker in a size to take you deep or shallow as you prefer for the location and conditions. First, pass the line through the slip sinker and tie on the hook. Second, push the point of the hook into the center of the end of the worm head and thread it about ½ inch into the center of the worm body. Next, bring the point of the hook out of the body. It should be about ½ inch back from the head. Now pull the eye and shank of the hook back through the worm body until the eye end of the hook disappears into the worm about ¼ inch. Lastly, push the point of the hook into the worm just past the barb. Now you have a straight worm that's virtually weedless.

66. Tweaking the Texas Worm Rig

Some experts refine this rig by pushing the hook point all the way back through the body so that the point lies just beneath the surface of the bait. Eventually, your worm fishing will lead to many different and exciting ways to fish worms and soft-plastic baits. But the good old Texas Rig will still be one you can count on. Two of the best places to learn all about worm fishing are the Bass Pro Shops and Cabela's Web sites.

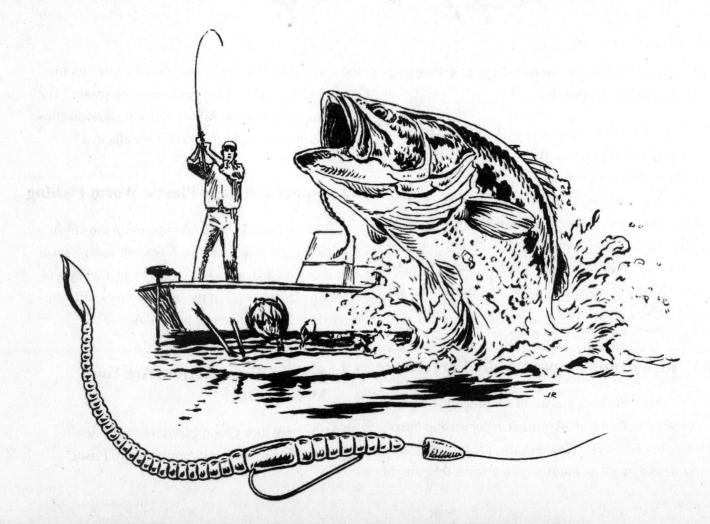

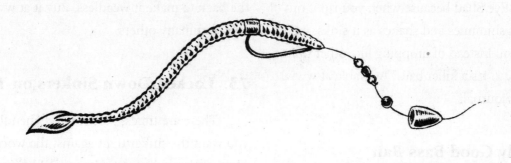

67. The Deadly Carolina Rig

The ubiquitous Texas Rig is rivaled by the Carolina Rig for bass-catching effectiveness. Basically, the Carolina Rig differs by having the bullet sinker positioned up the line, instead of on the nose of the soft bait as in the Texas. This makes the soft-plastic lure or worm sink slower and float behind and above the bullet sinker. The lure or worm moves freely with an enticing action. The Carolina Rig is so effective that many top anglers never bother to use the Texas Rig at all. Many tournament anglers keep one rod loaded for action with a Carolina Rig all set up.

68. Setting Up the Carolina Rig

Here's how to set up the Carolina Rig as related in the book *Advanced Bass Fishing* (1995), by Dick Sternberg: "Make a Carolina Rig by sliding a 1-ounce bullet sinker and a glass bead onto 20-pound mono or 30-pound Spectra, tying on a Size 10 barrel swivel, then adding a 3-foot, 12-pound mono leader. Attach a 3/0 HP hook for a lizard, 2/0 for a French fry (small worm) or crawworm. The glass bead keeps the sinker from damaging the knot, and makes a clicking sound. The lighter leader prevents losing the entire rig should the hook get snagged." The preferred tackle for rigging the Carolina varies, and you can see a variety of ways to make the rig on Internet fishing sites. On Google, try "Carolina Worm Bass Rig."

69. Buy This Book and Catch More Bass!

The title says it all: *Advanced Bass Fishing: Tips and Techniques from the Country's Best Guides and Tournament Anglers*. But what makes Dick Sternberg's book so useful is that the pages deliver on the promise of the title. The techniques are so well presented in detailed photographs and drawings that you will be able to put the best "insider" bass fishing techniques to work next time you go fishing. Published by The Hunting and Fishing Library (1995), the book listed on Amazon for $21.50 at this writing and less, used, at other Internet sites. Search the Internet, find it, buy it, use it. You'll start catching bass like never before.

70. Kevin VanDam's Early Season Tactics

At Strike King Lure Co. and on their Web site, *No Tiger!*, pro Kevin VanDam is held in the highest regard of professionalism. And with good reason: VanDam has won just about everything in tournaments and keeps on doing it. In an interview on his placing third in difficult conditions in the February 2007 tournament at Lay Lake near Montgomery, Alabama, VanDam said, "My primary bait was the new Strike King Red-Eye Shad, a lipless crankbait. I was fishing a crawdad color with gold and white on the edge of the grass at Lay Lake. When the water's cold, as it was at Lay Lake, lipless baits like the Red-Eye Shad can really be effective . . . I fished the Red-Eye Shad because when you rip it out of the grass and it shimmies and shakes as it sinks, it actually swims down, instead of dropping like other lipless crankbaits do. . . . It's a killer bait." Available at www.strikeking.com/journal.

71. A Really Good Bass Bait

The YUM Money Minnows, from www.lurenet.com and tackle dealers, have been attracting a lot of attention from pro bassers. I now have them in my own tackle box and can report great success in using them, especially in the "Sight-Fishing" episodes covered elsewhere in the bass section of this book. I've been using the 3 ½-inch version in bluegill colors, but there are plenty of others to choose from. Rig it Texas style with an extra-wide-gap, offset worm hook or a shank-weighted swimbait hook—and make it weedless. The lure has a belly slot. I turn the hook up through it and out the top of the bait, then set the hook lightly into the back to make it weedless. Good instructions for using the weighted hook and getting the lure deeper are on the www.lurenet.com site. My personal use with this lure has me convinced that you'll catch more bass by using it.

72. Tie On a Strike King Zulu

The Strike King Zulu has become one of my favorite lures for fishing weedless in all kinds of bigmouth cover. It's soft plastic at its best, catching fish and holding up well after the tussles. I rig it with the hook coming out the top and turned to nestle just enough under

the back to make it weedless. Buy it at www.basspro.com and many others.

73. Locked-Down Sinkers on Texas Rigs

There are times, particularly when flipping, when you want the sinker tight against the worm or soft-plastic lure you're using, instead of having the sinker slide. You can do this by pegging a toothpick alongside the sinker to hold it against the lure. So many anglers are doing this now that bullet sinkers are available with locking devices to hold it to your plastic bait.

74. Try a Tricked-Up Dinger

The YUM Dinger worm, from www.lurenet.com, is a hot bass lure everywhere, but pro Tim Horton of Muscle Shoals, Alabama, has come up with a new tactic for using it, according to a report in *Field & Stream*, May 2006. For flipping, getting the lure down through tangles and limbs, Horton rigs a 5-inch Dinger Texas-style with a 4/0 hook and no weight. He clips off the hook from a ¼- to ⅟₁₆-ounce ball-head jig with a keeper collar, and slips the jig's collar into the Dinger's tail. Now the Dinger is ready to dive tail-first down into the big-fish lairs.

75. When Schooling Fish Won't Hit

It's really frustrating when schooling bass are tearing the water apart, but they won't hit your lures. Perhaps the fry they're on is smaller than you've been accustomed to imitating. Drop down in lure size to see if they'll start hitting.

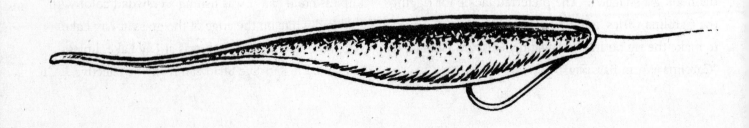

76. Try Clear Plastic for Schooling Fish

Clear plastic lures can be effective for schooling bass because the fish don't see them well enough to tell they're bogus. Working them fast helps also.

77. The Floating Worm: Fun and Good

Floating plastic worms, made to stay on top or sink far slower than normal plastic worms, have arrived in bass fishing with a big-bucks bang, winning tournaments here and there and catching bass for anglers who like topwater fishing. Bass Pro Shops, www.basspro.com, carries them in their own brand, the Gambler brand, and two types of floating worms by Berkley Gulp. You should check other sites as well, remembering that not all plastic worms are true floaters. Rig them Texas-style, with a 3/0 light wire hook, a small swivel, and 12 to 15 inches of leader.

78. Skipping Floating Worms

Do you know how to skip a floating worm? You should, it's fun—just like skipping rocks on the water when you were a kid—and you catch lots of bass to boot. Picture a deep, dark lair back under some overhanging trees, or under a dock. The only way you can get a worm in there is to skip it over the water like a flat rock. It's not hard to do with a floating worm. Practice it on open water until you get the touch. Then start skip-ping your floating worm back in there where the bass are waiting.

79. High-Tech Gear Can Be Loads of Fun

"He who finishes with the most toys *wins*," goes the old adage. In modern bass fishing, the toys are endless, from underwater devices to counters on reels to tell you exactly how much line you've got out. Throw in some awesome motors and boats strong and fast enough to master both speed and distance over any body of water, and you've got a lot of toys to play with on any day's fishing. Even if you don't catch a fish, you can have fun with your dials, gauges, and flashing lights.

80. When High-Tech Goes Wrong

Be careful not to become the type of bass fisherman who seldom makes good catches because he can't resist cranking the motor and heading for greener pastures—in other words, playing with his toys. After a few casts in any spot, he announces, "They're not here. Let's race on!" And he does.

81. Here He Comes! Now What?

When you see a fish following your lure as you retrieve, but not moving in for the strike, what do you do? Slow down your retrieve, speed it up? I once

asked that question to popular TV fishing and sports personality Grits Gresham. Grits replied, "It doesn't make a bit of difference. Whichever one you do will be wrong." Well, there's a lot of truth in what Grits said, but with heart pounding, and even hands shaking, in anticipation, we've just got to do *something*. Here's my play: First try slowing down the retrieve. If that doesn't work, try speeding it up. That's about all you can do.

82. When Spring Bass Become Active

"One of the most frequently asked questions thrown my way during guiding is, 'When do bass first become active in the spring?' My standard answer for people in the northern states is that bass become active as soon as the water is soft enough for the bait to sink. In the South, it's as soon as the water temperatures become consistent in the mid to upper 40s."

—Pro guide Troy Jens, Lake Guntersville, Alabama, in the article "A Great Spot for Spring," on the Web site www.lurenet.com.

83. Catching the Year's Earliest Bass

"Dragging jigs and bottom draggers at a snail's pace in deep water is not the answer to big cold-water spring bass. These bass are after shallow baitfish, and my favorite baitfish imitator for these springtime cold-water periods is the Cotton Cordell Super Spot."

—Pro guide Troy Jens, Lake Guntersville, Alabama, in the article "A Great Spot for Spring," on the Web site www.lurenet.com

84. Working Early-Spring's Deadliest Lure

When bass are staging for the spawn on breaklines from 4 to 8 feet deep, close to deeper water, pro guide Troy Jens of Lake Guntersville, Alabama, likes to go

after them with the Cotton Cordell Super Spot. He uses the ½-ounce Super Spot and works it just fast enough to stay above the bottom. One reason he likes the bait is because it can be fished from very slow to super fast. Writing for the Web site www.lurenet.com, Jens says he uses the Super Spot from ice-out through water temperatures in the 40s. "As the water warms into the 50s, I begin fishing the tops of the humps and ledges and I begin moving further back into the creeks."

85. Floating Worms: Make Sure They Can

Not all plastic worms are real floaters. The genuine floaters are chemically designed and made to resist sinking. They do sink, but very, very slowly, and they ride above the sinker when pulled along the bottom—even when attached to a hook. Make sure you're getting the real deal, real floating worms.

86. Hooking Up Your Floating Worms

If the hook you use on a floating worm is too heavy, you'll be defeating the reason you are using a floater. A 3/0 or 2/0 that's thin and wire-like should be just right. Drive the hook through the worm, then back it up to make it weedless.

87. The Deadly Jerkbait Pause

"The . . . technique for cold water is working a jerkbait over steeply sloping banks in very cold water and long points during a warming trend. Using a Smithwick Rogue or XCalibur Jerkbait or Twitch Bait, make long casts, crank the bait down, and begin a jerk-jerk-pause retrieve. Many pros say that it's the pause, not the jerks or twitches, that is the key to this technique. Do not get in a hurry. Vary the duration of your pauses from just a second or two to excruciatingly long waits of up to a minute."

—Lawrence Taylor, www.lurenet.com

88. The Lure That Got Away

Every March, in the first teasing springtime weather, when it was still too cold to catch bass in several places where I lived as a young man, one lure—a yellow Heddon Tadpolly—produced fish almost every afternoon I went out. Working very, very s-l-o-w-l-y in the shallows, the Tadpolly's enticing wobble brought up springtime lunkers in a way no other lure has ever matched. An old saying goes, "When you find something you really like, buy several, because they're sure to stop making it." So true. Today, the Heddon Tadpolly is gone—except on eBay, where it is a popular collector's item.

89. Lure Action, Not Color, Counts Most

". . . I am convinced that color is not as important as action."

—A.D. Livingston, *Fishing for Bass: Modern Tactics and Tackle*, Lippincott, 1974

90. Do Lure Colors Really Matter?

"So far I haven't been able to make rhyme or reason of why a bass will hit a certain color at a particular time. But that does sometimes seem to be the case. Yet, I wonder."

—A.D. Livingston, *Fishing for Bass: Modern Tactics and Tackle*, Lippincott, 1974

91. Bass Expert's Favorite Lure Colors

"There are exceptions, but I generally use black (or dark) lures in murky water and shiny lures in clear water. I also tend to use black early and late in the day . . . shiny when the sun is high and bright, black when fishing deep, and shiny when I am fishing shallow."

—A.D. Livingston, *Fishing for Bass: Modern Tactics and Tackle*, Lippincott, 1974

92. Smallmouths on the Rocks

In his wonderful autobiography, *My Life Was THIS BIG and Other True Fishing Tales*, Skyhorse Publishing (2008), by Lefty Kreh with Chris Millard, Lefty not only points out the importance of fishing the rocks to catch river smallmouths, he puts a great deal of emphasis on the angle of the cast. Presenting the fly from the wrong side of the rock will not result in strikes because of the unnatural drift of the fly (much the same as in "drag" in presenting trout flies). For instance, a rock with current on both sides will fish better when the cast and the drifting fly are on the same side as the current. A fly cast across the rock to reach the current on the other side usually will not work.

93. When Smallmouths Go Berserk!

Smallmouth bass have a tendency to sometimes follow a fish you're playing. When this happens in clear water, you'll see that you're on a honey hole and know it's the place to keep fishing.

94. When Smallmouths Tease You!

When smallmouth bass make some passes at your lure, but don't hit, drop down to a smaller size lure. You'll probably get a strike.

95. Reaction Strikes: Take 'Em When You Can

When bass are on the feed, searching for food like predators on the prowl, they are, of course, striking out of hunger. But many strikes occur when the bass is just sitting there, finning easily, not feeding at all. A case in point might be a bass lying under a log, or in a stretch of lily pads. A crankbait or other lure that suddenly flashes past sometimes elicits a savage strike that comes out of pure instinct to attack available prey.

It's as if your lure woke up a sleeping bass. It doesn't happen all the time, but when it does, count yourself as fortunate.

96. River Sloughs: Don't Miss Them

Those deep bends, elbows, and sloughs just off the main flow of a river cry out to be fished hard. As Ray Bergman reminds us in *Fresh-Water Bass*, Knopf (1946): " . . . these backwaters are inclined to be somewhat weedy and stumpy with fallen trees helping to foster the feeling of wildness. The situation is enticing . . . Alluring pockets, deep looking holes, and enchanting little caverns formed by stumps and logs . . . "

97. Surface Plunkers: The Sweet Feel of "Real"

Everybody wants to catch fish on surface lures when they are hitting. The trick is to make those plugs look like fish swimming and feeding on the surface. Working these baits is all a matter of feel. Only the feedback, the muscle memory, of your hands and arms can tell you how it's done. Here's Ray Bergman on the subject, from *Fresh-Water Bass* (1946): " . . . you can't just throw it out, reel it in and expect it to do its stuff. [*Chug, splash, bob, wiggle*, like live fish.] To do this you jerk hard but use a short movement. One make of lure requires more jerk than another."

98. Darter Plugs: The "Extra" Surface Baits

Not all surface plugs are in the plunker and popper variety. Darter plugs, for example, have a deadly up-and-down motion. They should be in your tacklebox right alongside the plunkers. As Ray Bergman says in *Fresh-Water Bass* (1946): "When this lure is handled correctly with a twitch and pause it acts very much like a crippled or badly injured minnow. That is, it darts

slightly under the surface speedily and quickly, and then just as suddenly gives up and comes to rest on the surface."

99. When the Wind Blows

Fishing in the big wind can be very tough, not necessarily because the fish aren't biting, but because the waves and the wind slapping your line and lure make it very difficult to present the bait with the proper action and speed—not to mention getting it into the proper location to start with. Ray Bergman, in *Fresh-Water Bass* (1946), reminds us we can still catch fish: "I do believe that when you can handle your lure correctly in the wind the fish will take, other factors being equal, regardless of the direction of the wind."

100. Lucas on Bass

If you have a few years on you and love bass fishing, you may be familiar with the name Jason Lucas. He was angling editor of *Sports Afield* magazine from the late 1940s until right at the time when I came to *Sports Afield* in 1967 as an associate editor. Lucas was gone from the magazine before I had a chance to work with him or meet him, but I was very tuned in to his reputation and work. Ted Kesting, *Sports Afield*'s editor-in-chief in the mid-1940s, when the magazine was headquartered in Minneapolis, became acquainted with a man who could catch bass consistently, in all seasons, even in hard-fished waters. And, most importantly, the man could write! Jason Lucas became Angling Editor soon after Kesting discovered him, and built an aura of bassing skill by fishing almost every day—in one case fishing for bass for an entire 365-day straight run. Lucas came along before bass boats and sophisticated electronics. He was a skilled angler, however, with the curiosity to experiment and learn everything about bass fishing he could. Today, the best of his words survive in the book *Lucas on Bass Fishing*, originally published in

1947 by Dodd, Mead, and Co., and available today at www.amazon.com and other sites in a paperback edition published in 2005. You can find copies of the used original hardcover on the Internet.

101. Think Brown for More Bass

"Nearly all of the bottom-feeding fish which bass eat are of a dirty-brown color, with dirty-white or dirty-yellowish bellies. So, as might be expected, a dirty-brown plug often seems to get them down here when nothing else will."

—Jason Lucas, *Lucas on Bass Fishing*, Dodd, Mead, and Co., 1947, reprinted since

102. Looks Are Deceiving

"It is impossible to judge the merits of a lure from looking at it, or seeing its action in the water . . . There's but one good way to find out how well they'll take a certain lure—try it on them!"

—Jason Lucas, *Lucas on Bass Fishing*, Dodd, Mead, and Co., 1947, reprinted since

103. Uncle Homer: My Bassing Hero

Among the many pleasures that came my way when I was editor of *Sports Afield* magazine in the 1970s, none were more intense than working and fishing with Homer Circle, my Angling Editor. "Uncle Homer," as we all fondly called him, is a man of extraordinary talent and immense kindness.

In his 90s as this is being written, Homer has been elected to several angling Halls of Fame. Some of his best articles—and glimpses into his vast knowledge of bass fishing—can be found in the book *Bass Wisdom*, available in a Lyons Press paperback version from www.amazon.com.

104. Never Underestimate a Bass' Vision

"I watched the large yellow butterfly as it 'flitted' along the canal bulkhead 18 inches or so off the surface. I just happened to glance its way as it neared an old dock that emerged from the

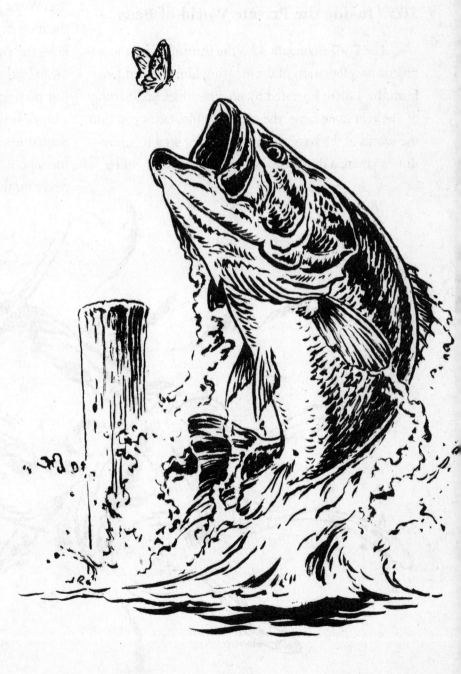

cement-walled shoreline. The water's surface erupted and a 3-pound largemouth shot toward the flapping morsel. The bass' aim was off and it crashed back into its environment, no fuller for its experience. The happening, however, further reinforced my belief that largemouth bass have very good vision. The presence of the air-born butterfly was not detected through the bass' sense of smell, sound (lateral line), or taste. It was seen . . . "

—Larry Larsen, *Bass Fishing Facts* (1989)

105. Inside the Private World of Bass

The DVD *Bigmouth 35* is the thirty-five-year anniversary celebration of the amazing film by Glen Lau from the 1960s. Narrated by no other than Rod Serling of *Twilight Zone* fame, the one-hour film takes you into the world of the bass as you have never seen it before—unless you're a diver. Lau is also a great angler, and a close buddy of Homer Circle, and you can count on their combined expertise for ideas that will definitely help you catch more bass. Available at www.amazon.com.

106. Sight Fishing for Largemouths— Step One

As the great Yogi Berra once proclaimed, "You can observe a lot just by watching." Truer words were never spoken when it comes to largemouth bass fishing. When the water is still and quiet—usually early in the morning or at dusk, especially in late spring or early fall—the sight and sound of minnows on the move mean bass are in attack mode. Those minnows aren't just playing around. They're about to be gulped into a bigmouth's gullet, and they're trying to leave Dodge. Sometimes you'll even hear or see the bass slash into the school, or see big swirls. Your tackle should be ready for the next step.

Use a weedless lure when working the lily pads for largemouths.

107. Sight Fishing for Largemouths—Step Two

Your electric motor has just ceased humming, or you've carefully laid down your canoe paddle. You're drifting into the area where you saw or heard minnows on the run, or a bass swirl or strike. Your chosen lure (which we'll cover in Step Three) is ready. Ahead of you are lily pads, half-sunken logs, or a brush-choked shoreline. Here, in this moment and position, is where most anglers fail. Either they move too aggressively and spook the fish, or they make casts that are too far out in the open water. They're thinking the bass will come roaring out of the cover and strike. While it's true that sometimes happens, don't count on it. The cast must go as close to the cover, or even into it with a weedless bait, as possible. Right here is where casting ability shines. Putting that bait right into every nook and cranny is the key to getting a strike.

108. Sight Fishing for Largemouths—Step Three

There are about a zillion lures that will catch fish in this situation, but I have a couple of favorites, and it's my book, so here we go: I'm positively in love with two soft-plastic baits in the swimbait or jerk bait category. (No, I do not get them for free. I buy them, like you.)

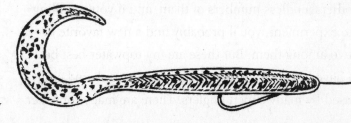

The Mann Hardnose and the Strike King Zulu have been absolute killers for me and my buddies in sight-fishing situations. Actually, they're good baits all the time. You can swim them and jerk them and expect savage strikes. We fish them with the Texas Rig, minus the sinker for the sight-fishing situations. With the hook embedded properly, they're virtually weedless. As with other recommendations, check Bass Pro Shops and Cabela's.

109. Time to Walk the Dog

Everybody wants to catch bass with topwater lures—and why not? When conditions are right, and bass are feeding on or near the surface, there's nothing like the explosive strike of an aggressive bass. You can fish topwater lures many ways, including the famous "Walk the Dog" technique of slowly working it over the surface. You can pause it, twitch it, or just let it lie there, waiting. Then slowly move it a foot or so, then pause, wait, and twitch once again. When the strike comes, you will know it!

110. Forget Top Water When the Time's Not Right

As stated elsewhere in this book, fishing top water is often a fruitless, fishless exercise in futility. When the bass just aren't feeding on the surface, all you will get up there is casting practice.

111. Proven Topwater Lures

When the time and conditions are right for top-water fishing, the seven lures featured here are the ones you can absolutely count on to get strikes. Yes, there are others, endless numbers of them, and if you're willing to experiment, you'll probably find a new favorite or two among them. But these are my topwater best bets. I have seen them in action and witnessed them being used by many expert anglers. There are many topwater

lures out there that are far less expensive than these. Quite frankly, in my opinion, they are not as good. These are the best. Fish them and have fun!

1. Rapala Skitter Pop

An absolute killer bait from the famous maker of wooden lures. This was Rapala's first-ever topwater lure, and it's a great one. The plastic cupped lip produces a "spitting" action. An assortment of color finishes, 2 to 2 ¾ inches, at $7.99 from Cabela's as this is written. The Skitter Pop will catch both largemouth and smallmouth bass wherever they swim. Available at www.cabelas.com.

2. Rebel Zell Rowland Pop-R

Moving down in price to $4.99 from Bass Pro Shops is this popular plastic bait, aka "The Pop-R King." Many good anglers who don't want to fork over the extra buck for the wooden Rapala fish the Rebel Pop-R. In four color finishes, at 2 ½ inches, the Pop-R is a lure you can count on. Available at www.basspro.com.

3. Arbogast Hula Popper

A favorite for decades—because it works. When the Hula Popper doesn't get strikes from surface feed-

ers, you're probably in for a very slow day of surface action. You can pop it, walk it, let it rest, and tremble it. It comes in a variety of finishes. Costs $4.99 at Cabela's.

4. Heddon Lucky 13 and Baby Lucky 13

Created in 1920, the Lucky 13 has been catching bass ever since. Today's versions, the Lucky 13 (3 ¾ inches) and Baby Lucky 13 (2 ⅝ inches), produce resonating sound and a weaving body action for a variety of gamefish, especially bass. Cabela's lists both at $4.99. Fish the Baby version for smallmouths.

5. Arbogast Jitterbug

This lure has been a mainstay in the tackleboxes of bass addicts for decades. The back-and-forth, plodding, popping action represents live prey struggling, and bass on the feed gobble it with fury. It costs $4.69 to $4.99, and comes in 2- and 3-inch sizes, in a variety of colors. As with several other topwater baits, failure to get strikes with a Jitterbug does not bode well for your surface fishing that day.

6. Heddon Zara Spook, Super Spook, and Super Spook Jr.

Heddon's Zara Spook was one of the first—if not *the* first—topwater, Walk the Dog lures. It's still catching fish today, and costs $4.99 at Cabela's. The Super Spook is an upgraded version of the Zara, and at $4.99 is a solid choice for a variety of fish. The Spook Jr. is also $4.99 and is the choice for smallmouths and picky largemouths.

7. Lucky Craft Sammy

Ready to spend $10 for a single lure? If you're really hungry for topwater action, and nothing else seems to work, the Lucky Craft Sammy might save your day. At $9.99 (on sale) and $13.99 to $15.99 regularly priced (Cabela's), the Lucky Craft Sammy has a lot of new technology going for it and consistently gets strikes. If you can afford it, and are not afraid of losing it to a big fish or

submerged log, give it a try. Comes in a variety of colors, 2 ½ to 4 inches.

112. What Hook Size?

"Always match your hook size to the head diameter of the soft-plastic bait you're using. Example: On an 8-inch plastic worm use either a size 4/0 or 5/0 hook; on a 4-inch worm, a size 1/0 to 2/0 hook."

—Bill Dance, *IGFA's 101 Freshwater Fishing Tips and Tricks*, Skyhorse Publishing, 2007

113. How Bill Dance Beats Windy Days

In his book *IGFA's 101 Freshwater Fishing Tips and Tricks*, Skyhorse (2007), bass guru Bill Dance described his favorite strategy for coping with windy days. He uses heavier jigs and lighter line. With the wind causing you to have poor control of your drifting boat, the faster your bait gets down, the better. "Seconds can make the difference in success or failure," Dance says.

114. Smallmouth Savvy: Go Deeper With Jigs When You Have To

J.B. Kasper's outdoor column in the *Trenton Times* (N.J.) is always excellent, but he hit a home run with readers in his piece on July 31, 2009. Kasper described his annual trip to New York's legendary Thousand Island area. Arriving at Caiger's Country Inn, in Rockport on the Canadian side, where he has always enjoyed great fishing, Kasper found high water and lower water temps (low 70s in shallow water) that made the fishing in shallow water very poor. "It became evident," Kasper says, "after about two hours that the bass simply were not there. A switch to fishing jig-plastic bait combination of 20- to 30-foot drop-offs off rocky points put us into fish." Kasper used jig-heads dressed with hellgrammites and Slugos. "Swimming plugs and crankbaits were ineffective, mainly because we could not get them down to where the fish were holding."

115. Fishing the Legendary Devil's Horse

In these pages, you hear so much about fishing soft-plastic lures directly in the cover that you may get tired of hearing about it. But it's the truth: Soft-plastics, rigged weedless, plunked into and fished directly in the weeds, sticks, and pads, catch the bass. You can, however, still catch bass on the old standby surface baits like Smithwick's Devil's Horse, with props fore and aft, by working it on the edges of cover at dawn's early light. Baitfish leave deep water to forage in the weeds and cover at night, returning to the deep after dawn. If you're going to fish the edges, dawn is the time to do it. And the Devil's Horse, or lures like it, should produce some action.

116. The 1 Million Tactic

That's what *Field & Stream* magazine in June 2008 called the tactic that won pro Scott Suggs the big prize in the 2007 Forrest Wood Cup at Lake Ouachita in Arkansas. As reported by Bill Heavey, Suggs yo-yoed spinnerbaits just above the thermocline. In summer, bass often drop down to the cooler layer of water just above the thermocline. The thermocline is where the water is much colder but lacks oxygen. Just above the thermocline, bass can suspend in water that's cooler than the surface areas and still have plenty of oxygen. To find the thermocline, you need to get a high-tech depth finder, call a local dive shop (if there is one), or note carefully the depths where you're finding fish. You won't make a million bucks, but you'll catch more bass.

117. A Bassing Blog You Shouldn't Miss

Of all the excellent articles and blogs available on the B.A.S.S. site at www.sports.espn.go.com/outdoors/

bassmaster/index, *Charlie Hartley's Bass Wars*—found directly as this is written on www.sports.espn.go.com/outdoors/bassmaster/news/story?page=b_blog_Hartley_2009—has become one of my favorites. A successful businessman in Ohio with his Signcom, Inc., designing, manufacturing, and installing commercial signs, Hartley hits the tournament circuits hard and shares his experiences on the B.A.S.S. site. His articles are archived, so you can see them all, from 2008 on. He is sponsored by Venom Lures, www.venomlures.com. Hartley led the first day of the 2009 Bassmaster Classic and became something of an instant celebrity in bass fishing. Hartley knows bass, and he knows bass fishing tournament competition, and he shares what he knows brilliantly. You will not only enjoy reading Hartley, whether you are interested in tournaments or not, you will end up catching more and bigger bass.

118. Red Hooks, Bleeding Baits—Are They For Real?

In his excellent blog www.richlindgren.com, tournament angler Rich Lindgren shares both his skills and accounts of the competitions. He is an observant, serious angler with lots to say. In a report on the on-going trend toward using "bleeding" baits and red hooks, he said, "Granted some of these bleeding baits are a little overdone, but the adding of red coloring and bleeding spots is a trend that is not going away soon. In general I am a big fan of sprucing up my baits with touches of red. . . . I think the red hook gives the fish a target, so if you have a red hook on the front, you hook more fish on the front hook."

119. Add Red for More Strikes

Sharing his further thoughts on red hooks, veteran tournament angler Rich Lindgren, in his blog, www.richlindgren.com, says he feels adding red hooks and touches of red on lures triggers strikes from bass that are

only following and then turning away at the last instant. He adds red to not only crankbaits and topwater lures, but to spinnerbaits, buzzbaits, and jigs as well. You can add red hooks and colors to your favorite existing baits. "All in all," says Lindgren, "the color red is not going to make you an instant pro, but it can turn a good day into a great day and get you those extra bites . . . "

though, and now, surfing the Web, I find that Bass Pro Shops—www.basspro.com—has a new entry in the race for the world's most realistic frog imitation. It's the Tru-Tungsten Mad Maxx Frog, so real it looks like it's about to jump through my computer screen. It costs a hefty $8.49 a pop. Will it catch bass? Well, if looks could kill . . .

120. Fake Frogs: How Fine Are They?

One of my favorite titles from old issues of *Sports Afield* was "Fake Frogs Are Fine." Like many other bass anglers, I have always been fascinated by frog imitations, spinning, bait-casting, and fly fishing. They look so real! How can any bass resist them? Well, in my own case, they resisted them with no problem. Most frog imitations just haven't paid off for me. I keep trying,

121. Waders Not Required

Wading wet, doing without waders, makes a lot of sense in high summer on smallmouth rivers and creeks (and even some trout rivers). At first you might be a little cold, but you'll quickly adjust to the conditions and find a certain freedom of motion you lack with waders. You'll need good wading shoes, of course.

122. Casting to Bass Cover

A cast that lands more than a foot away from bass cover is a wasted cast.

123. When the Water's Falling Too Fast

When fishing rivers for bass, especially big rivers, the periods after heavy rains when the water is falling ultrafast will often cause the bass to move out into the depths and suspend. They'll stay there until the flow stabilizes.

124. Oxygen Content is Crucial

"Oxygen content is far more important than water temperature in locating fish during August and early September. Bass are willing to endure water temperatures in the high 80s providing there is ample oxygen."

—Mark Sosin, "How to Read Bass Water You've Never Fished," *Sports Afield*, April 1975

125. Find the Oxygen, You'll Find the Fish

"Certain banks will have ample oxygen, while others won't hold enough to support life. You can work down a bank and read three parts per million on an oxygen meter. Then, only a quarter mile away, the meter will show eight or ten parts per million on the same bank. That's where the fish will be and it may only last for 100 yards or so. Once you run out of oxygen, you must locate the next zone."

—Mark Sosin, "How to Read Bass Water You've Never Fished," *Sports Afield*, April 1975

126. Double Your Fun With Two Jigs

Deep-jigging for smallmouths is always a reliable tactic, but don't forget to take the trouble to add a second jig to your line. Fish a heavier jig on the end of your line, with a lighter jig of another color attached to a dropper about 18 inches up the line. A Perfection Loop Knot will work nicely for the dropper, or some other type if you have a favorite. Don't be surprised to find yourself battling a pair of smallmouths at times. Sometimes a hooked bass creates a frenzy among its mates in a school.

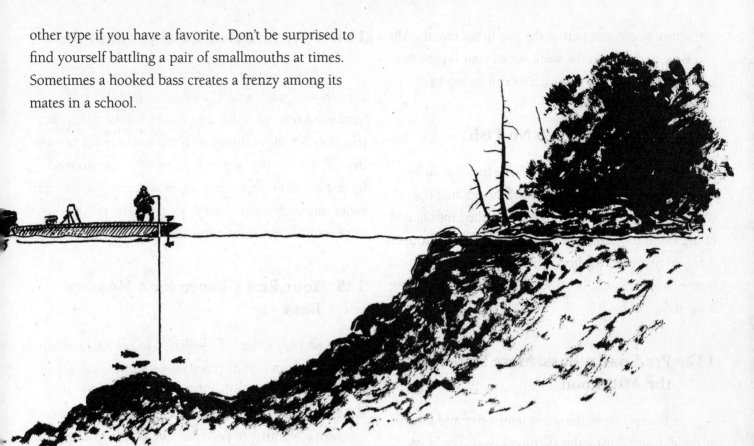

127. Add Some Venom to Your Lures

The Ohio company Venom Lures (www.venomlures.com) offers an excellent array of largemouth and smallmouth lures and accessories. They also sponsor B.A.S.S. professional Charley Hartley, whose blog on the B.A.S.S. site at www.sports.espn.go.com/outdoors/ bassmaster/index is one of the best around. I especially like Venom's Drop Shot Minnows. The 4-inch model is my favorite.

128. It's Not a Strike, It's a Slurp!

In a revealing article in *Sports Afield* in December 1971, Angling Editor Homer Circle went to great lengths to show readers that bass actually do not strike a lure, they suck it in, even when they're taking topwater baits. Armed with this knowledge, you should have better feel and touch fishing plastic worms.

129. How Bass Slurp Prey

Homer Circle continues on how bass strike: " . . . when a bass decides to take an object into its mouth, it does not have to seize it like a dog. Instead, it only has to get close to the object, open its mouth, and simultaneously flare its gill flaps in a pumping action. Instantly, water rushes into the bass's mouth and out the gill vents, literally sucking the object into the bass's mouth."

130. Setting the Hook on Slurping Bass

In his article on how bass strike, in the December 1971 issue of *Sports Afield*, Homer Circle went on to explain how the fact that bass suck in their prey should affect your action on setting the hook on a plastic worm: "When a bass takes such a free-sinking worm, it nearly always sucks it all in. Therefore, you can stop all this guesswork about how long to let a bass run. He's got worm, hook, and part of the line in his mouth. All you have to do is reel the slack out of your line so you can bust him. And do it now, later can be too late!"

131. Quick Pull, Then No Fish

What's going on when you feel a bass has picked up your worm, yet you set the hook on nothing but water? Chances are the bass simply grabbed the tail end of the worm to keep it from moving away, then dropped it as you tightened the line. The fish never sucked the worm into its mouth, because the angler kept it moving away too quickly.

132. Pre-Spawn Bass: More Strikes in the Afternoon

In the spring, as the water temps rise into the 50s at midday and during the afternoon, you should get more strikes from fish moving into warmer waters. On a cold morning when fishing is slow, if the water temps are slowly climbing, you can reasonably look forward to afternoon action. Don't go home at lunch.

133. Staging for the Spawn: Early Spring's Best Bassing

Reporting in his blog from Falcon Lake, Texas, in early February 2008, veteran pro Charley Hartley described the rewards of fishing bass as they are staging for the spawn. " . . . they're biting jigs thrown right into the bushes off the secondary points. The bass are staged on the last turn in front of the spawning bays. And when I mean staged, I mean they're everywhere. Like I said, they're hitting jigs today, but to tell you the truth they'd probably hit just about anything you throw in there. They're hungry and not at all shy."

—*Charley Hartley's Bass Wars*,
February 5, 2008 on the B.A.S.S. site at
www.sports.espn.go.com/outdoors/bassmaster/index

134. Why Live Bait Catches Giant Bass

Live bait—such as shiners, minnows, and even sunfish—are such a deadly attractor to bass for two important reasons. First, and most obvious, is the fact that they are the real prey bass are accustomed to feeding on. But equally important, and often overlooked by anglers who use them in open water, these live baits swim into and underneath thick pads and cover where big bass lurk and lures never go.

135. Your Best Chance for a Monster Bass

If you are fortunate enough to locate a hole where a big bass resides, your surest way to get the lunker will be using a live sunfish. Not too big, not too small, a 4-incher is about right. Hook it up top, at the dorsal fin, with a Number 6. Feed out line to let the bait swim into the hole . . . then wait.

136. Picking the Right Hook for Plastic Worms

Picking the right hook size for the plastic worm you're using is simple. Basically, it's big worm, big hook; small worm, small hook. For a 7- to 8-inch worm, a 3/0 or 4/0 hook will be just right, while a 1/0 will be too small and a 6/0 too big. For a 5- to 6-inch worm, use a 2/0 hook. For finesse worms under 5 inches, use 1 and 1/0. Now all you have to do is to make sure they're sharp.

137. Rigging the Expensive Trout Lure

The thought of losing the expensive swim baits so popular with western bass anglers is downright scary. To make sure your Huddleston Deluxe Trout Lure is rigged properly go to www.bassresource.com and check out the detailed, step-by-step article and photos by "Fish Chris" Wolfgram, under the "Articles" and "Bass Lure Techniques" sections.

138. Those Super-Shallow Crankbaits

"Crankbait addicts can be so pleased with their big-lipped, deep-diving lures that they sometimes forget the effectiveness of lipless or super-shallow crankbaits," says Don Wirth in his basspro.com article "The Inside Scoop on Super-Shallow Crankbaits." Baits like Mann's 1-Minus and the Bomber Square A are deadly swimming slowly through patches of water in or alongside tight cover.

139. Knocking on Wood

Wirth continues on the same subject, "You're probably thinking, 'Run a $6 crankbait through a brushpile? No way!' But a properly presented super-shallow diver is a deadly alternative to a jig or spinnerbait in this snaggy cover." He recommends using a short, underhanded pitch past the brushpile or other cover, then, " . . . reel s-l-o-w-l-y until you feel the bait contact the cover." Stop your retrieve the instant the bait touches something, and it will float upward, clearing the obstruction. Start retrieving again and hang on for action.

140. Crankbait Snagging Remedy

"Clip the leading hook from each set of the trebles on your crankbaits to reduce snagging in tight cover."

—Don Wirth, "The Inside Scoop on Super-Shallow Crankbaits," www.basspro.com

141. Jim Porter's Guide to Bass Fishing

One of my favorite Web sites for bass articles and products has become *Jim Porter's Guide to Bass Fishing*, www.stickmarsh.com. The site has innovative lures for bass and panfish, and Porter's articles are solid with experience and usable information.

142. Bass Lures Don't Come Easy

Be aware that those pretty and expensive bass lures that tempt you in the shops and catalogs aren't overnight creations. The lure business is highly competitive, and much research and testing goes into every creation. Every curve and shape, every ounce of weight, affects the way the bait will swim.

143. How to Choose a Crankbait

There are so many crankbaits out there that choosing a winner can be a bit confusing. They may all look the same, but the bill makes the difference. Long bills dive deeper, wide bills give more side-to-side action, and rounded bills give a steady wiggle.

144. Crankbait Action: The Wrong Stuff

You can't expect a long-billed crankbait, designed to dive and fish deep, to perform well for you in a shallow-water patch of weeds. Every lure has a purpose, a job to do. Think about that before you tie one on and put it to work. What, *exactly*, do you want it to do in the existing conditions to catch fish?

Before you tie on a lure, figure out exactly what you want it to do.

145. Soft-Plastic: The Bass Won't Let Go!

In his excellent blog, *Jim Porter's Guide to Bass Fishing* at www.stickmarsh.com, in an article on fishing soft-plastic jerkbaits, Porter debunks theories that bass spit out plastic baits: " . . . Unless you scare the bass with a sudden jerk on the line or letting him pull the line too tight, a bass normally WILL NOT drop that soft-plastic lure. It doesn't LOOK, SMELL, nor TASTE like real food to the bass. But if he thinks it is trying to get away in some manner, he just won't let go." Porter goes on to describe how to fish his company's soft jerkbait, the "RIPPIN' Stick."

146. Sea Anchors on Bass Boats

Saltwater anglers know all about sea anchors and drift socks to hold their boats better in the tides and currents. Savvy bass anglers know about them too—and use them to cut down on the drift in strong winds. Cabela's and Bass Pro Shops have them.

147. A Largemouth Angler Fishing for Smallmouths

There's one important thing to remember when you're an experienced largemouth angler heading out for smallmouth for the first time: downsizing! With few exceptions, lures for smallmouths are smaller than your favorite largemouth baits.

148. Pass the Watermelon

In the *BASSlog Blog*, where he keeps tabs on things like moon phases and best lures of the pros, B.A.S.S. pro Richie White reports that favorite soft-plastic colors are green pumpkin, watermelon, and watermelon/red fleck. Other good choices are black/blue, junebug, black, red shad, and blue fleck. For diving crankbaits, the leaders are shad, baby bass, blue/chartreuse, white, firetiger, and green/orange. Shad is the best color for jerkbaits. Check out White's *BASSlog* at www.sports.espn.go.com/outdoors/bassmaster/index.

149. Bass Turned Off . . . Then Turned Right Back On

In his wonderful and now-mellow book, *Fresh-Water Bass*, Knopf (1946), the legendary Ray Bergman describes experiences when he learns that largemouth bass wise up to certain lures. He was using a white surface plug in a week's fishing, and each day his catch became smaller and smaller and finally stopped altogether. His companion suggested going to live bait. "But I didn't want to fish with live bait. I wanted to fish with plugs. I put on a green underwater one and used that, and I started to catch bass again. This seems to show clearly that these bass had become wise to the white plug."

150. It's Gobies for Lake Erie Smallmouths

"For Lake Erie smallmouths, there is one overwhelming choice: the goby. Gobies are nonnative fish that were introduced into the Great Lakes from the discharge of ballast water by ocean-going vessels. These fish are small but voracious feeders and are outcompeting many native species, such as perch, for food. On the positive side, the goby has created a tremendous forage base for smallmouth bass and the brown fish are bigger and badder because of it."

—Tony Hansen, "Drop-Shotting Smallmouth Bass," on the Bass Pro Shop Outdoor Library, www.basspro.com

151. The Single-Worm Trick for Bass

Bluegill and crappie anglers are sometimes surprised when the tug on their line turns out to be a hard-pulling, fighting largemouth bass in the 1- to 2-pound class. When bluegill fishing, you can make this unexpected treat happen more often by using a single earthworm hooked right through the middle. Set your float to let your worm dangle at various depths, and you'll catch a bass. I don't know why this single-worm trick works, but it does.

152. Destination: Lake Erie

Lake Erie is, without a doubt, one of the greatest smallmouth destinations in the world. Some say it's the absolute greatest. It's big water, so you have a lot of planning and preparation to do, but the resources for the fishing—guides, lodges, tackle shops—are all there.

153. Coping With Surface Lure Splash-Down

While bass will sometimes strike lures the instant they hit the surface—and even grab them right out of the air—most bass-fishing experts put their faith in letting their surface plug or bug rest on the water a few moments before starting the retrieve. The theory is that the bait splashing down will frighten fish in the immediate vicinity, even make them swim off some distance. Let the bait sit until well after the ripples spread away and die out completely, then give the bait a twitch.

Then do some more twitching. Then, as you retrieve, try slow crawls with wiggles, violent jerks and pops, or whatever seems to be working.

154. Getting the Touch with Plastic Worms

"He [the plastic worm expert] knows by the delicate sense of feel that he has discovered which type of bottom cover his worm or eel is dragging over. That's right, he can tell by the feeble feel transmitted by his line what substances—hard, soft, tall, short, or snaggy—his lure is approaching, in, or coming off of."

—Homer Circle, *Sports Afield Fishing Annual*, 1972

155. Plastic Worms in the Strike Zone

" . . . all fishermen who crawl worms and eels over bottom cover will tell you their biggest bass, and most of their bass, grab the lure *immediately after* they feel it crawl over and drop off a branch, weed, log or other obstruction."

—Homer Circle, *Sports Afield Fishing Annual* , 1972

156. Study-Time with the Bass Professor

Doug Hannon isn't called The Bass Professor for nothing. He has spent his life studying and catching largemouth bass in general, but specializing in big bass—really big bass, the 12- and 15-pounders. You see Doug on various TV fishing programs, but his headquarters is his Web site, www.bassprofessor. com. You can learn a heck of a lot about bass fishing by visiting with Doug there, including all the info on his Snake lures that catch monster bass and the new spinning reel he has developed that eliminates those troublesome loops that can mess up your fishing. Doug also has a terrific book, written with W. Horace Carter. It's called *Hannon's Big Bass Magic*, and you can get it from Doug's site and places like www.amazon.com. I bought the book and have devoured every page with great relish.

157. Doug Hannon on Making Bass Strike

The Bass Professor, Doug Hannon, is a firm believer in the contradictory viewpoint that bass feed more in the day than they do after dark, but that the average angler will catch more and bigger bass by fishing late and at night. Behind Doug's belief is this logic explained in his book, *Hannon's Big Bass Magic*: "The darkness covers up an angler's presence and, most of all, his mistakes . . . I feel that bass have long since become conditioned to the fact that man spells danger. My studies show that only one in ten bass which sees a lure will strike it and that one makes a mistake . . . At night . . . close inspection is more difficult for a fish, and he may strike without any investigation."

158. Moon Up Early—Great Fishing

" . . . I am convinced that lunar influences have a big impact on bass and also that they will strike more frequently on those nights when the moon comes up in the evening before the sun goes down."

—Doug Hannon, *Hannon's Big Bass Magic*

159. Doug Hannon's Moon Phase Choices

In his book *Hannon's Big Bass Magic*, Doug Hannon says that studies of world record catches in the 1970s revealed a definite correlation with his favorite moon phases to fish. Those are the three days on each side of a full moon and dark moon. It's interesting to note that these same moon phases are the favorite of legendary angler Stu Apte, who discusses them in another section of this book.

160. Good Bass Fishing Close to Home

Sometimes it's possible to ignore a lake that's close to your home, simply because it looks as if it's harboring too much activity. But when you really consider the people using the lake, and come to realize that they're mostly swimmers, kayakers, sailboaters, and float tubers—not fishermen—you may find you've got a good fishing spot all to yourself. Not on weekends, but during the week, especially at dawn.

161. Fishing Tidewater Bass

"The trick in fishing tidal waters is to fish the right spot at the right time. Mostly, the bass turn on when the tide first starts to move. It doesn't make any difference if the water's rising or falling, just so it's moving."

—*Charley Hartley's Bass Wars*, March 28, 2009, on the B.A.S.S. site at www.sports.espn.go.com/outdoors/bassmaster/index

162. Another Tidewater Tip

"The water will move first near the mouth of a creek or bay. Fish there for a few minutes and then, when the bite drops off, go back further into the tributary and fish another spot as the water starts to move. If you're quick you can fish several places that way every time the tide moves."

—*Charley Hartley's Bass Wars*,
March 28, 2009, on the B.A.S.S. site at
www.sports.espn.go.com/outdoors/bassmaster/index

163. The Carolina Rig as a Search Bait

Mark Hicks, in an article "Carolina Rigging," *Bass Times Tips and Tools*, November, 2008, reports that "Jared Lintner, an Elite Series pro from Arroyo Grande, California, regards the Carolina-style setup as a search bait." Lintner won several tournaments fishing California lakes to depths of 60 feet with a ¾-ounce Carolina Rig matched with a 6-inch PowerBait Lizard, "Now," reports Hicks, "Lintner's favorite setup is 20-pound-test fluorocarbon line, a ¾-ounce tungsten sinker, two 8mm glass beads, and a 3/0 Gamakatsu hook knotted to the end of a 3- to 4-foot-long, 8- or 10-pound-test fluorocarbon leader."

164. Positively Swimbaits

The swimbait surge is one of the latest bass-fishing buzzwords, resounding from tackleshops to boats, coast to coast. These are realistic-looking, mostly soft-plastic designs made to swim in fresh or salt water. They are among the more expensive lures (some of them *very* expensive), and if they didn't catch bass and win tournaments you would not be hearing so much about them. Both Cabela's, www.cabelas.com, and Bass Pro Shops, www.basspro.com, offer good selections.

165. A Swim Bait Nation

The swimbait lure option has spread across the nation like wildfire, and the Western-oriented site www.swimbaitnation.com makes the most of it with articles and reports from pros and amateurs on using swimbaits. In the clear waters of the West, a lot of bassers have caught onto the fact that bass love eating stocked trout. There are swimbait trout imitations that cost a bundle (how about $40 to $50 for the Huddleston Trout or the Baitsmith Magnum Trout?) but catch big bass and win tournaments. One of the sites mentioned for these swimbaits is www.basstackledept.com. The hunt is on to break George Perry's World Record (22 pounds, 4 ounces).

166. California, Here I Come

A lot of good fishing information and tips related to California fishing is available on the site www.calfishing.com.

167. A New Worm to Shake Up Your Bassing

Bassmaster Elite pro Jeff Kriet has earned a great reputation for his deep-water results in lakes like Kentucky, Oneida, and Clarks Hill. He fishes with quite an arsenal, but in particular likes drop-shot fishing and shakey-head worm fishing. Kriet has lately been cashing in (literally) on using his shakey-head techniques with the worm of his own development. It's the Jeff Kriet Squirrel Tail Worm, sold on www.bigbitebaits.com. What's unique about Kriet's worm is the thin, limber tail that literally dances every time the shakey head is pulled or bumps something. Kriet combines the worm with his Big Bite Shakey Head Jig, ⅛-ounce 75 percent of the time and 1/16 the rest. See the article "Shakey Details Matter," according to Kriet on www.bassfan.com.

© Pat Ford 2010   This largemouth hit a jig worked along a mild dropoff.

168. A Favorite Worm Rig

I have run the details of Col. Dave Harbour's favorite, shallow-water worm rig in several magazines, and I have fished the rig with great success in varying waters—from northern smallmouths to southern swamp bigmouths. Here's the rig, what Harbour called "The Super Rig": Start with a soft 6-inch, straight-tail purple worm, such as Crème's Wiggle Worm, Dave's worm of choice. Hook two No. 5 or 7 black snap swivels together, then add a leader of 14 inches the same test as your line. The worm is not hooked Texas-style; instead, thread the hook from the head deep into the body, then out, leaving the body pushed up over the eye of the hook. This gives the worm a humped position that really works.

169. If You're Not Drop-Shot Fishing . . .

If you haven't given drop-shot fishing a try yet, you're missing out on a great fishing technique. The variations on the technique are many, and you can have a lot of fun experimenting with them. Right here, however, I will keep it simple and explain a basic rig that will catch bass—not to mention walleyes and panfish—wherever you fish. Basically the rig is another wrinkle in the "Bottoms-Up" fishing trend. At the end of your line is a tungsten weight, say ¼ or ⅜ ounce, hooked to the line with a snap swivel so you can change the weight as the depth demands. Tied with a Palamar knot 12 inches or so up the line is a No. 2 Wide Gap hook. Put your worm or jig on that hook, and you're in business. You can add a swivel above the hook if you wish. Hook your worm through the nose or through the body wacky-style. Drop it straight down and jig it, pull it along the bottom, experiment until you find what's working.

170. Bill Dance: Pull That Worm, Don't Reel It

Over the years, TV personality and celebrity angler Bill Dance has frequently recommended fishing a Texas-rigged plastic worm. He likes darker color worms early and late, and transparent worms in the middle of the day. He fishes the worm by letting it drop to the bottom, then pulling on the worm by raising the rod from a 45-degree angle to vertical. Then he reels up the slack. The worm is "pulled" with the rod, not reeled. Reeling is only for taking up slack.

171. How to Lose a Bass Tournament

In tournament fishing, catching lots of bass doesn't matter. It's the total weight of your five fish at weigh-in time that puts you in the money. For most of us anglers, a 2-pound bass is a nice fish. But in the vast majority of tournaments, catching five 2-pounders isn't going to be good enough. You've got to turn your back on those spots and find bigger fish most of the time. As in all fishing, there's no such thing in tournaments as "all the time."

172. Find the Other Boats, Find the Fish

Some tournament anglers, in the frenzy of competition, don't have the time to find bass on their own. Their strategy is to find where other boats are fishing

Grassy, brushy shorelines are always good spots for bass.

© Pat Ford 2010

and join the party. The next time you're on the water, keep an eye out for congregations of boats. If you're not catching fish where you are, then get over there!

173. Hitting the Pro Circuit, Part One: Dreams and Realities

Dreaming of becoming a professional bass angler, competing in tournaments for big bucks (and perhaps even making it to the Classic and winning a bundle)? Well, before you do something foolish like quitting your job or taking out a second mortgage on your house, read the blog where one of the best professionals tells it like it is—costs, sponsors, the hard work, the "real" rewards. We're talking about *Charley Hartley's Bass Wars* blog, archived on the B.A.S.S. site at www.sports.espn.go.com/outdoors/bassmaster/index. In his reports of September 10, 18, and 28, 2008, and October 2, 2008, Hartley gives the clearest, no-nonsense look at the

© Pat Ford 2010   Some tools of the trade.

realities of turning pro of any site we've seen. No matter whether he is writing advice on tournaments or simply giving you tips on lures and strategies, Hartley is worth reading every time he posts a new report.

174. Hitting the Pro Circuit, Part Two: Bring Money!

"Let me make something clear: I have never—not once in thirty years—tried to discourage anyone from turning professional and following their dream. I followed mine and wouldn't expect any less from anyone else. But there are financial consequences to the decisions we make."

—Charley Hartley's Bass Wars,
October 2, 2008 on the B.A.S.S. site at
www.sports.espn.go.com/outdoors/bassmaster/index

175. Hitting the Pro Circuit, Part Three: Assessing Your Chances

"So, when you analyze your skills realize that there are thousands of club champions and hundreds of anglers who have won big charity tournaments. Lots of guys can catch bass. That's not the test. The test is skill coupled with fanatical perseverance, a single-minded purpose, a love of the sport, and the marketing ability to make it all work financially."

—Charley Hartley's Bass Wars,
October 2, 2008 on the B.A.S.S. site at
www.sports.espn.go.com/outdoors/bassmaster/index

H. More Bass Tactics

WADE BOURNE

Bass

Bass fishing is more complicated than fishing for sunfish or crappie, partly because of all the different types of bass tackle and lures. Bass are still members of the sunfish family, however, and they share certain behavior characteristics with bluegill and crappie. Anywhere you're likely to catch these latter fish, you're apt to find bass, since they all hold around the same types of structure.

Let's begin with the simplest technique. You can catch bass on a long cane or fiberglass pole, but you need a stronger pole than you used on bluegill, and your line should be at least 12-pound test.

Tie on a slip-bobber rig with the bobber set at around 3 feet. Use a 1/0 or 2/0 steel hook. Add a light sinker 6 inches up from the hook. Then bait this rig with a gob of nightcrawlers or a live minnow hooked through the back.

Drop your line near likely fish-holding spots, but don't leave it in one place for more than 2–3 minutes. If a bass is there, it'll usually take the bait. When you get a bite, wait for the bobber to disappear before setting the hook. Then pull the fish quickly to the surface and land it.

When using the long-pole method, work your way around the pond, being careful not to let the fish see you. They are skittish when they're in shallow water, and they'll spook easily.

While this long-pole method is a good one, most experienced fishermen go after pond bass with casting or spinning tackle and artificial lures. Casting allows you to reach targets farther away and also to cover more water. Many artificial lures will catch pond bass, but my three favorites are topwaters, spinnerbaits and plastic worms.

Try topwaters early in the morning, late in the afternoon or at night (during summer). Use topwaters when the sky is overcast, especially when the surface is calm. In warmer months, I prefer poppers and propel-

Sometimes you have to wade right into cover to reach the big ones.

ler baits that make a lot of noise and attract bass from a distance. In early spring, I like a quieter floating minnow.

Cast topwaters close to weeds, beside logs, along dams or anywhere you think bass might be holding. Cast past a particular object, then work the bait up to where you think the fish are. Allow the bait to rest motionless for several seconds, then twitch it just enough to cause the slightest ripple on the water. This is usually when the strike comes!

If a spot looks good, but you don't get a strike, cast back to it several times. Sometimes when bass are "inactive" (aren't feeding), you have to arouse their curiosity or agitate them into striking, and repeat casts may do this.

At times, though, bass just won't strike a surface lure. If you don't get any action on a topwater lure in 15 minutes, switch to a spinnerbait and try the same area. Keep your retrieve steady, and try different speeds (fast, medium, slow). You might try try "fluttering" the bait— allowing it to sink momentarily after it runs past a log, treetop or other cover. This can trigger a strike from a bass that's following the lure during a steady retrieve.

Don't be afraid to retrieve a spinnerbait through brush and weeds. If you keep reeling while it's coming through cover, this lure is virtually weedless. You may hang occasionally (use strong line with these baits so you can pull them free), but you'll get more strikes by fishing the thick stuff.

Plastic worms are what I call "last resort baits." Bass can usually be coaxed into striking worms when they won't hit other lures, and plastic worms can be worked slower and through the thickest cover. They're also good for taking bass in deep water. Plastic worms are top prospects for midday fishing in hot weather.

For pond bass, use a 4-7 ½-inch plastic worm rigged Texas-style with a ⅟₁₆ -¼ oz. sliding sinker. (The heavier sinker is for deeper water.) Cast it right into cover or close to it. (Make sure the point of the hook is embedded inside the worm.) Then crawl it slowly

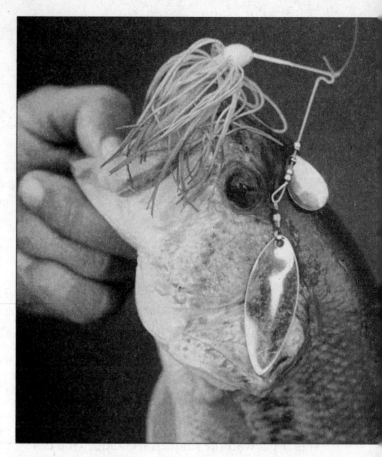

A spinnerbait is a super-productive lure for catching bass in ponds and small lakes. This is an easy lure to use. Simply cast it and reel back with a steady, medium-paced retrieve. Most strikes come around cover where bass hide to watch for prey.

through the cover, lifting it with the rod tip, then allowing it to settle back to the bottom.

When fishing lily pads, brush or other thick vegetation, cast to openings and pockets. Cast off points, ends of weedbeds or riprap, and corners of piers. These are places where bass are likely to hang.

If you don't get action in the shallows, and you suspect the bass are deeper, it's time to change tactics. Since you can't see underwater, you must locate structure by interpreting what you can from the surface. Find a gully feeding into the shallow end of the pond. Then try to imagine how this gully runs along the pond bottom, and cast your plastic worm along it. This can be prime bass-holding structure.

A second deep-water strategy is to cast a plastic worm into the deep end or along the dam, then crawl it back up the bank. The third option is to simply walk along the bank and cast at random, hoping you'll locate bass along some unknown structure under the water. In all cases, however, it's very important to allow your plastic worm to sink to bottom before starting your retrieve. When casting to deep spots, if you get a bite or catch a fish, cast back to that same spot several more times. Bass often school together in deep water.

There are other baits you might use in special situations. Many ponds have heavy weedbeds or lily pads. You can fish them with a topwater spoon that wobbles over plants and attracts bass lying underneath. Leadhead jigs tipped with a plastic trailer (grub, crawfish, etc.) can be hopped across bottom when searching deep-water areas. Diving crankbaits are good for random casting into deep spots.

A variety of lures can be used to catch stream bass and smaller panfish. Spinners, diving crankbaits, topwater minnows and plastic worms and tubes are all deadly on fish that inhabit small moving waters.

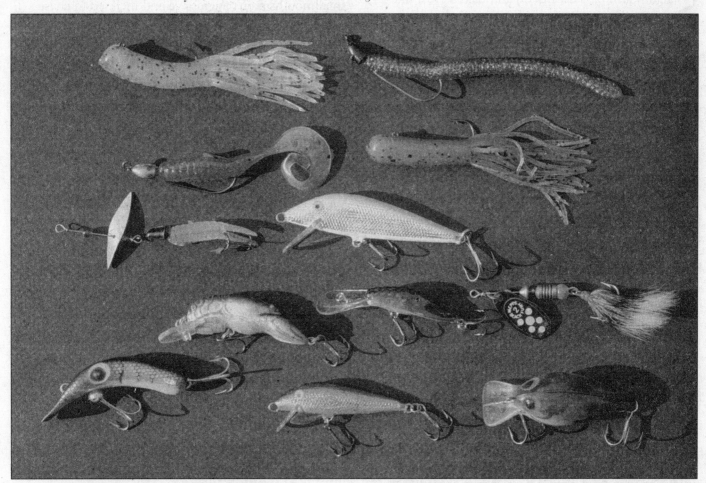

G. Flyfishing for Bass Tips

TOM ROSENBAUER

Flies to use for smallmouth bass in rivers

Smallmouth bass eat insects and baitfish just like trout, and you can fish for them with your standard trout flies. But that's not as effective and certainly not as much fun as getting them to chase bigger bugs. A smallmouth's number one prey is crayfish; thus any streamer with lots of action and stuff wiggling at all angles to look like the claws and legs of a crayfish will drive them wild. Bead-Head Woolly Buggers with rubber legs, Yellow Muddler Minnows, and patterns with rabbit strips all appeal to smallmouths. Throw in a few patterns that look more like a baitfish, such as a Clouser Minnow or a White Zonker, and you'll have the streamers covered.

Another favorite smallmouth food is the hellgrammite, a large black larva of the dobsonfly. A black Woolly Bugger or large black stonefly nymph with rubber legs will do for them. Fish these dead drift, with or without a strike indicator, especially on days when smallmouths aren't aggressive and inclined to chase streamers.

Don't rule out surface poppers, though. Smallmouths will investigate small bass bugs, often hanging back for a full minute before smashing them, but there is nothing more thrilling than catching a frisky smallmouth bass on a bug. Even if you come upon a smallmouth sipping delicate mayflies on the surface, you can often convince it to go for a bigger mouthful and inhale a bass bug that is ten times the size of the mayflies it's eating. And there is no better surface bug for smallmouths than the cone-shaped chartreuse popper with rubber legs known as a Sneaky Pete.

The Woolly Bugger is one of the best flies for river smallmouths.

Smallmouth Bass

How to find a bass and panfish pond close to home

It's silly to wait for a trip to Montana or Alaska to enjoy some fly fishing. Anglers who have fished throughout the world still thrill to the dawn rise of a largemouth bass to a popper in a suburban golf course pond. And the many species of sunfish swirl eagerly to small poppers and regulation trout flies, making you feel like a hero. I would be willing to bet there is a pond within five miles of your house that holds some bass and panfish, no matter where you live. Even the ponds in Central Park are packed with eager bass and panfish just waiting to inhale a fly.

Here's how to find one: Pick the pond closest to your house that is *reasonably* accessible. ("No fishing" signs on golf course ponds are only meant to be obeyed during the day, and dawn raids on these places will evoke thrills you forgot when you reached puberty.) When spring flowers begin to bloom (this might be March in Florida or May in North Dakota), begin scouting the shoreline for saucer-shaped nests made by bass and panfish as they clean a place on the bottom prior to laying eggs. The spots typically show up as a light spot or a clean area of gravel in an otherwise muddy bottom. Now you know fish live there. Catch-

Chances are you won't have to travel far to find a pond filled with bass or sunfish.

ing them is simply a matter of trying a small surface bug or a size 10 Hare's Ear Nymph.

After spawning is over in a few weeks, the fish will stay close to the shallows, but in midsummer they might spend most of their time deeper, in the middle of the pond. But don't worry. They still come close to shore to feed at dawn and dusk, when you can sneak in without getting caught.

Small Fry - Largemouth Bass

How to find bass in a pond or lake

You *can* catch largemouth and smallmouth bass anywhere the Bassmaster folks can catch them with conventional tackle, but you probably won't bother, because catching bass with a fly sometimes involves fishing a sinking line in twenty feet of water. Most of us prefer to catch our bass on the surface or close to it,

where we can fish a floating line. Casting and picking up a floating line is a pleasure instead of a chore. Bass ambush their prey, so when fishing for them in shallow water you will seldom find them far from dense weed beds, logjams, piles of big rocks, or docks. Largemouths prefer dense mats of lily pads, cattails, and other aquatic weeds, and they will be *in* the weeds, not just close to them. A weedless fly helps. Sometimes they

won't move more than a few inches from their ambush point, so you should cast right into the nasty stuff. Smallmouths prefer rocky bottoms. Look for them close to submerged logs and large boulders, especially close to a place where shallow water quickly drops off into the depths.

How to fish a bass bug

Whether fishing for largemouth bass, smallmouth bass, or sunfish, you should begin by fishing a surface bug slowly. Slow enough that you get impatient. Bass are infinitely more patient than you. The natural tendency is to cast the bug and begin moving it as soon as it hits the water, like something trying to get away. Bass prefer prey that is struggling, and most animals that struggle twitch a few times, then rest motionless.

So cast your bug and don't move it. Strip in enough line to come tight to the fly but not enough to move it. Then wait until all the rings around the fly disappear. Don't worry about a bass losing interest, as they often approach potential prey and eyeball it for a

full minute before making a decision. Time and again, a bass will wait until everything gets quiet and then suddenly pounce on a fly that is totally motionless. After you've waited so long you can't stand it, give the fly a single twitch. Move it about an inch. Then wait again. Continue this way until the fly is close enough to pick up for another cast.

This twitch-and-wait strategy is by far the most productive way to fish a bug, but if it doesn't work, by all means try others. If the water is deep, sometimes three or four abrupt twitches followed by a long pause bring bass up from deeper water when they hear the commotion. You can also try a steady retrieve, where you keep the fly moving and never let it pause. Experiment until you find the right formula, and it will work for you throughout the day.

How to fish a bass streamer

Largemouth bass seldom chase a fly aggressively as they are ambushers—sprinters, and not long-distance runners. When you fish a sinking bass fly, move it slowly and steadily, and when presenting a subsurface fly to bass try to position your cast so that nearly your

A deer hair mouse and a cork popper, two very popular bugs for largemouth bass

Typical subsurface streamers used for bass

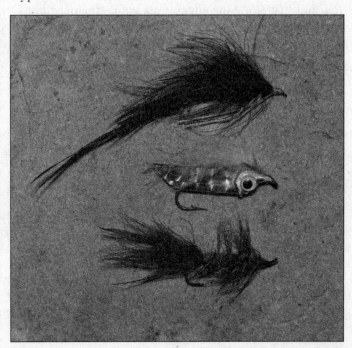

Try to position your boat so you can cast parallel to shore; this will let you retrieve your fly through the most productive water, for the longest time.

entire retrieve moves the fly along near cover. In other words, if a big log sticks out into a lakeshore, don't make a cast at 90 degrees to the log, because only the first foot or so of your retrieve will be appealing to bass lying in ambush. Instead, position yourself so that your fly will swim along parallel to the log, presenting a tasty morsel to a lurking bass throughout its progress.

Get that streamer in the middle of the thick stuff, too, not just along the edges. Cast your streamer right into the lily pads, drawing it over the surface of the pads, letting it sink into the holes between them. Even with a weedless fly you'll get frequent snags, but if your fly is not in deep cover it won't be fishing where largemouths feed.

Smallmouth bass are found more often amongst rocks and logs than weeds, so here you should try to fish your fly so that it rides just above piles of large rocks on the bottom, or off rocky points and cliffs. A weighted fly like a Clouser Minnow is deadly on smallmouths, and these heavy flies should be fished with a strip and then a pause that lets the fly sink. Smallmouths usually pounce on a fly that is sinking or just

beginning to rise after it has sunk, so watch your line for any twitch or pause because a big smallmouth may have just inhaled your fly.

Picking the right leader for warmwater fly fishing

Bass are not leader-shy, and even a fly line landing on top of one seldom spooks it. For largemouth bass, the leader should be as heavy as you can find, and if you can get the leader through the eye of the fly you've gone as light as you need to. Big bass flies are very wind-resistant, and a short, stiff leader helps turn them over, so a leader of between six and seven and a half feet long with a breaking strength of fifteen to twenty pounds is about right. You'll appreciate that heavy leader when yanking a big largemouth out of aquatic salad, too. Smallmouths live in clear water and are slightly spookier than largemouths, so a nine-foot leader that breaks at twelve pounds will straighten the smaller flies used for them and will land even a world-record smallmouth with ease.

Trout

A. Trout Introduction

WADE BOURNE

Several trout species inhabit North American waters and are very important sportfish. They live in many different types of waters, from small brooks to huge lakes. Some trout are natives; others are raised in hatcheries and released into suitable waters. Trout are cold-water fish and lively fighters when hooked. They have sweet, delicate meat. Because of their wide availability, natural elusiveness, fighting qualities and good flavor, these fish are highly sought by anglers.

The U.S. and Canada have five major trout species: rainbows, German browns, brook trout, cutthroats and lake trout. Six other species found in localized areas are Apache trout, Arctic char, bull trout, Dolly Vardens, Gila trout and golden trout.

Rainbows are so-named because of the pink streak down their sides. Native to western states, this fish has been stocked into streams, ponds and lakes throughout much of the U.S. and lower Canada. Today the rainbow trout is probably the continent's most important cold-water sportfish. The world-record rainbow trout (42 pounds 2 ounces) was caught in Alaska in 1970.

The German brown trout is a European native that has been widely stocked in suitable American waters.

Lake Trout

Cutthroat Trout

These fish have dark or orange spots on their sides. Many anglers consider them to be the wariest, most difficult trout to catch, making them extremely popular among sport anglers. Browns tolerate slightly higher water temperatures than other trout, so they can live where some of the other trout can't. The world-record brown trout (40 pounds 4 ounces) was taken in Arkansas in 1992. (When the angler who caught this fish died, he had the taxidermy mount of his world-record brown buried with him.)

Brook trout are native to the eastern U.S. and Canada, though they have been transplanted into other areas. They have light, wormlike markings along their backs. They also have small blue and red dots along their sides. "Brookies" are probably the easiest of all trout to catch, and they are the best to eat. The world-

Brook Trout

record brook trout (14 pounds 8 ounces) was taken in Ontario in 1916.

Cutthroat trout are found mainly in the western U.S. and Canada. Their name comes from the red markings behind and under the lower jaw. Their sides are dotted with small black spots. Like brook trout, they are not too difficult to catch, and they're delicious to eat. The world-record cutthroat, weighing an even 41 pounds, was caught in Nevada in 1925.

Lake trout are what their name implies: residents of large, cold-water lakes from Canada south through the Canadian shield lakes of northern and Midwestern states. Lake trout also live in many western lakes where water temperatures don't exceed 65° F. Lake trout are silver-gray in color, and they have deeply-forked tails. The world-record lake trout weighed 72 pounds and was caught in Canada's Northwest Territories in 1995.

Trout feed on a broad variety of larval and adult insects, minnows, worms and crustaceans. In streams, trout spawn in shallow riffles where they build nests (or "redds") in gravel.

B. Stream Life with a Trout

DAVE WHITLOCK

Part I

Stream trout live in an incredibly different environment than you and me. When I began experiencing their world as they do, my respect and knowledge of them increased greatly, and so did my success in fly fishing for them. To accomplish this, I enter their world and quietly spy on them. To submerge in the chilling 50 to 65 degrees Fahrenheit water where trout live, and to see and breathe there, I equip myself with a neoprene wetsuit, hood, gloves and booties, weight belt, face mask, snorkel, and swim fins.

When I first put on all this gear, I feel as if I'm in some sort of spacesuit. But as soon as I go below the surface and into the stream's swift current, the equipment restrictions seem to disappear. I'm now truly in a different world and suddenly my emotions and heart rate rise rapidly. I feel the pressure of the transparent liquid atmosphere against my face and body, and it quickly becomes comfortable and almost soothing.

Trout swimming in a clear, sunlit stream can see shallow objects and colors clearly; distant objects fade into the color of the water.

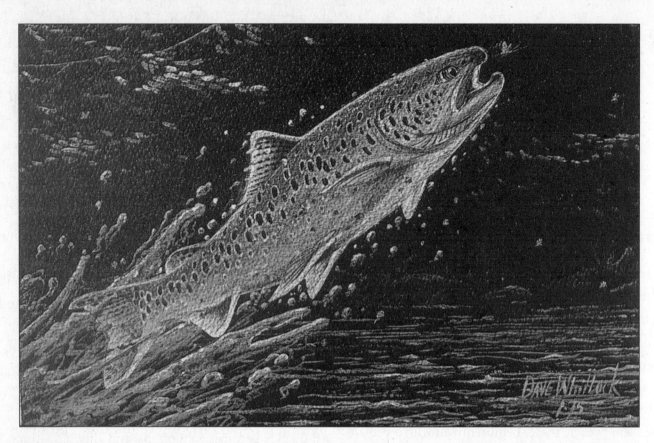

Amazingly, trout can see objects like small insects flying in the air above them through a small distorted window, and they have the ability to leap through that surface and catch them. They also use this same ability to detect airborne and land dangers.

Sounds that seem greatly amplified surround me and as I stare, wide-eyed, I can see colors and objects clearly for six to ten feet. Objects farther away are in hazy focus and muted colors, eventually forming a blur in the water's turquoise-green tint. Everything seems to be rushing toward and past me. Even shafts of light in the water column and the bottom below me seem to race by. After a minute or so my body begins to warm up, my heart rate slows, and my breathing becomes slower and deeper.

At a distance I see the first trout. It appears to be a shadowy green form gliding just off the bottom. As quietly as I can, I move closer. The fish begins to take on more body and color details. Then at a point determined by the trout's caution of me, I can move no closer. Its 10-inch or so length seems in constant, effortless motion as if it were soaring above and into the water's current using some invisible energy source. Yet for me to remain in a position to observe it, I must kick hard with my fins and hold tightly to the bottom rocks.

But then, of course, my body is neither shaped nor lubricated to eliminate the water's force and friction as the trout's is so well-designed to do.

When I'm in the environment of trout, I never cease to be amazed by and learn from them. As the minutes pass, I become less emotional and begin to see the fish and their world more objectively. I begin to see more like a trout. I can best describe the experience as being in a watery wind storm with the unrelenting force of the current and with all sorts of tumbling objects that suddenly appear out of the upstream haze and speed toward and past me. Leaves, twigs, strands of algae, stems of aquatic plants, silvery pearls of air bubbles, insects . . . all drifting and tumbling in one direction and in all levels of the water column.

Looking at the stream surface from below gives me the illusion that I'm watching a time-lapsed sequence of swiftly moving skyscapes. But there's something drastically different about the sky roof of the stream. I can only see a relatively small irregular circle of very distorted blue sky, clouds, and shoreline trees. And most of the underneath surface of the stream is an equally distorted reflection of the stream bottom!

If this is what a trout sees when it looks upward at the stream surface, how can it see objects moving above the surface well enough to leap through the surface and eat them? My most educated guess is that trout have extremely keen eye and body coordination and that they are "in the zone" all of the time. I'm so often amazed as I watch trout magically leap through and above a heavily riffled, fast-moving stream surface to snatch flying caddis, mayflies, damselflies, and dragonflies . . . and even my dry flies! Trout seem to have a sense that biologists have yet to discover. If you've viewed the water's surface from below, you'd probably agree that it seems like trout have extrasensory perception.

When I'm lucky enough to find several trout holding just off the bottom, I am always transfixed by their behavior and their curiosity to the objects drifting toward them. The younger fish are the most active, zooming forward, right, left, down, or up to meet the objects at least halfway. Older trout are much less excitable and much more conservative with their observations as well as the distances they will move to intercept drifting morsels. More on that later.

Trout's Sight Below and Above the Surface

1. Light rays penetrate surface of stream through a 96-degree arch angle. This is usually known as the trout's surface window.
2. This surface window is distorted by how wavy or rough the surface.
3. The area blind to trout varies 10 degrees from surface (plus or minus 10 degrees) according to how smooth the surface.
4. If the surface is smooth, trout cannot see objects at a 10-degree angle above the surface.
5. Surface area beyond the 96-degree cone of vision is a reflection or mirror of the bottom.
6. Trout can see objects clearly in the water column.

My advice to anglers: Always keep in mind that stream trout live in a constantly moving watery atmosphere, and they have highly evolved senses to detect and catch foods. Get into the water with them so that you can visualize their world as they experience it. Through that understanding you'll become a more successful angler.

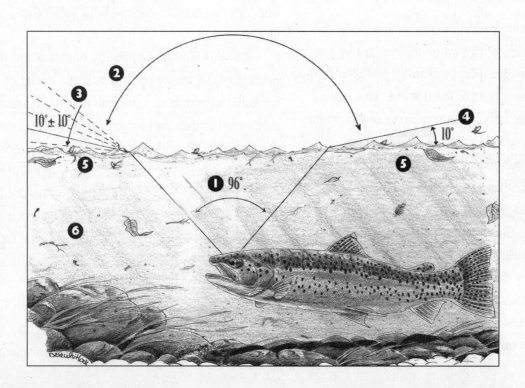

Stream Life with a Trout

DAVE WHITLOCK

Part II

The surface reflections of a trout stream reveal some of its subsurface secrets, and one of the most intriguing and perplexing is the variation of water speeds from top to bottom. As water flows down the gradient of a steambed, it moves with variable speeds depending on the degree of the gradient and the friction it encounters as it flows downhill. The steeper the gradient, the faster the water moves by a particular point. At the same time, as the water moves by that point, the speed of the vertical column of that water can vary considerably from the surface down to the stream bottom. It's very important to understand these vertical speed variations to better comprehend the reasons that fish live and feed where they do and how best to present and fish your flies.

Vertical current speeds, or current speeds from the top to the bottom of the water column at one point, may vary from, for example, three miles per hour at the surface to nearly zero next to the bottom. This variation is a simple function of water moving fastest where there is the least friction, which is at the surface where air offers the least resistance. As water encounters water and the resistance of the non-moving objects of the stream bottom, it slows down. The rate of slowdown is proportionate to the roughness or irregularity of the bottom. For instance, sand will offer much less resistance to water flow than will coarse rock, large rubble, or bottom-rooted aquatic plants.

Because trout often look for the most comfort and food with the least amount of effort, they tend to rest on the bottom or suspend close to the bottom where the water current is slowest. Most of their natural foods, such as aquatic insects, crustaceans, and minnows, also choose to live in this zone. The angler who can present and fish his or her flies effectively in this lower portion of the water column will catch trout more consistently.

That sounds pretty simple for successful fishing except that the subsurface stream has its own form of four-letter word, "drag." In this case it's called "vertical drag." If you think the horizontal drag control in dry fly fishing is complicated, add to those surface considerations the current speed variations that the underwater fly, tippet, and leader experience. Wild trout can be just as particular about dragging subsurface flies as they are about surface dragging dry flies! So to be successful with nymphs, emergers, and streamers on your floating lines, it's essential to control both surface and subsurface drag.

Careful mending of the fly line's tip and floating portion of the leader upstream of the tippet or indicator helps to counteract the pull on the line from the surface. The finer and longer the tippet you can use, the faster the fly will sink into the slowest zone while offering the least vertical drag. The water resistance of the fly itself also helps to slow the pull on the fly from above, much like a sea anchor. Extra weighting, such as split shot on the tippet, will slow the downstream drift caused by the more rapid water movement higher in the vertical current column.

Just before I began writing this chapter, I witnessed an eye-opening demonstration of how vertical drag can affect the success of a fly's performance. Two

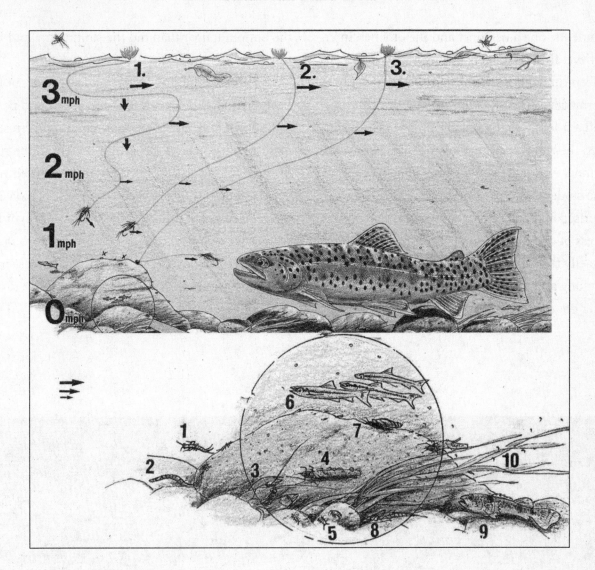

Can you identify the aquatic trout foods shown in the enlargement?

1. mayfly nymphs
2. leeches and aquatic worms
3. crayfish
4. cased caddis larva
5. scuds and sowbugs
6. minnows
7. snails
8. stonefly nymphs
9. sculpins and darters
10. midge larva and pupa

The top diagram page shows vertical current speeds and their effects on trout, trout foods, and subsurface flies.

Current speeds are proportional to the stream's gradient and the friction that water is subjected to as it moves downstream and encounters air, water, and stationary objects. Generally, the fastest current will be at the surface, slowing vertically as the water nears the stream bottom.

Trout in a particular area of a stream, especially in riffles, pockets, and runs, will hold just off the bottom where current flow is modestly slow. Most aquatic trout foods live in this area for the same reason.

When presenting a nymph to a feeding trout, anglers should remember that vertical drag especially affects how a subsurface fly sinks and the speed and direction it drifts to the fish:

1. A long, thin tippet presented in a slack coil or pile allows the weighted fly to sink faster than a straight tippet presentation.
2. The fly will have drift speed proportional to the extent of the vertical drag that the tippet encounters between the surface strike indicator and the fly. The arrows show the extent of drag and where most occurs (at surface and mid-depth).
3. A weighted fly and split shot combination will allow the fly to sink into and drift through the feeding zone better and help reduce vertical drag.

of my students, one a beginner and the other an intermediate-level fly angler, were fishing a very swift 2 ½-to 3-foot-deep run with a size 6, olive, Nearnuff Sculpin. The intermediate student, who was first through the run, used a 5-foot, No. III sinking-tip line. The beginner fished the run next with a full-sinking, No. IV line. The beginner, using the sinking line, took 10 rainbows while the student with the sink-tip caught only one! I was surprised and amazed at the drastic difference in the success of one form of sinking line over the other using exactly the same fly in such shallow water. Then, after thinking about it, the reason became clear: The full sinker got the fly deeper into the slow layer next to the bottom longer than did the sinking tip, and without much interference from surface drag.

Those wonderful, larger, wild stream trout like to have their food delivered to them, as often as possible, right down where they are most comfortable resting on or suspended just off the stream bottom in the riffles or runs. In that position, within inches of their heads, is a constant, fast-moving conveyor belt of oxygen and food. Placing and drifting a fly on this conveyor belt with as little vertical drag as possible, so as to match the belt's speed, will ensure you consistent success in catching quality trout.

C. 30 Trout Tips

KIRK DEETER and CHARLIE MEYERS

1. It Starts with the Grip

In golf, nine out of ten swing flaws can be traced to your hands and how you hold the club. The same is true of the fly cast. It starts in your grip. You want to be firm, without over-clutching the handle. The line goes where the rod tip directs it to go, and your grip dictates the direction of the rod tip. Because of this, line your hand up so that it can control how the rod flexes. Hold your thumb on the top of the grip, then snap those casts. If you visualize looking "through" your casting thumbnail, odds are that the line will unfurl right through that window. —K.D.

A good, consistent cast begins with a firm grip.

2. "10 and 2" Is Too Little, Too Late

Many fly-casting instruction books tell you to imagine casting as if your rod moves along an imaginary clock face, with the forward cast stopping at ten o'clock on the imaginary dial and the backcast stopping at the two o'clock position. That's correct, *in theory*. In reality, when casting, most people are oblivious to the positions of that imaginary clock. What feels like two o'clock on the backcast may actually be four o'clock. When I guide, I change time zones and suggest to clients to go to one o'clock on the backcast. For whatever reason, most people achieve the ten o'clock–two o'clock mechanics if they're thinking 10 and 1. Try it—you'll see what I mean. —K.D.

3. Don't Get Cocky

The number-one mistake most novice fly casters make is going back too far on the backcast. The only tipoffs are the noises of line slapping the water or the rod tip scraping the ground behind them. This happens, more often than not, because the caster is allowing his wrist to cock too far back. As it relates to fly casting, the wrist-versus-arm equation is a difficult balance to describe. Remember this: The arm is the engine; the wrist is the steering wheel. Yes, sometimes it's "all in the wrist," but that pertains to matters of aiming the cast, not powering it. When you let your wrist power your cast, you will inevitably crash. If you have a problem with your wrist over-cocking, there are a few simple fixes that will help you capture the right feel. One is to get a large, thick rubber band, wrap it around your casting wrist, and then insert the rod butt inside that rubber band when you practice

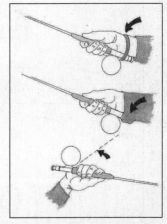

casting. If you find that the rubber band is flexing too much, odds are you are breaking your wrist too far. If you are wearing a long-sleeved shirt, tuck the rod butt inside your cuff. It will have the same effect, and it will tell you when you're cocking your wrist too far on the backcast. Even seasoned anglers will tuck the butt end of their rods inside their shirt cuffs now and again to help them regain their stroke. —**K.D.**

4. Watch That Thumb

Many people are frustrated when their line bunches and dies on the forward cast. This is usually caused by going too far with the backcast, which creates an open loop. The best tip I've ever heard for correcting this came from Dan Stein, a guide on the Bighorn River in Montana. He simply suggests that you keep your casting thumb in your peripheral vision at all times. Lose sight of your thumb, and you're going back too far. Simple as that. —**K.D.**

5. See the "U"

Watching how your line behaves during the cast will tell you if you're making mistakes. It's tricky to self-diagnose the exact nature of a problem, however, and even harder to make the fix. Before you get bogged down in complicated physics lessons, try watching your casts from a fresh perspective. Dan Wright taught me this exercise: To help develop the proper feel for a cast,

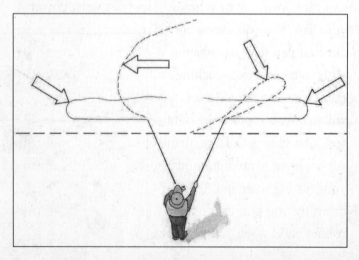

first tilt your rod sideways and cast from waist or chest level on a flat plane above the ground. Use a measuring tape stretched straight along the ground as your benchmark. Start with small flicks of line, maybe 15 feet long. As you look at the line shooting back and forth, you'll be able to see and feel both good U-shaped loops and tailing loops. Make both forward and backward casts from a dead stop. Eventually, link those casts together. Build line length gradually. As the good loops become uniform and systematic, you'll be able to lift that cast 90 degrees over your head, still watching, and feeling, how the line shapes. If you tail, start over. The key is keeping the tempo even. Good loops grow in distance with practice. —**K.D.**

6. Too Much, Too Soon

Perhaps the most common casting error, apart from breaking the wrist on the backcast, comes at the very beginning. Many anglers begin applying full power on the pickup, starting with the rod parallel to the water, while there is still slack line on the water surface. This immediately creates an extremely large loop while failing to properly load the rod. The angler spends the remainder of the cast sequence fighting to tighten the loop, eliminate wind resistance, and build line speed. Most often, he never recovers. An effective cast begins by stripping in *excess* line, then smoothly lifting the rod tip to ten o'clock. This places the rod in position to load while setting the stage for a short, quick power stroke. Remember: The shorter the power stroke, the tighter the loop and the more powerful the cast. —**C.M.**

7. Roll 'Em Easy

I find that I roll cast on a river at least three times for every overhead cast I make. When you get the roll cast down and you learn to use the water to load your rod, you'll find yourself spending less time and energy thinking about casting. In turn, you'll be more focused on reading the water and finding fish. The roll cast is important for two other reasons. First, it's a stealthier approach and is less likely to spook fish than false casting overhead. Second, it's your go-to option when there are bushes or other obstacles behind you, where they'll likely foul up a backcast. What's the key to a good roll cast? Same as with any other cast—gradually accelerate the rod, building speed and resistance, then stop, change direction, and unfurl the cast forward. A common mistake people make is to start that roll cast with too much loose line on the water and the rod tip pointed straight at the sky. Instead, retrieve with the rod tip from a low position, with noticeable tension on the line as it slices through the current. When the moment is right (and you'll develop a feel to know when), lift the rod tip skyward and snap the rod forward, unfurling an on-target cast. —K.D.

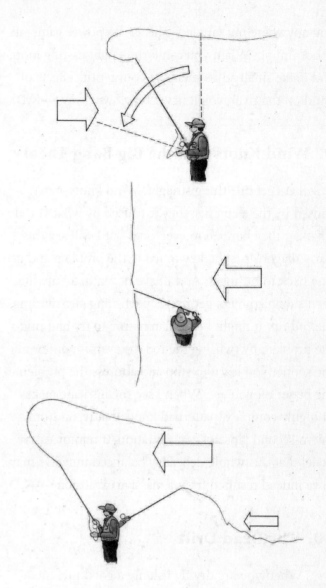

8. Make Friends with the Wind

The windiest place I've ever fished was the redfish flats of Aransas Bay, Texas. It was there, as I was struggling with a flapping fly line, that guide Chuck Naiser called a halt to the action, gently placed his hand on my shoulder, and said, "Son, you're gonna have to make friends with that wind, or else come back here in July when it calms down . . . but all the locals are busy then, chasing down the chickens that blew out of the barnyard." The point was well taken, and using the wind to your casting advantage is especially important for the trout angler who has learned the hard way that breezes whipping through the canyon can mess with the best intentions.

For a right-handed fly caster, the perfect wind is a gentle one coming over the left shoulder, because it keeps your line and flies pushed away from your head at a safe distance. When the wind howls from the right side, tip the top of your rod at a raised angle over your left shoulder, still powering the stroke from your right side. When the wind is directly behind you, shorten and power that backcast high, allowing the fly line to kite up with the wind's force.

If you go too far back, or break your wrist, and let that rod tip dip blow the kite plane, the wind will pile-drive the fly line into the water behind you. But do it correctly, and you'll reap the same rewards as the golfer who finds added driving distance with a tailwind. And the most intimidating wind of all—the one that blows right in your face—might actually be your ally. After all, your backcast is where you load the power in the rod, and a stiff breeze will help straighten the line behind you. To transfer that energy through the teeth of the wind, make a slight adjustment to finish your forward stroke lower.

In other words, if you normally stop the rod at 10 and 2 on the imaginary clock face, shift to 9 and 1, stopping higher on the backcast, and driving lower on the front. Remember, punching the rod won't get you anywhere but tangled. This isn't a power game; it's about timing. When you can form a tight casting loop, and make small adjustments to counter the effects of wind on the river, you'll never be blown away. —**K.D.**

9. Wind Knots and the Big Bang Theory

Let's get one thing straight: Wind knots aren't caused by the elements; they're caused by what you do. It's okay, they happen to everyone. But I will say this: Early diagnosis is the key to fixing the problem and getting back to business. And I have never, in all my life, seen a tangled mess get fixed by whirling and twirling the rod tip. It might be human nature to try and undo the problem by twirling the rod in reverse motion, but the sooner you learn to stop and address the problem, the better off you are. When I see the intricate mazes of highly complex, patterned knots that result from a micro-second lapse of concentration, it reinforces my belief that this whole delicately balanced universe may have indeed resulted from a massive explosion. —**K.D.**

10. The Dead Drift

When you are dry fly fishing, a good presentation always starts with a good drift. And a good drift is usually a dead drift, meaning the fly is traveling in exact connection with the current.

I once walked up on a guide friend and his client on a gorgeous Colorado afternoon, a day when insects were swarming and the fish were happy.

"What are they eating?" I asked.

"A good drift," he said, smiling. And to prove the point, he showed me the size 14 Royal Trude his guy was fishing with. I'd seen a lot of bugs that day, but nothing that looked quite like that. The secret to a good dead drift is casting upstream and letting your fly float with the current. Drag, when the fly line is caught by the current, causing tension that moves the fly unnaturally, and "micro-drag," when the leader does the same thing, will inevitably turn fish off.

Try to keep as little fly line on the water as possible. When the fly is moving from upstream down at a straight tangent, drag is less of a concern. But when you are casting at an angle to the current, keeping the line off the water is smart; failing that, always keep the fly line upstream from the flies. —**K.D.**

11. The Swing

You're fishing nymphs in a run, and just as you get ready to lift up and make another cast—bang—you get a hit! It happens all the time. What you just did is hook a fish on the swing. As the line straightens out down current, the flies inevitably lift toward the surface, which looks exactly like insects emerging. Trout love eating those bugs.

Many people have lost touch with the art of wet fly fishing and swinging bugs subsurface. In my family, we had a rule that the little kids had to fish the river with wet flies, so they'd work the water going downstream. When you got big enough, you were allowed to

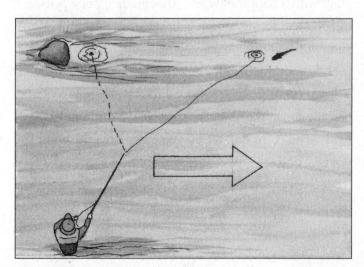

turn back into the current and start working dry flies upstream.

I always thought that Grandpa made that rule to keep the kids dry. I'm starting to see an ulterior motive: We caught a lot of fish that way, and learned the value of the swing. —K.D.

12. When in Doubt (Set the Hook)

Always curious about the mysteries of trout fly fishing, Jack Dennis took an underwater camera into a local stream to discover what really happens when anglers made presentations to fish beneath the surface.

Among his more revealing discoveries: Anglers failed to detect 40 percent of the strikes they received using conventional nymphing techniques, particularly with indicators.

The reason? Invariably, the problem was too much slack in the line. Dennis found that fish feeding actively on a plentitude of insects floating past their noses seldom moved much; rather, they simply held their position and opened and closed their mouths. In such situations, anglers generally failed to realize when a trout had taken the artificial fly.

In feeding situations with fewer insects, when trout drifted up or darted sideways to take the artificial,

The key to hooking fish when nymphing is to get the slack out.

the line often moved sufficiently for the angler to detect the strike.

One solution to a light bite is to get as close as possible to the fish, eliminating as much loose line as possible. But the ultimate cure for missed strikes is keen concentration, setting the hook at the slightest pause in the drift. Make the hook set quick and short, keeping the fly down in the target area if you don't connect. —C.M.

13. No Clear Indication

The decision to use a strike indicator for nymphing is usually a matter of preference rather than necessity. You can catch fish either with or without an indicator, whether it's a balsa bobber, piece of yarn, or a large buoyant fly.

Success generally depends upon conditions. Short-line nymphing without an indicator often works best in a swift, deep run where you can get close to the trout. Often, you'll feel the strike directly and quickly, an advantage over the delay caused by slack line common with indicators.

On the other hand, an indicator helps deliver a good presentation at a greater distance and offers a good visual for those who need or desire it. Should you choose an indicator, select a system that allows for quick depth adjustment, a critical element in presenting the fly in different locations as you move along the stream. Reluctance to change depths may be the most important reason for nymphing failure.

One variable is beyond dispute: In a strong wind, get rid of the indicator. It's like trying to cast a kite, plus it catches the wind when on the water, accelerating the speed of the drift. —C.M.

14. The Down-Current Hook-Set

As a guide, I often see people make great casts and drifts, then yank the fly out of a trout's mouth when it hits. The problem is that they try to set the hook in an upstream direction.

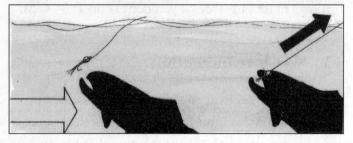

Trout face into the current 99.9 percent of the time. They eat things that float toward them. If a trout eats a bug (dry fly or nymph) that is floating toward it, why on earth would you think it's a good thing to rip that fly back upstream? The whole point of fly fishing is to set that J-shaped hook into the trout's mouth, and that can only happen if you set the hook down-current (not downstream . . . *down-current*).

It seems as if our instinct tells us to lift, flick, and pull upstream with every take. Before you make your next cast, take a minute, watch the way the current is moving, and then plan to set the hook down-current in the same direction of the current flow. This will increase your success-to-net ratio tenfold.—**K.D.**

15. **Getting to the Bottom of Things**

The month: January. The river: Colorado's Roaring Fork. The challenge: getting flies down to sluggish trout holding close to the bottom in extremely cold water. Three anglers tried a more conventional approach, drifting bead-head nymphs with a couple of split shot while furiously mending line to neutralize a steady current. Each caught an occasional fish, working hard for their strikes. A fourth companion seemed to have a trout with every second cast, chortling at the obvious discomfort of his far-less-successful friends.

Closer inspection revealed his novel and highly effective approach. His flies were heavily weighted with tungsten wire and a tungsten bead, with about the same specific gravity as a ship's anchor. He also pinched two larger split shot to his leader. The truly novel ingredient was the balsa indicator, much like an antique panfish bobber, that was large enough to stay afloat above all that weight. With this rig, our friend kept his offering dead-drifted in the zone much longer than anyone else, and he had the fish to show for it.

Such a weighty assembly isn't for everyone, but when trout are hugging bottom, it gets results. —**C.M.**

16. **Stack Mending for Drifts**

As long as your flies are floating naturally, and the drift is good, there's no rule against making multiple mends to cover lots of water. In fact, in big rivers, like the Colorado at Lees Ferry in Arizona, and up on Oregon's Deschutes, stack mending for long drifts is a smart way to fish.

Make your cast, let your flies settle, then make your mend. As the flies float downstream, make another mend, feeding more line as you go. Then another. And another. Mete out line gently by wiggling the rod tip to feed line through the guides; at the same time, don't get caught with so much slack that you cannot set the hook when your indicator stalls 50 or 60 feet away from you. It can be tricky. The key is making many small, gentle mends as you feed your line through the run. —**K.D.**

17. **Fish Like Changes**

The best lesson I ever learned about locating trout in a river came from a tuna captain. Fishing with Steve "Creature" Coulter, 40 miles off Hatteras, North Carolina, I stared out at the horizon and asked him how in the world he went about finding fish in the open ocean. "It isn't so hard," he said, smiling. "It's just like trout fishing."

For the record, Creature might be one of the most decorated big-game fishermen on the Atlantic seaboard, but his closet fishing passion is chasing trout with flies. "How do you figure that?" I asked, perplexed by the comparison.

"Fish like changes," he said. "Changes in currents, changes in depth, changes in water color, changes in structure. If you find a patch of sea grass floating in the open ocean, that's a structure change, and you'll find fish under it. If you find a place where currents converge, baitfish will school there and bigger fish will follow them. Reefs, wrecks, and rock formations attract fish too, as do underwater ridges and canyons."

Apply that thinking when you go to the trout river. Look for changes in currents, where swift water meets slow water; changes in structure, where rocks and trees create holding water; changes in depth, like shelves and pools; or changes in color, which usually signals a depth or structural transition.

"It's all pretty much the same," Creature told me. "You trout guys can walk or row a boat to find those changes, but you're essentially doing the same thing a tuna boat captain does in the ocean."

Find the changes, find the fish. —**K.D.**

18. Rock On

That rock in the middle of the river or jutting off the bank should always get your attention. Why? Because that slab of granite affects the flow of the river, altering the current and creating subtle microcurrents around it. From downstream,

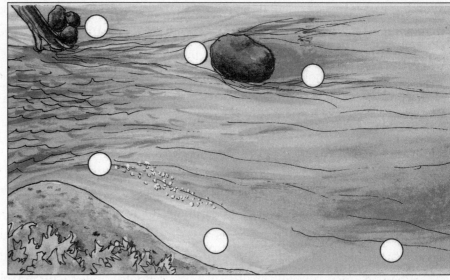

White circles indicate changes in current, depth, water color, and structure—all likely spots to hold trout.

you'll be able to see two distinct current lines to the right and left, where the water folds around the rock. Eventually, those currents merge like the bottom point of the letter "V." That's where cast number one should land, at the bottom of the "V."

Your next casts should be right up the two current seams. The fish will usually be where the fast water meets the slower water. That dead spot right behind the rock might also be worth a cast or two, although the fish usually don't tuck their noses right onto the stone.

Think about it. The food is washing downriver, packed into that seam where the current meets the slower water. The fish could swim out into the heavy

water, but that takes energy, and the insects there are moving by at a quicker pace. If you were a fish, wouldn't you hang out where you have to use as little energy as possible to hold your position, especially when the buffet is churning right there? —K.D.

19. Nervous Water

Bonefish guides are always looking for patches on the water with telltale ripples that reveal movement under the surface. They call it "nervous water" or (in Mexico) "agua nerviosa."

When fish move through shallow water in schools, they make a subtle disturbance that reveals their presence, even when their fins do not beak the surface.

This is also true with trout, especially in flat water like slowmoving spring creeks and lakes. It's always worth looking for nervous patches of surface water when you are figuring out where to make your first cast. —K.D.

20. Where Would You Be?

When reading water, ask yourself this simple question: *If I were a trout, where would I be?* Understand that your life revolves around three things: eating, not being eaten, and making little fish.

In the context of fly angling, the eating part is most important. Playing the role of trout, you understand that you primarily eat insects and smaller fish. You know that you'll find more of both closer to the banks, so that's a good starting point to choose where you want to hang out in the river. The insects you eat come in all forms: nymphs, emergers, adult bugs hatching, adult spinners falling to the surface to lay eggs, terrestrials falling into the river, and so forth. You know that mayflies, for example, like to lay eggs on gravel bottoms, and that that is where nymphs, emergers, duns, and spinners are likely to concentrate.

Currents also concentrate insects. Bugs get trapped and collected in the seam where fast water

bumps up against slow water, for example. You (the trout) want to be near that seam, in a place where you aren't expending more calories to swim than you can consume.

At the same time, you don't want to become calories for another predator. You want to find cover in those rocks or under that log. Lacking thick cover, my exit strategy is to go to deep water. There has to be a place where I can escape to the depths when I'm threatened.

Making little fish is another matter. We spawn on gravel. Hopefully the angler reading this book won't mess with me when I'm on a spawning bed.

The more you ask yourself, "If I were a trout, where would I be?" while you are on the water fishing, the easier reading water becomes. Thinking like a fish will make places and targets pop out before you cast. You'll overlook fewer targets, and catch more trout. —K.D.

21. Make Big Water Small

Most of us started fly fishing on small streams. They're easy to wade and easy to read. You have that one log sticking out in the current, scouring the river bottom, and you can guess there's a good chance that Mr. Brown Trout might be hanging around it.

But what do you do when you get on a big, wide river, like the Madison, the Bighorn, the South Fork of the Snake, the Green, the Colorado, or the Delaware?

Among the guides I've fished with on these rivers, from Patty Reilly in Wyoming to Bob Lamm in Idaho to Joe Demalderis in New York, they all say that the key to reading them is to make big water small.

By that, they mean taking a river that's 50 yards wide and mentally dividing it into five 10-yard-wide sections. If you're wading upstream, start with the 10-yard section that's closest to the bank. Look for fish first. Now look for changes in structure—a rock, a log, a dropoff. Also look for changes in currents. Is there a spot where fast water meets slow water? Look for a depression in the bottom. If you've found the changes, make your casts: 10 casts, covering all the hotspots on your radar.

Nothing happened? Move out from the bank to the next 10-yard-wide section of water. Look for the same things—current breaks, structure, dropoffs—and cover them with solid casts.

Nothing happened? Move toward the middle and repeat the process. Do this until you can't wade any deeper (if you're wading big rivers, it usually is too deep to work all the way across), and until you feel you've made enough casts.

Next, wade upstream and start the process over. Make big water small in your mind. Divide and conquer, always working from the bank outward. —K.D.

22. Follow the Bubbles

One early morning, while dry fly fishing a trico hatch on Montana's Missouri River, guide Pete Cardinal checked me up, then told me to stop casting and watch the water. We were working a seam where fast water, colliding with a slow pool, was creating a foamy bubble line. At times, that bubble line would disperse and spread out in wide fronds of white, wispy water. At other times, the currents converged and collected hatching insects in a tight, white highway that ran straight through the run. Until Pete pointed it out, I hadn't noticed that the fish were keyed into this system. When the currents dispersed or collapsed, the fish didn't rise. When the foam line formed a hard seam and collected those tiny mayflies, the trout began slurping away at the surface. The lesson? Follow the bubble line. When you see a pronounced foam or bubble line on the surface, there's a very good chance that trout will be underneath it, and feeding. —K.D.

23. Seeing Is (Not) Believing

Among the most important, yet least understood, aspects of sight fishing is the role played by refraction.

Put simply, the fish we think we see 20 feet away in shallow water will actually be closer and deeper than it appears. It will also seem larger than it really is, which may be where all those fish stories get started. —C.M.

24. Use an Attractor Fly

One of the best lessons I learned from scuba diving with trout came from watching them react to attractor flies. To set the scene, I had a buddy fishing a two-fly dry-fly rig. The lead fly was a size 12 Stimulator—a big ugly bug that might look like a terrestrial or a stonefly, although its basic mission is, as the name implies, to stimulate a rise. The second fly, trailed 18

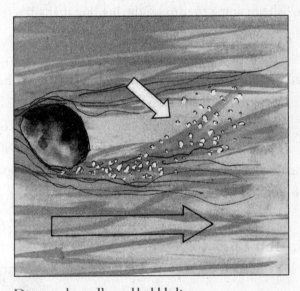

Dispersed or collapsed bubble line.

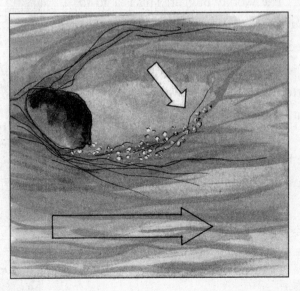

Tight bubble line.

inches off the hook shank of the first, was a size 18 Blue-Winged Olive, meant to match the natural *baetis* flies that pop up on the surface now and again.

As I watched the fish from below the surface, time and time I noticed them swim up to check out the larger fly, then catch view of the smaller fly and go eat it. The lesson is that if you are fishing two small dry flies, you won't draw their attention as consistently as you would by using an attractor dry fly.

The same applies to nymph fishing, particularly in swift currents or in tinted water. Your first should be a big ugly bug—maybe a hot pink San Juan Worm or a size 14 Flashback Pheasant Tail. Your trailer fly should be something smaller, perhaps a size 18 Barr Emerger. The fish are going to turn on the big bug that attracts their attention. Sometimes they'll eat it, but usually they'll pass on it in favor of the smaller fly. And they won't eat the smaller fly as consistently if you don't have an attractor bug drawing them in in the first place. The attractor fly really only works when you are prospecting and when there isn't a consistent hatch coming off. When you're fishing a prolific hatch, don't mess around with attractors. —**K.D.**

25. Ten Flies to Never Leave Home Without

The Woolly Bugger: This is a go-to trout-producing streamer that can be fished effectively on lakes and rivers.

The Pheasant Tail Nymph: A generic pattern, it represents a wide range of immature mayflies.

The Prince Nymph: This is probably the best all-around attractor nymph pattern you can use.

The Parachute Adams: A generic-looking adult mayfly, when wet its gray body can effectively match many insect species.

The Pale Morning Dun: A midsummer staple on many rivers, east and west, this is the mayfly pattern that matches insects with pale bodies (yellow, pink, cream).

The Copper John: Another attractor nymph, it's valued as much for its weight and sinkability as for its flashy profile.

The Elk Hair Caddis: Use this dry fly on any rivers where caddis hatch in large numbers.

Black Foam Beetle: It won't sink, and it's a killer pattern for fish keyed on terrestrials, anywhere.

The Barr Emerger: Pale Morning Dun or Blue-Winged Olive varieties fool the most selective trout.

The Muddler Minnow: It's a streamer and grasshopper, all in one. —**K.D.**

26. Firmer Footing

There's no stepping around it: At times our angling success will depend upon how well we wade. Whether it's a brawling British Columbia steelhead river or a slippery brook, the ability to reach the right position may be the most important factor in catching that special fish.

In a similar vein, the ability to wade with confidence has much to do with our overall enjoyment of the experience onstream, whether we catch anything or not.

The fact is, it's practically impossible to enjoy fishing if every step along a rocky streambed leaves us afraid of a dunking. Fear shouldn't be a part of the angling experience.

Good equipment is the first step to safe wading. It begins with a solid sole for gripping rocks. Either rubber or felt soles work fine, though you must thoroughly clean felt after each day of fishing, so you don't carry invasive species to other waters. If the stones of your favorite streams also come with a slick coating of algae, as is often the case with nitrogen-enriched tailwaters or other altered environments, buy boots with studs that can bite through slime into the rock.

Once you've acquired the proper gear, including a stout wading staff, relax, bend your knees, and enjoy. —C.M.

27. Mark That Line

We've all made the mistake of removing a perfectly good line from a spool, then forgetting to mark its weight and design. The result is a drawer full of mystery lines that otherwise could be put to work. Lefty Kreh devised an ingenious coding system, using a waterproof marker and a series of dots and dashes, that lets him identify each line. You can also take a strip of masking tape and write down the proper identification on a storage or spare reel spool. Devise a system and use it, or else you're going to have a bunch of useless line on your hands. —C.M.

28. Shadow Casting

The deadly combination of bright sunshine and a calm surface creates line shadows that spook fish. One way to avoid this is to position your cast so the line's shadow doesn't pass over the fish during delivery. When this isn't possible, or when the sun is directly overhead, consider using a roll cast instead. Measure the distance so that only the monofilament leader passes over the fish. —C.M.

On sunny days, take extra care not to line a fish when you're casting.

29. Tap the Rod

Here's a slick trick that will impress your fishing friends and make life easier: When moving from one spot to another, always keep the fly line-to-leader connection pulled through the tip top of your rod. Trying to pull the knot through the end guide in a hurry with bent rod on the stream is a pain, and is also a good way to break the tip.

With the knot through the tip top, hang your bottom fly on a guide halfway up the rod, drape the leader around the reel seat, and reel in the slack so the fly line connection remains outside the guides.

When you are ready to fish, undrape the leader from behind your reel, let the line hang free, then give a gentle tap or two on the top of the rod, just above the cork handle. The slight vibration will pop the fly off the guide, and your line will fall into the water. No reach-

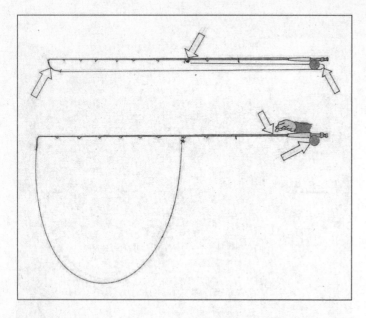

ing up the rod and picking the flies off (or sticking your fingers). Let it hang, give it a tap, and you're good to go. —K.D.

30. Be Ambidextrous

The more you develop your casting and reeling abilities with your "off" hand, the better fly fisherman you'll become. Here's a simple way to start developing a cast with your non-dominant hand, shared by guide and writer Kim Leighton on the Yellowstone River years ago:

Cast as you normally would, using your dominant hand, but as you do this, gently cup the reel with your off hand. This will build a sense of timing and tempo that you can eventually transfer from one hand to the other. If you're only able to develop a casting ability with your off hand that is 25 percent of your good one, you'll still better off when you find yourself in a tough spot where the river, cover, and currents make an opposite-arm delivery your only viable option. —K.D.

D. 25 Trout Tips

TOM ROSENBAUER

1. Pick a rod by line size

The first decision about picking a fly rod has nothing to do with your height, weight, strength, location, or casting skill. The physical weight of a fly rod is also insignificant. The first thing to decide is what line size you need. Every fly rod made is designed for a specific line size (although some may handle several with some adjustment in casting style). These sizes are based on the weight in grains of the first thirty feet of the line, regardless of whether the line floats or sinks, because it's the weight of the line bending the rod that lets you cast. Luckily, you and I don't need to memorize these grain weights because all fly-fishing manufacturers use a number system that ranges from 1 through 15, where each line size correlates to a grain weight. It's used by every maker of fly rods throughout the world.

The smaller the number, the lighter the line. Lighter lines, in sizes 1 through 4, deliver a fly with more delicacy. They cast small flies and light leaders best, but don't cast as far as

heavier lines and don't handle the wind as well. As lines get heavier, in the 5 through 7 range, they lose some delicacy but gain in their ability to deliver larger flies and longer casts, and you won't have to fight the wind as much. These middle sizes are most often used for trout and smallmouth bass. Sizes 8 through 10 are considered the basic rods for long casts, big flies, and lots of wind, and are the sizes most often used by saltwater, bass, and salmon anglers. But they splash down heavier and won't protect a light tippet as well as the lighter rods. When you get into line sizes 11 and heavier, you're really looking at a rod designed to fight big fish, because once you get to a 10-weight rod, you've probably maximized the distance you'll get and going heavier

Just by looking at this small stream with clear water you can expect that a 4-weight line would be about perfect.

only gives you more power to turn the head of a big tarpon or shark.

Fortunately, the flexibility of the rod needed to throw each line size corresponds perfectly with its purpose. Rods designed for lighter fly lines are very flexible, so it's easier to play a trout on a two-pound tippet with a flexible 4-weight rod. If you fish a leader with a two-pound tippet on a 9-weight rod, you'll most likely break most fish off on the strike because the stiffer rod is not as good a shock absorber, and besides, fishing a heavy 9-weight line on top of spooky trout will send most fish running for cover before they even see your fly. Playing a small trout on a 9-weight rod is not much fun, anyway, because the rod will hardly bend against the wiggles of a ten-inch fish. And playing a ten-pound redfish on a 4-weight might be fun for a few moments, but the lighter rod just does not have the strength to land a big fish sounding under a boat, something a stiffer rod will do with ease.

2. How long should your rod be?

I once asked a tournament caster if there was an optimum rod length for casting, ignoring all the other

To manipulate a fly line over these tricky currents, a fly rod nine feet long or longer would be the most efficient tool.

tasks we ask of a fly rod. Without hesitating, he answered "eight and a half feet." The physics of fly fishing are not easily understood, and air resistance, line weight, loop shape, and line speed all come into play, so I won't begin to theorize as to why eight and a half feet is the optimum length. But if all you ever wanted to do was cast out in the open with no wind, and had no conflicting currents to worry about, you'd want an eight-and-a-half-foot rod.

But fishing is much more than casting. In small, brushy places, an eight-and-a-half-foot rod gets tangled in the brush as you walk from one spot to another, and the wider casting arc of a longer rod offers overhanging trees more chances to snatch your fly and leader. A rod that is between six and seven and a half feet long is better for brushy streams, with the really short ones best for almost impenetrable woodland brooks, while rocky mountain streams with wider banks, where if you can get midstream you have plenty of room in front of and behind you, allow rods up to eight feet long before they get clumsy.

Rods longer than eight and a half feet are best for bigger waters. It's easier to keep your back cast off the ground behind you with a longer rod, they are better at making casts over fifty feet, and when you need to mend line or hold line off the water to prevent drag, those extra six inches make a surprising difference. Nine-foot rods seem to be the perfect length for saltwater fly fishing and give a great balance between making longer casts and the ability to play a large fish. It's actually easier to play large fish on a shorter rod as opposed to a longer rod, though, and that is why 14- and 15-weight rods for huge sailfish, marlin, and tuna are usually made in eight-and-a-half-foot lengths. They don't cast as well as nine-footers, but these species are typically teased close to the boat with a hookless plug or bait so casts longer than fifty feet aren't needed.

Really long rods, ten feet and over, are best when tricky currents require the angler to manipulate the fly line once it hits the water. Because the swing of a fly is so important in salmon and steelhead fishing, and these fish are often caught in very wide rivers, two-handed rods up to fifteen feet long are sometimes used with special casts called spey casts that can pick up sixty or seventy feet of line and deliver it back on target without false casting and without the line ever going behind the angler.

3. How to pick a reel

For fish like smal trout, panfish, and bass, a fly reel is simply a line storage device. It keeps your line neat and orderly when you walk to and from fishing, and also keeps excess line from tangling at your feet and around the clutter that fishing boats seem to attract. Nearly all of the reels you see are single action, which means that one revolution of the handle moves the spool around once. Unlike spin fishing or bait casting, where you retrieve line after each cast and a multiplying action comes in handy, it's not needed in fly fishing. In the past, automatic reels with springloaded spools and multiplying reels with gear systems were made, but these reels proved to be heavy and clumsy, not to mention difficult to maintain in good working order.

Smaller reels don't need strong drag tension, either. All that's needed is enough tension on the reel to prevent the line from back-lashing on the spool when

A narrow arbor trout reel on the left compared to the heavier, large arbor saltwater reel on the right.

you pull some off, and perhaps some light tension if a bass or trout pulls a few feet of line when fighting. This tension might be provided by a simple click mechanism composed of a spring and a small metal triangle called a pawl, that engages teeth on the reel spool, or it can be from a small disc drag system. The main considerations when looking for a small reel are how nice it looks and how much it weighs, as the more expensive reels are lighter and more attractive than the less expensive entry-level reels.

Many fish run a hundred yards or more when first hooked. Big trout, salmon, steelhead, and most saltwater species will yank from five feet to a hundred yards of line during a battle, and it's difficult to put tension on a reel by grabbing the fly line with your fingers, as it is neither precise nor uniform, and grabbing a fly line when a fish is running usually leads to a broken leader. These fish require a mechanical, adjustable break system or drag to help you tire them; otherwise they'll just swim away until they steal all your line and backing. Fly reels for these species employ a disc drag system like the brakes on your car, and these drags are most often made with a cork or plastic disc against the aluminum frame of the spool. These bigger reels also require extra capacity for the one hundred to four hundred yards of backing you'll need. Thus, when looking for a reel for these species, check the capacity to make sure it will hold the line size you have plus the maximum length of backing you'll need.

In big-game fishing for tarpon, marlin, sailfish, or tuna, where the fish run as fast as a car and may keep up the pace for hundreds of yards, drag strength is critical, as is the ability of the reel's design to dissipate the heat generated by the friction of the drag surfaces. In the middle of a battle with a marlin, lesser fly reels get so hot they smoke and then seize up completely. There is no way for a consumer to tell if a fly reel is up to this challenge, and the only way to assure yourself of a reel that will hold up is to buy a large, expensive big-game reel with a first-class reputation.

4. Picking the right waders

When picking a pair of waders, regardless of what other decisions you make, the most important point is the correct fit. Waders should be loose enough to let you do deep-knee bends without constricting your movement so you'll be able to step over logs or climb a steep bank once you get to the river, but they also should not be excessively loose, as baggy waders present more resistance to the current and will also wear more quickly because the fabric chafes and eventually wears through. Buy waders at a store where you can try them on, or carefully study the size chart on a Web site and buy from a retailer that offers easy return privileges if they don't fit.

Get breathable waders. Clammy waders can ruin your day, and although those thick neoprene waders may look warm, your body condensation stays inside them all day long. (Besides, you can wear layers of fleece inside breathable waders and stay just as warm.) And you only have to wear neoprene waders once on a 90-degree afternoon under the blazing Montana summer sun to realize you made a big mistake.

Waders come in two basic styles: boot foot and stocking foot. With boot foots, the boot is an integral part of the wader and you just slip them over your socks. Some have laces for extra security and some are just plain rubber boots. They are the easiest waders to put on if you aren't very nimble. Stocking foot waders, which incorporate a breathable upper with neoprene booties, require a separate wading boot. They give you a lot more flexibility, so if your foot size does not correspond to what is common for your height and weight, your chances of getting a better fit are greatly increased. You can also pick a lightweight wading boot for travel or a heavier boot for more support on long walks or rocky streams.

5. What fly line should you use for starting out?

Your first fly line should be a tapered line of the size called for on your rod. And it should float. When you look at fly line designations, you'll see something like this: "WF5F." The first two letters represent the taper, which is less important and is covered in the section below on weight forward versus double taper lines.

Even in deep water, you can fish with a floating line by adding weight to your leader and adjusting your presentation.

The boot-foot waders on the right come with boots already attached and are ready to use. The stocking-foot waders on the left will need a pair of separate wading shoes.

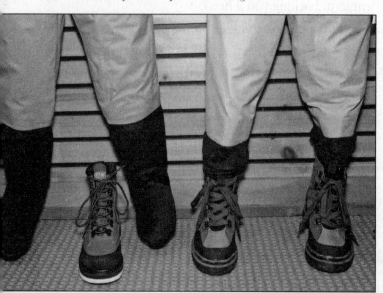

The middle number is the line size, and it must match the designation on your rod. The last letter, F, tells you the line floats, which is what you want.

Why is a floating line so important if you won't fish many dry flies? First, it's much easier to pick up a floating line off the water when you're casting than a sinking one, because you have to lift all of the line free of the water when making a cast, and getting a submerged line moving and above the water with a single back cast is difficult. Next, you can fish nearly every kind of fly—floating or sinking—with a floating line because you can use a weighted fly or weight on your leader to sink a fly, but you can't fish a dry fly with a sinking line. Third, floating lines land much lighter on the water, and when you're starting out, you'll need all the help you can muster to keep your fly line from landing on the water too hard.

For trout fishing, I use a sinking line less than 1 percent of the time, and could probably live without ever using one. A floating line is also the basic line for Atlantic salmon, bonefish, redfish, and bass, so I'm not just suggesting this line for the novice. Unless you fish for saltwater fish in deep water or fast currents, or fish for trout in lakes in midsummer after they go deep, you may go for years without feeling the need for a sinking line.

6. How do you cast in the wind?

The combination of wind and fly fishing scares many people away, but with a few basic tips you can easily fish in winds up to about twenty miles per hour. Above that it does get pretty hairy. Here are some guidelines for casting on windy days:

- Keep your casts short. Spend more time getting close to fish. Fish are not as spooky on windy days so you can afford to creep right up on them.
- Cast side-armed instead of directly overhead. The wind is lighter closer to the water, and by casting at 90 degrees to the vertical you keep the fly and line farther away from your head.
- With a tailwind, put more energy into your back cast and aim it higher, and put less energy into your forward cast. With a headwind, reverse the process.
- If you have a crosswind, try to make sure the crosswind does not blow the fly across your body. Turn around and cast, or change positions.

Side-arm casting

- Shorten your leader and tippet and try to use flies that are less windresistant.
- On long casts with a light wind, I would rather cast into the wind that with it. I find that a wind behind me pushes my back cast below the tip of the rod and ruins my forward cast. I find it easier to let the wind help me on my back cast, and then I overpower the forward cast.

Turning your cast to the side on a windy day will give you better control of your line.

7. How do you increase the length of your casts?

Most fish of all types are caught at forty feet or less, but eventually you'll need to reach out and touch a distant spot, especially if you do any fishing in salt water. The first thing to remember is that excessive false casts, which are the normal response to a long cast, are counterproductive. The more your line is in the air, the greater the chance you'll eventually screw up. Take your time and slow down. Hold some loose line in reserve, either in big coils or in a stripping basket. Increase your false casts to about thirty-five or forty feet, which is where the rod really begins to flex and pick up energy. Make no more than three false casts. On the last one, release the excess line and aim your rod tip slightly higher than you would on a shorter cast, to help the extra line clear the guides on the rod.

Increasing your false casts to about forty feet and holding some line in reserve will help you make longer casts.

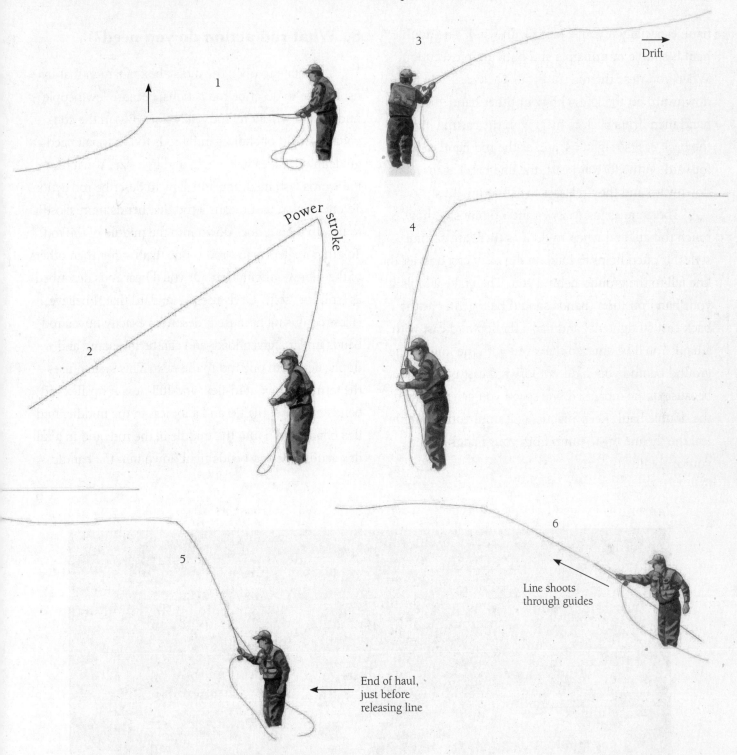

Remember that as you increase the length of line you cast, your timing will be a bit slower because it takes longer for the line to straighten behind you. Also, raise your arm up above your head and increase the length of your casting stroke. On a short cast, the rod should move mostly up and down. On a long cast, you should add length to your stroke by moving the rod back and forth in addition to up and down. Yes, you

will go beyond that sacred two o'clock position you learned from your uncle, but you need the longer casting stroke to move the longer line.

Most people can cast well up to fifty or sixty feet (depending on the rod and the caster) without adding a double haul to the mix. However, to increase your line speed (and the amount of line you can shoot on each cast) you'll eventually want to learn the double haul, especially if you're faced with wind. The double haul is simple in principle and difficult in execution. When you raise the rod into your back cast, you haul downward on the line with your other hand. The line hand then drifts back to meet with the casting hand as the back cast straightens, and as the rod hand moves forward on the forward cast, the line hand again hauls downward and then releases the shooting line.

There are as many styles and opinions on how much to haul and when to do it as there are casting styles. It often helps to haul on the back cast and let the line fall to the ground behind you. Then take a look at your hand position (hands should be together as the back cast straightens) and make the forward cast with a haul. You'll be amazed that even with the line on the ground behind you, a decent forward cast is possible because of the increased line speed you generate with the double haul. Keep practicing it until you suddenly feel the fly line try to jump from your hands—then you've got it.

8. What rod action do you need?

I hesitate to open the messy box of jargon that fly fishers use to describe rod actions, because few people understand what a fly rod really does. But in the convoluted world of choices in fly rods today, we all need guidelines besides just length and line size. You'll hear the words fast, medium, and slow to describe rod action. To one person, fast means a rod that bends more close to the tip than it does down into the middle of the rod. To other anglers, a fast rod is one that's stiffer than others of the same configuration. Or you'll hear rods described as "still" or "soft." Orvis uses a standard that, I believe, is less confusing because it describes exactly how a rod bends under a given load, and can be measured and duplicated from one rod to the next. This system uses the terms tip-flex, mid-flex, and full-flex. A tip-flex rod bends mostly at the tip and a lot less in the middle, mid-flex bends down into the middle of the rod, and in a full-flex action, the rod bends right down into the handle.

In a small mountain stream like this, a full-flex action will load the rod better on short casts.

Obviously there are degrees of each action, but putting rods in those broad terms is enough. So what do these terms tell you about what the rod will do for you? A tip-flex rod develops higher line speed and tighter casting loops, which means it is a rocket ship that will shoot a lot of line. It also has more reserve power for long casts, and most anglers feel this action has better accuracy on long casts. A full-flex rod is great for short casts and light tippets; because the rod bends so much it acts as a superb shock absorber. It's also more fun with small fish because the rod bends so easily. A mid-flex rod, naturally, is somewhere in between and is a great compromise between close-in accuracy and power for distance.

You might find you like one action type for all your rods. That's fine; one of the actions just might fit your personality and casting style. For instance, if you are a type-A person you might always want a tip-flex rod, and if it takes a life-threatening situation to get your pulse going, you might want a laid-back full-flex rod all the time. I prefer a tip-flex for saltwater fishing where I know I'll have a lot of wind and will be forced to make frequent long casts. For small-stream trout fishing I like a real full-flex action. For basic trout fishing I like a mid-flex. Fortunately, reliable fly shops will let you "try before you buy" so if you're not sure, you can experiment with different actions before you decide on the right one for you.

9. Why does your fly keep hitting your line?

Fly casters often get frustrated when the fly catches the rod, fly, or leader on its path, and this happens most often on the forward cast. The first thing to check is the wind—make sure you don't have a crosswind blowing the fly into your rod. With no wind to blame, the most common reason for this problem is a closed or "tailing" casting loop.

To understand what happens on a bad loop like this, you have to first see what happens on a good loop.

Examining your own casting loop is tough. You're not at a good angle to see what's happening. My advice is to watch a good caster in action, either live or on a video. You see that a good casting loop on the forward cast looks like the letter J turned on its side, or a candy cane. As the forward cast unrolls, the bottom of the loop gets longer and the top gets shorter. In a good cast, the top loop always stays above the bottom loop. A tailing loop happens when the top of the loop drops below the bottom, and the fly catches on the line.

Tailing loops can be tough to correct, and the only therapy is practice. Some casters respond better to knowing what their hand and arm are doing wrong, and others find it easier to correct problems just by thinking about the rod and line. A tailing loop is usually caused by the caster using too much wrist on the

Tailing loop fly hits radar line

A good tight loop

A nice loop like this one won't catch on itself.

forward cast, too soon. The weaker wrist muscles are better at giving the forward cast that final crisp snap, so when you make a forward cast, try to initiate the cast with your forearm and follow up with a wrist snap. If you find it easier to relate to what the rod and line are doing, remember that the tip of the rod has to get out of the way of the line quickly, and the best way to do this is to concentrate on pointing the rod straight out in front of you, at waist level, as quickly as possible.

10. Why does your line pile up on the water?

The flip answer to this question is, "You are doing something wrong on your cast," but, truly, almost anything you do wrong will give you puddles of line instead of a nice straight cast. However, two errors are the most likely suspects. First, examine a bad cast and determine if the line is piling right in front of the rod

tip, or if it's slamming on the water some distance out from your position.

Line piling right in front of you is almost always caused by a poor back cast and then not putting enough quick power into the forward cast. When you practice casting, turn around and watch your back cast *every time*. Not putting enough power into the back cast, or dropping the rod tip too far behind you, dumps the line below the tip of the rod so that it can never form a good casting loop on the forward cast. Once you are able to drive the line up and behind you so that the line at the end of the back cast is straight and parallel to the water, it's a simple matter to point the tip of the rod quickly in front of you. It's hard to make a bad forward cast with a great back cast.

Line slamming into the water, surprisingly, does not come from too much power on the forward cast. It comes from aiming the tip of the rod *at* the water rather than straight out over the water. If the tip of your rod

Great casters make full use of the rod's bend to develop casting energy.

never drops below a horizontal angle on the forward cast, you can put as much power as you want to in the cast—your line will never slam on the water.

11. Which direction should you move when fishing a stream?

Before you decide which direction to fish, you should have a basic strategy in mind. Will you be fishing primarily with a dry fly, nymph, wet fly, or streamer? Dry flies are best fished at an upstream angle to prevent drag, and because dry-fly fishing is usually practiced in shallow water where fish can see the sur-

face, working against the current keeps you behind the fish, in the blind spot in their rear quarters. Swing a wet fly or a streamer on a downstream angle, and by working slowly downstream, you can cover all the likely water by swinging the fly across the current, taking a few steps downstream, and repeating the process.

You can fish nymphs at almost any angle you can think of, depending on water conditions and the rig you're using. The most popular way to fish nymphs is across-stream, casting on a slight upstream angle, so when fishing them you can move either upstream or downstream. If the water is shallow it's a good idea to work upstream, as you would with a dry fly, so you can

This angler is swinging a wet fly downstream, making a few steps between each cast so he covers all the water.

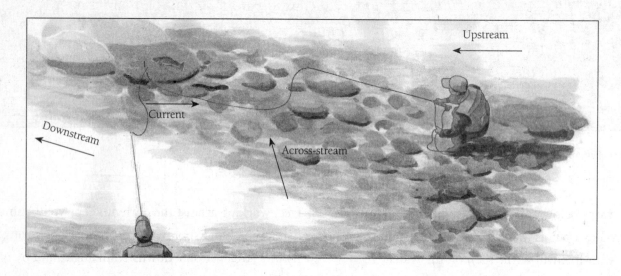

sneak up on the fish. If the water is swift and it's too much work to constantly fight the current, you may prefer to move slowly downstream.

12. How to land a fish without losing it

Most fish are lost at the strike or during the final moments of landing. The rest of the stuff in between might be exciting, but it's not where many fish are lost.

To be sure of landing a fish, the best approach is to have a buddy with a net, preferably the long-handled variety so your assistant doesn't have to get so close to the fish or swipe the water for the fish. In a current, get your buddy downstream of your position, and once the fish gets in close, move your rod tip off to the side and downstream while the net handler holds the net under water. As soon as the fish passes above the net, a quick upward sweep captures it with a minimum of fuss.

Swiping at a fish with a net is a quick path to a broken leader.

Without a friend with a net, assuming you have one yourself, try to lead the fish upstream of your position with the tip of the rod, reach out and place the net under water, and then let the fish drift back in the current and lift the net under the fish. If you find yourself without a net and connected to a very large fish (or a fish that won't fit into the puny net you're carrying), the best approach is to beach the fish. Scan the shore for a shallow beach where you can lead the fish until it gets into water so shallow that is has to turn on its side. Once it does, you can back up and slide it easily into shallower water where it can't move at all.

During a close-quarters battle, whether from a boat in deep water or in a current while wading, remember that a fish can only swim in the direction its head is pointing. It is not easy merely to crank in a big fish, and it requires a lot less force to just turn the fish's head. Keeping the rod high over your head and pointed directly at the fish gives the fish only one option—to swim away from you and down, and any time the fish gains distance from you the fight will be longer. Keeping your rod to one side or another leads the fish back and forth, but it has to swim on an angle toward you if you keep its head pointed in your direction.

The best way to land a big fish in fast water is to have someone hold the net underwater and lead the fish over the top of the net.

13. What is drag and how do you stop it?

The easiest way to describe drag is to demonstrate when it is absent. Throw a twig into moving water and watch how it floats—it moves at the mercy of each little micro-current on the surface, never cutting across currents of different speed. This is how an insect drifts. Few insects have the power to swim contrary to any amount of current, and the movements they do make are tiny hops and pirouettes, not enough to throw off a wake. A fly that creates a wake telegraphs a message to a feeding fish that the object in question is not food because it does not behave like the rest of the insects.

When attached to a leader, a fly can streak across currents when the leader or line is in a different current than the fly. This will happen, eventually, on every cast you make, and avoiding drag is merely ameliorating what must happen when something is attached to a floating object. Drag can be very overt, when you can see the wake from thirty feet away, or it can be minuscule, arising from tiny current threads and invisible to

an observer just a few feet from the fly. But trout can always see it.

The best way to avoid drag is to fish in uniform currents and cast straight upstream. If the line and leader float at exactly the same speed as the fly, drag won't develop until the fly is almost even with your rod tip. But fishing straight upstream is often not practical or even desirable, because on a long drift it puts your fly line right on top of the fish. So most times when fishing with a dry fly or nymph we cast at an angle that is somewhere between straight upstream and directly across the current. At this angle you'll often get a decent drag-free float for four or five feet. However, you'll often be faced with trout feeding in slow water along the far bank and fast water between you and the fish, so without some tricky moves you might get only an inch of drag-free float. Here are some of the tricks to use, either alone or in combination:

- Change positions. Often just moving a few feet will give you a longer drag-free float.
- Instead of fishing quartering upstream, fish quartering downstream. If you can, also make a quick mend upstream just before your line hits the water. This is called a reach cast, and that upstream arc in your line has to invert before the fly drags.
- Add an extra-long tippet to your leader. The tippet will land in loose coils, which will have to straighten before your fly begins to drag.
- Make a sloppy cast. By this I don't mean one that slams on the water, but an underpowered cast of controlled sloppiness that throws big piles of slack line on the water. You'll have to cast more line than you think you need because some of your line will be taken up in the loose piles on the water.

14. What is the best way to wade a fast river?

People drown every year while wading in rivers. Most of these accidents are preventable. The first

Slow current
or
Dead water

Fast current

Fly drags

The best way to fish a treacherous river like this is to shuffle your feet slowly, keep your profile sideways to the current, and never wade downstream when you don't know what's below you.

rule is to always wear a wader belt. Waders with air trapped inside them are quite buoyant (no, you won't float upside down and drown; Lee Wulff proved that eighty years ago by jumping off a bridge while wearing waders) and by keeping the belt tightly cinched around your waist, you'll hold a lot of air inside. Besides, in a moderate spill you'll only get wet from the waist up.

In addition, keep these tips in mind to avoid an accident:

- When crossing fast water, always angle upstream. You will be sure you can retrace your steps to safety, whereas if you wade downstream in fast current and find yourself pushed into a deep hole, you may not be able to retreat.
- The best places to cross are in riffles and the tails of pools, where the water is shallowest.
- Keep your profile sideways to the current to present less resistance to the water.
- Use a wading staff, which adds amazing security and balance to your wading. If you don't have one and need to cross some raging currents, find a hefty

stick to use as a temporary staff. It's like growing a third leg.

- Shuffle your feet along the bottom, making sure your forward foot has a secure spot before moving your other foot forward.
- Look for patches of sand and gravel, which typically show up as lighter spots on the bottom. They are much easier to negotiate than rounded boulders. (It goes without saying that you should wear polarized glasses so you can see below the surface better.)

15. Where should you hold your rod tip after casting?

A good cast requires a nice follow-through of the rod tip, with it ending up comfortably at waist level, parallel to the water. This is especially important when practicing, as there seems to be a natural tendency to then point the tip back up to about the ten o'clock position. I think this comes from those of us who learned to fish with a spinning rod before we learned fly casting. But this causes problems most times, as when the tip is up there swinging in the breeze it moves the line backward from where you just carefully placed it with your cast, and it leaves a big loop of line in front of you to be shoved around by the wind.

In all cases when fishing in still water, saltwater or fresh, your rod tip should move down to the surface of the water after casting. Here you have more control over your fly line, and in fact some bonefish guides recommend that you put the tip just under the surface of the water and keep it there when retrieving your fly. When fishing moving water, if you are swinging a fly downstream or making a long cast in uniform current, then again your rod tip should be held low. However, if you're fishing in places with lots of swirling currents, or

A low rod tip like this keeps your line under control, especially when fishing a streamer.

if the place your fly lands is in a different current lane than where you're standing, it makes sense to hold the rod higher—high enough to keep the different current between you and your fly isolated from the fly line.

16. Do you have to match a hatch to catch trout?

Unlike humans, trout do not like variety in their diets. Feeding exposes them to predators, and eating something novel that may or may not provide useful calories could be a waste of energy. So they eat what is safe, which means familiar or abundant prey. Of course they do experiment or they'd never find a new source of food, but if a recognizable morsel is available they'll invariably choose it.

So when a particular species of insect is hatching in great numbers, trout may pay attention only to something that is similar in size, shape, and color,

ignoring everything else. In that case you will do best trying to match the hatch. However, during the course of most days trout feed on a number of species of insects, crustaceans, and baitfish, and in that case they'll

There are times when your fly has to be close to the natural, as this Sparkle Dun is to the natural mayfly. But many times it's not as critical, especially when a number of different insects are on the water.

strike a wide variety of flies as long as the flies are within a range of what they've eaten recently. For example, several weeks after a killing frost has retired all the grasshoppers for the season, I've been able to tempt trout with a grasshopper imitation. From my experience I've found that trout keep the memory of a prey item as "safe" for about three weeks.

Sometimes there may be several insects hatching at the same time and trout may be picking off all of them. In that case, chances are if you fish a fly that looks at least close to one of the bugs you see on the water and your presentation is realistic, you'll do okay. So unless trout are feeding heavily and there appears to be only one insect present, you may not have to worry about matching the hatch.

17. Where to find trout around rocks

The natural place to look for trout around a big rock in the middle of a river is behind the rock, where the fish are protected from the brunt of the current. However, the force of the current also digs a trench in front of a midstream rock and along its sides, and a cushion of low-velocity water also builds up in front of a rock. Trout will lie in all of these places, so when fishing around big rocks it's important to make accurate casts behind a rock first, then a few casts to each side,

and finally in front of the rock. By starting downstream behind the rock first you'll avoid spooking trout in front of the rock with your fly line.

18. Getting started in nymph fishing

In most trout streams, nymph fishing is the most reliable way to catch trout. Surface feeding exposes trout to predators, so unless enough insects cover the surface to make this risk worthwhile, trout stay deeper in the water column and pluck food at their level. The best way to get started in nymph fishing is with a strike indicator, because not only will it let you see when fish take your fly, it will also give you an idea of where your fly is drifting, and whether your artificial is dragging across currents in an unnatural way.

Try to keep your initial nymph rig as simple as possible. Tie a weighted nymph or a beadhead pattern to the end of your tippet and then attach a strike indicator on the upper part of your leader. The indicator should be one and a half to two times the water depth up on your leader because the fly seldom hangs straight down, and you want your fly to be suspended a few feet off the bottom. Cast at an upstream angle and watch the indicator like a heron stalking fry in the shallows. If it hesitates, wiggles, or darts upstream, set the hook

Current

The Copper John is one of the most popular nymphs used, and features a wire body, brass head, peacock feathers for the thorax, and partridge feathers for the legs.

instantly—it's easy to miss unseen strikes to a nymph, so better safe than sorry.

Nymphs seldom drift as deep as you think, so if you don't hang up on the bottom on a dozen casts, you are probably not fishing deep enough. To get deeper, either move the strike indicator higher on your leader or add a couple split shot to the tippet about ten inches above the fly. Once you feel comfortable with a nymph rig, add a second fly by tying sixteen inches of tippet to the bend of the upper hook and adding a second fly to this piece. Two weighted flies often help you get deeper without adding shot to the tippet, and you can fish two different patterns to find out which one the trout prefer.

19. How do you know what insect the fish are taking?

Whenever you see trout rising, it's important to figure out what insects are *on* the water, not what bugs you see flying. Often, one type of insect is hatching while another variety is migrating upstream, and the ones most visible to you may not be on the water at all. This is particularly common with caddisflies, because these moth-like aquatic insects, while very important to trout, live for weeks after they hatch and migrate upstream in clouds that sometimes obscure the far bank. If you see caddisflies in the air, moving purposefully upstream in a straight line, chances are they're migrating. If you see them flying in a slow, erratic pattern, or if you see them bouncing on the water's surface, they are more likely to be hatching or returning to the water to lay eggs, and thus available to the trout.

Often you'll find a large insect hatching along with smaller, more abundant ones. It's natural to pay more attention to the bigger fly (and perhaps also wishful thinking because big flies are easier to see), but if the smaller flies are more abundant, the trout may be eating them and ignoring the big juicy ones. It doesn't make

You can tell a lot about what a trout is eating by the way it rises. This brown trout (can you spot it just to the left of the rise?) is probably taking something very small or an emerging insect in the surface film because the rise is very subtle.

sense to us, but when trout zero in on one insect they may ignore all others, despite how good the big ones look.

Try to watch a fish rising to see what it takes. This is not as easy as it sounds, but if you can find a fish that is rising steadily, focus in on that spot until you can figure out what the fish are taking. Some anglers carry a pair of pocket-sized binoculars just for this purpose. If you see a fish rising to what appear to be invisible insects, there are three possibilities:

1. The fish is eating tiny, dark insects that are too small to see from your vantage point. Try a small, dark fly.

2. The fish is eating insects that ride low in the surface film. These could be spent mayfly spinners, egg-laying caddisflies, ants, or beetles. If it's evening, try a size 16 Rusty Spinner (this fly imitates a ton of mayfly spinners and is a good bet anywhere in the country). If it's during the day, try a size 18 ant or size 14 beetle.

3. The fish is eating emerging insects just under the surface. If you don't see any bubbles along with the rise form, this is often the case. Fish an emerger, or don't false cast your dry fly so it drifts just under the surface.

20. How much do you need to learn about insects?

The thought of learning entomology scares many would-be fly fishers as it dredges up memories of high-school science class. Is it helpful to learn a little basic aquatic entomology? Absolutely, because different groups of aquatic insects have different life histories and different behavior, and knowing, for instance, that most stoneflies crawl to the shallows to hatch and don't ride the current when hatching might save you from need-

may flies — adults, larva or nymph

caddis flies — adults, pupa

midges — adults, midge pupa

stone flies — adults, larva or nymph

lessly fishing a stonefly dry fly, even if you see a lot of them in the air.

As you learn about these insects, you naturally learn more about their life history, and when you understand the behavior of trout *prey* as well as trout, you'll develop a canny instinct for predicting what the fish will do next. My advice is to learn at least to identify the four most important orders of insects and then learn a little about their life histories. These four orders are mayflies, caddisflies, stoneflies, and midges. Learning to identify the adults in the air and the larvae when you turn over rocks in a river is not hard and may even add to your enjoyment and appreciation of all aquatic life.

- Mayflies fly slowly after they hatch and look like sailboats on the water and tiny butterflies in the air. The nymphs have threadlike gills along the abdomen.
- Caddisflies skip and bounce on the water when hatching and look like moths in the air. Most caddis larvae build cases of stones and sticks, although some common species don't build cases. These "free-living" larvae usually look like green or tan grubs. All caddisflies have a brief pupa stage between the larva and adult stages that is not often seen but is very important to trout.
- Stoneflies are clumsy fliers in the air, and two pairs of wings are visible as they fly. The nymphs are flat with thick legs and tails, and crawl onto rocks along the shore to hatch.
- Midges are tiny insects with only one pair of wings and look like gnats in the air and on the water. The larvae look like tiny worms and are often bright red or green. Like caddisflies, they have a brief pupa stage and the pupae are typically dark brown or black and very appealing to trout.

21. How to decide what nymph to use

It's pretty easy to figure out what fly to use when fish are rising because you often observe what insect the

If a little olive mayfly nymph is the most common one you see when sampling the stream bed, choose your imitation accordingly.

fish are eating. However, if you suspect trout are feeding underwater on nymphs, the clues aren't so obvious. One of the first things to do is to turn over some rocks to see what kind of aquatic insects are present. The best rocks to check are flat ones in riffled water because these are more hospitable for larvae. Many nymphs migrate to the shallows before hatching, so check the rocks closest to shore. Better yet, carry a small aquarium net and stir up a small bit of gravel and stones with your feet, holding the net just downstream to pick up the animals that get dislodged. The reason this is better than just turning over rocks is that some insects bury themselves in the gravel or silt and don't live on the underside of rocks, and seining in this way may turn up crustaceans like crayfish or baitfish like sculpins.

Now it's a simple matter to poke through your fly box for a fly that is about the same size and color as one of the critters you've dislodged. The most abundant one is your best bet, even if it isn't the biggest, juiciest one you see. If that doesn't work, try an imitation of the next most abundant creature.

If all else fails, just try some of the most popular artificial nymphs until you find one that works. Over the years, flies get popular because they work well in trout waters throughout the world, as the insects from a trout stream in New Zealand are not that different from the bugs in a California mountain stream. You can't go wrong with a size 14 Beadhead Hare's Ear, a size 12 Prince Nymph, or a size 18 Pheasant Tail Nymph. One of those will work most days in any trout stream in the world.

22. Reading currents to find trout

Behavioral studies of trout have shown that they prefer current speeds of about ten to twelve inches per second, which is about the speed of a slow walk. Try pacing it out with your foot. However, while they like to lie in water of this speed, they also like to be on the edge of a faster current, because the faster the current, the quicker food is brought to them. Thus the best place to find trout is where fast currents meet slower water, known as a seam. You can see these obvious breaks on the edges of fast surface currents, but there are also hidden seams below the surface.

Hidden seams are found on stream bottoms with rough texture, because each rock on the bottom makes turbulence and slows the downstream progress of currents. Thus, a piece of water studded with large boulders will hold more trout than one with a smooth sand or

This angler is fishing to the other side of a distinct seam where fast water meets slower current.

gravel bottom. The friction of water running along a bank creates a seam as well, and here, too, a bank with a rough or uneven shoreline will hold more trout than a smooth bank where the current runs swift and unbroken.

Changes in depth also create hidden seams. Any place deep water meets shallow will be likely to hold feeding trout, as long as the shallow side is at least eight inches deep. Trout will feed in surprisingly shallow water if not disturbed, and if threatened they can quickly dart back into the depths to hide.

23. Setting the hook on trout

The hooks used in most trout flies are small and very sharp. Trout jaws are almost the perfect medium for sinking a hook, and if you have trouble setting the hook, the problem could be your reflexes—but it could also be the fish. Trout quickly detect the fraud in our flies, and unlike when caught with bait, they eject a fly in a flash. If you don't set the hook the moment a trout takes your fly, you'll miss the opportunity. They won't wait around gumming your fly until you get your act together. Striking to a trout is simple—just raise your rod tip enough to take all of the slack out of your line and tighten the line until you feel resistance—no more, or you can risk breaking the tippet.

Setting the hook on trout is a matter of just lifting the tip of the rod enough to tighten the line.

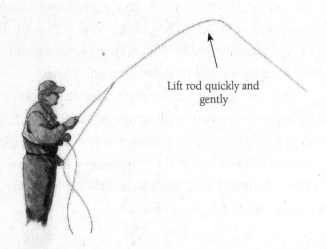

Lift rod quickly and gently

If you keep missing fish and are sure you're striking quickly enough, it may be the trout and not you. A trout that moves to a dry fly but changes its mind at the last minute because it doesn't like the fly or sees it suddenly begin to drag still has forward momentum and can't put on the brakes quickly enough. What happens is that the trout splashes at your fly with its mouth closed. We call this a refusal, and it means you were close but not close enough. Change your casting angle to avoid drag or try a fly one size smaller if you think you are getting refusals.

Trout also chase streamers, and sometimes seem only to want to move that obnoxious, gaudy thing out

of their territory. They sometimes just bump the fly or even throw a cross-body block at it without connecting. Try fishing the same fly slower or faster, which seems to be more productive than changing flies.

24. What is a mend and when should you do it?

In most dry fly and nymph fishing, the best presentation is a dead drift, which means the fly moves at exactly the same speed as the current, no slower and no faster. When swinging a wet fly in the current for steelhead, salmon, or trout, the best presentation is usually obtained by having the fly line in a straight line as it swings in the current. And when fishing a sinking-tip fly line, it's important to keep the floating portion of your line from pulling on the weighted part because the floater will draw the sinking part back to the surface. Forty feet of fly line cast across several different currents never behaves the way you want it to, and this is where mends come in handy.

Making a mend is easier than deciding when and where to use one. If you make a cast straight across a uniform current, you'll see that the line in the middle

Current causes fly to drag

Throw an upstream mend to stop drag

Current

of the cast begins to move downstream faster than the line that is held close to the rod tip, and faster than the fly and leader, which are slowed down by resistance to the water. As a result, as the line swings round, the fly begins to accelerate like the end of a whip. A little acceleration at the end of a swing is sometimes desirable, but left unattended it's too abrupt to appeal to most fish. By reaching out with the rod and making a quick flip upstream, you can straighten the fly line, or actually move the arc upstream in a mirror image of itself, depending on how much you want the swing to slow down or how deep you want your sinking-tip fly line to descend.

There may be times when you want a downstream mend, especially when your fly lands in fast water and the current between you and the fly is slower. In this case you mend in the opposite, downstream direction. Mends can be done with a stiff arm, a quick flip of the wrist, or a combination of the two. The more line you have to mend, the longer your rod should reach and the higher you'll have to reach with the rod. It doesn't matter how you do it as long as you move the line without moving the fly.

25. Where will you find trout in a lake?

When faced with a flat expanse of water with no current, even experienced fly fishers panic. Lakes are not as easy to read as rivers, trout can be anywhere because there are no currents to keep them pinioned to one spot, and in lakes you have both geography and depth to worry about. Local knowledge is best, but there are a few tips that can help you narrow down the possibilities.

- Scan the lake surface with binoculars for rising fish early in the morning or right before dark. Chances are any trout that are hungry will come to the surface then looking for hatching insects.
- Inlets and outlets are always hotspots in lakes. Trout spawn in moving water in spring and fall, and inlets bring in hatches of insects.
- In the cold water of early and late season, look for trout in shallows where the water is warmer than the depths.
- Springs coming into a lake will attract trout in both cold and warm water, as springs are warmer than

Inlets and outlets are always hotspots in lakes.

lake water in the early spring and colder during the summer. If springs aren't obvious, put a thermometer on a long string and take temperatures close to the bottom at various places.

- Submerged weed beds hold more insect life than sand or rock bottoms, so look for trout close to aquatic vegetation.

E. 229 Trout Tactics

LAMAR UNDERWOOD

1. The Biggest Key to Fly-Fishing Success

"Too many anglers spend too much time worrying about fly pattern and not enough thinking about presentation."

—Ted Trueblood,
"Fish and Fishing" Department,
Field & Stream, May, 1947

2. *Field & Stream's* Trout "Ultimate Lure" Survey Winners

In what it called the "Ultimate Lure Survey," published in March 2008, *Field & Stream* magazine asked 1,000 of its hard-core readers to name their favorite lures. The winners for the Trout category were:

In-Line Spinners, 65%, Mepps Aglia

Spoons, 15%, Little Cleo

Jigs, 9%, Marabou Jig

Soft-Plastics, 6%, Berkley Gulp! Worm

Plugs, 4%, Original Rapala

3. Learning from the Great Blue Heron

Beautiful to look at, the great blue heron is universally disliked by trout anglers who see the bird as a poacher on their favorite fish—especially after they have seen ugly holes in the backs of trout. Stop to consider the heron's fishing tactics, however, and you might see your own catches improve dramatically. Regard the heron as it lands in a likely spot, wades into position, then stands rock-still as the minutes go by—minute after minute, patiently waiting, for as long as it takes. Emulate this strategy on water holding trout that are either feeding or lying in the current. As you try to approach the trout and get into good casting position, they will spook. The trick is to get into position and, just like the heron, get your fly ready in your hand, get enough line out to cast, keeping it and your rod tip low and away from the fish, and wait . . . and wait . . . and wait. Sooner or later the fish will go back to feeding or lying in the current where they were before. Bingo.

4. Fastest Fly-Fishing Course Ever

In a Web site centered around fishing Pennsylvania's legendary spring creeks, such as the Letort, www.limestoner.com writer Gene Macri comes up with what he titles, "How to Get 10 Years Fly Fishing Experience Immediately." Macri's system is based on studying the surface of your favorite spring creek with binoculars. You will see the bugs, what they're doing and not doing, and the trout, what they're doing and not doing, in a way you've never imagined.

5. Meeting the Late Summer Challenge

"The big hatches are over, trout are well-fed and spooky. What's going to bring them to the surface? The answer may surprise you. . . . Anglers bombard the water with hoppers when another insect is far more important. That insect is the beetle. Scientific studies reveal that terrestrial beetles are three to seven times more common in trout diets than grasshoppers . . . most anglers don't imitate them, so trout haven't seen a plethora of fake beetles."

—Jeff Morgan, in the article "Meeting the Late Summer Challenge," www.westfly.com. Get Morgan's new book *The Oddballs: Productive Trout Flies for Unorthodox Prey,* Amato Publications, 2010, at www.amazon.com. Also check out his previous book, *Small-Stream Fly Fishing,* Amato Publications, 2005.

6. Need More Convincing? It's Beetles for Trout

"I became a beetle addict after seeing how well they work on highly pressured summer trout water such as the Henry's Fork, the Yellowstone region, the Green River, and the many streams in the Missoula area. No other patterns brought the consistent success and confident rises that beetle imitations elicited."

—Jeff Morgan, in the article "Meeting the Late Summer Challenge," www.westfly.com. Get Morgan's new book *The Oddballs: Productive Trout Flies for Unorthodox Prey,* at www.amazon.com. Also check out his previous book, *Small-Stream Fly Fishing.*

7. How Expert Jeff Morgan Searches New Water for Trout

"Most anglers have little confidence in a pair of Size 20 nymphs in a 200-foot-wide trout stream. To overcome this reluctance, use tiny nymphs behind something a little meatier, such as a Pupatator. [The Pupatator is Jeff Morgan's buggy-looking nymph creation.] My standard 'starting' rig on new waters is a Size 8 Pupatator, a Size 16 rusty or olive beadhead Hares Ear, and a Size 20 Blue-Winged Olive nymph, Brassie, or scud. This allows me to cover an array of foods in a spectrum of colors and sizes. Once one fly outshines the others, I can then retool my approach with whatever the trout are keying on."

—Jeff Morgan, in one of the regular articles he writes for www.westfly.com

8. Where Trout Are Always Hungry

Small streams that flow into some of the best wilderness streams don't have the amounts of food and insect life of the large rivers. The water is swift, and the trout will quickly grab prey floating into view. Some

In fast water, even big trout will grab prey that comes floating by.   © Stu Apte 2010

anglers mistakenly think these trout are stupid, but they're not. They're just hungry. Use floating flies like Royal Coachmen, Stimulators, and Humpies.

9. Make Your Dropper Fly Expendable

When tying a dropper leader to a dry fly or strike indicator, make the dropper in a lighter strength than your main leader. When you hit a snag, you're better off losing the dropper fly instead of your whole rig.

10. Dropper Fly Length for Dry Flies

When it's to be tied to a dry fly, most experts and top guides prefer dropper leaders in the 18-inch range. Much shorter, and you'll be fishing too shallow. Much longer, and you might as well be using a strike indicator instead of a dry fly.

11. Long Live the Long Rod

It's easy—and somewhat fashionable—to fall under the spell of trout anglers who preach the gospel of using the shortest rod possible. They point to its ease of casting under trees and brush, and to the sense of feel you get from a fighting fish. Long rod disciples are out there, however, arguing that short rods leave too much line on the water, more than you can handle with ease. One of the best of the Long Rod contingent was Leonard Wright, superb angler and writer, who once did an article in *Sports Afield* called, "Long Live the Long Rod." (February 1974). In it, Wright said, "The most overrated piece of fishing equipment in America today is the short fly rod."

12. Tying on the Dropper Leader

Most trout guides tie the dropper leader to the bend of the dry fly hook. Some tie it directly to the eye of the dry fly hook. My personal choice is to use the bend.

13. The Dry Fly as a Striker Indicator

Whether your dry fly is one to search the water, or one to match a specific hatch, make sure it's large enough, and buoyant enough, to give your dropper leader and nymph a good floating platform, visible throughout its drift. If your dry fly is too small, or your nymph too large and heavy, you'll defeat your entire purpose.

14. Ted Trueblood's Dyed-Leader Experiment

Back in September 1951, Ted Trueblood wrote a remarkable, ground-breaking article for *Sports Afield*. In the story, called "A New Theory of Flies and Leaders," Trueblood described dyeing his leaders in the kitchen sink to imitate string moss, which did not seem to spook trout in his rivers. He experimented with green and brown dye with pinches of blue. A few days later he went to Silver Creek. He caught and released 21 trout on 2X. He went on with his experiments and found that, "In most waters I found I could hook fish on tippets a full size larger, and occasionally two sizes larger, than before." In the article, which has been reprinted in the book *Sports Afield Treasury of Trout Fishing*, The Lyons Press (1989), Trueblood also has some startling observations on flies trout take. "Except during the spawning season, all activity of trout is governed by two overwhelming stimuli: fear and hunger. They are hungry most of the time, the severe cold season excepted." Trueblood maintained that trout will take almost any fly, as long as it looks like something to eat and they aren't frightened by the leader.

15. The Spell of the Mayfly

"Mayfly adults provide a lesson in life. In no other insect is the adult stage so brief and with such singular purpose. We must appreciate its qualities as we might a sunset, for too quickly will it be gone. And we must appreciate, also, that a whole sport has grown up around it."

—Jay Cassell, "Mayfly Artistry,"
Sports Afield, May 1982

16. Blue Ribbon Flies

Every year when I'm in the deep clutches of winter, I enjoy receiving the catalog from Craig Mathews

Blue Ribbon Flies out in West Yellowstone, Montana (www.blueribbonflies.com.) They always come up with some new flies that snag my attention, and I particularly enjoy reading Mathews' rundown of his experiences in the previous season. Mathews and his associate, John Juracek, have some great books and DVDs, along with detailed maps for fishing the Yellowstone area.

17. Where Are the Hatches?

Among the lessons about trout fishing that have cost me considerable gobs of both time and money, one of the most important has been the realization that even on those rare days when hatches occur, they do not happen everywhere. Don't expect the entire surface of the river to burst with emerging caddis and mayflies. Hatches occur—*when* they occur—in scattered sections of the river, in varying water types. A riffle, a smooth glide, a deep pool—all might harbor hatches at different and varying times. You might have great fishing in hatches at one small section of the river at dusk, then meet your buddy at the truck later and learn that he saw nothing—no rises. Big rivers or small streams, that's the way it goes.

18. Upstream with Dries, Downstream Nymphs and Streamers

Stu Apte loves trout fishing almost as much as he does fishing for tarpon and bonefish. His favorite strategy is to fish part of a big river or small stream upstream with dry flies, then take a break and rig for nymphs and streamers and fish back downstream. This system can be particularly effective when you're fishing dries early in the morning, then switching to nymphs and heading back downstream as the sun gets overhead.

19. Big Sky Fishing Web site

The name rings with promise—Big Sky Fishing. And the Web site, www.bigskyfishing.com, delivers with superb information and coverage of high-country rivers and lakes.

20. Fish the Skwala Hatch for Openers

You would think that my years in magazine editing, particularly those at *Sports Afield* and *Outdoor Life*, would have seen me working with writers on the Skwala hatch out in the high country, but I missed it. Many top guides and anglers have not been missing out, however, and on rivers like Montana's Bitterroot this hatch of stoneflies in March (lasting into April) signals the beginning of some serious trout angling. The hatches are sparse and localized, but the action is good in pockets when you find them. This is cold weather fishing, of course, so wear gloves, base layers, the works. Check outfitters and guides all over the high West to learn how you might cash in and kick off your season. Flies include Olive Stimulators and Skwala Stones and custom patterns like the Designated Hitter Skwala Stone from The Fly Shop, www.theflyshop.com.

21. Visiting The Fly Shop

Located in Redding, California, The Fly Shop is one of angling's premier spots to find everything you need, from flies to great destinations. Their catalog is second to none, and their Web site, www.theflyshop.com, has it all. I particularly like their flies—always some interesting new patterns there.

22. Trout Pellet Fly—The Real Thing

You may risk being scorned, laughed at, even cursed at, but at times you might be so fed up with your lousy luck fly fishing for trout that you feel like nuking them. That's when you long for a fly imitating trout food pellets. Now you can buy one—at The Fly Shop, www.theflyshop.com. Their Pellet Fly is listed under Stoneflies and Attractors, Size 10, $1.75 at this writing.

23. Trout Pellet Fly—The Reasonable Facsimile

A fly that you use all the time can actually be a pretty good imitation of a trout pellet. It's the Muddler Minnow, which, in its small sizes, has a predominate, bulbous head that looks very pellet-like. Whether you're thinking "Trout Pellet" or not, the Muddler in small sizes is a terrific fly to fish, dry or sinking.

24. How to Spot Nymph Takes

"The fish in the tail shallows were nymphing, and they hovered just under the surface, drifting forward restlessly in the current when they took something in the flow. Their mouths would open lazily, expelling water past their gills, and flashing white each time they intercepted a hatching nymph."

—Ernest Schwiebert, "The Mill at Longparish" in *Death of a Riverkeeper*, Dutton, 1980

25. Small Stream, Small Backpack, Big Day

Do everything you possibly can to find a small trout stream tucked away among the hills and mountains—the Appalachians, the Rocky Mountain high country, the New England ranges, the midwest forests, the northwest peaks. Once you find a stream that's just right, lots of clean water and trout (most of them won't be big, but so what?), completely isolated, enjoy it to the hilt as often as you can by strapping on a small backpack that has everything you need for a full day's fishing, pick up your light rod, and go. If you've never done this, I hope you give it a try. Someday you'll thank me!

26. Fish Streamers in Small Streams

Writer, fly tier and creator, and expert angler Jeff Morgan says in his book *Small-Stream Fly Fishing*,

Small streams can give up some surprisingly big trout.

Frank Amato Publications (2005), that his favorite technique for fishing streamers in small streams is "sinfully easy." He crimps a split-shot near the eye of his fly and uses a floating line with 8 feet of 4X tippet. The fly is fished straight downstream. For other Jeff Morgan tips, see his archived articles at the WestFly Internet site, www.westfly.com, and see his newest book, *Productive Trout Flies for Unorthodox Prey: The Oddballs,* Frank Amato Publications (2009). See Amazon for listings of Jeff's other books.

27. Traver Award Story Collection

Those who share my interest in great writing will be applauding *Fly Rod & Reel* magazine's first collection of stories that have been recognized over the years in the Robert Traver Award competition. Published by Fly Rod & Reel Books in 2009, the softcover book called *In Hemingway's Meadow* includes eighteen original tales of fly fishing. Since 1994, the award has gone to stories and essays in honor of the late John Voelker, who used the pen name Robert Traver on such trout classics as *Trout Madness,* St. Martin's Press (1960), and the best-selling novel *Anatomy of a Murder,* St. Martin's Press (1958). The title of this collection references the "meadow" where Hemingway's "Nick" camped in his immortal story, "Big Two-Hearted River," and is from the award-winning story by Jeff Day. The book was edited by Joe Healy. You can find it at places like the fly-fishing site, The Book Mailer, www.thebookmailer.com, Barnes & Noble, and Amazon, or by going to www.flyrodreel.com.

28. Strike Indicator Flotation Help

You help your dry flies float with a little flotation spray or powder, so remember to do the same to flotation devices like strike indicators.

29. Fishing Small Streams Behind Other Anglers

It's frustrating, but there it is: Another angler is ahead of you on the stream. Unless you're going to leap frog far ahead of him (not just the next pool), you're better off doing two things: 1) Rest the water for a few minutes, if you can; and 2) Use different tactics than the angler ahead of you, provided you can see what he's doing. If he's fishing a dry fly, go to nymphs and streamers. If he's ripping streamers through the pools, try a dry fly with a nymph dropper.

30. Small Streams and Sink-Tip Lines

Handling awkward sink-tip and full-sink lines on small streams is unnecessary. Use tiny split-shot or beaded sinking flies to get down when you have to.

31. What's That on Your Dropper?

In his outstanding book *Small-Stream Fly Fishing,* Frank Amato Publications (2005), Jeff Morgan questions the wisdom of putting certain flies on your dropper attached to a dry fly. Since your attached nymph will be riding 18 to 24 inches (the preferred length of the dropper leader) below the surface—not on the bottom—the nymph being used should represent a fly found in mid-currents, not on the bottom. The flies Jeff says he avoids for using on the dropper—because they're bottom-dwellers—are "stonefly nymphs, caddis larvae, midge larvae, sowbugs, fish eggs, aquatic worms, crane fly larvae, and most scuds."

32. Give Small-Stream Trout Your Best Shot

Fish small trout streams slowly and carefully in an upstream direction. Keep your casts short, popping

your fly into tiny pockets. Short, accurate casts are everything.

33. Finding and Fishing the Seams

Seams are places in the river current where a slight change-of-pace in the flow occurs between fast water and slow water. Imagine a rock in the stream. Think of the water rushing past on both sides as the fast lanes. The slow or still water behind the rock and directly in front are the slow lanes. Between the fast and slow lanes will be seams of intermediate flow, perfect for trout to ambush prey.

New York – Pennsylvania fishing guide Gary Edwards took this big brown that hit an ant pattern in the middle of a sulphur hatch.

© Jay Cassell

34. Don't Miss the Trout Bum

His book of essays called *Trout Bum* started the John Gierach surge in angling reading popularity some years ago (the book has been republished several times since), and by now the surge has turned into a tsunami of books, all of which should be on your list for reading pleasure. Gierach not only takes you fishing with him in his home Colorado waters, but everywhere else where the fishing is interesting, even when it's not always good. Gierach is the "everyman" trout writer, with engaging prose that makes you feel like you've met a friend for life. His books are everywhere, and likely some are in your local library.

35. On Sinking Lines: Drop Down One Size

Maine outdoorsman, writer, and painter Tom Hennessey gave me a tip on buying a full-sinking fly line—not a sinking tip or high density sinking, just a regular sinking line. Tom said he's had better luck with sinking lines by dropping down in size one weight. For example, if your rod's an 8, he'll buy a 7 sinking line. It will cast much, much better, says Tom.

36. Are the New Fluorocarbon Leaders Worth It?

The fluorocarbon leaders cost a lot more than the traditional nylon. Are they worth the extra dough? You get greater strength, far less visibility. They're perfect for the conditions when stealth counts for everything in your trout fishing—low, clear water and super-wary fish. There are a lot of anglers sneaking up on trout with fluorocarbon leaders these days.

37. Spring Creeks: Superb Trout Destinations

Flowing up clean and cold from aquifers and chalk beds inside Mother Earth, twenty-four hours a day, seven days a week, 365 days a year, spring creeks are worth every hour and every cent trout addicts spend to find and fish them. Here are trout you can *see*, prolific insect hatches, and easier wading than the rough-and-tumble freestone streams. They are tough to fish, but . . . so what? You can find plenty of them in Pennsylvania, scattered throughout the upper Midwest and far West, and in England the chalk streams are angling destinations to die for.

38. Why Spring Creeks Are Tough

Running smooth and clear with no breaks or riffles to cover the sound of your wading or awkward casts, spring creeks are a challenge for any angler, especially the novice. They're fun, yes, but challenging. Veteran angler and writer Ted Leeson describes the situation in his wonderful book, *Jerusalem Creek,* The Lyons Press (2002): "Nothing about a spring creek hides your presence or want of skill, or a faulty presentation or the inadequacies of tackle or miscalculations of method."

39. When You Can't Match the Hatch

One of the most frustrating experiences in trout fishing is to find yourself in the midst of a big hatch of insects, with trout taking them eagerly, and you just can't seem to get the right fly onto them. This happens all the time with hatches like the tiny Tricos. Instead of letting frustration overwhelm you, try putting on a fly that totally changes the pace of what's going on. Use a No. 16 Royal Wulff or Fan-Winged Royal Coachman, for instance, or a buggy terrestrial imitation. And there's always room for the Adams, the go-to fly when nothing else is working. The Stimulator ranks high with go-to flies also.

40. When Spring Creek Trout Turn On

"Spring creek trout have a reputation for being moody, which often means they are difficult, but when

The farther you get from a road, the better the fishing is going to be.

they're in the mood to feast, almost nothing—not sloppy wading, not poor casting, not a ridiculous choice of flies—will dissuade them."

—Ted Leeson, *Jerusalem Creek,*
The Lyons Press, 2002

41. The Tuck Cast Takes More Trout

"I am nymphing a favorite run of broken water, using a weighted Perla Stonefly Nymph with a split-shot crimped to the leader 6 inches up to get it down quickly in the fast water. I use a tuck cast to further enhance the nymph's entry to the water. A cast developed by George Harvey and made famous by his friend, another local fishing fishing legend, Joe Humphrey."

—Chuck Robbins, writer and guide, in his Pennsylvania fishing days recalled in his first book, *Odyssey at Limestone Creek,* Tussey Mountain Publisher (1997). Chuck now guides and writes in Montana. See www. chuckngalerobbins.com

42. When Rain Is Your Friend

No one especially likes fishing in the rain—and thunderstorms are downright dangerous—but there are times when rain comes in just the right amounts at the right time to get trout moving and feeding. The rain washes all kinds of terrestrials and morsels into the stream, and the trout go after them with vigor. The only way you'll find out if it's a "good rain" or "bad rain" is to be out there. Chances are you'll have the stream to yourself. And, whatever you do, don't miss the spots where other streams or runs pour into the main river.

43. Fishing the Back Door to Yellowstone

The town of West Yellowstone—home of guides and tackleshops and the main entrance to Yellowstone National Park and its angling treasures—is not the only game in town. On the other side of Yellowstone, to the east, lies Cody, Wyoming, on the Shoshone River and entryway to the Shoshone National Forest and the eastern side of Yellowstone. Cody has the Buffalo Bill Museum and is home to Tim Wade's North Fork Anglers, headquarters for fishing the Shoshone rivers and the park. Their site is www.northforkanglers.com. They have everything you need to crack into the Yellowstone region's backside.

44. Where the Road Leaves the River

Some fishing tips seem so simple—like sharpening your hooks—that most people probably ignore them. A simple one that I hope you will not ignore is this: Fish where the road leaves the river. Walk to where the crowds don't go, and you will be rewarded with better trout fishing. Most people will not walk there. They just won't do it. At a health club I sometimes go to for workouts, I watch in fascination as people maneuver and jostle their cars into parking positions close to the front door. All that so they don't have to walk a couple hundred feet across a big parking lot. Walking . . . to do the very thing they came to the club for, getting exercise. It makes no sense. Neither does not walking into the woods to fish where you can't see the road. But that's what people do.

45. Sulphurs: The Year's Best Fly Hatch

In the West they have the glorious Pale Morning Dun hatches that fill the air with greenish-yellow bugs. In the East and upper Midwest, the highlight of the springtime hatches sees the arrival of a similar mayfly—the Sulphurs, most in the genus *Ephemerella* in various sizes with other Latin subtitles for those who take their fishing and fly-tying with textbook correctness. Where I fish, mostly in Pennsylvania and New Jersey, the hatches begin in mid-May, a week or so after the storied Hendricksons have played out. The party goes on until late in June, with the fishing getting tougher as it progresses.

46. Making the Most of the Sulphur Hatches

The Sulphur hatches bring out anglers by the droves on eastern and mid-western trout streams. Try to catch the earliest Sulphur hatches you can to beat the crowds. Look for cloudy and rainy days to be the best for Sulphurs. As the hatch goes on, look for the best action to occur from late afternoon into the evening, almost dark.

47. When the Sulphurs Have Competition

Sulphurs aren't the only mayflies you'll see in late May. They come at the same time that Green Drakes, Brown Drakes, and Gray Drakes can be on the water. A friend returning from Spruce Creek in Pennsylvania, where he had gone to fish the famous Green Drake hatch, told me he did not do well until he figured out that the trout were rising to the Sulphurs, not the few Green Drakes showing.

48. The High-Country's Forgotten Early Season Fishing

"Most destination anglers don't travel to the West during the off-season . . . I have recurrent dreams about the spring Baetis (Blue-Winged Olive) hatches along the upper Bighorn near Thermopolis, Wyoming, and the innocent, chubby rainbows and browns that rise freely to them. The pods of 18-inch trout that begin their first surface-feeding frenzies on the Missouri, alone and unmolested by boats and anglers, beckon. The newly restored Madison River with its reliable pre-runoff flows and its superb wading flats and reliable hatches are high on my list of destinations, as is the lower Henry's Fork around Ashton and other streams nearby. I have never hit a Mother's Day hatch on the Yellowstone, or a giant stonefly or *Skwala* hatch either.

But they are on my list of sparkling experiences that lie ahead."

—John Randolph, Editor, *Fly Fisherman Magazine,* in the article "Spring Hatches," in May 2004.

49. My Big Sulphur Hatch Mistake

I once wrote a story for *Sports Afield* called "Mid-Stream Crisis." It's about, among other things, being slap in the middle of a great Sulphur hatch coming off just at dusk. A big fish broke me off. I had no reading glasses, no penlight or even flashlight, and I simply could not see well enough to tie on another fly. How can you call yourself an experienced angler and be so unprepared? Fish were rising and taking all about me as I sloshed out of the stream, excited, but sad in defeat.

50. Fly Line Colors: They Do Matter

"When Brian Clarke and I were engaged in writing *The Trout and the Fly,* we carried out many experiments with underwater cameras on fly lines . . . This proved, at least to us, that dull colors such as green or brown were far less fish scaring . . ."

—John Goddard, *John Goddard's Trout-Fishing Techniques,* Lyons and Burford, 1996

51. The Secret of Timing Trout Feeding Activity

In his wonderful book *The Ways of Trout,* The Lyons Press (1985), the noted angler and author Leonard M. Wright, Jr., culminated years of research by nailing down the period when you can expect maximum trout feeding activity. The secret: the time when the water temperature is rising faster toward the optimum of 63 degrees. At 63 degrees, feeding activity slows, the blitz is over. Reveals Wright, "Fish feed best when the

temperature gradient toward the optimum is steepest." Wright found the reverse to also be true, fishing rising when the temperature is dropping back toward 63 after being much higher for hours.

52. Falling Barometer: Look Out Below

" . . . I have never recorded an 'active,' much less an 'aggressive,' rating for lights feeding during a low or falling barometer." ("Lights" being Wright's feeding pellets used on his home Never-sink River to study trout feeding habits.)

—Leonard M. Wright, Jr., *The Ways of Trout,* The Lyons Press (1985)

53. Fly Rod Casting Techniques You May Never Master, But Should

In his book *John Goddard's Trout-Fishing Techniques* (1996), the noted British author John Goddard outlines why and how the following fly-casting techniques can help you catch fish. There are 13 very specific casts, ranging from "The Parachute Roll Cast," through such casts as "The Deep-Water Tuck Cast," "The Wet-Fly Swing Cast," "The Puddle, Pile, or Parachute Cast," "The Storm or Wind Cast," "The Bow and Arrow Cast," and "Curve Casts." As you can see, the skill of casting with a fly rod can be a never-ending learning and experience process.

54. Why Are All Those Trucks Parked Over There?

The surest sign a certain stretch of a trout stream or creek is a real hotspot for action is to see a few trucks or SUVs parked at a nearby opening in the woodlands. Such a visual tip means a lot more than the free advice you get in tackleshops.

55. Upstream Wading Made Easier

In a strong current, wading upstream is best done with sideways steps. Lean your whole body into the flow slightly.

56. Tests on Fluorocarbon Tippets

Noted Pennsylvania trout author Charles Meck did some serious testing on fluorocarbon leader tippets with his Patriot dry fly. What conclusions did he draw? "First, fluorocarbons appear to work. Second, use the finest fluorocarbon leader you can. Of course, there's a tradeoff: If you use 6X and 7X you're more likely to break off heavier trout."

—Charles Meck, *Fishing Limestone Streams*,
The Lyons Press, 2005

57. More About Fluorocarbon Tippets

Continuing Charles Meck's fluorocarbon tippet tests: "I did not catch any trout on the dry fly in that very clear water until I used a 5X fluorocarbon tippet. I caught even more trout on the Patriot dry fly when I used a 6X fluorocarbon. I feel confident that had I used a 7X fluorocarbon leader I would have done even better."

—Charles Meck, *Fishing Limestone Streams*,
The Lyons Press, 2005

58. Buying Flies Before You Go

It's fun and easy to get into stocking up on trout flies just before you make a big, long-anticipated trip.

If it's to be a guided trip, however, do the family exchequer a favor and hold up on the flies until you arrive on the scene. Chances are the guides will have plenty of the ones you'll really need.

59. You Can Bet on Beetles

To catch more trout on flies, concentrate on fishing beetle imitations, particularly June Bugs, not only in high summer, but throughout the season, from spring into winter. You can spend all the time (and money) you want trying to imitate the famous mayfly and caddis hatches, but beetles are what the trout are feeding on most of the time. Reporting in a fantastic article in *Field & Stream,* September 1955, called "Mr. Botz and The Beetle," Angling Editor A. J. McClane discussed stomach contents taken from brown trout caught in New York's Catskill Mountain streams in April, May, June, and September. Beetles, far and away, were the insects being digested. Make beetle imitations a mainstay of your trout fly offerings, and you'll catch more fish. And don't forget that many superstar flies like the Muddler Minnow may be mistaken for beetles by trout, along with other popular flies as well. McClane adds, "There's no doubt in my mind that some of our standard wet-fly patterns, such as the Silver Doctor, Leadwing Coachman, and Black Gnat are mistaken for beetles by the trout." McClane also puts the Royal Coachman in the same fish-taking category because of its appearance under certain light conditions.

60. Barbless Hooks Make More Sense

Required in many trout streams, barbless hooks have a lot going for them in every form of light-tackle fishing, fresh and salt water. First, they are easy to extract when the angler sinks one into his hand or body. Second, they are easier to extract from the fish, allowing your catch to be released and live to fight another day. Finally, they sink deeper than barbed hooks, making most hookups just as effective as barbed hooks.

61. Barbless Hooks: How to Know They're Legal

There are so many trout streams today that require barbless hooks, anglers need to be doubly on the alert to make sure the flies they are using in these waters are legal. Even after the barb has been mashed down with pliers, the hook may not pass the test. What tests? Fishermen in many states are confused over this issue and are asking for legal guideposts. One state, Arkansas, spells out its definition in the 2007 *Trout Guidebook* as, "Crimped completely, the hook is smooth and will not snag when passed through cloth." That sounds pretty clear. If it will not pass through cloth without snagging, it's not legal. Until a better uniform definition comes along, that one sounds reasonable.

62. Making Your Hooks Barbless

For large bass lures, you're probably going to have to file the barbs down or replace the sets of hooks with new barbless ones (readily available, see separate sources). For trout flies, the procedure is simpler, but there are right and wrong ways to go about it. The correct way is to fit the point and barb of the fly straight into the head of the pliers. (Do not turn the hook crossways to the pliers.) Mash down carefully, working around the barb until it has been smoothed flush with the hook shaft. You might find it easier to use a special set of pliers for holding the fly, and another, more precise one for mashing the barb.

63. Where to Obtain Barbless Hooks

As this is being written, there are already several makers of barbless hooks for both fly fishing and fresh and salt water light-tackle fishing. By the time the book is in print, due to the rapidly growing interest in the subject, the list will no doubt be much longer. Check the Internet by Googling "Barbless Fish Hooks." At present, for treble hooks one of the easiest ways to change hooks on your favorite bass baits is to go to the *Boundary Waters Journal* site, www.boundarywaters-journal.com. The magazine has been offering sets of treble hooks since barbless hooks became the law in the Quetico. Another site is www.QueticoFishing.com.

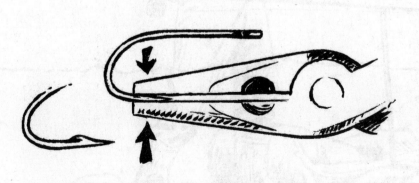

Familiar hook manufacturers who have been active in the barbless area include Gamakatsu and Eagle Claw and Umpqua for barbless flies.

64. Wading Staffs Make Sense

Falling down while wading and fishing isn't fun—on any kind of water, small creeks or big rivers. You'll get hurt, break or lose some tackle, or at least get wet, possibly very wet. Small streams have rocks, slippery and rounded. Large rivers have powerful current, and sometimes, as a bonus, slippery and rounded rocks. If you're a geezer, you already know darn well you need a wading staff. If you're coming onto geezer age, you're probably thinking about using one. If you're young and strong, you probably think wading staffs are for geezers only. Wading staffs, clipped to your fly vest, whether homemade or store bought, make life so easy. If your legs are in the least unsteady, try using one. You'll never go wade fishing again without it.

65. A Common Mayfly Frustration

Perhaps nothing in fly fishing is so frustrating as to finally be on the water while a big mayfly hatch is coming off, and the trout just aren't interested. I personally have seen such inactivity on the Brodhead in Pennsylvania when the long-awaited Hendrickson hatch was underway and the trout were lying doggo—not interested in nymphs underwater or the duns that were floating on the surface like a fleet of galleons. The textbooks all say that when the trout aren't on the duns, they'll be taking the nymphs down below, or the emergers in the film. It wasn't happening. The day was cold and dull, and nobody was catching fish. What to do? You tell me!

66. Try Tailwater Trout at "High Tide"

In an interesting article in *North American Fisherman*, August/September 1992, well-known outdoor

writer Dr. Jim Casada says he's had better luck fishing tailwaters when they were running full. Most anglers don't fish then because of the high water and all the canoists and floaters. But Casada says he could always find some wadeable water, out of the main stream, and catch lots of trout there—alone.

67. You Can Count on the Griffith's Gnat

Ernie Schwiebert was the first—or certainly one of the first—to write about the Griffith's Gnat in the original version of his book *Nymphs*, Winchester Press (1973). Since then many famous anglers and writers, and countless legions of anglers, have gone on to embrace this remarkable fly, one of the best midge imitations ever. The fly imitates the midge characteristic of sitting on the water with only its hackle fibers touching, not the body. The imitation resembles a single midge or an entire cluster of tiny ones. Expert angler and author Gary Borger says he favors Size 16 generally, but has plenty of others ready. For picky fish, he sometimes trims the hackle and lets the body rest on the water.

68. The Key to Early Season Success

"It pays to add or subtract weight as necessary to keep the flies down near the bottom. Especially in cold water, trout are reluctant to move up in the water column."

—Writer and Montana guide Chuck Robbins, www.chuckngalerobbins.com

69. Get Out of That Rut

"You've got to keep switching gears. The worst thing is to keep plugging away with something that isn't working in the first place."

—Writer and Montana guide Chuck Robbins, www.chuckngalerobbins.com

70. Fishing Cold, Early Season Water

"Streamers fished slow and deep, with or without a nymph trailer (18 inches or so is about right) often provide a wake-up call for spring trout. Vary the presentation pattern, add or subtract weight, until you find the right combination—then stick with it until the trout tell you otherwise. Many times just a subtle variation—size, color, add a shot or two—does it. Other times, it's more a presentation thing. For instance, start by casting down and across, let the fly(s) swing around; next cast bounce the rod tip a few times during the swing; then toss in a hand-twist retrieve. Next pick up, strip off a little more line and do it again, only this time use a short-pause, long-strip, pause, retrieve. No dice. Add a little more weight, change patterns, and repeat same. In a general sense, the colder the water, the slower the retrieve."

—Writer and Montana guide Chuck Robbins, www.chuckngalerobbins.com

71. Try Egg Patterns for Fall Trout

Trout egg patterns, especially in the fall, consistently take trout, if my experiences and those of my trout-fishing friends are any indicator. These flies need to be bounced right along the bottom, and it's very hard to tell if you have a bite or have ticked a rock. Sometimes the trout take the fly and spit it out so quickly that you can't react. In clear water it is sometimes possible to see the fish's mouth flash white as it takes the fly. Look for lots of strikes, a few hook-ups.

72. The Czech Express Has Arrived

When Czech fly-fishing teams started winning trout tournaments (yes, there *are* fly-fishing tournaments), American anglers began tuning into their techniques with intense vigor. Today Czech nymphing is so popular and taking fish so effectively that the flies are sold by many dealers (www.cabelas.com; www.theessentialfly.com), articles and videos are posted on popu-

lar sites, and entire books are available on the subject. (See *Czech Nymph and Other Related Flyfishing Methods* by Karel Krivanec at www.amazon.com.) Basically, Czech nymphs are great-looking flies tied extra-heavy to sink fast. The rig to fish them consists of a strike indicator and a triple-dropper setup, each dropper about 10 cm. The heavy Czech nymph is tied to the middle dropper, then your favorite traditional nymphs to the other two. This is high-stick nymphing, with short casts and the high rod immediately following the indicator downstream.

73. When Brook Trout Ponds Come to Life

Those cold, black-water wilderness lakes—called ponds in Maine—hold brook trout in sizes and numbers to dream about. Yet, under the long days of bright sun in June, they can seem to be absolutely lifeless. There are no rises, and no matter how hard you fish with streamers, strikes are few—or none. Then, between sunset and dark, the big Green Drakes start emerging, and trout—big trout—start slashing the water everywhere. Here's how Arthur MacDougall, Jr., described the experience in his wonderful *The Trout Fisherman's Bedside Book,* Simon & Schuster (1963): "We had to wait all afternoon . . . . When the sun set, and the wood thrushes began their ventriloquial harmonies, the trout began to rise. As if by summons, they were everywhere all over the pond. And these were brilliantly colored trout, fat, quick, and strenuous."

74. The Fly Hatch That Loves Bad Weather

"I have fished little Blue-Winged Olive hatches that have continued for hours on rainy days. Show me a cool, inclement, drizzly afternoon in April and May or September and October and I'll show you a heavy hatch of little Blue-Winged Olives."

—Charles Meck, *Fishing Limestone Streams,*
The Lyons Press, 2005

75. Those Splashy, Leaping Rises

When trout are leaping clear of the water in splashy rises, they are probably chasing emerging caddis.

76. Casting to Rising Trout

Yellowstone area expert and outfitter Craig Mathews on his favorite way to cover fish rising to duns or emergers: "I like to use a short, set-length cast—never more than 15 feet. This allows me to pick up and recast after the fly has traveled just enough beyond the fish that I can do so without spooking him and can get back out to him without false casting or stripping in slack."

—Craig Mathews, *Western Fly-Fishing Strategies,*
The Lyons Press, 1998

77. Trout on the Move

In his book *Western Fly-Fishing Strategies,* Lyons Press (1998), expert angler and outfitter Craig Mathews cites a biologist's report that cutthroat trout from Yellowstone Lake have been tracked migrating 6 to 8 miles between the lake and the Buffalo Ford area in a single day. Similar activity occurs on the Lamar River, Mathews adds, and other smooth-water rivers in the area. "An area that produces one day can be void of fish the next," Mathews says.

78. Random Casting: It Won't Work on Spring Creeks

"Generally, blind fishing a spring creek where there is no surface activity is unproductive and accomplishes little but spooking trout," says Yellowstone area expert author and outfitter Craig Mathews in his excellent book, *Western Fly-Fishing Strategies,* Lyons Press (1998). Mathews adds that an exception occurs when terrestrials or damselflies are active.

79. Try Joe Brooks' Broadside Float

The legendary angler and writer Joe Brooks did an article for *Field & Stream* in May 1961, called "The Broadside Float." In it, he reported having great success holding his streamers broadside to the current as they drifted downstream. He manipulated the streamers into the broadside presentation using line mends. Brooks felt the broadside float gave the trout a better view of their prey.

80. Leave Those Stressed Fish Alone

In high summer, you may be lucky enough to fish trout water that still has fish around. But if you find them all schooled up in pods at spring holes, that's a sure sign the temperatures have them under great stress. If you catch and release one of these fish, it may not survive the ordeal. Leave them alone until cooling rains and lower temperatures bring the stream back to normal.

81. Casting with Either Hand

Like great baseball players who can bat from either side, trout anglers who can cast left- or right-handed have a tremendous advantage. Even if you're a righty, and your left hand feels like a foreign object, try to get out there and practice. It will pay off with far more fish caught.

82. Fish Nymphs and Emergers With Upstream Casts

Yellowstone author and guide Craig Mathews, in his book *Western Fly-Fishing Strategies*, Lyons Press (1998), on fishing nymphs and emergers: "An upstream dead drift is the most productive cast for larger trout." Mathews says that anglers who float their nymphs down and across, mending occasionally, take smaller trout. They do it because it's an easy way to fish.

83. Stream Wading Rule One

Take short steps when wading your trout stream, big or small waters. And don't step on rocks that might roll under your feet.

84. Netting Your Trout

Making wild swipes at the water with your net is a sure way to knock a trout—big or small—off the line. Jabbing at the fish tail-first is another bad move.

The right way: Submerge your net, pull the fish over it headfirst, and lift. You've got him!

85. A Fly Fisher's Creed

"When fishing's fast, move slow! When the fishing's slow, move fast. Above all, keep moving."

—Chuck Robbins, author and fly-fishing guide. Check the Web site he maintains with his wife, Gale, for his blog, articles, and information on books, www.chuckngalerobbins.com.

86. Fly Fishing Beyond the Basics

"Beyond mastering the basics—casting, wading, reading the water, fly selection, etc.—the hardest thing for beginners to grasp is to keep moving, making the first shot count, then move on."

—Chuck Robbins, author and fly-fishing guide. Check the Web site he maintains with his wife Gale for his blog, articles, and information on books, www.chuckngalerobbins.com.

87. Fly Fishing Rule One

"Regardless of the rig—streamer, nymph, dry—strive to make each cast different. Lengthen the cast, move a step or two, change the angle, change the retrieve, etc. The *only* exceptions are when casting to visible fish—rising, feeding, resting underneath cover, whatever."

—Chuck Robbins, author and fly-fishing guide. Check the Web site he maintains with his wife Gale for his blog, articles, and information on books, www.chuckngalerobbins.com.

88. Get That Nymph Down

"Most urgent [in nymph fishing] is to add whatever weight necessary to keep the nymphs on the bottom. A wise man once observed, 'The difference between a great day nymphing and a skunking is often one measly split-shot.'"

—Chuck Robbins, author and fly-fishing guide. Check the Web site he maintains with his wife Gale for his blog, articles, and information on books, www.chuckngalerobbins.com.

89. No Hatch to Match? It's Time for Nymphs

Advice for fishing western rivers from a top guide and author: "Lacking a hatch, it's tough to beat a pair of nymphs rigged 5 or 6 feet or so below a strike indicator. Limited to just two patterns, a No. 10 Pat's Rubber Legs and a similar-sized red San Juan Worm would be my picks though my nymph box contains a good selection of beadhead and standard nymph patterns—Prince Pheasant Tail, Hare's Ear, Micro-May, Bloody Mary, Copper John, etc., in a variety of sizes and variations."

—Chuck Robbins, author and fly-fishing guide. Check the Web site he maintains with his wife Gale for his blog, articles, and information on books, www.chuckngalerobbins.com.

90. When Summer Trout Move Out

During extremely hot weather, the real dog days of summer, you may not find trout bunched at the mouths of spring creeks entering your river. Look for them up the creek itself. They'll be very spooky, but they'll be there. Realize that many trout anglers do not fish during times like this, when the fish are under stress.

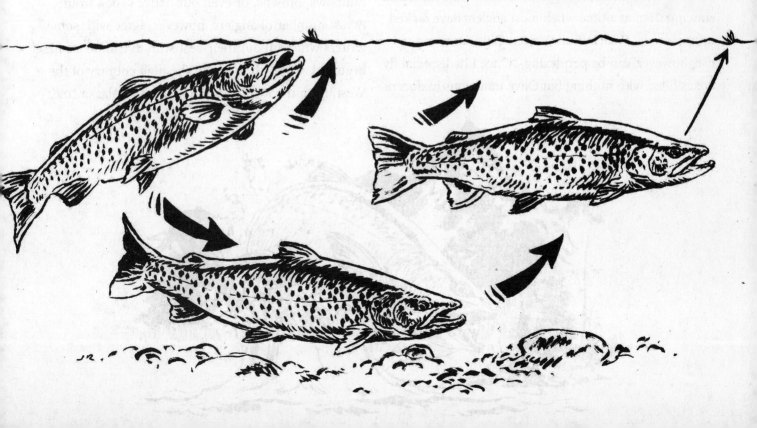

91. Where Trout Hold and Where They Rise

When trout are in holding water, they fin slowly, suspended, facing into the current. When they rise to take a fly, the splash or tiny swirl you see will usually be a little downstream of their holding lie. They take the fly, then swim back into their holding position. Keep that in mind when targeting your cast.

92. Fish Big Boulders on Both Sides

As soon as most trout anglers take up the sport, they learn to expect trout to be lying in the pockets behind boulders. The front sides of boulders also contain pockets, and the trout love them.

93. John Merwin on Blue-Winged Olives

In an article called "An Olive Afternoon: Problems and Solutions in Autumn Trout Fishing," on the *Field & Stream* Web site, veteran writer and angler John Merwin relates dealing with the ubiquitous Blue-Winged Olive hatches which take place in autumn over much of America. And, as Merwin describes, the Olives are enticing trout at a time when most anglers have racked up their rods. Which Blue-Winged Olive imitation to use, however, can be perplexing. "Once I had special fly boxes filled with nothing but Olive imitations in dozens of different styles. Fishing a just-right imitation became an obsession. I've finally decided there isn't one. Just about anything will work sometimes. Nothing works all the time." Available at www.fieldandstream.com.

94. John Merwin's Blue-Winged Olive Fly Choices

John Merwin has reduced the sometimes-bewildering process of "Which Blue-Winged Olive should I use?" to easy choices that catch fish, especially in the autumn. "In the past couple of years I've settled on four fly patterns, one of which will almost always work during a hatch of little Blue-Winged Olives. Exactly which of the four will work seems to change not only from day to day but also during a single afternoon. These are a Pheasant-Tail Nymph, an RS2 Emerger, a CDC Olive Emerger, and an olive-bodied spinner—all in Sizes 18 through 24." Available at www.fieldandstream.com.

95. Why You Should Fish for Cutthroats

In angling literature and popularity, the cutthroat sometimes does not get the respect of the popular rainbows, browns, or even our native brook trout. A vast number of anglers, however, agree with some writers who pull out their best stuff in tribute of these beautiful, wild fish found in the high country of the West, from the Rocky Mountains to the Alaska coast-

lines. Here's Frank Dufresne at his best in a *Field & Stream* article, "Trout Trouble," May 1955: "I've never known the right words to do justice to a cutthroat trout . . . It's not that they fight so savagely as some other gamefish . . . Could be it's that wild Alaska water they live in, the amber-tinted, foam-flecked stretches winding in the midday gloom of valley bottoms where the logger's ax has never chopped a hole to sunlight. . . . Good chance it's the company they keep, because bear, deer, and timber wolves are their neighbors."

96. Give Trout Unlimited Your Support

Since July 1959, Trout Unlimited has grown to 450 chapters with 150,000 serious and avid anglers. Their work with stream restoration and trout conservation has been a national treasure. There are lots of benefits for joining. Check them out at www.tu.org.

97. Seeing Trout: Rule One

"Perhaps the most common factor that betrays the trout is its movement. So imprint this upon your mind: *movement equals fish.*"

—John Goddard and Brian Clarke, *Understanding Trout Behavior,* The Lyons Press, 2001

98. Weeds: The Trout Stream Signpost

Weeds in trout streams are like signposts that say, "Fish Here!" Weeds not only provide cover for the trout, but for the food the trout needs to live.

99. Fishing Trout Stream Weeds

You'll find trout lying in the calmer water at the heads of weed patches, under the weed patches themselves, and downstream where the constant sweeping of the weed arms have eroded the streambed.

100. You Have to Be Sneaky to Catch Trout

Your approach to trout stream pools, and your very first casts, mean everything to your ultimate success. Careless approaches and careless casts will spook trout, sending them bolting from the pool, or—and this happens more often—alert trout that something is amiss. Once alerted, they may not strike for some time. You'll be thinking, "They're not biting today." But that's not the case at all.

101. When Your Fly Is Snagged

When your fly snags on the bottom or on a rock or limb in a trout stream, *do not* pull back hard in an attempt to free it. Instead, use a Roll Cast, which will pull the fly in the opposite direction and often free it.

102. The Roll Cast: A Fly-Fishing Must

Not only is the Roll Cast useful for freeing your fly from snags, in many situations you will not have room behind you or to the side for a backcast. That's where the Roll Cast will pay big dividends for every moment you've spent learning it.

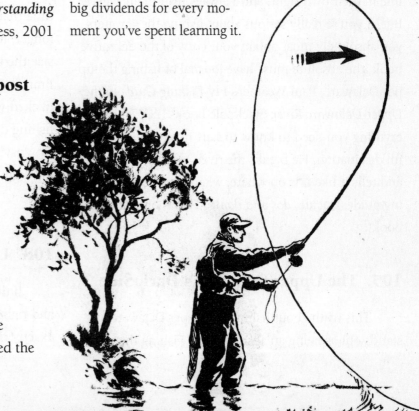

103. The Upper Delaware: The Big East Trout Mecca

Its call is irresistible to the myriad of fly fishermen who live in the greater New York and Philadelphia areas—and beyond. The upper Delaware in the vicinity of Hancock, New York, about 300 miles from where it enters Delaware Bay, is the source of New York City's drinking water and about 80 miles of trout waters. The upper Delaware's three stems—the West Branch, the East Branch, and the Main Stem—are often called the East's answer to the storied trout fishing in the American West. The Delaware is the longest undammed river east of the Mississippi. Fittingly, its upper reaches are the homes of myriad wild trout. But they are challenging to fish, as many anglers will attest.

104. How to Start Fishing the Upper Delaware

Articles are constantly appearing in popular fishing and outdoor magazines that focus on the difficulties of the wild trout fishing in the upper Delaware, in the vicinity of Hancock, New York. These tomes are fine in their own right, and I always read them eagerly. But, if you're really serious about fishing these waters, you absolutely must obtain your copy of the definitive book, the absolute must-have journal of fishing the upper Delaware. Paul Weamer's *Fly-Fishing Guide to the Upper Delaware River,* Stackpole Books (2007), has everything you need to know to start fishing this wonderful destination. He breaks the rivers down by sections, and tells it like it is on where, when, and how—including guides, tackle, *dos* and *don'ts*. This is one fantastic book!

105. The Upper Delaware's Dark Side

This truth about fishing the upper Delaware stands out as being an absolute fact: Fishing the water for opportunistic feeders during the day gets you nothing—most of the time. The fly hatches, and all the action, take place at the end of the day. Stretches where you would swear there are no trout during the day come alive with rising fish.

106. When the Upper Delaware is Bight

Bright, sunny days on the upper Delaware are tough to fish, with the action occurring at dusk only. The fish are super-sensitive to the light and the dangers that come from above, like the large numbers of eagles and ospreys that abound in the area. On a bright sunny day you may be in for a long boat ride, with splendid scenery but not the hatches and rising trout you came to find.

107. Which Upper Delaware Branch to Fish?

The realities of picking one of the three upper Delaware branches to fish can be summed up this way: The West Branch, the top water, is smaller than the Main Stem, and much more crowded in mayfly time than the lower waters. The Main Stem is larger, longer, has more places to fish, but considering its size the trout are more spread out than on the West Branch. The East Branch is smaller than the other two, packed with trout, but access is a major issue, and the fishing depends on the water being released from the Downsville impoundment. Of course, if you're booking a guide, he will know which branch is fishing the best.

108. Upper Delaware Guided Days

If the fish are really on, and the weather is cloudy and right for hatches, you may hit the upper Delaware exactly right with a guided float and have a day or two

for the books. If these conditions do not exist, you probably have booked a long and expensive boat ride.

109. Blind Casting the Dry Fly

"Riffles [on New York's upper Delaware] break the surface and help disguise leaders and tippets in the chop. I have caught a lot of trout by blind casting dry flies upriver in the upper Delaware's riffles, but very few while casting upriver in the pools."

—Paul Weamer, *Fly-Fishing Guide to the Upper Delaware River,* Stackpole Books, 2007

110. Surface Feeders: Three Casts and Out

"Once I find a rising fish and slowly move into the proper casting position, I cast only three times for each

time the fish rises. If the fish hasn't eaten my fly by the third cast, I stop casting and watch and wait until the fish rises again."

—Paul Weamer, *Fly-Fishing Guide to the Upper Delaware River,* Stackpole Books, 2007

111. The Dry Fly Fished Downstream on Big Rivers

Although upstream stalking and casting is the tradition for dry fly fishing, many shrewd anglers who fish big-water rivers like the Delaware in the East and the upper Missouri in the West favor a downstream cast. They get into position a good distance above the fish and slightly to the side. They cast quartering downstream to the rising fish, then mend the line upstream to get a straight downstream line-leader-fly float—without drag.

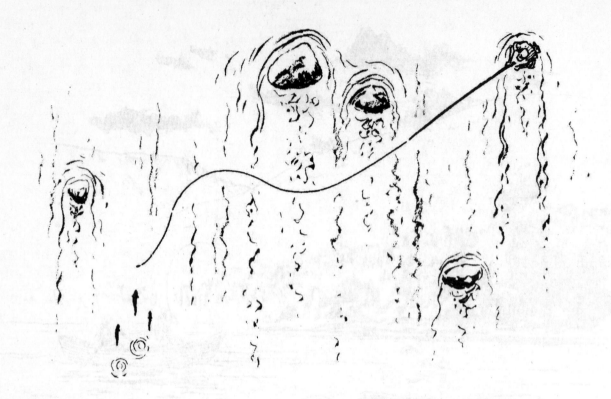

112. Streamers Need Speed

"Many anglers strip their streamers too slow. It is impossible to strip a streamer faster than a trout can catch it."

—Paul Weamer, *Fly-Fishing Guide to the Upper Delaware River*, Stackpole Books, 2007

113. Streamers: The "Go-To" Flies

"What kind of an artificial can be used at all times and anywhere, whether flies are hatching or not? The streamer or bucktail, of course, the development of which in the 1930s represented a major breakthrough in trout fishing."

—S.R. Slaymaker II, *Tie a Fly, Catch a Trout*, Harper & Row, 1976

114. Dry-Fly Purist Bunk

When you check out a dry fly "purist"—the flyfisher who says, "It's a dry fly, or nothing"—you'll often find he doesn't do any nymph fishing simply because he can't do it.

115. Ripping Streamers

Sometimes the only way to get into position to work streamers through likely looking water is from the downstream side, casting upstream. Then you have to remember that your fly is floating toward you very swiftly with the current. To get any realistic movement at all on the fly you need to be retrieving line so fast that the act has come to be called "ripping streamers" by many fly fishers.

116. Nymph Fishing: Cast Up, Fish Down

"In my method of fishing the nymph, one casts upstream but *fishes* down. The purpose of the upstream cast is to give the nymph time to sink before one commences to attempt to control and fish it. For this reason, the position for the first cast to any stretch should be some yards upstream of any suspected fish. You will work down to him on succeeding casts."

—Charles E. Brooks, *Nymph Fishing for Larger Trout,* Crown Publishers, 1976

117. And Still Champion: The Muddler Minnow

The Muddler Minnow has probably made more "Best Fly" lists than any other. Why? Because it catches trout. You can find it in every fly shop and fly-fishing catalog, in many hook sizes. You can dress it and fish it dry on the surface; you can work it down and across like a streamer; and you can let it bounce along the bottom like a nymph. Like the Woolly Bugger, the Muddler Minnow belongs in your fly box.

118. Delaware Rainbows Are Special

"Delaware rainbows are genetically different, something special—a 14-incher can put you into

backing. And because it's got plenty of space and food, every fish has the potential to be 20 inches."

—Famed Catskill and upper Delaware (New York) angler Ed Van Put, quoted in J.L. Merritt's *Trout Dreams: A Gallery of Fly-Fishing Profiles,* The Derrydale Press, 2000

119. Tactics of an Upper Delaware Legend

"I catch a lot of fish in the last thirty minutes of the evening. It's not exactly night fishing, because there's still a little light. I call it 'dark' fishing. You can't see the fly anymore, but you can see the rises. Cast ahead of them, and if the fish stop rising hold your cast until they start coming up again."

—Famed Catskill and upper Delaware (New York) angler Ed Van Put, quoted in J.L. Merritt's *Trout Dreams: A Gallery of Fly-Fishing Profiles,* The Derrydale Press, 2000

120. Don't Strike That Trout Too Soon

Upper Delaware rainbows take surface flies deliberately, and many anglers are spurred into a hair-trigger strike that misses the fish. "You've got to strike the rise, not the fly. Even if I can see the fly, I try not to look at it."

—Famed Catskill and upper Delaware (New York) angler Ed Van Put, quoted in J.L. Merritt's *Trout Dreams: A Gallery of Fly-Fishing Profiles,* The Derrydale Press, 2000

121. The Ed Van Put Fly Selections

"While Ed Van Put is reputed to fish the Adams exclusively, a glance through his fly box belies this. If no fish are rising, he said, he may search the water with a Chuck Caddis, a Henryville Special, or a Cream Variant. For nymphs he favors the Zug Bug, and he occasionally fishes downstream with traditional wet flies like the Royal Coachman and Cow Dung."

—J.L. Merritt on famed Catskill and upper Delaware (New York) angler Ed Van Put in *Trout Dreams: A Gallery of Fly-Fishing Profiles,* The Derrydale Press, 2000

122. A Deadly Nymphing Technique

In his book *Trout Dreams: A Gallery of Fly-Fishing Profiles,* The Derrydale Press (2000), Jim Merritt describes fishing techniques of many legendary fly fishers. This excerpt on Chuck Fothergill, famed for his angling prowess in Colorado's Roaring Fork and Frying Pan rivers, describes Fothergill's deadly nymphing technique. What follows is an absolutely deadly way of fishing a nymph. You'll find it to be one of the most productive of the tips in this book: "Using a floating line with a leader weighted with several twisted-on lead strips, he quartered a short cast upstream. He held the rod high, his arm angled like the Statue of Liberty's, and kept it that way through most of the drift. As the line drew abreast of him and continued downstream, he followed it with the rod, which he lowered gently to maintain a drag-free float. At the end of the drift he lifted the rod, swinging the nymph toward the surface. Probing the run carefully, he was quickly into a fat rainbow which leaped explosively and stripped line off the reel as it charged downstream."

123. A Fly That Will Live Forever

Al Troth tied his original Elkhair Caddis from the hairs of a bull elk, then later switched to the cow elk, bleached for greater visibility. First tied in 1957, the Elkhair has joined the ranks of flies such as the Muddler Minnow, the Adams, and the Pheasant Tail nymphs as standard fish-takers. Troth says that besides caddis, "It'll imitate stoneflies, little hoppers, any number of things. The trout ate it in 1957, they eat it now, and they'll eat it twenty years from now."

—Al Troth, in J.L. Merritt's *Trout Dreams: A Gallery of Fly-Fishing Profiles,* The Derrydale Press, 2000

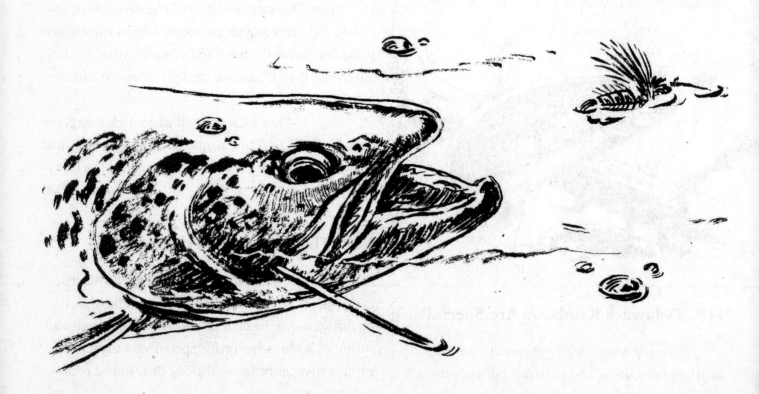

124. Heads-Up Nymph Fishing

"Some 98 percent of mayfly nymphs come to the surface head up. For most imitations, therefore, it's not a bad idea to weight the upper third of the hook."

—Famed Pennsylvania angler Joe Humphreys, in J.L. Merritt's *Trout Dreams: A Gallery of Fly-Fishing Profiles,* The Derrydale Press, 2000

125. Hitting the Hatch at Prime Time

"The easiest time to catch rising fish is at the beginning and end of the hatch. Early in the hatch you'll find a lot of juvenile fish, but as the hatch gets heavier, the bigger fish appear, and a pecking order starts to prevail."

—Famed angler and author Al Caucci, in J.L. Merritt's *Trout Dreams: A Gallery of Fly-Fishing Profiles,* The Derrydale Press, 2000

126. Where Trout Are Feeding

"Consider the current as an underwater cafeteria line, only instead of the fish moving to the food, the food comes to the fish."

—Dick Galland, "Master Basic Nymphing," in *Fly Fisherman Magazine's* "Nymphing for Trout" booklet

127. Current Seams: Where the Trout Are

"Then consider a trout's other requirements in moving water—relief from the current and shelter from danger—and you'll know where to begin. Target the edges of eddies, slower-water seams, and deep runs that are close to the main current. Trout swim out, take a food item, and return to cover."

—Dick Galland, "Master Basic Nymphing," in *Fly Fisherman Magazine's* "Nymphing for Trout" booklet

128. Add Weight Before Changing Flies

"If you find yourself fishing a spot that looks ideal, but you are not getting strikes, add weight to make sure the fly is on the bottom before changing flies."

—Dick Galland, "Master Basic Nymphing," in *Fly Fisherman Magazine's* "Nymphing for Trout" booklet

129. Saying No to Strike Indicators

"Today there is an implied presumption that if you fish a nymph, you must use a strike indicator . . . Though indicators are a necessity in certain situations, they are a handicap in other circumstances . . . On

some heavily fished streams, the fish learn to associate the glowing orange ball with a threat and they become reluctant to feed."

—Jim McLennan, "Nymphing Without Indicators," in *Fly Fisherman Magazine's* "Nymphing for Trout" booklet

130. Other Strike Indicator Negatives

Despite their popularity, strike indicators do have certain negatives: They splat down on the surface when cast . . . they drag on the surface, causing the fly to drift at an unnatural speed, usually too fast . . . they present the fly at a fixed depth, instead of getting it to the varying depths of the stream . . . they sometimes catch the wind on casts, making accuracy difficult.

131. Fly Stories: An Orvis Treasury

One of the many things I like about the Orvis site, www.orvis.com, is "Fly Stories" in the flyfishing section. These are short tales told by anglers of various flies they have used—and the fly decisions that were made and what happened. It's great stuff.

132. Gary LaFontaine: His Endless Legacy

Before losing a courageous battle with Lou Gehrig's disease (ALS) at the age of fifty-six, Gary LaFontaine became one of fly fishing's greatest anglers, authors, fly tyers, and ambassadors of sportsmanship. His books include *Caddisflies, Fly Fishing the Mountain Lakes, The Dry Fly: New Angles,* and *Trout Flies: Proven Patterns.* He is featured in several DVDs and co-authored many fishing guides in book form and pocket form. Living in the Montana high country, and fishing there and all over the world, Gary built a legacy that can be best experienced at the site dedicated to his name: www. thebookmailer.com. Here you will find gear from the LaFontaine private label, plus books, DVDs, and fishing guides from scores of authors and sources. A newslet-

ter is available. LaFontaine Private Label, PO Box 1273, Helena, MT 59624-1273; 800-874-4171.

133. Fishing the High-Country Lakes

If you're thinking about doing a pack trip into the high-country lakes of the great western mountains, you'll want to read a copy of the late Gary LaFontaine's *Fly Fishing the Mountain Lakes,* Greycliff Publishing (1998). The book is available from the site honoring Gary, www.thebookmailer.com. The book is packed with details on everything from planning and packing, to specific mountain lake fishing techniques. Gary loved this type of fishing so much that he became quite an expert on what to pack in—and how to do it—including his decision to always take a kick boat, no matter what packing challenges it created.

134. When an Entire Pod of Trout Are Rising Right in Front of You

Standing opposite a pod of rising trout, as can happen on the best rivers, will likely set your heart racing and your fingers trembling. Now's the time to be cool, however. A cast right into the bunch will probably scatter them in a frenzy. Try to get into position below the pod, downstream from it, and cast toward a fish on the outside. If he's hooked, and you can keep him from running into the pack, you may pick off a couple more doing the same thing.

135. Best Way to Fish Mountain Lakes from Shore

In his book *Fly Fishing the Mountain Lakes,* Greycliff Publishing (1998), available from the site www.thebookmailer.com, the late Gary LaFontaine describes his favorite technique for fishing from the shore in mountain lakes as "Multiple Roll Casts." He starts with three Roll casts *short* of the drop-off. Next three are *right on* the drop-off. Then five casts *beyond* the drop-off. The slowly advancing fly seems to excite trout lurking in the depths.

136. The Pack Boat for Mountain Lake Fishing

In his book *Fly Fishing the Mountain Lakes,* Greycliff Publishing (1998), available from the site www.thebookmailer.com, the late Gary LaFontaine describes in detail his favorite gear and techniques. An interesting aspect of his decision on what to pack in is revealed here: "A flotation device—for me it has to be an inflatable kick boat, not a float tube—gives the fly fisherman access to all the areas of a lake that the crowds don't fish." LaFontaine was willing to use whatever means possible—goats, alpacas, Ilamas, horses—to pack in everything he needed. If he couldn't manage a kick boat, he carried a lightweight backpacker's float tube.

137. Mountain Lakes: The Gifts from Above

"One of the secrets of mountain lakes is that the vertical winds, not horizontal ones, deposit most of the food on the water. The other secret is that trout in these lakes, given a choice, prefer to feed on the surface." This tip comes from the late Gary LaFontaine in his book *Fly Fishing the Mountain Lakes,* Greycliff Publishing (1998). He's referring to the anabatic winds that "rush up the mountain slopes like the air up a chimney." He continues, "Look for upslope winds on warm afternoons." With these tips, you can easily see why you would be foolish to plan a backpack adventure in the high Rocky Mountain lakes without reading Gary's book. You can obtain a copy at www.thebookmailer.com.

138. Pairing the Hatch

In his book *Fly Fishing the Mountain Lakes,* Greycliff Publishing (1998), the late Gary LaFontaine describes his technique of picking off a feeding fish when a multitude of bugs are on the water. He watches the direction the fish is feeding, picks up the next most-likely insect, then places his cast an inch or so in front of the natural. Focused on the natural, but with a sudden new opportunity in front of it, the trout usually takes Gary's fly. You can obtain Gary's books at www. thebookmailer.com.

139. Best Days to Fish a Mayfly Hatch

In his classic *A Summer on the Test* (1924, republished by Nick Lyons Books/Winchester Press in 1984), the English writer John Waller Hills takes dead aim at picking the best days to fish the big mayfly hatches of his beloved Test River and other waters. "My experience has been so unvarying, that if I were told I was to have only two days fishing during the period, I should choose my days with every confidence . . . By the fourth day (since the main fly hatch began) trout have acquired the taste of the newly hatched fly and are taking it confidently . . . the big fish are moving by then . . . This is the first great chance, the fourth day. And the next is the twelfth day, by which time the fly is going off and trout know it, and are making the most of the short time remaining."

140. Early Season Fly Hatches

Here's the legendary English writer John Waller Hills on early season hatches in his classic book *A Summer on the Test* (1924, republished in later editions): "So I finished up with eight fish: a good day. . . . Now these two days were the opposite of each other; the first, fine and hot, produced hardly any fly and two fish, and the second, bitterly cold, showed an immense hatch and four brace of fine trout. Never, never believe that cold weather hinders fly. You will hear it, always and everywhere; but it is not only untrue but the reverse of truth. Except at the very beginning of April, you get more fly on a cold day than on a warm." Of course, Hills was speaking of his English hatches, but you can apply his wisdom to your own waters.

141. A Very Special Tip for Fly-Fishing Beginners

In this quote, the legendary English writer John Waller Hills in his classic book *A Summer on the Test* (1924, republished in later editions) is speaking of dry fly fishing in particular, but his intention to "clear the air" applies to all forms of fly fishing: " . . . what I want to impress on any reader who is not a dry fly fisherman is that dry fly fishing is much easier than it sounds. There is a conspiracy of anglers, started by Halford [the English expert and writer] and carried on with increasing momentum by later writers, to make out that the art is so dreadfully obscure that none but the gifted should attempt it. The perplexed beginner, poring over the great masters, reads of the accuracy and delicacy required . . . how a single mistake is fatal, how he must be able to recognize at a glance each of the hundred and one insects on which trout feed . . . He despairs of reaching this level . . . He is completely misled. He believes what is egregious nonsense. The sport has its difficulties, and they are not small; but in the first place anyone with ordinary ability can surmount them, and in the second the price paid for failure is not nearly as great as writers would have us believe. You can make heaps of mistakes and yet kill plenty of fish on a difficult river and a difficult day. . . . believe me, it is not nearly as hard as it sounds."

142. Wade in Carefully, Stop Spooking Trout

I watched a guy wading into the Missouri River, his rod and fly ready. Clearly, he was looking out in the current, where several rainbows were rising in a nice pod. What he didn't realize, or take time to discover, was that there were many more fish holding in the current right by the shore. He waded into them, intent on the distant pod. The fish bolted away, taking the pod fish with them. It pays to not be in such a hurry. Look trout water over very carefully before wading ahead.

143. How an Expert Plays Big Trout

"Let a large trout get his head down and he will dictate the fight, but keep his head up and he cannot

Watch the water before wading in. Many times, trout will be right at your feet; wade in without looking, and you'll spook the whole pool.

run effectively. You will quickly realize how much easier it is to control a fish on the surface, and to bring the battle to a rapid conclusion."

—John Goddard, *A Fly Fisher's Reflections,*
The Lyons Press, 2002

144. Big Trout in Weedy Water

"I learned early on—and painfully!—that when fishing for trout of 4-pound-plus in weedy water, it is a question of holding on as soon as you set the hook, or the fish is as good as lost."

—John Goddard, *A Fly Fisher's Reflections,*
The Lyons Press, 2002

145. Stay Out of the Trout's Rear-Vision Mirror

In studies with English author Brian Clarke for the book *The Trout & the Fly,* noted angler and author John Goddard reached the conclusion that trout have superb 45-degree vision to the rear and recommends the following tactic to cope: " . . . try positioning yourself opposite or even slightly upstream of any trout rising

very close to the surface and cast to him from this position as I think he will be less likely to see you, but do remember to avoid any sudden movements and where possible cast sideways with a wrist movement to avoid moving your arms."

—John Goddard, *A Fly Fisher's Reflections,*
The Lyons Press, 2002

146. Nymph Fishing Made Easy

The greatest discovery in the history of fly fishing—as far as float-fishing guides in the high-country West have discovered—is nymph fishing. Not the classic nymph fishing of most American trout streams, spawned from English experts like Frank Sawyer and company, but using a couple of nymphs tied in tandem below a strike indicator that floats on the surface. That strike indicator—they come in all different shapes and sizes—is nothing more than an elaborate bobber. Picture this: You started out years and years ago fishing with a bobber. Now, you've got the money and time to book a top guide on one of Montana's top streams, like the Big Horn or Beaverhead, and you're floating along in the raft chunking out a stretch of fly line (yes,

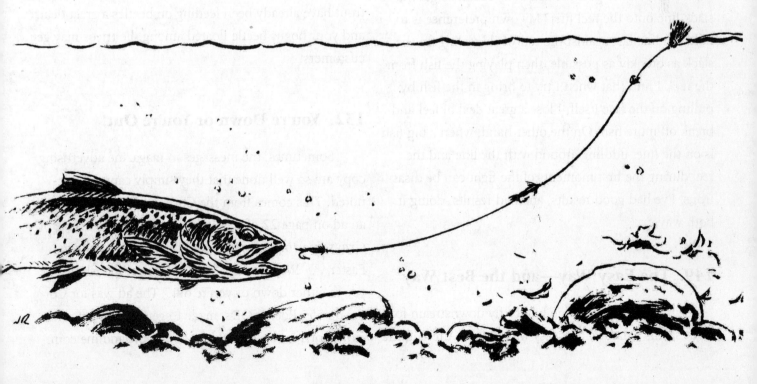

"chunking" is the right word, not "casting") with a couple of weighted nymphs tied to a "bobber"—aka, "strike indicator"—riding the current. Okay, you're having fun, catching trout. I have no problem with that, so long as you see the irony.

147. How to See More Trout

"Trout are dim, uncertain and nearly invisible. You learn after a time where to look and what to look for. You must not expect to see a whole trout, outlined as solidly as though lying on a fishmonger's slab; any fool can see that: but what you have to train yourself to pick out is a flicker, a movement, a darkness, a luminosity which if you stare at it hard enough will resolve itself into a shadowy form."

—The legendary English writer John Waller Hills in his classic book *A Summer on the Test* (1924, republished by Nick Lyons Books/Winchester Press in 1984)

148. Play That Fish from the Reel?

You'll usually have some loose line in your hand when you hook a trout, and now the question becomes whether to pull the fish in by hand, or get the slack line onto the reel first? My own preference is to hold the line fast against the rod while reeling up the slack as quickly as possible, then playing the fish from the reel. I find that when I try to bring in the fish by pulling on the line itself, I lose a great deal of feel and break off more fish. On the other hand, when a big fish is on the line, fiddling around with the line and the reel during the first moments of the fight can be disastrous. I've had good results, and bad results, doing it both ways.

149. The Easy Way—and the Best Way

Fishing your spinning lure or fly downstream for trout seems a natural and easy way to fish. After all, the fish are lying facing into the current, where your bait or fly is headed directly to them. Fishing upstream, however, gives you the advantage of stealth, sneaking up on the fish.

150. The Right Times to Fish the Wrong Flies

There's an old trick that sometimes really does work when you're into rising trout and just can't seem to get them interested in your imitations. Switch to an easy-to-see fly like a No. 14 Royal Wulff or an Adams, and you might be surprised by the results.

151. A Trick for Fishing a Tough Hatch

In high summer in the East and on some Rocky Mountain rivers like the upper Missouri, the hatch of the tiny tricothrids (trico) is a landmark event, luring fly fishers who try to match the hatch. Despite the fish-rising activity, trying to get a fish interested in your tiny (No. 22) fly is quite a challenge. Some experienced anglers claim a change-of-pace is needed here. They go to a terrestrial, an ant, or a beetle. When the tricos come, trout have already been feeding on beetles a great deal, and your bogus beetle floated among the tricos may get customers.

152. You're Down or You're Out!

Sometimes, the messages in magazine advertising copy are so well done that they simply cannot be ignored. This comes from the Cortland Line Company in an ad on page 22 of the February-March 2004 issue of *Gray's Sporting Journal*: "Get down. . . . Way down. . . Faster. . . . Way faster . . . In this type of fly fishing, you're either down or you're out." The ad was for Cortland's 555 Rocket QDs, made to get your fly into the strike zone faster. Available at www.cortlandline.com.

153. Rocks and Trout: Pinpointing the Lies

"The trout likes the upstream sides of rocks, logs, and . . . other solid objects . . . for exactly the same reasons that he likes the tops of hatches: because he has a splendid view of what the current is bringing him; and yet is cushioned from the weight of the water."

—John Goddard and Brian Clarke, *Understanding Trout Behavior*, 2001

154. Trout under the Bridge

"Any fisherman with more than a morning's experience knows that the water beneath a bridge is a likely lie for a trout; and often, for a big trout. It is that rare phenomenon, the 'complete' lie . . . The narrower a section of the river is, the deeper it will be . . ."

—John Goddard and Brian Clarke, *Understanding Trout Behavior*, 2001

155. The Devilish Smutting Rises

In the United Kingdom, anglers call it a curse. The legendary "smutting rise" occurs plenty in America, too. It happens when trout are feeding in the surface film on tiny larvae and pupa of midges. Often only tiny rings show on the water as they suck in the flies. Reach for the smallest Griffith's Gnat you can tie on.

156. What Color Leader?

The question of whether or not your leader should be a certain color—or no color at all—has been around trout streams for a long time, even back when you had to dye your own leaders if you wanted them colored a certain way. Here are a few choice words from the legendary A. J. McClane, from his fishing column in *Field & Stream,* November 1949: "I have made dozens of leaders dyed with methylene blue, potassium hy-droxide, malachite green, Bismarck brown, tea, coffee, and iodine. Aside from messing up the sink, they left no other mark in fishing history. . . . I much prefer an opaque or nearly translucent material, the kind commonly labeled 'mist,' for all fishing above surface or below."

157. The Perfect Small-Stream Trout Rod

Opinions abound on the subject of the perfect rod for small-stream trout fishing. Here's one you can take to the bank: You want a short rod, 7 feet, to handle the overhanging limbs and close brush along the sides of the stream. You must have a fast, powerful tip. It will get your short line out fast and sure. You want all this in the lightest rod you can find, one that comes alive in your hand. You'll enjoy every cast, and the feel of a fighting fish will be your ultimate reward. The long-rod advocates will cry "Foul!" at this opinion, claiming to

© *Jay Cassell*

In small streams like this, it pays to go with a shorter rod. You'll avoid snagging your fly in the trees, and instead keep it in the water, where it's supposed to be.

have more control with the longer stick. To each his own. In small streams, go with the short rod and keep your fly and line in the water instead of the trees and bushes.

158. Upstream or Downstream?

You've got your favorite creek or stream all to yourself for a change. What's it to be: upstream or downstream? The usual method is to fish your floating flies in an upstream direction, while fishing nymphs and streamers downstream. There's not a thing wrong with that game plan.

159. The Most Important 10 Inches in Trout Fishing

"Scientists have found that most of the trout taken on nymphs are within 10 inches of the river bottom . . . That's where the food is, and because the food is there and the current runs more slowly, there'll be a lot of fish there."

—Lefty Kreh, with Chris Millard, *My Life Was THIS BIG and Other True Fishing Tales,* Skyhorse Publishing, 2008

160. Midsummer, Low-Water Conditions: Go With a Dry Fly

Author and trout expert Leonard M. Wright, Jr., was a writer I respected and felt privileged to publish when I was editor of *Sports Afield* magazine. In one, "Give Summer Trout a Moveable Feast," he went against tradition in urging anglers to use a dry fly fished with a twitch for midsummer trout. Wright reasoned that in midsummer, daylight hours, the nymphs and other bottom-dwellers were hiding under rocks, emerging only at dusk and night. "The main food supply most of the day is made up of insects that have flown or tumbled onto the surface and these, trapped in the rubbery surface film, are carried downstream on top of the water," Wright wrote in the article, republished in his book *Fly Fishing Heresies,* Winchester Press (1975).

161. Twitch Your Midsummer Dry Fly

"To catch a loafing trout's attention (in midsummer) and to gain his confidence, your dry fly should move—and move as a living insect does. This means a small movement, not a great plowing wake. And it should move in an upstream direction. For all stream-

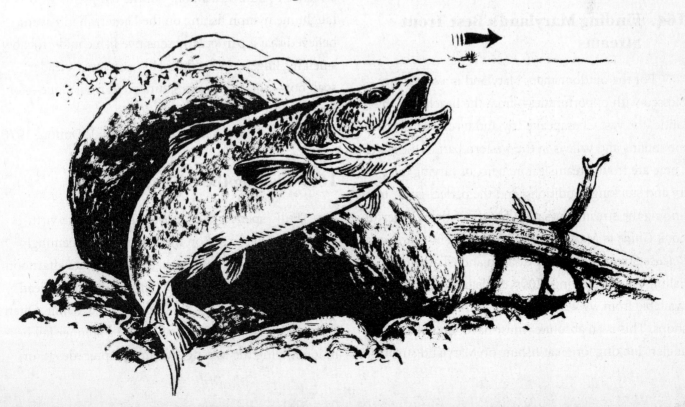

bred flies, whether hatching out or returning for egg-laying, move in an upstream direction."

—Leonard M. Wright, Jr., *Fly Fishing Heresies,*
Winchester Press, 1975

162. Leonard Wright's Summer Dry Fly Technique

" . . . you break with tradition and cast your fly in an across-and-downstream direction, when you give it a tiny twitch it will lurch upstream. Then let it float free again as long as it will."

—Leonard M. Wright, Jr., *Fly Fishing Heresies,*
Winchester Press, 1975

163. Your Summer Trout Fishing Will Improve

"A fly twitched slightly on the surface will raise trout all day long on the much-neglected pools and long flats where the dead-drift nymph or dry fly would seem very dead, indeed."

—Leonard M. Wright, Jr., *Fly Fishing Heresies,*
Winchester Press, 1975

164. Finding Maryland's Best Trout Streams

For the outdoorsman, Maryland is a state truly blessed with opportunities—from the beaches of the Atlantic, the vast Chesapeake Bay and its environs, to the mountains and valleys in the western part of the state. There are trout streams galore here, of varying quality and stocking conditions, and the perfect guide to finding the stream that's right for you is the wonderful book *Guide to Maryland Trout Fishing: The Catch-and-Release Streams,* by Larry Coburn and Charlie Gelso, Falling Star Publishing (2006, updated regularly). It's available from www.amazon.com and many tackle shops. This is an absolute "must-have" book for trout anglers looking for great fishing on Maryland streams.

165. A Trout Stream Where Legends Were Created

Maryland's Big Hunting Creek, not far from Frederick and a stone's throw from the famous Camp David, retreat of presidents, is the stream where legendary angler Joe Brooks and others started the Brotherhood of the Jungle Cock group in the 1940s, teaching fly fishing to youngsters. There is a Joe Brooks Memorial in the upper section of the stream, which still ranks as one of Maryland's most interesting and beautiful to fish. See the book *Guide to Maryland Trout Fishing: The Catch-and-Release Streams,* by Larry Coburn and Charlie Gelso, Falling Star Publishing (2006, updated regularly).

166. The Drift of the Dry Fly

"The line of drift of the naturals is important to presentation too, and the fly must be placed to duplicate its route."

—Ernest Schwiebert, *Trout,* E.P. Dutton, 1978

167. Are Your Hands Poisoned?

"It is not fully known if trout and grayling are as sensitive to odor as salmon, but the old ghillie who taught me nymph fishing on the Lauterach in Bavaria believed that a particularly sensitive fish could probably smell his fingers on his flies. His secret was a leader soak box—thick felt pads saturated in trout slime—for his nymphs."

—Ernest Schwiebert, *Trout,* E.P. Dutton, 1978

168. Fishing the Spinner Rises

"Fully spent and exhausted spinners are virtually impossible to see on the water. Many seemingly unexplained rises of fish, particularly in late afternoon and evening, are triggered by large numbers of dead or dying spinners lying flush in the surface film. Often the only method of identifying such a spinner fall lies in identifying the mating swarm that precedes it, or observing the dwindling flight of male spinners that remain over the water."

—Ernest Schwiebert, *Trout,* E.P. Dutton, 1978

169. Stay On Watch for Sipping Rises

"Always pay particular attention to the fish which are sipping under the banks, and don't be deluded into the notion that because you see a fish make more break on the water than a minnow would, that he is a minnow, for he is quite likely to be a three-pounder."

—Francis Francis, *Book of Angling,* 1867, as referenced by Ernest Schwiebert in *Trout,* E.P. Dutton, 1978

170. Small Rise, Big Trout

"It is strange how quietly a big fish will often take fly after fly, close to a bank, with only just his upper lip pushed into the surface to suck in the victim."

—Francis Francis, *Book of Angling,* 1867, as referenced by Ernest Schwiebert in *Trout,* E.P Dutton, 1978

171. Schwiebert's Fly Line Color Choices

In his magnum-opus, *Trout,* E.P. Dutton (1978), legendary angler and writer Ernest Schwiebert discusses the improved visibility of bright and white fly lines, saying they're great for photography and watching your line. But, for serious fishing: "Yet, I still use a dark mahogany-colored line for the difficult, hyperselective fish on my home waters in the eastern mountains, and I feel it has been more effective on the shy fish of our famous western spring creeks. Fishing deep I prefer darker colors . . . Pale colors are unwise in a sinking line that works deep among the fish and is viewed laterally against the adjacent colors of the bottom."

172. Eliminating Drag: The Key to Successful Dry Fly Fishing

From the moment anglers make their first cast with a dry fly, they start learning that drag is the great boogeyman of dry fly fishing. You'll see it often, and you'll hear about it everywhere fly fishers gather. Drag occurs when the current pulls the fly line and leader downstream from the fly, dragging the fly across the water, leaving a large, small, or even miniscule wake. It doesn't look natural, and the fish know it, and won't hit it. The late George Harvey, Penn State angling instructor, author, and an angler of legendary talent, made studies of drag with an intensity few have equaled and came up with some useful ideas on defeating it. He writes about it all in his book *Techniques of Trout Fishing and Fly Tying,* Lyons & Burford (1990): "I have seen anglers stand in one spot and change flies for over an hour and still never take a fish," Harvey says. "On many occasions, by moving just a step to the right or left the angler could, on the next cast, eliminate drag and take the trout on the original pattern."

173. Eliminating Drag: The George Harvey Solution

In a lifetime of studying drag and its deadly impact on dry fly fishing, the late, legendary Penn State angling professor George Harvey came up with some real answers. He decided that "perfect" casts were not the answer. The problem, he felt, lay in the leaders. When leaders straightened, a dragging fly was the result. He came up with a formula that would allow a leader to fall in S-curves, giving the fly a longer drag-free float. He started by going against the universal heavy-butt requirement of the times. He wrote about it in his classic, *Techniques of Trout Fishing and Fly Tying,* Lyons & Burford (1990): " . . . I do not use the heavy-butt leaders . . . I want the S curves in the leader to progressively get longer from the fly to the line. The heavy-butt leaders will not give you this progression . . . If you use this design for your dry-fly fishing, you will increase your catch by at least fifty percent." Here is the design Harvey recommended for a hard nylon 9.5-foot leader with 5X tippet: Starting with the nail knot, 10 inches of .017; 20 inches of .015; 20 inches of .013;

20 inches of .011; 12 inches of .009; 12 inches of .008; 18 inches of .007; 22 to 30 inches of .006. Although not butt heavy, Harvey's leaders were constructed with stiff monofilament in the first four butt sections, then soft mono in the rest of the leader. Of course, there are many more details on constructing and using such leaders in George Harvey's book. Remember: We are talking dry fly leaders here, not leaders for nymphs and streamers, which need to straighten so you can follow the drift of the underwater fly by watching the end of the leader or the strike indicator.

174. Buying George Harvey S-Curve Leaders

No, you don't have to tie those George Harvey leaders to cut drag by 50 percent, like George Harvey promised—unless you want to. You can buy them from Frog Hair, the Gamma Technologies company that makes and sells leaders, tippets, and fly flotation dressings (excellent ones, I might add). Look for the Dry Fly Slack Line Leader with George Harvey's picture on the cover of the sleeve. Frog Hair offers 4X, 5X, and 6X tippet sizes in 11 ½ feet. I bought mine on www.amazon.com, but you can find other sites, including the excellent site www.feather-craft.com. Or Google "Frog Hair Leaders" or go directly to Frog Hair, www.froghairfishing.com. The leaders are knotless and are said to represent the requirements for the desirable S-curve that beats drag. Instructions for casting are on the back of the sleeve.

175. Gary Borger's S-Curve Drag-Free Ideas

Author and angler Gary Borger came up with a way to tie S-curve leaders with fewer sections (and fewer blood knots) than in the George Harvey method. He offered his ideas in his book *Presentation,* which is out of print and sells on Amazon and other sites for more than $225. In the book, Borger has optimum leaders for

nymphing and other techniques as well. Perhaps someday an enterprising publisher will reissue the book.

176. Bottoms-Up Tactic for Finicky Feeders

When trout don't seem to be hitting and are probably hugging the bottom, particularly in lakes, try using a fast-sinking fly line, a short leader, 6 feet or so, and a floating fly like a Muddler Minnow or a Woolly Bugger. Your line will go along the bottom, with the fly trailing behind and above.

177. Choke-Up for Short, Tough Casts

Baseball players choke up on their bats, golfers choke up on their clubs. Fly fishers ought to choke up on their fly rods when making short, difficult casts under or between branches of overhanging bushes. Move your casting hand all the way up on the rod itself, several inches above the cork, for more control. Try it in practice. You'll be surprised at how effective this can be.

178. Make Dropper Rigs Your Wintertime Project

Why waste precious time on the stream tying the two-fly rigs that are so popular and effective today? Make it a wintertime project. Pick your floater dry fly, tie a leader 18 inches or so to the shank of the hook (some prefer to tie it into the eye of the dry fly hook), and tie a nymph to the leader. Store them in small plastic bags. When you're on the stream, all you have to do is tie the dry fly to your leader, dress it for better floating, and start catching fish.

179. Joe Humphrey's Best Nymph Tactic

In fishing upstream, to get a weighted nymph down and keep it down before the current drags the line and pulls the nymph back up, Joe Humphrey recommends what he calls the Tuck Cast. To make it, he stops the rod suddenly on the forward stroke at the 10:30 position by having the last two fingers of the casting hand pulling and the thumb pressing. Humphrey says, "It's a quick, squeezing action." The nymph is made to tuck back under the leader and drop to the bottom before drag sets in on the line. It's all in his book, *Joe Humphrey's Trout Tactics,* Stackpole (1981).

180. Joe Humphrey's Trout Tactics

The successor to George Harvey, the late legendary Penn State angling professor whose writing and influence has been widely felt in the world of fly fishing, particularly dry fly fishing, Joe Humphrey has emerged from the Penn State fly fishing classes as one of Pennsylvania's finest trout fly fishers ever. He holds the Pennsylvania record for the largest trout ever caught on a fly, a brown weighing 15.5 pounds, in 1977, and is a master angler who shares what he has learned. His book *Joe Humphrey's Trout Tactics,* Stackpole (1981), is a loaded with skills that will help any angler take more trout.

181. Taking the Temperature for Trout

The price of the gear mentioned may be out of date today, but the advice is not: " . . . a five-dollar thermometer can make more fishermen better fishermen than any other single piece of equipment."

—Joe Humphrey, *Joe Humphrey's Trout Tactics,*
Stackpole, 1981

182. The Right Temperatures for Trout

The renowned flyfisher Joe Humphrey, in *Joe Humphrey's Trout Tactics,* Stackpole (1981), has read stream temperatures on thousands of trips, including many with the Penn State "trout professor," the late George Harvey. In his book, he cites the importance of temperature in trout fishing: "A trout's metabolism increases with the rise in water temperature. When its metabolism

increases, the trout's demand for food is greater." Humphrey goes on to name 58, 59, 60, and up to 65 degrees as the "up-and-at-'em" temperatures for all trout species. He warns, however, " . . . these temperature ranges are *general* guidelines, and exceptions occur." See Joe's fantastic book for more details on the temperatures that will help you catch more trout.

183. Setting the Hook on Nymph Strikes

"There's an instant of tightness in the normal dance of a leader in current that indicates a trout has mouthed the fly—however briefly or gently—and you can tell, the way you can tell from the sound whether a guitar string has been struck by a musician or say, bumped by the tail of a passing dog."

—John Gierach, *Trout Bum*, Simon & Schuster,
1986

184. Trout on the Edge of Town

The Little Lehigh is one of Pennsylvania's treasured limestone creeks, with beautiful cool water pumped up by Mother Earth every day of the year. Located in Allentown, in a beautiful park, the Heritage section of the water is a mile or so of fly-fishing-only water from Hatchery Road off Route 309. Headquarters for anglers here is the Little Lehigh Fly Shop, www.littlelehigh-flyshop.com, 610-797-5599, located on Hatchery Road. The river is a treasure to behold, whether you are fishing or just having a picnic, as many Allentown folks and tourists do, with trout in plain sight all up and down the river. The trout are skittish as hawks, very difficult to approach and catch. You'll see lots of anglers here, few having hookups. Still, if you are longing to see some wild trout rising to flies right in front of you, give the Little Lehigh in Allentown a try.

185. Special Tactics for Giant Trout

When catching some of the biggest trout in the river is your objective (as opposed to my usual pursuit

of just wanting to catch lots of representative fish and get lots of action), you've got to use big-fish tactics. That means focusing on the deepest, darkest pools with big nymphs and streamers and getting deep. Sure, lots of big trout are caught sipping tiny flies off the surface.

If you're lucky enough to find them, tight lines! But in the main, you've got to fish down and dirty to lure out the big trout.

186. My Crazy Giant-Trout Morning

The theory of special tactics for giant trout came into play for me one June morning on a private stretch of Pennsylvania's Spruce Creek owned by friend Sylvia Bashline. Fishing with writer Nick Sisley, I studied a fine deep pool where the water pressed against a cut bank back in the shadows. I pulled out an olive land-locked salmon fly, about 4 inches long, tied it on, and

cast. The instant I pulled the streamer into the shadows, several fish flashed in the pool, and I thought, "Oh, boy!" In the next instant, a pike-sized fish bolted up through the pool with the fly in its mouth. It was a brown trout, huge, powerful, the trout of my dreams. Somehow, I managed to land the fish. Nick took a picture or two, and we measured the beast at 25 inches and released it. As you can imagine, this encounter is one of my favorite trout memories.

187. Use a Glove to Fish the Tangles

When trying to wade the edge of a trout stream that's flowing through tangles of branches, vines, and assorted gremlins that stop your progress, you'll be better off if you have a work glove on one hand to help clear your way. It's crazy how a single branch will find your landing net if you let it.

188. Three High-Desert Trout Destinations

Mentioning the word "desert" doesn't exactly conjure up images of trout, but when you make it read "high desert" you've got a whole new ballgame. That's especially so in central Oregon's high desert country, where private lakes and river stretches offer trout-fishing opportunities of the highest quality. Three of the best are the Grindstone Lakes at www.grindstonelakes.com; Lake in the Dunes at www.lakeinthedunes.com; and the Yamsi Ranch waters, which include the Williamson River, at www.yamsiflyfishing.com. If you're ready to book some really good fishing and lodging, check them out.

189. Snake River Triple Play

The words Snake River bring to mind mountain men, beautiful high country, and battling trout. Places like Idaho's legendary Henry's Fork of the Snake come to mind, as do remote sections of the South Branch of the Snake, which flow through wilderness beyond the roads. Three destinations in Idaho's Snake River area have linked together their Web sites so you can click onto the kind of fishing that interests you most. The three sources that interconnect on guides and lodging in the area are the well-known Mike Lawson's Henry's Fork Anglers at www.henrysforkanglers.com; South Fork Outfitters at www.southforkoutfitters.com; and South Fork Lodge at www.southforklodge.com.

190. B.C. Wilderness Adventures Fishing

From Kim Sedrovic's Fernie Wilderness Adventures lodge, in the remote mountains at Fernie, British Columbia, trout anglers get top-notch action wading or floating rivers like the Elk. The scenery has been described as breathtaking in articles in sporting magazines such as *Sporting Classics*. And there are trout there to match the surroundings. Orvis endorsed. See www.fernieadventures.com.

191. Fishing the Housatonic

Fly-fishing the popular Housatonic River in Connecticut can be greatly enhanced by a visit to Housatonic River Outfitters at www.dryflies.com. They've got everything you need, and everything you need to know, to meet the hatches and catch trout here.

192. Fit for a King

"The flesh of the trout is a rare delicacy that comes from one of nature's most tender and perishable creatures. . . . By far the best time to enjoy your trout is beside the waters where they are caught. Take a fry pan along and some bacon or shortening, and a little cornmeal and salt, and have yourself a feast fit for a deposed king—or an ulcerated millionaire. But first take a trout. . . ."

—Robert Traver, *Trout Madness*,
St. Martin's Press, 1960

193. Winter's Gift: The Secret Spring

"Two weeks ago, when it was thirty below, steam rose from the creek behind our home, from the riffle above the bridge. I'd never noticed it before . . . Then I realized there must be an underwater spring in that section of the creek. . . . and now I know where I can catch trout in extremes, whether in late August or the last week of November."

—John Barsness, *Montana Time*,
Lyons & Burford, 1992

194. A Mistake-Proof Fly

"In western lakes a No. 8 olive Woolly Worm is never a mistake."

—John Barsness, *Montana Time*,
Lyons & Burford, 1992

195. Have You Got The Touch?

"There is no substitute for fishing sense, and if a man doesn't have it, verily, he may cast like an angel and still use his creel largely to transport sandwiches and beer."

—Robert Traver, *Trout Madness*,
St. Martin's Press, 1960

196. The Upper Missouri: Fly Fishing's True Paradise

There are people who would say I should not be telling you about this particular angling destination. They lament that the place has received far too much publicity already, and that tattletales like Underwood should be thrown into irons for revealing secrets. I don't see it that way, but be warned that what you are about to learn can change your life, bend and skewer your schedules and priorities toward new directions. It's happened to many people before you, people who long to fly fish on spring creeks—the clear, cold slick reaches of water boiling out of Mother Earth 24/7 at the same temperature and filled with healthy, hungry trout. The Upper Missouri river is not a spring creek, but it might as well be. From its water release at Holter Dam near Wolf Creek, Montana, down past the fly fishing and lodging headquarters at Craig, eight miles downstream, and on down for scores of miles below that, the Missouri flows smooth and cold. It is filled with rainbow and brown trout and fly hatches to dream about. The Upper Missouri is the kind of water that makes people contemplate giving up their jobs and seeking employment in Helena, not far away. Those who can afford it look to buy vacation homes

© Stu Apte 2010

Stu Apte displays a Missouri River trout.

and cabins there. Some of my friends in the eastern United States, where I live, treasure the Upper Missouri for fall "cast and blast" vacations, combining bird hunting with trout fishing there. There are books galore, maps, and information sites. We shall get to some of them here.

197. Fishing the Upper Missouri from Wolf Creek

The Fly Shop at Wolf Creek, Montana, is a great place for hitting the river along the eight miles from the Holter Dam release to the town of Craig. The Fly Shop, at www.wolfcreekoutfitters.com/flyshop, not only has guides but also rents drift boats and float tubes and is adjacent to motel facilities. Phone, toll free, is 866-688-7688.

198. Headhunters on the Missouri

The little town of Craig, Montana, is a larger village than its Wolf Creek counterpart, upstream, and hosts lodging, guides, and outfitters for fishing the Upper Missouri. Headhunters Fly Shop, www.headhuntersflyshop.com, is just a short cast from the river at Craig and is a full-bore operation for guides, boats, rentals, gear, lodging, and information. Craig is a colorful stop for the fly fisher, including a bridge over the river right in midtown, a railroad crossing, and ample watering holes to discuss trouting adventures.

199. The Upper Missouri's Trout Shop

Located among other fly-fishing operations in the thriving metropolis of Craig, Montana, on the Upper Missouri is The Trout Shop, a complete guiding and outfitting service where you'll find just about everything you need to enjoy fishing this fabulous river. Visit their superb Web site at www.thetroutshop.com to see what it's all about, then pay them a visit in person. You may never leave.

200. Flyway Ranch Missouri Access

For those who think the "city life" in Craig and Wolf Creek might be a little intimidating, there's the Flyway Ranch located between the two towns on the Craig River Road. The ranch features lodging right on the bank of the river. Visit their Web site at www.flywayranch.com or call them at 406-235-4116.

201. Schwiebert on Jackson Hole Cutthroats

"Bob Carmichael taught me about cutthroats in Jackson Hole [Wyoming] . . . *Young man,* he rumbled with failing patience, *When you know enough about this part of the country to have an opinion about the fishing—you'll know there's cutthroats and there's cutthroats. . . . These fish ain't no pantywaists—they're Jackson Hole cutthroats!"*

—Ernest Schwiebert, *Trout,* E.P. Dutton, 1978

202. Schwiebert on Jackson Hole Cutthroats, Part Two

"The fish worked steadily all along the current tongues, and when I finally hooked one it was a whitefish. *Forget your matching the hatch!* Carmichael always ragged me unmercifully. *Fish these big variants right in the rips—and you'll learn something about real cutthroat fishing!'*

—Ernest Schwiebert, *Trout,* E.P. Dutton, 1978

203. The Secret Weapon for Green Drake Hatches

"While the big news on Limestone Creek (a fictitious name for a Pennsylvania spring creek) is always the coming of the giant Green Drake, the best fishing is usually with one of the various sulfurs. It's no secret and a favorite saying of local veterans that the best Green Drake pattern is usually a Size 16 Sulfur."

—Chuck Robbins, *Odyssey at Limestone Creek,* Tussey Mountain Publishers, 1997

204. Alaska Tactics Come to New York

Ever see and hold one of the Mouse Flies recommended for the big rainbows in Alaska? Well, before the rainbows get totally focused on salmon eggs once the great salmon runs go into full swing, the Mouse Fly is considered a primary weapon, especially early and late in the day. At this time of year—dead winter—when I am inclined to dreaming of doing great things, I have decided to give the big Mouse Fly, complete with its curly tail, some quality time on New York's upper Delaware. I'll fish it just at dark, through a pool where I have reasonable expectations of raising a fish. Might work! Can't hurt!

205. That West Yellowstone Pose

"So we assume that recognizable West Yellowstone pose: modest, seasoned, and ever so slightly self-satisfied. The implication being, yes, I guess we do know a thing or two about fishing around here, and, no, we don't really care to go into it. If nothing else, we know how to fit in here. We understand that the less you say about fly fishing, the more people will assume you know."

—John Gierach, *Dances With Trout*, Simon & Schuster, 1994

206. The Trout Stream You Cherish Most

"Most of the fishermen I know—even those who think of themselves as Sportsmen with a capital S— have a creek like this somewhere in their lives. It's not big, it's not great, it's not famous, certainly it's not fashionable, and therein lies its charm. It's an ordinary, run-of-the mill trout stream where fly-fishing can be a casual affair rather than having to be a balls-to-the-wall adventure all the time."

—John Gierach, *Sex, Death, and Fly Fishing*, Simon & Schuster, 1990

207. Rookie Error: He Missed It!

When I first got into trout fishing, coming to the sport from a southern fishing background, I was quick to attribute missed hits as, "He missed it!" Or, "I snatched it away from him!" Of course, what I was seeing was a classic refusal rise. I just didn't know what it was.

208. The Approaching Cold Front: It's Hot Stuff

When a summer cold front is approaching, with thunderstorms threatening, your fishing can turn into a real frenzy of action for a while. You'll have to eventually take cover, however, or die!

209. The Cold Front Has Passed. What Next?

The first couple of days behind a real cold front, with the wind rising and temperature dropping, can challenge even the most experienced anglers. You can bail out for home, or hang in there and give it your best shot. If you do stick around, plan on fishing deep and slow.

210. The Catch-and-Release Code

"Game fish are too valuable to be caught only once."

—Lee Wulff, *Lee Wulff's Handbook of Freshwater Fishing*, J.B. Lippincott, 1939

211. Guaranteed: More Trout Spinning Small Streams

Dunking worms in deep holes for early-season trout in your favorite stream is relatively easy—as long as other anglers don't take over your hole. Spinning the entire stream, working your way carefully from pocket

In early spring, it's tough to beat mealworms as a trout bait.

to pocket, is a lot more fun and will produce lots of trout, provided you are a skilled caster. The ability to cast light spinners and baits into pockets with accuracy separates the trout anglers who limit-out from the ones who come up empty. They just can't cast. We're talking about all kinds of delicate casts, underhand flips, sidearm throws under brush, things like that. It's not distance; it's accuracy that counts. The only way to obtain this skill is to practice, practice, practice. You'll catch lots of trout if you do.

212. The Strong Pull of Bait Fishing

"Bait is a connection with rivers that no other method of angling quite reaches. We are visual animals; although we use all our other senses to some extent . . . Bait fishing allows us to see through touch, like a coyote sees through his nose."

—John Barsness, *Montana Time,*
Lyons & Burford, 1992

213. Best Bait for Early-Season Spinning

Hitting your favorite local trout stream when it's stocked with fish in early season is a coveted rite of spring. An absolutely deadly bait—even better than worms—is the mealworm, the larva form of the mealworm beetle. Find a baitshop that carries them, and you are in business. You can also order them live right off the Internet at places like Cabela's, www.cabelas. com. (They'll keep in your fridge.) Place a No. 6 or 8 bait hook about three-fourths of the length of the beetle. Notice that stuff will be oozing out of the beetle, creating a fantastic fish attractor. Use a single split-shot to get the bait down. Many anglers like a barrel swivel about 18 inches above the hook to prevent twists. Mealies stay on the hook fairly well. Cast them into pocket water, in front of boulders, around their sides, into deep holes, down through riffles. Using ultralight spinning gear, mealies, and a rig like this, you're going to catch lots of early-season trout.

214. Small Spinners for Small-Stream Trout

If you are a good caster, you can do very well on early season trout in small streams by using ultralight spinning tackle and the smallest, lightest in-line spinners your rig can handle. Mepps, Panther Martin, and Blue Fox are some favorites, but there are many others. The bigger and heavier the spinner, the bigger and deeper the water it takes to fish them without them hanging up constantly. You want the lightest spinners your stream can handle, working them into pockets and under overhanging cover. Casting and retrieving these spinners in a small stream is an art unto itself, as challenging as fly fishing—but a lot more productive most of the time.

215. The Downstream Swing: Your Spinner's Strike Zone

When your spinner is swinging on the downstream arc of your cast, just before it swings across the current and the line straightens out below you, don't be in a hurry. Far from it, realize that the next several seconds may bring the strike you've been waiting for. Alternate between little jerks and steady pulls as it swings across. When it's downstream directly below you, keep it still for a moment, then start a careful retrieve.

216. Small-Stream Spinning: The Real Art

The real magicians of small-stream spinning—the guys and gals who catch most of the trout—avoid snagging by careful manipulation of their line with a subtle sense of feel in their rod hand. They don't make long casts; you might even say they don't cast at all in the true sense of the word. Instead, they make little flips and tosses, putting the small spinner into the holes with backhand and sidearm moves. They also match the size and weight of the spinner to the conditions, and often

hold their rod high on the retrieve to keep the lure from snagging the bottom. A good formula to remember: Flip the spinner out rod-low and retrieve it rod-high, watching the line carefully to make sure your little Mepps isn't about to snag up.

217. What Color Spinner Blades?

As in everything about fishing, there are no absolute rules regarding which color to choose for your spinner blades. However, a great many successful anglers like to use bright, silver-type blades on bright days. Use gold blades on dull or dark days.

218. Adding Weight to Your Spinner

When adding split-shot to your line to get your spinner deeper, place the shot several inches above the spinner, not on the spinner's nose. Placing it on the nose will interfere with the spinner's action.

219. Fish the Woolly Bugger with Spinning Tackle

Tie on an olive Woolly Bugger streamer, place enough split-shot to make the cast about 8 inches up the line, and fish it just as if you were using a fly rod. Whether or not to use a weighted beadhead fly, or the unweighted, depends on the current and depth you're trying to fish. Olive Woolly Buggers in various weights and sizes belong in your kit with your Mepps and other in-line spinners.

220. Fishing the Big, Slow Pools

When you're lucky enough to get a big slow pool all to yourself on your trout stream, don't make your first casts to the backside. Start by making a series of Fan Casts to the nearest part of the pool, gradually working your casts to the backside. You'll really be covering the water that way.

221. Keep it Simple and Fun

We talk elsewhere in this book about the importance of catching fish when you take kids fishing, making sure they get action. One of the best ways to do that on early season trout streams is to use a simple bait-keeper hook, like a Size 8, perhaps a split-shot and barrel swivel about 12 inches up the line, and a bobber. You can use a light spinning outfit, or even a plain long graphite pole or fly rod. Your bait will be one of the many Berkley Powerbaits, a glowing, scented trout tantalizer you carry in a small jar: www.cabelas.com. If you can find a good spot, the kid will see the bobber start dancing, then go under, and you'll have a fishing partner for life.

222. Try a Different Spinner Lure

If you feel that the trout in your local streams are being pounded too hard with traditional in-line spinners like Mepps and Panther Martins, consider going to an alternative. Two excellent choices are the Spin-A-Lure and Lil' Jake Lure, both wobblers with tantalizing action. Available at www.cabelas.com. Work them the same way you do in-line spinners.

223. Spinning with a B-17

B-17 makes fantastic lures in sizes and weights for both fly fishing and spinning for trout and bass, and just about everything that swims. They're expensive compared to your average spin-bait, but wait until you see and try them. Don't be put off by the unusual name of their Web site, www.b-17swimsuit.com.

224. Small Spinners Reveal Trout Locations

When using small spinners for trout, keep an alert eye on the lure as it swings through a pool or behind the rocks, especially on your first cast into a hole. Even when they do not hit, trout often respond to a spinner by a flashing movement.

225. The Deadliest Trout Spinner?

The Colorado spinner is thought to owe its origin to a man named John Hildebrant, who, in 1899, put a hole in a dime, attached it to a hairpin shaft, and started catching trout. In much-improved forms, it's been catching trout ever since. The late Ted Trueblood, angling editor and columnist for *Field & Stream,* in his *Angler's Handbook,* "Thomas Crowell" (1949) as calling it "The most deadly trout lure ever devised for fishing in the United States . . ." He added, "In various sizes it will catch all other kinds of gamefish." Fish the Colorado with line as light as possible, and with just enough weight on your line to make the cast. Although some experts do not like baiting the Colorado, I personally have had great success with trout using a Colorado spinner sweetened with a worm.

226. Spinning with Small Jigs Takes More Trout

If you want to catch lots of trout during early season when the water's cold and the streams are a little high and off-color, leave your fly rod in the truck and go with light spinning tackle. Use tiny jigs tipped with live bait or soft-plastics like Berkley's Power Nymphs. Small hair jigs work too.

227. Matukas and Spinners: A Deadly Combo

A Web site called Jerry's Flies, www.jerrysflies. com, is where I first started reading about Matuka spinner flies. Combining a Matuka streamer with a spinner creates a lure you can count on to get trout moving in whatever pool you work it in. Matukas, which I believe originally came from New Zealand, have been a favorite of trout fly fishers for years. Combined with a spinner, they are even more effective. Before Woolly Buggers came along, the Matuka was my go-to fly for searching the water. I like olive.

228. Sweeten Your Trout Spinnerbait

No need to send your Mepps or other spinner lure out there all by itself. Where legal, you can sweeten your trout fishing spinner lure by tipping it with a piece of earthworm. It spoils the action of the spinner a little, but you'll catch more trout. They love worms. The fly-fishing-only crowd hates all this, but what the heck . . . you're out to catch some trout. This will help

you do it. Maybe someday you'll get into fly fishing. Right now, you'll be eating trout.

229. Spinning Tricks for Trout

You don't hear much about "spinning the bubble" these days, but it's still an effective way to catch trout on streams or lakes where all-tackle fishing is allowed. Tie your spinning line to the kind of ball float that you can get water into to add weight for casting with flies. Set your leader from the float to the depth you think will bring strikes, and tie on a nymph. Cast upstream, downstream, or across and let your rig float down through trout lairs. You'll catch fish.

F. More Trout Tactics

Lakes, Ponds, and Reservoirs

Trout are generally thought of as fish of streams and large lakes. However, they can also live in cool-water ponds. Northern beaver ponds are great places for wild brook trout, and spring-fed manmade ponds can sustain stocked rainbows.

Trout do not relate to structure the way warm-water fish do. They roam a pond or small lake and are likely to be found at any depth. The best way to find them is to walk the bank and try different areas. You can catch trout on either natural bait or artificials. Use spin-cast or spinning tackle and 4- or 6-pound test line. For fishing natural bait, you can use either a bobber rig

A boat is a definite help in fishing a large lake or reservoir. Anglers who can move around and fish away from the bank have a better chance of success on these larger waters.

or a very light slip-sinker rig. Bait with a night crawler, grasshopper, commercially preserved salmon eggs, or whole kernel corn. Use a #8 short-shank hook.

If you prefer artificials, stick with tiny crankbaits, sinking spoons, in-line spinners (probably best), and minnow lures. If you're casting a lure that sinks, use the countdown method to fish different depths.

How to Fish Large Lakes and Reservoirs

Large lakes and reservoirs are some of the most popular and accessible fishing locations. Most are public waters with boat ramps, piers and other facilities to accommodate fishermen. They usually have large, diverse fish populations, and offer many opportunities for anglers.

What's the difference between a lake and a reservoir? A lake is made by nature, while a reservoir is made by man. Natural lakes are plentiful in the northern U.S. and Canada, in Florida, along major river systems (oxbows), and in the Western mountains.

Natural lakes come in several forms. Some have rounded, shallow basins with soft bottoms. Others are very deep with irregular shapes and bottoms that include reefs, islands and other structure. In many natural lakes, vegetation grows abundantly in shallow areas.

Natural lakes vary in age and fertility—measures of their ability to support fish populations. Some are relatively young and fertile, while others are eons old and somewhat infertile.

Reservoirs exist throughout North America. These are impoundments formed by building a dam across a river and backing up the floodwaters. Dozens of reservoirs have been built across the continent in the last 50 years to control floods, and generate electric power.

In most cases, the bottoms of reservoirs were once farmlands or forest. The water covers old fields, woodlands, creeks, roads, and other features that, when submerged, became structure.

Reservoirs are divided into two categories: upland and lowland (or mainstream). Upland reservoirs were built in highlands or canyons. They are typically deep and wind through steep terrain. Their coves and creek arms are irregular in shape.

In contrast, lowland reservoirs course through broad, flat valleys. These reservoirs are wider and shallower than upland reservoirs and typically have a long, fairly straight trunk with numerous smaller tributary bays.

The fertility of a reservoir often depends on how fertile the area was before it was flooded. Lowland reservoirs impounded over river bottoms are highly fertile, especially if trees were left standing when the area was flooded. As the trees decay, they release nutrients that support fish. Upland or canyon areas are less fertile, however. This is why upland reservoirs seldom support fish populations as dense as those in lowland reservoirs.

Analyzing Large Lakes and Reservoirs

It's easy for a beginning angler to stand on the bank of a large lake or reservoir and feel overwhelmed. There's so much water and so many places where fish can be. Start by adjusting your attitude. Since there's more water, there are more fish, so your odds of success are roughly the same as when fishing a pond or smaller lake.

That's exactly how to approach this situation! It's impossible to fish an entire large lake or reservoir. So choose one small part of it, approach it like a pond or small lake, and use the same tactics. Whether they live in large or small waters, fish react the same to similar conditions in their environment. The basics still apply, and the same tactics work in large waters and small. The main difference is that, since they aren't confined in

Ethics & Etiquette

Ask First.
Don't trespass. Never go on private property without permission. If you find a place you'd like to fish, seek out the permission of the landowner.

small ponds, the fish have more freedom to roam, and may migrate from one area to another depending on the season, food supply and other factors. Therefore, when deciding where to fish on a big lake, you have to pick the right small part.

How do you do this? Ask a nearby tackle store operator where the fish are biting. Watch where other anglers are fishing. Try to determine if the fish are shallow or deep. Learn the depth where they're biting. Use whatever information you can to get an overall picture, then key in on a location.

One aid that all anglers should learn to use is a topographic map. A "topo" map shows water depth and contour changes on the lake bottom. You can look at a topo map and find drop-offs, reefs, flats, creek chan-

nels, sunken islands and other types of structure. You can use the map to find these special areas where fish are likely to hang out. For instance, if a tackle store operator tells you crappie are spawning around the shoreline in shallow bays, you can locate shallow bays on your topo map, learn how to get to there, then go fish them.

In essence, topo maps are road maps to hot spots. Get one for the lake where you plan to fish and begin studying it.

Streams and Rivers

Trout are found in cold-water streams throughout much of the U.S. and Canada. Some are native to their

This stream angler is doing everything right. He's casting up-current, and retrieving his lure back through a deep hole with cover. There is a good chance he will get a strike.

home waters while others have been raised in hatcheries and stocked.

Fly-fishing is a popular, effective way to take trout, but I don't recommend it for beginners. I suggest sticking with light spinning tackle until you build your angling skills. Then you might "graduate" to fly-fishing in the future.

Stream trout are very elusive fish. Get too close, make too much noise, wear bright clothes, or drop a lure right on their heads, and they'll dart away. Instead, you have to stay back from feeding zones, remain quiet, wear drab-colored clothes, and cast beyond where you think the fish are.

Trout hold in similar areas as smallmouths. They prefer eddies adjacent to swift water where they can hide and then dart out to grab passing food. During insect hatches, trout also feed in open runs with moderate current.

Since most trout streams are clear, rig with 4-to 6-pound test line. Then tie on a small in-line spinner, spoon, floating minnow or crawfish crankbait. Cast these lures around rocks, logs, weeds and other likely structure bordering swift water. The heads of pools can be especially good early in the morning and late in the afternoon. Also, trout love to feed after dark.

Natural baits are also effective on stream trout. Night crawlers, salmon eggs, grasshoppers and minnows are good bets. Canned corn or small marshmallows will tempt bites, especially from hatchery-raised trout. All these baits should be fished on the bottom with a very small hook (#12) and a split shot clamped 10-12 inches up the line.

How to Fish Large Rivers

Earlier in this chapter I mentioned that fishing large lakes is like fishing small ponds in terms of basics. The same comparison can be made between small streams and large rivers. Big rivers are just little streams that have grown up. They are more complex, however, and contain a much broader range of fishing conditions.

Large rivers are the most diverse of all waters. They contain a wide variety of fishing locations: eddies, bluffs, dropoffs, shallow flats, feeder streams, backwater sloughs, tailwaters, deep and shallow areas, and swift-flowing and calm water. Rivers also hold all species of freshwater fish and North American large rivers offer a smorgasbord of fishing opportunity.

As with small streams, large rivers are also divided into two types: warm and cold water. Most rivers in North America are the warm, deep variety, supporting sunfish, bass, white bass, catfish, walleye, etc. Many are dammed into "pools" to provide enough deep water for navigation.

In contrast, cold-water rivers are typically shallow and swift, flowing through mountainous areas and usually hold various trout species.

Large rivers are most often fished from boats, though you can fish successfully from the bank, especially below dams or in backwater sloughs and oxbows. But whichever method and location you choose, large rivers are topnotch fisheries that beginners and veteran anglers can share and enjoy.

Analyzing Large Rivers

As in small streams, current determines fish locations in large rivers. Understanding current and being able to read rivers is essential to fishing them.

Current in large rivers may be more difficult to figure out. In small streams you can see the riffles and swift runs, but in large rivers the current may appear equal from bank to bank. Look closer, though, and you'll see signs of current breaks. Points of islands, jetties, dam tailwaters, river bars and mouths of tributaries are all areas where current is altered, and are prime spots to catch fish.

Most fish in large rivers usually hang in eddies or slack water. Sometimes they prefer still water bordering strong current where they can ambush baitfish washing by. At other times they seek quiet backwater sloughs.

Besides current, three other variables in large rivers are water level, color, and cover.

WATER LEVEL—Rivers continuously rise and fall, depending on the amount of rainfall upstream. The level of the river is referred to as its "stage," and this can have a direct bearing on fish locations. Many times, when a river is rising and its waters are flooding surrounding lowlands, fish move into these freshly-flooded areas to take advantage of a banquet of worms, crawfish and other food.

COLOR—Large rivers vary greatly in water clarity. While the main channel area may be muddy, backwaters can be clear and more attractive to fish. Or, entire river systems may be muddy or clear, depending on recent rains. Most fish species feed better in clear rather than muddy water.

COVER—Fish react to cover in rivers the same way they do in other bodies of water. Species such as bass, crappie and sunfish usually hold in or close to cover. Structure provides hiding places and a shield from current.

So when "reading" a large river, be aware of current (especially eddies), river stage, water color, and structure. You will encounter a broad range of combinations of these conditions that may confuse a beginning fisherman. But by following the advice in the remainder of this section, you can be assured that you're on track and that you can, indeed, mine large rivers of their fishing riches.

Techniques for Fishing Large Rivers

Many techniques for fishing large rivers are the same for ponds, lakes and small streams. Therefore, the key to catching fish from rivers is finding them and then applying the fundamentals of tackle, bait and fishing methods.

Many large cold-water rivers offer very good trout fishing. Deep runs can harbor lunker browns,

Many cool-water streams in North America support abundant trout populations – both natives and stockers. The best way for beginners to catch these fish is casting tiny spinners or natural bait into holes below swift runs.

rainbows and cutthroats. These trophy fish are very wary, so they're hard for beginning anglers to catch. However, smaller trout can provide plenty of action for beginners who use basic techniques and who are careful not to spook the fish.

As in small streams, current is the most important factor in deciding where to try for trout in large rivers. The concept is simple. Current funnels food into predictable areas, and the fish hold in or around these areas where the pickings are easy. They'll lie in the shadows and then dart out and grab a morsel as it drifts by.

Pools below riffles or waterfalls are prime feeding locations. So are eddies behind rocks, logs or anything else that diverts current. Undercut, shaded banks on outside bends of the river are prime hiding places for trout as are holes below the mouths of feeder creeks.

On rivers, fish natural bait the same way as in small streams.

The trick is to study the current for places next to the flow where trout can lurk and watch for food.

Fish these spots with the same lures recommended for stream trout: spinners, spoons, floating minnows and small crankbaits. Always cast upstream and retrieve your lure back with the current. Decide exactly where you think trout should be and pull your lure close to this location.

Use natural bait the same way as in small streams. Worms, minnows, grasshoppers and salmon eggs will take native trout. Whole kernel corn, cheese, and small marshmallows are good for stocked trout. Fish these baits with a small hook and a split shot crimped a foot above the hook. Make a quartering cast upstream from where the trout should be. Then reel in slack line and feel for a bite as the current carries the bait along bottom. Set the hook at any unnatural bump or pressure.

© Jay Cassell

Mid-sized streams (above) often yield big-sized trout (below).

Walleyes

A. Walleye Introduction

WADE BOURNE

The walleye is a member of the perch family. It gets its name from its large, glassy, light-sensitive eyes. While walleye average 1-3 pounds, in some waters they grow to more than 20 pounds. Many walleye experts consider fish over 10 pounds to be trophies. The world-record walleye, weighing an even 25 pounds, was caught in Tennessee in 1960.

Many anglers highly prize walleye for its table quality. Its meat is white, firm and mild-tasting. Because of this eating quality and its abundance in many waters, the walleye is a favorite among anglers wherever it's found.

Walleye are native to cool, clean lakes, reservoirs and major rivers of the central U.S. and much of Canada. They have also been stocked in both eastern and western waters outside their home range.

Walleye spend most of their time in deep main-lake/river areas where there is good water circulation, but they also frequently feed on shallow flats and close to shore. They normally move into these areas in low-light periods such as night, dawn, dusk, cloudy days or when vegetation or muddy water shields them from bright sunlight. A walleye's main food is small baitfish, though it will also feed on insects and small crustaceans and amphibians.

Walleye are early spawners. Their spawning run starts when the water temperature climbs above 45° F. Walleye in lakes spawn on shallow flats with hard, clean bottoms. In rivers, walleye spawn below riffles in pools with rock or sand bottoms. In river-fed lakes and reservoirs, an upstream spawning run is the rule. When spawning, one large female walleye can lay several hundred thousand eggs.

One characteristic of these fish is especially pertinent to beginning anglers: they have sharp teeth! Fishermen who stick a finger into a walleye's mouth will get a painful surprise. Instead, they should be gripped across the back.

Walleye

Sauger

Sauger

Sauger are closely related to walleye, and many people confuse them because of their similar appearance and habits. But there are two easy ways to tell them apart. Sauger have dark, saddlelike blotches on their backs (as opposed to the walleye's smooth golden scale pattern). Also, sauger have dark spots on the main dorsal fin. (A walleye's dorsal fin is spot-free.)

Sauger don't grow as large as walleye; they seldom reach 4 pound. (The world record sauger – 8 pounds 12 ounces – was caught in North Dakota in 1971.) The sauger is a river fish, though it also lives in river impoundments and some natural lakes. Its range includes the Mississippi Valley west of the Appalachian Mountains and north to James Bay in Canada. Sometimes sauger are found co-existing with walleye, but they're more tolerant of dingy water than walleye. This means sauger can thrive in slow-moving, silty streams where walleye can't survive.

The sauger's feeding and spawning habits are very similar to those of walleye. This fish is also prized by anglers for its fine table quality. And like walleye, sauger have sharp teeth which should be avoided by anglers.

B. Walleye Tactics

WADE BOURNE

Lakes and Reservoirs

Walleye are traditionally deep-water, bottom-hugging fish, but they will frequently feed in the shallows. The determining factor seems to be light penetration into the water. Walleye don't like bright sunlight. But on overcast days, at night, when shallow areas are dingy or wave-swept, or when heavy weed growth provides shade, they may hold and feed in water no deeper than a couple of feet.

Walleye may be the ultimate structure fish. In deep areas, they hold along underwater humps, reefs and drop-offs on hard, clean bottoms, especially those with rock or sand. They prefer water with good circulation and rarely concentrate in dead-water areas like sheltered bays or coves. Walleye will move in and out of feeding areas.

Walleye spawn when water temperature climbs into the mid-40° F range, and this is a good time for beginning anglers to try for these fish. (Check local regulations, as some states maintain a closed season on walleye until after they spawn.)

Look for shallows or shoal areas with gravel or rock bottoms that are exposed to the wind. Sloping points, islands, reefs, and rock piles close to shore are

Large rivers are among the most diverse of North America's waters. Big rivers have a broad range of fish and structure where fish concentrate. Look for bass, after spawning, off points that lead into submerged feeder creek channels.

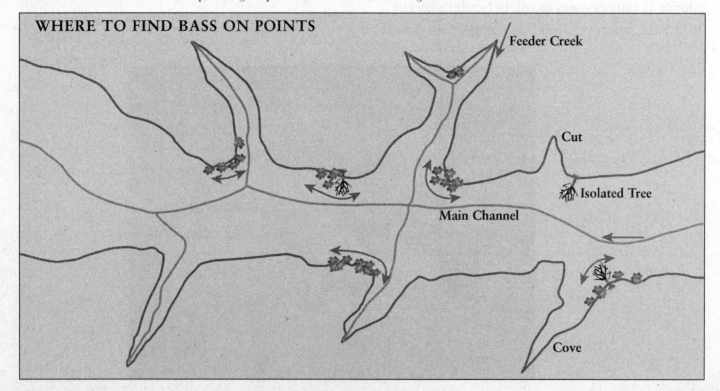

WHERE TO FIND BASS ON POINTS

high-percentage spots. Fish them during low-light periods: dawn, dusk and at night.

Try a slip-bobber rig baited with a night crawler, leech or live minnow in these areas. Adjust the bobber so the bait is suspended just above bottom. Try casting shallow areas with jigs tipped with live minnows or shallow-running crankbaits.

In early summer, walleye can be caught along weedlines and mid-lake structure, both requiring a boat to properly fish them. When fishing weeds, cast a small jig ($\frac{1}{16}$ or $\frac{1}{8}$ ounce) tipped with a minnow right into the edge of the weeds, then swim it back out. Work slowly along the weedline. Pay special attention to sharp bends in the weedline or areas where the weeds thin out. (This technique will also produce bass, crappie and pike.)

Fishing deep structure can be a needle in a haystack situation, so it's best to stay on the move until you locate fish. If you see other boats clustered on a small area, they're probably fishing productive structure. Go there and try drifting a night crawler on a slip-sinker rig. Move upwind of the other boats, and let out enough line to hit bottom. Then engage your reel and drag the night crawler across bottom as you drift downwind.

A bite will feel like a light tap or bump. Release line immediately, and allow the fish to swim off with the bait. After about 20 seconds, reel up slack, feel for the fish, and set the hook.

This is the standard way to fish for lake or reservoir walleye, but there are other good methods. Bottom-bouncing rigs trailing night crawlers or minnows can be productive along deep structure or submerged points. This is the same principle as using the slip-sinker rig. Let your line down to bottom, engage the reel, then drag the rig behind you as you drift or troll. A slip-bobber rig drifted across this structure is also a good bet.

As you fish deep structure, it's a good idea to have a floating marker handy. If you get a bite, throw out the marker, then come back to this spot after you've landed your fish. Walleye are school fish, so there are probably more in the same area.

Beginners should try two other simple approaches for walleye. First, find a rocky shoreline that slopes off quickly into deep water. Fish this from dusk to around midnight, either with live bait (slip-bobber rig) or by casting floating minnow lures. Second, cast into areas where strong winds are pushing waves into shore. This wave action muddies the water and walleye move right up to the banks to feed. Cast a jig and minnow into this roily water. Either walk the bank or wade the shallows, casting as you go. Pay special attention to the zone where muddy water borders clear.

Streams

River walleye and sauger collect in fairly predictable places. They spend most of their time out of current, so look for them around islands, rock jetties, eddies below dams, etc. They usually hold near the edge of an eddy where they can watch for food.

Trophy walleye like this one can be caught from many of North America's big lakes and reservoirs. These fish usually stay in deeper water and hug bottom structure. Sometimes, though, when feeding and water conditions are just right, they will move up into shallow vegetation or close to shore.

The best river conditions for catching walleye are when the water is low, stable and relatively clear. Walleye continue feeding when a river is rising, but may change locations in response to high-water conditions. When the river gets too muddy, or when the water starts dropping again, walleye generally become inactive and hard to catch.

Tailwaters below dams are the best places for beginners to catch river walleye. Some fish stay in tailwaters all year long, but the biggest concentrations occur during winter and early spring. Walleye may hold close to dam faces or behind wingwalls. They like to hang along rock ledges, gravel bars or other structure. But again, the key is reduced flow.

Boat-fishing is best for catching river walleye. Use a jig tipped with a live minnow, matching your jig weight to the amount of current. In slack water, a ⅛-ounce jig is heavy enough to work most tail-water areas. Float or troll through likely walleye locations, vertically jigging off the bottom. Or anchor and cast into eddies, holes and current breaks. Let the jig sink to the bottom, and work it back with a lift/drop retrieve. At all times, work the bait slowly. Set the hook at the slightest bump.

A good technique for bank fishermen is casting crankbaits or jigs tipped with minnows along riprap banks in early spring. Walleye spawn along the rocks downstream from dams when the water temperature climbs into the mid-40° F range. Cast parallel to banks, bump crankbaits off the rocks, or swim jigs just above them.

In summer and fall, look for walleye farther downstream, along riprap banks, jetties, gravel or rock bars, mouths of tributaries or sloughs, or deep eddy pools at the edge of current. Cast jigs or troll live-bait rigs through deeper areas, or cast crankbaits along rocky shallows.

This river walleye was caught in the white water right below a dam.

C. Walleye Tactics

LAMAR UNDERWOOD

1. White-Water Walleye Holes

In summer when walleyes go deep and may be tough to find in schools on the reefs, the current below the rapids on lake outlets can usually be counted on to give up some fish. They have everything they need here: plenty of oxygen, food coming their way, and cover to hide.

2. A Deadly Summer Walleye Lure

The jig-and-spinner combination lure has been catching walleyes—and other fish—a long time, but sometimes a new and successful wrinkle of tinkering with a jig-spinner comes along. Writing in the Spring 2009 issue of the *Boundary Waters Journal*, Darrel Brauer's article, "Walleyes for Dinner," reports on

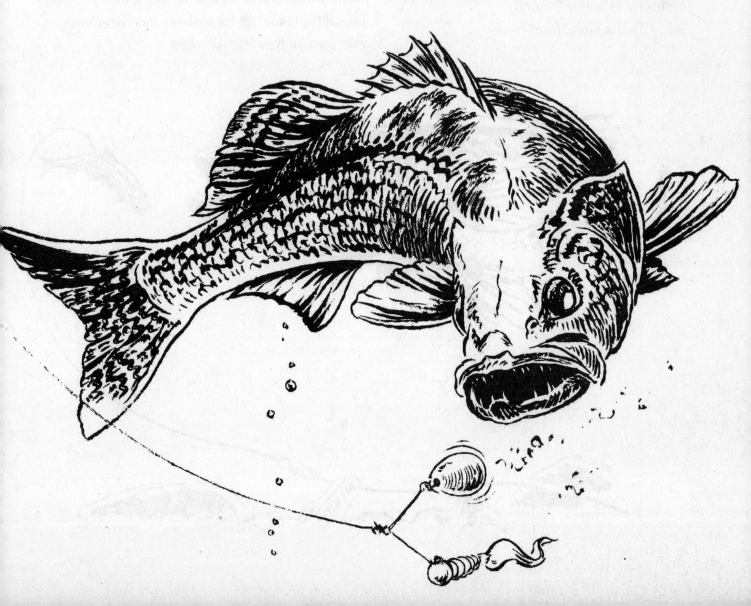

finding a winning combination for trolling for finicky summer walleyes in about 8 feet of water: "The precise specifications are: begin with a Betts Spin Size 3 gold spinner, add a ¼-ounce Eagle Claw saltwater jig dressed with a pure-white 4-inch Berkeley PowerBait grub. Not only is this combination effective when trolled down to about 12 feet, it is absolutely deadly when fished in the current below rapids and falls."

3. *Field & Stream's* Walleye "Ultimate Lure" Survey Winners

In what it called the "Ultimate Lure Survey," published in March 2008, *Field & Stream* magazine asked 1,000 of its hard-core readers to name their favorite lures. The winners for the Walleye category were:

Spinners, 54%, Erie Dearie
Jigs, 19%, Jig With Mister Twister
Minnow-Type Lures, 12%, Original Rapala with
Smithwick Rogue second
Crankbaits, 9%, Rapala Shad Rap
Soft-Plastics, 3%, Berkley Gulp! Minnow
Spoons, 3%, Dardevle

4. The Rig That Worked Magic—And Still Does

The legendary Lindy Rig put today's Lindy Tackle Co. on the map. It's especially good for fall walleyes, reports Brian McClintock in the September 2007 issue of *Field & Stream*. Hook a 6-inch minnow or chub behind the dorsal fin with a No. 2 Octopus hook. The leader is 36- to 42-inch 10-pound test connected to a barrel swivel. Now comes a ⅛- to ¼-ounce slip sinker that will slide and bounce along the bottom. For more fish-taking Lindy tips for walleyes and everything else, visit www.lindyfishingtackle.com.

5. Northland Tackle Free Booklet

Northland Fishing Tackle, www.northlandtackle.com, is loaded with great walleye baits and information—as well as all other freshwater gamefish—and features a free 96-page catalog and fishing guide.

6. Walleyes for the Frying Pan: Beware the Cholesterol Police

You will not find many anglers who don't rank the walleye as No. 1 in the frying pan. For my taste, the fillets should be fried, even deep-fried. Yes, the docs will call this a heart-stopping meal, and that might keep you away. But . . . what the heck. How often do you do it? Some of the best meals I've ever had in my life have been shoreline lunches with walleye and pike fillets fried in a pan that the guides had first used to fry great slices of bacon as soon as they got the fire going. The Cholesterol Police were shouting in my ear, but I dug in with great gusto. Life's too short to miss this kind of culinary experience.

7. Putting Flasher Spoons to Work

On Lake Huron's Saginaw Bay, Mark Gwizdala was having a slow afternoon with his usual trolling lures and tactics. He started thinking of the ways other anglers use flashers for salmon and trout. He tied on a flashy spoon and in-line weight about 5 feet ahead of a spinner with a night crawler. Bingo! Mark's success that

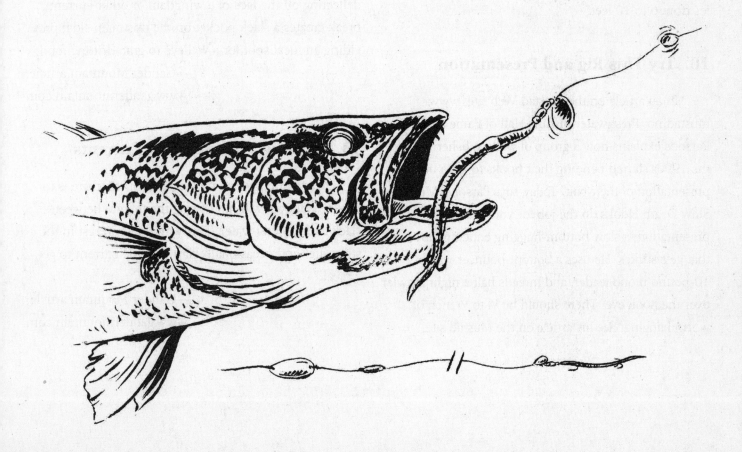

day has spread to anglers all over the Great Lakes trolling for suspended walleyes, and even into other techniques for bottom bouncing. The flasher spoon attracts the fish's attention, the lure and bait close the deal.

—Reported by Dave Scroppo in the article "Master Class for Walleyes," on the Outdoor Life Web site www.outdoorlife.com

8. A Trick for Cold-Water Fishing

Walleye expert Jeff Murray, writing in *North American Fisherman,* said that he favors fishing for cold-water walleyes with an inflated crawler hooked right in the nose so that it swims lazily through the water in a straight line.

9. Live-Bait Rig for Taking More Walleyes

A simple rig to catch more and bigger walleyes is to use a slip-sinker system, with a sliding egg or bullet sinker in front of a barrel swivel, with a leader that varies from 6 to 10 feet.

10. Try This Rig and Presentation

In an article on the Mustad Web site, www. mustad.no, Freshwater Fishing Hall of Fame angler Gary Parsons explains how a group of walleye fishermen in the 1990s started bending their hooks to get a unique presentation of their bait. Today, says Parsons, Mustad's Slow Death Hooks do the job for you in a deadly finesse presentation, a slow bottom-hugging enticing move that gets strikes. He uses a bottom-bouncer weight, 10-pound mono leader, and threads half a night crawler over the hook eye. There should be ¼ to ½ inch of worm hanging. See his article on the Mustad site.

11. Focusing on River Walleyes

"Walleyes will tolerate a slight current, but seldom will you find them in fast water, unless there is some type of cover to serve as a current break. When searching for walleyes in rivers, you can immediately eliminate a good share of the water because the current is too swift. Just how much current walleyes will tolerate depends on the season."

—Gander Mountain article, www.gandermountain.com

12. Overlooked Walleye River Hotspots

"You can find river walleyes in slack pools, in eddies, or downstream from some type of current break like an island, a bridge pier, or a large boulder. But many anglers make the mistake of fishing only the downstream side of obstructions. For instance, walleyes usually hold just upstream of a wingdam, a rocky structure intended to deflect current toward the middle of the river to keep the channel from silting in. Current deflecting off the face of a wingdam or other current break creates a slack pocket on the upstream side, providing an ideal spot for a walleye to grab drifting food."

—Gander Mountain article, www.gandermountain.com

13. Reading Walleye River Currents

"Current edges are to a river what structure is to a lake. Walleyes will hold along the margin between slack and moving water. This way, they can rest in the still water and occasionally dart into the current to get a meal."

—Gander Mountain article, www.gandermountain.com

Pike

Muskellunge,
Northern Pike, Pickerel

A. Muskellunge, Northern Pike, Pickerel

Muskellunge

Many anglers view the "muskie" as the supreme freshwater trophy fish. Muskies are top-of-the-food-chain predators. They are never very numerous in any body of water. They grow huge in size.

They're hard to get to bite, but when they do, they fight savagely. Muskie anglers often cast for hours or even days without getting a strike. When they finally do hook one of these fish, however, they experience one of the most difficult and exciting challenges in all of fishing. Muskies are the wild bulls of the water, and it takes great skill and dedication to land them consistently.

The muskie is a member of the pike family. It is found in natural lakes, reservoirs and streams/rivers in the Northeast, upper Midwest and southern Canada. This fish requires cool, clean water.

The muskie is cylinder-shaped, and it has a long, powerful body. Its sides are usually yellow-tinted and marked with dark blotches or bars. This fish has a flat, duck-like mouth and very sharp teeth! It feeds mainly on smaller fish, but it will also attack birds, small muskrats and other hapless creatures that enter its domain.

Muskies typically stalk their prey alone in shallow water, around reeds, rocky shoals, quiet eddy pools in streams, and other similar spots. During warm months, they feed more in low-light periods of dawn and dusk. On cloudy days, however, they may feed anytime. One of the very best times to fish for muskies is during fall when they go on a major pre-winter feeding binge.

Muskies live many years and frequently grow beyond 35 pounds. The current world record, weighing 67 pounds 4 ounces, was caught in Wisconsin in 1949.

Since the muskie is such a vicious predator, nature has a way of keeping its numbers down so other fish have a chance to survive. The muskie is a late spawner (water temperature in the mid-50° F range). The fish that survive, however, grow to rule over their home waters. The only predator to big muskies is man.

MUSKELLUNGE

PIKE

Northern Pike

It would be fair to call pike the "poor man's muskie." Members of the pike family, "northerns" are much more numerous than muskies, and they are easier to catch. By nature, pike are very aggressive, and they often attack any bright, flashy lure that swims by.

Pike inhabit natural lakes, reservoirs, rivers and streams throughout the northeastern and north-central U.S. and most of Canada. They thrive in warm, shallow lakes or river sloughs with an abundance of water weeds.

The pike's body is shaped like a muskie's: long and round with the same flat, pointed mouth and sharp teeth. Its color is dark olive on the sides with light, wavy spots. Its belly is white. Pike can grow over 20 pounds. Because they're so vulnerable to fishing pressure, big ones are usually found only in lakes off the beaten path. The world-record pike (55 pounds 1 ounce) was caught in Germany in 1986.

Pike spawn in quiet, shallow areas when the water temperature climbs into the 40° F range. After spawning, they linger around weedbeds, especially those close to sharp underwater contour changes. They are not school fish by nature, but they will cluster together if their food source is concentrated. Like muskies, they eat almost anything that swims, floats or dives. Most of the pike's diet consists of fish, and they will attack prey up to half their own body size.

When hooked, a pike is a strong battler, rolling on the surface and shaking its head from side to side. It isn't the most desirable table fish because of its many small bones, but anglers can learn to remove these bones during cleaning. The meat of the pike is white, flaky and tasty.

Pickerel

These toothy predators are a mini-version of pike and muskies. Their sides are covered with a yellowish

CHAIN PICKEREL

chain pattern on a green background. They're aggressive strikers, and they give a good fight on light tackle. Most pickerel range from 1-3 pounds, but can grow larger than this in southern habitats. The world-record chain pickerel, caught in Georga in 1961, weighed 9 pounds 6 ounces.

The grass and redfin pickerels rarely reach a foot in length. The redfin is found along the Atlantic coastal plain in small creeks and shallow ponds. The grass pickerel's range is primarily in the Mississippi and Great Lakes drainages.

Pickerel spawn in shallow weeds as water temperatures reach the high 40° F range. Pickerel are active in cold water, and the best seasons for catching them are late fall, winter and spring. They feed primarily on small fish, so active lures like spinner-baits, in-line spinners, spoons and floating minnow lures work well on them.

Pickerel love to lurk in weedbeds (above). Subsurface minnows (below) are always a good bet.

B. Pike Tactics

Lake and Reservoirs

Pike fishing is best in spring, early summer and fall, when these fish are in quiet, weedy waters. They are normally aggressive, attacking any moving target. Look for pike in bays, sloughs, flats and coves that have submerged weedbeds, logs or other "hideout" structure. Pike like fairly shallow water—3-10 feet.

Pike can get big, and even small ones are tough fighters, so use fairly heavy tackle. (Use 12-20 pound line.) They have sharp teeth that can easily cut monofilament. For this reason, always rig with a short steel leader ahead of your lure or bait.

Find a place that gives you access to likely cover. Cast a large, brightly-colored spoon next to or over this cover. You can cast from the bank or wade-fish, staying on the move to cover a lot of water. If you have a boat, motor to the upwind side of a shallow bay and drift slowly downwind, casting to clumps of weeds and weed edges. Retrieve the spoon steadily, but if pike don't seem interested, pump the spoon up and down or jerk it erratically to get their attention. Other good lures for pike are large spinnerbaits, in-line spinners, large floating minnows, and wide-wobbling crankbaits.

Live-bait fishing is extremely effective. A large minnow suspended under a fixed-bobber rig is almost irresistible to pike. Clip a strong 1/0 or 2/0 hook to the end of a wire leader. Add a couple of split shot above the leader. Then add a large round bobber at a depth so the minnow will be up off bottom. Hook the minnow in the lips or back.

Cast this rig to weedlines, pockets, points or other structure. Then sit back and wait for a bite. When the bobber goes under, give the fish slack as it makes its first run with the bait. When the pike stops, reel in slack line, feel for the fish, and set the hook hard!

Rivers

Use the same tactics, tackle and baits for pike in large rivers that you would use in large lakes and reservoirs. The only difference is locating these fish within the river system.

The best places to look for river pike are in backwaters. They often hold in sloughs, marshes, tributaries and oxbows away from the main channel. Cast to logs, brush or other shallow cover.

As in lakes and reservoirs, river pike are most active in spring, early summer and fall. A bonus time to fish for pike is whenever a river is rising and flooding adjacent lowlands. If you stay on the move and make a lot of casts, you're likely to enjoy some first-rate pike action.

C. Muskellunge, Northern Pike, Pickerel Tactics

LAMAR UNDERWOOD

1. On the Hunt for Pike

Northern pike, and their smaller cousins, chain pickerel, are masters of the art of ambush—fierce predators roaming the water in wolf packs. They're not always around, and sometimes they don't seem to be on the bite, but if you're fishing good pike or pickerel water, you should be in for prime action. Weedy, still-water bays with deeper "escape" water nearby are where you should find the fish.

2. When Pike Attack

"The greediness of pike knows no bounds," wrote Sergei Aksakov in *Notes on Fishing* back in 1847. Nothing has changed. As an example, note that when you're casting in good pike water, you might see a sudden swirl some distance from where your lure plunks down on a cast. "Spooked one," you think to yourself. No sir! You haven't spooked anything. That pike has just launched his attack. Get set for a strike!

3. A Fish of Wildness

Pike are similar to brook trout and lake trout in that their prime environment is the great north country. If you haven't been there, you owe it to yourself to do everything you can to plan such a trip. From Minnesota's Boundary Waters Area and the adjoining Quetico, up through all the vast reaches of the Canadian wilderness, wolf packs of pike patrol through the cold, clean waters. This is the land of spruce, white pine, and birch; of loons calling from across the lakes; of beavers, otters, and mink; of moose and black bear. If your heart cranks up a notch or two when you think about country like this, and the fish that swim there, you'll know you've just got to go.

4. Playing Those Pike

Despite their great size and fierce disposition, northern pike sometimes seem on the sluggish side when you're playing them. Then it happens: The pike sees the boat. It's a whole new ball-game now; time to hold on to your hat. The pike will pull the trigger,

your rod will bow into a hoop, and you'll know you're in a fight.

5. Pike and Pickerel for the Frying Pan

Despite their vast number of bones, pike and pickerel make absolutely delicious fried meals. The trick is to slice off the fillets with surgical skill—and a sharp fillet knife—and extract the long Y bones. Then pick through the remaining slab of clean meat for stray bones and get ready to fry 'em up.

6. Hang On to Your Hat

When fishing for pike and pickerel, watch for swirls in the water nearby just as you start your retrieve. No, you haven't spooked a fish. On the contrary, a pike or pickerel has his prey—your bait or lure—in his sights and is moving in for the kill. Get ready!

7. Northern Pike: Here, There, Everywhere!

Because they are found in so many northern latitudes, making them a Holarctic fish, northern pike can claim the distinction of being the most widely distributed freshwater fish in the world. (Now wait! Don't try to tell me you knew what Holarctic meant!)

8. Fly Rod Pike? Go Right Ahead

Because I have been fortunate to travel to fishing camps in both Canada and Alaska, I have been able to tangle with northern pike on a fly rod on several occasions, sometimes alternating between fly rod and spinning gear in the same boat. While pike aggressively hit big streamers under the right conditions, I feel the action is faster and sportier using light spinning tackle and lures. Some anglers go all *ga-ga* to say they caught a fish on a fly, and if that's your bag, go right ahead.

9. They Love Their Pike in Great Britain

As much as Americans and Canadians cherish their northern pike and its fishing, you have to hand it to the Brits for downright adoration of this fish. The excellent Web site of the Pike Anglers Club of Great Britain will show you what I mean: www.www.pacgb.co.uk/.

10. The Perfect Pike Spoon or Spinner

The perfect pike spoon or spinner is the one that will wobble, flash, and give the most action at the *slowest* retrieving speed.

11. Give the Devil a Chance

Like many another fishing "seniors," I caught my first northern pike—and a lot since—on the classic Eppinger Dardevle—red-and-white stripes on the front and flashing, silvery nickel on the back. Today's models, and all the assorted imitators, come in many different colors, but I always have the itch to tie on the red guy.

12. Sound Off for Northerns

Letting pike know there's prey in the water by splashing down lures and baits—and running spinner-baits alongside weedy lairs—has been an excellent technique just about forever. However, a new twist worth trying comes along every now and then. On the site of the Twin Lakes Outfitters, Nakina, Ontario, www.twin-lakes-air.com, they're talking about doing The DareDevil Slap. That's a name taken from the original Eppinger Dardevle, and the tactic is to cast the lure very high over your target zone, then jerk your line toward you when the bait's 2 or 3 feet above the water. The

sound of the spoon slapping the surface triggers vicious pike attacks.

13. Team a Rapala with a Dardevle

Among the northern pike fishing techniques on the Web site of Twin Lakes Outfitters, Nakina, Ontario, www.twin-lakes-air.com, an idea that looks really good is to use a worn-out Rapala with a perfectly good Dardevle. Take the hooks off your broken Rapala, then attach it to a black steel leader. Attach another leader to the back of the Rapala with a spring-slip-ring, then attach your Dardevle (or whatever you want to use). The Rapala will get the pike's attention, and the Dardevle will complete the deal.

14. The Fish of 10,000 Casts

The muskellunge (muskie) isn't called the "The Fish of 10,000 Casts" for nothing. That number may be exaggerated; nevertheless, the muskie is indeed a trophy fish and not easy to come by, especially on artificial lures. They can be caught, however, on both lures and live bait, but the top guides who know how to do it will never call it easy.

15. The Oldest Muskie Story Out There

To illustrate how difficult muskellunge fishing can be, this old anecdote has been around for a long time. Guy asks his friend, "How was your muskie trip?" His friend replies: "Oh, it was fantastic! In five days' fishing, we had three follows."

16. Why Those Big Mossback Muskies Are Different

Writing in his "Fresh-Water Fishing" column in the November 1945 issue of *Sports Afield,* Angling Editor Cal Johnson noted that the term "mossback" really fits the muskellunge—make that *big* muskellunge. When muskies go 30 to 60 pounds they have a coating of dark, slimy vegetation on their backs. Small or medium muskies don't have the "mossback" look simply because they do not spend the time lurking in the dense vegetation that the big fish do.

17. Muskies Prowling for Prey

Big muskies feed on big baitfish. In the November 1945 issue of *Sports Afield*, Angling Editor Cal Johnson reports on seeing a 6-pound walleye taken from the stomach of a 35-pound muskellunge. "The very large muskie is quite inactive and moves about very little," Johnson said. "He will go on a hunting expedition every so often and stalk and capture a large walleye pike, redhorse or big black sucker, swallowing them whole. Then he swims alongside some submerged log . . . or other piece of cover and lies perfectly still for several days until the food is digested." No wonder big muskies are so hard to catch.

Lures used to catch pike

Panfish

A. Sunfish, Crappie, Yellow Perch

Sunfish

To biologists, "sunfish" is the family name for several species, including bass, crappie and bluegill. However, to most anglers, "sunfish" is a collective term for bluegill, shellcrackers (redear sunfish), pumpkinseeds, green sunfish, longear sunfish, war-mouth and other similar species that southerners call "bream." These are the most numerous and widespread of all panfish. They are willing feeders, which makes them easy to catch. They're also scrappy fighters, and they're delicious to eat. This is why sunfish are extremely popular with beginning anglers. It's a safe bet that a sunfish was the first catch of the vast majority of North American fishermen.

Sunfish live in warm-water lakes, reservoirs, rivers and ponds throughout the U.S. and southern Canada. They spend most time in shallow to medium depths, usually around weeds, rocks, brush, boat docks or other cover types. They feed mostly on tiny invertebrates, larval and adult insects, worms, small minnows and other prey.

Sunfish are capable of reproducing in great numbers. One adult female will produce tens of thousands of eggs in a single season. Because of this, many smaller waters experience sunfish overpopulation. The result is lots of little fish that never grow large enough to be considered "keepers" by fishermen. However, in waters where there are enough bass and other predators to prevent overpopulation, some sunfish species will average a half-pound in size, and some individuals can exceed a pound.

The bluegill is the most popular sunfish. The world-record bluegill was caught in Alabama in 1950. It weighed a whopping 4 pounds 12 ounces!

Crappie

Crappie are widespread and abundant in many waters, and they're prized for their delicious table quality. They average larger in size than sunfish, and they are fairly easy to catch. These are reasons why millions of anglers target these fish each year.

Bluegill Sunfish

Black Crappie

White Crappie

Yellow Perch

Actually, there are two crappie species: white and black. Differences between these species are minor. One apparent difference is as their names imply. Black crappie have darker, blotchier scale patterns than white crappie, which usually have dark vertical bars.

Both these species live in natural lakes, reservoirs, larger ponds and quiet, deep pools of medium-to-large streams. Crappie occur naturally from southern Ontario to the Gulf of Mexico in the eastern half of North America. They, too, have been stocked into numerous lakes and rivers in the West. Black crappie are typically found in cooler, clearer lakes, while white crappie inhabit warmer lakes that are dingier in color.

Traditionally, most crappie fishing occurs in the spring, when these fish migrate into quiet, shallow areas to spawn. When the water temperature climbs into the low-60° F range, they begin laying eggs in or next to such cover as reeds, brush, stumps, or man-made fish attractors built and sunk by anglers.

After spawning, crappie head back to deeper water, where they collect in schools and hold along sunken creek channels, weed lines, standing timber, sunken brushpiles and other areas where the lake bottom contour changes suddenly or where deep submerged cover exists. Expert crappie anglers know that these fish can be caught from such areas all year long, though they must employ some fairly specialized techniques to do so.

Crappie feed mainly on small baitfish and invertebrates. In some lakes, they average a pound or more in size; crappie over 2 pounds are considered trophies. The world-record white crappie weighed 5 pounds 3 ounces and was caught in Mississippi in 1957. The

world-record black crappie weighed 4 pounds 8 ounces and was boated in Virginia in 1981.

Yellow Perch

Along with walleye and sauger, yellow perch are members of the perch family. These fish average 6-10 inches long, though many lakes only have stunted "bait stealers" that are smaller than this average.

Still, yellow perch are very popular since they are delicious to eat. The world-record yellow perch (4 pounds 3 ounces) was caught in New Jersey in 1865.

The yellow perch's natural range extends throughout the Northeast, Midwest and Canada (except British Columbia). It lives in all the Great Lakes and inhabits many brackish waters along the Atlantic Coast. Yellow perch have also been stocked in many reservoirs outside their natural range. These fish thrive in clean lakes, reservoirs, ponds and large rivers that have sand, rock or gravel bottoms. They also abound in weedy, mud-bottomed lakes, though these are the type spots where they tend to run small in size.

Yellow perch swim in schools and feed on minnows, small crustaceans, snails, leeches and invertebrates. Adults spend most of their lives in deep water, usually moving shallow to feed, mostly during daylight hours in areas exposed to sunlight.

These fish begin spawning when the water temperature climbs into the mid-40° F range (mid-50s in the southern part of their range). Yellow perch often make spawning runs up feeder streams; they also spawn around shallow weeds and brush.

B. Sunfish Tactics

WADE BOURNE

Sunfish

Bluegill and other small sunfish are my choice for someone just starting out in fishing. These are usually the most plentiful fish in ponds and small lakes, and they always seem willing to bite.

In spring, early summer and fall, sunfish stay in shallow to medium-deep water (2-10 feet). In hottest summer and coldest winter, they normally move deeper, though they may still occasionally feed in the shallows.

Small sunfish love to hold around brush, logs, weeds, piers and other cover. On cloudy days or in dingy water, these fish often hang around edges of such structure. This is true during the early morning and late afternoon. But during the part of the day when the sun is brightest, especially in clear-water ponds, sunfish swim into brush or vegetation, under piers or tight to stumps and logs. On sunny days, they like to hide in shady areas.

If possible, get out early to fish for sunfish in a pond or small lake. Take a long panfish pole or light-action spinning or spin-cast rod and reel spooled with 4- or 6-pound test line. Tie a fixed-bobber rig with a long-shank wire hook (#6 or #8), a little split shot, and a bobber.

(Remember to balance the weight of your split shot and bobber!)

For bait, try earthworms, crickets or grasshoppers. Thread a small worm up the shank of the hook, or use only a small piece of night crawler. A whole cricket or grasshopper is the perfect-size bite for a bluegill.

Next, adjust the bobber so your bait hangs midway between the surface and the bottom. If you can't see bottom and you don't know how deep the pond is, begin fishing 2-4 feet deep. If you don't catch fish, experiment with other depths.

A fallen tree or log can form an ideal hiding place for bass, sunfish, and other species. Be sure to carefully scout a small lake or pond for such underwater structure.

Let's say you think sunfish may be holding around weeds growing close to the bank. Drop your bait in next to the weeds. The bobber should be floating upright. If it's laying on its side, the bait is probably on bottom. In this case shorten the distance between the bobber and hook so the bait will suspend above the bottom.

Be careful not to stand right over the spot you're fishing, especially if the water's clear. The fish will see you and become spooky. Sometimes it's better to sit on the pond bank rather than stand. Wear natural-colored or camouflage clothing and avoid making any commotion that might scare the fish.

Sunfish will usually bite with little hesitation so if you don't get a bite in a couple of minutes, twitch your bait to get the fish's attention.

Carefully select locations to place your bait. Keep it close to cover, and if the fish aren't biting well, look for openings in cover where you can drop the bait without getting hung up.

If you're not getting bites, try something different. Fish around another type of structure. If you've been fishing in shallow water, try a deeper area. (Don't forget to lengthen the distance between your bobber and hook.) If the pond has a dam, drop your bait close to it.

If there is an overflow, aerator or fish feeder, try around those.

Most anglers who pond-fish walk the banks, but you have two other options. You can fish from a small boat to cover more water, or you can wade-fish. This technique is especially good in ponds with a lot of brush, cattails or similar cover. In warm months, you can wade-fish in old pants and tennis shoes.

Remember to "think structure." Don't drop your bait at some random spot in the middle of the pond and then sit and watch your bobber for an hour. Keep moving until you begin catching fish. Then slow down and work the area thoroughly. Once you find a productive spot, stay with it as long as the fish keep biting.

A special opportunity exists during spring when sunfish are spawning. They fan nests in shallow water (2-5 feet deep) around the banks and especially in the shallow end of a pond. Often you can see the nests. They're about the size of a dinner plate, and they appear light against the dark pond bottom. Usually, many nests will be clustered in the same area.

When you see these "beds," set your bobber shallow and drop your bait right next to them, trying not to spook the fish. You're probably better off casting into the beds rather than sneaking in close with a long pole.

There's little difference in fishing for sunfish in small ponds or in large lakes. Catching them is a simple matter of figuring out their locations and then getting a bait in front of them.

In spring, sunfish migrate into shallow areas to spawn, so look for them in bays and pockets along wind-protected shorelines. Before spawning, sunfish hold around brush, stumps, weeds, rocks or other structure in 2-8 feet of water. Then, as the water temperature climbs into the mid-60° F range, sunfish will move up into 1-4 feet of water and spawn in areas that have firm bottoms - gravel, sand, clay.

Long poles or light-action spinning or spin-cast tackle will take these fish. Use fixed or slip-bobber rigs with wiggler worms, crickets or a small hair jig tipped with a maggot for bait. When fishing around cover, keep your bait close in. When fishing a spawning area, drop the bait right into the beds. (When fishing a visible sunfish spawning bed, try the outer edge first, then work your way to the center. This keeps fish that are hooked and struggling from spooking other fish off their beds.)

If it's spawning time and no beds are visible, fish through likely areas and keep moving until you start getting bites. If sunfish are around, they'll bite with little hesitation, so don't stay very long in one place if you're not getting any action.

After spawning, sunfish head back to deeper water. Many fish will still hold around visible cover, but they prefer to be near deep water. Two classic examples are a weedline on the edge of a drop-off and a steep rocky bank.

Ponds and small lakes are plentiful throughout North America, and many offer very good action on fish that rarely see baits or artificial lures. These diminutive waters are great places for beginners to learn the basics of this sport.

Besides a bobber rig, another good way to take sunfish is "jump-jigging," which involves casting a ¹⁄₁₆-ounce tube jig around weeds or rocks. Use a very light spinning outfit. Slowly reel the tube jig away from the cover and let the jig sink along the edge. Set the hook when you feel a bump or tug. This technique requires a boat, since you have to be over deep, open water casting into the weeds.

Docks, fishing piers and bridges are good locations to catch post-spawn sunfish. The water may be deep, but usually the fish will be up near the surface, holding under or close to the structures. Don't stand on a dock, pier or bridge and cast far out into the water. The fish are likely to be under your feet! Set your bobber so your bait hangs deeper than you can see, then keep your bait close to the structure.

Sometimes you have to experiment with different depths to find where sunfish are holding, and you should change location if you're not getting bites. Once you find the fish, work the area thoroughly. Sunfish swim in big schools after spawning, and you can catch several in one place.

One special sunfish opportunity exists when insects are hatching. If you can find insects swarming over the water and fish swirling beneath them, get ready for some hot action! Just thread one of the flies onto a small hook, and drop it into this natural dining room.

C. Crappie Tactics

WADE BOURNE

Crappie

Fishing for crappie in ponds and small lakes is similar to fishing for bluegill and sunfish. Always fish close to structure and stay on the move until you find fish. The primary difference is the bait you use. Crappie prefer minnows over other natural baits, and they readily attack small jigs and spinners.

Long poles are a favorite with crappie fishermen. Many crappie experts quietly skull a small boat from one piece of structure to the next, and use a panfish pole to dangle a float rig with a minnow or jig in next to cover. They ease their bait down beside a tree or

One secret to fishing ponds and small lakes is to keep moving until you locate fish. A small boat will enable an angler to cover more water and prime fish locations.

piece of brush, leave it for a moment, pick it up, set it down on the other side, then move to the next spot. In small lakes and ponds, crappie scatter throughout the shallow structure, and this "hunt-and-peck" method of fishing is very effective. This is especially true in spring, when the fish move into shallow cover to spawn. You can also use this method while wade-fishing or fishing from shore, if the structure is within reach.

Another good crappie technique is to use a slip-bobber rig with a spinning or spin-cast outfit. Hook a live minnow through the back onto a thin wire hook (#2) or through the lips on a lightweight (1/16 or 1/32 ounce) jig. Then cast this rig next to a weedline, brush-pile or log.

If you don't get a bite in 5 minutes, try somewhere else. If you get a bite, don't yank if the bobber is just twitching. Wait for the bobber to start moving off or disappear beneath the surface before setting the hook. Crappie have soft mouths, so don't set too hard, or you'll rip out the hook. Instead, lift up on your pole or rod, and you should have the fish.

If you don't catch fish shallow, try deeper water, especially during hot summer months or on bright, clear days. Adjust your bobber up the line and drop your bait right in front of the dam or off the end of a pier. Try casting into the middle of the pond and see what happens. With this method of fishing, 6-10 feet is not too deep. There is less certainty in this technique, however, because you're hunting for crappie in a random area.

To cover a lot of water, cast a 1/16-ounce jig or a small in-line spinner. After casting, count slowly as the bait sinks. After a few seconds, begin your retrieve. Try different counts (depths). If you get a bite, let the bait sink to the same count next time. You may have found the depth where crappie are holding. This technique is called the "countdown" method of fishing with a sinking bait.

When retrieving the jig, move it at a slow to moderate pace, and alternate between a straight pull and a rising/falling path back through the water. With the spinner, a slow, straight retrieve is best. Crappie will usually bite if you pull either of these baits past them.

Crappie follow the same seasonal patterns as sunfish, except slightly earlier. When spring breaks, crappie head into bays and quiet coves to get ready to spawn. When the water warms into the low-60° F range, they fan out into the shallows. They spawn in or around brush, reeds, stumps, logs, roots, submerged timber, artificial fish attractors or other cover. Crappie spawn-

ing depth depends on water color. In dingy water, they may spawn only a foot or two deep. But in clear water, they'll spawn deeper, as far down as 12 feet. A good depth to try is 1 to 2 feet below the depth at which your bait sinks out of sight.

Minnows or small plastic jigs are good baits to try. Drop them next to or into potential spawning cover. You can do this from the bank, from a boat, or by wade-fishing the shallows. Lower the bait, wait 30 seconds, then move the bait to another spot. When fishing a brush pile, treetop or reed patch, try moving the bait around in the cover. If you catch a fish, put the bait back into the same spot to try for another. Stay on the move until you find some action.

After crappie spawn, they head back toward deeper water, where they collect along underwater ledges, creek channel banks and other sharp bottom contour breaks. This is where a topo map can help. If

Don't let the size of a lake or reservoir intimidate you. Fish do the same things in big lakes that they do in small ponds. Bass, bluegill and others often hang around rocky banks.

you're fishing from shore, look for spots where deep water runs close to the bank.

Then go to these areas and look for treetops, brush, logs or other visible cover. Fish these spots with minnows or jigs. Or, if there is no visible cover, cast jigs randomly from shore. Wait until the jig sinks to the bottom before starting your retrieve. Then use a slow, steady retrieve to work the bait back up the bank. Set the hook when you feel any slight "thump" or when you see your line twitch.

Fish attractors are another good crappie opportunity. Many fish and wildlife agencies sink brush or other cover into prime deep-water areas to concentrate fish. These attractors are then marked so anglers can find them. They may be out in a bay or around fishing piers or bridges. Dangle minnows or jigs around and into the middle of the cover. You'll hang up once in awhile, but you'll also catch fish.

Fall may be the second best time to catch crappie in large lakes and reservoirs. When the water starts cooling, they move back into shallow areas, holding around cover. Troll slowly through bays, casting jigs or dropping minnows into likely spots.

D. Yellow Perch Tactics

WADE BOURNE

Yellow Perch

Yellow perch spawn in early spring when the water temperature climbs into the high 40° F range. They head into a lake's feeder streams or shallows, and during this migration, they are extremely easy to catch.

A fixed- or slip-bobber rig is a good choice for perch. Use light line (4-8 pound test) and a #6 long-shank hook. Add a small split shot and bobber, bait with worms or live minnows, and drop the bait into shallow areas around cover. If you don't get quick action, try somewhere else.

After the spawn, these fish return to main lake areas. Smaller fish hold along weedlines, and jump-jigging is a good way to take them. (Refer to the "Sunfish" part of this section.) Larger perch move onto reefs, ledges and deep points, and hang close to bottom. They may hold as deep as 40 feet.

Again, ask bait dealers about good deep-water perch spots. When you find one, fish it with a two-hook panfish rig. Bump your bait along bottom to attract strikes. If you catch a fish, unhook it quickly and drop a fresh bait right back into the same spot. Other perch will be drawn by the commotion.

E. Sunfish, Crappie, Yellow Perch Tactics

LAMAR UNDERWOOD

1. Springtime Fun Guaranteed

For a mixed-bag springtime catch of crappies, bluegills, perch, walleyes, bass—you name it—fish a small jig, sweetened with a minnow hooked upwards through the lip, and use a sliding bobber at your preferred depth. Experiment to find the depth where you're getting strikes and enjoying the pulls and fun that make you feel like a kid again. Use ¼-, ⅛-, or ¹⁄₁₆-ounce jigheads, with white or yellow soft-plastic grubs, such as Kalin's Triple Threat (Bass Pro Shops). Your preferred float, stick, or bobber should be on the small side to be sensitive to tentative cold-water hits.

Lamar Underwood holds up a crappie he took on jig.

2. Watch Those Spinner Blades

That spinners for panfish need to be small is fairly basic know-how, but often overlooked is the need for the spinner blades to be thin, therefore turning easily and quickly at the slightest and slowest pull.

3. When the Big Bluegills Spawn

"Regardless of where you live, bluegills generally start spawning just about when largemouth bass are finishing . . . If conditions are favorable they might even spawn several times a year."

—John Weiss, "Panfish Secrets the Bass Experts
Won't Tell,"
Sports Afield, October 1973

4. Look to Deep Water for Big Bluegills

Among the many landmark articles writer John Weiss did for *Sports Afield,* one of my favorites was his extraordinary "Panfish Secrets the Bass Experts Won't

Tell," which appeared in the October 1973 issue. As he often did, John Weiss gave serious panfish anglers lots to think about and tricks to try from what he learned fishing with expert Norm Saylor in a fully rigged bass boat at Lake Eufaula, Alabama. An experienced, deep-water, structure bass angler, Saylor used spinning-rod tactics exclusively in his search for big gills. Saylor's Strategy: If your favorite lake—or the one you're fishing—has any big bluegills, they're going to be in deep water most of the time. At different times, the big gills will move out of deep-water sanctuaries, using established migration routes, to reach their feeding areas. Then, back they go to deep water. To find them, you have to crack into their deep-water sanctuaries, just as in bass fishing.

5. Finding the Beds of Bull Bluegills

Continuing John Weiss' revealing look at the tactics of angler Norm Saylor: "Drifting along any shoreline, it's easy to spot the honeycomb appearance of several clusters of spawning beds," Norm explained. "But

I look for mammoth concentrations where there might be as many as fifty beds in one small area. This first part is duck soup, and most anglers look no farther. They break out their fly rods and have a ball with 6-inch-long fish, not realizing there might be a group of 1 ½-pounders only 50 yards away." Working deep and deeper toward bars and a submerged island, Saylor and Weiss eventually locked on a concentration of bulls and took eleven, with the smallest going 1 pound even and the largest exactly 2 pounds, a trophy bluegill anywhere.

6. Ever Hold a True Bull Bluegill?

"If you have never witnessed firsthand a bull bluegill in the 1½ or 2-pound category, it's quite an awesome sight . . . Usually, the bulls are much darker in color than their smaller counterparts, sometimes taking on an almost black color . . . The average length of these bulls is about 12 inches. Even the trophy bluegills seldom exceed this length . . . Now hold out your hand, palm-up. With a bull bluegill lying in your hand and his nose just covering your middle finger, your entire hand should be covered. His mammoth tail section will extend down your forearm, completely covering the band of your wristwatch."

—John Weiss, "Panfish Secrets the Bass Experts Won't Tell," *Sports Afield,* October 1973

7. The Biggest Bluegill Ever!

"The world-record bluegill of 4-pounds-plus was only 15 inches long. As the bulls reach maturity, they gain practically all of their weight in girth and breadth, not length."

—John Weiss, "Panfish Secrets the Bass Experts Won't Tell," *Sports Afield,* October 1973

If you want big bluegills, the trick is to go deep.

8. A Deadly Sliver of Plastic Worm

In a February 1972 article in *Sports Afield,* frequent contributor Col. Dave Harbour published the results of some really serious panfish lure experiments. He found he caught more panfish, and far bigger ones, by adding a tiny sliver of a white plastic worm. His No. 1 bait was a tiny lead-head black-and-white nymph with a No. 10 hook. He cut the sliver of worm the same length and size of the nymph and hooked it so most of the worm was off the hook, wiggling. "I don't pretend to know why the weighted black-and-white nymph tipped with white worm is such a lethal big bull bluegill magnet . . . but the worm sliver sure transformed the nymph into a dessert bottom-hugging bluegills couldn't resist."

9. A Super-Star Panfishing Tactic

Writing in the April 1972 issue of *Sports Afield,* Angling Editor Homer Circle described one of the deadliest panfishing rigs he had ever seen. It simply consisted of a No. 1 Indiana spinner blade, super-polished and delicate to turn at the slightest movement, with a couple of beads up the line for weight and a No. 6 Eagle Claw hook baited with a sliver of flesh cut from the side of a panfish. The strip was 1¼ inches long and tapered like a minnow, from a starting width of ¼ inch. The angler who developed the method back then, Dave Goforth, said, "The spinner calls 'em, and the meat gets 'em."

10. *Field & Stream's* Panfish "Ultimate Lure" Survey Winners

In what it called the "Ultimate Lure Survey," published in March 2008, *Field & Stream* magazine asked 1,000 of its hard-core readers to name their favorite lures. The winners for the Panfish category were:

Jigs, 40%, Jig with Mister Twister
Spinners, 33%, Beetle Spin
Soft-Plastics, 15%, Berkley Gulp! Earthworm with
    Berkley Power Grub second
Minnow-Type Lures, 8%, Original Rapala with
    Rebel second
Crankbaits, 2%, Rattlin' Rapala
Spoons, 2%, Dardevle

11. Which Crappie Is That?

Because the crappie is such a popular and widespread fish—famous for both the action and in the pan—much confusion exists over crappie identification. White crappie, black crappie, calico bass—three names, but, whoops, there are only two fish, two real crappies. The white crappie is the most common and widely distributed. The black crappie is the fish sometimes called "calico bass," although at times you will also hear the white crappie called "calico bass." It's very confusing, but throw out the "calico" label and you have the two fish everybody catches and loves to eat—white crappie and black crappie. The dorsal fins of both fish are different, but the easiest way to distinguish between the white and black crappie is by noting that the spots on the white crappie are arranged in neat vertical bars, while on the black crappie they are scattered randomly along the sides of the fish.

12. Fly-Fishing Bonus: Bluegills on the Bed

When bluegills are bedding—the time varies greatly from area to area—fly fishing for these hard-fighting panfish really comes into its own. After you spot the smoothed, rounded patches of the spawning beds, cast a nymph on a light leader into the spots and let it sink onto the beds. A bluegill will pick it up, take it off the bed, and then spit it out. The fish are not feeding, only housekeeping.

13. Don't Lose That Fish

They don't call crappies "papermouths" for nothing. Those lips with the wide section of thin membrane mean that you can never be sure of a fish until it's in the boat. Crappies, even big ones, are not powerful fighters, but what they lack in power they make up for in suspense, since your hook can pull loose at any moment. I've seen some crappies-to-die-for lost right at the net or hand when the hook broke through the lips of the "papermouth."

Black crappies have randomly scattered spots on their sides.

14. Catching Slab-Sided Bluegills in Midsummer

In the heat and blazing suns of high summer, you probably won't have much luck catching the really big bluegills by fishing your usual spots—shoreline cover, stumps, fallen trees. The occasional good fish might be taken early or late in the day, but mostly the pickings will be slim. Still, provided your lake has a healthy bluegill population, the slab-sided fish you covet can be found and taken. Instead of target casting to cover, fish for them deep with 1/16- or 1/32-ounce jigs, straight over the sides of the boat. Yes, straight down! Slowly work the jigs up and down at various depths and locations until you find the fish. Note the level where you've finally hit the schools of big fish, and you'll be in business with a close-up of the fish with the jig in the corner of its mouth.

15. Fishing the Deadly Lau Loop

Back in 1975, when I was editor of *Sports Afield*, Angling Editor Homer Circle came through with many articles on advanced skills, sometimes working with his friend, the legendary guide-turned-filmmaker Glen Lau (producer of *Bigmouth* and others). One of the best presentations from this talented combo was an article on fishing deep for summer bluegills by using a method that is a virtual pioneer on today's drop-shot fishing. The irony is that the "pioneer" method is better than today's—because it used Glen Lau's knot, which is a great improvement over the Surgeon's Knot or Palomar Knot used in today's drop-shot rigs. Homer and Glen came up with a rig consisting of a weighted jig fly (or small jig) on the end of the line, then a dropper 8 inches above, and another 6 inches above that. Each dropper was 2 inches long, using very tiny mono. The dropper

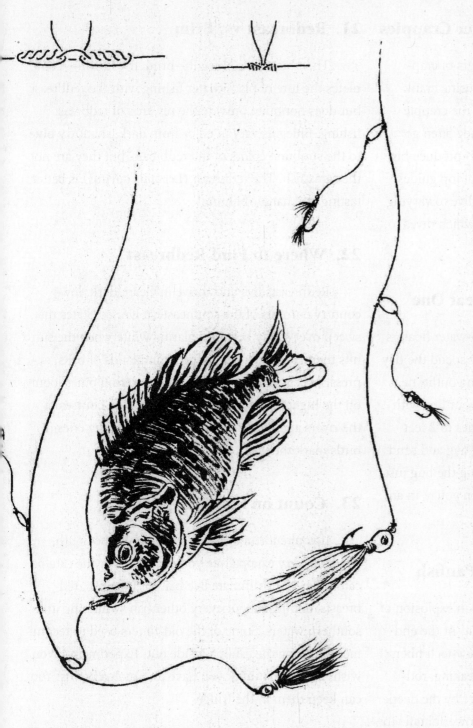

16. Go Deep With Sponge-Rubber Spiders

Those sponge-rubber spiders that look and feel real enough to bite you will catch far, far bigger bluegills if you wrap some lead wire around their heads. They're made to be fished on top, but that's seldom where the big 'gills are hanging out. They're deep. You've got to find them, then get your spider down to them.

17. Catching Big, Summer Yellow Perch

Yellow perch are prime targets for anglers everywhere, but especially in the Great Lakes region where they grow big and fat. Veteran angler Steve Ryan explains how to cash in on the action in the article "Summer Perchin'" on the Lindy Tackle Web site, www. lindyfishingtackle.com: "Lake Michigan's fishery has changed considerably over the last several decades but the methods for catching these tasty fish remain the same. Crappie spreaders, Lindy rigs, jigs, and slip floats will catch you a limit of perch no matter where you fish. These rigs are nothing more than bait delivery systems designed to present live bait to fish in the most effective means possible." Ryan likes to set up his rigs with minnows when the water is cold, then night crawlers or softshell crawfish when the water temperatures top the mid-50s. See his article for more details.

was attached to a ⅛-inch Lau Loop, which had a more-sensitive feel and presented the fly more enticingly. Homer and Glen used very tiny 18-inch ice-fishing rods rigged with three guides and Ambassadeur reels. The flies were No. 12s to 16s and dropped straight down to the bottom. They were deadly when jigged and retrieved simultaneously. With a little imagination, you can put together a similar rig today and customize the tactics with various mini-jigs and flies. It's deadly on deep panfish.

18. Try Crankbaits for Summer Crappies

If you're not happy with the numbers of crappies you've been getting in summer, try using crankbaits. Especially on larger waters, where the crappie schools roam around a lot, and where they often go deep, crankbaits either cast or trolled can produce big crappies for you. Some favorite models of top guides include the 2-inch Bandits in sizes that dive to varying depths, and Rebel's 2-inch Deep Vee-R, which dives to 8 to 10 feet.

19. Turn a Bad Day into a Great One

When your favorite fly rod and top-water floaters are producing absolutely no strikes, why spend the day flailing the water? Pick up a light spinning outfit, tie a one-quarter-ounce sinker to the end of your line with a dropper leader 1-foot long tied 18 inches to 2 feet above the sinker. Tie on a No. 8 floating bug and send your rig down where the fish are. Dancing the bug just off the bottom is especially effective when you're in an area where the bream are concentrated.

20. Tribute to a Very Special Panfish

To the eye, the redbreast sunfish is an explosion of color, shaped like a living sunrise portrait. At the end of a light rod or pole, whether cane or new-tech fibers, the redbreast's runs to escape are line-breaking, rod-bending displays of power, made effective by the deep, slab-sided body and the sweeps of the powerful tail. To the palate, the white, firm fillets of fried redbreast are delicious to a point that defies description. As a card-carrying Georgia boy from the heart of redbreast country, along the banks of the Ogeechee River, I have spent most of my life far from my beloved river, but its siren call has always pulled me back. I return to Georgia to find, catch, and eat redbreasts every chance I get—with corn dodgers on the side, thank you very much.

21. Redbreast vs. Brim

The ubiquitous bluegill—brim, if you will—completes the lure of black-water fishing with the redbreast, but does not quite provide the rewards of redbreast fishing. Bluegills vary in color from dark, shadowy blue to the sunburst colors of the redbreast, but they are not the same fish. The redbreast (*Lepomis auritus*) is better tasting and harder fighting.

22. Where to Find Redbreast

Redbreasts live and thrive in clean, dark, low-country currents of the southeastern United States that sweep over sandy bottoms, glaring white when the sun hits them, and through boggy swamplands of oaks, cypress, sweet gums, and magnolia. Towering pines loom on the higher ground along the serpentine courses of the rivers and creeks, where the never-ending cries of birds mark the flow.

23. Count on the Catalpa Worm

If you're fortunate enough to live in the South, treasure every catalpa tree you can find. For the catalpa caterpillar is the ultimate live bait for bluegills, redbreasts, and just about every other fish swimming in southern waters. Some of the old-timers used to recommend turning the catalpa inside out. Experiment if you wish, but I don't think you have to. Catalpa bonus: You can keep them in the fridge.

24. Cricket Know-How

Crickets are a mainstay of panfishing with live bait—and a mainstay of bait shops—but they come off the hook easily and you'll be plagued by minnows and tiny fish constantly stealing your bait. They're best used when you're after *big* panfish.

25. Hooks for Bream: When You Want Them to Straighten Out

One popular theory on choosing lines and leaders for panfish, especially bream, is to use very light leaders in still water so that the bait falls in a soft, lifelike manner, as if dropping from a tree. In current, or areas so filled with stumps and limbs that you're bound to hook into them, use a very strong leader and springy, light hook that will straighten out with a strong, steady pull. That way you won't keep losing your whole rig in the stumps.

26. Use Slip Bobbers for Crappies

We want to find crappies fast. Today! Now! One of the best ways to do it is to use two rods, with sinkers and baits for two different depths, and using slip bobbers. These bobbers allow every cast to return to its previous depth, saving time and putting you on the fish faster. Once you've found the depths the fish are taking on a particular day, you can set your bobber and forget it. The Betts "Mister Crappie" Slippers at www.basspro.com are good ones, as are the Cabela's "Easy-On Slip Bobbers," www.cabelas.com.

27. Bait-Keeper Hooks Do a Better Job

You may have fished for years with great success using regular hooks, but if you're a live bait angler you're going to do much better with today's bait-keeper hooks. They keep your bait on the hook much longer, thereby catching more fish.

28. Fry 'Em Up—Southern Style

Panfish fillets are great, but this old Georgia-raised boy likes the whole fish, deep-fried. Scale them, gut them, cut off the heads (being careful to save that big hunk of meat just behind the head), and slide them into the fat. I'm willing to put up with the bones to get every morsel of this delicious meat.

F. Crappie Fishing by the Seasons

KEITH SUTTON

Spring

Crappie invade shallow-water haunts along the banks of lakes, rivers and ponds during the spring spawning season. This makes them much easier to find and catch than during other seasons and results in more anglers fishing for crappie during this period.

The following tips, however, will improve your fishing success throughout the spring—before, during and after the spawn.

Spring is a season of bounty for crappie anglers. When these panfish are in the shallows on their beds, it's often easy to catch dozens in a short time.

When spring weather turns rainy, crappie often move from deep to shallow water, making them easier to find and catch.

1. Watch the Weather

Successful prespawn anglers know how crappie react to changing weather patterns. This season has lots of bumps, starts and backups. Warming trends are interrupted by sudden cold fronts. Crappie migrate from deep water to shallow and back several times before settling into spawning patterns.

The best fishing usually is toward the end of warm spells. One clue is a cold front approaching after several warm days. During this time, male crappie start fanning in shallows. Females also move shallow, looking for food. Therefore, focus fishing efforts on shallow waters where spawning will occur.

When a cold front hits, crappie return to deeper waters, holding near distinct bottom structure where light penetration is minimal and winter cover is abundant. If conditions are sunny and windy (typical after a cold front arrives), wave action cuts light penetration, and crappie remain near mid-depth structure. Several days after the cold front hits, the wind calms, allowing greater light penetration and driving crappie to deeper structure and cover.

If weather remains sunny and begins warming before the passage of another cold front, crappie gradually begin migrating back to shallow waters. Rainy weather, especially a warm rain, sends them scurrying to shallow reaches.

Consider all these factors when selecting areas in which to focus your fishing efforts.

2. Try Tailwaters

Don't overlook the opportunity to take loads of spring crappie in the tailwater below a big-river dam. River crappie often move upstream in early spring, searching for spawning sites. When they reach a dam, they mill around for a while, and you have an excellent chance for extraordinary catches. A jig/minnow combination often outproduces a jig or minnow alone in this situation. Cast around wing dams, boulders, lock walls and other current breaks where crappie can rest and feed.

3. Remember Hotspots

As crappie are caught and removed from a spawning bed, other fish move in to take over prime nesting sites. Therefore, fishing may continue to be good at a single site for many days throughout the spawn.

4. An Inconspicuous Marker

Crappie on beds often get spooked and disappear. If you wait 15 or 20 minutes and come back, chances are the fish will be in the same spot. But if you use an ordinary marker buoy to mark the spot, someone else is likely to see it and beat you to the punch. Instead, tie a piece of brightly colored yarn around a stick-up or weed stem near the bedding area. That way, only you will know the location of the hotspot.

5. Cut It Off

You're less likely to frighten skittish crappie if you turn off your outboard well before reaching the spot you want to fish. Drift into position, or use a trolling motor to cover the last few yards to your fishing area.

6. No Motor At All

In some situations, even the sound of a trolling motor can scare crappie off their nests. Avoid this by using a small paddle to scull your boat from the front seat. This is much quieter and may provide the edge you need to get closer. A cane pole or jigging pole is great for this style of fishing. If you're adept at sculling, you can keep on the move until crappie are found,

fishing different spots all the while. And when employing one of the 10- to 20-foot featherweight poles now available, you can keep your distance to avoid spooking these edgy shallow-water fish.

7. Go Weightless

If you're fishing with live minnows and crappie seem especially watchful, don't weight your bait. Use a thin-wire Aberdeen hook on a 6 ½- foot spinning rod matched with a long-spool, easy-cast reel full of 2- or 4-pound-test mono. With this rig, you can easily cast the unweighted minnow 50 feet or more. Hook the minnow through the back and cast toward likely hiding spots. The minnow should struggle near the surface for a short time, attracting nearby crappie. Then as the baitfish tires, it begins sinking, still wiggling enticingly. Crappie can't resist.

8. Slider Time

Any angler targeting spring crappie in dense cover also should consider fishing with Charlie Brewer Weedless Crappie Sliders. These unique lures are to crappie fishing what plastic worms are to bass fishing. When properly rigged, with the hook point of the special-made jighead buried in the grub, they can be worked through almost any cover without hang-ups. Cast and retrieve them around stumps and logs, work them like jigs in brush or fish them beneath a slip float in weedbed pockets. There's simply no better snag-free lure for fishing spring hideaways.

9. A Little, Not a Lot

Jig/minnow combos are great spring crappie-catchers, too, but often too bulky for fishing tangles. You'll still have an edge, though, if you tip your jig with a tiny piece of minnow instead of the whole thing. The added smell/taste increases your catch when finicky crappie avoid plain jigs.

Tilt your motor up and paddle to avoid spooking cagey spring crappie.

10. Plugs & Flies

Topwater plugs and flies don't make good crappie lures most of the year, but slabs in skinny spawning waters can see these lures more easily than fish in deeper water. Sponge-rubber spiders, popping bugs and little plugs such as Rebel's Bumble Bug and Big Ant make little disturbance when cast to bedding areas and often draw reaction strikes from fat male crappie guarding their nests.

11. Tube Time

A float tube, or belly boat, provides a great means for slipping up on spring crappie in backcountry oxbows, small ponds and other waters with no boat ramp. Or don some waders and go right in. An ultralight spinning rod and a few Crappie Sliders are all you need to nab slabs anywhere they hide.

12. Return to Deeper Water

Spawning may continue until the water temperature reaches 70 degrees or more. As soon as crappie leave their beds and shallow-water fishing takes a nosedive, look for fish in the same staging areas where

Male crappie guarding nests often nab tiny plugs like Rebel's Big Ant.

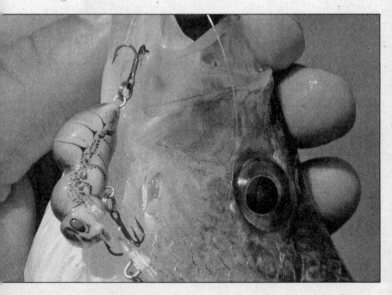

they were found just prior to the spawn, places such as points, creek channel edges and drop-offs bordering shallow flats.

Summer

During hot weather, crappie fishing gets tough . . . unless you know the secrets for summer success. These tips could help.

13. Try Bottom Fishing

When you know the thermocline's depth, look for areas where crappie-attracting structure covers the

Some crappie anglers quit fishing after crappie spawn, but summer is a season of plenty, too, if you know where to look for crappie and how to entice them.

bottom at that depth, then bottom-fish a live minnow. Thread a slip sinker on your line, and below it, tie on a barrel swivel. To the swivel's lower eye, tie a 3-foot leader of light line tipped with a crappie hook. Add a minnow, then cast the rig and allow it to settle to the bottom. When a crappie takes the bait, the line moves freely through the sinker with no resistance to alert fish to a possible threat.

14. Pumping Iron

Summer crappie often suspend in 10 to 20 feet of water around the branches of standing submerged trees. To reach them quickly, lower a small jigging spoon on a tight line directly down through the branches. Give the spoon a short upward pull at every 3 feet of depth. Crappie often inhale the lure as it falls, and you won't know one is on until you raise your rod tip.

15. Attract Minnows, Attract Crappie

When fishing is slow during daylight hours, try an approach that duplicates the use of a crappie light at night. A light attracts insects, which in turn attracts minnows. But minnows also are attracted by chumming with dry dog food, bread crumbs or similar offerings. Scatter the chum by handfuls in several shallow-water areas, then move back to the first place you put chum and drop in a minnow. Fish each consecutive spot and see if your catch rate doesn't improve. Often, it will.

Hot-weather crappie often hide in the confines of dark cypress hollows.

16. Scale Drop

Here's another "chumming" method to try when fishing is slow. Save some scales from the next crappie you fillet. Rinse them and store inside a sealable container filled with water. Carry the container on your outings, and if things get slow, drop a few scales in the water above inundated cover. Crappie blow out the scales of baitfish as they eat them. As the scales fall, they flicker and catch the eye of crappie, which often will move toward them to investigate. A jig or minnow presented on a tight line in the vicinity of scales you drop may get hit.

17. Cypress-Water Tips

Cypress-shrouded lakes and bayous tend to be shallow, which allows the water to reach excessively high summer temperatures. When the temperature exceeds their comfort level, crappie get lethargic and tough to catch. There's one place, however, where crappie still find comfort—inside hollow cypress trees.

The best trees have small to medium openings to the interior, thus excluding most outside light. Don't drop a minnow or jig inside the tree, but dangle it enticingly just outside the opening. Crappie will dart

out when they see your offering, then usually rush back inside. Use heavy line, set the hook quickly and try to keep the fish outside the hollow so it doesn't tangle you.

18. Side-trolling

When trolling for summer crappie, try positioning your trolling motor(s) so they pull your boat sideways. This allows you to move in a very slow, controlled fashion so you can mine deep structures more efficiently.

19. Fish Storm Fronts

Summer weather tends to be stable, with minimal effects on crappie activity. But when conditions are such that afternoon thunderstorms are popping up day after day, plan an outing that allows you to fish just before a storm hits. Don't be on the water during periods of lightning or high wind. But if you can do it safely, be fishing when the clouds start to thicken and the wind picks up. Just before a storm hits, crappie often move to surface strata and feed actively. The action may last only a few minutes, but during those few minutes, you may catch more fish than you will the rest of the day.

20. After the Storm

When a summer storm ends, look for crappie in the thickest available cover—buckbrush, willow thickets, etc. Allow the wind to blow your boat against the cover. Use a long pole to work a jig into the brush, then fish little pockets most folks miss. Fish the jig with little movement, and work each hole thoroughly.

21. Drop a Drop Bait

A great lure for jumbo summer crappie is a tailspinner like Mann's Little George or Strike King's Sand Blaster. These often are referred to as "drop baits" because they sink very quickly. They're ideal for catch-

ing crappie on deep channel drops, humps and ledges. Freeline the lure to the depth where fish show up on your sonar, then retrieve it at a fast clip for hard reaction strikes.

22. Dock-walking

On bright sunny days, crappie may move fairly shallow if they can find overhead cover that shades them from bright rays. Boat docks, fishing piers and swimming platforms provide such cover, but anglers in boats

Drop baits like Mann's Little George sink fast to quickly reach deep summer crappie.

may fail to get bites because crappie can see them. These same fish may bite, however, when the angler walks on the wooden structure and fishes from above. Crappie get used to foot traffic on these structures and seldom spook, so the quiet overhead approach often works when a bait presented from a boat won't. Let the wind drift a minnow or jig suspended under a bobber into the shade beneath the structure. Or try fishing a small jig vertically through wide cracks in boards over the shadiest water.

23. Slingshotting

Slingshotting, also called shooting, is another way to get at summer crappie hiding beneath man-made structures such as docks, piers and boathouses. This technique uses a short fishing rod like a slingshot to catapult a crappie jig into the shady area beneath the structure.

Use a 4½- to 5½-foot, medium-action rod outfitted with a spincasting reel or an autocast spinning reel

that allows you to pick up the line and flip the bail at the same time. A 1/32-ounce jig is right for most situations, and you're better off using solid-body jigs when slingshotting because they stay on better than tube jigs. Pinch the jig carefully between the thumb and index finger of your free hand, pull the rod back like a bow, aim and release the lure, letting it fly beneath the structure. With some practice, you can slingshot a small jig 15 to 20 feet under a dock or boathouse where big crappie are hiding.

Prepare for a strike as the lure falls. It helps to use highly visible line so you can see slight line movements that signal a taker. No hits? A slow retrieve close to the bottom frequently produces.

24. Care for Your Catch

Summer crappie placed in a stale livewell or on a stringer in hot surface water soon die and become soggy. For good-eating fish, take along an ice chest

For the best eating, place crappie on ice to keep them fresh.

containing several inches of cracked ice. Drain melted ice frequently to prevent your fish from sitting in water. The result is firm, fresh fillets that have the delicate, delicious flavor for which crappie are famous.

Fall

Autumn is a golden season for crappie fishing fans. Summer's crowds have vanished. Lakes, ponds and rivers shimmer beneath canopies of vermilion and amber leaves. Summer-fattened crappie are in prime condition, offering exciting possibilities for action-hungry anglers.

This season offers some of the year's best crappie angling if you learn some tips that will help you find and tempt these silvery panfish. Read on, and you will.

25. Try Bluffs

Fall crappie often hold near steep vertical bluffs along the shoreline that allow quick movement from shallow to deep water and vice versa. This time of year, however, they may be anywhere between the bottom and the surface, making them difficult to pinpoint. Start

In water discolored by turnover, crappie usually hold tight to cover, so anglers should present baits and lures very close to cover objects such as stick-ups and stumps.

by looking at the water clarity. If the water is discolored, light penetration will be restricted, and crappie will move shallower. Thus, the angler should begin by fishing shallow reaches first. If the water is clear, bright sunlight will drive most crappie into the depths or under heavy cover. In this situation, fish first around deeper hideouts. Efficiently check all depths until a crappie is caught, then work that depth thoroughly for additional fish.

26. Back Out with the Fish

When fishing a reservoir that has current caused by power generation, it pays to observe changes in the amount of current. Crappie may be in as little as 4 to 5 feet of water when current is minimal, but when power generation increases and current is stronger, crappie will move out to structures 10 to 20 feet deep. In the latter situation, work offshore cover, positioning your boat directly above and dropping minnows straight down. Or back off and cast ⅛-ounce jigs dressed with tubes or curlytail grubs.

27. Get to the Point

If the water level starts dropping fast due to power generation, try fishing points using small spinners. Retrieve the lure with an up-and-down motion, or buzz it along the surface and allow it to "die" and fall right beside the cover. Position your boat in deep water and cast toward the shallow part of the point, or vice versa.

28. Use Some Scents

When an autumn cold front passes, you may entice persnickety crappie to bite by adding liquid, gel or solid scent products to your lures. These often enhance the number of strikes you get when crappie are finicky. The fish will hold on longer, too, increasing your chance of getting good hooksets.

rises and other prominent bottom structure. Fish them with a rig made by tying a ⅜- to ½-ounce bell sinker at your line's end. Place a snelled hook 12 inches above the sinker on a dropper loop, then tie a 1/16-ounce jig directly to your line 18 inches above the hook. Bait the hook with a lively minnow, then drag the rig across the bottom near the rock pile until you catch a crappie. When you find your quarry, position your boat right over the strike zone and switch to a vertical presentation, which will help you avoid spooking other crappie.

31. Cedars and Shad

Not all crappie hold on deep structures in late fall. Many follow schools of shad into the backs of feeder

Use a slip-bobber rig to work minnows over shallow cedar brush piles for hot fall action.

Adding a scent product to your lure may increase hookups with sometimes fussy fall crappie.

29. Fish Windward Shores

Wind can be an important factor in determining where you're most likely to find early-fall crappie. Wind pushes tiny invertebrates that minnows and other baitfish eat. If there's a westerly wind for a couple of days, an east-shore area could hold the most fish, or vice versa. Consequently, you should always give wind-hit areas your full attention.

30. Rock and Roll

During late fall, as aquatic vegetation dies, crappie often move to deep rock piles. The best are associated with humps, outside channel bends, saddles between

creeks, holding in 4 to 6 feet of water along the edges of channel breaks. If you can find cedar brush piles in such areas, chances are you've found a mother lode of crappie. Work them with a stationary slip-bobber-and-minnow rig, or use a vertical tightline tactic with jigs.

32. Try Bream-like Lures

In ponds and small lakes, crappie often stay fat and healthy by eating a diet heavy on juvenile sunfish. In these waters, particularly those with clear water, your fall catch rate may soar if you fish with lures resembling tiny bream in color and/or shape. Jigs with some combination of red, gold and green colors work especially well in this situation, as do small sunfish-imitation crankbaits and spinners with gold blades and brightly colored bodies.

33. Return for Wayward Suspenders

At times, your fish finder may pinpoint a bit of key structure—an isolated stump, for example, or a rock pile—that is void of crappie. When you find such areas, slowly circle around that spot and look for suspended fish. If you find them, make note of the struc-ture's location, then return to it later. You might find that these previously inactive crappie have moved onto the structure and begun feeding.

34. "See" Edges Out of Sight

Fall crappie often hold along creek-channel drop-offs and other edge areas. You can fish such a location better if you mark it with several buoys. Locate the drop-off with sonar, then slowly follow the edge. Throw out a marker buoy each time you cross a certain depth—10 feet, for instance. Continue placing the buoys, about 20 feet apart, until you've used them all. Now you have a visible image of the edge and can fish it more thoroughly for crappie.

35. Soft-Plastic Minnows

Although often overlooked by crappie anglers, realistic soft-plastic baitfish lures such as the Banjo Glitter Minnow and Snag Proof's Moss Master Swimmin' Shad are dynamite on fall crappie. They not only come in a variety of sizes and colors, but they're weedless as well, allowing you to place them right in the middle of thick cover where crappie are likely to be.

Salmon, Steelhead,
and Shad

A. Introduction

JAY CASSELL

Salmon, Steelhead, and Shad

These three gamefish have little in common, except for one important trait: They all spend most of their lives in salt water, and enter fresh water solely to spawn. (The exception to this is the landlocked salmon, which lives its entire life in fresh water.) After spawning, steelhead, shad, and Atlantic salmon return to the salt, where they recuperate, fatten up, then go back up freshwater tributaries to spawn again the following year. For Pacific salmon – chinook, coho, sockeye, chum, and pink – spawning is a one-time occurrence. After spawning, these fish die.

Angling for Atlantic salmon takes place primarily in the Canadian Maritime provinces, though some Atlantics are fished for in remote parts of the northeastern U.S. Angling is mostly done with fly rods, with most fish being returned to the water after being caught. The fish is considered a great prize by many, as its stocks have been seriously depleted by commercial fishing and the building of dams, mostly in the 1800s, across many spawning tributaries. A trophy Atlantic might weigh 30 pounds, though most caught average in the teens.

Angling for landlocked salmon is done in streams, rivers, and lakes in the northeastern U.S. in particular. Both fly fishing and spinning are accepted methods for catching these smaller cousins (three pound average) of the Atlantic salmon.

Steelhead, originally natives of the northwestern U.S., were transplanted to the Great Lakes in the 1970s, where they adapted to their new environment. Instead of making runs to the salt, they live in the depths of the big lakes and run up tributaries to spawn. Such well-known streams as the Pere Marquette in Michigan and the Salmon River in New York are popular destinations for anglers from across the country. A fifteen-pound steelhead is considered a trophy anywhere, though some individuals may top 20.

Pacific salmon, found in the Pacific Northwest, as well as in British Columbia and Alaska, were also transplanted to the Great Lakes, where many – and, in particular, chinooks and cohos – have continued

Coho Salmon

to thrive. In the Great Lakes, these gamefish are taken in the tributaries and well as in the lakes themselves, depending on the time of year. Fly, spin, and bait casting gear is all used to great effect. In the Northwest and Alaska, Pacific salmon are caught in salt and fresh water, by both commercial fishermen and recreational anglers. Alaska has become a holy grail for many anglers, who trek north each summer for the chance to catch salmon fresh from the sea, on a variety of gear. Pink salmon generally run two to four pounds while Chinooks, or kings, are at the other end of the spectrum, with some monsters hitting the ninety-pound mark. Many exceed thirty pounds.

The final species in this section, the American shad, is found on both the West and East coasts. The fish is found up and down the Atlantic seaboard, with particularly strong fisheries found in Florida's St.John's River and Pennsylvania's Delaware River. Angling is done in the spring, when the fish make their spawning runs. In a reverse of what happened to steelhead and Pacific salmon, the American shad was transplanted to the West in 1871, with initial stockings occurring in California's Sacramento River. Sportfishing now occurs from Baja, California, up the coast to Cook Inlet in Alaska. Angling methods run the gamut of tackle, although shad darts and spinning gear is the tackle of choice for most fishermen after these hard-fighting gamefish. A typical shad will weigh two to five pounds.

In this section, you'll find valuable information on how to catch all of these elusive species.

B. Salmon, Steelhead, and Shad Tactics

LAMAR UNDERWOOD

1. Experts Only Need Apply

"These big rainbows are extremely secretive—almost never being seen before they're hooked. That makes it difficult even for expert anglers to puzzle out their habits, and almost impossible for the beginner."

2. No Beginner's Luck Here

"Nine out of ten captured steelhead are taken by fishermen who have landed such fish before."

3. The Truth About Atlantic Salmon Fishing

My friend Jim Merritt, one of the finest anglers I know and author of many articles on the subject, raises an interesting point about Atlantic salmon fishing: "With about a zillion books on trout fishing tactics, why are there only a few on Atlantic salmon fishing tactics? Is it not because fly fishing for salmon—both Atlantic and Pacific types—basically consists of making a cast quartering upstream and then letting your fly swing

down and across? You might put a few mends in your line, straightening it out or getting a deeper drift and swing, but basically that's it. Cast after cast." Jim's dead right.

4. Those Mysterious Landlocks

Landlocked salmon, so coveted for ice-out fishing in Maine and Quebec, have backgrounds shrouded in certain mysteries. Were they descended from the Atlantic salmon, as some scientists believe, trapped in inland waters by geological upheavals long ago? Or is the Atlantic salmon simply a breed of landlock that wandered downstream long ago? Anglers looking for springtime's first pull from a battling fish probably could care less, but they do appreciate the gift of one of the gamest (and tastiest) fishes that swim.

5. Landlocked Salmon: The Source

Although they have been successfully planted in watersheds like Maine's Moosehead and Rangeley Lakes, landlocked salmon were originally found only in the basins of the Presumpscot, Piscataquis, Penobscot, and St. Croix Rivers of Maine and the upper reaches of the Saguenay River in Quebec, where they are known as *ouananiche*.

6. Fishing Out the Swing

With your fly, lure, or bait swinging over a steelhead lie, then straightening out downstream, let the line hang for several moments before starting your retrieve. Sometimes, particularly in colder water, steelhead will follow the lure and not take until they have examined it thoroughly.

7. Find and Fish the Holding Water

You'll spot inexperienced steelhead anglers a mile away: They'll be fishing the entire river, every run and hole. The veterans have learned that the river can be divided between traveling water and holding water. That will cut the fishable areas down to about 15 or 25 percent of the river. Holding water will have the current, depth, and cover that are just right for resting and sticking around for a while. Traveling water is just that: water that you should travel through on your way to better spots. Learning to read the water takes time and experience. For outstanding advice on the subject, see the article "Reading Water: A Little Science and a Lot of Opinion," by Andy Batcho, on the Washington Council of Trout Unlimited site, www.troutunlimited-washington.org.

8. When You Can't Move That Fish

It's an enviable position to be in, but it can be frustrating: You've hooked a big salmon or steel-head, and he's into a pool he likes and you can't budge him—without breaking your leader or rod. Sometimes, as a trick of last resort, banging on the end of the rod butt with the palm of your hand will get the fish moving. This doesn't always work, but sometimes it does.

9. Where the Fish Are Lying

"The water was a tailout, the lower end of a pool at the top of a long rapid. Black [Dennis Black, Umpqua Feather Merchants] explained that steelhead usually move quickly through a rapid, then rest in the quieter holding lies above it. Once he pointed them out, I could see the shadowy forms of five steelhead hanging in the current."

10. Pool Etiquette: It Makes Sense

There are violations all over the map, but *there is* a correct way to share the fishing in a steelhead or salmon pool where several anglers are gathered. Starting at the top of the pool, make a cast that allows your fly to swing down and across the hotspot or strike zone. Next take a step downstream and make another cast. Keep repeating the steps and casts until you reach the bottom of the pool, then go back to the top and start over. Of course, this assumes you are fishing with considerate sportsmen and women. You will on occasion run across a complete jerk and idiot who wants to camp on the best water and keep it for himself. When that happens, it's time for a diplomatic conversation.

11. Great Lakes Steelhead Fighting Qualities

"After catching 25-pound fish on the Kispiox, skating dry flies for surface-feeding steelhead on the Dean in British Columbia, and catching thousands of Great Lakes steelhead, I can tell you this: There is no difference between a hot Western fish and a hot Eastern fish."

12. Low and Slow for Winter Steelhead

Winter steelhead take slowly and deliberately. A fly whipping past over their heads isn't going to be chased. Nor will a lure or bait rig. Whatever method is used, you've got to get your bait on the bottom, where the fish are hugging, and move it slowly. The winter steelhead angler who isn't getting hung up probably isn't catching many fish.

13. Best Landlock Salmon Flies?

"I have caught more salmon [landlocked salmon] with a Black Ghost streamer than any other fly. And the Gray Ghost comes next. . . . Because they are superior, as lures, or because I have spent more time fishing with them than with other patterns?"

14. A Good Day on Black Salmon

As has been shown elsewhere in this book, and as you will learn elsewhere in print and on the rivers, Atlantic salmon fishing is a big and expensive gamble, but well worth it in the minds and hearts of the faithful. For some, one idea that lessens the odds is to go for the so-called "black salmon" on New Brunswick's Miramichi River during the period April 15 through May. It is then that the spawned-out, fall-run fish which have stayed in the river all winter, still fasting under the ice in deep pools, start their run back to the sea. They are rather gaunt, compared to their condition when they made their run from the sea in the fall, and they are called, "black salmon" or "slinks" because they are rather dark and lean compared to summer fish. Many salmon anglers consider the practice of fishing for these fish to be a low-life practice, far beneath the dignity of the lofty Atlantic salmon gentry. Others say, "Hold on. This is great fishing, with fish much bigger and stronger than you might think. They jump, they run, they fight like Atlantic salmon should." These anglers catch lots of fish too, not the paltry numbers from regular salmon fishing. Rates at the Miramichi camps that offer this fishing are sensible, and the chances for success great. Check out some of the Miramichi salmon camps on the Web and make up your own mind if "black salmon" fishing is for you. A caveat: This is cold, bundled-up fishing with a full sinking line and big streamers worked deep and deeper.

15. The Truth About Grilse

I am fortunate to have fished at many Atlantic salmon camps, where the talk was always of grilse weighing an estimated "five or six pounds." In his book, *Fly Fishing Heresies* (1975), the late Leonard M. Wright, Jr., nails the subject once and for all: "Having weighed and measured well over 100 grilse from several rivers, I can cite the following figures with confidence: Grilse average 33 inches long and weigh a shade under 4 pounds."

16. Buck or Roe? You'll Feel the Difference

The male shad, the buck, leaps more and makes flashy runs. The roe, the female laden with eggs, the

one you're after, makes your rod and line feel as if perhaps you've hooked the bottom. Then the "bottom" begins moving and pulling hard and steady, and you know you're in for a fight.

17. How to Get More Salmon Strikes

Leonard M. Wright, Jr., was a keen student of all forms of fly fishing for trout and salmon, with vast experience in fishing for both. From his Atlantic salmon experiences, he became convinced that most salmon casts resulted in the fly passing over and past the fish, too shallow and too fast. The speed and depth of the fly became critical issues to Wright, and he went to a method of fishing his salmon flies "low and slow." Wright says, "Many times I have heard salmon anglers claim that . . . the most killing part of any presentation

occurs during the last part of the swing when the fly is straightening out below them." Wright became convinced that the catch success when the fly "is straightening out below them" was due to the speed having been too fast in the earlier parts of the presentation. Only in the last critical moments was the speed of the fly right for the salmon to take a look.

18. The Leonard Wright Salmon Cast

As described above, Leonard Wright liked to fish his salmon fly "low and slow." To do so, Wright cast out and across and began *mending his line upstream constantly* to get the end of his fly line and the fly in a straight, downstream drift. In his great book *Fly Fishing Heresies* (1975), Wright references legendary Miramichi River angler Ira Gruber, who reportedly said,

A good-sized Atlantic salmon: a true trophy in anyone's book.

" . . . if half the fishermen made their flies swing slower and fished them down deeper there'd be darned few big salmon left in this river."

19. The Hardest Fish to Predict

Everybody knows that in Atlantic salmon fishing, even after months of planning and dreaming, you might arrive at your river and find: 1) The fish aren't in yet. They're still holding offshore, waiting for the right water levels and temperature; 2) The fish have come and gone; 3) The water is high, and staying high, and the fish are running the river, not staying in pools; or 4) The water is low, hot, and the fish are dour, holding in some pools but taking absolutely nothing. In this instance, it may start to rain on your final day in camp,

and when you return home you'll be subjected to the phone call that exalts, "Just after you left . . ."

20. Facing Atlantic Salmon Disappointment

Just back from my favorite Atlantic salmon river in New Brunswick, a 1,000-mile drive from my home in New Jersey, I am still nursing my utter disappointment in not getting a single strike in three days' fishing. Nor did my three companions. The river was high in continuous rain, stained, and the fish were running the river to the upstream pools. That's Atlantic salmon fishing. You drive 1,000 miles. The fish swims 5,000 miles, maybe more. Your visits to the river don't coincide. The only best-laid plans with worse odds is to try to change planes for a connecting flight in Chicago or Atlanta.

21. Why Salmon Hit Flies

It's an old, old argument, with opinions from all sides, so I might as well weigh in with my own. The question before the House is: "Since they are not feeding when they enter rivers to spawn, why do salmon hit flies?" Experts of every stripe have discussed the subject, in print, and I must side with Lee Wulff in believing that salmon take the fly due to a flash of memory from their years in the river as a parr. When certain conditions are absolutely right—the speed of the fly in the water, the slant of light on the fly's colors, the temperature—a salmon urged by some inner biological need to be "on the take" will hit a fly.

22. A Salmon Remembers

When Atlantic salmon fishing, one often hooks and reels in tiny parr that have eagerly attacked the fly. Years later, when the salmon returns from the ocean depths to its home river, memories of its years chasing flies will be strong enough to cause a response to your bogus fly if . . . and it's a big IF . . . the bite is on and conditions are right. A "taking fish" can be hard to find.

23. Check Out Newfoundland and Labrador

Two of the great destinations for brook trout and Atlantic salmon are Newfoundland and Labrador. Check out the Newfoundland and Labrador Guides Association at www.nloa.ca.

Since they aren't feeding when on spawning runs, why do Atlantics hit flies? Many believe it's because they remember eating small baitfish when they were parr.

24. Hook a Salmon, Break a Rod

Alaskan guides have told me that they probably see more rods broken by chum salmon than any other types. The chums come in just before, and with, the silvers, and they can be big—topping 20 pounds. Add mint condition, fresh from the salt, and you've got a fish that will take you deep, deep into the backing. When trying to "horse" such a big fish in the final stages of the fight, many anglers over-stress the rod by pulling back hard just as the fish launches a final desperate run.

25. When the Bite Is On

When fishing for Atlantic or Pacific salmon there are certain times when the fish are in a taking mode, "on the bite," as anglers love to say. When this happens, for whatever reason—barometer, temperature, light, moon phases, whatever—have your line in the water and keep fishing hard. It won't last!

26. When Salmon Strike

The strike of the Atlantic salmon is one of fly fishing's most treasured moments. Alas, it can be a short-lived moment if you react too quickly and pull the fly away from the fish. If your nerves are steady enough, the salmon will usually hook itself. Raise the rod slowly, feel the line tighten, and get set for a battle royal. Many salmon are hooked during idle moments when the angler is looking away or talking to a companion. A hair-trigger reaction to a strike is not the way to go.

© Jay Cassell   A spawning sockeye salmon, taken in Alaska's Kenai River.

27. Two Salmon Strikes

On the previous cast, a fish had swirled near the fly. Now, as my Green Highlander swung down through the pool, my senses were keyed on hair-trigger. A sudden flash, and I reacted as the water boiled then broke in a missed strike. "Rest him a bit," the guide suggested, and we did just that. When I got the fly back on the same float, a pair of black ducks banked overhead, suddenly and dramatically. I couldn't take my eyes off them and was so engrossed when the strike came. Even before I thought to raise the rod, the fish was on, the reel screaming, and we had a hookup. That's often the best way to handle a salmon strike: by doing nothing!

28. Ernie Schwiebert's Salmon-Fishing Advice

The late Ernie Schwiebert, a dear friend and one of the great angling authors, once told me that he believed that the strike of an Atlantic salmon on any particular cast stems from the *previous* cast. "That's the cast when you caught its attention," Ernie said.

29. Landlock Fever: A Springtime Malady

"Although spring fever is contracted easily by sportsmen up here in my home state of Maine, there are a variety of seasonal tonics that will at least arrest that annual affliction. For some, one dosage of dipping smelts will bring their temperatures down. For others, though, the sure-cure prescription of taking trout from big-feeling brooks may have to be refilled several times. There are, of course, those whose allergies and addictions require special medication. Not the least among them are the stalwarts whose worse fever begins to subside at the words, 'ice out,' but whose cure will not be complete until they are trolling streamer flies for landlocked salmon."

30. The Perfect Landlocked Salmon Fly

"The streamer fly is to landlocked salmon fishing what the double-barreled shotgun is to bird hunting . . . Their names alone—Green King, Nine-Three, Gray Ghost, Pink Lady, Supervisor—are good for what ails you."

31. Focusing on Landlocks

"With the exception of the Mickey Finn, Parmacheene Belle, and a few other patterns, the colorations of most streamer patterns are subdued—suggestive of smelts. Greens, grays, black and white barred with black predominate. As is the case with all fishing flies, streamers that are heavily dressed catch fishermen, those on the slender side catch fish. And you may know better than I that there are times which landlocked salmon lust for them."

32. She's Quite a Lady!

"Years ago, the angler became enamored with Lady Amherst when she charmed his first Atlantic salmon . . . Her crowning accomplishment occurred on a mist-shrouded May 1 morning at the Bangor Salmon Pool when she lured the 'Presidential Salmon' off its lie. . . . Like all classic salmon flies, the Lady Amherst is a work of art. For that reason, it is seen most often nowadays in framed displays, where among Jock Scotts, Silver Wilkinsons, and Dusty Millers, to name a few, it represents what is considered to be the epitome of the fly tier's art."

33. The Landlock Salmon Fly Retrieve

"Trolling streamers is an art mastered by few . . . the accepted rule is that the feathered lures should be fished fast and 'on the rocks.' In that regard, a saying attributed to old-school masters of the art is, "A streamer should be fished fast enough so's you'd seriously doubt that a salmon could catch it.'"

34. Same Spot, Same Lures, Different Results

When you see two boats working on a shad holding pool or run, slinging shad darts, and one boat is taking fish while the other is getting casting practice, you can bet heavy money the losers are not fishing deep enough. If your dart is not heavy enough, you won't get down to the fish.

35. A "Must-Read" Shad Book

If you're a serious shad fisher and you've never read John McPhee's *The Founding Fish,* Farrar-Straus-Giroux (2002), do yourself a favor and grab a copy

This Delaware River shad was taken on – what else? – a shad dart.

Trolling with hookless crankbaits, and shad dart trailers, is a good way to find out how deep the shad are. These two came from the Delaware River, in Pennsylvania.

from Amazon, Barnes & Noble, or your library. The natural history of this great American fish, the angling techniques being practiced today—it's all there in some of the richest prose you'll ever engage.

36. Fluttering, Flashing Shad Lures

When I caught my first shad as a teenager on Georgia's Ogeechee River, experiencing for the first time in my life a fish's pull that actually made my wrist ache, we were trolling slowly upcurrent with Tony Acetate silver spoons. Today, fluttering, flashing spoons and lures seem to have been pushed aside by shad darts, but they are still effective choices, trolled slowly, upstream, just as we did years ago. Rig with swivels to prevent line twists.

37. A Clever Way to Troll for Shad

Here's a technique that can be particularly effective on a river like the Delaware in New Jersey, Pennsylvania, and New York. Troll with rods out on both sides of the boat, using bass crankbaits with the hooks removed. An 18-inch leader attached to the crankbait has a shad dart. By running various crankbaits at different depths, you can find the level where the shad are holding and keep your shad darts right in the strike zone.

Catfish, Bullheads, Carp

A. Catfish, Bullheads, Carp—Introduction

WADE BOURNE

Catfish

Catfish will never win a beauty contest, but they are beautiful, indeed, to millions of North American anglers. These whiskered fish live in warm-water rivers, ponds, lakes and reservoirs throughout much of the U.S. and southern Canada. Catfish are willing biters, and they're spirited fighters when hooked. They're also very good fried and served with French fries and hush puppies!

There are three common American catfish species: channel catfish, blue catfish and flathead catfish. All have a host of local nicknames.

Channel catfish have olive-blue sides fading to silver-white bellies. They also have small dark spots on their backs and sides. Channel cats live mostly in rivers or lakes with slow to moderate currents. They are the smallest of the three catfish species, rarely exceeding 25 pounds. The world-record channel cat weighed 58 pounds even and was caught in South Carolina in 1964.

Blue catfish look very much like channels, except they don't have spots on their backs and sides. They grow larger than channel catfish. Blue cats occasionally exceed 100 pounds. The world-record blue cat weighed 116 pounds 12 ounces and was caught in Arkansas in 2001. Blue catfish thrive in big, slow-moving rivers such as the Mississippi, Ohio, Tennessee and Missouri. They gang up in tail-race areas below dams on these rivers.

Flathead catfish are so-named because of their appearance. The flathead's mouth is long and flat, and its lower jaw is slightly longer than its upper jaw. Its back and sides are mottled brown tapering to a lighter belly. Flathead catfish live in a variety of waters, though they prefer current and clean water. The world-record flathead cat weighed 123 pounds and was caught in Kansas in 1998.

All three of these species share certain traits. They have a slick, scaleless skin and feature eight barbels (whiskers) around the mouth. The barbels contain highly-developed smelling organs, which the fish use to sniff out and "taste" various foods. Catfish have one of the most highly developed senses of smell of all fish. Sometimes catfish rely more on their sense of smell to find food than their sense of sight.

Flathead Catfish

Bullhead Catfish

Blue and channel catfish eat worms, insects, bait-fish, crawfish, invertebrates, wild seeds, and a long list of other foods. Flathead cats, on the other hand, feed primarily on living foods - baitfish, crawfish, etc. Many catfish feed more at night than during the day. They feed mainly on the bottom, though they will move up and forage near the surface if a good feeding opportunity exists there.

Catfish spawn in late spring, after the water temperature reaches 70° F. Females lay eggs in holes in the bank, under logs, among rocks, or in other spots that offer some protection from current and concealment from predators.

Bullheads

Bullheads are members of the catfish family, and are often assumed to be small catfish. There is one easy way to tell them apart. Bullheads have rounded tails (flatheads have rounded tails like bullheads, but are recognized by their long, flat mouth.)

There are three common species of bullheads in North America: black, brown and yellow. Their range covers most of the U.S. and southern Canada. They live in a variety of waters, from small ponds and marshes to large impoundments and rivers. Three

other species (snail, spotted, and flat bullhead) are found in the Southeast.

Bullheads prefer quiet, warm waters, and they usually hang close to bottom. They are highly tolerant of pollution and low oxygen content, which means they can survive in many waters where other species can't live.

Bullheads are usually much smaller than catfish. They rarely grow larger than 2 pounds. The world-record black bullhead weighed 8 pounds 15 ounces and was caught in New York in 1951. The world-record brown bullhead weighed 6 pounds 5 ounces and was caught in New York in 2002. The world-record yellow bullhead weighed 4 pounds 4 ounces and was caught in Arizona in 1984.

Bullheads share many of the same feeding and spawning habits as catfish. They're favorites of many panfish anglers, since they're plentiful and usually bite when other species won't.

Carp

Jay Cassell

Although many freshwater fishermen have certain gamefish that they like to fish for, above all others, the reverse is also true: Many freshwater anglers also have certain gamefish that they simply don't like, for one reason or another. And for whatever reason, the carp often falls into the latter category. Some feel the carp is ugly; others disdain its sporting prowess; still others look down on its unwillingness to hit artificial lures, instead preferring homemade concoctions such as doughballs or cornmeal.

Despite this, the carp does have a following, and it's growing. Think about it; Carp grow huge—up to 25 pounds in many waters; they're abundant; and they are able to survive in murky or even polluted waters that would kill other gamefish. In the past 10 years or so, fly fishermen have also discovered that yes, carp will hit certain flies. Expect to see more of anglers "sight fishing for northern bonefish" in the coming years.

B. Catfish, Bullhead Tactics

WADE BOURNE

Ponds and Lakes

Catfish and bullheads spend the most time on or near the bottom of small ponds and lakes, so this is where you should fish for them. While they prefer deep water, they may move up and feed in the shallows from time to time. In either location, fish directly on bottom without a float or just above bottom with a float.

While you move a lot searching for sunfish, crappie and bass, fishing for catfish and bullheads calls for a pick-one-spot-and-wait-'em-out method. These fish find their food mostly by smell and you have to leave your bait in one place long enough for the scent to spread through the water and for the fish to home in on it.

It's possible to fish for these species with long poles, but I prefer spin-cast or spinning outfits so I can fish farther off the bank. I take at least two rods. I pick a spot on the bank close to deep water. Then I cut a forked stick for each rod and push it into the ground next to the pond's edge. I cast out my lines, prop my rods in the forked sticks, and wait for something to happen.

Carefully examine small ponds for features that provide fish holding areas. The map below shows typical features encountered in a farm pond, such as sunken timber and brush piles, shallow weed beds, and a submerged creek channel.

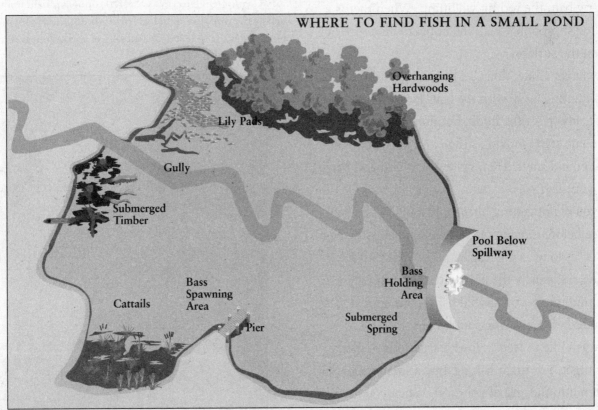

WHERE TO FIND FISH IN A SMALL POND

Overhanging Hardwoods

Lily Pads

Gully

Submerged Timber

Cattails

Bass Spawning Area

Pier

Bass Holding Area

Submerged Spring

Pool Below Spillway

When using two rods, I tie a bottom rig on one and a slip-bobber rig on the other. This gives the catfish or bullheads a choice of a bait laying on bottom or hanging just above.

Catfish grow much larger than bullheads, so if catfish are your main target, you need larger hooks. I recommend a #1 or 1/0 sproat or baitholder hook. If you're fishing for bullheads, select a smaller #6 hook. If you're trying for both species, use something in between - a #2 or #4.

Catfish and bullheads will eat the same baits. Earthworms or nightcrawlers are two favorites. Chicken liver, live or dead minnows, grasshoppers and a wide variety of commercially-made baits also work well. With all these baits, load your hooks. The more bait on them, the more scent you have in the water, and the more likely you are to attract fish.

Cast your baited lines into deep water. With the bottom rig, wait until the sinker is on bottom, then gently reel in line until all the slack is out. With a slip-bobber rig, set the bobber so the bait is suspended just above bottom.

Now, just relax and wait. When a fish takes the bottom-rig bait, the rod tip will jump. When there's a bite on the slip-bobber bait, the bobber will dance nervously on the surface.

If you get a bite, don't set the hook until the fish starts swimming away with the bait. Pick up the rod and get ready to set the hook, but don't exert any pull until the line starts moving steadily off or the bobber goes under and stays. Then strike back hard and begin playing your fish.

If you're not getting bites, how long do you stay in one place before moving to another? Probably the best answer is "as long as you can stand it." The best cat-fishermen are usually the ones with the most patience. But at a minimum, you should fish in one spot at least 20 minutes before moving somewhere else.

Catfish like to feed in lowlight periods of dawn, dusk or night. For night fishing, buy a small metal bell and fasten it to the end of your rod. When you get a bite, the bell will ring, indicating that a fish has your bait.

Big lakes can hold big catfish, and the best time to catch them is in late spring during the spawn. These fish move to the banks and look for holes and protected areas to lay their eggs.

Look for banks with big rock bluffs, riprap, etc. Catfish like to spawn in rocks. Fish around these areas with fixed or slip-bobber rigs baited with gobs of wiggler worms or nightcrawlers. Set your float so the bait hangs just above the rocks. Use medium strength line (10-20 pound test) and a steel hook (#1-3/0), since the possibility of hooking a big fish is good.

After they spawn, catfish head back to deep-water flats and channels. Normally they spend daylight hours deep, and move up at night to feed in nearby shallows. Find a point or other spot where the bank slopes off into deep water, and fish here from late afternoon well into the night. Use a bottom rig, baited with worms, cut bait, liver, commercial stink bait, or other popular catfish baits.

U.S. Geological Survey (USGS) topographical maps, such as the one shown below, provide detailed information about the bottom features and shorelines of lakes, rivers and impoundments.

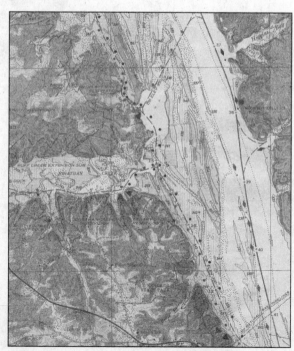

Another easy and productive method for taking catfish is called "jug fishing." This method requires a boat and 25 or more milk or 2-liter soft drink plastic bottles. Tie strong lines of 4-6 feet onto the jug handles or around the spouts. Tie a 2/0 steel hook on the end of the line, and add a split shot or a clincher sinker 6 inches up from the hook. Bait these lines with minnows, fish guts, or other catfish bait, and throw the jugs overboard on the upwind side of a lake or bay. The wind will float the jugs across the water, and catfish will be drawn to the bait. When a jug starts bobbing on the surface, move the boat in and retrieve the fish.

Bullheads normally stay in warm bays that have silty or muddy bottoms. Like catfish, they hold deep during the day, but move up shallow and feed from late afternoon through the night.

The technique for catching bullheads is the same as for night-feeding catfish, except you need lighter tackle. A spinning rod, 6-pound test line and a #3 hook are a good combination. A small split shot should be clamped on the line a foot up from the hook. Worms are good bait for bullheads.

Rivers and Tailwaters

Catfish and bullheads are plentiful in most large warm-water rivers. In the daytime, catfish stay in deep holes and channel edges, while bullheads prefer shallower backwaters. At night, both roam actively in search of food.

The best time to try for these fish is just after sundown. Fish for catfish along bluffs, tributary mouths, flats bordering the channel, or the downstream side of rock jetties. Try for bullheads in mud-bottom sloughs.

For catfish, use stout tackle and a bottom rig. Sinkers should be heavy enough to keep the bait anchored in current (1-3 ounces). Hooks should be large and stout (1/0-3/0 steel). Live minnows, worms, cut bait, liver or any traditional catfish bait will work. Cast the rig and allow it to sink to the bottom. Prop the rod in a forked stick jammed into the ground and sit back and wait for a bite. Serious catfish anglers fish several rods at once. They stay in the same spot for several hours, waiting for the fish to feed.

A rock bank will offer red-hot catfishing during spawning time, especially if the rocks are out of direct current. Fish these spots with a fixed or slip-bobber rig, adjusting the float so the bait hangs just above the rocks.

River catfishing can be phenomenal in dam tailwaters - a collection point for fish. Tailwaters contain baitfish, current, dissolved oxygen, and bottom structure where fish can hold and feed.

The best way to fish a tailwater is to work eddies close to the swift water that pours through the dam. If you're bank fishing, use a bottom rig and cast into quiet waters behind wing walls, pilings or the dam face. If the bottom is rough and you keep hanging up, switch to a slip-float rig adjusted so the bait hangs close to bottom.

A better way to fish tailwaters is from a boat, floating along current breaks while bumping a two-hook panfish rig off the bottom. Use enough weight so your line hangs almost straight under the boat. Make long downstream drifts, up to a quarter-mile or more, before motoring back up to make another float. Don't lay your rod down since big catfish strike hard, and can yank it overboard.

Another special catfishing opportunity occurs right after a hard rain. Look for gulleys, drains or other spots where fresh water is rushing into the river. Catfish often move up below these inflows and feed furiously. In this case, use a fixed or slip-bobber rig and dangle a bait only 2-3 feet under the surface in the immediate vicinity of the inflow.

Fish bullheads in rivers the same as in large lakes and reservoirs. Light tackle, worms and a bottom rig or bobber rig are hard to beat.

C. Catfish, Bullhead Tactics

LAMAR UNDERWOOD

1. Giant Catfish: You Need Help

The biggest catfish—we're talking 20 to 30 pounds and higher—are caught on the bigger rivers, from deep holes. Fishing these waters, particularly where impoundment water is being released, can be treacherous. Think about hiring a guide before you tackle it on your own.

2. Finding and Catching More and Bigger Catfish

My friend John E. Phillips is a prolific and engaging writer whose prose has enhanced many magazine pages over the years. Not only are his articles excellent, but he is the author of several books, including *The Masters' Secrets of Catfishing*, available from John's Night Hawk Publications Web site, www.nighthawkpublications. com. Click on "books," then go to "fishing books."

3. Chum Them Up with Dog Food

"Use an ice pick to punch two dozen holes in a can of inexpensive dog food. The day before you fish, sink the can of dog food on a rock, clay, or sandy bottom without mud . . . To chum cats in quicker, purchase the more expensive dog food packed in gravy . . . By the time you fish the next day, the dog food should have chummed the cats to the spot where you want to catch them."

—John Phillips, "John's Journal," Night Hawk Publications, www.nighthawkpublications.com

4. Favorite Baits for Blue Cats

"For whopper blues, stick to fish. Big catfish almost exclusively eat other fish. Use whole fish, 4- to 6-inch-long strips or meaty chunks," reports John M. Felsher in "Big Game Sport on a Small Budget," on a www.cabelas.com Field Guide Story. Some of the largest blues hit "mere morsels," he says. Felsher notes that some guides prefer skipjack herring, cut into chunks or filleted. The fillet is hooked one time with the hook exposed and undulates in the current. Catfish can't resist it.

5. A Good Basic Catfish Rig

To fish your catfish bait right on the bottom, use an egg sinker, barrel swivel, 20-inch leader, and No. 6 hook.

6. Fish the Mussel Beds

Wherever you can find freshwater clams or river mussels, consider them to be catfish magnets. As these critters die and are washed off the shells, catfish will be on them. No clams? Then use spoiled shrimp or live worms.

7. Use Dog Food in Small Ponds

"When you fish small ponds or little lakes, use cheap, dry dog food to chum up catfish. Anchor your boat and every two to three minutes throw a handful of dog food out in the water . . . bream will show up first, allowing you to catch a mess of bluegills and shellcrackers. In a short while, the catfish will begin to come to the chum . . ."

—John Phillips, "John's Journal," Night Hawk Publications, www.nighthawkpublications.com

8. Switch to Catfish for More Fun

"I used to specialize in fly fishing for smallmouth. But as I've gotten older, I've turned to catfishing. It doesn't take as much effort, and I can just about always count on getting a few." (Other southern anglers can do the same in the small creeks and rivers near their homes.)

—Buffalo River, Tennessee, angler Joe B. Sweeney, in the Wade Bourne article "Lazy Days: Small Streams and Southern Catfish," Bass Pro Shops Outdoor Library

9. Best Water for Small-Stream Catfish

"Most people think catfish hang in deep, quiet holes. This may be true of the bigger ones, but smaller cats feed in shallow, swift areas. I'm talking about runs that are 2-3 feet deep and exposed to direct current. Also, a spot is better if it has a clean gravel or clay bottom instead of a mud bottom. Catfish hold around cover (logs, treetops, rocks, and so on) in these areas and move out into the current to find food. In fact, they feed a lot like a bass."

—Buffalo River, Tennessee, angler Joe B. Sweeney, in the Wade Bourne article "Lazy Days: Small Streams and Southern Catfish," Bass Pro Shops Outdoor Library

10. Baiting Up for Small-Stream Catfish

Buffalo River, Tennessee, angler Joe B. Sweeney says "catfishermen can bait with any range of cut-up fish pieces, crawfish tails, stink baits, worms, insects, etc. However, he has narrowed the bait choice to three top performers: red worms, chicken livers, and catalpa worms." Sweeney says the best way to keep chicken livers on the hook is to run the hook through a thumb-sized piece two or three times.

—Wade Bourne, in the article "Lazy Days: Small Streams and Southern Catfish," Bass Pro Shops Outdoor Library

5. The Bluefish Frenzy: You've Got to Be There

Whether you are out for the pan-sized blues called "snappers" in bays and coves, or the 15- to 20-plus pounders called "slammers" just offshore, you're in for rod-bending, tackle-busting action like few fishing trips can provide. And despite the complaints of those who don't like to eat them, many of us bluefish addicts think they're great on the table, especially when freshly caught. Even if you live in Kansas or Iowa, put bluefishing on your list of Things To Do Before You Die. By the way, if you're a trout fisherman and thinking of taking that small reel along, forget about it! A bluefish will blow it to pieces in one run.

6. Chumming: The Saltwater Action Creator

When you experience chumming for saltwater gamefish on charter trips or with friends who are showing you the way, you'll quickly learn to appreciate this fun and deadly way of fishing. Anchored in a likely spot for waves of moving fish or over a mother lode of suspended fish which are happy to not be going anywhere, you'll be grinding and chopping small baitfish, clams, and other delicacies and feeding the gunk into the tides. Once a long "slick" is established, work your jigs or baited hooks into the "hot zone" and hang onto your hat. Chumming is saltwater's light-tackle heaven.

7. Keep It Quiet!

As related by distinguished writer John Hersey in his classic bluefishing book *Blues*, Knopf (1987), we have no less a sage than Aristotle to remind us that noise frightens fish. He related, ". . . for they are observed to run away from any loud noises like the rowing of a galley." They will also "run away" from a variety of intrusions committed by anglers, such as banging tackleboxes and gear in the bottom of the boat and slapping the sides of a craft with oars or paddles.

8. You Know the Fishing's Really Lousy When . . .

You know the fishing's really lousy when the kids you've brought out start saying, "Can we go back and catch more bait? That was really fun."

9. If It Ain't Chartreuse . . .

In a *Sport Fishing* magazine poll of charter skippers by Doug Olander to find their favorite lure colors, in the all-important inshore fishing group, chartreuse was the strong winner—once again proving, "If it ain't chartreuse, it ain't no use!"

10. Great Easy-Chair Fishing

You can do a lot worse things with your time and money than spending them on *Sport Fishing* magazine and its Web site, www.sportfishingmag.com. The magazine is packed with articles on all types of saltwater fishing, from going for flounder in bays to taking on giant marlin offshore. There's information galore here, on techniques, gear, and destinations. The magazine can literally be the ticket to some of the greatest fishing of your life.

11. More Great Easy-Chair Fishing

Competition among magazines is good for readers. In the saltwater realm, *Sport Fishing* magazine is rivaled by *SaltWater Sportsman*, which has everything about fishing the briny one could possibly ask for. The magazine's Web site is www.saltwatersportsman.com and you will be rewarded by visiting it. You'll find how-to on everything, along with tons of videos and destination ideas. I've noticed that *SaltWater Sportsman* sometimes gets letters from readers in places like Kansas, who are fascinated by their magazine links to the strange and amazing world of fishing the salt. The pulling power of the oceans is strong.

12. Focus on Saltwater Fly Fishing

The magazine *Fly Fishing in Salt Waters,* with its Web site at www.flyfishinsalt.com, is one of my favorite sources for good ideas and information on fly fishing in the briny, from inshore tidewaters and flats, out to the deep waters where the big ones roam. The magazine will not only make you a better angler, it will send you to places where you'll find fly-fishing action to dream about.

13. Storing Leaders and Pre-Tied Fly Rigs

In a technique tip from *Sport Fishing* magazine's Web site, reader Bill Hallman explained his idea of storing leaders on plastic tubes wrapped on a plastic coat hanger, two tubes on the top arms, one on the long bottom. Secure the leaders to the plastic with toothpicks. Fly-fishing rigs with dropper nymphs tied to a dry fly can be kept this way as well.

14. Bluefish Seeing Red

Back in 1972, when I was editor of *Sports Afield,* Stephen Ferber, a friend in the process of building his own publishing company, wrote a tremendously informative article on bluefishing for the *Fishing Annual.* His top tip was one worth remembering today: "The color that takes the most spring blues is red. . . . I won't come right out and say that Gene Hendrickson was the first to use the red plugs for bluefish, but it is possible. . . . He had rigged red plugs to each of the outriggers, a blue one to one stern rod and a yellow feather to the other. After two hours of trolling, he caught twenty-one blues—eighteen on the red lures. Now he carries a can of fluorescent-red spray paint on board for use when his plugs get too chewed up, or for changing, say, a silver non-producer into a bluefish killer."

15. When the Blues Are Running

"A school of blues can send panic hundreds of yards forward of their path as they wheel and turn en masse on feeding forays, making terror-stricken baitfish jump through the water's surface like a volley of arrows . . . He is a fierce predator, savagely running down and chewing up anything in his path—including other blues."

—Stephen Ferber, *Sports Afield Fishing Annual,* 1972

16. An Extra Bluefish Danger

When landing bluefish, "The one constant danger lies in the lure itself. Remember, there are nine hooks in each plug. The chopper jumps, twists, shakes, and thrashes after he's brought over the side. In many occasions, you'll have more than one hooked blue in the boat at the same time—so getting one of those barbs through the finger is a real possibility even for the most experienced of men."

—Stephen Ferber, *Sports Afield Fishing Annual,* 1972

17. Great Autumn Surf Fishing

In October and November along the Atlantic coast, reports J.B. Kasper in his *Trenton Times* outdoor column, storms push a lot of clams into the wash along the beaches, making them the bait of choice the first few days after a big blow. Kasper says to look for some of the best movements of stripers and blues " . . . just after the new and full moon, especially when the top of the tide occurs around sundown and sunset."

18. When the Mackerel Run

When the mackerel tide flows north along the Atlantic coastline every spring, and anglers enjoy the year's first big run of fish, many of the mackerel-fishing faithful do not realize that these little torpedo-like speedsters are part of a great tribe of saltwater battlers, including tuna, marlin, and sailfish. The mackerel is also related to the albacores, bonitos, giant kingfish, wahoo, and the Spanish and cerro mackerels. The mackerel is the smallest of all his relatives, but anglers don't mind a bit when the action begins.

19. Surf Fishing's Scouting Report

Next to seeing fish breaking and knowing exactly where the action is (instead of guessing where it might eventually happen), try to get a look at your stretch of beach at extreme low tides. Study where even the smallest cuts and channels show on the bottom. That's where you're likely to get strikes when the waves move in, bringing the fish with them on a rising tide.

20. Fish the Ebb-Tide at Night

"By and large, we found the early ebb the most fruitful time to fish . . . Many fishermen forget that bass are night feeders . . . If you wish to catch bass by daylight, fish when high water comes at morning and evening."

—Wyman Richardson, *The House on Nauset Marsh*, W.W. Norton, 1947

21. Two Critical Rules for Stripers in the Surf

"He used to catch a lot of bass, and may well have taken more fish off that beach than anyone else. However, we chose to attribute this rather more to his observance of . . . Rule 1: Be there when the fish are biting. Rule 2: He catches the most fish who does the most fishing."

—Wyman Richardson, *The House on Nauset Marsh*, W.W. Norton, 1947

22. The Joys of Full-Moon Fishing

When you're on the beach for stripers and blues when the moon is full, or nearly full, and the skies are reasonably clear of clouds, you'll enjoy night fishing with almost-daylight visibility.

23. Heed the Call of the Surf

If the call of the surf—the breaking waves, the flowing tides, the onshore and offshore birds with their flights and cries, the great vastness of sky and salt-scented air—means anything at all to you, I'd like to give you a shove, not a nudge, toward getting into surf fishing. In autumn, in particular, when the crowds have mostly gone and the fish are at their best, on the move, the great surf-fishing beaches like those in New Jersey can provide magical angling days. With your daypack—food and beverage, even something to read if you like—and your tackle, you're all set. The very best way to get into it is to hire a guide a couple of times, let him show you the gear, the techniques that work best—before you blow a lot of money on the wrong stuff. There are also many clubs and associations, or perhaps you have a friend who can show you the ropes and tools. Most of the people who are really crazy about surf fishing have found they don't have to catch a lot of fish to have a good day on the beach. Of course, catching fish is what really makes surf fishing exciting. Just beachcombing won't cut it. Two of the best books to get you into the mood of surf-fishing are David DiBenedetto's *On the Run,* Morrow (2003), and Roy Rowan's *Surfcaster's Quest,* The Lyons Press (1999).

24. Lefty Kreh's "Miracle" Saltwater Fly

"Lefty's Deceiver is now used around the world in salt water (although it is a popular freshwater pattern as well). Without being boastful, I think it's accurate to say that the Deceiver and the old Clouser Minnow are two of the most imitated saltwater flies in the sport." [Editor's Note: Lefty Kreh's Deceiver was honored by the United States Postal Service in 1991 by being chosen to illustrate a 29-cent postage stamp. Lefty says he is very proud that the caption doesn't read, "Deceiver," but instead reads, "Lefty's Deceiver."]

—Lefty Kreh, with Chris Millard, *My Life Was THIS BIG and Other True Fishing Tales*, Skyhorse Publishing, 2008

25. The Standard Fly Casting Method Doesn't Work

"In the standard method the angler basically brings the rod from 10 o'clock back to about 2 o'clock and then back to 10 o'clock. After trying the technique for a while I began to realize that it was not the best, most efficient way to cast a fly line."

—Lefty Kreh, with Chris Millard, *My Life Was THIS BIG and Other True Fishing Tales*, Skyhorse Publishing, 2008

26. The Lefty Kreh Fly Casting Technique

"Through trial and error I gradually learned to take the rod way back behind me and make longer backcasts and longer forward casts. I also abandoned the high-hand vertical style of the standard method and adopted a much lower position, a more horizontal profile for my arm. As I began to refine my technique I found that I was not only making longer, more accurate casts with tighter loops, but I was doing it with far less effort than the old 10 to 2 method demanded."

—Lefty Kreh, with Chris Millard, *My Life Was THIS BIG and Other True Fishing Tales,* Skyhorse Publishing, 2008

27. Lefty Kreh's Fly Casting Revolution

"In March 1965, I wrote an article detailing my new technique in *Outdoor Life*. Many people view that article as a landmark in the evolution of the fly cast. To this day, however, many critics see it as outright heresy, an affront to the traditions of the sport. And therein lies one of the great blessings and burdens of the sport: Tradition."

—Lefty Kreh, with Chris Millard, *My Life Was THIS BIG and Other True Fishing Tales,* Skyhorse Publishing, 2008

28. The Importance of Casting Lefty's Way

"The old-fashioned 10 to 2 technique is adequate for that limited type of fishing [small-stream trout fishing]. . . . That technique does not work well when you are fishing for larger fish with larger flies on heavier lines over larger, windier bodies of water. As a result, most people who learn traditional casting technique while fishing for freshwater trout can't perform in other conditions."

—Lefty Kreh, with Chris Millard, *My Life Was THIS BIG and Other True Fishing Tales,* Skyhorse Publishing, 2008

29. Mystery of the Galloping Bass

"Not infrequently a school of bass will harry bait without actually feeding. On such occasions they will often roll almost clear of the water or flip their tails way out. We call this galloping—'A galloping bass never bites'—and very disappointing it is, too."

—Wyman Richardson, *The House on Nauset Marsh*, W.W. Norton, 1947

30. A Pocket Full of Good Fishing Luck

As are all the Orvis Pocket Fishing Guides, the hand-sized *Pocket Guide to Flyfishing for Striped Bass and Bluefish*, by Lou Tabory, is a quick-read, superbly illustrated guide to the skills you need to master to fly fish the briny. Available at www.amazon.com.

31. Bluefish: Power x Two

"I'd rather have two mad bluefish on the same line in a cold ocean than catch all the sailfish and marlin ever made. The only thing I know of that's better is a frisky Atlantic salmon in a cold Canadian stream, on about six ounces of fly rod."

—The Old Man in Robert Ruark's *The Old Man and the Boy,* September Song, 1953

32. Fantastic on the Table

Of all the great fish to have on your plate—particularly fried, yes deep-fried—the snook ranks near the top of my list, with some others, of course, including crappies, bluegills, catfish, walleyes, and red snapper.

33. Why Focus on Snook?

"The snook, or robalo, is closely related to the basses, although this silvery fish with a greenish or brownish back is more streamlined than any bass and has a distinctive coal-black lateral line and a long pointed head with protruding lower jaw. . . . The snook averages about 4 pounds but the world's record weighed over 50 pounds . . . a real demon on the end of a light fishing stick."

—Col Dave Harbour, *Sports Afield Fishing Annual,* 1972

34. Fighting Qualities of Snook

"As an old snook expert who should know, Tom Bonsall described this challenging fish as 'shy as a brown trout and as powerful as a tarpon.' The snook is one fish that will find the weakness of any man or his tackle in 10 seconds."

—Col Dave Harbour, *Sports Afield Fishing Annual,* 1972

35. Those Special Boat Shoes

When you're new to saltwater fishing and going on a friend's boat for the first time, it's standard courtesy to check in advance on your footwear. You don't necessarily have to have the most popular, expensive kind, but you want to make sure yours aren't going to put skid marks all over the place.

36. Beware Those Teeth!

One thing you definitely do not want to do when fishing salt water is to join the long, long list of anglers whose fingers and hands have been slashed open by bluefish teeth. When landing and unhooking bluefish, beware those teeth! The "handle with care" sign is definitely in play.

37. Hit Those Points—Hard

"Points that protrude at an angle to the beach can be ideal fishing locations. Fish the flowing water along the bar's inside edge."

—Lou Tabory, *The Orvis Pocket Guide to Fly Fishing for Striped Bass and Bluefish,* The Lyons Press, 2001

38. Surf's Up, Fly Fishing's Down

"Conditions are ideal for fly fishing when the surf along the steep ocean beaches is less than 3 feet. An increase of 1 foot in wave size increases the fishing difficulty by three times."

—Lou Tabory, *The Orvis Pocket Guide to Fly Fishing for Striped Bass and Bluefish,* The Lyons Press, 2001

39. Favorite Place to Fish

"If I could fish only one water type, it would be a creek or small river flowing into deeper water. I like places that you can cast across when the flow spills into 6- to 10-foot drop-offs."

—Lou Tabory, *The Orvis Pocket Guide to Fly Fishing for Striped Bass and Bluefish,* The Lyons Press, 2001

40. Fishing the Right Place at the Wrong Time

"Fishing a good spot under the wrong conditions is like lacing up your ice skates in July."

—David DiBenedetto, *On the Run: An Angler's Journey Down the Striper Coast,* William Morrow, 2005

41. Striper Book Destined to Become a Classic

If you love striped bass fishing, or even have a notion that makes you want to try it, an absolute must-have book is David DiBenedetto's *On the Run: An Angler's Journey Down the Striper Coast,* published by William Morrow (an imprint of HarperCollins) in 2005. The book is so well-written that reading it seems to transport one to DiBenedetto's side as he fishes for stripers on the great fall migration run, from Maine to North Carolina.

42. Summer Stripers Are Night Feeders

"The stripers had yet to show their fall colors, so I concentrated my efforts at peak feeding times, the happy hours of dawn and dusk and throughout the night. At these times, stripers rely on their excellent night vision to ambush unsuspecting prey."

—David DiBenedetto, *On the Run: An Angler's Journey Down the Striper Coast,* William Morrow, 2005

43. Go Slow for Stripers at Night

"To catch a striper at night, you need to reel agonizingly slowly. Old-timers like to say, 'Reel as slow as possible, then reel twice that slow.'"

—David DiBenedetto, *On the Run: An Angler's Journey Down the Striper Coast,* William Morrow, 2005

44. Bluefish and Striper Migration Differences

Striped bass basically migrate north along the Atlantic coast in the spring, then south in the fall. Bluefish migrate from Atlantic depths offshore to preferred inshore areas in the spring, then fade back into the depths in the fall and early winter.

45. The Fall Striper Migration Run

The great fall striper migration run, a virtual living river of fish along the Atlantic coast, from Maine to North Carolina, takes place within a mile or so of shore. It varies with the run of the baitfish. Where the baitfish go, the stripers follow—from areas well offshore right up to the beach.

46. Misjudging Late-Fall Fishing

As a landlubber sensitive to temperature changes and the advent of winter, you might feel that those cold late-fall, early winter days have shut down the fishing. Perhaps it has, in fresh water, but the sea temperatures take time to drop, and fishing along the coast can be red-hot just when you're thinking the weather has turned too cold.

47. The Good Old Chum Line

" . . . Dad and I also chummed grass shrimp along the coast for striped bass and tide-running weakfish . . . The trick was to drift a pair of tiny shrimp back in the chum slick at the same rate as the tide was flowing."

—Mark Sosin, *The Complete Book of Light-Tackle Fishing,* The Lyons Press, 1979

48. You'll Need a Gaff on the Jetties

"A longer gaff is important when fishing jetties, as it's often dangerous to scramble down to the water in order to land a big fish. Jetty regulars carry longer gaffs strapped to their backs so they're not impeded when walking."

—Al Ristori, *The Complete Book of Surf Fishing,*
Skyhorse Publishing, 2008

49. Sand Fleas: The Kind You Like

When you hear saltwater vets refer to sand fleas, they're not talking about insects that swarm and bite like regular "fleas." As Al Ristori tells us in his excellent *The Complete Book of Surf Fishing,* Skyhorse Publishing (2008), sand fleas are tiny crabs that scurry back and forth along the surfline and can be caught by hand. They make good bait for all kinds of saltwater denizens, particularly for that gourmet's delight, pompano.

50. Great Surf Fishing Starts Right Here

Al Ristori's *The Complete Book of Surf Fishing,* Skyhorse Publishing (2008), is the perfect starting point for getting into this rewarding and challenging fishing experience. From tackle to techniques, Ristori gives aspiring surf anglers all the solid, no-nonsense information they need to catch the fish that roam along the beaches. A legendary angler and writer from New Jersey, Ristori has fished many of the world's greatest beaches, and knows firsthand everything he writes about. When I look at his pictures of tarpon and snook in the surf beside the Parismina River in Costa Rica, I have to smile. It was there a leaping 90-pound tarpon knocked me overboard and broke my foot back in the 1970s. Al was there when it happened.

51. Rigging Up to Bottom Fish Live Bait

"The best all-purpose rig is what I call the basic bottom rig. The sinker comes off one arm of a three-way swivel on a short length of leader and the hook is attached to the other arm via a leader. The leader varies

in length, but for many situations, I like at least 3 feet. You can make it shorter when necessary."

—Mark Sosin, *The Complete Book of Light-Tackle Fishing,* The Lyons Press, 1979

52. Spring Means Mackerel

They're sometimes called "little warriors," and the fishing fleets all along the Atlantic coast will be rigged and on the move for mackerel in March and early April. New Jersey, Long Island (especially Montauk), and points north usually get fantastic runs of little warriors that bring the first taste of spring to winter-weary anglers. Check your coastal listings and climb aboard. The action is fast, friendly, and rewarding.

53. Stripers in the Surf: Six Top Lure Choices

In his Fishing Column in *Field & Stream,* May 2008, John Merwin named his six top lure choices for stripers in the surf: 1) Bucktail Jigs, ¼ to ½ ounce, white tipped with red pork-rind strip, black after dark: www.basspro.com; 2) Slug-Go soft-plastic jerkbait. Available at www.lunkercity.com; 3) Kastmaster wobblers: www.acmetackle.com; 4) Bomber Magnum Long A plug: www.bomberlures.com; 5) Super Strike Super "N" Fish Needlefish Plug: www.superstrikelures.com; 6) Pencil Popper (Stan Gibbs): www.gibbslures.com.

54. Give Sea Trout Your Best Shot

Sea trout answer to many names, including spotted sea trout, speckled trout, and specks. In the mid-Atlantic saltwater regions, sea trout never achieve the box-office status of striped bass and bluefish, even though they are eagerly sought and caught at times. Head on down through the Carolinas and on around the coasts to the Gulf states and Texas, and you'll find where the sea trout really come into their own. Sea

trout are outstanding on the table, one of the best. Best baits and lures include live shrimp worked over grassy flats in water 6 feet deep, over oyster bars, and at the mouths of tidal creeks.

55. The Tides Are the Key

"In salt water, the fish are on the prowl much more than they are in lakes or streams. Tides play a vital role in their existence and their body rhythms are tuned to this cycle. Saltwater angling looks much easier than freshwater sport to those who have never tried it, but figuring out where fish might be on a stage of the tide isn't always the easiest thing to do."

—Mark Sosin, *The Complete Book of Light-Tackle Fishing,* The Lyons Press, 1979

56. Gulls and Terns Taking It Easy

Okay, you were expecting a blitz, gulls screaming and diving, showing you stripers and blues tearing the water and baitfish to pieces. Instead, all is quiet, and the only gulls you see are sitting on the water, resting. Before you head for another spot—or go home—consider that the birds may just be taking it easy for a spell while the baitfish have gone back deep, taking the blues and stripers with them. The area is definitely worth checking out on sonar or just by watching or trying some casts for a while.

C. Techniques

AL RISTORI

This is another subject that could fill up a book all by itself. It's also necessary to detail it to specific areas and fisheries. Here, I'll review the techniques which I feel are particularly important and of fairly universal importance.

Deep Trolling

Surface trolling is relatively basic and easy to learn. However, the volume of fish feeding at the surface is rarely more than a fraction of what may be available lower in the water column. Getting down to those fish while trolling can be accomplished in a number of ways, though all require quite a bit of time, expense, and effort, plus a commitment to master the technique.

Wire line and Luhr Jensen planers are two means of getting down to where fish feed most of the time.

Wire-line rigs are often trolled from outrodders in order to spread the lines and prevent tangles that can be a disaster with wire. Bunker spoons also work better in that fashion.

The easiest and most direct is trolling with wire line or leadcore. It must be noted that wire line trolling is not legal under IGFA rules, but leadcore is approved. Wire is far more efficient than leadcore in cutting through the water to achieve depth without weight and is the better bet in strong currents. Leadcore is easier to use but, due to its bulk, works best in shallow waters and where there isn't much current. The general rule with single-strand wire at the relatively slow trolling speeds used for striped bass and bluefish is to let out 100 feet of wire to attain 10 feet of depth. Thus, if you're trolling in 22 feet, 200 feet of wire should put your lure right where you'd normally want it—two feet over bottom where any feeding fish can see it but you won't be hanging up or catching weed. Of course, all this isn't quite as simple as it sounds, since the skipper must be alert to adjust for a variety of conditions. For instance, a larger wave, a boat wake, or a sudden increase in current at a rip can momentarily "stop" a boat trolling at slow speed—which is all that's required for the wire to drop to bottom. Getting hung up with wire means you'll have to bring in any other lines that are out and run back uptide ahead of the hang to pull

Live sardine hooked through the nose so it can swim and attract predators.

Wire can be marked to determine depth by wrapping material such as vinyl tape at 50-foot intervals.

Stan Blum with kingfish trolled with a downrigger off Fort Pierce, Florida.

in the opposite direction. Lures will usually pull free in that fashion. If not, run the boat over the spot and maintain headway while pulling on the leader by hand. That's why I use long leaders attached to the wire with an Albright knot so they can be reeled onto the spool.

Handling wire is a big problem for beginners. Both the more flexible monel and the less costly stainless steel have virtually no stretch and tend to jump off the spool rather than lay on it like other lines. The trick to streaming wire is tension. First, clamp your finger on the spool before taking the reel out of gear. Then strip the leader out past the knot or swivel so nothing will catch in the guides. Wire can now be streamed slowly under thumb pressure, which is reduced as more is out and tension increases. If there are no other lines in the water, all of this can be accomplished in a flash

by speeding up the boat. If wire has to be paid out at slow speed, the angler must also stop it with his thumb several times in order to prevent weighted lures from falling to bottom.

How do you know how much wire you have out? Unless you buy a wire marked by the manufacturer

(Malin was trying to perfect that product as this book was written), it's necessary to mark the wire by hand. By far the best bet for beginners is to buy the wire at a tackleshop and have them mark it. In areas where wire is commonly used, marinas with lots of sportfishing docks will have a dock with marks at 100, 150, 200, and 250 feet. Unless you're fishing very shallow waters, there's no need to place a mark before 100 feet. However, should you be regularly working a spot that only requires 75 or 125 feet, make a mark at that spot. Indeed, if that's the only place you'll be using wire line, forget the marking entirely and attach to your backing at that point. If there's no dock marked out for you, the alternative is to lay the line out on your lawn after putting it on the reel and measure the spots to be marked. Remember that the long length of leader doesn't count for depth.

Many materials can be utilized for marking wire. Coated colored wires within phones are very good, but I usually employ vinyl tape, which can be purchased on a card at about $1 for five rolls in different colors. The rolls are too wide, so I pull off some tape and strip them in half before wrapping the pieces on my wire. Be sure there aren't any edges exposed, as these will catch in the guides and slide. Tape rarely lasts more than half a season, but is easy to replace once you get used to it. Any system of marking will work as long as you remember the code. I generally use the same color for a single mark at 100 feet and a double mark at 150 feet. I use another color with a single mark at 200 feet and a double at 250. Using the double marks rather than another color is important at night, as then you'll have to feel the marks when setting your line. Though some trollers use only 150 feet and add drails to get deeper, I always employ the entire 100 yards and avoid drails, which sink like a rock if you make a mistake while trolling and require handlining of the leader. In order to get down farther, I slow down or make wide turns. All of this can be avoided with leadcore, which comes with the braid pre-colored with a different color every 10 yards.

Planers may be used in conjunction with mono or braided lines to attain depth without getting involved in wire or adding equipment to the boat. In many cases planers are so efficient that commercial fishermen use them while trolling with handlines. The main drawback from a sporting viewpoint is that long leaders must be used, which require lots of handlining in order to get the fish to boatside. In addition, the heavy tension involved makes it mandatory to place the rod in a holder rather than holding it if you care to do so with wire or lead core. There are many sizes and types of planers, and the angler must find one suited for his form of fishing, as each is limited to reaching certain depths and many can't be trolled at higher speeds without tripping. Rather than rigging them directly onto the line, they can also be rigged separately on a heavy line attached to the boat with the line then set in a snap on the planer. Of course, that doubles the work involved as the planer must be brought in after every hit.

Downriggers are very efficient at bringing regular mono or braided lines into the depths, and provide a big advantage in depths greater than those which can be attained by wire line or planers. On the other hand, downriggers also require a substantial investment and lots of effort on the part of the skipper and crew. Basic downriggers consist of a reel filled with cable, clutched cranking handle, boom, and pulley. The lure or bait to be run from any sort of conventional or spinning tackle is run out the desired distance from the ball and then attached to a release clip on the cable. The ball is then lowered to the desired depth, and when a hit occurs the line will pop out of the pin so the angler can fight the fish unimpeded and on tackle as light as he cares to use. Adjusting the tension on the release clip is critical with light tackle so the line will pull free on the strike rather than breaking.

Getting that tension correct can be a problem as speed increases in order to avoid having to constantly reset lines that pop free without a strike. Though the amount of cable streamed is displayed on the downrigger, determining just where your lure is requires some

Dead baits must lay out properly in order to look natural and not spin. When a second hook is called for with large baits, the first must still be placed in front with the second less than a length away as not to create a bend, which will cause spinning. These fluke baits are a smelt and squid strip combo and a whole squid (which swims backwards).

"Doormat" fluke like long fillet baits from other fluke, sea robins, and so on, but the first hook must be at the head with a stinger set so it won't cause the bait to spin.

guesswork as the forward movement of the boat raises the standard 10-pound ball considerably. The net result is that, depending on speed and current, you may be trolling at only half the depth indicated on the downrigger. This problem can be overcome by experience, but it will take experimentation. You can also try a Z-Wing, which is a combination of planer and weight that can be used to hold lures at greater depths with an outrigger or by itself on a length of rope to facilitate relatively fast trolling. Many skippers at Zihuantenejo, Mexico, use Z-wings and often bail out with a bait trolled about 20 feet below the surface on slow days when billfish aren't showing.

Downriggers should be retrieved whenever a substantial fish is hooked, as there's a good chance of losing a battle should the mono touch or get tangled in the downrigger cable. If backing down becomes necessary, the cable must also be kept away from the props. Expensive electric downriggers simplify the problem of having to hand crank downriggers every time a fish is hooked or missed, or a pin opens up. However, they also require more complicated boat rigging.

Baiting Up

Placing bait on a hook may seem too simple a matter to be discussed here, but it's probably the most frequent error committed by the casual angler—and I often see the same errors made by those who should know better. The general rule is simple:

Secure the bait so it flows out naturally rather than spinning in the water. That applies whether you're drifting, casting, trolling, or even just bottom fishing. Thus, if you're utilizing a baitfish with a single hook or a treble, that bait must be hooked in the head. If the bait has a mouth that opens easily, such as an anchovy, it should be hooked through the jaws. Using a strip bait, the hook must be placed as close to the leading edge as possible while still providing a firm grip—and the end is best trimmed. All of this is intended to prevent the bait from spinning and looking unnatural. Even in bottom fishing, a poorly hooked bait will spin in the current. A bait that flows off instead of being bunched is more attractive and leaves more of the hook available to penetrate. Not only do bunched-up baits tend to turn off all but the hungriest of predators, but they result in twisted leaders which further compound your problems. Fortunately, most predators hit at the head of a bait, and no matter how long your bait is they should be hooked with the single hook. Those toothy fish noted for cutting off baits (especially king mackerel,

Plug-cut herring are standard among Pacific Northwest anglers who mooch for salmon. These baits are rigged to provide a slow, controlled spin.

wahoo, and barracuda) may require a second hook, but the connection at the head is still required. One way to get around adding a second hook is to rig with a long-shank hook inserted far back in the bait while securing the eye inside the head so it will trail out properly.

An exception to the rule about baits not spinning is provided in the Pacific Northwest, where salmon fishermen do exactly the opposite by making their herring baits spin. The plug-cut herring involves cutting the head of a small herring off at an angle and then rigging a two-hook rig around it so it will spin when slowly retrieved or mooched (trolled very slowly). That controlled spin has proven very effective over the years. Another exception involves hooking live baits in areas other than the head for drifting or casting. Inserting the hook in the back or tail creates a different swimming action and often triggers strikes when baits hooked in the head are ignored or just played with. I learned that

lesson while giant tuna fishing out of Gloucester, Massachusetts, during the 1970s, when a single giant swimming through our slick refused not only our dead baits but also live mackerel and harbor pollock that we had jigged before leaving the harbor. After much frustration, and having tried everything else, I changed the hook in a harbor pollock from the head into the tail area, and that foot-long fish barely got below the surface before the 800-pound giant engulfed him.

Another important point about baiting involves not burying the hook. Very few gamefish see enough

Circle hooks are hard to bait, but their efficiency and the lack of harm to fish being released makes them ideal for most bait fishing.

Capt. Ron Hamlin developed techniques for rigging billfish trolling baits that ensure live releases. This is a mullet rigged with the circle hook on top of the head to allow penetration.

hooks to become "hook wary," as anglers often say. On the other hand, many fish are able to discern unnatural presentations. The weight of the hook plus the leader and any swivel will cause a hooked bait to sink faster and look different. Getting around that problem is often vital to success, but it's rarely the sight of the hook that is the vital factor. However rigged, the hook must either be exposed or unencumbered for the strike. Tuna fishermen can get away with hiding hooks in butterfish by rigging them so the hook is in the soft belly with the point just coming through the thin belly skin so it will pull through immediately. With other baits it may be possible to run the hook just under the skin, but in every case the object should be to present a natural-looking bait with the hook positioned to set immediately in the fish rather than getting caught back in the bait. Not only are hook-ups with ordinary fish missed due to hooks buried in baits, but several times I've seen anglers lose mako sharks after battling them for 20 minutes or more before finding that the hook was caught back inside the bait all the while—and the mako just didn't want to give it up!

The use of circle hooks is becoming more common, as they are more efficient for hooking most fish when using bait, and are far superior in preventing gut-and-gill-hooking, which results in heavy mortality among released fish. The problem with circle hooks is baiting them. Some manufacturers have tried to get around this by angling the circle slightly, but that also results in more swallowed hooks catching in the stom-

ach. The concept involves letting the fish turn away with the bait before coming tight. Captain Ron Hamlin started the use of circle hooks in Guatemala in order to cut down on the mortality of Pacific sailfish, which are all released. Not only was that accomplished, with bleeders now being rare, but the catch rate actually went up. During one three-day trip there I was able to hook and eventually release 24 out of 25 sailfish strikes by simply lowering the rod tip to the fish and reeling tight before lifting (not striking) the rod. It isn't always that efficient, but circle hooks can make you a more successful as well as a more responsible angler in many fisheries. I've already found that to be the case in chunking and clam chumming for striped bass, and while using both worms and grass shrimp for weakfish. Though the toothy bluefish almost always cuts off hooks tied to mono leaders, I had about a 50 percent success ratio with even them while using bunker chunks intended for stripers. Since the hook pulls toward the jaw, blues have a hard time getting to the leader if they don't cut it off on the initial hit.

Chumming and Chunking

Chumming may well be the most effective and universal technique for catching a wide variety of species ranging from bottomfish to tunas. Billfish are among the few that don't seem particularly attracted to chum, but even they are caught occasionally in slicks. Chunking is a form of chumming in that chunks of bait are used rather than ground chum, and the two methods are frequently combined.

Just about anything can be used for chum, but oily fish make the best ground chum. Nothing can beat the menhaden for that, as they are the most abundant and

Ground chum brings a blue shark to boatside, and is also standard for other sharks, school bluefin tuna, little tunny, bonito, and reef fishing.

A quicker means of rigging balao with circle hooks under the jaw, as developed by Mike Murray.

oiliest fish along the Atlantic coast and in the Gulf of Mexico, where millions of pounds are taken each year by purse seiners for reduction into fish oils and meal. Menhaden (also known as mossbunker, bunker, porgy, and fatback) are also netted in vast quantities for bait and chum. Party boats in the Metropolitan New York/ New Jersey area have heavy-duty meat grinders aboard with which to create their own fresh chum. Most anglers are able to buy frozen ground chum (generally in five-gallon buckets or smaller cans) or even in dried form. Where menhaden aren't available, mackerel, bluefish, herring, and other oily species will do. Most Florida anglers obtain chum in the form of frozen logs, which are created from a variety of ground-up fish and scraps. Chum logs can also be created from other baits more suitable for various species. For instance, winter flounder aren't fish eaters, so chum is formed from ground clams to which corn kernels and/or rice are often added for additional attraction.

Ground chum can be used in either fresh or frozen form. Fresh chum is ladled over the side either full strength or mixed with water to make the supply last longer. Frozen chum is hung in the water by

some means (the simplest is to overturn the can into a mesh bag and tie it overboard) and slowly dissipates. In either case, the idea is to create a slick on the water and a scent trail that will lure fish to your boat. That slick will usually be obvious, especially on a rough day, but can't be seen when frozen chum is dropped to bottom in a chum pot to attract bottom feeders such as flounder. Chumming with ground bait is probably the most common means of fishing for sharks, and the primary weapon for party boats in the New York/New Jersey Bight area seeking bluefish.

Menhaden are chunked for striped bass, bluefish, red drum, and other bottomfeeding game fish.

Chunking is very similar except the chum is presented in the form of chunks of baitfish rather than ground bait. Menhaden, herring, mackerel, butterfish, and many other small, abundant, and inexpensive fish are used in that fashion for species that don't rely on scent very much. It's generally best to cut chunks smaller than those used for bait, but also to adjust according to the size of fish. For instance, bluefin tuna anglers seeking schoolies use small chunks of butterfish while those trying for giants prefer large chunks of menhaden, which are not only more attractive but also discourage the schoolies. Whereas even very large sharks will swim around in slicks looking for something to eat, tunas generally zip right through a slick and will only stick around if chunks are being swept back to them. Key West guides are able to chunk such glamour species as tarpon, permit, and cobia as well as snappers by obtaining shrimp boat "trash," the by-catch of shrimp trawling, and dribbling small cut or whole fish and shellfish astern. For tarpon, use trash consisting mostly of small fish, while for permit try to find "crabby" trash. Another unusual but very effective chunking material is the waste product of clam processing plants—the bellies. Striped bass, especially schoolies, would rather eat the bellies in any case, and that bait is especially effective when squeezed to release the juices when being used as chum on top—as well as when used in a chum pot.

The basic method of chunking involves throwing a good quantity when first arriving at a fishing spot, and then settling down to a slow, but steady dribble so as to attract without filling the quarry. This can be done at anchor or on the drift, depending on the situation. Chunks may also be mixed with ground chum, especially if there's no worry about attracting sharks or bluefish, and a chum pot is often dropped to bot-

Author fought this giant tuna on Stellwagen Bank off Gloucester, Massachusetts, while Larry Cronin ran the Boston Whaler and wired the fish before the author placed the straight gaff.

Butterfish serve as both bait and chunking material for tunas and bluefish.

tom with chunks when chunking in relatively shallow waters for stripers with bottom rigs. Whereas a strong current is an aid in spreading a chum slick, it can be a problem for chunking as the chunks move away too quickly or don't sink to bottom near the boat when you're seeking bottom species. In such areas it's best to get started at the beginning of a tide and "salt" the area astern with chunks. Cut back on chunking as the current increases and throw them forward so as not to be chunking for any boats anchored downtide of you. A means of getting chunks where you want them involves placing them in a weighted paper bag and lowering it to the bottom on a line before a snap of the line breaks the wet bag and deposits the chunks where they'll do some good.

Once fish come into a chum slick or chunk line they'll frequently stay there and refuse to spread to others even yards away. Therefore, it's important to be the first on a spot. Alternately, you can try the same area late in the day or at night when there may be little or no competition. Fresh chunks with slime intact are always better than frozen ones, though there's rarely any big difference when fish are really turned on. Indeed, I've had some of my hottest striped bass chunking while using solidly frozen menhaden chunks, which actually act like individual chum pots as they thaw.

Chumming can also be done with live baits, and that's the norm on the west coast where live anchovies and sardines can be bought in quantity. Live baits are flipped around the boat and will usually stay there in order to seek protection from tunas, wahoo, barracuda, yellowtails, and other large gamefish. Some fishermen pinch baits in order to have them swim erratically and create more attraction. Chunks can be used in combination with live baits as long-range skippers out of San Diego discovered when they tried the time-honored east coast chunking technique and found that large yellowfin tuna often preferred chunks to live bait.

That's hardly surprising since tunas are conditioned to feed on just about anything dead falling through trawler nets or being thrown over by draggers and shrimp boats.

The use of tiny live grass shrimp as chum for weakfish goes back many decades in bays along the Mid-Atlantic coast. They are dribbled astern a few at a time and lines can be baited with several of the shrimp or with other baits such as seaworms. Once established, grass shrimp chum lines usually produce so many weakfish that tiny lures such as shad darts and small bucktail jigs are just as effective. Stripers and tautog are

Wiring an 800-pound class tiger shark from the Reelistic offshore of Indian River, Delaware.

Capt. Bob Montgomery leaders a cobia over a wreck in the Gulf of Mexico out of Key West as another follows.

Leader men must be alert with fish that may jump at boatside, as this tarpon is doing to Capt. Robert Trosset at Key West.

Author leaders a black marlin off Panama before release. Billfish often spit out their stomach during a fight, but swallow them back.

among other species attracted by grass shrimp chumming.

The one constant involved in chumming is the need for water movement. There normally must be some flow, though in areas of strong currents fishing is often best at the beginning or end of the tide when the current isn't too swift. Slack water is occasionally productive when the fish have been turned on before the current slacked. Movement is particularly critical in sharking, as those fish are spread over large areas rather than concentrated on a particular piece of bottom or dropoff. When there's no movement the chum falls straight down and anglers have to hope that a shark will be swimming their way. On the other hand, with good wind and current the slick will spread over miles and bring curious sharks within range of baits near the boat.

The End Game—Gaffing, Netting, and Tagging

While fighting fish is the most important aspect of the sport, the fish of a lifetime could be lost if the angler isn't prepared for the end game. There are a few general rules to keep in mind while preparing to boat a fish. Most important is getting a good shot the first time. All too often there's panic at the wrong moment as

gaffs or nets are being swung wildly and to no good effect—frequently resulting in the loss of the fish. There's rarely any reason to make a desperation stab. Anglers who overpower large fish and then attempt to boat a "green" fish are asking for trouble and frequently get it. Mako sharks are particularly dangerous and have wiped out many a cockpit while sending anglers scrambling for safety. Fish should be fought to the point where they can be led alongside for an attempt at boating that leaves little to chance. Wherever possible get the angler forward of the gaffer. If leader must be handled in order to bring the fish within reach, the leader man should be in between. Either the angler or leader man should literally present the fish, broadside if possible, to the gaffer so he has a clear shot at the head or shoulders. Do this as smoothly as possible in order not to panic the fish. A key factor in not losing fish at boatside is keeping their head in the water. It often takes only a little shake on some slack to dislodge a hook from the hole it's worn during a fight.

In big-game fishing the boat is usually kept in gear at very slow speed in order to maintain tension and plane large fish along the surface. Anglers on drifting or anchored boats must be alert to any movement by the fish and be prepared to dip the rod tip in order to clear props and rudders. In open boats it's best to work larger fish off the bow where a sudden move under the boat will rub the line only over bottom paint instead of line-

Gaffing a giant tuna at Prince Edward Island. The wire man should bring the fish within reach of the gaffer so he can get a good shot in the head.

Billing a black marlin in Panama.

cutting metal. Try to bring the fish alongside upcurrent or uptide so there will be less chance of it diving under the boat. Wherever possible, move with the fish so as not to end up with an angle forward or aft and a consequent lack of control.

One of the most common mistakes by small-game anglers is reeling a fish almost to the tip of the rod. That leaves the fish far from the person trying to boat it, and can lead to rod breakage. Bring the fish only to about a rod length and then lift the rod to slide it toward the mate. Try to avoid gaffing fish farther back than the shoulder, as you won't have as much control and will be ruining meat. Especially avoid gaffing toward the tail, as large fish are extremely difficult to control in that fashion. The gaff should be placed over the fish and brought back in one motion, which will also swing smaller fish into the boat in a single sweep. In the case of large fish which are notoriously wild when gaffed (especially dolphin and cobia), there must be a clear area behind the gaffer to an uncovered fish box so the fish can be deposited and the top replaced in an instant while everyone available sits on the cover to make sure it doesn't get knocked off.

Special care must be taken with billfish and sharks, which can do a lot of damage as they surge forward or jump. The head should be slightly forward of the gaffer when it's hit and pinned quickly against the boat if possible. I prefer to hit sharks in the gills, as

gaffs often bounce off their tough skins. Small billfish and all those to be released are billed (be sure to use gloves to avoid tearing your hands up) rather than gaffed. This is another tricky proposition since everyone must be alert to a last second jump that could drive that bill through flesh. Never get directly in front of a bill when preparing to grab it, but rather slide it slightly past you and reach down to grab sideways with both

Netting of striped bass is becoming more popular now that 90 percent are released by anglers. Lou Truppi will find that can be a problem with treble-hook plugs.

Mike Ristori demonstrates there's no problem netting big stripers such as this one caught by Pete O'Connor on a bunker chunk at Shrewbury Rocks, New Jersey.

Jay Cassell's blue marlin is lifted alongside Hawaiian Tropic off Key West for removal of hook. This position is dangerous, as the marlin could push forward and do damage with its bill.

hands. Though long leaders permit the capture of large fish long before they can be fought close to the boat, they represent a great danger both to the person leadering and anyone else who may get caught in the slack leader should the fish take off again. Wherever possible, I prefer using short, or wind-on, leaders and having the fish reeled to the boat where leader handling is either not necessary or only requires a pull in order to present the fish for gaffing.

Standard straight gaffs with shafts four to eight feet are used in most cases, but in big-game fishing it's often best to utilize flying gaffs in which the head detaches under pressure when the fish is struck. The detached head is secured by a heavy line to a cleat and, hopefully, any jumping that the fish might do will be 20 feet away instead of in the boat. A maximum of 30 feet of gaff rope is permitted by IGFA rules, which also limit the overall length of gaffs and nets to eight feet and prohibit the use of harpoons. Flying gaffs are used primarily for large billfish and especially for sharks, which tend to roll when hit and will tear a straight gaff out your hands if they do so. Tuna, even giants, only move forward

and don't jump, so they can be handled with a heavy straight gaff.

Gaffs heads come in a variety of gaps, varying from two to 16 inches, between shaft and point. While large gaps are best for big fish, it's very difficult to gaff smaller fish (especially those with roundish bodies such as wahoo) with such gaffs. Much smaller sizes are far more effective with such fish, and gaffs can even be fashioned out of large fish hooks with the barbs filed or bent down and then wrapped on a fiberglass shaft. There are also smaller hand gaffs with very short shafts that are used in small boat situations for lip gaffing large fish and pinning them to the side of the boat while a hook or lure is removed prior to release. Those gaffs may also be carried by surfcasters to aid in beaching fish. Bridge and pier fishermen seeking large fish utilize a bridge gaff that consists of a very large treble attached to heavy cord that's lowered to a fought-out fish laying on top by running it through a shower curtain clip over the fishing line. A quick snatch once the bridge gaff is alongside the fish allows the fisherman to handline the catch up to his platform rather than taking a chance on breaking off by trying to lift with the fishing line. Naturally, bridge gaffs should never be used on fish that are to be released.

The most important point to remember in netting fish is only netting from the head. Trying to push a net through the water at the tail of a fish is a recipe for disaster as the fish will sense the net and dart away—frequently breaking taut lines or pulling hooks.

Even more so than with gaffs, it's vital that the angler bring his fish to the netter on the surface for a very measured lifting with a slightly forward motion. Wild stabs or digging underwater with nets almost never works. Nets come in many sizes, and the angler should obtain one or more suited to his style of fishing. Small nets are easiest to use when boating small fish, while the largest hoop sizes are best for salmon, halibut, large fluke, and striped bass. Avoid using nets for sharp-toothed fish as they not only ruin nets but might even cut through before you get them aboard. Also don't

Fish without significant teeth can be lifted aboard with a lip-lock, as demonstrated by Al Malanga.

use nets when fish are hooked on plugs bristling with treble hooks. You may well end up with a treble in the net while the fish hangs outside the mesh ready to shake off—and then you'll still have to spend time trying to get those hooks out of the mesh before resuming fishing. Few anglers use rubber nets, but they do eliminate problems with toothy fish such as bluefish.

The best bet in a release situation from small boats is using a long enough length of heavy mono or fluorocarbon leader so most fish can be lifted aboard without worrying about gaffs or nets. Even when keeping fish, that method avoids most of the mess as there are no gaff holes to create bleeding. Smaller fish can be swung aboard with heavy enough tackle, but once again the angler must not reel almost to the tip as that will result in a fish hanging in the air and, quite possibly, a broken rod. Reel the fish to within a rod length and lift your rod to swing the fish toward your waist in one smooth motion.

Many fish can be handled from small boats by simply grasping them with a lip lock, just as freshwater bass fishermen do with their favorite quarry. I use that method with striped bass that are too large to swing aboard. Their jaws result in rough fingers, but rarely any cuts. Fish with teeth or those so heavy that they require more than a lip lock can be handled with a gill-cover grip when subdued at boatside. Be sure you place your hand under the gill cover and not into the gill rakers, which will shred your skin and also possibly kill a fish intended for release. Fish with narrow and rigid tail sections can be grasped from that end. That works well with tunas if you can get at the tail; because the tuna lacks an air bladder and therefore has to keep swimming in order to live, grabbing the tail section can be a challenge. Jacks are easy to handle by the tail, but it's best to wear gloves to avoid being cut by their scutes.

Tagging adds excitement to release fishing. In the case of smaller fish, they can be handled on deck as a tag is inserted by hand. Putting a cloth over their eyes tends to calm them down just as is the case with birds

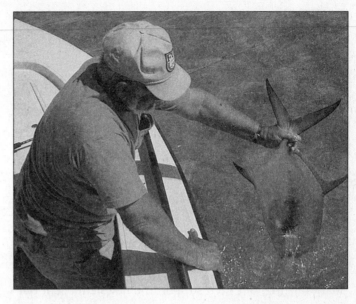

Capt. Harlan Franklin lifts a permit from the flats at the Marquesas out of Key West by grabbing the tail.

With its bill pointed away, this hook can be removed from the marlin, but if it doesn't come out easily, the fish will be better off if the hook is clipped for a quick release.

that get hooked. Tagging sticks are used on large fish that must be left in the water. AFTCO makes a nice commercial stick, or anglers can create their own with a broomstick and a hose clamp to hold the pin provided by National Marine Fisheries Service tagging programs. Most tagging is done by scientists, but volunteer anglers are the prime source of tagging in several programs. Jack Casey started tagging sharks during the 1960s at the old U.S. Fish and Wildlife Service Lab at Sandy Hook, New Jersey, but after the creation of the National Marine Fisheries Service that program was shifted to Rhode Island. Sportsmen not only do most of the shark tagging, but even support the newsletter sent out to participants. Those who are active in sharking can obtain free tagging kits from NMFS Cooperative Shark Tagging Program, NOAA/NMFS Lab, 28 Tarzwell Dr., Narragansett, RI 02882. Billfish and tuna anglers are urged to get involved with the Cooperative Game Fish Tagging Program, NOAA/NMFS Lab, 75 Virginia Beach Dr., Miami, FL 33149 in the Atlantic—and the same program at NOAA/NMFS Southwest Fisheries Center, P.O. Box 271, La Jolla, CA 92038. Anglers joining the American Littoral Society enjoy the unique opportunity to tag any saltwater fish of their choice by buying

ALS tagging kits. Those tags are applied by hand with a needle. Contact American Littoral Society Fish Tagging Program, Sandy Hook Highlands, NJ 07732, phone 732291-0055.

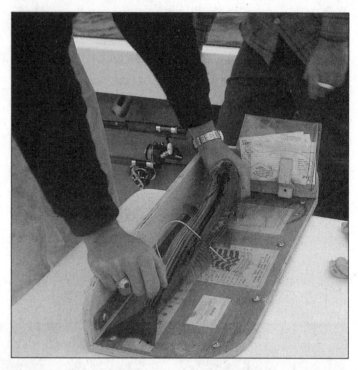

Capt. Al Anderson of Point Judith, Rhode Island, has the tagging of school stripers with American Littoral Society tags down to a science.

D. Surfcasting Strategies

AL RISTORI

All the information provided in this book won't do any good unless you actually get down to the surf and start putting that knowledge to use. It's fine to understand the theory, but that's no substitute for time on the beach. While most of that time probably won't be productive in terms of fish caught, it could be invaluable in learning what must be done in order to be a successful surfcaster.

Perhaps the most important thing you can do is to make friends in the area you'll be fishing. Most surfcasters are friendly, and quite willing to help those politely asking for information. It's not just what is, or isn't happening now that's important, but also whatever pearls of wisdom can be garnered about what's occurred recently or usually happens at this time of year or under various conditions, plus the techniques involved. Years of experience can be poured out at no cost to those who

On steeper beaches, fish without teeth, like this striper, can be landed by grasping them by the lower lip. (Joe Blaze photo)

Rich Rusznak lands a bluefish with classic fly-rod form on a gently sloping beach. (Joe Blaze photo)

are good listeners and demonstrate the requisite desire to learn. There's just no substitute for such information, and it's relatively easy to come by.

Joining a local fishing club with lots of surfcasters is another means of getting a leg up that will save lots of trial-and-error. Also patronize tackle shops specializing in surfcasting. Your purchases will bring valuable information from the owners who have a financial interest in your success, and you'll also have another opportunity to mix with anglers who may be of help. Never be afraid to ask questions, and don't forget to reciprocate. Should you stumble across something of value, be sure to pass it on to those you're receiving information from or you'll soon see your sources dry up.

Even when nothing much is going on along the beach, productive time can be spent observing the lay of the land at various stages of the tide and under varying weather circumstances. When a run of fish does occur, you'll be much better situated to take advantage of it.

For instance, as noted in the chapter on reading the surf, there are sloughs that will consistently hold fish even though they may be hard to spot on a high tide. Those spots may stand out at low water, and that knowledge could make all the difference at other stages of the tide when they might not be obvious.

Tide is a critical factor when fishing the surf as even small changes in water level can make all the difference. Sand bars that are too shallow on lower tides become a great attraction once covered by enough water, especially so when there's enough wind or high enough seas to produce white water on the bar. The area you ordinarily fish may not have enough water at low tide to hold fish. Yet, there could be another spot not too far away that features a sharp drop-off and is actually better at low tide because that small deep area tends to concentrate fish. By acquiring this information you can fish various areas at different stages of the tide and maximize your opportunities.

Weather forecasts are important in determining where you focus your efforts. Of course, they're not always right in terms of wind force. However, knowing the wind direction and how high the waves are will be a big help. After a while you'll learn what areas are best on various winds, and whether they're fishable in big seas. Some of the most memorable days on the surf occur during bad weather, but there are also occasions when the water is so discolored or full of weed that there's little

Different shorelines call for revised tactics. Here the author works the jetty wash, which corrals bait and makes it vulnerable to feeding fish. (Joe Blaze photo)

Angler uses the action of the waves to work fish toward the beach. (Joe Blaze photo)

This is what it's all about: Ristori shows off an early morning striper that his a plug along the jetty at Sea Girt, New Jersey. (Joe Blaze photo)

hope. These are things you'll have to learn in your area by putting in the time.

Keep a log of your fishing on a daily basis. Over a period of time you'll be able to look back and put together some sort of pattern for particular spots under various conditions. This will help maximize your opportunities to be at the right place at the right time, which is the bottom line in consistently catching fish from the surf.

While there is no substitute for having a network of friends to keep you informed of fish movement, it's also important to follow news reports in local fishing columns and radio or TV shows, where they're available. Just keep in mind that everything you get from

With the right touch and deft timing on the part of the angler, this striper landed itself on the sand. (Joe Blaze photo)

Indeed, it was a bent rod that put me on fish a few years ago after having suffered a minor stroke. My doctor wouldn't let me drive, but my wife surprised me one morning by offering to drive me to the surf. It was later in the morning than I'd ordinarily leave, and I had no expectations when we pulled up to a favorite street ending in Bay Head on the Jersey Shore. There were only a few birds picking around and no signs of fish, but the lone angler on the beach had a bent rod. I scrambled back to the car, grabbed my rod and a metal lure, and proceeded to release lots of school striped bass by casting blind into surf that showed no signs other than those casually picking birds. I would never have made a cast there if it hadn't been for that single bent rod, but I ended up making my wife late for work because the stripers wouldn't stop hitting, even as the sun got higher in the sky. Fortunately, her boss is a surfcaster and appreciated the fact that I couldn't leave them biting!

Angler body language can also be helpful as just observing concentrations of fishermen, and how hard they're working an area is a clue as to whether something has been going on and might recur. I even check the surfcasters' body language when boat fishing, keeping an eye out for anglers ganging up instead of spreading themselves out along the beach.

While conditions during a storm may be unfishable, the beginning of a storm is one of the best times to be on the beach. Adjustments may have to

those reports is a day old, and much of what happens on the surf is a mere flash in time. There are periods when fishing is good for days, particularly during migrations, but more often the blitz one day will not be repeated the next day, even if conditions remain the same. Nevertheless, that's still your best bet to get into a hot bite and you must be ready to follow it up. Staying in bed and waiting for the call that it's happening again may cost you your best opportunity of the season.

Though most surfcasters dream of being all alone on the beach when the fish of their choice is chasing bait into the wash, other anglers can be a big help in locating fish. I make no bones about the fact that one of my principle methods of locating fish along the surf involves watching for bent rods or anglers walking into the wash to land or release their catch. That's often a more reliable clue than bird activity and bait concentrations.

Often stripers will feed very close to the beach in the trough formed by a drop-off in the bottom. Rich Rusznak has presented his fly parallel to the waves so the fly remains in the trough longer. (Joe Blaze photo)

It can be frustrating to watch those schools move along without being disturbed, but sooner or later the predators will take their toll and you've got to be patient enough to wait them out.

Storms can also present an opportunity for exceptional bait fishing as shellfish are uprooted and smashed on the beach. That happens along the Jersey Shore when a northeaster creates waves that fill beaches with surf clams. As those clams die, open up, and are washed back into the surf, striped bass feed on them right along the drop-off and become easy targets for anglers who pick up fresh clams at their feet and fish them just yards away from where they're standing.

The timing of your efforts in the surf must be attuned to those of the fish you're seeking. Though most game fish feed both night and day, some are more active at certain times. The low light periods of dawn and dusk are traditionally the most rewarding for most predators, especially when that time of day coincides with the

be made in terms of heavier tackle in order to cast lures or bait into the wind, but game fish are apt to be feeding close to the wash as the surf is building.

Though the immediate aftermath of a storm may not be the best time to fish the surf, your best opportunity could occur shortly thereafter.

Especially during the spring and fall, storms trigger migrations of bait fish. That, in turn, attracts the game fish that feed on them.

Jerry Fabiano takes his time convincing a striper to leave the deeper water beyond the drop-off. (Joe Blaze photo)

desired tide and weather conditions. Without knowing a thing about an area I'm fishing for the first time, that's when I'll be trying rather than during the middle of the day or at night.

After Dark

Surfcasting at night presents challenges not faced during the day, but can be the most effective way to catch some species under particular conditions. Bait is a most important consideration in determining when to fish. For instance, if predators are feeding on migratory schooling bait that moves during the day, they're not apt to feed actively at night. On the other hand, if bait is scarce during the day, it's likely that predators will be seeking whatever they can find in the dark.

Night fishing is actually quite pleasant under the full moon, and that's usually a good time to try it. The dark of the moon presents more challenges. In some areas, there's a problem with phosphorescence that lights up your lure and makes it look unrealistic. You'll have no problem following it under those circumstances, but when that condition is absent you may find yourself reeling your lures right up to the tip of the rod. Though a long leader with a knot that interferes with your cast is annoying, it can be a help at night, as you feel the knot hit your tiptop and know when to slow the retrieve.

Fishing your lure right to the beach is important during the day as many hits occur right at the drop-off and even more important at night when fish are even less reluctant to strike in just inches of water. Be sure your drag is set light enough to prevent both a break-off and ripping out hooks with a fish thrashing on only a few feet of line. At that point, with the fish hitting so close, you may only have to back up a couple of steps to beach the fish!

Some anglers are very sensitive about lights being shined in the water at night, so it's good form to only point a flashlight toward the beach when removing hooks or changing lures. Actually, most fish are attracted to steady lights at night. Lights from shore-side piers and restaurants, and even street lamps attract bait, and predators tend to hang around the shadow lines. On the other hand, flashes of light might spook them.

Do everything slowly and surely at night. Even simple things, such as completely closing a snap after changing lures, can be fouled up. Shuffle your feet while wading in order not to step into a hole or over a drop-off; and, in tropical areas, shuffle to stir up rays before they remind with their barb you that you have stepped on them. Check landmarks as you walk onto a beach, and plan your return.

Bob Noonan fishes Barnegat Inlet because he knows that at dusk predator fish are often feeding heavily. (Joe Blaze photo)

Sometimes the best strategy is simply being in the right place at the right time. This angler hits pay dirt at dawn. (Alberto Knie photo)

It's very easy to get confused after dark, especially if you've been walking up and down the surfline.

While most of us are happy to have our feet solidly planted in the sand, there are some venturesome anglers who extend their range by wearing wet suits. That's become quite common at Montauk Point. Long Island's eastern tip on the south side features many boulders close to shore, and wet suit anglers swim out to them for a perch that puts them tight among the striped bass they seek. Needless to say, only strong swimmers should attempt that extreme fishing which also requires the finest reels that will stand up to being completely submerged.

Landscape and hazards of Montauk take on a different dimension once the sun goes down. Know the area you are fishing and move carefully when fishing after dark. (Alberto Knie photo)

E. 25 Saltwater Flyfishing Tactics

CONWAY X. BOWMAN

1. How to choose a basic saltwater outfit

Getting started in saltwater fly fishing can seem like an overwhelming task, but it isn't complicated. It's most important to buy the right rod and reel for the type of fishing you'll be doing. The East Coast striper fly fisherman will require a very different outfit from what a West Coast surf perch fisherman needs, and the guy interested in catching redfish in the Louisiana marsh will need a vastly different rig from the angler casting to bonito off a jetty in Southern California. Here are my suggestions:

The Rod

Choose a seven- or eight-weight rod. This is the perfect starter rod for the beginning saltwater fly fisher, heavy enough to punch a fly into a stiff wind, yet light enough to cast all day. Technically, you could use a heavy trout rod, but ideally you want to use a saltwater rod because it's made of materials that can handle salt, sand, and generally tough conditions.

The Reel

A good direct-drive reel that can hold a minimum of 200 yards of thirty-pound Dacron

A basic rod matched with a quality reel is a good starting point for a beginner.

backing will work well in most saltwater fly-fishing situations. Currently, fly reels designed for saltwater fishing are more than adequate in handling fish up to fifty pounds. Buy an extra spool to hold your shooting head.

Fly Lines

Here is what you'll need:

1. A basic weight-forward (WF) floating line matched to the weight of your fly rod. The WF floating line is a great all-around fly line for sight-casting in shallow water. Don't get confused by all the marketing of "saltwater tapers," "bonefish tapers," or "redfish tapers." Such lines are for more advanced, specialized fly fishers, not beginners.

2. A weighted shooting head. A combination of a weighted front taper and an intermediate running line, this is ideal for subsurface fishing or fishing rip currents from the beach. When fish are feeding below the surface, the shooting head will keep your fly in the hit zone longer. A 250- to 300-grain should be sufficient for most situations. The grain weight equals the sink rate of the fly line, so a 250- to 300-grain line will sink between five and eight inches per second. This is plenty of sink rate to get you down to feeding fish.

2. Saltwater fly rod length

The standard nine-foot fly rod works best in many saltwater fly-fishing situations. It provides the angler with enough length to keep his fly line high off the wa-ter while backcasting and is effective when fighting fish in shallow water.

Many beach fly fishermen prefer a longer fly rod, something in the ten- or eleven-foot range. The added length assists in keeping the fly line safely above the shoreline structure on the backcast. This also allows for the shooting and/or weight-forward section of the fly line to extend beyond the rod's tip section, providing much-needed assistance in shooting the fly line as well as extending the length of the cast.

For bluewater fly fishing, a shorter rod (eight to eight and a half feet) works best when fighting a fish in deep water. A stiff butt section is especially important for putting pressure on a fish when reeling it in from deep water. It also saves the angler a trip to his chiropractor for an adjustment on his sacrum.

A shorter rod is best when you're fishing for bluewater fish such as tuna, sharks, and billfish.

3. What makes a good saltwater fly reel?

A good saltwater fly reel should be made from first-grade aluminum bar stock, have a slightly over-sized handle that can be easily cranked while fighting a fish, and, most important, have a strong drag system.

The drag system is the heart of a good saltwater reel—it is essential in controlling the powerful surge of a gamefish that's determined to escape. A disk drag system of cork, Rulon, or graphite will stand up to the long, strong fights of saltwater gamefish. Many of the stacked-disk-drag fly reels on today's market are outstanding and require little special maintenance. The cork-drag reel has the most powerful drag system; however, such reels require a bit of TLC. Oiling and lubricating the cork drag are essential to retaining its excellent action.

For both synthetic and cork fly reels, back off the drag at the end of each fishing day or if the reel is not to be used for a long time. This will help preserve the drag and keep it working in top form on future trips.

A quality saltwater fly reel is a smart investment.

4. Drag setting for saltwater fly fishing

Proper drag settings are essential for saltwater fly fishing. A proper setting can spell the difference between landing and losing the fish of a lifetime. Unlike conventional or spinning reels—on which the drag is usually preset and not adjusted during the fight—the fly reel

Palming the reel gives the angler more control when fighting a fish.

drag can be manipulated by applying pressure to the reel with palm or fingers, giving the angler more control over the amount of pressure needed throughout the fight.

To set the drag, take your fly reel and tighten the drag so there is only light tension on the reel as you pull off line with your free hand; then tighten the drag until you feel resistance.

Begin fishing using a light drag. Once you have a fish on and the fight has begun, apply needed pressure by palming your reel—however, apply the pressure carefully so you don't break the tippet. Don't be surprised if you lose a few fish as you learn this method. It takes time and practice. Eventually, though, knowing when and how to apply pressure will become instinctive.

5. Using intermediate lines

Intermediate lines don't float and they don't sink rapidly. When you cast them out onto the water, they will sink very slowly, which makes them perfect choices when casting to fish feeding just below the surface (one to five feet) or in slightly deeper channels. You can use these versatile lines in situations as varied as casting to bonefish feeding off a reef in a channel or to West Coast yellowtail feeding just below the surface in the middle of the ocean.

An intermediate fly line is perfect for fishing along reef channels.

When choosing your rod and corresponding fly line, base your choice on the type of fishing you intend to do, as a heavier intermediate line, such as an eight, will sink faster than a lighter line, such as a five.

In addition to getting the fly in the hit zone, the slick coating on an intermediate line will let you put extra length in your cast.

6. Using a sinking line

The best saltwater fly fishing usually takes place below the surface, whether you're fishing near shore or offshore. Fish such as tuna, dorado, bluefish, and stripers will often feed in deep water, requiring anglers to get their flies deeper into the water column. This requires the use of a full-sinking line or sinking shooting head.

Full-Sinking Line

Full-sinking lines are rated Types I through V, I being the lightest and V the heaviest. If you are casting to fish only a few feet below the surface, a Type I or II shooting head will work fine. However, if the fish are feeding twenty feet down, the Type V would be your line of choice. The entire fly line is weighted, and is approximately one hundred feet long.

Once mastered, the integrated shooting/sinking head is a joy to cast.

Integrated Sinking Shooting Head

These are my favorite sinking fly lines. The first twenty-six feet of these lines are weighted, and the rest is monocore running line. Due to the slick surface of the monocore running line, these fly lines cast like a dream. Additionally, since all the weight is loaded at the front end of the line, the momentum of the weighted section helps extend the distance of your cast. These lines are rated in grains, from 150 to 800 grains—150 is the lightest, 800 the heaviest. An 800-grain line will work most effectively to fish to thirty feet.

Lead-core Line

In depths over twenty-five feet, lead-core lines are usually the best choices. Because they sink so quickly, they work well when you're fishing from a drifting boat and when you're dealing with strong currents. They are typically twenty feet long, and are attached with a loop-to-loop connection to a monofilament running line. The weight of the lead-core line and the thin diameter of the mono running line allow these lines to get down faster when compared to the other types of sinking fly lines. However, they can be difficult to cast—not only that, but the mono running line has a tendency to coil while casting.

7. Does fly line color matter in salt water?

Today's fly fisherman can buy fly lines in a wide variety of colors. Before settling on a color, consider its advantages and disadvantages. If you buy a brightly colored line, for example, you'll be able to follow a hooked fish's position in a fight. On the downside, many fish, especially those found in shallow, clear water, are skittish and easily spooked by brightly colored line.

Fly lines in natural colors (light blue, tan, or light green) are wise choices in most situations. Such colors make it easier to match the line color to the surround-

Fly lines in light blue, tan, or light green are good choices for salt water.

ings in which you plan to fish. On overcast, low-light days, gray and green lines are good choices; clear, sunny, blue-sky days seem best served by light blue lines; in rocky areas or light brown sandy waters, tan should be considered. Remember that one color does not suit all conditions.

8. Backing: weight and quantity demands

Losing a big saltwater gamefish after it is hooked and decides to head for the horizon is, in many instances, the result of filling your reel with backing that is either too short or too light.

Twenty-pound backing is a good choice for most inshore saltwater fly-fishing situations, while thirty-pound backing is better suited for larger bluewater gamefish.

Since many inshore saltwater gamefish will make initial runs of seventy-five to one hundred yards before they turn and settle into fighting mode, your fly reel should hold a minimum of 175 yards of twenty-pound Dacron backing.

Twenty- and thirty- pound Dacron backing are good choices for a saltwater fly reel.

Bright colors allow you to see where your fish is going during the fight.

For bluewater fly fishing, a minimum of 300 yards of thirty-pound Dacron or gel-spun polyethylene is standard. Big bluewater gamefish such as tuna and marlin will run off 200 yards of backing before you have time to say "Come back and fight like a man!" These fish can also dive to great depths, thus making essential an abundant supply of backing.

9. Best color for backing?

The phrase "getting into your backing" arouses excitement through a saltwater fly fisherman's being each time he hears it. There is nothing more exciting than witnessing one hundred yards of backing slicing through the water, pulled by a bonefish, tarpon, sailfish, or marlin. When this happens, the color of your backing is essential for tracking the fish's direction: Is it swimming at an angle, or is it sounding? Sooner or later, every saltwater fisherman is going to experience this.

High-visibility backing will help you determine how to fight a fish. For instance, when tarpon fishing it is important that you are able to turn a fish's head during the fight, a move aimed at keeping the tarpon off balance and assuring that it is brought quickly to the boat. Just as important, high-visibility backing allows the angler to

track the fish's direction and keep applying pressure in the direction opposite from where it wants to go.

The best colors? I prefer bright yellow or bright orange, both highly visible backings regardless of weather conditions or water color.

10. Use a net in salt water

The fish net is not just for stream or lake fishing; it's also a useful aid in safely catching and releasing saltwater gamefish. It helps you control a fish, remove the hook from its tooth-filled mouth, and then release it without causing it harm.

If you are a catch-and-release fly fisherman, employing a net is easier on the fish once it is brought to boat or shore. Handling the fish can be harmful to it, as your hands tend to remove the fish's protective slime coating, leaving it susceptible to bacterial and fungal infection after it's released.

The standard trout net may be a bit small, but there are many great medium to large nets on the market. Select a net that suits the fishing you have planned.

Using a net can help tame an unwieldy gamefish.

Smaller nets are suitable for Southern California's surf perch and corbina; larger nets are needed for tackling species such as Gulf Coast redfish or East Coast stripers. Use only nets that have black rubberlike webbing,

as the soft, slick texture will not harm the fish. Forget about using grandpa's old aluminum net with the green polypropylene webbing. These nets do the fish more harm than good.

11. Polarized sunglasses

Whether you're stalking bonefish on the flats or sight-casting to tuna offshore, your most important piece of equipment, next to the fly reel, is quality polarized sunglasses, which eliminate glare from the water's surface. Drugstore sunglasses? Forget them. All they do is make you look sharp. A pair of high-end polarized glasses is well worth the money.

The variety of polarized lens color choices can be confusing, so here are a few guidelines in selecting your glasses:

1. For shallow flats, beaches, and marshes: amber lenses

Good polarized sunglasses will help you pinpoint more fish.

2. For deep water, offshore waters, and bright sunlight: gray lenses
3. For softer light, glare, and cloudy days: yellow, light rose, or amber lenses

Frame styles vary greatly, but function and coverage are the major concerns. Choose a frame that provides good coverage over the eyes, as well as in the temple area. Look for frames that do not let in light peripherally (from the side of the head), and choose a frame that will remain comfortable throughout a long day of fishing. Consider lightweight frames with arms that don't pinch behind the ears.

In the past, most anglers chose glass as a lens material. Glass is durable and relatively scratch-resistant, although it's heavy. Nowadays, outstanding synthetic lens materials such as polycarbonate and SR-91 are good alternative choices. SR-91 is strong, light, and has superior light transmission and clarity. Wearing glasses with SR-91 lenses all day isn't as much of a burden on your nose.

Eyewear is a personal choice. Whether you're a hipster or lean more toward the traditional styles, the important things to remember are lens coloration and eye coverage. Oh, and don't forget a lanyard for your glasses. It would be a shame to lose your expensive pair of shades to the deep blue sea!

12. Proper footwear for fishing

If I could fish barefoot, I would; however, this is not practical in many saltwater situations. A good pair of fishing shoes is as important as your favorite fishing hat, shirt, or sunglasses. It's important that your feet are properly shod for any occasion.

On the Skiff

When skiff fishing, a firm-soled running or deck shoe works well, but with modifications. The first thing I do when I put on a pair is to tuck in the laces snugly, leaving no exposed dangling ends. Fly lines can hang up on anything, but loose laces always seem to be at the top of the list. I know some fly fishers who are so concerned with this problem that they run duct tape around their shoes to keep the laces covered. And don't forget: No black soles!

Sandals? I would leave them at home. Like shoelaces, the straps on sandals pose another problem in line hangup.

Flip-flops, if you are so inclined, are an acceptable and comfortable option, as they have no line-grabbing laces or straps. On the downside, they offer little support for your feet.

On the Beach and Flats

There are hundreds of different types of practical shoes that will fit your needs on fishing trips. Select a shoe with high ankle support, a firm and solid toe, and

Proper footwear protects your feet when walking on coral reefs.

stiff arch support. Since you'll be wading in a variety of bottom conditions, including mud, soft sand, hard sand, and even coral reefs, select a shoe that has a thick sole to prevent punctures. If you fish with a stripping basket, you can use sandals because there is less chance of your line getting snagged on the straps of the conventional wading shoe.

Rocks and Jetties

If you fish from rocks and jetties, heavy-duty wading boots are not only comfortable, but provide great support. If you choose not to wear waders, then wear two pairs of socks in the boots for a better fit.

13. Develop a good backcast

Being able to lay out thirty or forty feet of fly line behind you is a skill you need to master. Fish can materialize behind you as easily as they can in front of you, and a quick, accurate backcast will improve your chances of catching them.

You can make the backcast in the same manner as the forward cast. First make a forward cast, allowing the line to lie on the water, then pick up the line and shoot it behind you. This move is called the water haul; instead of coming forward with the forward cast, you now allow the fly line to lay out behind you in the area where you spotted the fish. You can proceed with stripping the line from there, just as you would if the fish were in front of you.

14. Casting into a crosswind

Throwing a fly in a crosswind or a following wind off your casting arm's shoulder is perhaps fly fishing's most troublesome cast. I have seen many casts blown and fish missed because of an angler's failure to properly execute this cast. No matter where you fish in the salt, you will, at some point, be tested by a crosswind or following wind.

When you're placed in this trying situation, the Belgian or helicopter cast is your most effective cast. This cast should be executed quickly, with a minimum of backcasts. When winds become erratic and disagreeable, as is their habit on salt water, this cast can be the great equalizer to a seemingly insoluble problem.

To do it, first make a high backcast; then, make your forward cast a high overhead cast (liken your casting arm to a helicopter's blade as you make the transition from side cast to forward overhead cast).

With practice, you can easily master this cast. Whether you are fishing on the flats, the beach, or the open ocean, it will give you confidence when you find yourself dealing with winds.

15. How to hook fish that follow your fly all the way to the rod tip

It's very frustrating when a gamefish follows your fly practically to the rod tip, but refuses to strike. There is, however, an easy way to get a picky fish to take your offering. I call it "sweeping the fly."

When a fish has followed the fly to within a few feet of your rod tip (usually you'll have five to ten feet of line outside the tip), lower your rod tip and make a sweeping motion as if you were going to make a sidearm back-cast. Don't pull the fly out of the water— just keep it moving. On the sweep, the fly will move smoothly through the water, doing a great impersonation of a fidgety baitfish attempting to escape a predator. This move enjoys a high percentage of success. The trick is to exercise control over your emotions and not to pull the fly from the fish's mouth if it strikes. The hook-set is always very close to you, so be prepared to let the fish run, which means managing the line as it shoots through the guides.

A fly retrieved like an injured baitfish provoked this striper into striking.

16. Know your birds

In fishing, there are many visual indications that fish are on the bite. One of the easiest and most reliable signs to identify is bird activity.

Some species of birds are better indicators than others, and you don't have to be an ornithologist to recognize the better ones; a basic knowledge of the bird kingdom will do. Let's look at the birds and how they rate in priority and importance to successful fish finding.

The best fish-locating birds of all, terns work diligently in searching for baitfish. If you spot them picking and fluttering in an area, that's a good sign that gamefish are working baitfish. Terns often fly ahead of a school of gamefish, picking up baitfish that have been pushed to the surface.

Pelicans: The big daddies of the seabird world. Though not as agile and swift as terns, pelicans will tell you where the main bodies of baitfish and gamefish

Keep an eye on bird activity.

are. Pelicans will dive with abandon into the center of a bait ball, filling their mouths with as many baitfish as possible. By habit, pelicans will not allow a bait ball to relocate too far from them. So if you spot a pelican positioned on the water, you can be sure that bait and gamefish are in the area.

Gulls are the scavengers of the sea. Seagulls are opportunistic feeders that will feed on anything, from popcorn to anchovies. Their presence is a good sign that baitfish are about, but they can hoodwink even the best fisherman by diving on anything they can eat, including everything from plastic bottle caps to sardines. Keep that in mind when turning to gulls to find fish.

17. How to retrieve a saltwater fly

If you are using a fly that imitates the movements of a baitfish, try to observe the behavior patterns of the actual baitfish. How fast are they swimming? Are they swimming in schools or small groups when being chased by gamefish? Are they stunned by gamefish be-fore being eaten as they are sinking or, in fishing lingo, "on the fall"? Most injured baitfish swim in frenzied motions, so quick, short retrieves are generally the best. In conditions where the baitfish are lazily swimming about, try slower, longer strips to get your adversaries' attention.

Baitfish always swim into the current, so when fishing from a drifting boat, cast your fly upcurrent, then let it sink and drift in the current. At the end of the drift, as the fly swings behind the boat, allow it to gyrate, lifelike, in the current for a few seconds before beginning stripping. This technique often results in a strike, so hang on!

Crabs or Shrimp

If you're attempting to imitate a crab or shrimp, make short, small strips so the fly looks like it's scurrying along. This move usually gets a fish's attention. If you spot a gamefish eyeing the fly and beginning to approach it, stop stripping and allow the fly to sit motionless. Wait a few seconds, move it again in short spurts, and get ready!

Think like a baitfish.

18. The best rod angle for fighting fish on the flats or in shallow water

In trout fishing, we are taught to keep the rod high while fighting a fish. This accomplishes two things: First, it protects the light tippet, and second, it keeps the fish's head up, preventing it from moving into the current or deeper water. In saltwater fly fishing, however, we are using heavy, strong tippets that are virtually impossible to break, and enable you to exert maximum pressure when fighting a fish. To do this, employ a low rod angle and use the rod's butt section to do the fighting for you. When you're hooked up to a saltwater fish in shallow water, the higher the rod angle, the less pressure you put on the fish. Lowering the rod's angle will allow you to use the fly rod's butt section, allowing for more pressure on the fish.

Use a low rod angle for maximum pressure when fighting fish in shallow water.

19. The two-handed strip

Some saltwater fish react to a fly that is stripped as fast as possible. Tuna, barracudas, roosterfish, amberjacks, and yellowtail are good examples. These guys prefer a fly that moves like a racing car. If the fly isn't imitating a fleeting baitfish, and if it suddenly stops or even pauses, these fish will turn and swim away.

The two-handed strip is the perfect retrieve for these situations. This retrieve enables the fly to be stripped through the water without breaks or pauses, as happens with the conventional one-handed strip. The

Use a two-handed strip to imitate fast-moving bait.

drawback to using this retrieve is that you have to place the rod under your arm, which makes it almost impossible to lift the rod tip for a strike. Instead, you have to use a strip-strike.

For a successful two-handed strip, do the following:

1. After the cast, place the rod under one of your arms.
2. Point the rod tip down, keeping the tip in the water at all times.
3. Begin the strip by pulling the fly line with your hand at the first stripping guide.
4. Repeat this with the other hand.
5. There should be a continual motion, changing hands with each strip. Vary the speed of the fly as you strip it through the water.
6. Strip the fly all the way to the boat and repeat; if you feel a hit, give your line a solid strip-strike.

This is a great technique for blue water as well as nearshore fly fishing.

20. Choosing the correct baitfish fly

Picking the correct flies is one of the keys to catching fish. This can be a daunting task for the beginning angler, as most tackle shop fly bins are filled with huge numbers of flies in all shapes, sizes, and colors. Here are some basic guidelines.

Baitfish Patterns

I believe that a sparsely dressed baitfish pattern is preferable to a bulked-up, flashy fly because it looks more natural. I've also found that gamefish are far less selective when presented with a sparsely dressed fly. The fly is only a hint of what the fish is feeding on, and it often elicits a reflexive striking action. When gamefish do strike, they usually zero in on the fly's oversized eye, which closely resembles the large eyes of baitfish such as sardines, pilchards, and anchovies. For them, focusing on that eye results in fewer lost meals.

Sometimes less is more.

Color

Natural colors work best. Olive greens, browns, tans, and whites are all great color combos for baitfish patterns. Also, carry a selection of blue-and-white, red-and-white, and chartreuse-and-white flies, for those times when a bit more flash is called for.

Size

Fly size depends on what type of fish you're pursuing. In most saltwater fly-fishing situations, you'll need baitfish patterns that range from a small anchovy pattern in size 6 to a large sardine or pilchard pattern in size 2/0. Remember, it's all about matching the size of the baitfish that fish are feeding on.

21. How to find fish in blue water

Finding fish in blue water may seem to be a daunting task. The ocean is huge, and big gamefish such as tuna, dorado, sharks, and marlin can cover great distances in a matter of hours. But with good eyes and a little common sense, you can indeed find these fish in open blue water.

You may find other locals searching the kelp for fish.

The first clue to locating fish in open blue water is bird activity: working terns, gulls, and pelicans. Locate the circling and diving birds, and you'll find fish nearby. If you see birds floating on the water, you should fish the area anyway, as a raft of birds may indicate that baitfish and gamefish are in the area, just not actively feeding at that moment.

Once the birds and bait are located, look for gamefish agitating the water's surface in pursuit of baitfish. The gamefish will push the baitfish up from the depths, forcing the prey to explode out of the water, an activity easily spotted at long distances. When this happens, the birds will also be going crazy, diving into the melee to pick off baitfish at the surface.

If you don't see any birds, look for structure such as floating kelp paddies or weed lines. Baitfish like to congregate underneath these structures for shelter, and where there are baitfish . . . there are gamefish! Pull up next to these floating structures and cast a fly out along the edge. Make a few strips and see if anyone is home. Sometimes you can even see the fish stacked up underneath the structure.

22. How to find fish in the surf zone

The surf zone is a great place to start saltwater fly fishing, whether you're targeting stripers on the East Coast or corbina on the West Coast. This bewildering area of crashing surf, rips, rock piles, and sandbars can be intimidating to the uninitiated. Don't let it get to you! These two simple clues about surf zone structure will help calm your doubts.

Rip Currents

Fish that live along beaches love structure, especially rip currents. These are small channels, usually twenty to thirty feet wide, created by waves washing on shore and then needing someplace to get back out to

Extreme low tide is a good time to check out structure that is normally underwater.

sea. These riverlike indentations run perpendicularly through the surf zone. Fish congregate on the edges or even within the rip to feed on baitfish, crabs, and shrimp. Rips can be very productive on both incoming and outgoing tides, and can be found along the edges of reef structures, alongside pier pilings, and randomly along sandy beaches.

Potholes

Where you find rip currents, you'll also find potholes, which are dark indentations located from a few feet to a few hundred feet from the shoreline. When you're observing a beach at low tide, try to remember the locations of potholes. Fish will stack up in them when the tide rises and covers them with water. They will, however, change location as the sand moves around.

23. How deep is a fathom?

This may sound strange, but this is a question I hear more than any other question when guiding in salt water: How deep is a fathom?

The question may seem irrelevant; however, if you ever have to read a nautical chart, you'll notice that most charts record depths in fathoms, not feet.

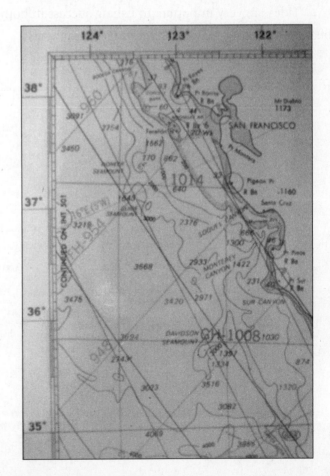

Understanding how to read a chart can help you in navigating a channel, finding a secret hot spot, avoiding a sandbar, and, most important, getting back to the dock at the end of the day.

Here are some useful conversions for reading a nautical chart.

1 fathom	= 6 feet
1 nautical mile	= 1.2 miles
1 knot	= 1.2 mph
1 meter	= 3.3 feet

24. Most productive tides: Rising and falling tides

I remember fishing off the beach when I was a boy, and noticing that once the water along the beach began to churn, I began catching fish. It was as if someone had turned on a switch, causing the water to come alive with baitfish, bird life, and hookups. A few years later I figured out that the ocean turbulence and activity were the result of a changing tide.

Tides are very important to fishing success in both offshore and inshore waters, dictating where the fish will feed, and when they will feed. Being familiar with the tide's ebb and flow will improve your chances for success, no matter where you fish.

Marshes, Flats, and Beaches—Tides Transport Bait

I find the rising tide to be the optimum time to fish. Flood tides bring in new water filled with baitfish, shrimp, and other forage for gamefish to feast on. The gamefish will herd the bait into tight groups. Like the bad guys in a Western flick lying in wait for the good guys, the gamefish lie in wait to ambush the bait as it moves into nearshore areas, using the shoreline as a trap.

Falling tides that flush out marshes, estuaries, and flats can prove beneficial to the saltwater fly fisherman, as gamefish predictably will wait in deep channels and holes, and on sandbars for a seafood buffet being swept toward them.

As the tide falls, the receding water pulls small, tasty creatures out of the rocks and marsh grass.

Rising tide brings in an abundance of baitfish and crustaceans.

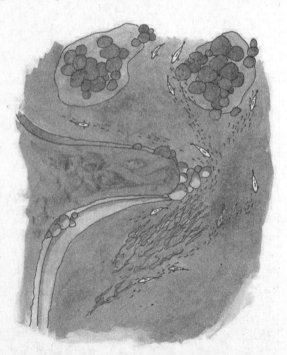

Offshore—Tide-creating Currents

Fishing offshore tides is different from fishing nearshore tides. Instead of the flooding and draining effect that tides have on inland flats and marshes, offshore tides are more about the movement of water, or current. This water movement is generated by both tide and wind. And the greater the current, the better the fishing. How does this occur? As water moves over offshore structure, drop-offs, rock piles, and even floating kelp rafts, the currents push the bait into tight groups, making them easier prey for predatory gamefish.

Tides and Moon Phase

Tidal movements correspond with the moon phase, with the most extreme tides occurring during new and full moons. Fishing during these times is usu-

Full and new moons produce strong tidal movements, which concentrate the bait.

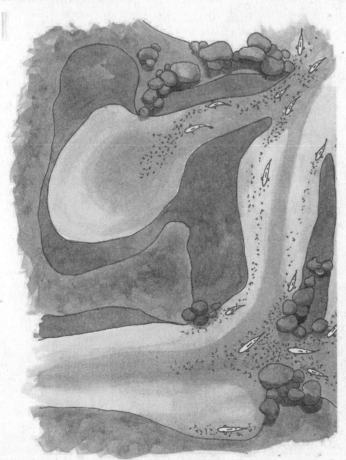

ally most productive. Keep in mind, however, that a full moon allows fish to feed all night. When the moon is full, fishing at dusk and dawn is often most productive.

Remember: The more tidal movement or current (water moving in, out, or in a certain direction), the better the fishing!

25. Learn from your guide

A good guide can provide you with a wealth of the information you need when fly fishing unfamiliar waters. His time spent on the water, logging hundreds of hours, studying the characteristics of different gamefish, and honing fly-fishing skills are almost guaranteed to make you a better angler. When you go to a different location and want to fish, hiring a guide is a worthwhile investment. Once you have enlisted his assistance, pay attention: Listen and learn! You might be a fly-fishing whiz on Montana's Beaverhead River, but you will find that saltwater fly fishing is entirely different from fly fishing in fresh water. Don't bend his ear with stories about your skills as a freshwater angler. You are there to learn from him, not vice versa.

Find a good guide and you may make a lifelong friend in the process.

Ice Fishing

Ice Fishing Introduction

JAY CASSELL

Once hunting seasons close down in the north, there's not much for outdoorsmen to do until spring. They could, of course, spring for airfare and head to Florida, the Gulf Coast, or even Hawaii. But for those more inclined to stay closer to home, ice fishing is the name of the game. And if you haven't tried it, you should. With sonar, power augers, snowmobiles, plus ice-fishing shanties that have everything from stoves and heaters to televisions sets, ice fishing doesn't mean you have to freeze your butt off. It's even civilized! And on some lakes, like Mille Lacs in Minnesota, ice fishing villages pop up on the ice as soon as it's hard enough to hold enough weight. In the north, they know how to party hearty in winter.

Here you'll find a variety of tips and tactics that will help you catch fish through the ice. You just have to get there!

A. Ice Fishing Tactics

1. The Truth About Ice Fishing

"Ice-fishing isn't so much a sport as it is a way of positively dealing with unfortunate reality. I mean, you can wake up in the morning depressed because it will be months yet before you can fly fish in real, liquid water, or you can leap out of bed thinking, 'Oh boy! It's the height of ice-fishing season.' Or if not, 'Oh boy,' then at least, 'Okay.'"

—John Gierach, *The View from Trout Lake,* Simon & Schuster, 1988

2. Where the Fish Are

"Fish congregate under the ice, and do not spread out over the lake as in spring, summer, and fall. The deep holes are best, but these deep holes do not necessarily have to be in the middle of the lake."

—Charles J. Farmer, *Sports Afield,* "The Sound Approach to Ice Fishing," January 1975

If you spot a bunch of ice fishermen all jigging in the same general area, you can be sure that fish are in the area. Time to join the party!

3. Ice Fishing's Biggest Mistake

"The most common error I have seen in ice fishing is angling too far from shore. Think of the ice-covered lake as you would if you were covering it in a boat. Chances are you would not fish the middle of the lake, but rather you would cast to points, the drop-offs, and where streams enter the lake."

—Charles J. Farmer, *Sports Afield,*
"The Sound Approach to Ice Fishing," January 1975

4. When Panfish Move Deeper

As the winter deepens and the action slows on your favorite areas along the banks for catching panfish—bluegills, yellow perch, pickerel—you may not have to chase all over the lake looking for them. First check out the deep water just adjacent to the areas where you caught panfish in summer and then at the start of winter's ice fishing.

5. Keeping Those Precious Smelt Alive

"Smelt are hard to get and hard to keep. They can't take sloshing around in bait buckets and will not be alive just when you need them most. Some anglers put baffles in their bait buckets to stop that from happening."

—Tom Hennessey, outdoor columnist
for the *Bangor Daily News*

6. Modern Ice-Fishing Gear: The Key to Having Fun

"The snowmobile and power ice auger made ice fishing what it is today. In the days before these devices came along, ice fishing only called to the strongest and most hearty. All the equipment being used today—from power augers to rods, reels, and jigs—is amazing in what it can do to help you have fun days out on the ice, instead of drudgery and plain hard work. Check out the gear on the Internet, particularly at places like www.cabelas.com, www.basswpro.com, and www.gandermountain.com."

—Tom Hennessey, outdoor columnist
for the *Bangor Daily News*

7. Check Those Traps Frequently

"Checking traps frequently can produce action with the bait that leads to strikes. Lifting the bait to check it gives it movement, action, attracting fish. Once attracted, they may start biting."

—Tom Hennessey, outdoor columnist
for the *Bangor Daily News*

8. The Key to Taking Landlocks

"Landlock salmon move around the lake only a foot or two below the surface. Fish for them more shallow than other species."

—Tom Hennessey, outdoor columnist
for the *Bangor Daily News*

9. Catching Lake Trout through the Ice

"Best bait for lake trout (togue, to Maine folk) is a golden shiner or sucker, about 3 to 4 inches long. Make a cut just where the gills meet at the belly where there's an artery that will bleed. Find the bottom, then lift bait about a foot off it."

—Tom Hennessey, outdoor columnist
for the *Bangor Daily News*

10. Setting Drag on Ice-Fishing Reels

"Basically, you want your ice-fishing reel to have little or no drag. Often when fish mouth the bait and feel tension, they will drop it. Fishing with no drag, you can set the hook after they've run a bit and taken the bait."

—Tom Hennessey, outdoor columnist
for the *Bangor Daily News*

11. Best Ice-Fishing Rigs

"Use 6 to 8 feet of leader for deep fishing, less for the salmon, which move about only a foot or so below the ice. Use a swivel connected to line and use a No. 6 hook (or 4 sometimes). Use split-shot."

—Tom Hennessey, outdoor columnist for the *Bangor Daily News*

12. Using Smelt as Bait

"Smelt will swim around and around and twist line. They will come to the top if you don't have sinker."

—Tom Hennessey, outdoor columnist for the *Bangor Daily News*

13. Better Lure Action under the Ice

Imagine an ice-fishing lure so effective it gives you the ability to "cast" under the ice. Sounds pretty good, don't you think? So do writers Ted Takasaki and Scott Richardson, who wrote on the tactics of ice-fishing guru Dave Genz in the article "Ice Spoonin' Walleyes" in the Articles section of the Lindy Tackle Web site, www.lindyfishingtackle.com. Genz especially likes first-ice walleyes when the oxygen levels and temps are more to their liking and they're more aggressive. He goes after them with Lindy's Rattlin' Flyer Spoon, with the look, flash, and sound that brings in walleyes, especially late in the afternoon when other lures are losing their effectiveness. The design of the Rattlin' Flyer, say Takasaki and Richardson, like its predecessor, the Flyer, allows the lure to have a gliding action when dropped into a hole, covering the water much like a cast. Genz uses a stiff-tip rod (limber tips won't give the lure action) and suggests on fishing the lure: "Don't lift it and let it pendulum back below the hole. Drag it. Twitch it as you drag it. Now, you're almost fishing like you would fish in summer." If you're a serious icefisher or a serious wannabe, check out all the details in this excellent article and many others at the Lindy site.

14. Early-Ice Walleye Spots to Set Up

Points that lead to drop-offs have always been known as prime walleye spots to put your ice auger to

work on. Some experts tweak this idea with a further refinement: They choose the spots where the drop-off is the steepest, and is leading to the deepest part of the lake.

15. Working the Jig

The word "jigging" seems to be synonymous with ice fishing, and everybody seems to do it differently. Common knowledge, however, says to let the spoon or jig go all the way to the bottom, then lift it with a couple of cranks on your reel and keep it at that level as you make it flutter up and down.

16. Making Your Jig Even More Deadly

Bait fishermen with their tip-ups catch a lot of fish through the ice, but the method that's the most fun is jigging with a short rod. You can sweeten your jig by adding a minnow, hooked through the lips. The same rig is very effective in crappie fishing.

17. Better Way to Fish Jigging Spoons

"Jigging spoons usually have the hook on the fatter end and you tie your line to the thinner end. Reversing that will cause the lure to flutter more and keep it from dropping too fast."

—Larry Whiteley, OutdoorSite Library, Bass Pro Shops, www.basspro.com

18. Don't Let Those Fish Freeze

"Don't let your fish freeze out on the ice unless you have a way of keeping them frozen. If they thaw out and you refreeze them when you get home, they will lose a lot of their flavor."

—Larry Whiteley, OutdoorSite Library, Bass Pro Shops, www.basspro.com

19. Tackle for Hard-Water Bluegills

In an excellent article on the Bass Pro Shops OutdoorSite Library, Jason Aki explains his tackle for consistently taking bluegills. "An ultralight to light jigging pole between 2 and 3 feet coupled to a micro spinning reel with line-holding capacity of 100 feet of 4-pound test . . . ."

20. Lures and Rig for Hard-Water Bluegills

Continuing recommendations from Jason Aki in his article on jigging bluegills through the ice: "First off, line your rod with the lightest fishing line you feel confident in using, and then tie on a small spoon with the treble hook removed. Onto the bottom of the spoon tie a 10- or 12-inch leader of monofilament line and a small curved-shank hook. Onto the hook spear two to three wax worms or a dorsally hooked crappie minnow. The idea here is to have the spoon attract the bluegills' attention from a distance and the scent of the bait to get the fish to bite."

—Jason Aki, "Jigging Ice for Bluegill," OutdoorSite Library, Bass Pro Shops, www.basspro.com

21. Moving On to Better Things

"Small moves are tweaking your position on a piece of structure. They're 5- to 20-yard changes . . . Large moves are used to cover big distances. . . . Often it's better to move and try to find active fish than spend a lot of time with finicky fish. Sometimes, a few short moves will put you into biters, while some days are just tough bites."

—Tim Allard, "Ice Fishing a New Lake," OutdoorSite Library, Bass Pro Shops, www.basspro.com

22. Ice Fishing with Gander Mountain

We've mentioned the Gander Mountain mail-order and resource center elsewhere in this book, but their ice-fishing coverage deserves special mention. Tackle, gear, and information: it's a complete coverage. Check it out at www.gandermountain.com. The articles and tips are in their Resource Center.

23. Find the Fish with Sonar

"The sonar available to the modern ice angler is nothing short of amazing. In fact, many anglers don't even drill holes through the ice unless they first spot gamefish with their sonar. How is that possible? By simply pouring water on solid, clear ice and placing the transducer in the water, the unit can transmit and receive sound waves through the ice, allowing you to see the depth, weeds, and even fish."

—Gander Mountain article,
www.gandermountain.com

24. The Yellow Perch Challenge

Yellow perch are a universal ice-fishing joy. They're great on the table, they usually roam the waters in schools, and they are widely distributed over North America's best ice-fishing destinations. While perch can be easy to find at times, they can also be difficult, zigging while you're zagging and vice versa. Before you can catch them, you have to find them—and it's not always that simple.

25. Yellow Perch Lures of an Expert

In an excellent article on the Bass Pro Shops Outdoor Library, angler Tim Allard says he divides his baits between "search" baits, which are relatively big jigging baits and "finesse" baits, for subtle jigging on holes where he knows there are fish. Allard tries to attract perch with relatively big jigging baits like Northland's Buckshot Spoon, Blue Fox's Rattle Flash Jig'n Spoons, Bay de Noc's Swedish Pimples, and Lindy's Rattlion Flyer. For subtle jigging he names ice jigs like Lindy Little Joe and Northland's Super Glo.

Part 2
Tackle &
Knots to Know

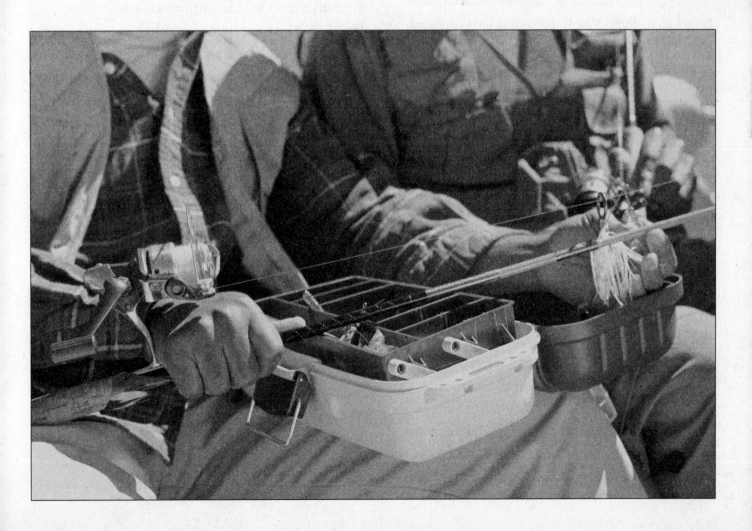

Tackle

STEVE PRICE

Rods

The first rods were tree limbs long enough to extend a line into a body of water and strong enough not to snap while the angler was playing a fish. By the 1850s, fishermen had attached three or four strips of flexible cane bamboo tips onto tapered poles made from such durable woods as hickory. As technology improved, so the amount of bamboo increased, culminating in the "classic" eight-strip laminated style.

Major innovations in man-made material happened after World War II. Fiberglass rods appeared, made by two techniques: one consisted of glass fibers impregnated in cloth that was wrapped around steel templates for size and taper; the other involved glass fibers wrapped around a light wood core and wrapped with a cellophane film before being heated. Although other rod materials are now more popular, some fishermen still prefer fiberglass' relatively greater "give," which produces a more sensitive feel for setting hooks. Fiberglass also survives in heavy-duty saltwater rods.

High-modulus graphite ("modulus" means "stiffness") is now the overwhelming material of choice for almost all kinds of rods. Invented in Britain for aerospace use and introduced into the fishing world by Fenwick in 1973, graphite offers two-thirds the weight and up to 10 times the stiffness of fiberglass.

Graphite is carbon fiber that comes from the residue of crude oil, post-refining sludge that is extruded into polyacrylic nitrate fibers. Through a series of baking operations, the fibers are carbonized and oxidized so the molecules become stiff graphite fibers.

The fibers are placed onto a supporting "scrim" layer (usually fiberglass), after which they go into a matrix of epoxy resin shaped for the desired length and taper. The graphite is then wrapped around a mandrel, or form; how the fibers are wrapped determines the rod's taper and other characteristics. Finally, the graphite is subjected to high-pressure compression to achieve its strength.

Very few graphite rods are made of pure graphite. A rod that is, for example, "95 percent graphite" contains 5 percent of another material, most often fiberglass. This is a common practice, since many rod-makers feel that pure graphite is too brittle.

The stiffness of graphite rods is described by their MODULUS expressed per square inch, or p.s.i., indicates that the blank was rolled under a substantial amount of pressure and the graphite was well bonded. Over the past several years, boron has been making a strong move to become an alternative to graphite. Although fans of graphite have serious reservations, other fishermen feel that boron equals and even surpasses graphite's sensitivity and durability.

Before the advent of man-made materials, rods made of bamboo were standard. Bamboo fly rods are now considered handsome vestiges of a bygone era, able to cast tight loops but very fragile in all but the most experienced of hands. Only a handful of anglers routinely use them, although they are displayed as collectibles by many more people. Craftsmen still turn out handmade cane rods, especially the fly-fishing variety. Even if you come across a bamboo rod in workable condition in somebody's attic, consider the species strictly of historical interest (translation: stick to the man-made, more affordable variety).

General Considerations

The flexibility of a rod's shaft (or "blank"), the manner in which it bends and how rapidly it straightens, determines its "action." In rods with "fast" action, only the top one-third flexes, while the entire shaft of a "slow" action rod does the bending. A rod described as having "progressive" action has a tip that bends more than the middle section, which in turn bends more than the butt end. In other words, a parabola instead of a circle.

As a general rule, stiff rods have faster action, which allows casts of greater distances and makes maneuvering a lure easier. A stiff fly rod tends to produce tighter line loops between the back- and the forecast. More flexible rods with slower action are preferable for more delicate presentations.

Rods used for plastic worm and jig-fishing tend to have firm tips for greater sensitivity and ease in setting the hook. Live bait, however, calls for a rod with relatively slow action, since too strong a "snap" will rip worms and other fleshly creatures off the hook. Bottom-fishing requires a relatively strong rod because bait is more likely to become caught on objects on the bottom.

The REEL SEAT is the part of the rod by which a reel is attached. Two sliding rings allow some degree of adjusting the reel's position along the grip. Another choice is a FIXED BUTT CAP with one sliding ring. Somewhat more popular are the UPLOCK (where the reel seat fits into a slot at the grip's top end) and the DOWNLOCK (the seat fits into a slot at the rod's butt end); in both instances, a sliding ring or screw holds the other end of the reel seat in place.

(Many surf-casting fishermen who don't want to take the chance of rough use and big fish tearing the reel off a rod simply tape their reels to their rods; they

An example of a downlock seat.

use the most durable packing tape they can find to secure the reel to a cork base, then leave the rig in place throughout the entire season.)

Whatever the style, seats made out of machined metal are more precisely and durably made than ones that are stamped. Nickel silver is prized for its self-lubricating quality, with aluminum a very acceptable alternative.

GUIDES, through which line passes along the length of a rod, come in two main styles. The single-foot variety is wrapped onto the blank by its sole projection. The two-foot's twin projections may make it twice as secure, but since the number of wraps by which guides are held in place are thought to affect a rod's action, many fishermen prefer single-foot guides, which require half as many wraps.

Silicon carbide is the most durable material for guides. It's also the most expensive, so aluminum oxide is more prevalent.

Although cork is the traditional material for handles (and remains so for pistol-grip rods), most baitcasting fishermen prefer an EVA foam composition. Foam is more durable and it offers greater "gripability," especially when wet.

Multipiece rods are joined together by ferrules. The open cylindrical end, called the "female," fits over the solid end, or "spigot" or "male."

"Pack" rods are designed for easy carrying while traveling. They consist of three (or four) to seven component pieces. Thanks to the strength of man-made materials, they are just as durable as one- or two-piece rods, and with little to no objectionable action.*

Also designed for ease of transportation, telescopic rods slide into themselves, like the shafts of folding umbrellas. Commonly used for saltwater fishing, they are found more infrequently as freshwater angling tools.

---

* Another example of a "pack" rod of sorts, as well as of tackle telemarketing, is the Pocket Fisherman. This rod-and-reel combo that folds into a small carrying case has been promoted by super-salesman Ron Popeil (of Veg-O-Matic chopper fame) in infomercials to the tune of 1.25 million sold.

Baitcasting Rods

The "right" length and weight of a baitcasting rod depends in large part on the weight of the particular lure that you plan to use. Manufacturers have grouped rods as listed in the following table:

	ROD LENGTH	LURE WEIGHT
	(IN FT.)	(IN OZ.)
Extra-Light:	6 to 6 ½	⅛ to ¼
Light:	5 ½ to 6 ½	¼ to ½
Medium:	4 ½ to 6	⅝ to ¾
Heavy:	4 ½ to 7 ½	¾ to 1 ¼

Rods that fall into the "medium" group are considered the best for all-around, general-purpose fishing. Bass fishermen favor them, while anglers after muskies and pike choose heavy rods. Light rods are best for panfishing.

You'll note that there's a fair amount of overlapping in rod lengths among the categories. That's because proper length is also a function of the kind of conditions you must cope with and the kind of presentation you're aiming for. A short rod delivers a lure in a relatively flat trajectory, which is essential if you're fishing in a heavily wooded area. On the other hand, and foliage permitting, longer rods tend to cast bait in a high arc.

Rods used for the technique known as FLIPPIN' (the "g" is almost never written, much less pronounced), or an underhand or "slingshot" cast, tend to be slightly longer than those intended for PITCHIN', which is an overhand or sidearm presentation. Both have a flexible tip. The rest of the blank, or its lower 80 percent, is stiff, in order to toss heavy bait a good distance (pitchin') and to penetrate heavy weed cover (flippin'). There is now a tendency to use the same rod for both techniques, with a compromise length 7 ½ feet.

Relatively short "pistol-grip" handles have a hook projection for the caster's index finger. The one-handed

Flippin' rods can easily double as pitchin' rods.

style is popular for baitcasting and is usually found on short (5 feet-6 feet) rods where, according to its fans, pistol-grips permit snappier and more accurate casts.

Pistol Grip.

The "triggerstick" handle is similar, in that it also offers index-finger support, but the handle itself is longer, usually long enough to accommodate a two-handed casting grip. Triggerstick handles are most often found on flippin' and pitchin' rods.

Length would be a handicap in rods used in ice-fishing. The typical rod used for that purpose is no

Triggerstick.

more than 3 feet in length; many ice-fishermen make their own rods from remnants of longer rods that have snapped.

Saltwater Rods

Subtlety of presentation is not much of a factor when surf-casting 50 yards to a bluefish or trolling for tarpon, so rods made of fiberglass and composite are found as frequently as those made of graphite.

Rods are designated according to their strength; specifically, the amount of force needed to bend a rod 90 degrees. The International Game Fish Association established the following classifications for trolling rods in conjunction with the organization's world record-keeping:

Ultra-Light: 6, 12, and 20 lb.

Light: 30 lb.

Medium: 50 lb.

Heavy: 80 lb.

Ultra-Heavy: 130 lb.

Without Limit: 130 to 180 lb.

To be recognized by the IGFA, these "classified" rods must be composed of two sections, either separable or one-piece. The rod blank itself (called the "tip") must measure a minimum of 40 inches with five guides plus the tip-top. The butt, or handle, cannot be longer than 27 inches. The tip may be made of fiberglass or graphite, while the butt may be made of metal or fiber and have a grip of cork, rubber, or other material.

Rods used for fishing from anchored boats (known as "bottom-fishing") usually measure 10 feet or less. The IGFA classifies these rods into 6-, 12-, 20-, and 30-pound weight categories.

Surf-casting rods are built for ultra-long casting, up to 200 feet or more. Medium-length rods are from 6 feet to 10 feet, while long rods measure between 10 feet and 15 feet. Most are made of graphite, fiberglass, or a composite.

Boat rods, those monster pieces of tackle used for blue-water fishing, are designated according to their line class, or the TEST STRENGTH of the line that is designed to be used on them. A rod with a line class of 20 pounds, for example, is meant to carry 20-pound line. Big-game rods, such as those used for tuna, range in length from 5 feet 6 inches to 6 feet and take line between 50 and 130 pounds.

Rods attached to downrigger trolling tackle measure about 8 feet and take 8- to 20-pound line.*

---

* A DOWNRIGGER is an electric battery-operated device that maintains bait at a predetermined depth. The fishing rod's line is snapped to a weight at the end of the downrigger's stainless-steel cable. The cable is lowered from the tip of the downrigger's 2-foot or 4-foot boom until the desired depth is reached. A footage counter on the downrigger indicates the depth of the weight. Using that data, the fisherman or boat captain can release or rewind cable to compensate for any changes in depth due to the boat's speed and the ocean's current.

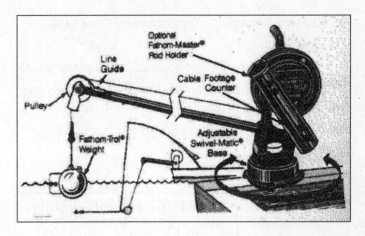

A downrigger. [courtesy Penn Reels]

When a fish strikes, the line is released from the weight, and the downrigger's motor rewinds the cable, returning the weight to the boom tip and out of interference range.

Playing a big-game saltwater fish generates a great deal of line friction against a rod's guides, so rods used for that purpose have roller (also called pulley) guides. Fishermen routinely inspect these guides, because a jammed pulley is worse than useless.

Spinning Rods

One of the advantages to spinning tackle is its ability to present lighter bait than baitcasting gear can. Accordingly, line thickness becomes relevant, as is lure weight. The following table tells that tale:

	LINE DIAMETER (IN MM)	LURE WEIGHT (IN OZ.)
Ultra-Light:	.005 to .008	1/16 to 5/16
Light:	.008 to .010	1/4 to 3/8
Medium:	.010 to .012	3/8 to 5/8
Heavy:	.012 to .013	1/2 to 1
Extra-Heavy:	.015 to .024	1 to 4

With regard to length, most freshwater spinning rods range from 5 ½ feet to 7 feet. The upper end of that spectrum is most effective for longer casts. There are also two-handed spinning rods for salmon and steelhead fishing that are 7 to 8 feet in length.

Saltwater fishing from boats calls for spinning rods between 6 feet and 10 feet that can cast lures weighing between ¾ ounce to 2 ounces.

Surf-casting spinning rods are divided into four categories:

	ROD LENGTH	BAIT WEIGHT
	(IN FT.)	(IN OZ.)
Super-Light:	8 to 10	¾ to 1
Light:	11 to 12 ½	1 to 2 ¾
Medium or Semi-Heavy:	13 to 15	2 ¼ to 3 ½
Heavy:	16+	3 ½+

Hardware

Unlike line coming out straight from a baitcasting reel, line cast from a spinning reel emerges in spirals. The guide on a spinning rod closest to the reel must therefore be large enough to accommodate the spiral, but it must also be small enough to keep the spiraling line from slapping against the rod. The other guides (more often single-foot than snake in style) progressively reduce the size of the spiral. That's why the guides on spinning rods diminish in size down to the smallest one at the tip-top. Ceramic-lined guides are best at dissipating heat caused by friction.

Spinning rods use three types of mechanisms to hold the reel. Sliding rings slip onto the reel handle to hold the reel in place by tension against the handle. A fixed-reel seat screws the reel in place; there is greater security, but the metal corners can chafe your fingers. A sliding-reel seat combines the first two devices and has the advantage of great comfort and security.

Not all spinning rods are designed for light tackle fishing. Many boat rods and surf-casting rods are big brawny members of that family.

Fly Rods

In baitcasting and spinning, the weight of the bait provides the force that carries the line during a cast. That's why such rods are described in terms of optimum bait weight.

In fly casting, however, the line moves because of its own weight is carried by the energy generated by the propelling force of the rod during the cast. Accordingly, rods are described in terms of the weight of the line that they are intended to hold.

The following broad classifications give an indication of which weights are designed for particular kinds of fly-fishing:

1-weight through 3-weight: for small trout and panfish sought with delicate presentations of tiny light flies on small, slow-moving streams.

4-weight through 6-weight: for general, all-purpose trout fishing.

7-weight and 8-weight: for relatively larger streams and lakes and for bass fishing (where more line weight is needed to "punch" heavier bass flies).

9-weight through 11-weight: for salmon and steelhead fishing, where casts between 40 feet and 70 feet are routinely needed on fast rivers. These weights are also appropriate for bonefish, permit, and small tarpon, especially on saltwater flats where ocean winds are an ever-present factor.

12-weight through 15-weight: for playing and landing such substantial deep-sea quarry as sailfish, tarpon, and tuna.

Somewhat muddying the waters is the ability of modern rods to accommodate slightly lighter or heavier line weight. Some anglers who want a bit more distance routinely use a line one weight heavier than the rod calls for: 6-weight line on a 5-weight rod, for example. By the same token, line that is one weight lighter produces slightly greater sensitivity (thinner line also cuts through wind better than line with a thicker diameter does).

As for action, the stiffer a fly rod, the further it will cast a fly. That makes sense, because a stiff rod can generates a faster action (think of it in terms of more "snap"). Faster action in turn generates higher line speeds, which produce greater distances.

Conversely, a more supple, or "slow," rod will toss a fly in more of a lazy lob, a characteristic that's desirable for more delicate presentations.

The action you'll want depends on the kind of fishing you'll do. Bear in mind that the vast majority of casts made for trout (bass and panfish too) are 25 feet and under, well within the parameters of a medium-action rod. The ability to throw a fly 70 feet or further is an enviable skill, but not something that a novice trout angler needs.

However, casts of from 40 feet to 70 feet are routine when coping with wind and longer distances across saltwater flats or salmon and steelhead rivers.

With regard to length, if you remember that a fly rod is, in John Merwin's phrase, a "flexible lever," you'll understand the physics of why longer rods are able to develop and deliver greater power. Unless they're confining their fishing to small streams with heavy overgrowth, novice fly-casters in pursuit of trout would do well to select a rod in the 8-foot to 9-foot range. A 9-foot length is appropriate for salmon and steelhead fishing.

A rod's weight is also a factor. The difference of an ounce or two may not seem like much when you're looking over a selection in a tackle shop or catalog, but even that small amount of weight will add up over a day on the water. All else being equal, most people select a lighter rod.

Hardware

The rule of thumb is one guide for each foot of rod plus the tip-top. That translates into a total of 8 guides for a 7-foot rod.

In his book *Advanced Fly Fishing* (Delacourt, 1992), Lefty Kreh points out that line that passes through the butt guide (the guide closest to the handle)

during a cast does not go straight through, but at an angle from below. A small butt guide restricts the amount of line that passes through in that fashion; Kreh prefers a butt guide that's slightly larger than a fly rod's other guides (16mm for 1-weight to 6-weights, 20 mm or 24 mm for heavier rods). As for the type of guide, Kreh argues that snake guides create less friction than the one-foot variety, and they weigh less too. The additional wrapping that a two-foot guide requires, he adds, has a negligible effect on a rod's action.

Fly rod handles, which are traditionally made of cork, come in a variety of shapes. The cigar is the most popular, although its tapered shape offers relative little support to the fisherman's thumb. The bulge at the top of the half-wells style of handle and the twin bulges of the full-wells offer far greater support, making them preferable for heavier tackle and bigger fish.

Heavier rods often have a fighting butt, a knob at the handle end that can be pressed against the angler's stomach and thus offer better leverage for fighting salmon, steelheads, and saltwater species. Such butts are de rigueur on two-handed "Spey" rods traditionally used for salmon and sea trout along British lochs and rivers.

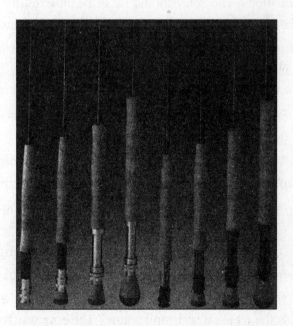

A variety of fly rod butts. The rods fourth and eighth from the left have fighting butts.

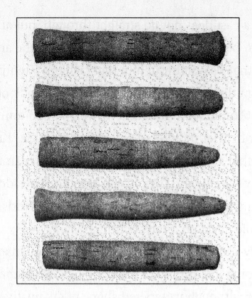

Fly rod grip styles. From top: Full-Wells, Reversed Half-Wells, Super Fine, Western, Cigar.

Before You Buy

Even within such categories as baitcasting, fly-fishing, and blue-water, quarry (that is, the species of fish you're after) and conditions will largely determine your choice of rod. As with other tackle, you can learn a great deal about what is appropriate through (1) magazine articles; (2) advertisements; and (3) word-of-mouth, whether from users or tackle shop recommendations. The latter should never be underestimated, since the best-selling "Ugly Stick" baitcasting rod owes its success to word-of-mouth as much as to Shakespeare's innovating advertising campaign.

When examining a rod:

1. Sight along its length, checking for straightness as you rotate the rod.

2. Are the guides lined up straight and are the wrappings secure? Whatever the style of rod, its wraps need an even coat of varnish to prevent the wrapping thread from coming apart and fraying.

3. If the handle is made of cork, is it solid and snug? Avoid cork that's dried and cracked, with lots of pits and gouges.

4. Is the reel seat snug and secure? The only way to tell for sure is to try it, either with a borrowed reel or one of your own that you brought with you.

5. How does the rod feel? You can cast a half-dozen rods of the same length, weight, and material but made by different manufacturers, and you might have six different reactions. The only infallible method of determining how well you like a rod is to conduct a hands-on trial. Rig a candidate with reel and line if you can, then take it outside and cast until you get a good feeling for the rod's particular properties and idiosyncrasies. If the seller won't let you rig the rod, insist on trying a number of "false" casts.

Then comes the matter of cost. How much should a good rod cost (or, put another way, why are some rods more expensive than others)?

Better materials and more careful craftsmanship cost more than cheaper materials and run-of-the-mill workmanship. A rod made of premium graphite, solid hand-machined fittings, and a defect-free cork handle will handle better, last longer, and look better than one that rolls off a mass-production assembly line. Sure, you can get away with a cheap rod, but if you're planning to make fishing a lifetime sport, not to spend a little extra (okay, sometimes a lot extra) for a rod that you can grow to know and use for many years is false economy.

Packaged "starter" sets that include a rod and reel cost less, but that's because the tackle tends to be the manufacturer's "bottom of the line." It's false economy. Similar to a would-be musician's starting out on a "learner" instrument, the kind of results that would encourage you to continue are difficult to come by; cheaply-made (i.e., inexpensive) rods lack the action and sensitivity that leads to immediate enjoyment and quick progress. If you're uncertain whether fishing will be a long-term sport for you, consider borrowing a good rod until you've decided whether you want one of your own.

Care and Maintenance

The greatest enemy of a fishing rod is human negligence. Car doors and windows, one fisherman ruefully pointed out, are the serial killers of the rod-destroying felons. Far better to invest in a carrier, either one that can be mounted like a ski rack on a car roof or, if the size of your vehicle permits, one that can carry rods on the inside.

A rod left on the ground can be stepped on. One left leaning against the sides of cars is likely to be caught by a gust of wind and blown underfoot or transported into the path of an oncoming vehicle. Similarly, a rod that juts out of a boat can be snapped by a passing log, boulder, pier, or another boat. A rod needn't be snapped in two to be harmed; a bent blank, reel seat, or one or more guides and ferrules will affect the rod's action and function.

Fly-fishermen learn to carry their rod butt end first, so in case they drop the rods, the tips and guides are protected. There's also less risk in snagging an overhead branch, a good reason for carrying any kind of rod in that fashion through wooded areas.

Toting more than one rod can be a handful, a problem to which multi-rod carriers are a solution. Carrying even one rod, especially when you break it down into its component pieces, is likely to produce a tangled line. The Rod Buddy™, composed of two rubber clamps, holds the rod pieces together, and it secures the line in the process (Marine Innovations, P.O. Box 21040, St. Catharines, Ontario L2M 7X2 Canada).

Cleaning a rod prolongs its condition and life. After removing the reel and breaking the rod down into its components, use a damp cloth to wipe away dirt, sand, vegetation, or any other debris. Saltwater rods deserve a more thorough cleaning. Fleece mitts (the kind used to wash car bodies) make good tackle cleaners. Dip one into soapy water and swab the rod, then rinse the rod in freshwater to remove all traces of corrosive salt. You may need to use a soft brush to remove dried fish scales, dried algae, and anything else that's stuck to the rod.

Then dry the rod with a clean, soft cloth, paying particular attention to the ferrules, guides, and reel seat. While you're at it, check to see whether guides and ferrules might have become loose or bent. If so, take the rod to a qualified person to make the necessary repairs.

Keeping a rod in a cloth sleeve keeps dust and other dirt off the rod. Storing and transporting a rod in a hard protective case greatly reduces the chance of its being stepped on, snapped, or otherwise trashed. If your rod didn't come with its case, you can buy one at most tackle shops or mail-order outlets. Or, you can make your own from a length of PVC pipe and two rubber stoppers.

A rod case.

Rod-Making Made Easy

"What's the best way to start?" we asked a half-dozen people who have some experience making their own rods. "Find a teacher," was the unanimous answer. That's not to say that making a rod is particularly difficult, but like most do-it-yourself projects, the guidance of a more experienced person saves time and eliminates wasted effort and its accompanying stress. And since rod-building involves using a number of specialized tools, whoever provides the instruction may own such equipment and let you use it, a good idea while you decide whether you want to make such a capital investment.

Finding a teacher should be no more difficult than inquiring at your local tackle shop; if the proprietor or sales clerk can't oblige, he or she often knows of someone who can. Or you can find someone through your local fishing club or chapter of Trout Unlimited, Izaak Walton League, B.A.S.S., or similar organization.

However you approach rod-building, you'll begin by selecting a blank, the heart of the rod. You'll base your choice on several factors: length, action, weight, and line or bait size. If you have a favorite rod, chances are good that you can get a blank made by the same manufacturer.

Other ingredients consist of a reel seat, a handle, ferrules, a set of guides, thread to wrap the guides, cement, varnish or another finish, and brushes with which to apply the finish.

The machinery that you'll need to buy or borrow are a rod-wrapper lathe and a slow-rotating drying motor that helps achieve a smooth glassy finish on your custom-made, handmade rod.

Most tackle shops, catalogs and angling-related websites (such as cabelas.com and basspro.com) carry the items you'll need

Reels

Reels used to be dismissed as being nothing more than a gizmo for storing line. Not any more, though. The array of reels found in all types of fishing demonstrates an effort on the part of the tackle industry to create high precision, durable instruments that perform an active and essential role in the process of playing and landing fish.

Two preliminary items: Whether a reel is designed for baitcasting (known in saltwater circles as a "conventional" reel), spinning, spin-casting, or fly-fishing, the concept of "drag" is central to any discussion of reels. DRAG is simply resistance, which translates into the amount of tension that a line (including a leader, if any) can take before it breaks. To prevent such breakage, reels contain drag mechanisms that automatically disengage the reel spool and thus release line when a certain pressure is reached.

The GEAR RATIO of a reel indicates the number of revolutions it takes to rewind a certain length of line. As a general rule, each revolution picks up approximately 5 inches of line, so that a reel with a gear ratio of 3:21 retrieves some 15 inches (4:1=20", 5:1=25", etc.).

Baitcasting Reels

The earliest recorded reference to a line-holding device mounted on the end of a rod is said to have appeared in the literature of third-century China, although a reel very definitely is pictured in a thirteenth-century print from that country. In 1651, Thomas Barker refers in his *The Art of the Angler* to a "wind, to turn with a barrel to gather up line."

Before the nineteenth century, revolving-spool reels were made either of wood or bronze in the English single-action style. The first modern American baitcasting reels were crafted by a succession of Kentucky-based watchmakers (why the Bluegrass State accounted for so much reel-making activity remains unexplained). An early and important innovation of that era was a gear mechanism that allowed several revolutions of the spool for each turn of the crank handle; when another watchmaker devised a 4:1 gear ratio, the first quadruple multiplier reel was born. Other advancements later in that century included click-and-drag springs and level-wind mechanisms.

A baitcasting reel, circa 1950.

What distinguishes baitcasting reels from those used in other types of fishing is the revolving spool from which the weight of the bait pulls the line. This ability to release the line at high speeds also gives rise to a major potential problem, that of BACKLASH, the bird's nest tangle of line that happens when a spool spins faster than the line is released. To eliminate that hazard, many reels contain magnetic "brake" mechanisms that limit the speed at which the spool revolves during a cast; the brake can be adjusted to reflect the weight of the plug or whatever other bait the reel is being asked to cast.

Another potential problem with baitcasting reels involves uneven line distribution during the rewind; too much line on one side or in the middle of the spool creates lumps that can interfere with the reel's action. The solution, developed during last century, is a LEVEL-WINDER DEVICE, an elongated loop that slides back and forth across the spool to ensure that the line lays even and flat.

A baitcasting reel with a level-winder. [courtesy of Abu Garcia]

Getting the bait out to where fish are is just one job of a baitcasting reel. Landing a fish is another task, and these reels, particularly for salt-water fishing, employ either of two kinds of braking systems against the drag produced by a hard-fighting fish. The STAR DRAG consists of a series of discs that increase or decrease pressure against the spool's drum. It's a durable system that is operated by one or two star-shaped wheels mounted between the reel casing and the winder.

A baitcasting reel with a star drag system. [courtesy Daiwa]

As its name suggests, the LEVER DRAG SYSTEM contains a single lever that exerts pressure against the reel drum. Many fishermen consider reels with this system more sensitive than those with star drags. Adjustable drags automatically downshift to a lower gear that is more efficient in fighting big fish (much as low gears on bicycles afford more power). Some surf-casting reels have two-speed retrieval systems for even more precise control.

In either case, both star and lever drags often need to be readjusted according to bait weight and conditions throughout the course of the day and often while a fish is being played and landed.

As for how initially to set the drag of a baitcasting reel, the standard practice is to hold the rod at a 45° angle and then press the bar on the reel that releases the line. Adjust the drag control so the plug (or whatever other bait you're using) descends slowly until it touches the ground. The plug shouldn't drop like a rock, just "slide," with no additional line coming off the reel once the plug touches down.

Ball bearings have become standard components of both saltwater and freshwater reels. They reduce friction for smoother rewinding under tension and at greater speeds.

Reels used for big-game (or "blue-water") ocean fishing might be described as "freshwater reels on steroids." Made of anodized aluminum or graphite for maximum resistance to corrosion, they are substantial pieces of equipment both in size (some weigh 10 pounds or more) and cost.

Some saltwater reels have attached electric motors, handy for rewinding line from depths of up (or down) to 300 feet, but are heavy to handle. That's why many ocean-going fishing vessels have shelves mounted along their railings to support these cumbersome attachments.

Tackle manufacturers continue to fine-tune baitcasting reel technology. For example, some now have levers that disengage the clutch lot to let out more line without requiring the angler to turn the reel handle, while gyroscope-style rotors reduce wobble while the line is rewound. Even handle knobs have been designed to be more ergonomically sound – their contours accommodate fingertips better than the round knobs did.

Spinning Reels

Fist developed in nineteenth-century Britain, SPINNING REELS were improved in Britain and France and introduced into the U.S. before World War II. The technique quickly grew in popularity when people discovered that the absence of a rotary spool meant the virtual elimination of backlashes. Moreover, with no rotating spool that needed a relatively heavy bait to activate it, spinning permitted the use of lightweight bait, ¼ ounce or even less; this greater range of bait was another major plus. Finally, fewer moving parts meant that spinning reels were easier, and therefore less expensive, to manufacture, and consumers certainly did not object to the lower price.

A spinning reel's components. [courtesy Penn Reels]

One would think that a spool with a very large diameter would be most efficient, since the larger the diameter, the less potential interference with the line during a cast. However, a diameter that is too large forces the escaping coils of line to become equally too large. The coils will then slap against the rod, robbing the cast of distance and accuracy.

The most popular type of line retrieval mechanism is the BAIL, a metal hoop across a spinning reel spool's face. One end is on the pick-up bracket, the other on

the rotating cup. The bail is opened manually by a flick of the angler's finger, then closes when the winding handle is cranked; the line moves along the bail until it reaches the roller and then onto the spool.

A system found on older reels is the AUTOMATIC PICK-UP ARM. It consists of a single curved arm that swings out of the way during the cast. As soon as the winder handle is turned, the arm strikes a cam and swings back to pick up the line.

A MANUAL PICK-UP is simply a roller on the revolving cup. The angler's forefinger slips the line over the roller. Because it has the fewest working parts, the manual pick-up is the least likely to fail.

Drag is adjusted by tightening or loosening the nut found either at the front of the spool or at the rear of the reel. A reel that has its drag adjustment knob on the front of the spool cannot accommodate the snap-off spools that make changing lines literally a snap. However, reels that have the knob on the rear can.

A spinning reel with a rear drag system. [courtesy Abu Garcia]

The ANTI-REVERSE LOCK is a ratchet that prevents a reel from letting line unwind, except for the drag mechanism. Most spin-fishermen keep it on all the time in conjunction with a properly-set drag (you can always flip the bail if you want to unwind line to a deeper depth). It's a particularly useful feature for such "single-handed" operations as netting a fish.

Whichever features you select, the choice of spinning reel should be based on line weight and line capacity. The following categories describe the range:

Ultra-Light: up to 8-lb. test
Light: 8- to 15-lb. test

Medium: 15- to 30-lb. test
Heavy: above 30-lb. test

Spin-Casting Reels

A SPIN-CASTING REEL is a spinning reel with a closed face. The enclosure is usually a rounded hood with a small hole on its face through which the line passes. The fisherman's thumb on a release button or knob on the back end of the reel controls the line during a cast: the moment pressure on the button relaxes, no further line is released.

With regard to line retrieval, a pin winds around inside the hood to settle the line onto a cup. Some reels have more than one pin, which makes for a faster rewind.

Friction and line capacity are the two main considerations of spin-casting reels. With regard to friction, monofilament is the line of choice; braided line creates too much resistance, while mono glides off the spool and through the hole. The hood makes line capacity somewhat restrictive, although not impossibly so.

Most "kiddie" fishing sets include a spin-casting reel. That's because spin-casting tackle is easier to use than a spinning rod and reel. Although you don't have the same accuracy of line control, since the release button is an all-or-nothing mechanism, a little bit of practice is all it takes for anyone can learn to gauge the amount of time the button should be held down to achieve a respectable cast.

That's not to say, however, that all spin-casting reels should be considered "kid stuff." More sophisticat-

Two spin-casting reels with thumb-release knobs.
[courtesy Daiwa]

ed features now include a 4:1 ratio retrieval, star drag systems and "power" handles for better grip.

Fly Reels

The first reels used in fly-fishing were wooden affairs inspired by bobbins. Technology took a giant step forward when in 1874 Charles F. Orvis was awarded a patent for a ventilated (that is, having holes in its sides), narrow-spool reel. Another more recent innovation was the exposed rim that permits braking by the palm of the angler's hand.

A fly reel. [courtesy Orvis]

Fly reels are categorized primarily according to the range of line weights that they are intended to hold. Reels designed for the lightest weights, 1 through 5, are necessarily smaller than those meant for salmon, steelhead, and especially deep-sea-fishing.

The weight of a fly reel becomes crucial to establish optimum balance. A reel that is too heavy means that the rod itself will feel too light, and that will interfere with line control while you cast. A reel that is too light, however, makes a rod feel too heavy, especially at its tip. This too creates casting problems. In the best of all worlds, a rod and reel will have their center of balance just in front of the grip.

Many fly reels adjust for drag by means of a single triangular pawl held by a spring against a geared wheel. Since pawls can slip and spring coils can lose their tension, a more precise mechanism is a padded disc that applies pressure against the spool, much as disc brakes retard an automobile's forward movement.

The least adjustable resistance control comes from the click ratchet, activated by an all-or-nothing on-off switch.

Resistance can be applied manually by letting the flat of your hand rub against a reel's rim. This is possible, however, only on a reel designed for "rim palming"; that is, one with an exposed rim.

Even the sound a reel makes can be a matter of choice. Some fishermen enjoy the loud clicks that a ratchet arrangement makes, especially the coffee-grinder "rat-tat-tat" heard when a big fish strips line off such a reel. Others prefer a more understated and harmonious sound. The only functional difference, some big-game anglers feel, is that clicking ratchet systems can deprive line tension of consistent pressure.

One sound that a big-game fly-fisherman doesn't enjoy hearing is that of a reel handle knob cracking against his knuckle. A big fish can yank line so hard and fast that the reel's spool will rotate in excess of 5,000 rpms.

ANTI-REVERSE REELS eliminate this danger; the spool rotates as the line goes out, but the knob does not.

A system of internal springs and gears characterize the "AUTOMATIC" FLY REEL. A flip of the lever (usually with your little finger), and the mechanism springs into action, pulling the slack in the line back onto the reel spool. Many anglers, especially who release lots of line fishing for salmon and steelheads, swear by automatics. Others who prefer greater human control sneer at them, citing poor drag control and relatively little line capacity with no backing.

More widely accepted examples of mechanical advantage are MULTIPLIER REELS. Their gear systems (typically, a 3:1 retrieve ratio) offer faster line retrieval, very much of an asset when trying to land any of the larger and hard-fighting freshwater or saltwater species.

Before You Buy

Whichever kind of reel you consider, you'll become aware that reels are precision instruments. Some,

however, are more precise than others, usually with regard to the materials from which they are made and the care and accuracy of the assembling process.

The finest quality reels are made from bar stock metal that is honed to exact specifications. Another method is to cast metal parts out of molds, a somewhat less expensive process. According to a March 1993 article in *Fly Rod & Reel*, the difference between the two techniques is "negligible" (or, put another way, a matter of personal bias). Other reels are molded from plastic or graphite, or mass-produced from stamped metal. One benefit of the lower end of this craftsmanship spectrum is that mass-produced reels tend to accept abrasion, bangs, and other traumas better than their handmade ultra-precision brethren…they just keep on clicking.

Some reels come only in right-or left-handed models. Others can be adjusted to be worked by either hand. But as Gary Soucie points out, switching hands on the rod after casting is hardly a big deal. You cast with your stronger hand and arm, so playing a big fish with that side of your body makes more sense.

With regard to material, brass or steel are extremely durable. So is such man-made material as graphite. Plastic, however "space-age" it may be hyped, remains at the fragile end of the spectrum.

Reels with thick coats of finish are more scratch-resistant than those with thin anodized or baked finishes. Reel feet that are screwed on are stronger than ones that are riveted. Plastic pawls tend to crack or wear out faster than pawls made of metal.

When inspecting a reel:

Look and feel for any imperfections

Check for loose, wobbling parts as you wind the reel, especially the spool and the spool release (and any spare spools that you're also considering buying.)

Test the drag system. Listen for clicks as you rotate the spool.

Make sure the spool is large enough to accommodate enough line for the type of fishing you plan to do. That's a particularly important consideration in "blue-water" ocean fishing, where a reel must be able to hold 400 feet or more of line (and if a fly reel, line plus backing).

Finally, confirm that any defects that occur during a warranty period will be corrected or the reel can be exchanged.

Care and Maintenance

Reels are precision instruments, so dropping or otherwise subjecting them to abuse won't do them or you any good. If you do drop a reel, immediately remove any dirt, sand, or other debris that may be clogging the mechanism. Make sure, too, that no screws have come loose or that, if it's a spinning reel, the pick-up bail is not bent.

A saltwater reel should be lightly rinsed in freshwater after each use to remove any traces of salt. If possible, remove the spool to remove any water trapped there. Dry the reel with a clean absorbent cloth, then apply a slight amount of reel oil on internal moving parts. After reassembling the reel, put just a drop of household oil.

The need to store and transport reels in cases is as important as it is for rods. Leather or cloth reel bags are designed for that purpose (plastic "zip-up" sandwich bags make a handy substitute). Padded reel cases are even sturdier. So are tackle boxes, in which many anglers keep their baitcasting and spinning reels safe and secure amid plugs, bobbers, hooks, and other gear.

Lines

The earliest fishing lines were strips of animal sinew, later replaced by pieces of twine or thin rope that were also knotted together into workable lengths. By the Middle Ages, braided or twisted horse-tail hair had become the material of choice. Silk was added until it finally replaced horsehair entirely. In order to make the line float, fishermen dressed it with oil or grease, and whether floating or not, line needed to be thoroughly dried after each use to retard rotting. Deep-sea fisher-

men favored another fabric, linen, which was braided or twisted into line.

The 1940s and 1950s saw several major technological advances. Sporting goods manufacturers realized that the extruded polymeric amide known as nylon, first used for parachutes and women's stockings, produced a thin tough line that was perfect for fishing (single-strand nylon is now known generically as "monofilament"). Other petrochemical materials, such as Dacron®, followed. Scientific Anglers was the first, in 1949, to coat synthetic line with a substance that caused fly line to float better and more durably than any silk.

Innovations of this decade include Du Pont's Kevlar™ and other so-called "super" lines. Amazingly strong and thin, they have changed almost all forms of fishing.

Baitcasting and Spinning Lines

Line used for these methods are either monofilament (a single strand) or braided from more than one strand of whatever material is used. These materials include:

NYLON: Monofilament, or single-strand nylon, offers all-around versatility. Its ability to stretch up to 35% is excellent for absorbing the recoil of a heavy plug or a fish's strike. It's also inexpensive and easy to knot, although knots in soft, waterlogged mono line have a tendency to loosen. There are disadvantages, though. The same ability to stretch means reduced sensitivity when a fish plays with or strikes bait. Mono's "memory," or its tendency to remain in coils (it "remembers" being coiled on a reel's spool), can adversely affect casting distance and accuracy. Moreover, any nick or knot dramatically reduces mono's strength, so the line must be constantly inspected and frequently replaced.

CO-FILAMENT: The core of co-filament is made of monofilament that is stiffer and stronger than standard mono, which is co-filament's outer layer. The result is a line with less "give" and memory and more abrasion resistance. Saltwater anglers favor co-filament for bottom-fishing.

DACRON®: Du Pont's trademark for its polyester fiber Dacron® stretches to a maximum of 10%, far less than monofilament. It absorbs less water and is less resistant to sunlight deterioration than nylon is. Many anglers favor Dacron® lines for trolling because of its high visibility and sensitivity to strikes. On the other hand, tying knots in Dacron® requires considerable care.

TERYLENE™: This polyester line approximates the characteristics of older silk lines, having buoyancy between nylon and Dacron®.

WIRE: Wire lines are primarily used for medium to deep trolling. Wire is sensitive (you'll feel every movement of your bait – and fish), strong, and abrasion-resistant. Although it has a tendency to twist, that can be overcome by using one or more swivels.

A single-strand line sinks faster than one that is multi-strand, a benefit when you're trying to get depth in a hurry, yet it is no less durable. Another variety of wire line, lead core, is made of Dacron® or nylon braided around lead wire; Gary Soucie points out that Dacron® stretches less than nylon and helps hold the line's shape when tension stretches the lead core (as it invariably does).

Of the materials of which wire line is made, stainless steel is the most popular for its strength and durability. A nickel-copper alloy marketed under the brand name Monel™ is a close second. Copper, which tends to corrode in salt water, is a better freshwater choice.

"SUPER-STRENGTH" FIBERS: A spungel polyethylene, Kevlar™ (a Du Pont trademark) is five times stronger than steel by weight. An example of its strength: Kevlar™ is used in bulletproof vests and as maritime cables to moor ships (a ¼-inch Kevlar™ rope has a strength of 6 tons). Thanks to the strength of Kevlar™ and such other similar fibers and brands as Spectra™ and IronThread™, the chance of losing a lure or a lunker due to line breakage has become virtually nonexistent. In fact, you're more likely to snap your graphite rod or straighten a hook that is snagged on a log than snap a braided super-strength line.

Among other properties of super-strength line is its smaller diameter, approximately one-third the size of nylon monofilament or Dacron®. Thinner lines create less drag, a particular useful feature when bottom-fishing where a line's "belly," or bow, detracts from the fisherman's ability to feel a strike. Despite their small size, these lines come in tests in the 30- to 130-pound range, although IronThread™ has come out with a 6-pound-test that is as thin as sewing thread.

Another plus is that super-strength lines have virtually no stretch. That allows a faster hook-set that takes less effort. Gone is the need for Herculean "jaw-breaker" hook-ups, thanks to the line's strength and less stretch (3%-5%, compared to monofilament's 20%-30% and often more). Super-strength line requires less line on your reel, since you'll be able to hook and hold a fish without its running all over the lake before you can bring it to your boat. Super-line also has no "memory" as nylon and Dacron® do, so the line gives bait better action. The line also lies limp in the water, without curling.

Why then, you might well wonder, would anyone choose such antediluvian line as nylon or Dacron® monofilament instead of this space-age braided marvel? First of all, there are times when monofilament's stretch is preferable. This stretchability allows a fish to take the bait deeper into its mouth even while you're setting the hook.

Then too, people have complained that superlines don't hold knots very well. In response, manufacturers have promoted special knots for this material, as well as a super-glue that is as strong as the line itself (you'll also need a super-sharp knife to cut the line; many standard clippers won't make a dent). Another objection is that it's relatively expensive compared to monofilament. On the other hand, it lasts longer than mono, so you won't need to replace it very frequently. Then too, you'll need less since any fish taken on super-strength line won't run all over the lake before you can haul it into your boat (some anglers use monofilament as spool-filling backing for their super-strength line).

Once you've decided on the material, you will need to decide between monofilament or braided line. Mono absorbs less water than braided line, and it produces less friction for longer casts. Because spinning lines need some stiffness so the line will "spring" off the spool, mono works better than braided line for that purpose.

However, braided line, which is limper than mono, is easier to cast off a baitcasting reel, and surf-casters tend to favor it for their revolving-spool reels. Some prefer nylon because it holds knots better than Dacron®, which, others argue, has less stretch and sinks faster and better for bottom-fishing.

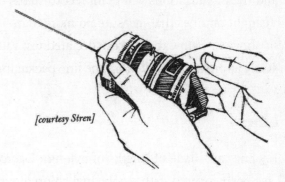

[courtesy Stren]

Filling a spin-cast/closed-face reel

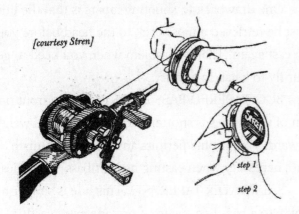

[courtesy Stren]

step 1

step 2

Filling a revolving-spool reel

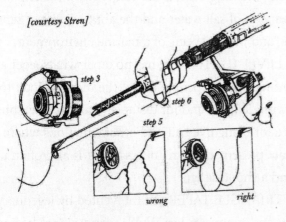

[courtesy Stren]

step 3

step 6

step 5

wrong

right

Filling a spinning reel

The thickness of a line affects castability. A heavy line will not cast well with a light bait on its end, nor will a plug or other artificial bait move with its intended action if it is towed on a line that is too heavy. By the same token, heavy bait will not stay attached very long when on light-weight monofilament line. Also, with regard to thickness, thicker lines tend to last longer, because there's more of it to resist abrasion.

Another element is the relationship between line and rod. A stiff rod needs a heavy line to perform, while a light rod needs a much finer line.

But, you may well ask, if modern super-strength "unbreakable" lines hold almost anything tied to them, why not routinely use a heavy test? The answer is that no matter what the material of which the line is made, the thinner the line, the easier it is to cast, the greater its sensitivity and the less visibility it shows to a fish. That's why experts counsel using the lightest line possible for appropriate conditions.

Moreover, to go after lake or pond fish that weigh under five pounds by using a line that tests at 10 times that weight strikes many people as the sporting equivalent of hunting squirrels with an elephant gun.

These are the reasons why, notwithstanding the availability of super-strength lines, many freshwater pond and lake bait- and spin-fisherfolk seldom venture byond the 10-pound to 12-pound-test range, with 20 pounds the maximum for pickerel and muskie anglers.

A line's test or breaking-point rating becomes an important factor for anyone who plans to go after a world-record catch. The International Game Fish Association rates and monitors manufacturers' test ratings, and the organizations will grant record status only to fish caught on lines that measure no more than 5 percent above or below the maker's declared test rating. Such IGFA approval is marked on the line packaging.

Fly Lines

Fly lines are made of lengths of nylon or Dacron® that have been covered with a polyvinyl chloride wrap. Fly lines come in a variety of types, each with its own properties for specific purposes.

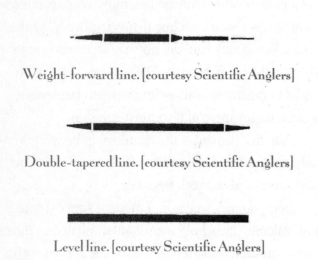

Weight-forward line. [courtesy Scientific Anglers]

Double-tapered line. [courtesy Scientific Anglers]

Level line. [courtesy Scientific Anglers]

WEIGHT-FORWARD (abbreviated WF) is the most popular line for general-purpose fly-fishing and is recommended as the easiest for novices to use. The first 30 feet are heavier than the rest of the line, which is known as the running line; the weight up front permits longer casts than those made on double-tapered lines. The thinner mid-section, however, makes roll-casting more difficult.

DOUBLE-TAPERED (DT), of which the first 10 or 12 feet are tapered, has a narrower and lighter front section than the one found on a weight-forward line. That enables a fly to be presented with greater delicacy. Making roll casts is easier too, since the heavier line behind lifts the front section off the water. Mending this type of line is also easier, again because of the heavier mid-section.

SHOOTING TAPER (ST), OR SHOOTING HEAD: This length of weighted line, usually 30 feet in length, is attached to a lighter running line by a loop. The weight allows maximum casting distance, which is especially useful when fishing in wide, fast rivers for steelheads and salmon. Line is stripped out preparatory to being cast, and to prevent it from drifting into tangles, the line is often kept in a shooting basket strapped to the angler's waist.

LEVEL LINE (see below) is typically used as running line, although monofilament is an acceptable substitute. If you choose mono, which is less expensive and sinks faster than level fly line, you'll want 20-pound test for line weight up to 7 weight, and 30-pound test above 7.

One drawback to shooting tapers is that the line must be retrieved almost back to the head before you can cast again. That's a problem when you need to get your fly to a fish in a hurry.

BUG-TAPERED/BASS LINES (BT): The front portion of these lines is shorter than in the normal weight-forward. That profile permits an additional "punch" that's necessary when casting heavier bass "bug" flies.

SALTWATER TAPER (ST): This line is similar in profile to a bass line, again to provide extra casting "punch." However, the line casing composition is more durable; the toughness is needed to resist the chemical reaction of salt water and the abrasiveness of sand, rocks, and other aspects of a marine environment.

LEVEL (L): This line has no taper whatsoever and, accordingly, many people find it the most difficult to cast with delicacy and for distance. Still, it's a reasonable choice for using live bait and other situations where a delicate presentation isn't necessary. It is also often used behind a shooting taper.

TRIANGLE TAPER (TT): Invented by legendary angler and innovator Lee Wulff, triangle taper begins with a 40-foot section tapered down toward the tip, behind which the line tapers back another 10 feet (that's what "triangle" refers to; the line's cross-section itself is round). This WF-DT hybrid thus encourages both casting for distance and with delicate presentations.

Specialty Lines

TARPON TAPER has a short front head and taper for accurate and delicate casts using a minimum of line.

Similar to bass taper lines, BONEFISH TAPER and saltwater taper also have short heads. These heads make delivering distance casts relatively difficult, but the line works better under windy conditions than a longer-casting line would.

Another classification of fly lines is in terms of buoyancy:

FLOATING (F): Floating lines, which have microscopic hollow glass "micro-balloon" beads in their coating, are essential for surface-fishing dry flies. A line that floats is easy to lift off the water surface and, therefore, to cast. In addition, it is the most versatile type of line, since it can be used in shallow water and, with the addition of a sinker or heavy fly, in deep water too.

SINKING (S): Sinking lines have tiny bits of weighted material in their coating. Used for wet flies, nymphs, and streamers, a sinking line is useful for fishing at depths and over long distances. It will keep a fly at a more or less constant depth in ways that a floating line with a sinker or weighted fly will not; the latter tends to pull the fly up with each tug or strip of the line.

FLOATING/SINKING (F/S): Better known as "sink-tip" line, its front portion (usually the first 6 feet), sinks while the rest of the line floats. Within this category of line is a range of speeds with the tip sinks:

SLOW SINKING: 1¼ to 1¾ inches per second (this and the following other rates will vary according to water conditions). Used when you want your fly to ride just below the water's surface.

FAST-SINKING: 2½ to 3 inches per second. For depths from around 5 feet and 15 feet.

EXTRA-FAST: 3½ to 4 inches per second. For depths from 15 feet to 20 feet.

Beyond these are the so-called "Super-Sinker" and "Super-Fast" types used in deep holes and in the sort of fast rivers in which salmon and steelhead are found.

INTERMEDIATE (I): This is in a sense a sinking line, but one that sinks so slowly that it tends to stay just below the surface. Many people find it useful on lakes or ponds when the wind creates a choppy surface.

Weight

The WEIGHT of a fly line is based on a standard computed in grains (not ounces) based on the weight of a line's first 30 feet (see chart below):

Fly rods are constructed to accommodate specific line weights, so your choice of rod will make selecting the proper line weight automatic. (For more on rod weights, see the section of fly rods, page 46.) Be aware, however, that most rods can handle a line weight one above or below the rod's designation; 6-weight line on a 5-weight rod will produce a bit more "punch."

You can now translate the arcane mysteries of fly line designation. A line marked "WF-5-F" translates into weight-forward, 5-weight, and floating.

Color

Whether fish respond to colors the way that other creatures do remains a subject of conjecture. Many fishermen feel that as long as a floating line rests on top of the water, color is irrelevant; fish seem to react more

Line Weight #:	1	2	3	4	5	6	7	8	9	10	11	12
Weight (in grains):	60	80	100	120	140	160	185	210	240	280	330	380

to shadows than to hues. Moreover, eye-catching colors from light pastels to bright neons are more visible to anglers, especially at dusk or during foggy conditions. However, as for sinking lines, the choice is for dark colors that act as underwater camouflage.

Backing

Unlike baitcasting and spinning line, fly line is not attached directly to the reel. A length of line called BACKING is used, and for two reasons. Backing fills up space on the reel's arbor to give the fly line a thicker base; the larger reel diameter means less rewinding is necessary to retrieve line. Backing also offers additional line, something of a safety margin in case a fish runs through all of the fly line.

Until recently, almost all backing was made of thin braided Dacron® or similar material. It ranged in test strengths from 12 pounds to 30 pounds, with 18 pounds or 20 pounds as the typical choice for most freshwater fishing. A heavier test is appropriate for saltwater game fish.

Lefty Kreh once suggested that 150 yards of backing is more than sufficient for any species of shallow-water fish. However, twice that amount and up to 400 yards is appropriate for billfish, tuna, wahoo, and large mackerel.

A new breed of backing appeared a few years ago. Made of super-strength material, it offers a thinner diameter that translates into more backing on a reel. Another benefit is greater strength than conventional backing. But, as Kreh was quick to point out in the same article, thin line (under 30-pound test) has the potential to dig into the layer of backing underneath it. The result is breakage when the line fails to unwind properly. To prepare level layers, thin super-strong backing must be wound on a reel with firm, even pressure and in smooth layers that extend from one end of the spool to the other.

Backing is attached to the reel spool by an over-hand knot and to the fly line by a nail knot. The "classic" way to measure the correct amount is a multi-stage process: (1) Wind the fly line, front end first, onto the reel; (2) join the back end of the fly line to the backing; (3) wind the backing onto the reel over the fly line until the spool is filled; (4) unwind everything (without tangling any of the line or backing); (5) tie the backing to the spool and rewind fly line-side-out.

Line Care

Nicks and chips in its outer core will not only weaken any fly line, but will diminish a floating line's buoyancy. Therefore, to practice your casting on a black-top driveway or a rocky field isn't the wisest of ideas. Neither is to cast a line that has no leader, since abrasion to the front of the line will weaken that section.

Floating line can be cleaned in warm water to which small amount of mild liquid detergent has been added. Wipe the line with a sponge, rinse in clear water, and wipe again with a clean sponge.

Liquid or liquid-soaked cloth cleaners wipe away dirt and restore a line's waterproof property. Silicon-based liquids and pastes designed to clean and polish automobile finishes work well for this purpose. Some cleaners contain Teflon™, which reduces friction against a rod's ferrules to produce longer casts.

Sound environmental practice includes disposing of used line properly. Whether an entire spoolful or just lengths, line can easily become a snare that birds and animals can't escape. Keep unwanted line with you and either incinerate it in your campfire or take it home.

An equally sound dental practice is not to bite off pieces of line after you've tied a knot. Line, and especially the new unbreakable variety, is strong enough to chip teeth. Use a clipper or a knife instead.

Leaders

A LEADER is a piece of line or wire that connects the line to the bait. Many bait and spinning fisherfolk simply dispense with leaders, preferring to tie their hooks or lures directly to the line.

That's good news for muskies, pickerel, and other species of fish whose razor-sharp teeth that can weaken or cut through even the strongest of super-strength lines. To reduce this likelihood, savvy freshwater anglers who pursue these species use leaders made of extra-heavy monofilament or wire. Which material to choose depends on the species you'll encounter and the conditions under which you'll fish. Monofilament leaders are strong, stretchy, flexible, and inexpensive. Wire, however, is essential if you're going after sharks and other heavy and tough deep-sea denizens. It is also more resistant than monofilament to sharp rocks and coral, and unlike mono, sunlight won't cause it to deteriorate. Among wire's drawbacks are the relative difficulty in handling it and the possible interference with the "natural" movement of the lure or live bait to which it is attached.

If you're going to use a wire leader, stainless steel is stronger than, and therefore preferable to, tin or brass, and a single solid strand is less obtrusive than braided (also called stranded) wire. For a more detailed analysis of types of wire leaders, see page 223 of *Hook, Line, and Sinker* by Gary Soucie.

The weight and energy of a big game fish can easily snap a line, which is why deep-sea fishermen use a SHOCK LEADER. That's a short (perhaps 2 feet long) length of monofilament that absorbs the concussive impact of a big fish's initial strike and ongoing fight.

There's a similar need in trolling to absorb the additional force produced by a fish striking against tackle on a moving boat. A MONO TROLLING LEADER may be up to 100 feet long to keep the bait or lure down deep.

RELEASE LEADERS developed in saltwater catch-and-release tournaments. They are short pieces of wire with a snap attached; the boated fish is released either by unsnapping the leader or cutting it. The procedure is based on the theory that a fish released with a hook and short length of wire in its mouth stands a far better chance of survival than one whose mouth has been mangled in an attempt to remove the hook.

In the realm of "package deal" leaders and hooks, SNELLED HOOKS have lengths of permanently-attached monofilament leaders. The theory is that the force used to set the hook when a fish strikes is absorbed along the hook shank instead of directly to where the line is tied to the hook's eye.

Other pre-tied rigs are more complicated affairs that mix hooks, leaders, spinners, snaps, and swivels in a variety of combinations. Some contain leaders that hold more than one hook, while others have metal arms that keep two or more leaders apart.

Fly Leaders

Unlike lures and live bait, flies cannot be attached directly to a fly line. Fly lines are too thick and heavy to allow a delicate casting presentation. Trout, in particular, are spooked by the splash of a line striking water, and all species react suspiciously when a fly is tied to line that to them must seem as thick as a ship's cable. The fly needs to be "distanced" from the line, and that's where leaders come into play.

The original fly leaders were lengths of braided horsehair, after which anglers used lengths of animal gut. Twentieth-century technology produced nylon, and monofilament leaders remain the material of choice.

Anatomically, a fly line leader is composed of three parts: the BUTT, or thick end, approximately 60% of the total leader length; a thinner mid-section of about 20%; and an even thinner TIPPET, to which the fly is tied, also about 20%.

Leaders come in two styles.

KNOTTED LEADERS are composed of three to eight sections of plain or braided monofilament of successively thinner diameter (the braided butt variety afford a bit of shock-absorbing "give" when a fish strikes.) An advantage is that broken or nicked sections can be accurately replaced. However, the knots that hold these sections together can become weakened with use. The knots also have a tendency to pick up weeds and other

Leader size:	0X	1X	2X	3X	4X	5X	6X	7X
Lb. Test:	15	12	10	7	5	4	2.8	1.9
Tip diameter:	.011	.010	.009	.008	.007	.006	.005	.004
Butt diameter:	.023	.023	.023	.023	.023	.023	.023	.023

debris, still another reason why not everyone uses this style.

The KNOTLESS, or plain, style of leader is a single strand of tapered monofilament. This material can stretch up to 10% or slightly more, so that too has a shock-absorbing property.

Leader thickness is expressed according to the diameter of their tippets. The calculation is based on the "RULE OF 11": the tippet size (expressed in a number followed by the letter "X") plus the tippet diameter equals .011. For example, a 6X leader's tippet measures .005 (6+.005=.011…"6" really means ".006").

The table at the top of the page indicates the dimensions and strengths of trout leaders sold under the Stren label.

Just as rod weight largely dictates line weight, the size of a fly (or nymph or streamer or bass bug) will determine the proper thickness of a leader. A fly should not only appear lifelike, but a leader must be able to "TURN OVER" properly, a phrase that means a leader's ability to go through all the phases of a cast and then settle on the water with neither too much nor too little force (a salmon-size streamer tied to a light leader will plop down, if it hasn't already snapped off during the back cast's crack-the-whip stage).

A rule of thumb helps us determine the correct leader thickness size. Known as the RULE OF THREE, it involves dividing the fly size by the number 3, with the result rounded off to the nearest leader size. For example, a size 16 dry fly would be suited to a 5X leader. However, some people still prefer to use the RULE OF FOUR, which provides a heavier leader that was preferable in the days before leaders were made of the more durable synthetic material of today.

Such rules are now made even more complicated by the advent of super-strong "fluorocarbon" leaders and tippets (purists put the word in quotes because the material is really polyvinylidene fluoride). The advantages are several, beginning with fluorocarbon's near invisibility, which spooks fewer fish. Fluorocarbon is also very resistant to abrasion and breakdown from exposure to sunlight (on the other hand, nylon and similar synthetics deteriorate from both ultraviolet light and age). And unlike nylon, which can lose up to 40% of its strength after two hours of use, fluorocarbon won't absorb water.

On the other hand, cost-conscious fishermen point out that fluorocarbon leaders are two to three times more expensive than those made of nylon.

Leaders come in lengths that range from 4 feet up to 15 feet for freshwater fishing, and even longer for saltwater (tarpon fishermen routinely use leaders that end in 100-pound-test shock tippets). For most streamside trout angling, 7½ feet and 9 feet are typical. Conditions and quarry are factors in determining the appropriate length. Fishing with a dry fly for wily trout on a large clear pond or slow-moving stream calls for a relatively long leader, to keep as great a "reality" distance as possible between line and fly. Windy conditions may call for a shorter leader, better for "punchy" casting. Shorter leaders will work well for bass and other less spooky species. They also let wet flies and nymphs go deeper. Thicker leaders can accommodate relatively heavy flies, such as bass bugs.

Leaders are attached to fly lines by knot or loop. The most frequently used knot is the nail knot. A "Chinese handcuff" loop (often in a bright eye-catching color that doubles as a strike indicator) is wormed onto the end of the line, then fastened by super-glue. A "square knot" over-and-under knot connects that loop with one on the end of the leader (some leaders are pre-looped, while others need one tied at the butt end).

These loop devices inspired an innovative interchangeable leader system, such as the one packaged by Orvis. "Mini Lead Head" attachments allow a floating line to be instantly converted into a sinking-tip line.

Changing or replacing a fly requires clipping off a piece of tippet, a process that reduces not only the leader's length but its taper. At some point the taper becomes inappropriately thick for the size fly you've been using. Replacing an entire leader is an expensive and time-consuming proposition, but there's an alternative: simply tie on a length of tippet material. That involves carrying a supply of spools in a variety of sizes. Many fly-fishing vests have a series of small pockets designed to accommodate tippet spools, or you can invest in a dispenser that has room for up to a half-dozen spools.

Leader and Tippet Care

Tippet dispensers, as well as leader wallets, prevent unwanted kinks, nicks, and tangles that weaken the monofilament material. No matter how you store or carry leaders and tippet material, monofilament should be kept out of the light, which causes the material to deteriorate, and extreme heat, which hastens that reaction even more.

Some anglers replace all their leaders and tippet material annually, although others claim they've had no untoward experiences with older material.

FLOATS, SINKERS, SPINNERS, SWIVELS, SNAPS, AND TACKLE BOXES

Floats

Floats (or bobbers, or bobs, or drifters, or strike indicators – call them what you will) are a mainstay of still fishing. The bait (usually live bait) remains suspended in the water waiting for a fish to come along. The fish strikes, the float jiggles, then disappears below the surface, and everybody knows there's a fish on the line. What could be simpler?

But fishing with a float isn't limited to the bare-foot-boys-with-cheeks-of-tan among us. Veteran anglers know that using a float is a good way to keep bait at whatever lake or pond depth at which fish are taking. Plus, having a visual cue that a fish is interested in your bait certainly helps knowing when to set the hook.

Evidence of the widespread use of floats and other strike indicators is the number of types and shapes of such devices. In addition to the most common red-and-white sphere secured to the line by a spring-operated hook is a bewildering array of shapes, sizes, and weights.

The appropriate size and shape of a float depends on the weight of the bait, water current speed, and wind conditions. For example, a fat round plastic bobber works in still ponds and lakes, but the drag that it creates may present far too much resistance for a fast-moving stream or river. That's where a long tin dart-like float made of ultra-light balsa wood would provide greater sensitivity.

As a general rule, tall and thin floats are more sensitive and offer less wind resistance. However, there is a point of diminishing returns; too sensitive a float when used with live bait will signal underwater activity whenever the minnow on your hook moves. Also, too light a float cannot accommodate a relatively heavy sinker, hook, and bait.

Sometimes, however, you will want to retard the speed of a float in a particularly fast-moving current. In that case, you would want to use a float that is weighted with lead shot.

HEAVY FLOATS also provide needed weight when you're trying to cast light bait a considerable distance, especially if you're using spinning or spin-fishing tackle.

TALL FLOATS, such as quills and barrels, are appropriate for choppy current conditions, riding high enough on the rough surface to be visible.

LONG STEMS also sink below surface drift and stay out of the wind.

Among other types of floats are DRIFT BOBBERS, submerged floats, that keep bait off the bottom.

SPINNING BUBBLES are made of clear plastic into which water can be poured to adjust the buoyancy; these are designed for casting.

So are POPPING CORKS, cigar-shaped wooden or plastic floats that make a splash or plop when cast and thus attract the more curious species of fish.

Floats are attached to lines by three methods. The above-mentioned spring hook is simple to operate, but the spring doesn't always stay tight enough to keep the line from sliding through. Other floats have an eye through which the line is threaded or a clip through which the line is slid and then slip-knotted.

SLIP FLOATS, with releasable stopper-like fasteners, make life easier in that regard: the fastener is released, the line length readjusted, and then the fastener reapplied.

Some floats attach to a line at both their top and bottom, but the more sensitive styles are fastened only at the bottom.

Floats range from several inches long and many ounces in weight to something as light and sensitive as a porcupine quill (yes, actual porcupine quills are used as floats). There's no hard-and-fast rule about appropriate size and weight for every situation; that's why carrying a selection in your tackle box is essential.

With regard to colors, floats traditionally have highly visible red tops, with brown as a good neutral color for bottom halves. Some floats add a yellow band between the red and brown. Its purpose is to indicate when a fish is biting at the bait from below; the bobber will rise, at which point you should set the hook.

High-tech has hit the float world in the form of battery-operated lighted floats that are especially useful for night fishing. One variety flashes a red light to indicate a strike; another blinks yellow until the float sinks, at which point the light becomes red.

Strike Indicators

Fly anglers have their own variety of strike indicators that they use for nymph fishing. One type is a small wooden float that threads onto the leader and is kept in place by a toothpick. Another is a small patch of synthetic fabric that sticks onto the line by means of adhesive backing. Becoming increasingly popular is a fluorescent-colored putty-like substance, a pinch of which is applied to the leader.

Or you can always tie a small length of colored yarn to your line, the way folks did in the old days.

Sinkers

Sinkers, or weights, are a staple item in all varieties of fishing where you want to get your bait down to the fish's level. Measured by weight in ounces (or fractions thereof), sinkers come in a variety of shapes. According to tackle authority Gary Soucie, the BANK SINKER should be considered the general all-around choice. The hexagonal teardrop shape produces the least amount of air resistance during a cast. It's also the steadiest in the air; other shapes wobble, which throws off attempts at accuracy. That shape also sinks faster and therefore is most able to come close to the spot where the fisherman intends it to go.

Among other popular shapes, the CLINCHER has wings at either end; the line passes through a groove along the body of the sinker and the sinker is secured in place when the wings are pinched around the line. Some of this style have rubber grips for better security. The TORPEDO is another of the fitted-or fixed-shape sinkers.

SLIP WEIGHTS, which are bullet-shaped, are an essential part of fishing with Texas- and Carolina-rigged plastic worms. The line is threaded through the hole that runs through the weight, and the worm's head fits snugly against the weight's concave base. Some slip weights have built-in rattles to attract bass and other curious species. EGG SINKERS also have holes that run through them.

CASTING SINKERS have swivel ends, while bank sinkers have eyes at one end of their teardrop shape. All these types are designed to slide along the bottom without being caught in weeds or other underwater snagging growth.

As the name implies, PYRAMID SINKERS are triangular in shape. They are intended to dig into the lake or ocean bottom and stay in one place.

BB-sized SPLIT SHOT WEIGHTS that pinch onto a line are used by both bait and fly-fishing. Fly anglers also use wraparound strips of metal, which are especially useful for getting and keeping a nymph along the bottom of a stream.

The choice of sinker shape is often determined by the bottom of the body of water. Mud, slit, sand, gravel, and other slick bottoms call for sinkers that can grip into the surface; the grapnel shape, for example, is effective under such conditions. On the other hand, uneven bottoms, such as rock piles, need a flat sinker that won't become wedged.

Trolling requires a weighted line to keep the bait or lure down deep and, equally important, to keep it stable. Such specialized trolling weights such as RUDDERS, FOLDING KEELS, and CRESCENTS reduce erratic movement in all planes.

Once upon a time, lead was the universal favorite material for sinkers. It's heavy and it's also cheap, so losing a sinker was no big deal. However, lead has fallen out of favor in some circles. Environmentalists cite numerous cases of wildfowl fatalities caused by ingesting lead shotgun pellets and lead sinkers. A movement to ban the use of lead sinkers entirely has received the support of many fishing and conservation groups, and some amount of federal legislation is expected over the next few years. Far better, conservationists say, is tin, bronze, and other nontoxic metals and alloys.

Spinners

We've encouraged spinners as an integral part of spinnerbait lures, but they can also be used on their own. Many fishermen attach a spinner to a simple hook rig as an attractor, either for bottom-fishing or trolling. If you do, remember as you select the blade shape that long thin blades tend to spin faster than short wide ones. Larger blades, which offer more resistance, sink more slowly than small blades, and they also turn more slowly.

Most spinners have built-in swivels. If not, you'll have to attach one yourself.

A single-blade spinner attached to a deer-hair plug.

A double-bladed spinner attached to a wet fly.

Swivels

Swivels, which prevent lines from becoming twisted, are widely used by live-bait fishermen. They are less frequently used with freshwater plugs, however, since a swivel can affect – and even negate – the action of some crankbait. On the other hand, surf-casters regularly use swivels and snaps with their plugs, since swivels are essential for shock leaders.

Swivels are also routinely used in trolling and drift-fishing, since line that is constantly being pulled through the water has a tendency to spiral. THREE-WAY and CROSSLINE SWIVELS have been designed for such use.

Swivels that include ball bearings, which reduce friction, are more efficient than those that have a sliding friction mechanism. BEAD CHAIN SWIVELS have the advantage of several rotating elements, so if one bead link jams, there are others that will still work.

There are two basic ways to attach a swivel. The one that has rings on both ends requires tying the line and/or leader twice (that is, once on each end). The other style of swivel has a ring on the top but a snap on the bottom; the snap facilitates changing leaders or hooks, a useful feature when you're in a rush to get your line back in the water.

Whichever you choose, buy the sturdiest you can find. Brass is the material of choice because of its strength, but just because a swivel is made of brass don't necessarily mean it's well machined. Cheaply made snaps tend to bend or snap when under pressure, and many an angler has regretted being penny-foolish after losing a good-size fish to a cheap swivel.

For the last word on swivels, including a discussion of how torque affects terminal tackle, see page 130 of *Hook, Line, and Sinker* by Gary Soucie.

Snaps

Snaps are a convenient way to change hooks and lures. They come in a variety of styles and sizes. The LOCK SNAP is most popular, primarily because its hole in the clasp case secures the ends of the snaps. Another favored style is the strong and lightweight ONE-PIECE, or DUO-LOCK. A favorite of saltwater anglers is the COASTLINE; its loop grows tighter under stress, but doesn't open. Other styles are the AMPERSAND, the BUTTERFLY, and the CONNECTING-LINKS.

Proper size will depend on thickness of line and/or leader and the size and weight of hook or lure. As a rule, use as small a snap as your tackle can accommodate; snaps that are too large tend to distract fish from the bait.

And as for strength and durability, steel is preferable to brass.

Tackle Boxes

The first tackle boxes were metal rectangular containers of the "toolbox" variety with one removable compartment tray. Most were secured by two or more hinged snaps on the front and by a built-in lock opened with a tiny key.

Boxes now come in many styles, most of which bear slight resemblance to the original:

TRUNK: several tiers of unfolding, stackable trays.

FLAT BOX: side compartments with transparent lids.

DRAWER BOX: up to four sliding compartments below a top compartment under the lid. One or more drawers may be designed to accommodate spinnerbaits.

HIP-ROOF: two facing tiers of up to three drawers that unfold away from each other when the box is opened. Additional items can be stored on the box's bottom compartment.

HANGING RACKS: deep boxes in which plugs and spoons hang on removable racks to prevent tangling and permit rapid drying. Most of these boxes have compartments for spare spinnerbait and buzzbait blades and skirts.

TACKLE TOTES: sturdy fabric tote bags with outside compartments and internal pockets and pouches. These spaces accommodate lures, scent bottles, reels, rain gear, and other essentials. Some totes have built-in vinyl pockets for storing plastic worms and other soft bait. Otherwise, separate vinyl binders and bags are available.

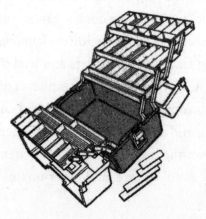

Trunk style. [courtesy Plano]

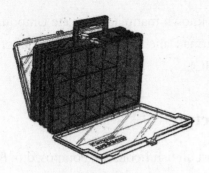

Flat-box style. [courtesy Plano]

Drawer-box style. [courtesy Flambeau]

Hip-roof style. [courtesy Woodstream]

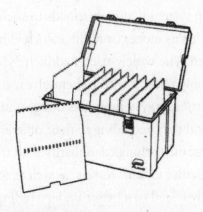

Hanging-rack style. [courtesy Plano]

Metal tackle boxes are now almost impossible to find; rugged, lightweight, and rustproof plastic has become the material of choice. Adjustable dividers make "customizing" shelves and drawers to accommodate individual items an easy matter. Boxes with flip-open tops allow reaching for frequently used items without the need to wade through other gear.

Before You Buy

How commodious a tackle box do you need? It depends on the amount of tackle you plan to carry. There are two approaches regarding tackle box sizes. One goes on the theory that "you never need it till you need it"; a box that can hold everything you might possibly need is worth the expense and the effort, since items left at home aren't very useful. The other approach is a variant of Parkinson's Law and states that "stuff expands to fill available space." Professional tournament fishermen carry large tackle boxes because their bait requirements are based on their knowledge of how to cope with very specific conditions. The rest of us don't have that kind of expertise, so it's far more sensible to carry only those lures, bobbers, etc., that you think you'll need.

The above debate becomes somewhat academic if you always fish from a boat that has lots of storage compartment space. However, if you're sharing a small boat with another angler or more, common courtesy dictates that you don't hog the storage space. The solution may be to own more than one tackle box of different sizes and use them according to particular situations and conditions.

Soft plastic worms, grubs, and similar bait are made of materials that can eat through certain plastics. If a tackle box isn't designated as "plastic worm-proof," you'll have to store such items in smaller boxes or bags inside the tackle box.

Smaller bags and boxes are also of great help in organizing a tackle box's contents. Hooks, jig heads, sinkers, small bobbers. . . . all can live in plastic containers. Some boxes have adjustable compartments.

Sturdy handles and latches are tackle box essentials. Imagine the feeling of seeing your box fly open and its contents spill all over the ground or, worse yet, into the water. Some fishermen take the additional precaution of snapping an elastic cord or cable around the box's girth just to make sure such accidents won't happen.

HOOKS

Found among the artifacts of northern European cultures, the oldest fish hooks were fashioned from acutely-angled twigs or, for greater durability, harder wood, the bones of animals, and the beaks and claws of birds. Whatever material these early hook-makers selected, they honed the end into a sharp point, often with a barb to prevent the fish from disgorging the hook (although some hooks were designed to ride perpendicular to the line and thus catch in a fish's throat). Some hooks had holes through which a line could be threaded and tied, while other required knotting the line around the hook's shank, similar to the way hooks are now snelled. As civilization's "ages of metal" developed, hooks were made of bronze and then iron.

The modern era of hook-making started in seventeenth-century England, where manufacturers of sewing needles diversified into producing steel hooks. The Great Fire that leveled much of London in 1664 dispersed many of that city's industries; needle-making was one, and its practitioners relocated to the Worcestershire town of Redditch. Until the beginning of the nineteenth century, virtually all hooks came from that town, of which the venerable firm of Partridge of Redditch remains a notable inhabitant (as they have been since the firm's beginning, all Partridge hooks are handmade).

As sport-fishing grew in popularity, other companies in other countries met the demand. O. Mustad, of Oslo, Norway, now the world's largest manufacturer, opened its doors in 1832, and the French firm of Veillard Migeon et Cie (abbreviated to VMC) started in 1910. Some 20 years later, the Denver-based Wright & McGill turned out its first Eagle Claw hooks. Among other well-known manufacturers are Umpqua and the Japanese firms Daiichi and Tiemco (the latter abbreviated to TMC).

Manufacture

Almost all fish hooks are composed of 80 percent or more carbon steel. The machine-made manufacturing process begins with malleable steel wire cut into pieces that are twice as long as the length of metal needed to make the hook. Both ends of the piece are sharpened by either mechanical or chemical means into points. The piece is cut in half, which results in two hooks. A barb is formed on the sharpened end and an eye on the other end, and then the wire is twisted into the desired hook shape.

The steel is cold-forged tempered for strength and durability. After this hardening process, the hooks are scoured to remove the oxide scale coating. One process, called chemical deburring or bright dipping, removes the outer layer of steel and so eliminates burrs and other rough spots for a smoother, sharper hook. A layer of lacquer or another finish comes next; bronze or blue-black color known as "japanned" are common. The process ends with a visual inspection and packaging.

Hook Sizes

A hook's size is based on its GAP, or the distance from the point to the shank measured perpendicular to the shank. However, anyone expecting to find a universal sizing system that corresponds to such absolute measurements as inches or millimeters will be sadly disappointed. The widely-used Redditch System and others are only relative within themselves, and even within a particular system, hooks designated as the same size will vary according to their different shape. As with most other things, familiarity with the products of particular manufacturers, as well as with hooks in general, will lead to a better understanding of this seemingly complicated subject.

As the size-number of a hook increases its actual size grows smaller, so that a 20 hook is smaller than a 10 hook. Not precisely half as small, but simply smaller, just as it is larger than, for example, a 24. Fly hooks are measured by even numbers (28 is the smallest), whereas hooks used for other types of fishing are numbered consecutively.

There are hooks larger than 1s, and they are designated by a number followed by a slash and a "0" (pronounced "aught"). These hooks grow in size as do their numbers, so a 4/0 is larger than a 3/0…here you will note that numbers above 1/0 run consecutively.

Hook Weight

Wire diameter or weight is expressed by a scale based on the letter "X" and the words "Fine" and "Stout," the latter describing the hook wire's relative thickness. The scale ranges from 1X to 3X. Fine wire, such as that used for dry flies, is easier to set in a fish's mouth, as well as better for keeping live bait alive. Stout hooks tend to be sturdier.

Eye Shape

The most common shape is the BALL EYE, a simple round circle. A TAPERED EYE, which grows narrow at its end, somewhat reduces the weight of a hook. Both the ball eye and the tapered eye often have gaps between the end of the eye and the shank, which some anglers feel increases the chance of fraying the line or leader.

To prevent this possibility, a LOOPED EYE is formed by the hook's wire bent into an eye and then doubling back along the shank; hooks for salmon and steelhead flies customarily are made this way.

A NEEDLE EYE, an elongated hole like the ones on sewing needles, makes it easy to push bait to cover the entire hook or beyond.

A FLATTENED EYE may have a small hole or even none at all. If there is no hole, the line or a leader will

be attached by means of a snell knot, which many people feel is less likely to fray and eventually break. Some hooks come with pre-attached leaders; a line of Wright & McGill "Eagle Claw" hooks is a classic example.

Finally, a BRAZED EYE is one that is coated with brass for additional strength.

Because the size of an eye is proportional to the size of the hook, threading line or leaders onto smaller

A snelled hook. [courtesy Eagle Claw]

hooks becomes a difficult chore for people with poor eyesight. However, Orvis has come to the rescue with its line of "Big Eye" hooks for sizes 16 and smaller.

Eye Position

There are three positions of an eye relative to the shank: RINGED, or parallel to the shank; TURNED-UP, and TURNED-DOWN.

The turned-up eye, which is used for traditional British trout, as well as salmon and steelhead flies, permits a relatively quick, rake-like penetration when a fish strikes.

On the other hand, a turned-down eye puts the hook closer to the line of penetration and is accordingly, more widely used, although some anglers feel that the turned-down eye of hooks size 22 or smaller interfere with the tiny gaps.

Shank Types and Length

The STRAIGHT SHANK runs in a direct line from the eye to beginning of bend.

The HUMPED SHANK has one or more humps that prevent a lure body from rotating.

Similarly, a BARBED SHANK has serrated projections that hold baits such as plastic worms more securely on the hook.

A STEP SHANK, or KEEL HOOK, is weighted so the hook rides upright to help avoid snagging on weeds.

Like the turned-down eye, a CURVED-DOWN SHANK is designed to bring the line of pull closer to the penetration point, while a CURVED-UP SHANK allows a faster, though shallower, penetration. Within these two categories are curves of a variety of angles, as the illustrations show.

If there is no other specific designation, a shank is considered standard length. Otherwise, there will be an "X" preceded by a number and followed by the words "Long" or "Short" (some types have names, such as the Carlisle, a long-shanked variety). That translates as follows; a "1X Long" has the shank length of the next larger hook size (a 12 would have the shank length of a 10), but would still have the gap width of a 12. By the same token, a 12 in "2X Long" would have the length of an 8, while a 12 in "2X Short" is as long as a 16.

8X Long is the longest size commonly available, and 5X Short the smallest.

The Carlisle [courtesy Mustad]

The Bend

The ROUND BEND, considered the "classic" shape, is a simple semi-circle that extends from the end of the shank to the point.

The SPROAT has a more elongated but uniformly rounded curve, while the LIMERICK and the O'SHAUGHNESSY have the sharpest angles of the bend directly behind their points.

The ABERDEEN has a round bend and a wide gap.

Points Types and Positions

Although the SPEAR POINT, the most common, varies in precise shape from manufacturer to manu-

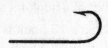

The Aberdeen. [courtesy Mustad]

The O'Shaughnessy. [courtesy Mustad]

The Sproat. [courtesy Mustad]

facturer, its point and barb resemble the flat edge of a spear head.

The NEEDLE POINT is ground on all sides for maximum "bite."

Despite its name, the HOLLOW POINT is solid, but is tapered into slightly concave sides for rapid penetration.

The KNIFE-EDGE POINT has a flat and wide surface, especially useful for big-game fishing.

The BARBLESS POINT has become particularly popular among catch-and-release anglers, who claim that the lack of a barb enhances penetration, despite the chance that a fish may be able to shake the hook more easily if it has no barb.

There are four point positions relative to the rest of the hook. The STRAIGHT POINT runs parallel to the shank. The ROLL POINT has only the point bent up toward the shank. In the BENT-IN POINT, a greater portion of the end of the hook loops out and then bends in, making disgorging the hook more difficult. Conversely, the KIRBY (named after a noted hookmaker and contemporary of Izaak Walton) or BENT-OUT POINT exposes the tip of the hook for faster penetration.

Although offset hooks may make deeper strikes in most species, they are more difficult to set in hard-mouthed fish and are more likely to bend when a big fish puts up a big fight. They also rotate while being trolled. Similarly, sharp angles in a hook's bend tend to weaken the hook, while perfectly round bends tend to open under stress.

Others

WEEDLESS HOOKS contain thin strands of metal or rugged filament that run from or just behind

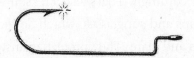

An offset worm hook. [courtesy Heddon/PRADCO]

the eye to above the point; when they work, and they don't always, the strand keeps the hook from becoming entangled. BAIT-HOLDING HOOKS are designed to hold live or artificial bait such as plastic worms. Some models have small projections that extend below the eye and provide an extra "finger" to grip the bait. Others have barbed shanks that do the same job, or spiral wiring along the shank that works well with dough balls and other soft bait.

DOUBLE or TREBLE HOOKS are clusters most often found on baitcasting lures and spoons. Although some people feel that multiple hooks just as easily snag a fish as hook one (and are therefore somehow less sporting), as Gary Soucie points out, they're widely used on plugs because they catch fish. That's also why they're routinely used by salt-water ice-fishermen. You should be aware, however, that doubles and trebles more easily catch weeds and other underwater obstructions, and they're harder to remove from a fish if your goal is catch-and-release.

Diametrically opposed to treble hooks is the PARTRIDGE TAG (for "Touch And Go") hook. Instead of a point it has a second eye, so that no fish is ever hooked. Just having a fish attracted to the bait – usually a fly – is satisfaction enough for the hook's users.

Salmon. [courtesy Mustad]

To Barb or Not to Barb

Some fishermen routinely remove the barbs from the hooks they use, while others buy only barbless hooks in the first place. Their reasoning: in addition to

Giant tuna. [courtesy Mustad]

Shark hook. [courtesy Mustad]

feeling that barbless hooks penetrate more easily, they contend that barbs tear larger holes in a fish's mouth than necessary. Fishermen who practice catch-and-release want to do as little as possible to jeopardize a fish's chance of returning safe and sound to the water. Losing an occasional fish that spits out or slips off a barbless hook, such people would argue, matters less than the fish's ultimate welfare.

On the other hand, there are those anglers who say a barbless hook is likely to slip out of the mouth of a fighting fish, only to be engaged again before the fish can completely eject the hook. A prolonged struggle can therefore result in several punctures, a recurrence that can be avoided by using a barbed hook that catches and holds only once. Moreover, expert anglers know how to remove a barb without causing damage by tearing away flesh.

The answer: If you plan to release a fish and don't think you're sufficiently skillful in removing barbed hooks, better fish barbless. Otherwise, the choice is yours.

Hook Care

How sharp should a hook be? A good indication of a sharp hook is one that will dig into the flesh of your finger or hand as you lightly drag it across. Another less hazardous test is to run its point across your thumbnail. Use as little pressure as possible, and if the point makes a scratch in your nail, the hook is sharp enough. If not, and even new hooks sometimes lose their razor-sharp edge during packaging and shipping, use a file to touch up the point. Carborundum files specifically designed for the purpose are available at tackle shops and through catalogs. Alternatives include carborundum or steel fingernail files, automobile ignition-point files, and even, for tiny hooks, the abrasive striking surface of a new matchbook cover.

Hooks used in saltwater fishing, particularly for species that have tough gristly mouths, need to be especially well honed. Fisherfolk after these species routinely sharpen their hooks, usually into a single triangle or a double-triangle "diamond" point. Electric hook sharpeners facilitate this process, and the devices are growing popular among freshwater bait anglers. Those people who use one need to be aware that heat from an overheated motor can weaken a hook's tempered strength.

Storing hooks can be as uncomplicated as keeping them in their original packaging, especially if they came in plastic boxes. Otherwise, they can be jabbed into a piece of cork or kept in special holders, although some people prefer airtight containers that retard rusting. Spring-tension racks for snelled hooks keep the leaders from becoming tangled, while form-fitting plastic covers prevent double and treble hooks on plugs and spoons from snagging other pieces of tackle.

Wherever you keep your hooks, don't forget before putting them away to rinse those that have been in salt water with freshwater, then dry thoroughly.

Hook Safety

No matter how careful you think you are, at some point in your fishing career you're going to be hooked. One day you may reach into your tackle box and yank out your hand, the victim of a bare hook ambush. Or you'll lose your grip as you're attaching a fly to your line, and its hook will become embedded in a finger. A fishing buddy may catch you in his back cast, or a sudden breeze can toss your cast back into your face.

Moral: fish hooks can be dangerous, so always treat them accordingly. That's also a reason why fishermen wear caps and sunglasses, which do more than keep off rays and glare. They protect against hooks, so please dress accordingly.

CLOTHING

Footwear

Many anglers, especially those who fish from a boat, favor athletic shoes of the jogging/sneaker type. Comfortable and relatively lightweight, they provide traction even when the boat's deck or its bottom is wet.

Shoes and boots of the style that's become generically known as "Bean boots" (after its innovator, the eponymous L.L. Bean) have waterproof rubber bottoms and leather uppers. They're especially good for walking along shorelines or over rugged terrain. A steel shank makes them durable, while molded heels and soft rubber or gum soles increase their comfort.

Knee-high "Wellie" style boots, with neoprene uppers and rubber lowers, also have a big following among anglers, especially those who walk along muddy shorelines. Those made by Muck and LaCrosse are especially popular.

Socks

Since few things are more uncomfortable than spending a day with cold and/or clammy or completely wet feet, the choice of socks is important. Polypropyl-

ene and silk both wick moisture away from the skin, which makes either fabric an excellent choice for a liner to be worn under cotton, wool, acrylic, or wool/acrylic socks, depending on the degree of warmth you seek.

Waders

Not all fishing requires working your way into position to meet the fish halfway. There are even anglers who wade but don't need special clothing, such as the bonefishermen who wear short pants or swimsuits while they work warm-water flats. But for those who challenge chilly streams and colder rivers and coastal surf, waders are essential for warmth and safety.

Waders come in two types. The one you'll need depends entirely on the type of water that you fish. Hip waders (also called "hippers") are designed for water that comes up no higher than pelvis-deep. Chest

waders are appropriate for deeper water. Although chest-highs can be rolled down to hip height when the weather and water level permit, many anglers don't like the excess material, and so owning both hippers and chest-highs makes some sense.

Within these types are two categories. The boot-foot wader contains an attached rubber boot. Its advantage is convenience, since you won't spend time lacing and unlacing wading shoes. But the boots tend to be heavy and bulky, qualities that give much-needed warmth and stability while surfcasting in the ocean. They also offer less ankle and heel support than separate wading shoes and boots do. That's less of a problem on smooth, relatively level surfaces (such as, again, when surf-fishing on sandy-bottom stretches of coastline) than when coping with the uncertain footing of a rocky-bottomed mountain trout stream or a rushing salmon river or a rocky surf.

That's a compelling argument for wading shoes, the kind worn with stocking-foot waders. They are made of synthetic uppers and felt soles. (In recent years, due to the spread of invasive species such as didymo, an algae-like substance that grows on stream bottoms and effectively kills off all other plant life, and hence, insect life, some companies such as Simms and Orvis have been offering boots with no felt [which can carry invasive species] and instead a sticky rubber type substance.) Some soles come with attached metal studs for easier and safer walking on muddy bottoms, although many angler prefer plain felt soles for rocky stream bottoms. The best wading shoes have a padded collar at the back, a sturdy tongue, solid eyelets, and a thick and sturdy sole. Although lacing shoes takes somewhat longer than slipping into their boot-foot cousins, that chore becomes somewhat easier for shoes with "speed lace" eyelets or bindings made of Velcro® strips.

The first waders were made of rubber. Some still are, and these are the type that some surf-fishermen continue to use. Lighter-weight nylon and other synthetics came next, and they remain the most durable (in the sense of tear-resistant) material. Multi-layered designs using waterproof and abrasion- and crack-resistant fabrics keep the wearer warm as well as dry; waders that retain body heat are a big plus on cold days and/or in frigid waters. Accordingly, and depending on the climate in which they fish, many anglers choose multi-ply materials that come in up to four layers. Among the strongest and most comfortable are a four-layer system composed (starting with the layer closest to the body) of a nylon liner, a closed-cell polyurethane foam, an insulator felt, and an insulating aluminum film covered by a waterproof polyurethane coating.

Stretch fabrics like neoprene revolutionized waders. Neoprene hugs the wearer's body and thus reduces the chance of water entering and collecting. Moreover, this form-fitting style traps and retains the wearer's body heat. And when temperatures rise to the point that insulation isn't welcome (and where water level permits), neoprene chest waders can be rolled down and worn waist-high.

Gore-Tex® is a fabric that is highly regarded for its "breathability"; it is composed of layers of billions of holes that are too small for drops of water to pass through, but large enough for human perspiration to escape. Despite the tiny holes, the fabric gets high marks for durability.

Why then choose a wader made of anything other than a stretch fabric? Cost is one factor; nylon and rubber are less expensive. Weight is another reason: single layers of nylon are far lighter and cooler for summer use, and they're equally durable in situations where there's little chance of snagging or otherwise puncturing the material.

The sizing of boot-foot chest waders is based on a combination of shoe size and inseam length, with the inseam measured from crotch to floor. (Some manufacturers also provide chest size and height and weight ranges for additional reference.) Inseams usually have a 4-inch range; for example, 30 inches to 34 inches for a size 8 foot. Stocking-foot sizes offer a slightly larger

range of inseam; in one instance, a wader that accommodates sizes 9 to 11 shoes has an inseam range of 30 inches to 36 inches.

However, since people come in all sizes and shapes and combinations of sizes and shapes, not everyone with a size 8 foot can comfortably wear an inseam in the indicated range, even when stretchy fabrics are involved. A comfortable fit is essential for ease of casting and lack of chafing. However, don't despair if you don't find your perfect fit on your first try. Different manufacturers make their waders in different shapes, so keep shopping around. Trying on waders before you buy a pair is always a good idea, but if that's not possible, dealing with a mail-order firm that has a good exchange policy is the next best course.

Many serious anglers have their waders custom-made. You send in your measurements, and the manufacturer tailors the garment accordingly. Custom-made waders are not inexpensive, but one devotee suggested that prorating the additional cost over four or five years of wear makes the expense less painful.

As for "extras," built-in knee-pads add comfort and durability, while hand-warmer front pockets are useful in cold weather. And far more than something in the "extra" department, women anglers have been pleased to learn that a number of manufacturers now offer waders specifically designed to fit the female form.

Certain accessories make wading easier and safer. Socks made of neoprene or another synthetic are worn over the foot of a stocking-foot wader; the sock's top folds gaiter-like over the boot-top to keep gravel and other debris out of the shoe.

Any chest wader that isn't form-fitting requires a wading belt. The belt straps tightly around the wearer's chest to keep out the water in case of a dunking, a serious matter because drownings have resulted from water-filled waders. A quick-release buckle is also of inestimable value in the unhappy event you need to get out of your waders in a hurry to swim for your life.

Unless your chest waders come with their own suspenders, you'll need a pair. Snaps are somewhat easier to attach but less secure than buckles or buttons-and-buttonholes.

Inflatable suspenders are activated by CO_2 cartridges and sinking. Also in the safety vein, cleats that strap onto wader boots or shoes (think of chains on auto tires) give considerably more traction than studded soles do. The most widely used brand is "Corkers," which has become something of a generic name for the item.

While not exactly part of your wardrobe, a wading staff can save your day (if not your life) in the event you need to cross difficult water. The wood or metal one-piece types are strong but can be unwieldy when not being used. The folding variety has the advantage of being able to be worn on your belt when not in use.

What to wear under waders depends on the climate and how much you want to avoid the clammy clutches of evaporating perspiration. Polypropylene or silk socks and underwear wick moisture away to your next layer of clothing, usually a second pair of wool or cotton socks. Polar fleece wading pants don't ride up under waders, thanks to their elastic foot stirrups. Otherwise, most fishermen find that sweats, long johns, or jeans work perfectly well.

Wader Care

The best way to prolong the life of waders, no matter what the material, is to keep them high and dry. Waders that are tossed in a corner are prone to suffer scrapes and other abrasions and punctures. Any residual moisture invites mildew and other unwelcome flora and fauna. Boot and wader hangers are specifically designed for storage and drying.

No matter how tight the fit, some amount of water will seep into wading shoes. Most people don't mind putting on wet shoes, since the wader's stocking foot comes between feet and the shoe itself. If, however, dry shoes are an imperative, a circulating-heat boot drier will speed things up considerably.

Despite the best care, holes will happen at some point in a wader's life. Punctures in rubber waders can be patched, and those in nylon waders can be taped with industrial-strength self-adhesive tape. Although neoprene has a tendency to self-seal small punctures, special cements are available, often as part of repair kits that include detailed instructions. Soles wear out faster than the rest of wading shoes do, and replacement kits give shoe bottoms a new lease on life.

Transporting waders is easier with a wader pack. Its mesh sides or top expedite drying, and the carpet pad that's part of most packs is a blessing to bare feet when changing in and out of shoes in the middle of the great outdoors (that is, a carpet of pine needles isn't such a blessing).

Pants

Many fishermen wear plain ol' jeans or cargo pants with pockets for such gear as pliers and knives. Rear pockets are secured by Velcro® flaps, a useful feature to keep possessions out of Davy Jones' locker.

Short pants are appropriate for fishing the flats along the Florida Keys and other warm places. Quick-drying and cotton-soft Supplex® has become the material of choice for shorts and for long- and short-sleeved shirts. However, since Supplex® tends to trap perspiration, some garments are treated in a process known as Intera, which draws moisture along the cloth's surface to increase the rate of evaporation.

For those days that you can't decide between long pants and shorts, you might try "zip-off" pants: zippers that run around the trouser legs at mid-thigh instantly convert the garment into shorts.

Shirts

The most essential consideration for any fishing shirt is that it not restrict movement. That's why they are cut to be generously roomy, especially around the armholes.

Shirts should also have collars that can be turned up to protect against the wind and the sun's rays. Some anglers favor button-down collars, which won't flap in the breeze but can always be unbuttoned and turned up.

Sun rays that are reflected off water produce particularly nasty burns. Long-sleeved shirts, which offer protection for your entire arm, are traditional. Button-tabs on some models secure the sleeves when you want to roll them up.

All types of fishing require lots of items that you'll want easy access to. That's why fishing shirts are made with a plethora of pockets (even if you wear a vest, you'll never complain about having too many pockets).

Vests

Before there were fishing vests, anglers carried their gear in their pockets or in small bags worn over their shoulders. Then the legendary Lee Wulff had a better idea, and the fishing vest was born.

The fishing vest – and because Wulff was best known as a fly-fishing guru, we'll begin with the fly-fishing vest – is marked by pockets. Big pockets, little pockets, pockets on the outside and inside, and even on the back. That's to accommodate the myriad items to which a fly-fisher needs ready access. And that's "ready" as in "immediate," not "Wait a minute until I wade to shore, fumble through my bag, and then wade back."

The number of pockets varies from vest to vest, ranging from 8 up to 30 or more. Some pockets are closed by rustproof metal or plastic zippers, others by flaps secured by Velcro®, while still others have no flaps or fastenings at all.

How many pockets you require on your vest depends primarily on how much gear you plan to carry. Most novices (and many experts) need no more than 10 or 12 pockets to accommodate all their gear; one or two large expandable ones for fly boxes; a couple of oth-

ers for floatants and desiccants; others for leaders and tippet material (some vests have small inner pockets for individual tippet spools); and the rest for strike indicators, leader sink-gink, sunglasses, and fishing license. That doesn't include items that are carried on the vest itself by means of retractable wire "zingers" (usually, line nipper and hook-removing hemostat pliers, to name just two), as well as a landing net hanging down the back.

Other features can include one or more D-rings for attaching such items as a wading staff; a fleece patch for drying flies; Velcro® rod-holding tabs; buckle straps for carrying traveling rods in their tubes; and hand-warmer pockets on the front of the vest.

Vests come in varying lengths. Those that extend below the wearer's waist have room for the most pockets, but if you're going to wade in deep water, you may want to sacrifice space for one of the so-called "shortie" models.

The best-designed vests have deep armholes that permit unrestricted casting. Because a fully-laden vest will carry several pounds of gear, a bias-cut, non-binding collar will distribute pressure evenly against the wearer's neck. Some vests have padded collars for just that purpose.

As for material, cotton or a cotton blend is most common, with such synthetics as Supplex® providing even greater durability. Many anglers favor mesh for greater coolness and less weight, but you should be

A "shortie" vest. [courtesy Orvis]

advised that objects tend to become snagged in mesh faster than in solid cloth.

Since a bright-colored vest will alert fish to the wearer's presence, solid and somber hues like tan, olive green, gray, or camouflage are most popular and the most readily available. Even within that spectrum, green or tan is appropriate for anglers who fish where there's lots of background foliage. By the same token, gray or slate blue will reduce the visual effect of standing out against open sky.

If there's any question about size, opt in favor of roominess. Fishing in cold weather means that you'll wear your vest over a sweater or a jacket (or both), while roomy vests allow air to circulate on warm days whatever the season. Another argument for roominess in cotton vests is that cotton is likely to shrink after a number of dunkings-and-dryings.

Since just about everyone welcomes pockets, other anglers besides the fly-fishing variety wear vests. Those designed for baitcasting and spinning fans who spend a fair amount of time in boats often include flotation safety features, either built-in "life preserver" foam or an apparatus for inflation. The latter can either be the automatic inflating variety by which CO_2 cartridges are automatically activated, or the manually inflating type where the wearer blows into a valve (some automatics have this backup capability). Whistles attached to vests come in handy when there's a need to signal for help.

Fishermen who don't like the idea of vests, but do like their safety features, might consider separate flotation suspenders.

Alternatives to Vests

Harking back to the pre-Wulff era, gear bags are making a comeback (actually, they never left), especially those that can be worn around the waist.

Other choices include the chest fly box, the fishing belt with its large main compartment and five smaller ones, and chest or shoulder packs made by the likes of Fishpond and William Joseph.

Jackets

Among the styles of nylon-acrylic wind- and water-resistant jackets are those with built-in sweatshirt linings and hoods. At the top of the line is a bomber-style jacket with flotation foam. Another top-of-the-line fishing jacket was recently introduced by Columbia. With micro heating wires throughout, you simply plug it in with an ISB cord, let the coat charge, and then you have the option of having high or low heat for the day.

Fly-fishermen tend to favor fleece pullovers made of nonabsorbent, quick-drying, and breathable Polartec or Polarfleece.

Rain Gear

Since precipitation is capable of insinuating itself almost anywhere, the most effective foul-weather gear makes every effort to keep the wearer hermetically sealed against moisture. That includes such features as covered seams, elasticized or Velcro® cuffs, collar-flap tabs, and covered pockets.

With regard to fabric, synthetics have pretty much taken over where oilskin and rubber once reigned. Hypalon™ laminate is one popular fabric. So is a nylon/Supplex® combination with a Zepel™ anti-moisture repellent surface.

Gore-Tex® is as "breathable" for rainwear as it is for waders; the fabric repels rain but allows perspiration to escape.

Our British cousins, who are no strangers to rising damp, discovered that cotton impregnated with paraffin wax repels moisture in a major way. Wax jackets, originated by Barbour but now manufactured by several other companies, is particularly popular among the sporting set. Waxed cotton is not quite as waterproof as synthetics are, but the process does the job (and has a certain British field sports cachet for those who care about such matters). The paraffin wears off, so the garments must be periodically re-waxed, an odorous chore best done in a well-ventilated area.

Wading jackets for fly-fishing are waterproof (not just water-resistant), with large chest pockets and often a hood and a drawstring waist to keep out the elements. Many are light enough to be folded and carried in a vest's pouch pocket.

Headgear

Hats are essential, no matter what the climate or time of year. Hats retain body heat during cold weather, and they help prevent sunburn when the sun shines. Equally important, headgear protects against wayward flying fishhooks whatever the weather.

The choice of fishing headgear is as varied as the imagination of those who wear them. To those of you to whom image is everything, you can top off your individual "look" in any number of ways: floppy hats with cords that tie under the chin or caps with long bills in front and back (to keep the sun off your neck as well as your face) for the explorer/adventurer look; ten-gallon Western hats for the Rocky Mountain fly-fisher look; "Sherlock Holmes" deerstalker caps and tweed cloth caps for the English chalk-stream or Scottish or Irish salmon-river look; baseball-style "gimme" caps with or without logos or funny sayings for whatever

look they're meant to convey…the choice is yours. But please remember to wear a hat.

One hat that's growing in popularity among anglers is "The Tilley Hat," a canvas number that features a cord that runs over the crown and ties securely under the wearer's chin. A layer of closed-cell polyethylene in its crown enables the hat to float under most conditions should it part company from the wearer's head.

Gloves

Ray Scott, founder of the Bass Anglers Sportsman Society (familiarly known as B.A.S.S.) devised a glove he calls "The Udder Hand." Its latex rubber fingers and thumb give a good grip on slippery fish. The glove also provides protection against hooks and fish teeth. When not in use, it adheres to your belt by a Velcro® holder (available through Bass Pro Shop).

For ice-fishing or any other cold-weather angling, the neoprene Glacier Glove® has a curved-finger design that the manufacturer says provides comfort and flexibility. When the thermometer dips even lower, polypropylene liners can be worn underneath.

Fly-fishermen prefer finger-less wool or acrylic gloves. This style doesn't restrict dexterity or sensitivity (e.g., when stripping line) while keeping the rest of your hand warm.

Sunglasses

You may not consider sunglasses as clothing, but covering your eyes is just as essential to your comfort and safety as covering the rest of your body.

Water reflects ultraviolet radiation (UVR), particularly the more damaging portion of the light-wave spectrum designated as "UV-B." Exposure can cause an inflammatory reaction to the cornea and of the conjunctiva, the tissue that covers the inner eyelid and eyeball. The effect feels as though there's a foreign body in your eye, and occasionally great pain and spasm of the eyelid. Some ophthalmologists believe that prolonged exposure to UV-B results in cataract formation in the lens. That's why the regular use of sunglasses is recommended.

The American National Standards Institute devised a labeling system that sunglasses manufacturers voluntarily follow. There are three categories: "Cosmetic" glasses filter 70 percent of UV-B; "general purpose" filter 95 percent; and "special purpose" block 97 percent. Anglers can further reduce the amount of any type of UVR by wearing frames with side shields, brow bars, and nose shields.

With regard to color, brown lenses reduce glare on bright days, while amber improves vision on cloudy days or under dim light. Gray enhances true colors.

Polarized lenses do not change the amount of UVR filtered from direct sunlight, but they do filter light that is reflected off water. The resulting elimination of glare lets us spot fish more easily, particularly on bright days.

Better-made lenses increase vision and decrease eye fatigue. Most glasses are now made from unbreakable polycarbonate; the coating process that makes them scratch-resistant adds to the cost, but to most wearers the increased cost is well worth it. Photochromatic lenses, which grow darker or lighter according to available light, are also more costly than lenses that remain only one shade.

Among sunglasses specifically made for fishing are bifocals with magnifiers for close-up threading work on the lower half. Spring-hinge glasses let magnifying lenses pop up and out of the way when you don't need them.

Few things are more frustrating yet more avoidable than losing your glasses overboard. Cords that extend from earpiece to earpiece let glasses dangle around your neck when you're not using them. Elastic straps hold glasses in place. Take your choice, but use one of them.

Support Belts

Hours of standing and casting along a shore or from a boat tends to take its toll. One result is fatigue and pain in the lower lumbar region of the back, sometimes temporary but sometimes chronic. That's why several manufacturers took a cue from items worn by construction workers and others involved in heavy labor.

Elastic support belts designed for fishermen do in fact relieve lower back stress. Many users prefer the kind with built-in suspenders that keep the belt in place while the wearer is casting or playing a fish. Other models feature an adjustable belt that threads through trouser loops for the same purpose.

Support belts are even inching toward the "vest" category: Valeo, for example, makes one that includes a built-in tool pouch, D-ring, and accessory clip.

A. Basic Knots

LINDSEY PHILPOTT

All anglers have a few special knots for general situations and general use. This list of about a dozen knots in alphabetical order is one that I find is useful to remember and practice whenever I get a moment to twist a piece of line. If you can remember and practice these, you'll be better at remembering and using the other knots in the book. A word to the wise here: You will see many books referring to the strength of the knot being as much as a claimed 200 percent of the strength of the line. This is clearly nonsense, unless you know what they are talking about. What they are really claiming is that the knot does not break until 200 percent (or whatever number they give you) of the manufacturer's stated breaking strength of the line. This number is found by breaking dozens or perhaps even hundreds of samples of line in a testing machine, under rigorous conditions of quality control in a laboratory. All the breaking strengths are then added up and divided by the number of tests to provide an average number for the break strength. As with many things in the scientific world, the average is just a number—it is not a guarantee. A clever mathematics teacher once told me that, if I stand with one foot on the stove and the other foot in the refrigerator, on average I would be comfortable. Clearly these extremes are unusual, but they are still correct when talking about an average—you need to know how many tests were done, what the spread of numbers (highest to lowest) was and if the line was all from the same production batch.

It is not unusual to have strength tests that differ widely from each other—the mathematical term for this is standard deviation. This just means that some strengths are higher and some are lower than the average. Taken overall, the average strength of a piece of line can be beaten by (or not do as well as) any other piece of the same line, sometimes even from the same batch. So, when a knot is claimed to perform at 200 percent of the breaking strength (which is implying that the knot makes the line stronger) it just means that several people got lucky once or twice and tested the knot using line that was performing better than the manufacturer's tests had shown to be the average strength, or that the strength number was understated. Knots will almost make a line weaker, though in the case of some knots, such as the Bimini Twist, the line will break before the knot, if it is tied properly. The point at which the line will break is almost always at the point where it enters the knot, because this is where it is first bent out of shape by the knot, inducing tension on one side of the line and compression on the other. Sometimes a knot will break at a different point within the line and sometimes, as mentioned above, the line will break outside the knot altogether. These are normal variances and may even be expected. It does not mean that a knot improves the strength of the line. You will also occasionally have a line break where there was a defect in the line, which, with modern manufacturing methods, happens a lot less frequently than with the older types of line. Enough of the physics already—let's get on with the knots.

a. Arbor Knot

Before you can start fishing, you'll need this knot to secure the line to your reel. When tying extra-slippery, non-stretch lines to the arbor, put a piece of tape around the arbor first, so knotted line has something to bite into. Otherwise the entire spoolful is likely to rotate around the arbor under pressure. The Arbor Knot uses an overhand knot on the standing part of your line, backed up by another overhand knot like this:

1. Wrap line around your spool in a clockwise direction.

2. Tie an overhand knot around the standing part and slip the tag end through it.

3. Tie an overhand in the tag end and pull it tight.

4. Slide the completed knot down to fit snugly onto your arbor.

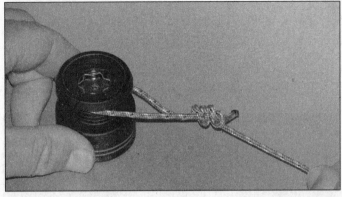

5. Put the spool back on the reel and start taking up line.

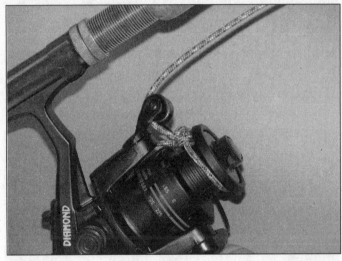

b. Bimini Twist

When you want to maintain your line at 100 percent of its rated break strength, the Bimini Twist is the knot to choose. When this knot is completed, the loop that results provides two strands that are used together, as if they were a single piece, when tying to another line or to a hook eye. Often the loop is clipped and the two strands are twisted together, and this twist is then used as a single line to make the next connection.

The trick to this knot is controlling the tension properly as the knot is formed. Practice this knot before setting out—there's nothing quite like the frustration of trying to tie a BT when the wind is blowing, and the boat is rocking.

1. Make a loop that is nearly twice as long as you need it and twist the loop 20 times around with your hand, while holding the tag end and the standing part together.

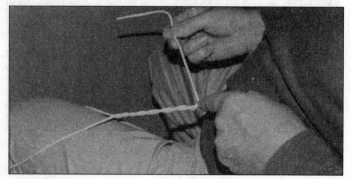

2. Place the loop around your foot and pull it up over your knee, then pull on both ends to twist the lines together and put the twist under tension.

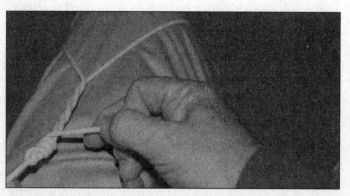

3. This step reverses the direction of the tag, rolling it down over the twist, heading back toward the loop. Release the tension on the tag end slightly and feed

the tag around the twists as they spin. At this point you can assist the rollover by straightening your leg to help the twisted portion spin, as you feed the tag smoothly down over the twists.

4. Then hold the last of the wraps firmly with your left hand while you tie a half hitch around one leg of the loop.

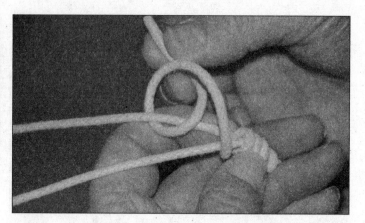

5. Then tie another half hitch around the other leg of the loop. At this point the knot should be stable.

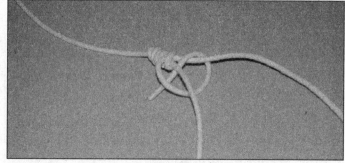

6. Now make a two-or three-wrap half hitch around both legs of the loop.

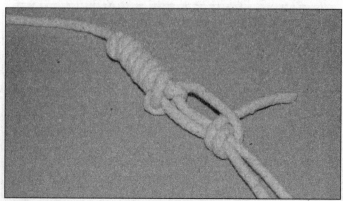

7. Pull the tag end tightly to snug up the finishing half hitches. Trim the excess, leaving a short tag so the half hitches do not work loose.

c. Crawford Knot

The Crawford Knot is a secure knot to use with a monofilament or Spectra leader, because the wraps develop the inherent strength you are looking for. It is a jamming wrap, relying on the tag end jammed into the space between the wraps and the eye on your hook. It can be difficult to fetch up securely unless lubricated well, but is a good knot to remember for a secure tie.

1. Pass the line clockwise through the eye and under the standing part.

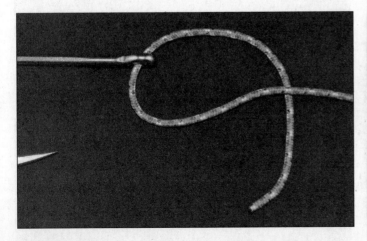

2. Wrap over both parts of the loop you just made, to the left, and tuck the tag end under both parts.

3. Bring the tag end over the two legs of the loop, this time to the right.

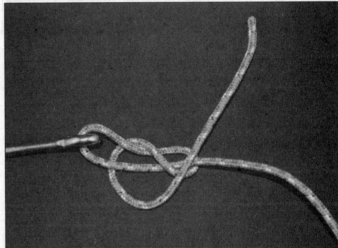

4. Tuck the tag end, from underneath, into the top loop.

5. Tuck the end back through the loop you first made by the eye.

6. Fair the knot and draw it down tight to the hook, lure, or sinker.

d. Improved Clinch Knot

This variation on the standard Clinch Knot has a small improvement in the last step, which makes it more secure in mono because of that extra pinch point.

1. Pass the standing part through the eye, clockwise.

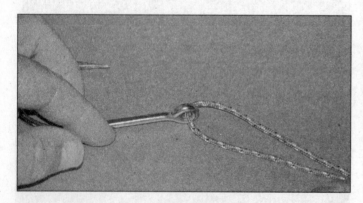

2. Form a loop over the standing part.

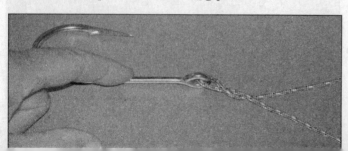

3. Make at least three more turns over the standing part, six for slippery line.

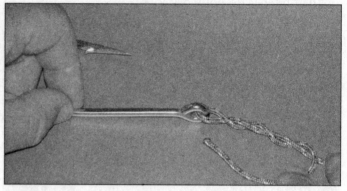

4. Pass the tag end UP through the loop by the eye.

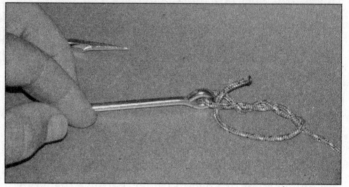

5. Pass the tag end DOWN through the tag end's own loop.

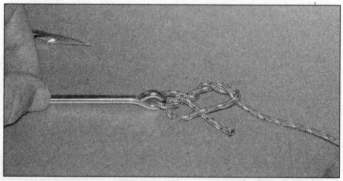

6. Gradually work the wetted turns together, pulling the standing part, and then trim the tag end.

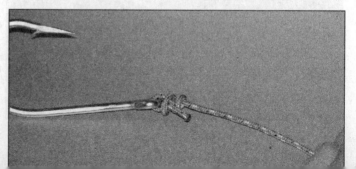

e. Jansik Special

This is a high-strength knot, especially favored by muskie fishermen. Its strength comes from the number of turns the line makes through the hook-eye. Those turns and their finishing wraps are important to spreading the load on the line, so don't skimp on them just because they are hard to make.

1. Make a loop through the eye, in a clockwise direction.

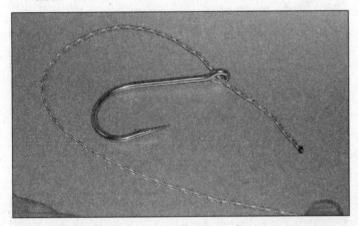

2. Bring the tag end through the eye again.

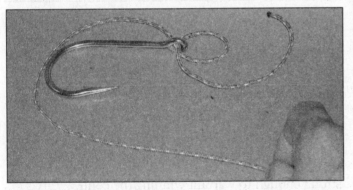

3. Bring the tag end through the eye a third time.

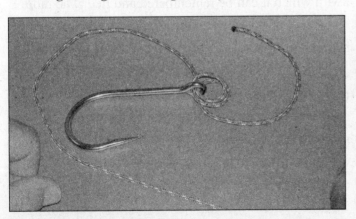

4. Start to wrap the two loops with the tag end.

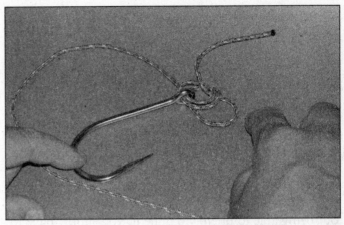

5. Complete three wraps around the loops with the tag end.

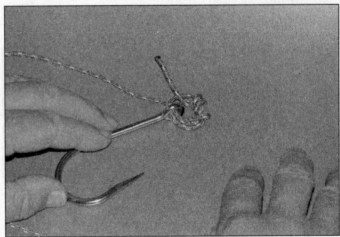

6. Fair the knot by pulling on the standing part, gradually working the two loops both through the eye until they are firm, and tightly holding the wraps from Step 5.

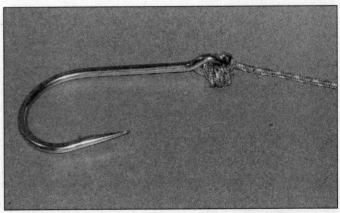

f. Offshore Swivel Knot

Fishing offshore requires that you use something really hardy and capable of taking a beating. A swivel attached to your double-line leader with this knot will stick like glue and never let go. It needs some care in tightening, but is well worth the effort to make it right. It gets its power from the fact that it has so many twists, from an old knot known as a Cat's-paw, in which each of the twists bears against the next twist, sharing the load throughout the hitch, a bit like a zipper, but without being able to unzip. To untie it, you simply have to wiggle the knot open a little and then reverse the direction of tying it.

1. Make a loop in the end of the leader or use a spliced loop if using Dacron braid.

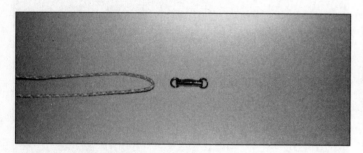

2. Pass the loop through the swivel ring.

3. Flip the loop back over itself to the left, leaving the swivel on the right.

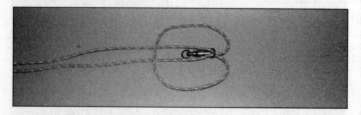

4. Turn the swivel back over itself to the right.

5. Repeat Stage 4 five more times (six in all).

6. Wet the knot thoroughly and draw the twisted loops slowly together, rolling the twists toward the swivel as you go.

g. Orvis Knot

The Orvis Company ran a contest to find the best line-to-hook knot. This knot, by Larry Becker of Waskom, Texas, was the winner. It is simple in construction, secure because it does not let go, and strong enough to warrant winning the contest. Orvis judges recognized it as a winner because of the ease with which it can be remembered and tied. The more I have looked at and used the Orvis knot, the more I am convinced that it is an extension of the Timber Hitch, a very useful and secure knot used in old squarerigged ships and on small day-sailor ships to attach a reefing line. Combine those attributes with the base figure eight around the standing part of your line and it is small wonder it was declared the winner. It is in any case a very secure knot.

1. Make a clockwise underhand loop through the hook or lure eye.

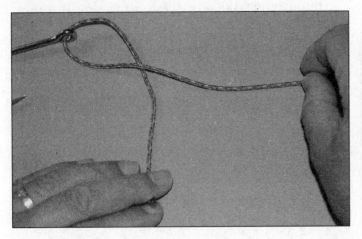

2. Bring the tag end over the standing part of the line to make a figure eight.

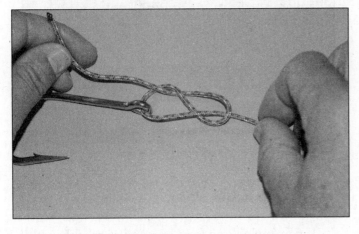

3. Start to make what appears to be a second figure eight, but keep wrapping the tag end around that arm of the first eight, one more time.

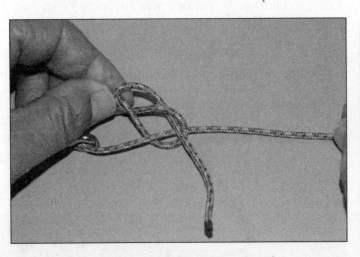

4. Now fair up the knot by tightening the wraps around the second eight and then pulling the first eight tighter.

h. Overhand Knot

Here is an interesting fact: did you know that two overhand knots tied in the same direction make a granny knot, or that two overhand knots tied first to the left and then to the right make a square knot? The overhand makes a helpful stopper knot—if you don't mind that it is usually permanent. It is also the basis for many of the other knots in this section, is a knot that can be tied by the wind, and may have been one of the first knots ever tied by primitive man. Shown are two distinct types of overhand knot, one left-handed and one right-handed. Both are correct—just be sure to use the same type each time.

1. (RH Overhand) Bring the tag end around over the standing part in a clockwise direction.

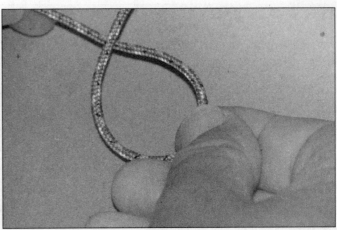

2. (RH Overhand) Tuck the tag end under the standing part and then through the loop you have formed.

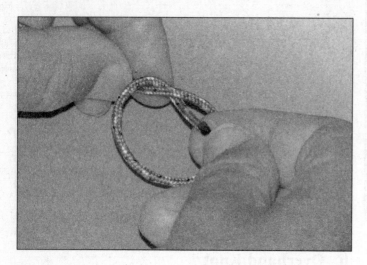

3. (RH Overhand) The completed knot, not yet faired up; leave the tag end sticking out about ¼-inch after fairing the knot.

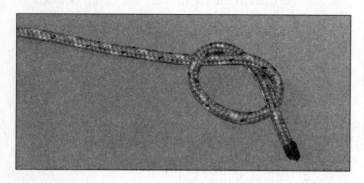

4. (LH Overhand) Bring the tag end around under the standing part, clockwise.

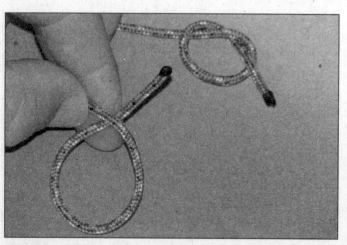

5. (LH Overhand) Seen here below the RH Overhand; tuck the tag end down into the loop and pull through from underneath.

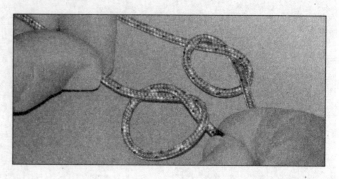

6. Here are the RH Overhand and the LH Overhand together before fairing.

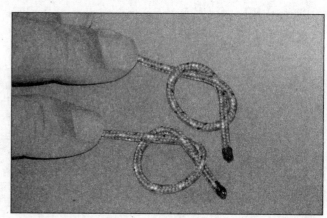

i. Palomar Knot

If you are looking for a knot to use reliably with braid line, this is it. The Palomar is easily tied, easily remembered and is very useful as a terminal knot for your gear. It can be tied using a loop (bight) or with a doubled line—either way, it will not come loose. A word to the wise—if you are tying a double or triple hook, don't use this knot, as the hooks are likely to get tangled in the loop at some point during the tying.

1. Bring a loop to the eye of the hook.

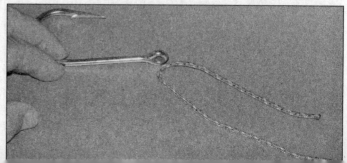

2. Pass the loop through the eye.

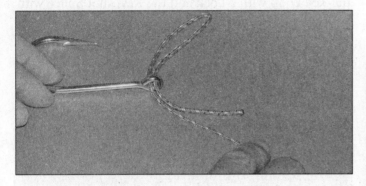

3. Make an overhand knot with the loop.

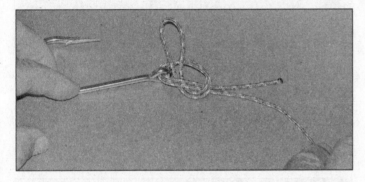

4. Pass the loop over the hook to pass behind the shank.

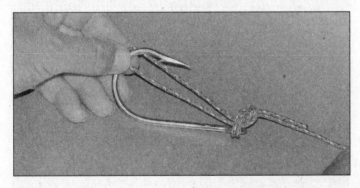

5. Fair the knot by pulling the overhand knot tight around the shank and then up over.

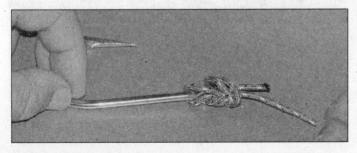

6. Pull the knot and eye, to tighten around the tightened overhand loop knot, then trim away the tag end.

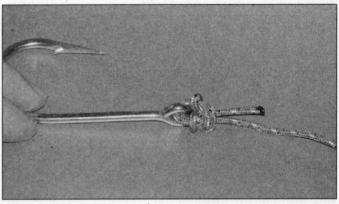

j. Snelling

Snelling is a word that was first used in print in the U.S. in 1893, when reference was made in Volume XXII of the February issue of the sporting magazine *Outing* to "well made, securely wrapped, double-snelled Aberdeen bend hooks." The origin of the word in Old English means quick or sharp, so I would guess that the name was given on account of the finished appearance of the hook shank being "sharp" when attached like this.

1. Pass the line through the hook eye and along the shank, then return, forming an overhand counterclockwise loop below the shank.

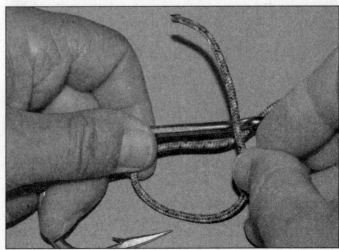

2. Make wraps around the shank and the upper part of the loop, until you have from four to seven wraps or more, depending on your line.

3. Fair up the knot by rolling it around the shank with your fingers, cutting away the tag end when you are satisfied the wraps are tight enough. Use a hook with a bent eye, NOT the type shown here.

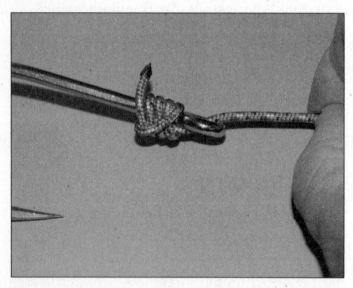

k. Albright Knot with a Lock

The Albright Knot has a great history, and it's a standby for tying light mono to heavier lines and leaders like heavy mono, singlestrand wire, or nylon-coated wire. It is trim enough to pass through the rod guides smoothly. The lock on this one brings a certain peace of mind to knowing that the tag end is not going to back out of the knot during a fight. It is sometimes known as the Key Loop with a Lock and the Key Knot Splice with a Lock.

1. Loop each line through the other (solid color is the lighter line; patterned is the heavier line or wire).

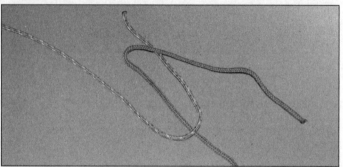

2. Start making turns around the legs of the loop, winding the lighter line back down the loop, over itself.

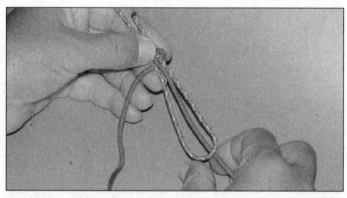

3. Continue wrapping . . .

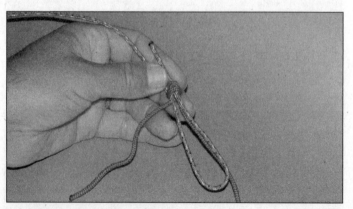

4. . . . until you have six turns, then tuck the tag end through the loop.

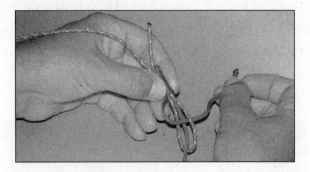

5. Then pull the loop through the wraps to capture the tag end. Make turns with the tag end around its own standing part and tuck it through the loop that has formed.

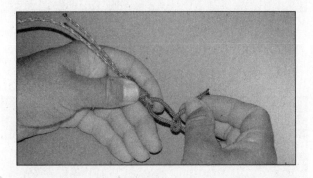

6. Pull hard on the tag end to make the turns snug against the loop end.

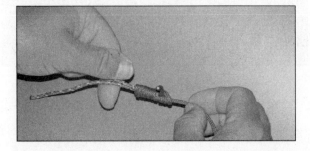

7. Here is what it looks like from the other side.

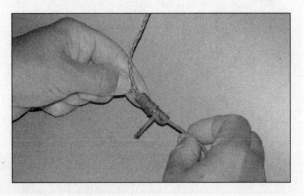

l. Blood Knot (Simple)

The simple Blood Knot is an elegant knot for joining lines of the same or similar diameter. Be sure to take the number of turns suggested, or you may find that the knot slips and comes apart. Lighter lines require more turns than heavier lines.

1. Lay the two lines together and overlapped about six inches.

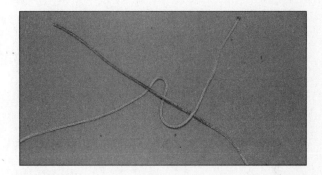

2. Pinch one line under the other (here the lighter line is pinched under) with its tag to the right and wrap it around the other standing part about four to six times.

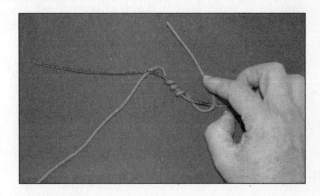

3. Tuck the tag end down between the two lines.

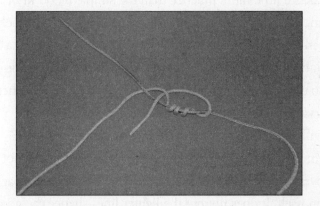

4. Repeat this with the other tag end, being sure to wrap in the opposite direction.

5. Tuck the second tag end through the wraps in the opposite direction of the first.

6. Form the loose knot up evenly and lubricate it with water or saliva, then pull steadily and firmly on both standing ends until the knot is formed. Tighten this knot with one steady pull. It is difficult or impossible to form properly unless it is tightened in one smooth operation.

m. Complex Blood Knot

I call this one the Complex Blood Knot because it takes a little more practice than the simple blood knot and because it is not really a Blood Knot; it only vaguely resembles it. It is used only when you want to attach a light line to a heavier one—the Blood Knot will not do it so easily, and this one is easy to remember. Don't bother trying to use it to tie two same-size lines together—it will just make for a bulky knot. The Complex Blood Knot is used to help make sure that the light line is not overstressed and that, where the heavier line bends back on itself, it does not cut the lighter line—hence the good

reason for doubling the lighter line. One more thing to add to the complexity; you could try leaving a dropper loop for a second hook instead of cutting away the light line loop where it passes through the center of the wraps. That way you get a two-for-one knot.

1. Make a bight in both lines.

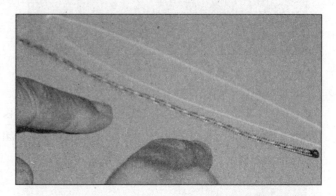

2. Start wrapping the heavier line around the lighter line.

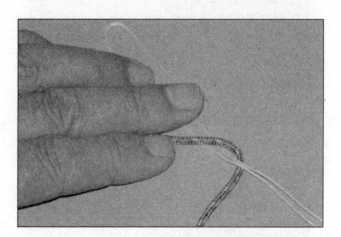

3. Bring the third or fourth (last) wrap between itself and the lighter line. This forms one side of the knot.

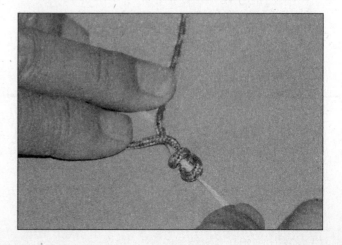

4. Now take the bight of leader and wrap it around the main line.

5. Tuck it over itself and down into the space where the tag of the main line sits. Be sure to tuck it OVER the main line tag as shown here.

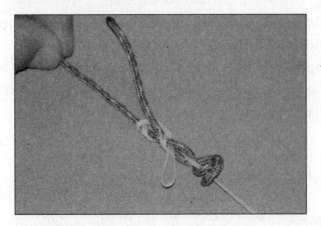

6. Draw the two lines apart, gradually rolling the leader bight tighter around the main line. If you need a loop at this point for a second leader, keep the leader bight, otherwise cut away the leader bight and the tag end of the main line to create a free-running knot. Coat with Pliobond if needed.

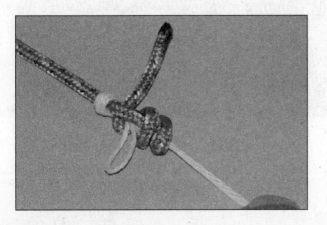

n. Huffnagle Knot

As with most knots where you want to join a light line to a heavy line, you have to prepare the light line first. Let's say that you are looking to connect a fly leader tippet to a good strong line, such as 80-pound test, or heavier. First, make a Bimini Twist in your light line. This double strand will be used to tie the knot to the heavier material. You will need to lubricate this knot to snug it down, and pliers to effectively tighten it.

1. With the heavier material, tie an overhand knot around the doubled strand of the leader.

2. Start wrapping the leader bight around the standing part of your main line, behind the overhand knot.

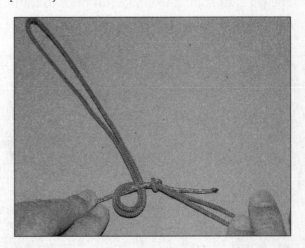

3. Tie an overhand around your main line using the bight of the leader and snug it down hard against the overhand already in your main line.

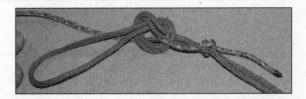

4. Wrap the leader bight several times (four or five) around the main line, being sure not to trap the bight under your wraps.

5. Pull the bight through and snug the wraps down against the leader's own overhand knot.

6. The tag ends should look like this prior to trimming.

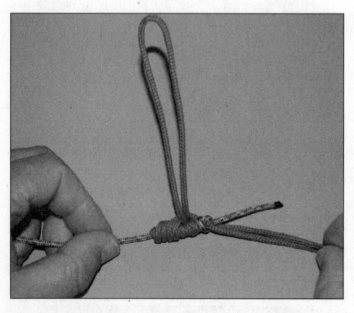

7. If you used a Bimini Twist to get your initial loop, fair the knot to get the BT's wraps down to the overhand knot. Otherwise, tuck the tag end of the bight under a half hitch to finish. Trim away both tag ends and coat with Pliobond.

o. Surgeon's Knot

This is an extension of the simple overhand knot that uses an extra tuck through the knot to develop, in the same way the Cat's Paw does, more friction by adding an extra twist. It is called the Surgeon's Knot as it is used in surgery to provide a better grip on the ligature to bring wound edges together.

1. Lay the two pieces of line next to each other, tag ends facing away from each other.

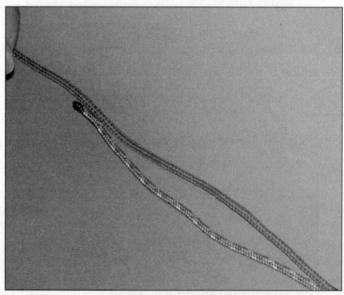

2. Make an overhand loop with both lines.

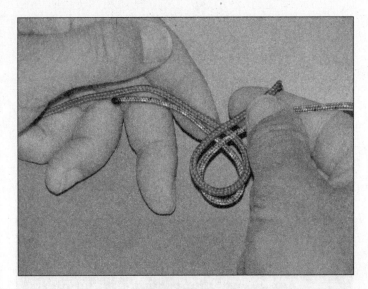

3. Make an overhand knot, left-handed or right, your choice (RH shown).

4. Double the overhand knot by adding another turn around the knot.

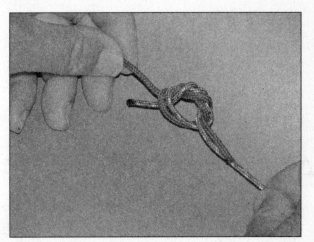

5. Fair the knot tightly, being sure to roll both parts toward each other—a little lubrication would help here.

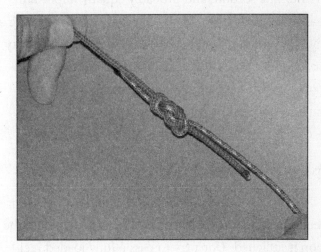

B. Basic Loops

LINDSEY PHILPOTT

Attaching a line directly to the hook involves passing the end of the line through the eye of the hook. Nothing very complicated or difficult about that, so why the need to know about putting a loop through the hook instead? One reason is that a loop spreads the load of the line over the eye of the hook (you are using twice as much line with a loop as you do with a single line), which lowers the load on the individual strands of line. The second, and probably equally important reason is security. You want your knot to stay in place on the eye of the hook. Loops develop greater security than regular knots and hitches. Try these few select loop-to-hook knots and hitches and see if they don't improve the security of your hooks.

a. Interlocking Loops

When you attach one loop to another, you will need access to one end of one of the lines to which the loop is attached. Don't try to pass a fully loaded reel and rod through a leader loop.

1. Two loops already made—use your favorites.

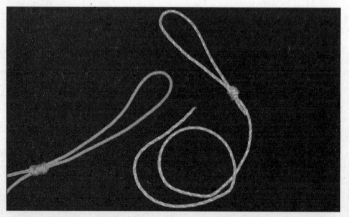

2. Insert the leader loop into the main line loop.

3. Take the other end of the leader and insert it through its own loop only.

4. Pull both loops away from each other and they should flip to look like this.

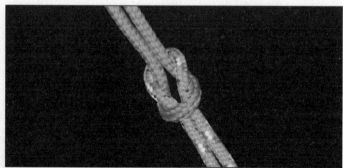

5. This is not quite perfect, but it will probably slip into place with pressure.

6. This configuration is weak and will cut through itself.

b. Duncan Loop

Alongside the Homer Rhode Loop and the non-slip Mono Loop knot, the Duncan Loop is a favorite among anglers for forming a strong loop that allows the hook or lure to swing freely. Under pressure, when fighting a fish, the loop will close, giving you a tighter and more secure knot. Be sure you make the wraps tightly.

1. Pass the tag end through the eye and make an S-shape.

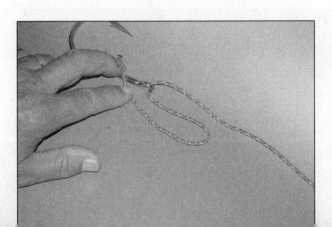

2. Wrap only one side of the S-shape with the tag end.

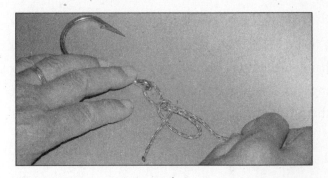

3. Continue wrapping until you have at least three turns.

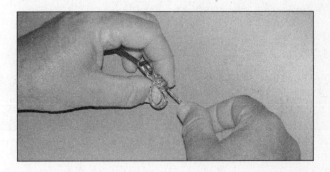

4. Pass the tag end through the loop you have formed. Adjust the loop to proper size by sliding the knot on the standing line, then tighten it in place by pulling on the tag end.

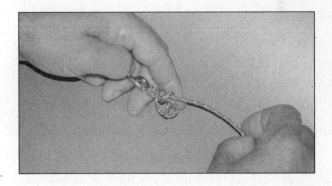

5. Here is the knot, tightened down to the hook—after a strike.

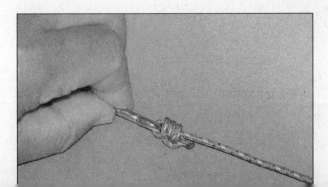

c. Egg Loop (aka Salmon Egg Loop)

Trying to get salmon eggs to stay in place can be a major headache unless you try this little trick. This handy device will provide you with a good solid seating and a built-in trap to keep things where you want them—on the hook.

1. Pass the tag end through the eye.

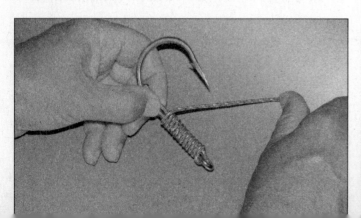

2. Lay the tag end along the shank and make turns of the standing part around tag end and shank.

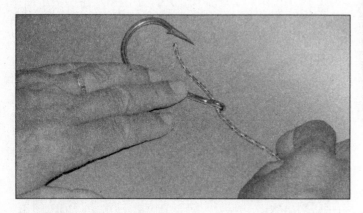

3. Keep making turns until you have at least seven turns.

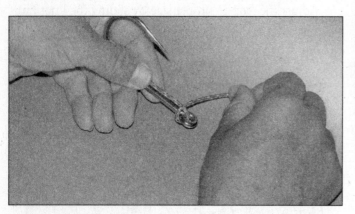

4. Make a loop with the standing part and pass the standing end through the eye, but keep it loose.

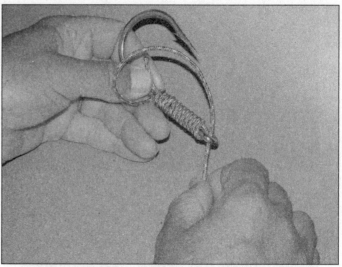

5. Make twists of the loop you just formed over the hook, trapping the tag end with your new wraps.

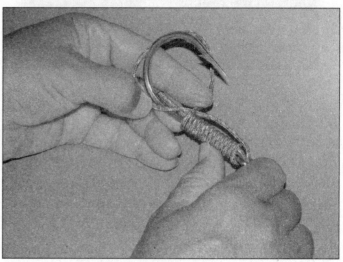

6. After three twists and wraps, stop and pull the standing part to tighten the wraps onto the tag end.

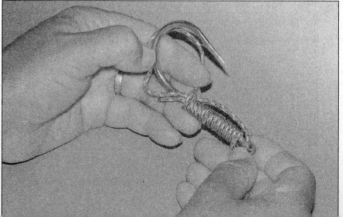

7. Tighten the standing part almost down onto the shank.

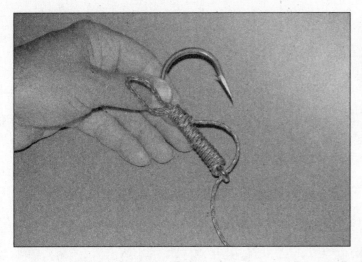

8. Now your hook is ready to receive the roe under the loop you created—the tension on your line will handily hold the eggs in place.

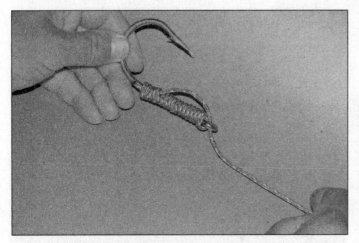

d. Homer Rhode Loop

This always makes me think about Homer Simpson, although of course he has nothing to do with Homer Rhode, the guide in the Florida Keys for whom the knot was named. This knot is also sometimes known as the Flemish Loop or the Loop Knot, for those who are not aware of Homer Rhode. The knot enables the lure to swing freely and it can be tied with mono or braided line, even plastic-coated wire if need be. Be sure to use pliers to make the turns tight.

1. Tie an overhand knot in the standing part and pass the tag end through the eye.

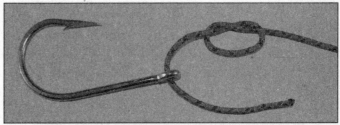

2. Pass the tag end through the loop of the overhand knot.

3. Make a second overhand knot around the standing part, using the tag end.

4. Tighten both overhand knots and slide them together to create the desired size of loop, and then cut away un-needed tag end.

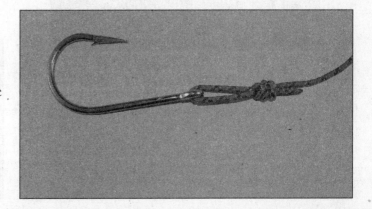

e. Mono Loop (non-slip)

Here is the third great stand-by. It is non-slip because of the wraps, so in light line or slipperier line, use more wraps.

1. First, make an overhand knot, but don't pull it tight.

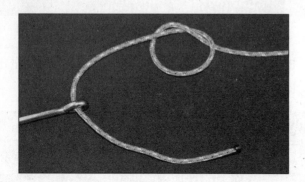

2. Pass the tag end through the eye of the hook and pass the tag back through the overhand knot the same way it exited the knot.

3. Wrap the tag end around the standing part three to five times, depending on what line you are using.

4. Bring the tag end back through the overhand.

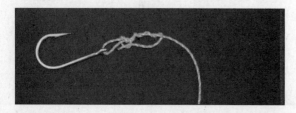

5. Fair up the knot and cut away the tag end as needed.

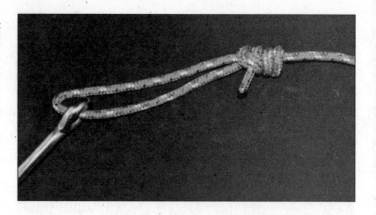

f. Perfection Loop (aka Angler's Loop)

This loop knot allows the slipperiest line, or even bungee cord, to be tied so that it will not slip.

1. Form a first counterclockwise underhand loop.

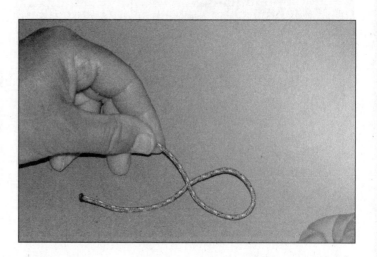

2. Continue to wind the tag end counterclockwise over the standing part to make the second loop.

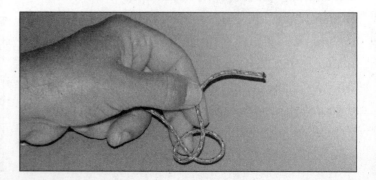

3. Position the tag end between the two loops and pull the top loop down through the lower loop . . .

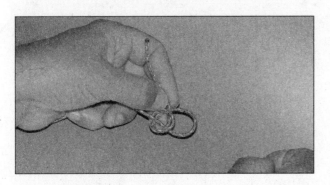

4. . . . trapping the tag end between the two loops. Tighten by pulling on the loop.

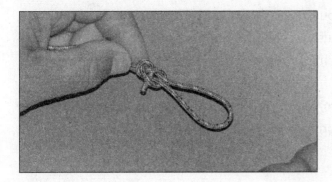

g. Surgeon's Loop

Like the Surgeon's Knot, the Surgeon's Loop will not slip in the slickest of mono or even PVDF—it stays put. For that reason you cannot expect to undo it very easily. This loop is known by several other names: Double Overhand Loop, the Two-Fold Water Knot, the Line Knot, and the Two-Fold Blood Knot. Nothing wrong with having a few extra names, just as long as you remember how to tie it, which is simplicity itself:

1. Make a loop.

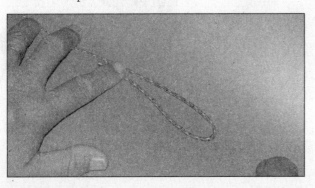

2. Start an overhand knot.

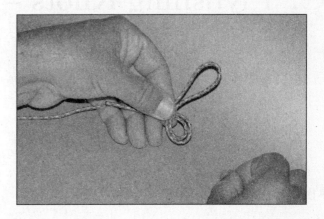

3. Make two passes through the overhand knot with the loop.

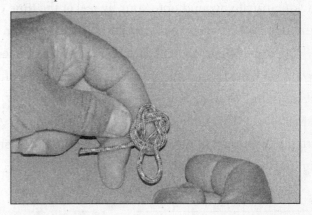

4. Pull tight—that's it.

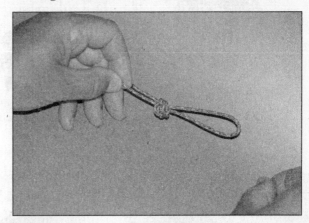

5. A view of the other side of the loop.

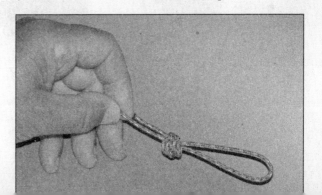

C. Flyfishing Knots – Backing to Fly Reel

CONWAY X. BOWMAN

Tying the backing to the fly reel

Many fly fishers don't know how to tie the backing to their fly reels. And why should they? Isn't backing usually wound onto your fly reel at the time of purchase? We have come to expect this courtesy from fly shops after buying a reel. However, if you ever need to change your fly line and attach new backing to your reel and find yourself miles from the nearest fly shop, being able to do it yourself will not only save you a lengthy trip to town, but will also afford you more fishing time.

Gel-spun and Dacron backing have a tendency to slip once they are connected to the fly reel's arbor. A good way to avoid this problem is to wrap a strip of blue medical or gaffer's tape around the arbor before putting on the backing. The tape's surface will create just enough friction to prevent the backing from slipping as you wind it onto the reel.

The Arbor Knot is a good knot for tying backing to your fly reel's arbor. It is simple to tie and very low profile.

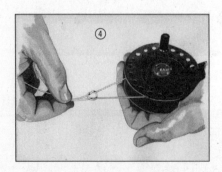

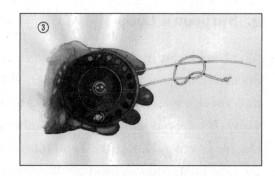

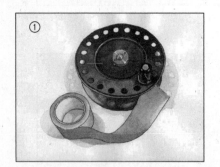

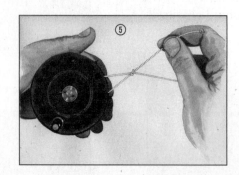

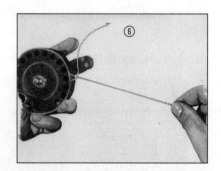

D. More Flyfishing Knots

GEOFFREY BUDWORTH

Nail Knot

(Also known as the tube knot)

Function

The nail knot joins a fly line to the butt section of the leader, as snelling attaches a line to the shank of a hook. Its name is said to have originated in the 1950s when a noted American fly fisherman named Joe Brooks learned the knot in Argentina using a horseshoe nail. Tying is done more easily, however, by means of a short length of drinking straw, a small diameter metal tube, or even the empty body of a ballpoint pen . . . hence its later name of tube knot.

Tying

Lay the ends of the fly line and backing line together, parallel, pointing in opposite directions, and begin a

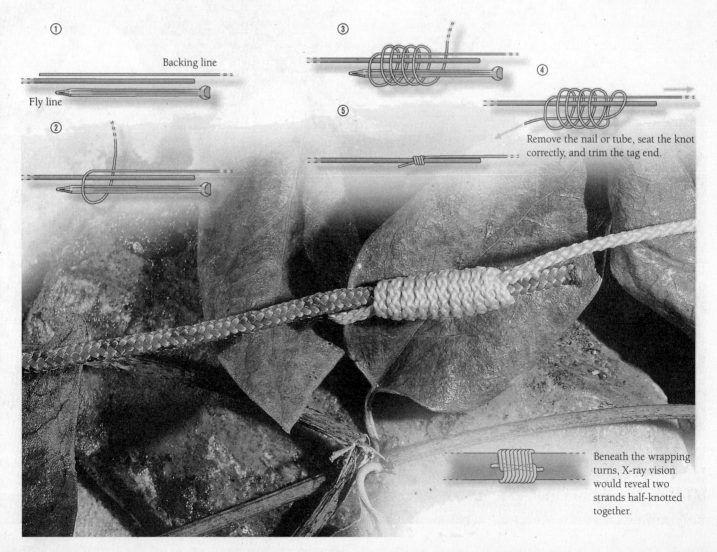

① Backing line

Fly line

②

③

④ Remove the nail or tube, seat the knot correctly, and trim the tag end.

⑤

Beneath the wrapping turns, X-ray vision would reveal two strands half-knotted together.

series of wrapping turns with the end of the backing line to enclose both the fly line plus a nail or tube (*figures 1–2*). Make at least five turns, then withdraw the nail and pass the working end completely through the space it has vacated within the wrapping turns (*figures 3–4*). If using a tube, pass the end through it before withdrawal, when the end will be pulled through at the same time. Tighten slowly so that the wrapping turns bed down neatly alongside one another, and finally tug both ends to tighten (*figure 5*). Trim the tag end.

Emergency Nail Knot

Function

Caught without either nail or tube, a nail knot can be improvised using a bight of spare line to pull the

working end through beneath the wrapping turns (not pictured).

Tying

Tie the knot as usual but include within it a bight of line. After the last wrapping turn, tuck the working end through the bight and pull the line out of the knot. Tighten and trim.

Asymmetrical Nail Knot

Function

Use this compact variant to join dissimilar thickness of mono.

Tying

Wrap the thicker line just twice around the thinner one and tie a curtailed nail knot—which is nothing more than a double overhand knot— (*figure 1*). Take eight turns with the working end of the thinner line

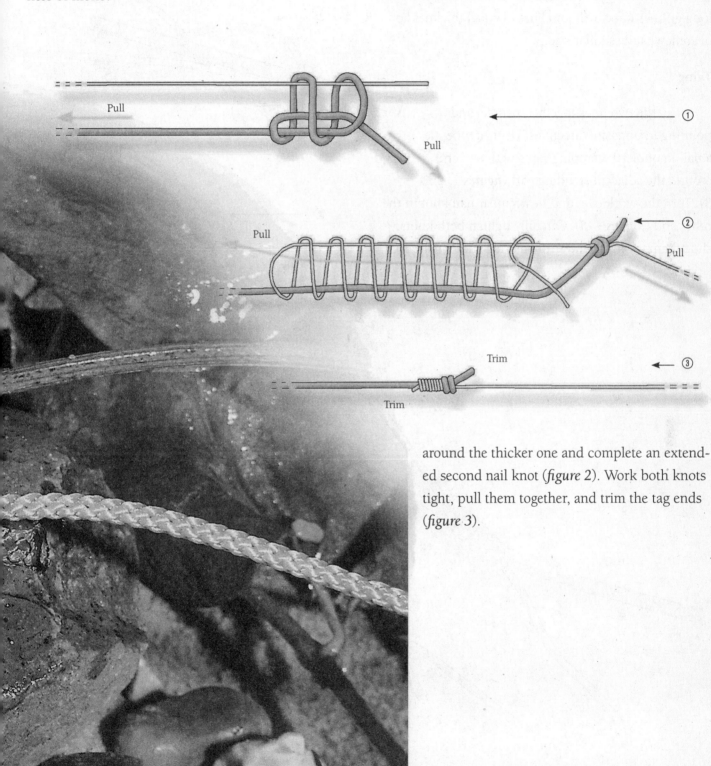

around the thicker one and complete an extended second nail knot (*figure 2*). Work both knots tight, pull them together, and trim the tag ends (*figure 3*).

Conjoined Twin Nail Knots

Function

In game or sport fishing, when maximum strength is required, this knot (which resembles an exceptionally long grinner knot) will join lines of equal thickness or of somewhat dissimilar size.

Tying

Lay the two lines together, parallel and pointing in opposite directions. Using a tube, tie a nail knot of 10 wrapping turns with one end around the adjacent standing part (*figures 1, 2, 3*). Turn the work over and tie a similar nail knot in the other end (*figures 4–5*). Carefully tighten both knots, slide them together, and trim both tag ends (*figure 6*).

1

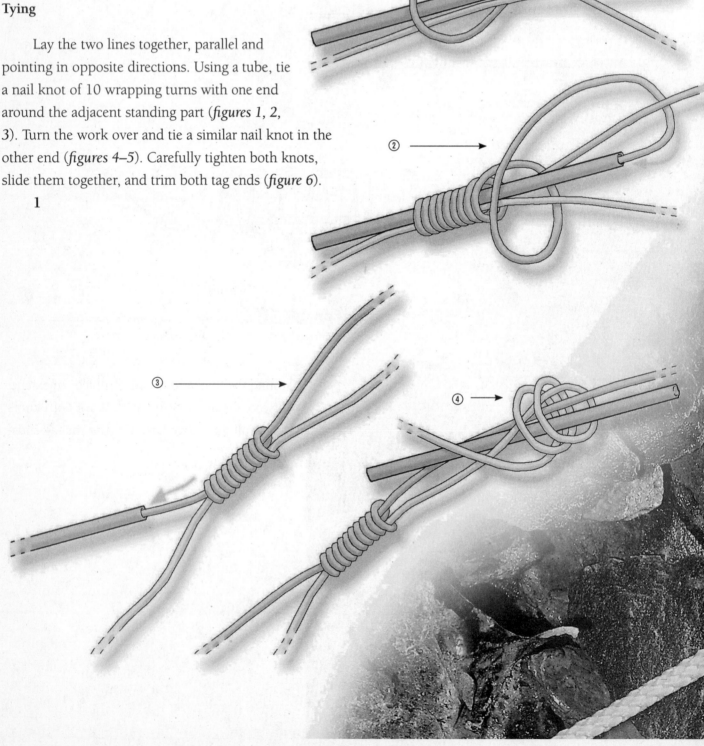

Nail Knot Loop

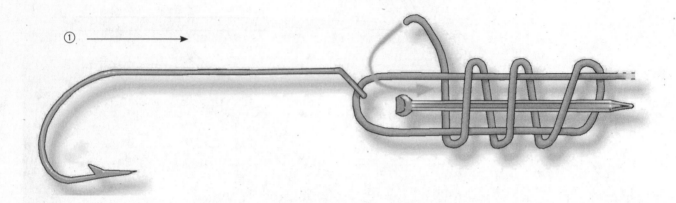

Function

For heavy lines and leaders, such as sea fishing shock tippets, this knot is used. Although it is a sliding noose (commonly known in rope and other cordage as the strangle knot), this tightly tied knot will hold firm enough to maintain a small loop that facilitates the free and realistic movement of a fly or other lure.

Tying

Pass the end of the line or leader through the hook's eye and lay it alongside its own standing part. Wrap and tuck a nail knot, using whatever aid is preferred or available (*figures 1–2*). Tighten the knot and adjust the loop to the required size.

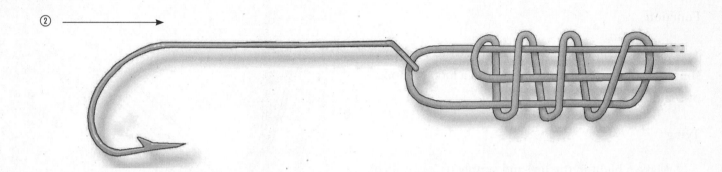

Reverse of knot

A Pair of Nail Knots

Function

Nail knots may be combined in pairs to create a simple seizing, in this instance to form a loop in mono or braid.

Tying

Make a bight in the line and simply tie a couple of basic nail knots following steps 3–5 on page 519.

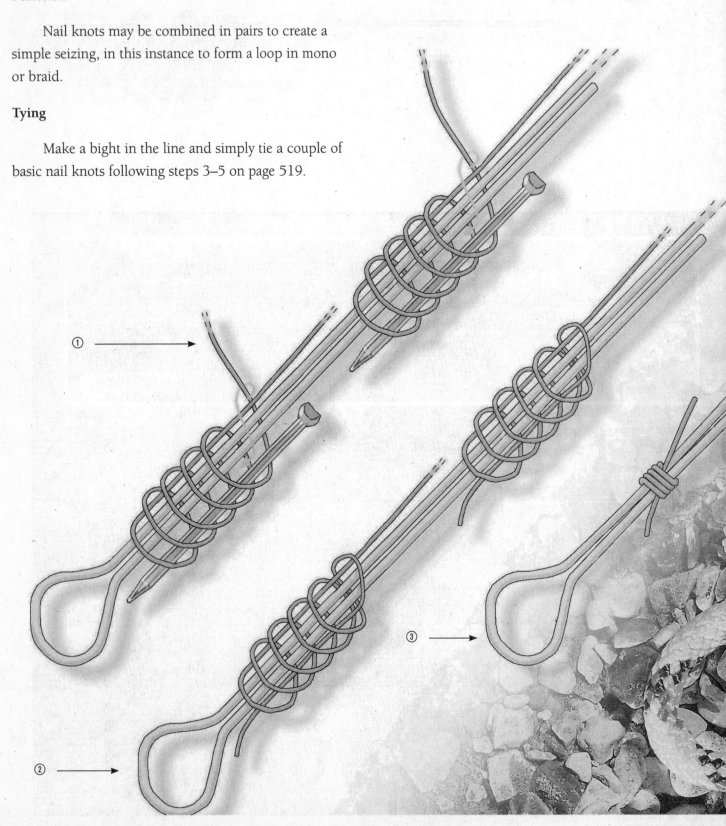

Needle Knot

Function

This modified nail knot makes a strong attachment for a mono leader to a fly line.

Tying

Push a needle into the end of the fly line, at a slight angle, so that it comes out again through the side. Then push the working end of the mono through the hole that has been made (*figures 1–2*). Slice the end of the mono leader obliquely for an easier passage. If the hole tends to shrink and obstruct passage of the leader's end, try heating the needle (gently) and—taking care to protect the hand—make the hole. Begin a series of wrapping turns with the mono, around the fly line, enclosing the needle (*figures 3–4*), and then pull the end through beneath the turns with the needle. Tighten and trim (*figure 5*).

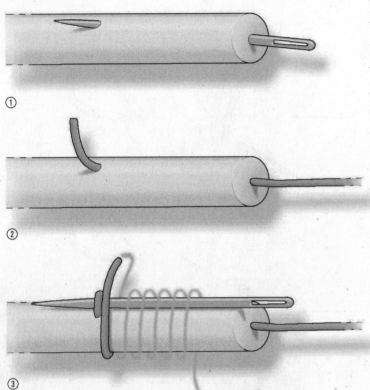

①

②

③

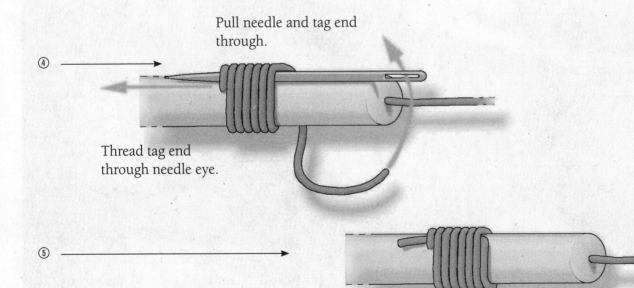

Pull needle and tag end through.

④

Thread tag end through needle eye.

⑤

Needle Knot Loop

(Or mono loop)

Function

Use this contrivance to facilitate frequent changes of leader and fly line.

Tying

Pass the two ends of a mono loop through a pre-made hole in the fly line—see the needle knot on the previous page for how to do this—then wrap both working ends together and tuck them to tie the knot (*figure 1*). Tighten and trim (*figure 2*).

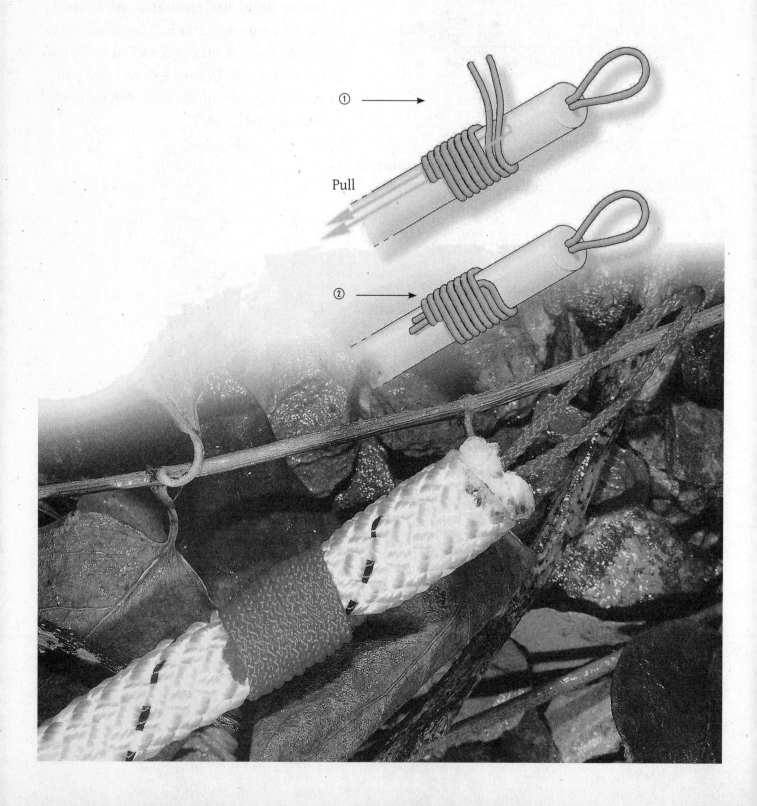

①

Pull

②

Specialist Fly Knot

Function

This is a kissing cousin of the clinch knot family. Promoted in the first instance by the Berkley Tackle Company, of Spirit Lake, Indiana, for use by fly fishers, it has proved just as effective with plugs and some other artificial baits.

Tying

Pass the end of the leader through the hook eye of the fly and double the working end into a long bight. Wrap four turns around both legs of the bight, then tuck the working end back through the loop nearest to the fly (*figure 1*). Tighten the knot, locate the resulting noose around the shank, and close it up alongside the eye (*figures 2–3*).

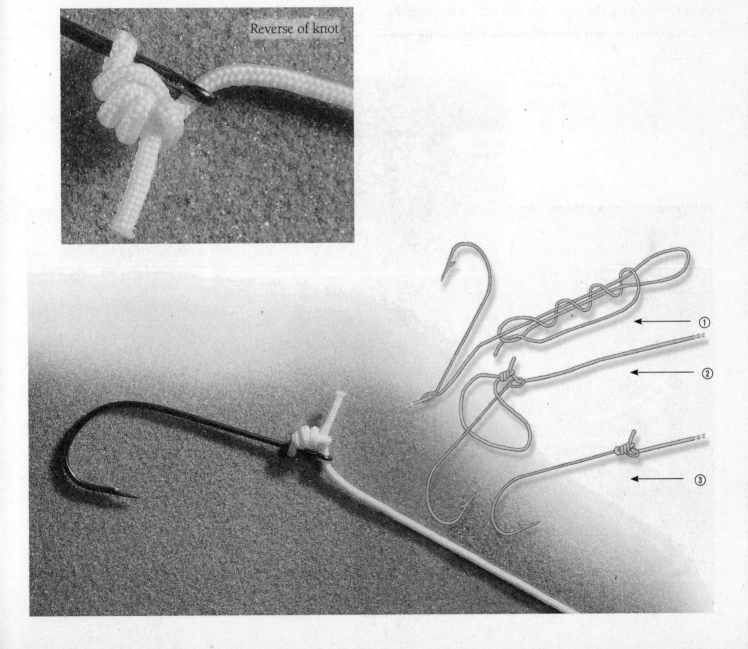

Reverse of knot

Trilene Knot

(Also known as the Berkley Trilene knot)

Function

Another offshoot of the clinch family, this knot is made stronger by having two turns through the eye of the hook, but it is not capable of being tied to very small hooks. It can be troublesome to tighten in lines of more than about 12 lbs (5.5 kgs).

Tying

Pass the working end twice through the eye of the hook, take four turns with it around the standing part, then finally bring the end back and tuck it through the two initial turns on the eye (*figure 1*). Flype to tighten (*figure 2*).

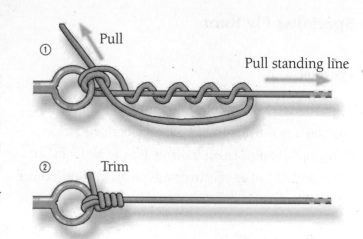

Reverse
of knot

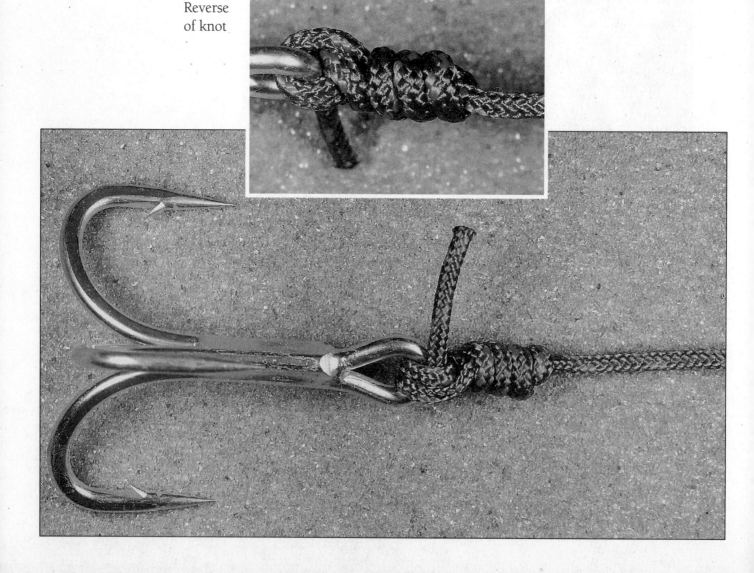

Improved Trilene Knot

Function

Akin to the improved clinch knot, it is no stronger than the basic Trilene knot but the extra tuck gives added security.

Tying

Tie a Trilene knot and simply tuck the working end back through the large loop (*figure 1*) before flyping and tightening the knot (*figure 2*).

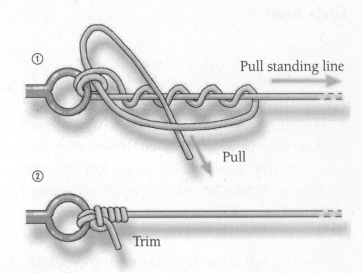

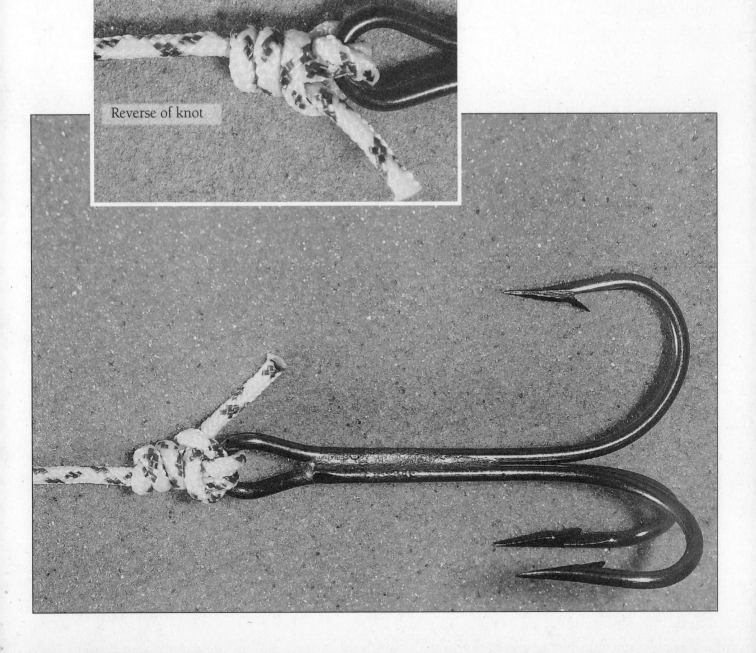

Turle Knot

Function

This vintage knot dates back to at least 1841 when
it was made popular by a Major Turle of Newton Stacey,
England, although he never claimed to have invented
it. No more than the simplest of nooses, it is outmoded,
but remains the basis for several more robust variants.

Tying

Pass the end of the fly line through the eye of the
hook and tie a simple noose (*figure 1*). Locate the noose
around the shank, beside the eye (*figures 2–3*), and pull
it tight (*figure 4*).

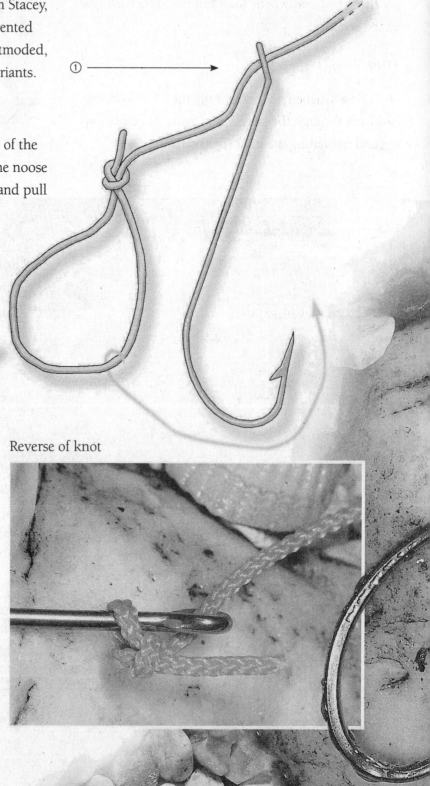

Reverse of knot

Two-Turn Turle Knot

Function

This stronger version of the Turle knot was first described in the April 1946 issue of *Fishing News*, having been devised and named by the angling author Dr. Stanley Barnes.

Tying

Pass the end of the line through the eye of the fly hook. Form first one, then a second loop, and include both within an overhand knot (*figure 1*). Tuck the hook and lure through both loops and tighten the knot around the shank close to the eye (*figures 2–3*).

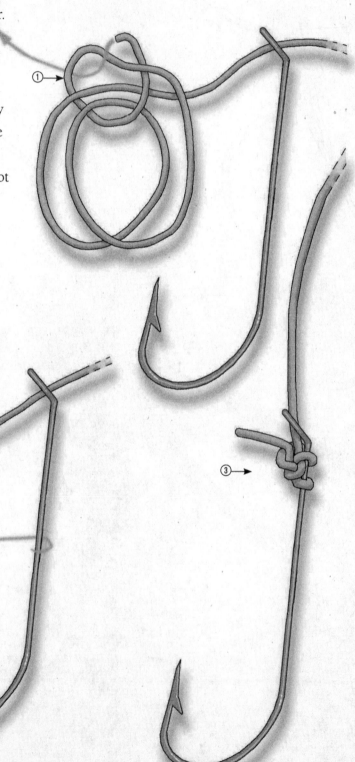

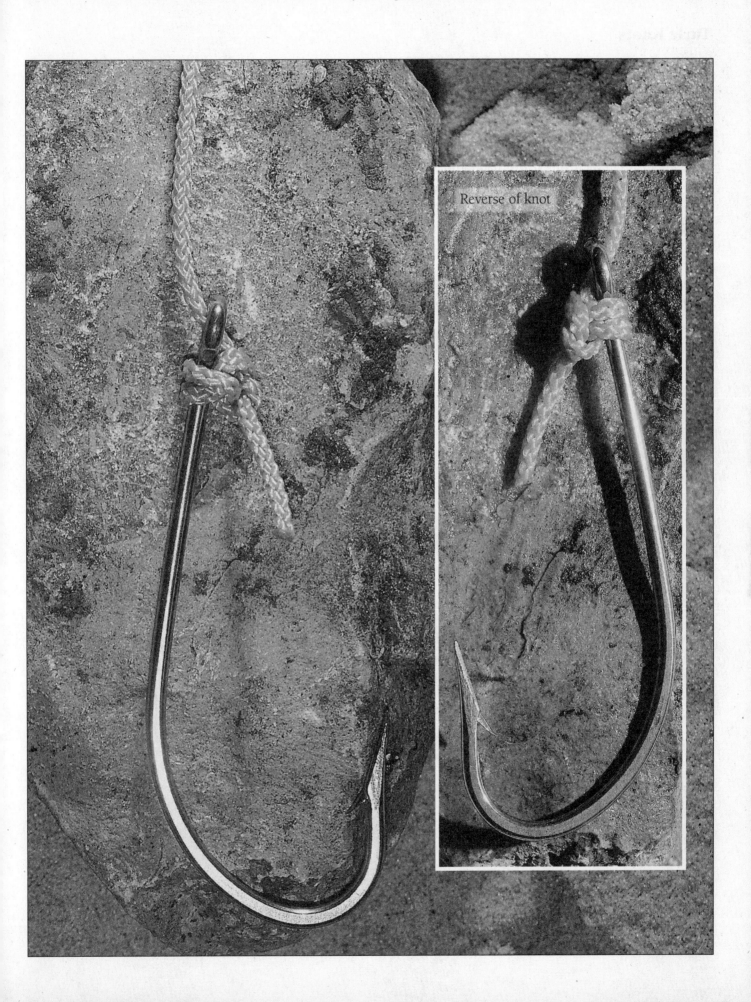

Reverse of knot

Turle Knots

(Reinforced)

Function

The weakness of both the basic and the double Turle knots lies in their simple overhand knot, both of which may be strengthened and rendered more secure.

Tying

The basic knot may be reinforced by tying a double overhand knot (*figures 1–2*) and, similarly, so may the double one (*figure 3*).

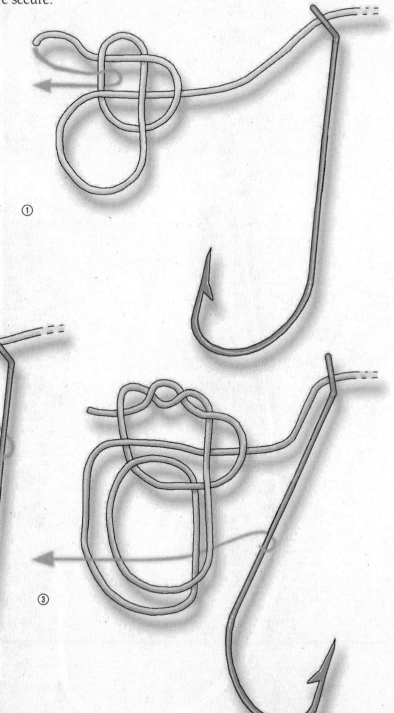

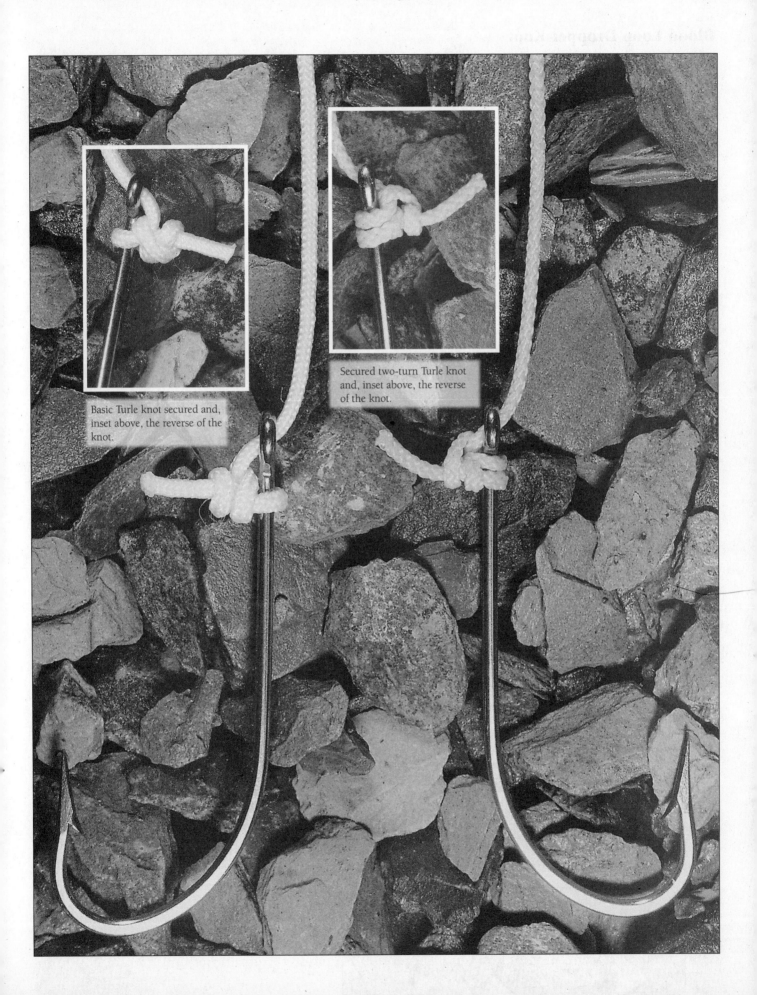

Basic Turle knot secured and, inset above, the reverse of the knot.

Secured two-turn Turle knot and, inset above, the reverse of the knot.

Blood Loop Dropper Knot

(Tied in the standing part)

Function

Standing out at right angles to the fishing line, blood loop droppers are for attaching extra flies (droppers) or additional sea fishing hooks and sinkers (weights) in a paternoster system.

Tying

Tie a multiple overhand knot in the standing part of the line and locate the central space or compartment (*figure 1*). Then simply pull the large loop or mouth of the knot down through it (*figure 2*). Partially tighten the knot until it flypes into a blood knot form, then fully tighten it (*figure 3*).

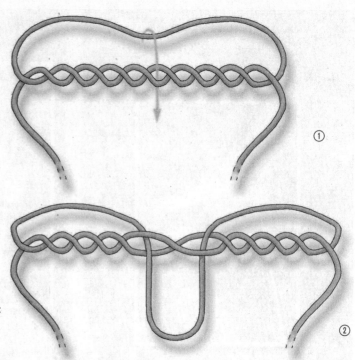

①

②

Reverse of knot

③

Front of knot

Blood Loop Dropper Knot

(Tied in the ends)

Function

This variant is used like the orthodox knot.

Tying

Tie a basic blood knot (either inward or outward coiled versions), and then merely tie the two ends together to create the required loop.

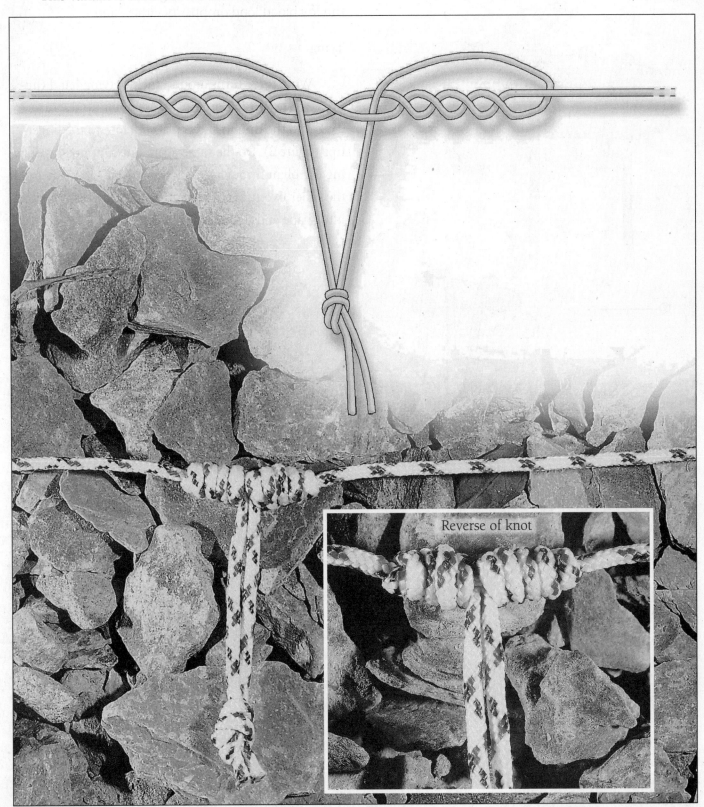

Reverse of knot

Alpine Butterfly Loop

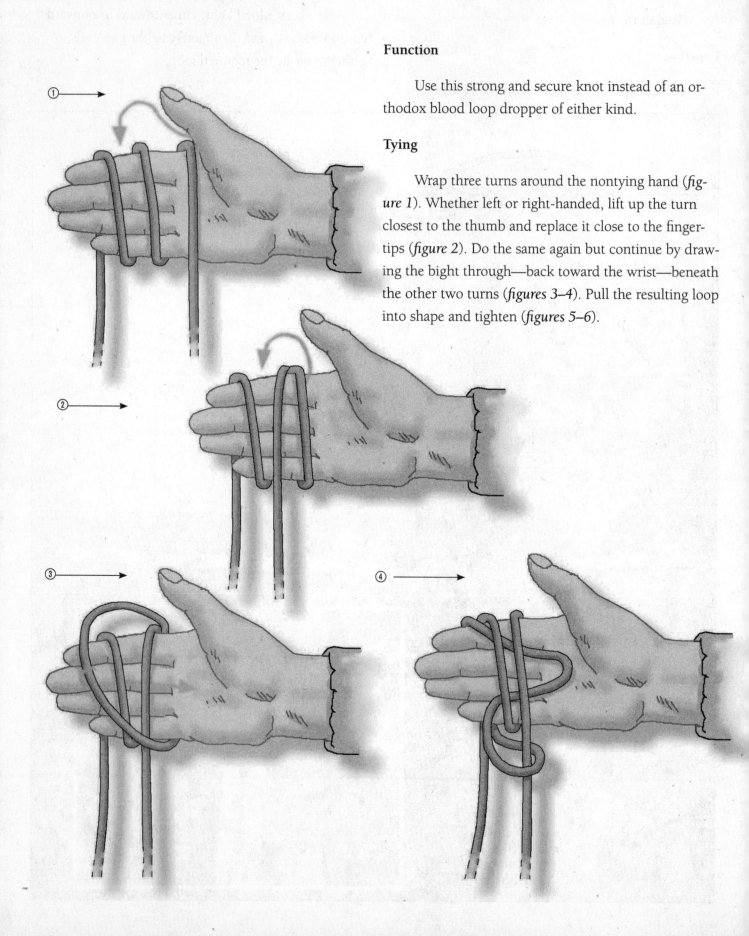

Function

Use this strong and secure knot instead of an orthodox blood loop dropper of either kind.

Tying

Wrap three turns around the nontying hand (*figure 1*). Whether left or right-handed, lift up the turn closest to the thumb and replace it close to the fingertips (*figure 2*). Do the same again but continue by drawing the bight through—back toward the wrist—beneath the other two turns (*figures 3–4*). Pull the resulting loop into shape and tighten (*figures 5–6*).

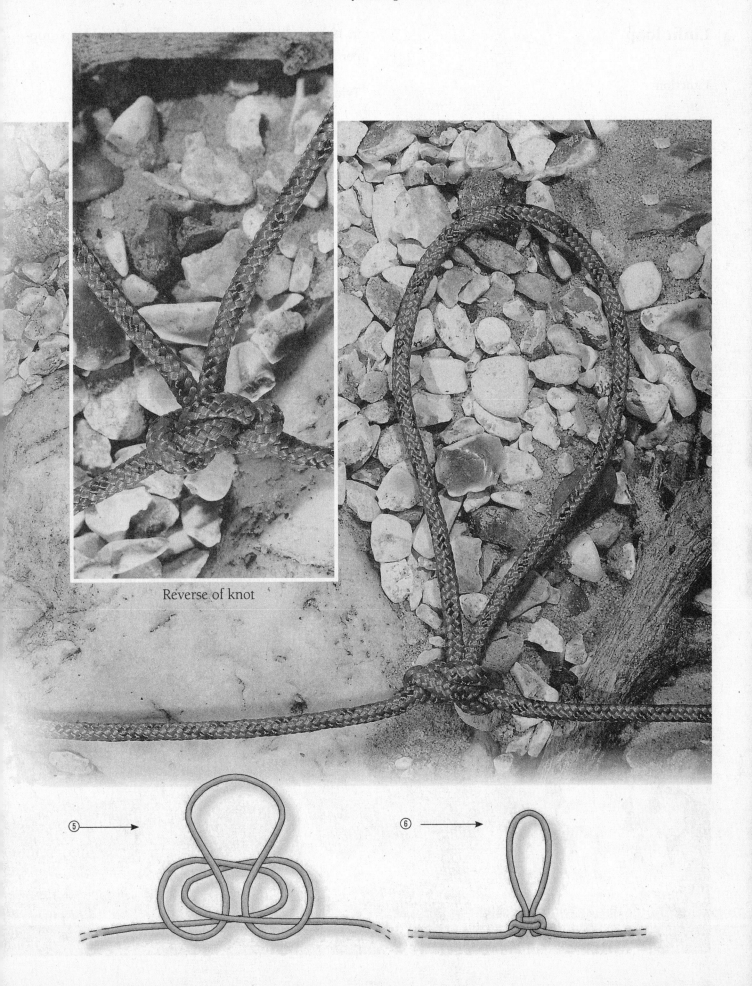

Reverse of knot

Linfit loop

Function

Like the linfit knot, this is another comparatively new fishing knot, invented by Owen K. Nuttall of Linthwaite, Huddersfield, England, which he published in 1986 as a robust alternative to both blood loop dropper and Alpine butterfly knots.

Tying

Make a large bight in the standing part of the line, bending it forward and down to form twin loops (*figure 1*). Impart a half-twist to each loop (left-hand

counter-clockwise, right-hand clockwise) and then partially cross right over left (*figures 2–3*). Pull the lower loop up behind all of the knot parts and make a final locking tuck through the compartment common to both upper loops (*figure 4*). Pull the knot snug and tight (*figure 5*).

Accessories

WADE BOURNE

Fishing is gadget-oriented! If you don't believe this, walk through a tackle store or sporting goods department and check out the products available. Beyond rods, reels, line and lures, there is a broad array of accessories designed to make fishing more efficient and convenient. But as the old saying goes, some are designed to catch fish, while others are designed to catch fishermen. Fishing gadgets will truly range from the practical to the outlandish!

Beyond a pair of basic rod/reel outfits and bait or lures, beginners need a small collection of other items to participate in this sport. Fortunately, this "must-have" list is small and relatively inexpensive—probably no more than $50 total.

Then there are many other accessories that are handy, but not essential. If you'd like to own them and can afford them, fine. They will likely add extra pleasure to your fishing.

And finally, there are the gimmicks that should be avoided. These are made and marketed to prey on beginners' lack of experience. These products usually come with unrealistic promises of success. Remember, nothing in fishing is guaranteed. If a product sounds too good to be true, it probably is. Save your money, and depend on using basic knowledge and practical products to catch fish.

Following are two lists. The first includes accessories that you should definitely purchase when getting into fishing. These are items that you will take and use on each outing.

The second list includes fishing accessories that are non-essential but which are practical and handy to have. These items can be purchased as your needs dictate and your finances allow.

A fisherman's tool is a must-have for anglers. Such a tool will be used frequently to tune lures, pry hooks from fish, change hooks on a lure, and handle other chores. Some tools include a hook sharpener, knife blade, screwdriver and other useful accessories.

Besides basic tackle, anglers need a small collection of accessories to participate in this sport. On the list of necessities are a tackle box, line clippers, needlenose pliers, polarized sunglasses and sunscreen. Non-essential-but-handy extras include a fishing vest, and for stream anglers, wading shoes.

Must-Have Fishing Accessories

TACKLE BOX/BAG—Every fisherman must have a tackle box or bag for toting tackle and gear. In essence, this is like a portable locker. It will carry such necessities as bait/lures, extra line, terminal tackle (hooks, sinkers, floats, swivels, etc.), and other small items.

I've actually fished with anglers who carried their tackle in small duffle bags, or even in paper bags. What a mess, especially when the paper bags got wet! To find something, these fishermen would have to stir around looking for it. This is why a hard plastic tackle box or soft-sided tackle packer is a good investment. They have compartments and storage boxes to keep tackle organized and accessible for quick location and use.

I recommend a medium-sized box (not one that's too large)! Select a box or packer that allows you to arrange compartments to suit your specific needs. Also, make sure your tackle box has a deep, roomy area to hold spare line, pliers, sunscreen and other extras.

As your involvement in fishing grows, you can continue adding tackle and lure boxes and arranging them for specific needs and/or species. My personal tackle packer is a soft-sided (cloth) system with individual plastic boxes, and I mix and match according to what type fishing I plan to do. I have several boxes of bass lures and tackle, one box with small jigs for panfish, another box of hooks, sinkers and floats, another box with streamfishing lures, another with catfish paraphernalia, etc. Then, when I'm going fishing, I choose the tackle box that I need for that day.

A sharp, thin-bladed fillet knife is useful when the time comes for cleaning and processing your catch.

FISHERMAN'S TOOL—This is a fancy name for needle-nose pliers. Some fisherman's tools also have a hook sharpener, line/wire cutter and other built-in features. The most frequent use of a fisherman's tool is prying hooks from fish, especially those that are embedded in the gullet. The needle-noses can reach deep into a fish's mouth and remove a hook safely and with minimal damage. Also, a fisherman's tool is handy for tuning lures, adding or removing a hook from a split ring and other tasks. The best fisherman's tools come with a handy belt holder.

LINE CLIPPERS—This is an angler's term for fingernail clippers that are used for cutting line. Buy line clippers with a lanyard for hanging the clippers around your neck. This keeps the clippers convenient for quick, easy use when changing lures, retying a frayed knot, etc.

FISHING CAP—Fishermen need a good cap to block the sun off their face and shade their eyes. Shading helps anglers see underwater to spot rocks, logs and fish. For hot weather, wear a mesh cap that's a light color—white or tan. In cold weather, you'll need something warmer. Also, for stream or pond fishing, a camo cap is a good choice.

POLARIZED SUNGLASSES—Sunglasses cut down on glare off the water, and polarized sunglasses actually allow you to see beneath the surface. They make it even easier to spot underwater objects that fish hang around, or to see fish themselves. Also, sunglasses protect eyes from flying objects, especially hooks. Keep sunglasses attached by a lanyard around your neck to keep from losing them when leaning over the water.

FISHERMAN'S TOWEL—This is a convenience item, but it's very nice to have when handling fish or messy live bait.

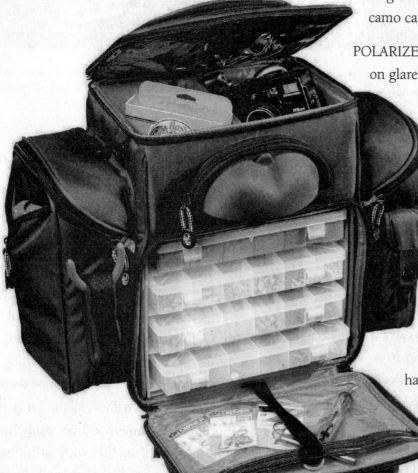

Every angler needs a tackle box or some type of storage system to tote his lures and accessories and to keep them organized.

A rainsuit isn't on the "must-have" list, but it's a very handy accessory for warding off rain and spray. Even wearing a rainsuit that's much too big is better than not having one when the sky opens up.

Having a towel keeps your pant legs from getting dirty. Consider purchasing a towel with a belt clip to keep it handy at all times.

SUNSCREEN—Having and using sunscreen is absolutely essential for fishermen. People who are in the sun a lot are at risk from skin cancer, which can be deadly. Before going fishing, apply sunscreen to all exposed skin (arms, hands, face, neck, ears, etc.) Use sunscreen that's at least 15 SPF, and higher is better.

FISH STRINGER—If you will be fishing from the bank or from a boat that doesn't have a live well, you will need a fish stringer to keep your catch. Stringers come in two types: rope stringer, and chain stringer. A rope stringer has a metal point on the end. The point is guided through a fish's gill plate and out the mouth, and individual fish slide down the cord on top of each other. A chain stringer has individual safety-pin snaps for holding fish. A chain stringer is better for keeping fish alive. Neither type stringer is very expensive.

Nonessential but Recommended Accessories

PFD (PERSONAL FLOTATION DEVICE)—Not many anglers wear a PFD when fishing off a bank, pier or bridge, but it's still a good idea, especially if you're not a strong swimmer. Also, a Coast Guard-certified PFD is required by law when fishing from a boat. (Always wear your life preserver when the boat is running. You don't have to wear it when the boat is not in operation, but it must always be in your possession.) One comfortable, convenient style PFD is the foam vest. Also, a new inflatable CO_2 type vest is extremely handy. It's so compact, you forget you have it on. But if you need it, you simply pull the lanyard, and the vest inflates instantly.

RAINSUIT—A rainsuit is obviously good for keeping you dry in a rainstorm. It's also good for shielding against spray when riding in a boat. The best rainsuits are made from waterproof, breathable fabric like Gore-Tex, but these are expensive. For starters, consider an inexpensive polyvinyl suit that comes in a small carry pouch.

FISHING VEST/TACKLE BELT—A vest or tackle belt is extremely handy for fishing streams or ponds where you will walk a lot. You wear your tackle instead of carrying it! You can store lures, tackle and accessories in pockets or compartments. Keep your vest or belt stocked, and you'll have everything ready when it's time to go fishing.

Fishermen using live bait need some way to keep their bait fresh and handy. A minnow bucket, cricket cage or worm box works for most, but anglers can go fancier, like this aerated cooler for holding goldfish for catfishing.

TOTE BAG—A tote or duffle bag is handy for carrying fishing accessories that won't fit into a tackle box. Any small bag with carry straps will do. By keeping all these accessories packed in one bag, you're not as likely to forget something.

This fisherman's tool includes needle-nose pliers, line cutters, knife blade, and multiple accessories ranging from bottle openers to screwdrivers.

LIVE BAIT CONTAINER—If you fish with live bait, you'll need a minnow bucket, worm box, cricket cage or some other container to keep your bait alive and healthy.

CAMERA—If you practice catch-and-release, a camera is handy for photographing trophy fish before you let them go. This way you can prove your big fish stories. A digital camera is best, since you can download images and email them to friends.

REEL REPAIR KIT—A small reel repair kit can be a lifesaver for in-the-field repairs or adjustments. I carry a kit that includes small screwdrivers (flathead and Phillips), an adjustable wrench, and a container of reel oil. I use my kit several times a year to work on reels and to handle other small maintenance chores.

LURE RETRIEVER—If you fish from a boat, a lure retriever can save a lot of money in lost lures. If you hang your lure on an underwater object, you can position the boat directly over the lure and use a retriever to free it. Lure retrievers come in two types: a heavy weight on a string, and a collapsible pole. The pole works better, but it's bulkier and more costly. A weight/string can be kept in a tackle box or tote bag. With either type, it only takes a few lures saved to recover the cost of the retriever.

If It Sounds Too Good, It Probably Is...

Every year I see advertisements for fishing products that sound too good to be true. They make outlandish claims of success. "Buy this product, and load the boat. Fish can't resist it!"

Keep your money in your pocket. As I said earlier, if a fishing lure or accessory sounds too good, it probably is. The secret to successful fishing is not buying and trying every new gimmick that hits the market. Instead, the secret to successful fishing is understanding fish habits and using a logical strategy to catch them.

Every angler needs a good fishing hat or cap. Many veterans prefer a hat that shades the ears and back of the neck.

This isn't to say that all new fishing products are hoaxes; far from it! Many new products have legitimate value in terms of making fishing easier and more successful. (When the depthfinder first appeared, many anglers were doubtful about this "electronic wonder," but it changed fishing forever.)

Still, don't buy new gadgets on impulse and expect them to produce instant results. If a new product is legitimate, it'll be around for a long time. Wait until the jury—more experienced anglers—returns a verdict. Watch for product reviews in fishing magazines and on TV shows. In some cases you can buy knowledge (via books, videos, magazines), but you can't buy experience. It takes both these things to become a successful fisherman.

Part 3
Boats and Boating

A. Boats, Motors and Boating Accessories

WADE BOURNE

I learned to fish as a small boy on the back seat of my dad's homemade johnboat. There was nothing fancy about it, but fancy doesn't have much to do with success. Dad's little boat got us on the water and took us to the holes where crappie lived. I remember days when we completely filled our cooler and had "extras" scattered along the boat's floor.

Not many beginners will enjoy the same learning opportunities. Most will start fishing from the bank, bridge or dock. But sooner or later, as your skills increase, you'll want to broaden your horizons and get out "on the water."

It's not that you can't catch fish around the banks. You certainly can, as we've noted in previous chapters. However, having a boat or some floating platform allows you to step up to another level in fishing. It opens a whole new world, allowing you to cover more water and be more versatile in your overall approach to the sport. In other words, a boat expands your fishing opportunities, and it allows you to increase your knowledge and fun.

Types of Boats

Fishing boats come in a broad range of designs and prices. High end bass boats cost in the mid-$30,000 range! On the low end are float tubes that start around $50. The expensive rigs are highly technical and ultimately functional, and someday you might decide to purchase one. But with this book's theme of keeping fishing simple, we'll stick to the fundamental, less expensive, easier-to-maintain models that beginning anglers are more likely to buy. These include johnboats, V-hulls, canoes, "bass buggies," inflatables and, again, float tubes.

An aluminum johnboat is a wise choice for beginning anglers who spend most of their fishing time on small waters. These boats are economical, portable and stable enough to provide a good casting platform.

Following are looks at each of these types of boats, the waters where they work best, and their advantages and disadvantages.

Johnboats

The aluminum johnboat may be the best all-purpose fishing boat for beginners. Johnboats have a flat bottom and a square or semi-V bow design. They are very stable and draw only a few inches of water, which enables them to traverse shallow areas. Johnboats were designed for streams, but a deep-sided, wide-beamed johnboat also adapts well to large open lakes. These boats perform well with outboard motors.

Johnboats come in a range of lengths, from 8 to more than 20 feet. However, the 12- and 14-foot models are most popular. These are light enough to be cartopped and carried to the water by two anglers. This means you can use a johnboat wherever you can drive close to a stream, pond bank or lakeshore.

Johnboats have three minor disadvantages: the flat hull provides a rough ride in choppy water; johnboats are clumsy to paddle; because of their all-metal construction, they are noisy when objects are dropped or banged against the sides.

But all in all, johnboats make very practical, relatively inexpensive fishing boats for beginners. Many anglers buy basic johnboats and customize them with seats, live well, carpet, rod holders, etc.

V-Hull

The V-hull is the workhorse of fishing boats. It's called "V-hull" because it has a V-shaped bow that tapers back to a flat-bottomed hull. This allows the V-hull to slice through waves, giving a smoother, safer ride in rough water.

Most are made of fiberglass or aluminum. Heavier fiberglass boats provide a smoother ride in choppy water. Most popular V-hull sizes are 12-18 feet. These boats are normally fitted with mid-sized outboards (25-100 horsepower).

A disadvantage of the V-hull is its weight. Larger V-hulls require trailers, and must be launched from ramps. They are awkward to paddle, but maneuver well with an electric motor.

These boats are the standard on big lakes and rivers because of their ability to handle rough water. As with johnboats, they are often customized with a broad range of accessories. Some models are equipped with console steering. Boat dealers sell a range of models, from basic no-frills boats to those with motor and accessories factory-installed. V-hulls are typically more expensive than johnboats.

Top-of-the-line bass boats are super fishing machines. They feature powerful outboards, a range of electronics, and the size and stability needed to fish big water.

Canoes

Canoes suffer from bad PR. Inexperienced canoe-ists believe these boats are too tippy for fishing. The truth is, certain models are very stable, and make excellent fishing boats for a wide range of waters. With only a little practice, beginners can handle a canoe and fish confidently from it.

Canoes offer anglers several advantages. They are relatively inexpensive and are extremely portable. They can be car-topped and carried to lakes or streams far off the beaten path. They are also ideal for small, urban waters where bigger boats are impractical or even disallowed. Canoes draw only inches of water. They are highly maneuverable and can be paddled through shallow riffles or bays. Also, some models can be outfitted with small outboards or electric motors for motorized running.

Canoes are made from several materials: fiberglass, aluminum, polyethylene. They come in square stern and double-end models. (Square stern canoes are best for using outboards or electric motors. Small motors may also be used on double-end canoes with a side-mount bracket near the stern.)

Fishermen shopping for a canoe should strongly consider a 16- or 17-foot model that has a wide beam and a flat bottom. This offers the greatest stability and versatility.

"Bass Buggies"

This type boat is also known as a mini-bass boat, but can be used for many different species. It is a rectangular, hard plastic casting platform supported by flotation arms running beneath both sides. Bass buggies come in one- and two-man models, ranging up to 10 feet in length. Most have molded-in seats, rod wells, battery compartments, etc. Most use an electric trolling motor but a few larger models accept a small outboard motor.

Bass buggies are mainly used on small, protected waters such as ponds, sloughs, strip mine pits and arms of larger lakes. They are highly maneuverable in standing timber, brush and other cover. They float in only a few inches of water. Bass buggies should not be used on large lakes or rivers with high waves or strong current.

Bass buggies are bulky, which means they aren't very portable. They must be hauled in a pickup bed or on a small trailer.

Inflatables

Inflatables are like rubber rafts, except today these "blow-up" boats are mostly made from PVC plastic. They come in a variety of sizes and shapes. The smallest models accommodate one passenger while the largest carry six people or more. These

Canoes are inexpensive, portable and easy to learn to paddle. All these features make a canoe a good choice for fishing on flowing waters or small ponds and lakes.

boats can be carried in a car trunk or SUV, backpacked to out-of-the-way waters and inflated on the spot. Portability is an inflatable boat's strongest advantage.

Inflatables have several disadvantages, however. They are more a means of water transportation than a true fishing boat. Their soft sides and bottom make them unstable for stand-up casting. Inflatables are subject to puncture from sharp objects, though most are constructed with separate flotation panels, so a puncture in one compartment won't sink the boat. Also, most inflatables come with easy-to-use repair kits. These boats are unwieldy to paddle, but some have a special motor-mount bracket that allows use of an electric motor or small outboard. One of the most attractive features of inflatables is price. They are very inexpensive. Two-man models start at around $50.

Float Tubes

The float tube (also called a "belly boat") isn't a standard boat like the others mentioned in this chapter. The float tube is a floating doughnut with a sewn-in seat and leg holes. An angler carries it to his fishing site,

steps in, pulls it up around his waist, then walks into the water. When he's deep enough for the float tube to support his weight, he propels himself by kicking with swim fins or special paddles attached to his boots. (Most float tube anglers wear waders, though they're not necessary if the water is warm.)

Float tubes are used to fish close to shore in small, quiet waters. They've very maneuverable, but they're slow. They're good for fishing in flooded brush, timber, patches of reeds or cattails or other similar spots that are difficult to reach by boat. Also, since float tubes are very quiet, they're good for slipping up on spooky fish.

Float tubes should not be used in strong-wind/open-lake situations. High waves can flip you upside down, and float tubes can be difficult to right. Again, these "boats" should be confined to quiet, close-to-shore fishing.

Float tubes are highly portable and fairly inexpensive. They come in basic or deluxe models. Deluxe models come with such features as zippered tackle holders, shoulder straps, an inflatable backrest and Velcro rod holders.

The V-hull is the workhorse of fishing boats. It's called "V-hull" because it has a V-shaped bow that tapers back to a flat hull. The V-hull is designed to slice through waves and provide a safe, dry ride in rough water.

Buying Your Fishing Rig

It's obvious now that, even with a simple fishing rig, you're looking at a sizeable investment. When it's time to go shopping, check around for a package deal. By buying a boat, motor, trailer, fish locater and accessories from one dealer, you have a better bargaining position for a discount.

Do your homework. Don't buy a rig without shopping around. Ask dealers for advice on what boat, motor, and accessories you'll need for where you'll be fishing. Check prices, collect literature, study it and decide for sure what you want before making any purchase commitment.

Boat dealers generally offer their best deals in late summer or fall, toward the end of the fishing season. At this time you're in a better position to bargain and wait for them to come down on price. Don't be in a hurry to buy your fishing rig. This is a big step, and you should proceed slowly and carefully.

Once you do take the step, however, you'll have graduated up to fishing's "high school." You'll have access to your chosen lake, river or stream's entire angling menu. No longer will you have to fish from shore and watch the boats go by. Now you can join them. The door will suddenly open to many new fishing challenges and experiences, more than you can experience in a lifetime.

Motors

Motors aren't absolutely necessary for fishing, but in many cases they certainly make the job easier. You must decide if you need a motor by the type boat you have and the water where you plan to fish. If you'll be using a small boat on remote streams, small ponds or lakes, paddles may be all the power you need. But if you'll be on larger waters where you'll have to cover more distance, or where winds or currents can be strong, a larger boat with a motor will be more practical and efficient.

Fishing motors come in two varieties: outboard and electric. Outboard (gas-powered) motors are more powerful and are used mainly for running long distances—getting from one spot to the next. Electric (battery-powered) motors are less powerful and much quieter. Their job is to ease the boat through the target area while the angler fishes. Electric motors are also used as the main power source on waters where outboards aren't allowed.

Outboard Motors

New outboard motors are expensive. Often they cost more than the boat they power. But anglers should view an outboard as a long-term investment. Modern outboards are dependable and easy to operate and will last many years if properly maintained.

Outboards range from 1.5 to 250-plus horsepower. Smaller motors are lightweight and portable. They attach to the boat's stern with clamp mounts. Larger motors are heavy, and they're permanently bolted onto the stern.

The main consideration when buying a motor is not to overpower the boat. All boats list maximum horsepower ratings either on the stern plate or in the owner's instructions. Never exceed these ratings—overpowered boats are unsafe to operate.

Electric Motors

Most electric motors fall into one of two categories: 12-volt and 24-volt. Twelve-volt motors are powered by one 12-volt battery. Twenty-four volt motors require two linked 12-volt batteries. The obvious difference between the two is available power, which is measured in "pounds of thrust." The 24-volt motor is much stronger than a 12-volt. Twenty-four volt motors are normally used on big boats that operate in rough

Outboard motors come in a wide range of horsepower sizes. Modern outboards are expensive, but they are good investments. They will last for years if properly maintained.

A clamp-on electric motor is a good choice for powering a smaller johnboat, V-hull or bass buggie. They are quiet so they won't scare fish, yet they are strong enough to maneuver a boat into the best casting position.

water. On smaller boats and quiet waters, a 12-volt motor is adequate.

Electric motors have different types of mounts and methods of operation. Some motors have "clamp-on" mounts with screws to tighten down on the sides or transom of the boat. Others have bow mounts that attach permanently to the front of the boat. Some electric motors are operated by hand, while others have foot controls that allow the user to run the motor while keeping his hands free to fish. Remote- and radio-control electric motors are available. Microchip technology is being used to upgrade electric motors each year, making them ever more "user friendly."

It is much more efficient for an electric motor to pull a boat rather than push it. A boat with an electric motor mounted on or near the bow is easier to propel and steer than one with an electric motor on the transom.

When shopping for an electric motor, you'll find models with many options and power ratings. My recommendation for a beginner's first electric is a 12-volt clamp-on model with 20-40 pounds of thrust. Remember that the heavier your boat, the more power you'll need to pull or push it. Also, electric motor shafts come in different lengths. Owners of johnboats, canoes and bass buggies will probably need motors with shafts that are 30 or 36 inches long. Owners of V-hulls may need a motor with a 42-inch shaft, since these boats have higher sides and are more likely to be used in rolling waves. Boat dealers can provide guidelines for choosing the right shaft length.

Fish Locaters

A fish locater is an angler's "eyes under the water." Its basic function is to show the bottom and objects between the surface and the bottom. Knowing water depth is important both from a safety standpoint and also for fishing efficiency. Fish locaters can show submerged structure: drop-offs, sunken channels, stumps, brush, rocks, weeds, etc. A good fish locater can even

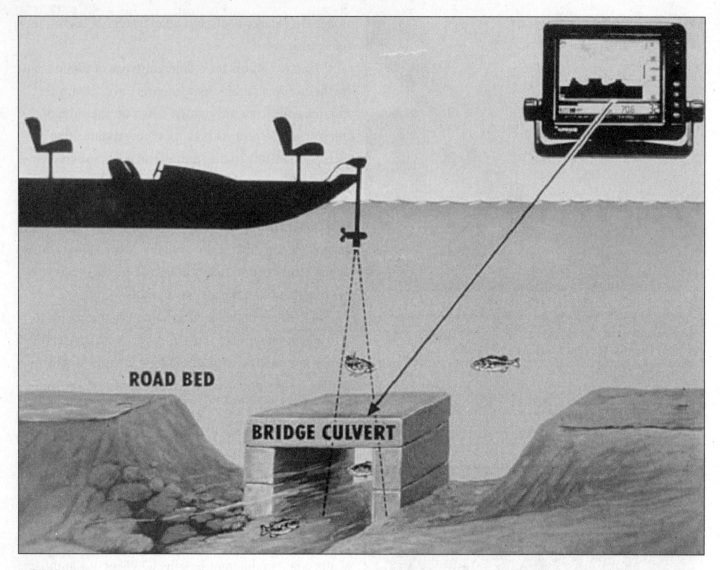

A fish finder's signal is interpreted as a grapic image on the LCD screen. The computer uses the transponder's signal to "paint" a picture of the bottom, features, and hanging fish.

tell whether the bottom is soft or hard, and can pinpoint concentrations of bait- and gamefish.

Even though a fish finder is fairly expensive (starting at around $75), it is considered an almost indispensable tool by serious anglers. I recommend one for all beginners who will be fishing away from shore on lakes and large rivers. A fish locater, properly used, will pay great dividends in terms of numbers of fish caught.

A fish locater is a sonar unit that sends out sound waves that strike underwater objects. Then the fish locater measures how long it takes the echoes to bounce back to the sending unit. The deeper an object in the water, the longer the time required for this roundtrip. The fish locater then translates this time into a distance

display, showing bottom depth and objects between the surface and bottom.

Most modern fish locaters are LCD units ("liquid crystal display") that actually draw chart-like pictures of what's beneath the boat. The latest technology includes different colors in this display to help users distinguish between fish and other underwater features. You can actually see fish you're trying to catch!

Boat Accessories

The boat, motor and fish locater make up the core of the fishing rig, but several other accessories are needed to complete the package. State and federal laws

A fish locater uses sonar to indicate depth and the location of underwater structure. An angler can analyze a body of water and discover the best fishing locations.

require certain safety equipment on all boats. Boats under 16 feet must carry a Coast Guard-approved flotation device for each passenger, paddle, some type of sound signal (whistle, air horn, etc.), running lights if the boat is to be used at night, and a fire extinguisher if gas is kept in an enclosed compartment. Boats 16 feet and longer must meet these requirements, plus the flotation devices must be wearable life preservers, and the boat must also have a throwable flotation device (cushion, safety ring, etc). For a full review of these requirements, contact your state water safety office.

Beyond these required items, you may consider a broad array of boat accessories: batteries and battery boxes, battery charger, landing net, anchor and rope, seats, fish basket, bilge pump, rod holders and marker floats. These and other accessories will complete your boat package and make your fishing easier.

Most bass boats use a stern mounted, gasoline powered outboard motor for travelling on lakes and rivers and an electric trolling motor, mounted near the bow, to maneuver around fishing spots.

There are two types of marine batteries: "deep cycle" and "quick start." Deep-cycle batteries release small amounts of electricity over extended time periods. They are used primarily to power electric motors. Quick-start batteries provide short, powerful bursts of electricity. They are intended for starting outboards and also for running electric accessories other than the electric motor.

Remember four tips for battery maintenance. First, always recharge your batteries immediately after use.

Don't allow them to sit discharged for long periods. Second, if your battery is not sealed, you can open the cell caps to check solution levels. Keep solution at recommended levels. Third, don't overcharge your batteries. If your batteries don't have charge indicators, use a hydrometer and check charge level as you recharge. Quit charging when the hydrometer reads "full charge." And fourth, during winter, charge batteries fully, then store them in a cool, dry place.

B. Flyfishing from a Boat

CONWAY X. BOWMAN

1. The boat as a clock

Imagine a clock lying on its back. According to my father, a World War II veteran, the United States Army Air Force used it as a directional system to help gunners pick up the positions of attacking enemy fighter aircraft. Now imagine your boat as a flat clock, its numerals used by your guide to direct your attention to a fish's position and where to aim your cast. Think of the bow as twelve o'clock, starboard as three o'clock, the stern as six o'clock, and port as nine o'clock. Understanding this system will contribute to your success in taking more fish, making your fly fishing more productive and pleasurable. My analogy may seem a bit farfetched, but as you progress as a saltwater fly angler, you will eventually hire a guide who will not only captain your boat but will also be a great source of information and suggestions. Almost all guides employ the clock system: When he says, "Tarpon at ten o'clock," you need to understand what he is saying and why, so you can act accordingly.

2. Fly-fish from a kayak

The kayak is a stealthy and effective vehicle to use for fly fishing, a means to access fishing areas where fish are normally easily spooked, such as flats, marshes, and kelp beds. In addition, a kayak is not only portable, but it requires a smaller investment than a flats skiff and is more environmentally friendly (no gasoline or motor oil required).

A properly equipped kayak can store a couple of fly rods, fly boxes, a BogaGrip (for holding fish by the lip, for hook removal), and even a push pole.

Using a kayak, you can stand and sight-cast on shallow flats, or paddle offshore to the kelp beds. If you feel uncomfortable paddling with a double-bladed

The kayak is an affordable way to explore backcountry waters.

paddle, then a pedal kayak may be more to your taste and abilities. Yet another option is a kayak with a small, battery-operated trolling motor, which lets you cover more water and even work into the wind.

On a kayak, the fly line can be stripped right onto the deck without your having to worry about hanging up on boat cleats or other obstacles.

A sea anchor will help you stay in position if you're fishing structure or around kelp beds. On the flats, a small anchor can help keep you in one spot.

If you do opt for a kayak, consider using a longer fly rod, preferably a nine and a half-footer. A rod this long will help keep your line off the water on your backcast and enable you to make longer casts.

3. Stand-up paddleboard? Why not?

One of the hottest new methods of angling for saltwater fish on the fly rod is from a stand-up paddle-board (SUP). Southern California fishermen have been fishing off their surfboards for years, but the recent SUP rage has created all sorts of venues for the more progressive saltwater fly fisher. Besides providing easier portability, the paddleboard gives you a better platform from which to spot, sneak up on, and cast to fish.

The SUP is an extremely versatile fishing platform, a craft you can launch anywhere, and all you need for transport is a cartop rack or a pickup truck. Much lighter than a kayak, the SUP is at home in shallow waters inaccessible by boat or in deepwater areas not frequented by the general public (simply toss it into a boat and take it where you want to go).

Outfit the SUP the same as you would a kayak, using a fishing box specifically designed for fly fishing, with a rod holder and places for your paddle, fly box, and other tackle. You can also build one to your own specifications.

If you use an SUP on a regular basis, you'll no-tice that your waistline will benefit. Paddling an SUP, whether kneeling or standing, is a great workout.

The SUP allows for better sight casting than a sit-in kayak.

Cancel that gym membership. Now you've got another excuse to go fishing . . . you're exercising!

As with kayak fishing, it takes some time to master the art of SUP fly fishing. You have to keep in mind, for example, that you will be pushed by the wind, so you need to be aware of your drift and compensate accordingly. Calm, glassy waters are best for the SUP, but offshore is not out of the question. In time, you'll really come to appreciate the benefits of an SUP.

C. Casting from a Boat

TOM ROSENBAUER

Casting from a boat

In one respect, casting from a boat is easier, especially if the boat is stable enough for you to stand in, because you have more elevation above the water, so it's easier to pick up line and it's easier to keep your back cast high. However, boats present their own challenges, and if you're prepared to deal with them, your time on the water will be easier.

First, most boats are full of cleats and seats and other gear that can grab your fly line when you make a cast. Try to remove as many obstructions as possible around your feet, or cover them with a wet towel or a piece of mesh if they can't be moved. Whereas most of us are pretty casual about where we strip our line when

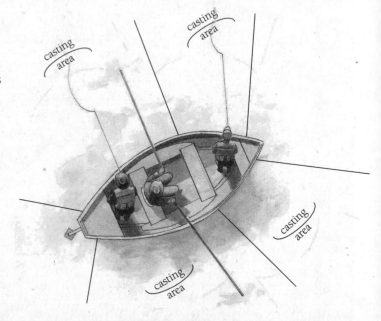

Ordinarily, the right-hander in the stern of this boat would be casting in the other direction so he could watch the other angler's back cast and not cast over the head of the guide in the middle. But all three of these guys are guides so they'll probably be OK.

wading, when casting from a boat it helps if you pay more attention to where each length of line is placed when you're stripping it in. Some anglers like to use a stripping basket in a boat, which is a device used to catch all your excess line after stripping it in. A plastic trash bucket can be used as a stripping basket in a pinch—just fill it with a little water to keep it weighted down and to keep your fly line slick.

You must also pay attention to the living obstructions in a boat. For instance, in a drift boat, where there is typically an angler in the bow and one in the stern with the guide sitting between the two, the territory over the length of the boat is a forbidden land—in other words, never cast straight in front of or straight behind a boat unless you want a very unhappy guide. And with two anglers casting at the same time, even if they are casting to different sides of the boat, it's very easy to tangle the back cast of one angler with the forward cast of the other. It's always the responsibility of the caster in the stern to watch out for trouble because the angler in the bow can't see what is going on behind him.

Part 4
Comfort and Safety

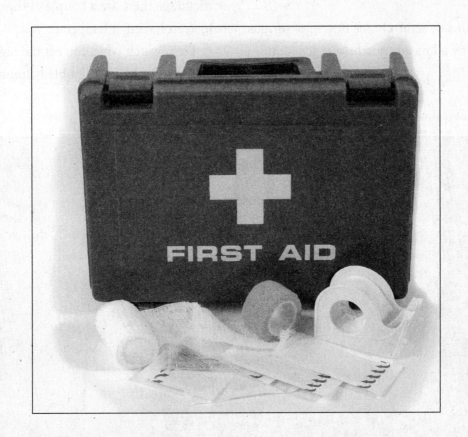

A. Fly Fishing Safety

CONWAY X. BOWMAN

1. Be prepared for a medical emergency

Many saltwater fly-fishing destinations are in beautiful but remote locations that have few or no medical services. If you get sick or hurt, you could be in trouble.

Before you leave for a trip, research the medical services that are available at your destination, and plan accordingly. Also make sure to pack a comprehensive first-aid kit, complete with antibiotics, pain relievers, bandages (and tape), diarrhea medicine, and insect repellent.

To ensure your safe return home in case of serious sickness or injury, by all means purchase evacuation travel insurance.

2. How to prevent seasickness

There is no worse feeling than being on the ocean and having your innards suddenly go into nauseous convulsions. You're the victim of a scourge that has plagued humankind since we first hoisted a sail on the ocean. Its common name is seasickness, though those who have suffered from it may also call it "sea death," as many folks would rather be thrown to the sharks to put them out of their misery. It isn't fun.

Without getting into the medical reasons behind seasickness, there are a couple of things you can do to help avert having it happen to you.

First, watch what you eat the night before you go fishing. Eat light. A double helping of lasagna with

Bug repellent is a must in most saltwater destinations.

Check the conditions before you head out.

some garlic bread and red wine on the side is going to sit in your stomach all night, and still be there the next morning.

If you eat light, yet still suspect that you're going to feel ill on the water, consider taking an over-the-counter medicine such as Dramamine or Bonine before you go out. Ear patches, wrist bands, and other medications can also be obtained, though in most cases you'll need a prescription from your doctor.

What has worked for many of my clients over the years is a teaspoon of pickled ginger, the kind you can get at your local sushi restaurant or Asian market. For

some reason, this remedy works almost all the time. If you're on the water and start to get an upset stomach, eat a teaspoon of ginger—you'll be amazed at the results.

One old-timer's method for curing seasickness is to look at the horizon or a landmark and avoid looking down, a move that usually triggers the nausea.

Another trick, used by one of my older fishing buddies, is to never go out on the ocean without a box of saltine crackers. Eating a few crackers always worked for him.

If all else fails, start the boat and motor into the wind. A breeze on your face will help you feel better.

3. Learn how to run a skiff

We talk so much about how to pick the right flies, cast into the wind, and fight fish, but we rarely cover the importance of being able to operate a skiff if called upon to do so.

It's simple. If you're on the water in a boat or skiff, miles offshore or somewhere on the flats, and your guide, captain, or fishing buddy is for some reason unable to run the skiff—perhaps due to illness or injury—it's critical that you know how to run the craft back to shore and safety. The chances are slim that this will actually happen, but you never know. It happened to me once, and I'll forever be thankful that I knew how to operate a boat.

One painless way to learn the basics of running a boat is to enroll in a boating and water safety class.

When heading out for a day on the water, make a point of familiarizing yourself with the skiff or boat's power unit. How does the motor start—with a key-controlled electric starter, or with a manual pull cord?

Does the boat or skiff have a center console with steering wheel, or is the motor moved by a tiller? Is

Knowing how to operate a skiff can be useful in an emergency situation.

there a kill switch that will deactivate the motor if the switch is detached from the key?

Where is the boat's GPS and navigation unit? Is it set to track back to the boat's launching point? Does the craft have a VHF radio? How is it operated and, in an emergency, how do you contact the Coast Guard?

And last, but hardly least: Where are the personal flotation devices and first-aid kit?

Familiarize yourself with all these aspects of boat operation, and you'll be able to return the boat and its passengers to safety if something happens to the boat's operator.

4. Sun protection

I know it looks great to have a tan, but in truth, that tan can eventually turn into skin cancer—and if you get melanoma, it can kill you. Here are some ways to keep those rays off your skin.

Sunblock

The recommended strength for sunblock varies. Some doctors say SPF 15 is adequate; many dermatologists say you should use nothing less than SPF 30. Whatever strength you decide to use, be smart and, during your day on the water and in the sun, take the time to reapply sunblock frequently, especially to your nose, ears, hands, and face—the parts of the body that take the brunt of the sun's rays. After application, be sure to clean your hands thoroughly so you don't get any sunblock on your fly or line. Gamefish can detect the odor and may spook.

Clothing

The best way to protect your skin is to completely cover your body with proven protective clothing. Most new outdoor wear is not only comfortable and functional, but has an SPF rating of 30-plus, which provides you with extra protection. These outfits come in an assortment of colors and styles for even the most fashion-conscious saltwater fly rodder.

Headgear

A hat is one of the most basic elements of sun protection. There is such a huge variety of hats available that it's largely a matter of preference. Some folks prefer the standard baseball cap, which provides moderate protection. Watch out for mesh trucker's caps, however, as the sun will penetrate right through the mesh. A widebrimmed hat that covers your ears as well as your head and neck is better for overall protection. Then there's the balaclava, which is currently very popular and can be worn completely over the face, on the neck, or merely on the head. Several versions are available, and can be adapted to hot, warm, or cold conditions.

Stay covered up to avoid the sun's harmful rays.

B. Comfort and Safety

LAMAR UNDERWOOD

1. Get That Hook Out

It can happen at any time, even when you're home and messing around with your tackle: You're hooked, and past the barb. You've got to get the thing out, and you don't want to head in for first aid or doctors. What to do? Well, this system works like magic, but you've got to have some nerve to pull it off. First, press down on the eye of the hook. Next, wrap a piece of string or cloth around the curve of the hook. Finally, while pressing down hard on the eye, give the shank a quick jerk. Put some antiseptic on the wound and go back to fishing. Caveat: Don't try this when hooked in vulnerable areas like the face. If you want to see this technique done visually before you try it, Google the words "fish hook removal." That will take you to several sites.

2. Waders and Drowning: The Big Myth

Despite long-time and widely held myths, waders and/or a wading belt cannot be the sole cause of you drowning if you fall into the river. The extra weight and cumbersome gear may make them feel as if they're dragging you down, but they're actually not dragging you down any more than your trousers or shirt. Swift currents, especially white water, can force you under, whether you're wearing waders or not. Lee Wulff proved all this by diving off a bridge into a river back in 1947 wearing full waders. He let the waders fill with water and floated downstream with his head up without a problem. If you fall in with waders on, keep your head up, get your footing as soon as you can, and slosh out of the water. Repeat: Keep your head up and don't

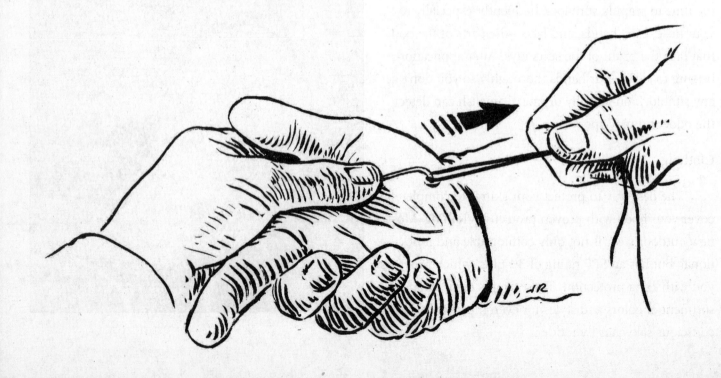

panic. The waders will not drown you. If you're still not convinced, wear your waders and hop into a swimming pool to see what it's like. Of course, we're assuming you know how to swim.

3. The Greatest Snakebite Kit

The best snakebite kit in the world is a set of car keys. Get to the hospital promptly, without panic or killing yourself or someone else on the way. If possible, carry the dead snake with you for certain identification that the bite is poisonous.

4. Lightning and Fishing

You can read a lot about lightning, learning interesting stuff, like the fact that instead of the old bromide of "never striking twice in the same place," it usually *does* strike twice in the same places. The thing to remember is that lightning can, and will, kill you very quickly if you're caught in a storm—or even on the edges of a storm—waving your rod around. No fish is worth the consequences. Take cover when a storm is approaching.

5. The Wind Behind the Rain

When the rain that has been plaguing your region for a day or two is coming to an end, and you're cheering the prospect of going fishing, be aware that with the passing front will come the wind. Be ready to fish in windy conditions. On big water, fresh or salt, you might not even be able to fish the way you want to—or even get out.

6. Stringer Danger!

In the deep South, where fishing in the black-water streams and swamps might yield a hefty stringer of bream, bass, and crappies, leaving that stringer waiting at the edge of the stream or lake while you make camp re-quires a note of caution. Before you reach down to pull it up, make sure a big moccasin or water snake hasn't paid your fish a visit. The cottonmouth is venomous, poison to you and me, while the non-venomous water snake can have a lousy disposition at times and ruin your day.

C. Fishing Safety

Several years ago I had one of my worst scares ever while fishing on my home lake. I was in my boat alone, casting for bass around a shoreline on the far side of the lake. I'd noticed storm clouds building to the west, and I'd heard thunder rumbling. But the fish were biting, and I allowed the excitement of the moment to overrule my good sense to get back to the boat ramp before the storm broke.

Winter fishermen should be prepared with gloves, face mask and good boots and socks. Anglers must be prepared for two special perils that this season brings. One is hypothermia—a lowering of the body's core temperature through rapid heat loss. The second danger is frostbite.

When I finally decided to head back in, I'd waited too long. When I was in the middle of the lake, a fierce wind struck, and it seemed as though my small boat and I were in the North Atlantic. Waves were as high as my head. Spray drenched me, and the boat started taking water.

I cinched my life vest up tight. My only hope of not swamping was to turn downwind and run with the waves. After an anxious 15-minute ride, I beached in a desolate cove, where I was stuck for a couple of hours while the storm passed. Rain poured down, and lightning popped! I sat huddled in a gully, soaked and miserable, but at least I was okay.

Overall, fishing is a very safe sport, but it does involve certain hazards. Some of these may be life-threatening, others only discomforting. The old adage "an ounce of prevention is worth a pound of cure" applies. If I'd started back to the boat ramp 15 minutes earlier, I wouldn't have wound up in such a predicament. If the angler down the lake had done the same, he'd probably be alive today!

Following is a look at safety considerations in fishing, at dangers which can arise and how to avoid or deal with them. We'll take them in order of seriousness: life-threatening first, then discomforting second.

Weather Perils of Fishing

LIGHTNING - Because fishing is an outdoor sport, you will experience different types of weather. This means that sooner or later you'll be exposed to one of the most dangerous of all natural killers: lightning.

Fishing has certain hazards. A combination of open water and high winds can swamp a boat if resulting waves get too high. Anglers should always watch the weather and be careful to avoid potential danger on the water.

Lightning doesn't get the scare publicity that tornadoes, hurricanes and other sensational weather phenomena do. But each year lightning claims more lives than all other weather-related accidents combined. Invariably, some of these victims are fishermen.

Kids learn at an early age that lightning strikes tall objects. Tallness is relative. A fisherman in a boat on a lake is tall in comparison to what's around him. The same is true about an angler standing on a flat, barren shoreline. In either case, if the fisherman is using a rod (particularly graphite), in effect he's holding a lightning rod, and he's inviting disaster.

The cardinal rule is never allow yourself to get caught where lightning is likely to strike. If you see a storm coming, get off the water or away from high areas or tall objects. The safest place to be is inside a house or vehicle. Don't stand under isolated trees or poles. If you get caught in an electrical storm, wait it out in the lowest spot you can find, and keep a low profile. If you get caught on the water and can't make it to shore, stow your rods and lie down in the boat.

HIGH WINDS - High winds are another weather peril for anglers in boats. Small boats and big waves are a bad combination. If you think the waves are too high, don't go out. If you are out and see a storm coming, head in. If you get caught in high waves and start taking water, forget about trying to get back to the dock or ramp. Turn and go with the wind. Let the waves take you where they may.

If you are in a boat that does swamp, stay in it rather than abandon it. Most boats today have level flotation, and even if they fill with water, they won't sink. Keep your life jacket cinched tightly, try to stay calm, and wait for someone to come to your rescue.

A hook buried in a hand is a quick way to ruin a fishing trip. Sooner or later most anglers will be presented with this dilemma. They have the choice of going to a doctor to have it removed or removing it themselves by using the "yank" method described in this chapter.

FOG - Sometimes you may be tempted to head out onto a foggy lake. My advice is don't go. When you can't see where you're going, you risk running into an unseen object or getting lost. Stay at the boat ramp until the fog lifts. You won't miss much fishing time, and you won't be taking unnecessary chances.

Also, keep a GPS or a compass handy in case fog rolls in. I have a GPS on my fish finder, and I also keep a small compass in my tackle box. Fog causes you to lose all sense of direction, and a GPS or compass can help you find your way back to the launch site.

HYPOTHERMIA - "Exposure" is the common term for hypothermia. This is a loss of body heat - typically caused by getting wet - that can eventually cause death. This is not just a winter problem. It can occur in other seasons, too. It's usually brought on by a combination of cool air, wind and wet clothes. Evaporation of moisture from clothing causes a rapid heat loss, and this leads to a drop in body temperature. If this drop is severe, death can follow.

The first sign of hypothermia is mild shivering. This is the body's way of trying to warm itself, and it's also a warning signal of trouble. If something isn't done to reverse this situation, the shivering can become uncontrollable, and the victim starts losing feeling in his arms and legs. His speech becomes slurred, and his thinking gets fuzzy. If his body temperature continues to drop (75-80° F), he will slip into a coma and possibly die.

If you or a fishing buddy starts shivering, don't ignore this signal!

It's time to take action. There are two things to do: (1) remove the cause of cooling (wet clothing); and (2) restore body heat. This can be done by replacing wet clothes with dry ones (especially a dry cap or hat), by drinking warm fluids (coffee, tea, etc.), by eating energy-rich foods (candy), and by warming next to a fire or some other heat source. You must stop the loss of body heat and restore it to a normal level. If the symptoms progress to uncontrollable shivering, get medical help fast. Remember, hypothermia is a killer.

FROSTBITE - Frostbite can be a threat to winter fishermen. In essence, this is a burn that occurs when skin is exposed to a combination of very cold air, moisture and wind. Circulation drops. The flesh becomes numb and freezes. Frostbitten toes or fingers turn white, and they're very cold to the touch.

Frostbite can be avoided by moving around, replacing wet gloves or socks with dry ones, holding numb fingers under your armpit, or holding a warm hand over an exposed ear, nose or cheek.

If frostbite does occur, don't rub it. Instead, place the frostbitten area next to warm skin, and leave it there to thaw. Seek medical attention.

The Danger of Drowning

Drowning is a constant danger to fishermen. Each year we hear tragic stories of anglers who have fallen out of boats or off the bank and were lost. This danger is easily avoided. Following are commonsense rules for making sure you won't become a drowning victim.

WEAR A LIFE PRESERVER. - Using a life preserver is the "ounce of prevention" I mentioned earlier. Very few anglers drown while wearing a Coast Guard-approved personal flotation device (PFD). Whenever you're in a boat, you're required to have such a preserver with you. You're not required to wear it, however, and this gets many lackadaisical fishermen in trouble.

Accidents happen when you least expect them, and they happen quickly. If you're not wearing your life preserver, and your boat suddenly overturns, you probably won't have a chance to put your PFD on. Always wear your PFD when the boat is running, and zip it up or tie it. Also, it's a good idea to wear it even when the boat's not running, especially if you're a poor swimmer. A vest-type preserver isn't bulky. It's comfortable, and it won't interfere with your fishing.

Or, perhaps a better option is an approved inflatable-type PFD that's worn like suspenders. If you fall out of the boat, a quick tug on a lanyard activates a CO2 cartridge that instantly inflates the PFD.

Bank fishermen should also consider wearing a PFD. Especially if you're fishing along steep banks, tailraces, docks, bridges or similar spots. Children should never be allowed close to such spots without wearing a securely fastened PFD.

DON'T OVERLOAD THE BOAT. - One of the worst incidents in my life was watching a duck hunter drown. Four grown men and a retriever were in a small johnboat motoring across the lake where my partners and I were hunting. Suddenly the boat capsized, and the men were in the water. One couldn't swim, and he went down in deep water before my hunting partners and I could rescue him.

The first mistake these men made was in not wearing their life preservers. They had PFDs in the boat, but they were of little use.

Their second mistake was putting too much load into too small a boat. Little boats aren't meant for heavy loads, especially when there's a chance of encountering high waves, strong current, etc.

How to Remove Embedded Hooks

Barb buried in / Line around wrist

Push down

Tighten up in this direction (do not pull)

Pull

Hook will pop up in this direction

Despite your best prevention efforts, sooner or later you or your fishing partner will likely be on the receiving end of a flying hook, or you'll sit or step on a hook. When this happens, you have a choice. You can go to a doctor and have it surgically removed, or you can pull the hook out yourself by the following method, which is simple and fairly painless.

You'll need two 18-inch pieces of strong twine. (Monofilament doubled over works well.) If the embedded hook is attached to a lure, remove the lure so only the hook remains. Run one piece of twine through the eye (hole) of the hook, and hold it snug against the skin. With the other hand, loop the other piece of twine through the bend of the hook (between the skin and the hook), pull out all slack, and get a strong grip. If you're doing this properly, the two pieces of string will be pulling in opposite directions.

Now, hold the hook eye firmly in place next to the skin. With the other string, yank up and away very suddenly and forcefully. Done properly, this yields a fulcrum movement that pops the barb back out the entry hole. Wash the puncture wound, treat it with antiseptic and apply a Band-Aid, then go back to fishing. Watch closely the next few days for any sign of infection, and if any appears, seek medical attention.

You never know when a boating accident will occur. Wearing a personal flotation device is like an insurance policy against drowning. PFDs should always be on and zipped up when a boat is moving, and it's a good idea to wear a PFD anytime you're on the water.

This lesson absolutely applies to all fishermen and other boaters. If you're going out on a big lake or river, be certain your boat is seaworthy enough to handle rough water. Sure, nobody intends to get caught in a blow, but unexpected storms can lead to disaster.

All boats are rated for maximum loads. Before you leave shore, figure the total weight that'll be in the boat, and don't overload it. Also, distribute the weight evenly throughout the boat. Don't concentrate the weight in one area.

DON'T DRINK AND BOAT. - The statistics tell a sad story. A majority of boating accidents involve alcohol consumption. Drinking and boating is just as serious as drinking and driving. (Many states now have laws against the former just as they do the latter.) The bottom line is, don't drink and boat! Also, don't ride with a boat operator who's been drinking.

AVOID KNOWN DANGER AREAS. - Tailwaters, dam intakes, rapids, waterfalls and other areas with strong currents or underwater objects pose special dangers to fishermen. Yet, some people fish these spots despite warnings to the contrary. Invariably some of them get into trouble. Never fish where posted warnings or your common sense tells you it's unsafe. Be alert to sudden water releases when fishing below dams. After a hard rain, avoid streams prone to flash flooding.

AVOID UNSAFE ICE WHEN ICE-FISHING. - Each fall a few anglers go out on new ice too early, or in spring they try to stretch the season by fishing on ice that is thawing and rotten. Both groups are pressing their luck, and inevitably some press too far. Incidents of fishermen breaking through thin ice and drowning are all too common and could be avoided if anglers would be more cautious.

Here's the rule to follow: two inches of new, clean ice is safe to walk on. Anything less is dangerous. Also, don't walk on ice when you see air bubbles or cracks.

Wading anglers should exercise special caution to avoid holes and dropoffs that could lead to stepping in over their heads.

Thin ice can turn an ice-fishing trip into a nightmare. Anglers should never test their luck by venturing onto ice that they have even the slightest doubt about being thick enough to support their weight.

When walking on new ice, have a partner follow a few feet behind, or you follow him! The person walking behind should carry a length of rope or a long pole to pull his partner out if he breaks through the ice. Take a long-handle chisel and tap in front of you to make sure ice is solid. But again, if there's any reasonable question that the ice is unsafe, don't go out on it!

Veteran ice fishermen follow other safety rules in the early and late season. They wear PFDs when walking on ice and carry long nails or pointed dowels in a handy pocket. If you break through, these can be used to jab into ice at the edge of the hole to pull yourself out.

The Dangers of Sunburn

Sunburn rides the fence between "discomforting" and "life threatening." A sunburn is certainly uncom-

fortable, though the pain is only temporary. Doctors now know, however, that overexposure to the sun's ultraviolet rays can cause skin cancer, and this can be deadly.

Pro anglers used to wear shorts and fish without shirts, and they had great suntans. Today, though, most pros have gotten the message. Many wear long pants, long-sleeved shirts, and caps with flaps to shade their ears and necks. On skin areas still exposed to the sun (back of hands, nose, cheeks), they apply a strong sunscreen.

Always apply sunscreen to exposed skin areas. Sunscreen should have an SPF (Sun Protection Factor) rating of at least 15, and 30 or higher is better. Sunscreen should be reapplied periodically when an angler is perspiring freely, since sunscreen will wash off the skin.

The Danger of Flying Hooks

There are three times when hooks "fly:" (1) When you're casting (or when your buddy is casting); (2) when you or he snatches a hung-up lure out of a shoreside limb; (3) when you or he is fishing with a surface lure, and you set the hook and miss. These "flying" hooks can be hazardous to anglers who happen to be in their path. Be alert when you're casting, and also when others are casting. If your bait snags on a bush or limb, don't get impatient and yank. Try to flip your bait out, and if it won't come, go get it.

Sunglasses or clear safety glasses will protect your eyes from flying hooks. I wear sunglasses during daytime fishing, and I wear safety glasses when night fishing. I particularly enjoy night-fishing with topwater lures for bass. Most strikes, however, are heard instead of seen. If the fish misses the lure, and you rear back with your rod, you've got a hook-studded missile flying at you through the dark.

Overexposure to the sun's harmful rays can cause skin cancer. When fishing in bright sun, anglers should wear long-sleeve shirts and broadbrim hats to shield exposed skin. Also, they should apply sunscreen (at least SPF 15) to backs of hands, neck and other exposed areas.

D. Crossing to Safety

KIRK DEETER

1. Crossing to Safety

There are ways to wade a river safely, and ways to ensure that you will get wet. Dale Darling, former owner of the St. Vrain Angler fly shop, has a few pointers for keeping dry. First, no matter how good your wading boots feel, you want to walk next to rocks, not on top of them. You never want to find yourself in a situation where your legs are crossed, or you'll lose your balance. Keep the toes of your boots pointed slightly upstream at all times to maintain balance. And when you're crossing the river in swift current, pick a destination point at a 45-degree angle downstream from where you start, and cross on an angle. If there's an obvious deep spot, avoid it by choosing a path of embarkation and debarkation from the river that starts at point A, upstream, and ends at point B, roughly 45 degrees downstream. As a rule, don't step into unfamiliar waters where you cannot clearly see your boots. Wear polarized sunglasses to help you see the bottom. And always cross the river downstream. When you fight the current by pressing upstream, you will inevitably lose the battle.

—K.D.

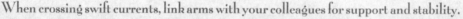

When crossing swift currents, link arms with your colleagues for support and stability.

Move slowly downstream; Shuffle your feet so you don't have any surprises.

If you had to cross here, would you cross above or below the riffles?

Part 5
Cookery

A. Simple Methods for Cleaning and Cooking Fish

WADE BOURNE

One of the real pleasures in life is "shore lunch"— beaching your boat and cooking and eating fish that you've just caught. Fresh fillets cooked over an open fire are always delicious. A morning of fishing guarantees a hearty appetite, and the fish will never be fresher or taste better. Throw in a skillet of home-fried potatoes and onions, baked beans warmed in the can, some shredded cabbage and cole slaw dressing, and some deep-fried hushpuppies, and you have a meal

Fish fillets never taste better than when cleaned, cooked and served up as shore lunch right beside the water where they were caught.

that rivals those served in the finest restaurants. Ah, the memories of shore lunches past!

For many anglers, eating fish is the end process and final reward in fishing. Fish are delicious, and they're more healthful than red meat, particularly when baked or broiled. There's a special satisfaction in sharing your catch with fishing buddies or other friends.

However, for fish to taste their best, they must be cleaned and cooked properly. This process starts the moment the fish is landed. First, however, let's discuss when to keep fish and when to release them.

To Keep or Release?

Catch-and-release is fishing for fun instead of for food. Releasing fish alive protects the resource against too much fishing pressure. Fish that are turned back alive can continue spawning, maintaining healthy populations, and providing fun and excitement for other anglers. Some anglers feel morally bound to release their catch alive, and they encourage others to do likewise.

So, is it okay to keep some fish to eat, and if so, when? Let's get one point straight. Fish are renewable resources. If managed properly, a certain number of fish can be taken from a population, and remaining fish can continue replenishing the population from one spawning season to the next. If certain criteria are met, anglers should feel no stigma in keeping fish to eat.

So, when is it okay to keep fish to eat, and when should you release them alive? There are two sides to this question: legal and moral. Legally, you may keep

The fresher fish are, the better they'll taste when cooked. One good way to keep fish fresh is to string them (when water temperature is cool.) Another good way is to kill fish quickly and deposit them on ice in a cooler.

your catch if you (1) have a fishing license; (2) take your fish by lawful methods; and (3) comply with creel and length limits.

Morally, the question of catch-and-release is a little more complicated. Some purists feel you should release every fish you catch. On the other end of the spectrum are fish hogs who keep every fish they get.

Simply stated, you should decide to keep or release your fish according to how plentiful they are and how heavy fishing pressure is. If fish are plentiful and pressure is light, it's okay to keep your catch. On the other hand, if fish are scarce or under extreme fishing pressure, anglers should release their catch—with one exception: a fish that's injured and will probably die. It's good conservation to keep these fish.

Remember back to my secret smallmouth stream? Let's use it as an example of how to decide whether or not to keep fish or release them.

This stream holds a healthy bass population, and I've never seen another angler on it. I fish it only twice a year, so I have no qualms about keeping enough fish for a couple of meals. The removal a small number of bass has no effect on the overall number of smallmouth in this stream.

But let's say the stream was suddenly discovered by other anglers, and fishing pressure became heavy. If I saw evidence of fishing pressure hurting the smallmouth population, I'd start releasing all my fish alive, and would encourage other anglers to do likewise.

As a general guideline, prolific breeders such as sunfish, crappie, perch, bullheads, catfish and white bass are less likely to be hurt by fishing pressure, so it's usually okay to keep these species. It's the bass, walleye, trout, muskies and other trophy fish that suffer most from fishing pressure. Depending on population and pressure in each situation, these are the species that should be considered for live release, especially the big female fish. These spawners are important in maintaining high population numbers.

If you do choose to keep fish to eat, keep the smaller fish; keep only what you need and release the rest. Even when fish are plentiful, don't be wasteful.

Caring for Your Catch

When you keep fish to eat, be sure they stay fresh. This guarantees they will retain their best flavor for cooking. If fish aren't kept fresh, the flesh becomes mushy and strong-tasting.

Filleting is a simple, easy way to prepare larger fish for cooking. Anglers using this cleaning method can quickly remove bones and skin from the meat. The first step is to slice the fillet lengthwise down the backbone, from the gills to the tail.

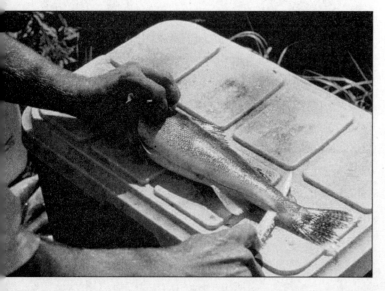

There are two ways to ensure freshness: keep fish alive or keep them cold. Fish may be kept alive in a fish basket, on a stringer or in the live well of a boat if the water is cool and well-oxygenated. Or, fish may be killed and placed on ice as soon as they're caught.

When you fish from the bank, a simple rope or chain stringer is the easiest way to keep your catch. Punch the point of the stringer up through the fish's mouth; then pull the stringer through the open mouth. Do not string fish through the gills. This makes it hard for them to breathe and could cause them to die. In hot weather, it's better to put fish on ice rather than trying to keep them alive on a stringer.

Dead fish that aren't placed on ice will spoil quickly. Check the eyes and gill color to determine freshness. If the eyes look clear and the gills are dark red, the fish are fresh. If the eyes are cloudy and the gills have turned pinkish-white, the fish are beginning to spoil.

Before putting fish in a cooler, give them a sharp rap with a blunt object (pliers, knife handle, etc.) on the spine just behind the eyes. This kills them quickly, which keeps them from flopping when placed in the cooler. Then place the fish on top of a bed of crushed ice in the cooler. Keep excess water drained away as the ice melts. Fish flesh gets mushy when soaked in water for an extended time.

Many anglers prefer to field-dress their fish before placing them on ice. This is done by cutting the gills and guts away with a small knife. These are the organs that spoil first, so this additional step helps ensure freshness.

Simple Methods for Cleaning Fish

Fish should be cleaned as soon after they're caught as possible. Don't leave fish in a cooler overnight. Clean and refrigerate them immediately. They will taste better, and you'll be glad you don't have to face this cleaning chore the next day.

There are a number of options for cleaning fish. They can be scaled or skinned with the bones left

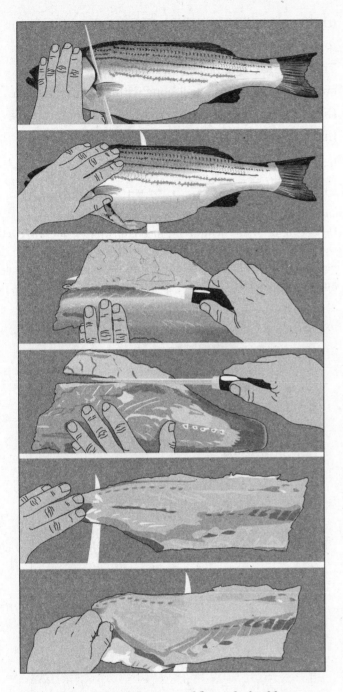

To fillet (1) Cut behind the pectoral fin to the backbone. (2) Separate the fillet, cutting toward the tail parallel to the backbone. (3) Cut off the rib section by sliding the blade along the bones. (4) Cut off the belly fat. (5) With the skin side down, begin to cut from the tail. (6) Cut the skin from the fillet with a sawing motion.

intact, or they can be filleted (meat cut away from the bones). It's up to each angler's preference. Usually small fish (bluegill, perch) are scaled and cooked whole, but even they can be filleted. When fish are filleted by a skilled cleaner, little useable meat is wasted.

Tools for Cleaning Fish

Any fish-cleaning method requires a sharp knife. I recommend one of the fillet knives sold in sporting goods stores. These knives have thin, sharp, flexible blades for fast, easy cleaning. A knife with a 7-inch blade is adequate for cleaning most pan- and gamefish.

One good alternative to a fillet knife is an electric knife. Run by batteries or power cord, an electric knife is a great fish-cleaning tool. Anyone can learn to use an electric knife to fillet fish with just a little practice. Of course, fish cleaners must be careful not to cut themselves, and this is an even greater concern with an electric knife.

Skinning is the preferred way for cleaning catfish and bullheads. After a large catfish is skinned, it may be cut into steaks for ease in cooking.

An inexpensive metal scaler with pointed teeth makes scaling fish much easier, but scaling can also be done with a metal spoon or a kitchen knife with a rigid blade. A fish-cleaning glove is optional; it protects your hand from nicks. A piece of ½-inch plywood makes a good cleaning platform, and you'll need two pans or buckets: one for the cleaned fish, and the other for discarded remains.

Fishermen also need "tools" for removing the fish smell from their hands. Commercial soaps are sold for this purpose. Also, rubbing your hands in toothpaste will remove fish smell. Then, a coating of lemon juice will add a refreshing scent. (Beware rubbing your hands in lemon juice if you have nicks or cuts!)

Scaling

Scaling is the process of scraping the scales off fish and then removing the heads and guts. The skin is left on, and all bones remain intact. Smaller sunfish, crappie, perch, walleye, bass, white bass and other species can all be scaled and cooked whole.

To scale a fish, lay it on its side. Hold its head with one hand, and scrape from the tail to the head (against the grain). The sides are easy to scale. The difficult spots are along the back and stomach and close to the fins.

After scaling, cut the head off just behind the gills. Then slice the belly open and remove the guts. The tail and major fins may be cut off if desired. Finally, wash the fish thoroughly to remove loose scales and blood.

Filleting

Many anglers prefer to fillet their fish for meat with no bones. Fish cleaned in this manner are easy to cook and a pleasure to eat. Also, when filleting is mastered, it's faster than scaling. Experts can fillet a fish in less than a minute. The only drawback is losing a small amount of meat in the filleting process.

To fillet a fish, place it on its side and hold the head with one hand. Make a cut behind the pectoral fin

(the fin behind the gill plate). This cut should be from top to bottom of the fish and as deep as the backbone. Then roll the knife blade toward the tail, and begin cutting parallel to the backbone with a sawing motion. (Keep the knife close to the backbone.) Done properly, this will cut through the ribs and separate the entire

Skinning catfish. (1) Grip the head and slit the skin on both sides just behind the pectoral spines. (2) Slice the skin along the backbone to just behind the dorsal fin. (3) Use pliers to peel the skin off over the tail. (4) Pull the head down, breaking the backbone, and pull out the guts. (5) Remove the fins with pliers and slice off the tail.

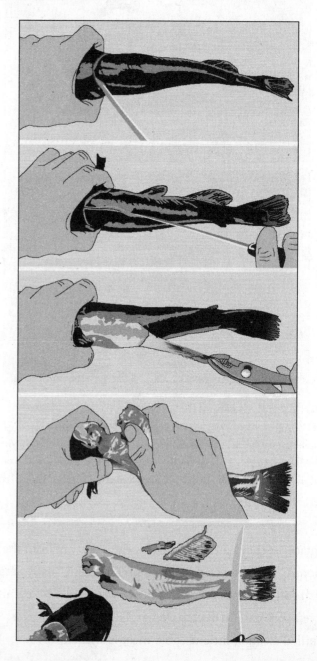

side of meat from the fish. Stop cutting just in front of the tail, leaving the meat attached to the body.

Next, lay the fillet back over the tail with the skin side lying flat against the cleaning board. Cut through the meat at the base of the fillet, but don't cut through the skin. Instead, roll the knife edge flat to the skin, and begin cutting between the skin and meat, separating the skin from the fillet. With a pulling-sawing motion, work the length of the fillet to separate the skin from the meat.

Now you have a side of meat with the skin removed, but the rib bones are still in the fillet. The last step is to cut around the rib section with the point of the knife to remove it from the fillet.

Each side of the fish is filleted in this manner. The end result will be two boneless slabs of meat, which should be washed and refrigerated immediately.

Skinning

Catfish and bullheads are covered by a slick skin instead of scales. These fish may be filleted as explained above, but many anglers prefer to skin and gut them. Catfish and bullheads may then be cooked whole, or bigger fish may be cut into steaks.

To skin a catfish, lay it on its stomach. Grip the head firmly with one hand, carefully avoiding the side and top spines, which can inflict painful puncture wounds. Slit the skin along both sides just behind the pectoral spines. Then slice the skin from the back of the head along both sides of the dorsal (top) fin to the point where the fin ends. Then, with a firm grip on the head, use pliers to grasp the skin at the point where these two cuts meet, and peel the skin back down the body and over the tail. Skin both sides in this manner. Then cut the head off, remove the guts, wash and refrigerate.

Simple Tips for Cooking Fish

Cooking and eating fish is the end result of the harvesting process. It gives me great pleasure to catch

fish, cook them and serve them to close friends. Following are simple tips for preparing fish.

FRYING—Frying is probably the most popular way to cook fish. Fish can be fried whole or in steaks or fillets. I prefer to fry fillets, and I cut fillets into chunks no larger than a couple of inches square.

Bread the fish before frying. Fish may be breaded with crushed saltines or corn flakes, bread crumbs, biscuit mix or commercial fish breadings. Far and away the most popular breading is yellow corn meal or a corn meal/flour mix. Either of these breadings fries to a thin, golden brown crust that doesn't overpower the taste of the fish.

I use peanut oil for frying fish, and I deep-fry them in a cast iron Dutch oven on a fish cooker. The secret to delicious, crispy fish is having the oil hot enough before you drop the fish in, and then keeping it hot as you cook. The ideal temperature for frying fish is 375° F.

Fillets are thin, so they won't take long to cook. Whole fish will take longer. When deep-frying, individual pieces are done when they float to the top of the bubbling oil. When pan-frying, cook the fish until they are golden brown; flip them over and cook them the same amount of time on the other side. Test for flakiness with a fork. When they are done, place them on a platter covered with paper towels to absorb oil, and serve them immediately.

BAKING—Baking is a healthy alternative to frying, and it is an almost foolproof method for cooking fish. Lightly grease the bottom of a baking dish. Arrange whole fish, fillets or steaks in the dish. Brush them with a mixture of melted butter and lemon juice. For variety, add garlic powder, Italian dressing, soy sauce or cajun seasoning. Put the lid on the fish or seal it with aluminum foil, and place the dish in an oven preheated to 375° F.

A standard-size baking dish of fish will bake in 15-25 minutes, depending on the size and thickness of the pieces. Baste the fish with the lemon-butter mixture

Storing Fish for Cooking

Fish can be kept in the refrigerator for 2-3 days without losing much freshness. However, if longer storage is desired, they should be frozen.

To keep cleaned fish (whole, fillets or steaks) in the refrigerator, blot them dry with a paper towel. Then place them on a plate covered with paper towels and wrap them tightly with plastic wrap.

To freeze whole fish, place them inside a plastic milk jug (cut the top away) or large frozen food container, then cover them with water. Tap the sides of the container to release trapped air. Use masking tape to label the container with the type fish and date they were caught. Then freeze.

To freeze fillets or steaks, place fish pieces in a double-walled Ziploc freezer bag (one bag inside another). Zip the inner bag almost closed, and suck all air out of this bag to form a vacuum seal around the fish. Then zip the inner bag closed. Do the same with the outer bag. The double thickness protects against freezer burn. Before freezing, label the outer bag with the type of fish and date they were caught.

Fish frozen in either manner described above will keep 6 months or longer without losing their fresh flavor.

To thaw whole fish frozen in ice, run tap water over the container until the block of ice can be removed. Place this frozen block in a colander or a dish drainer so melting water can drain. Thaw fish at room temperature. To thaw bagged fillets, place in a baking pan and thaw at room temperature. Cook fish as soon as possible after they're thawed.

---

once or twice while baking. Test for doneness by inserting a fork into the thickest part of the fish to check for flakiness. Do not over-bake fish; they will dry out. When the fish are ready to serve, baste them once more with the hot lemon-butter.

CHAR-GRILLING—More and more anglers are discovering the ease and good taste of charcoal-grilled fish. This simple cooking method takes little time and effort. It does require a grill with a hood or top to hold in smoke and regulate temperature. I prefer large fillets for grilling, but whole fish can also be char-grilled.

Light the charcoal and wait for the briquettes to burn down to an ash-gray color. Then add water-soaked hickory or mesquite chips for a smoky flavor.

When the fire is ready, spread heavy-duty aluminum foil over just enough of the grill to hold the fish. Then place the fillets skin-side down on the foil. Baste them with lemon-butter, barbeque sauce, Italian dressing or any other moist seasoning. Lower the top over the grill and regulate the air control so the charcoal will smolder and smoke at a low temperature. Baste the fish at intervals while cooking. Do not turn fillets; leave them with the skin down. Test for doneness by inserting a fork into the thickest part of the fish, and twist to see if the meat is flaky. Cooking time will vary depending on the size of fish and heat of the fire. Char-grilling fillets usually takes only a few minutes.

To char-grill whole fish, do not use foil. Place the fish directly on the grill or in a wire grilling basket. Turn the fish to cook an equal time on each side.

Summary

There are many other ways to prepare fish for the table. They can be used in soups, stews or gumbos. They can be pickled; flaked and used in cold salads; stuffed; served in casseroles; or embellished with a wide variety of sauces and garnishes.

Dozens of excellent fish cookbooks are available for anglers who would like to try more involved recipes.

Overall, fish are good for an angler's body and soul. They are truly a health food, and they are great fun to catch and prepare. That's why anglers who don't cook their catch should learn to do so. Through cooking and sharing your fish dishes with others, you get to enjoy them twice—once when caught, and once when served up as a gift to your friends.

Many anglers prefer filleting over other cleaning methods. Filleting produces boneless, skinless pieces of fish that are ready to be cooked.

B. Smoking Fish

CHRIS DUBBS and DAVE JEBERLE

Smoking Fish and Seafood

If someone happened to mention "smoked fish" at a party, what would you think of? An expensive, imported two-ounce tin of smoked Atlantic salmon, sliced thin? Or perhaps a dish of kippered herring served in mustard sauce at a plush wedding buffet?

Well, salmon and herring stand back! because any edible saltwater or freshwater fish can be smoked into a delicacy fit for the finest occasion and for the most discriminating palate.

While some individuals swear that "oily' salmon, herring, and whitefish provide the ultimate in smoked eating, others prefer "drier' pike, or bass, or panfish; it's a matter of personal taste. There's no doubting, though, that smoking, in addition to lending an exotic zest to standard dinner fish, will also salvage species usually considered inedible. Such trash fish as suckers and carp can be rendered into delicious main courses, and Pacific salmon, even after spawning has occurred and their flesh begins to deteriorate, may still be successfully smoked.

You needn't be an expert fisherman (but it helps) to procure fish suitable for smoking. Fresh and frozen perch, rainbow trout, haddock, cod, and red snapper are available year round at your local supermarket, and clams, oysters, and shrimp also smoke with distinction.

Fish Preparation

Fish may be prepared in several different ways for curing and smoking. Of course, removal of the internal

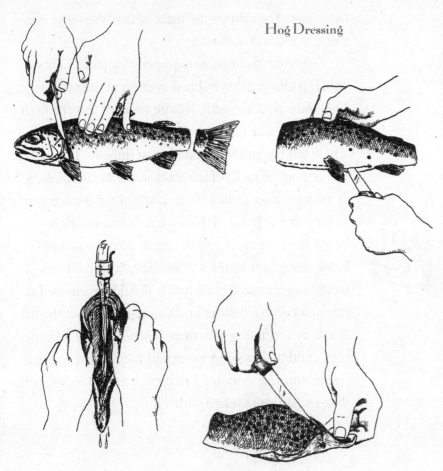

Hog Dressing

organs is always called for and should be accomplished as soon as possible. Small fish can be left whole if desired, with only their internal organs and gills removed.

Large fish will take quite a while to cure and smoke unless they are cut into smaller pieces. Dressing fish by any one of the following methods will greatly expedite the procedure and increase your chance of getting a thorough, uniform salt-and-smoke flavor.

Hog Dressing

Hog-dress fish weighing up to four pounds. Remove head and tail. Slit the belly and discard the entrails. Draw a knife gently along the top of the backbone, making a slight cut. Press on the fish to flatten it.

Fillet

Fillet fish weighing from four to ten pounds. Make a cut through meat to the backbone. Using the backbone as a guide, draw knife toward the tail, gently trimming each side of meat from bones with two separate cuts.

Steak

Cut steak from large fish weighing more than ten pounds. Slice cleaned and gutted fish crosswise into steaks of uniform thickness.

When preparing fish, always cut the head off below the gills. Gills on a fish spoil rapidly, and if not discarded will taint adjacent meat. Fins may or may not be removed, but be sure to scrape the dark nerve materials from beneath the backbone.

Don't bother scaling small fish like perch or crappies because you won't eat the skin anyway. Larger fish, to be cut into steaks or filleted and sliced, should be scaled to allow easy cutting.

Never remove the skin. Skin helps reduce shrinkage and retains precious oils during the smoking process, ensuring a moist and tender product.

Try to cut pieces of meat to a thickness no greater than one inch. Thicker pieces, or even large whole gutted fish, may be smoked, but the brine will take longer to work into the flesh, and the smoking time will have to be increased considerably.

Keep fish cool at all times; the flesh is tender and will soften if exposed to prolonged warm temperatures. When handling fresh or live fish, kill and clean as soon as possible, then rinse with cold running water, pat dry, and refrigerate.

Shelled seafoods, such as clams, oysters, and shrimp, acquire unique flavors when smoked. They may be prepared by lightly steaming or boiling. Remove clams and oysters from their shells and peel shrimp before curing and smoking.

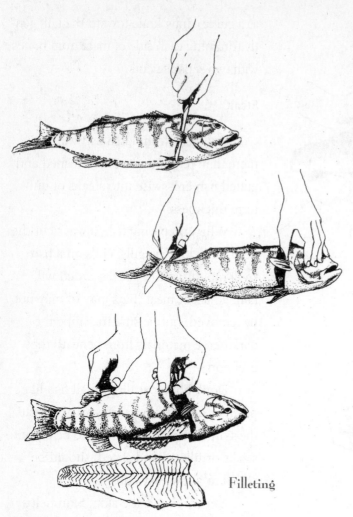

Filleting

Brine Curing

Prepare a brine solution. If you have prepared your fish as suggested earlier, they will require a brine cure of one to four hours. For one-inch-thick pieces, two or three hours should provide a medium cure. More or less time will raise or lower the salt content of the finished product. Very thin fillets may require as little as thirty minutes in brine to give them a mild cure. For curing larger, thicker pieces of fish, six to ten hours represents the range for a light-to-heavy cure.

Clams, oysters, and shrimp all require about thirty minutes brining.

Dry Curing

Quick Dry Cure

If you're especially eager to taste your fish, or simply don't have the time to wait for a brine cure, here's a faster way. The thinner the piece of fish, the more effective this method of curing.

After the fish has been properly prepared, a dry-cure mixture is gently rubbed over the entire surface. Care must be taken with delicate varieties that the flesh is not bruised or torn. Pat the mixture around bones where salt penetration is often most difficult. Lay the fish out on the racks of the smoker and begin smoking at a temperature from 150° to 170°F. After about thirty to forty-five minutes, a thick white liquid will have oozed from the surface of the meat. This is moisture being drawn out by the salt and heat. It contains dissolved salt and protein matter. It should be removed at this point with a basting brush so you can resalt the fish. Resalt by sprinkling with more of the dry-cure mixture, then continue smoking for an additional thirty to forty-five minutes, or until the fish turns a golden brown and flakes when it is pressed with a fork.

Standard Dry Cure

A standard dry cure can be accomplished by lightly rubbing dry-cure mixture onto the fish. Pat the mixture on the flesh so that a thin layer remains, then refrigerate the fish and allow it to cure for five to eight hours, depending on thickness and desired salt content.

Drying

After either method of curing, fish should be lightly rinsed in cold water and allowed to dry thoroughly before being smoked.

Smoking

Quick and Easy

Eager for smoked fish? Start with thin fillets. Sprinkle lightly with dry cure mix. Pop them into a pre-heated smoker for about one hour. If smoker temperatures have been high enough (150°-170°F), the fillets will be done, golden brown and flakey. If smoker temperatures haven't gotten that high, the fillets will still be nicely flavored but will require a brief cooking. Pan fry or broil.

Cook, Then Smoke

Fish may be taken right from the oven and placed in the smoker. Most fish will acquire a good smoke flavor in this manner after about two hours. Smoke at temperatures of 100° to 120°F. The meat will turn a golden brown and will taste great.

If salt flavor is desired, fish may be cured prior to cooking, then smoked for flavor.

Cold Smoking

If a mild smoke flavor is all you're after to liven up a favorite dish, use a brief period of cold smoking. One to four hours offers a mild-to-strong flavor that will hold up under cooking. Keep smoker temperatures low—around 70° to 90°F.

Hot Smoking

Lightly grease or oil the racks of the smoker to avoid sticking. Arrange the pieces of fish evenly on the racks, taking care none of them touch each other. Fillets should be placed skin side down.

Many fish caught from the shore are good for curing.

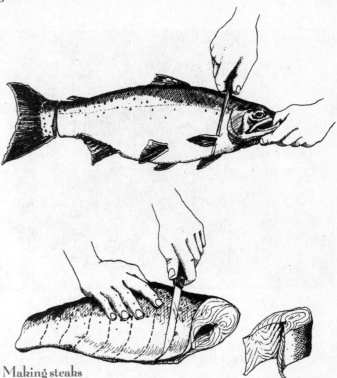

Making steaks

As with curing, there are too many variables to be able to give exact times for smoking. A temperature between 150° and 170°F will thoroughly cook and smoke a thin fillet within one hour. One-inch steaks might take six to eight hours.

It's best to check the fish periodically. Some lean fish dry out rapidly and may require basting. Brushing them with cooking oil, butter, or margarine will keep them moist. If you baste fish while using the quick dry cure, resalt them before further smoking.

When fish are done, they will be a pleasing golden brown. Large pieces, however, sometimes might appear done on the outside, but actually have not been thoroughly cooked. To test, simply press at the flesh with a fork. When it flakes apart under pressure, it's done.

Depending on how dry you want the finished fish, it can remain in the smoker even after it's been fully cooked to allow more moisture to escape.

Salmon

Because of the excellent quality of smoked salmon, it is worth lavishing a bit more attention on the preparation of this fish.

Seasoned fish cubes

To help retain the fresh flavor of this delicate meat, especially if it is to be stored for a while before smoking, be sure to remove the fat strip along the top (dorsal) fin line, and also the belly flap from each side, including the bottom fins.

A simple, yet reliable brine can be made from the following:

1½ pounds salt
½ pound (1 ⅛ cups) brown sugar
1 teaspoon onion powder
4 bay leaves, crushed

Allow thick salmon steaks to brine-cure for eight hours.

Wash and let dry.

Hot-smoke at about 170°F until flesh is flaky. At this point the meat will be moist. Many people prefer their salmon on the dry side. Allowing the fish to remain in the smoker for one or two additional hours will dry the meat more.

Salmon tastes best with a strong smoke flavor. Although it can be cold-smoked for a brief time to acquire a light flavor, and then included in some recipe, you'll be missing out on the fish's full taste potential. If you don't want to cook the salmon fully in your smoker

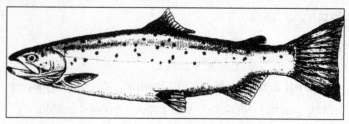

Atlantic salmon

because you have some exciting recipe waiting that calls for raw fish, then cold smoking is fine, but give the fish plenty of time to flavor. A minimum of four hours is necessary to bring out the best in salmon.

Carp

Many so-called trash fish can be smoked into culinary masterpieces. Only in the United States are carp considered lowly; in Europe and Asia these large-scaled fish are highly sought, and even raised as game and food fish.

The larger the carp, the better. Fillet it and cut into chunks or, if it is exceedingly large, hog dress it and cut it into steaks. Proceed with one of the brining and smoking instructions described in this chapter and you'll be hard pressed, when it's finished, to taste the difference from salmon or trout.

Smoked salmon

C. Fish Jerky

MONTE BURCH

Dried fish, in one form or another, has been a staple food of mankind for thousands of years. Whether living near fresh or saltwater sources, people have regularly dried a variety of fish as a way of preserving it for future meals. Native Americans on both the East and West Coasts, for example, smoked and dried salmon for winter use. This smoked and dried meat would often keep until the next season. The eastern and western inhabitants also pounded the dried fish into a powder and traded it with the Native Americans of the Plains. Fish drying on racks in the traditional method is still seen in the coastal native villages of Alaska and Canada. Dried fish was also extremely important in Europe. In northern Europe, dried codfish is still a common food in many households.

The Meat

It's recommended to use only lean-meat fish, including freshwater fish such as bass, brook trout, crappies, bluegills, walleyes, and perch. If using fresh-

Fish jerky or dried-salted fish has been a staple food source for many cultures. Fish with little oil or fat content, such as the largemouth bass shown here, are the best choices.

The Native Americans dried fish such as salmon split and hung over wooden frameworks.

water fish, it's important to use only fish that are fresh and completely free of parasites. Good choices in ocean fish include flounder, codfish, and even cuts of tuna that are free of fat. Oilier fish and those with a high fat content, such as snapper, mackerel, mullet, whitefish, carp, catfish, and pike, are not suitable for making into fish jerky. The high oil and fat content makes the jerky prone to spoilage. In many of these fish, it's almost impossible to trim off the fat, as the fat is evenly distributed throughout the flesh. If these fish are smoked, however, they can often be used with good results. In fact, smoked fish such as salmon and trout, although not technically a jerky because it is not dried, has long been a staple for many cultures and is a real delicacy.

Fish can deteriorate and decompose rapidly in heat as well as from the enzymes found in the flesh of fish. This is the main reason fish jerky should only be made of freshly caught and killed fish. The fish can be kept on ice a short period of time until you can make jerky from them. Fish should be free of slime, and the flesh should be firm with a slight fishy smell. Clean and fillet the fish as soon as you can to assure freshness. Make sure the fillets are well cleaned in fresh, cold, running water to remove any blood. Cut the fillets into ¼-inch-thick strips from 4 to 6 inches long. Do not make the strips any thicker or they will be hard to dry. If using small fish, such as bluegill, you may not need to cut the fillets into smaller strips.

To thoroughly kill any parasites present in fish, freeze the fish for at least 48 hours before curing or freeze the jerky after dehydrating.

Curing

Many types of fish used for jerky are commonly salt cured before dehydrating. This salt cure can be a dry or a liquid variety. Homemade cures can be used, or a number of cures are also available in retail stores. The follow-

Canning or pickling salt is used to cure the fish into jerky.

ing are two traditional methods. For a brine cure, use ¼ cup of fine pickling or canning salt to 2 cups of water. If this volume doesn't cover the fish, prepare more brine following the same proportions of salt and water. This amount will brine 1 to 2 pounds of fish strips. Make sure the salt is thoroughly dissolved in the water, and then pour the brine over the strips. Use a glass container, cover, and place in the refrigerator for 48 hours. This salt curing not only draws out the moisture from the flesh, but it also aids in preservation and concentrates the amino acids.

The fish must be filleted and then cut into strips about ¼-inch thick and 5 inches long. Panfish fillets can often be used whole. Pat the strips dry.

You can also use a dry brine, allowing the dry salt to work into the meat and bring out the moisture. Place a thin layer of salt in a glass pan or dish. Apply a coating of salt to each fish strip and place in the pan. Layer the strips in the pan, making sure all strips are well coated with the salt. Cover the dish with plastic food wrap or a tight lid and place in a refrigerator for 48 hours.

In either case, remove the strips from the curing container, rinse under cold water, and pat dry. Now you're ready to dry or dehydrate. Simple salting and drying doesn't produce a very tasty fish jerky. To add taste, lightly coat the strips on both sides with soy sauce, Liquid Smoke, or Worcestershire sauce before drying.

Fish Seasoning Mix

½ cup brown sugar
½ cup salt
1 teaspoon garlic powder
1 teaspoon onion powder
2 teaspoons white pepper

You can also make a seasoning mix to add flavor to the fish strips. Above is a typical mix. Mix together and allow the mix to set overnight in an airtight con-

Although salt alone will cure the meat, adding brown sugar, spices, and other flavorings adds to the taste.

Make sure salt, sugar, and spices are well mixed.

Spread the cure and seasoning mixture over the fish strips, making sure they are all well covered.

Place a layer of the cure and seasoning mixture in the bottom of a non-metallic bowl or pan, and layer the treated strips in place, adding additional cure and seasoning mix as needed. Cover and allow to cure in a refrigerator overnight.

tainer to blend the flavors. A pinch of powdered red pepper (or to suit) can be added to the mix if a hotter jerky is desired. Remove the strips from the original brine, rinse off the brine or salt, and pat dry. Coat the strips with the mix, and allow them to sit in the refrigerator for about 2 hours. Dry or dehydrate.

Cured Salmon

Fresh salmon
½ cup white sugar
½ cup brown sugar
1 gallon cold water
1¾ cups of Morton Tender Quick mix or Morton Sugar
    Cure (Plain) mix

An excellent cured salmon recipe comes from Morton Salt. Clean and eviscerate salmon. Remove head, fins, tail, and V inch from each side along the belly incision. For salmon weighing less than 10 pounds, cut into 3-inch steaks. Split steaks along the backbone, leaving skin on if desired. If salmon is greater than 10 pounds, cut into ½-inch steaks.

Prepare 1 gallon of brine for each 5 pounds of salmon using proportions of water, sugar, brown sugar, and Morton Tender Quick or Morton Sugar Cure (Plain) mix as listed. Completely submerge the salmon in brine, using a ceramic plate or bowl to weigh down the fish and keep it submerged. Cure in refrigerator for 16 hours. Remove salmon, and rinse it in cool water. Pat dry and cook as desired.

Salmon may also be smoked in an electric smoker, following the manufacturer's instructions. The salmon must be heated to an internal temperature of 160°F and held at this temperature for at least 30 minutes. Refrigerate if not consumed immediately.

Drying

In the past, fish was simply dried outside. Typically, the Native Americans split the salmon carcasses and hung them over wooden frameworks in the shade but

Wash off salt and seasonings and dry in an oven or dehydrator until the internal temperature of the jerky strips is 160°F.

in an area with good air circulation and quite often with a smoky fire beneath. You can also dry fish outside, given the right circumstances, but make sure it is well covered to keep away insects. A smoky fire can be helpful not only in the drying but in keeping insects away. Fish can be easily dried in a dehydrator by following the manufacturer's instructions. Fish jerky can also be dried in an oven. Place on wire racks over cookie sheets to catch the drippings. Set the oven at 150°F and with the oven door slightly open. Dry for about an hour. Then, turn the strips over and dry for another hour. Test the jerky strips. The finished jerky should be like red-meat jerky. You should be able to bend it without breaking. It should not be crumbly or crunchy. When dried properly, there should be no moisture on the surface of the jerky sticks. For safety, the internal temperature must reach 160°F.

Storage

Properly cured and dried, fish jerky should last for a long time in sealed containers in a cool, dry place. For safety, you may prefer to freeze and/or vacuum pack the jerky strips. Storing the prepared jerky in the freezer will also take care of any parasites.

Smoked Salmon

Fresh salmon
Hi Mountain Alaskan Salmon Brine Mix
1 gallon ice water

Although not an actual jerky, smoked salmon is easy to make with the Hi Mountain Alaskan Salmon Brine Mix. The brine mix is made with pure maple sugar. The package contains two bags of mix. Dissolve one packet in 1 gallon of ice water. The fish should be fresh and well chilled before curing. Immerse the fish in the brine solution, making sure it is well covered. Place it in a refrigerator for 24 hours. Remove the fish from the brine, rinse it well with fresh, cold water, and pat it dry. Let the fish sit at room temperature for about 30 minutes and then smoke it. Smoking time can vary depending on the type of smoker, location, outside temperature, and so forth. The fish should be smoked until the internal temperature reaches 160°F. If you cannot get fish to the desired internal temperature with your smoker, place it in the oven to finish once the desired color is reached.

Salmon Jerky

D. Fried Fish

RICK BROWNE

Baja-Style Fish Bites

Marinade:

¾ cup sour cream
1 tablespoon lime juice
½ teaspoon Mexene chili powder
1 pound red snapper fillets
1 cup flour
1¼ cups crushed corn chips
2 tablespoons melted butter

Heat frying oil to 375°F in Dutch oven or deep fryer
    pot.

Place 2–3 handfuls of spicy corn chips in a plastic bag, and using a rolling pin, crush them to crumb-like consistency. Pour the crumbs into a wide, flat bowl and set aside.

In a wide, flat bowl or Pyrex dish, mix the sour cream, lime juice, and chili powder with a whisk or spoon.

In another flat pan, dredge fish fillets in the flour, covering both sides of the fillets evenly.

Then soak the floured fish pieces in the marinade, again coating both sides well. Let the fish sit in the marinade for 1 to 2 minutes. Drain the excess marinade back into the bowl.

Now dredge the fish bites in the crushed corn chips, coating both sides well by pressing down on them with the back of a spoon while they are in the bowl.

Slip the fillets, no more than two at a time, into the hot oil and fry them until they are golden brown on both sides, about 3 to 4 minutes.

Serve fried fillets with a spicy tomato or fruit salsa on the side.

Serves 4

Beer-Battered Trout

6 brook or rainbow trout, ¾ pound each
2 cups all-purpose flour, plus 2–3 tablespoons
2 teaspoons baking powder
1 teaspoon salt
1 tablespoon mild curry powder
2 eggs, slightly beaten
2 cups warm beer
½ cup salad oil
oil for deep-frying
fresh parsley for garnish
lemon slices for garnish

Heat the oil to 375°F in deep fryer or Dutch oven.

Wash and pat the fish dry, then put them in a paper bag with 2–3 tablespoons of flour and shake until the fish is coated with flour. Set aside.

In a large bowl combine the remaining flour, baking powder, salt, curry powder, eggs, beer, and salad oil; whisk until the mixture is smooth. Dip the floured

fish into this batter, allowing the excess to drip back into the bowl.

Slip the fish into the oil and cook, turning once or twice, until golden brown on both sides, about 3–4 minutes. Remove fish from oil with a slotted spatula or frying basket. Drain on paper towels. Garnish with fresh parsley and lemon slices.

Serves 6

Dover Codfish and Chips

6 potatoes, approximately 1 ½ pounds

Batter:

½ teaspoon baking powder
1 ¼ cups flour
1 teaspoon salt
½ teaspoon white pepper
1 tablespoon vegetable oil
¾ cup beer
¼ cup cream (or whole milk)

3 egg whites
1½ pounds cod fillets
salt to taste
lemon wedges
malt vinegar for dipping
tartar sauce for dipping

Heat the oil to 350°F in a deep-fat fryer or Dutch oven.

Peel the potatoes and square each end and sides, then cut each into ¾" slices. Stack and cut them into ¾" sticks. Place in a bowl of ice-cold water to soak for 30 minutes to crisp them up.

Drain the potatoes; pat VERY dry using paper towels. Dip an empty frying basket into the oil (this prevents potatoes from sticking to it), then add the potatoes, and lower the basket into the oil. Deep fry the potatoes till just tender when pierced, and starting to brown, 3–4 minutes. Lift the basket out of the oil and drain the potatoes in a basket or wire rack. They are now partially cooked.

Sift the baking powder, flour, salt, and pepper into in a large, wide bowl. Make a well in the middle of the flour, add the vegetable oil and beer, and stir. Gradually add the cream (or milk) until well mixed. The batter will become elastic. Let the batter stand for 30 to 35 minutes, till thickened.

In a copper bowl, whisk the egg whites till stiffpeaks form. Gently fold the stiff whites into the rested batter, using a rubber spatula, until combined. Dip the cod fillets in the batter, turning to coat each piece thoroughly, and letting excess batter drip off into the bowl.

Using a slotted spatula, slide the fillets into the hot oil, turning once, frying 6–8 minutes until golden and crisp on the outside. Remove to a flat pan or baking sheet lined with paper towels, and keep the fillets warm in the oven (200°F) as you fry the rest.

After the fish has been cooked, place the potatoes back in the fryer basket and fry them till golden brown, about 1–2 minutes. Drain them on paper towels and place in 200°F oven to keep warm.

To serve, sprinkle the chips with salt, and decorate the fish with lemon wedges. Serve with malt vinegar and tartar sauce on the side.

Serves 6

Ol' King Cod

1 pound cod fillets

Batter:

1 egg
¾ cup flour
½ cup water
1 teaspoon salt
¼ teaspoon ground ginger
1 tablespoon sesame seed
½ teaspoon paprika
oil for deep-frying

Heat oil in Dutch oven to 375°F.

In a large bowl, mix the batter ingredients together, and let rest for 20 minutes to thicken. Thaw (if frozen) or rinse (if fresh) and pat dry the cod fillets. Cut into serving-size pieces and dip the pieces into the batter. Drain them briefly but make sure each piece is coated.

Deep fry the fish in 1" of oil in Dutch oven for 4–5 minutes each side or until golden brown.

Serves 4

Peanut-Cornmeal Fried Catfish

1½ pounds fresh or frozen catfish fillets

⅜ cup ground peanuts

⅔ cup yellow cornmeal

⅜ teaspoon salt

¼ teaspoon black pepper

¼ teaspoon ground red pepper

¼ cup milk

1 large egg, beaten

oil for deep-frying

Rinse the fresh fish and pat fillets dry. If frozen, thaw and rinse, then pat dry. Cut the fillets into 6 equal-size pieces.

In a wide, flat dish, combine ground peanuts, cornmeal, salt, black pepper, and red pepper. In a similar dish, combine milk and egg.

With your fingers, dip each piece of fish in the milk mixture, then roll in the nut mixture. Using your hand or a wide spoon, gently press the nuts into the flesh.

Meanwhile, in a heavy castiron Dutch oven or deep fryer, heat 2" of oil to 375° F. Fry 1 or 2 pieces of fish at a time, about 2 minutes on each side, or until golden brown.

Carefully remove the fish with a slotted spoon and place fillets on paper towels to drain. Keep them warm in a 200°F oven while frying up the remaining fish.

Serves 6

World's Best Eatin' Shark with Fresh Mango Salsa

2 pounds shark fillets (or haddock)
2 cups milk

Batter:

1 tablespoon butter
⅔ cup Hungry Jack biscuit mix
1 teaspoon salt
½ teaspoon granulated garlic
½ teaspoon chili powder
¼ teaspoon pepper
2 tablespoons flour

Skin the fish and cut it into 3" by 5" pieces. Wash them under cold running water and then pat them completely dry with paper towels. In a shallow pan or baking dish, soak the fillets in milk for 2–4 hours, drain, and discard the milk. Pat dry the fillets.

Heat oil to 375°F in Dutch oven or frying pot.

Melt the butter in a small pan. Mix the remaining batter ingredients in a shallow baking dish, and add the melted butter.

Put the shark fillets in a paper bag with 2 tablespoons flour, and shake until coated.

Drop 2 or 3 pieces of the fish at a time into the batter until they are well coated. Using a spoon or spatula, slip them into the hot oil.

Fry 4 to 5 minutes, or until golden brown, turning the pieces occasionally with a spoon to prevent their sticking together.

Serve with mango salsa.

Serves 6–8

Part 6
Good Reads

A. The Black Bass as a Gamefish

JAMES A. HENSHALL

"He is a fish that lurks close all winter; but is very pleasant and jolly after mid-April, and in May, and in the hot months." —Izaak Walton

Those who have tasted the lotus of salmon or trout fishing, in that Utopian clime of far away—while reveling in its aesthetic atmosphere, and surrounded by a misty halo of spray from the waterfall, or enveloped by the filmy gauze and iridescent tomes, sung idylls, chanted paeans, and poured out libations in honor and praise of the silver-spangled salmon, or the ruby-studded trout, while it is left to the vulgar horde of black bass anglers to stand upon the mountain of their own doubt and presumption, and, with uplifted hands, in admiration and awe, gaze with dazed eyes from afar upon that forbidden land—that *terra incognita*—and then, having lived in vain, die and leave no sign.

It is, then, with a spirit of rank heresy in my heart; with smoked glass spectacles on my nose, to dim the glare and glamour of the transcendent shore; with the scales of justice across my shoulder—*M. salmoides* in one scoop and *M. dolomieu* in the other—I pass the barriers and confines of the enchanted land, and toss them into a stream that has been depopulated of even fingerlings, by the *dilettanti* of salmon and trout fishers; for I would not, even here, put black bass in a stream inhabited by salmon or brook trout.

While watching the plebeian interlopers sporting in an eddy, their bristling spines and emerald sides gleaming in the sunshine, I hear an awful voice from the adjacent rocks exclaiming: "Fools rush in where angels fear to tread!" Shade of Izaak Walton defend us! While appealing to Father Izaak for protection, I quote his words: "Of which, if thou be a severe, sour complexioned man, then I here disallow thee to be a competent judge."

Seriously, from Izaak Walton to the present day, the salmon and trout of Great Britain have been sung in song and story as game-fishes, and it is sufficient to say that they deserve all the praise bestowed upon them. And as our ideas of fish and fishing have derived mostly from English authors, it follows that many American writers and anglers have been obsessed by their teaching, even down to the present day, as in dry fly-fishing.

Now, while we have in America the same salmon as in Great Britain, and several species of trout equally as good or better than the brown trout, we also have many other game-fishes equally worthy, and among them the black bass.

I feel free to assert, that, were the black bass a native of Great Britain, it would rank fully as high in the estimation of British anglers as either the trout or the salmon. I am borne out in this by the opinions of British sportsmen whose statements have been received without question.

W. H. Herbert (Frank Forester) writing of the black bass, says:

"This is one of the finest of the American fresh-water fishes: it is surpassed by none in boldness of biting, in fierce and violent resistance when hooked, and by a very few only in excellence upon the board." (*Fish and Fishing*, 1850.)

Parker Gilmore ("Ubique") says:

"I fear it will be almost deemed heresy to place this fish (black bass) on a par with the trout; at least, some such idea I had when I first heard the two compared; but I am bold, and will go further. I consider he is the superior of the two, for he is equally good as an article of food, and much stronger, and untiring in his efforts to escape when hooked." (*Prairie and Forest*, 1874.)

In regard to the comparative gameness of the black bass and the brook trout the following opinions of American anglers are added. Seth Green, one of the fathers of fish-culture and a lifelong angler for trout, among other fishes, has this to say:

"This is among the finest sporting as well as food fish in America. Bites fiercely at fly or trolling spoon; makes a vigorous fight for life, liberty and happiness, showing a perfect willingness 'to fight it out on that line if it takes all summer,' and at last when subdued and brought to the table does honor to the cook who prepares it, and pleasure to the palate that enjoys it." (*Fish Hatching and Fish Catching*, 1879.)

Robert B. Roosevelt, who, with Seth Green, was a Fish Commissioner of New York, and co-author of *Fish Hatching and Fish Catching*, and a notable angler for salmon and trout, says of the black bass:

"A fish that is inferior only to the salmon and trout, if even to the latter; that requires the best of tackle and skill in its inveiglement, and exhibits courage and game qualities of the highest order." (*Superior Fishing*, 1865.)

E. E. Millard, a veteran fly-fisher for trout for fifty hears, who has camped many summers on the famous Nipigon, and who is a true and faithful lover of the brook trout, has this to say in comparing the trout and the black bass as game-fishes:

"When the acrobatic bass approaches with every spine bristling it signifies fight, and he dies battling face to the foe—not that the trout tamely submits at the first prick of the steel; far from it. He is a fighter, though not a scientific one, having no appreciation of the finer and more artistic points of the game. He looks the fighter, having the neck and shoulders of the pugilist, but is rather too beautiful, which, however, does not always follow, and there is lacking a little of the Irish in his composition, though when put to the crowning test, he hangs on with bulldog tenacity, lacking only the resourcefulness of the smallmouth bass, the generally recognized champion of finny warriors, and of whom I can well believe that, inch for inch and pound for pound, he is the gamest fish that swims." (*Days on the Nipigon*, 1917.)

Now, while salmon fishing is, unquestionably, the highest branch of piscatorial sport; and while trout fishing

in Canada, Maine, and the Lake Superior region justi-
fies all the extravagant praise bestowed upon it, I am
inclined to doubt the judgment and good taste of those
anglers who snap their fingers in contempt of black
bass fishing, while they will wade in a stream with
brush and logs, catch a few trout weighing six or eight
to the pound, and call it the only artistic angling in the
world! While they are certainly welcome to their opinion, I think their zeal is worthy of a better cause.

The black bass is eminently an American fish, and
is truly representative in his characteristics. He has the
faculty of asserting himself and making himself completely at home wherever placed. He is plucky, game,
brave, and unyielding to the last when hooked. He has
the arrowy rush and vigor of the trout, the untiring
strength and bold leap of the salmon, while he has a
system of fighting tactics peculiarly his own.

Among anglers, the question is often raised as to
what constitutes a game-fish, and what particular
species are to be considered best among game-fishes.
In coordinating the essential attributes of game-fishes,
each inherent trait and quality must be duly and
impartially considered. Their habits and habitat; their
aptitude to rise to the artificial fly; their manner of
resistance and struggle for freedom when hooked; their
finesse and intelligence; and their excellence as food
must all be taken into account and duly weighed.

The black bass is more advanced in the scheme of
evolution, and exhibits traits of a higher organization
than either the salmon or trout. It is worthy of note that
the highest development of fishes is shown in those
with spiny-rayed fins as in the black bass, striped bass,
channel bass, etc., while those of a lower development
have soft-rayed fins as in the salmon, trout, whitefish,
pike, etc.

In the animal creation the highest intelligence
is exemplified by the parental instinct or care of the
young. This is shown in the highest degree among
mammals, next among birds, in but few reptiles, and
scarcely at all among fishes. In the two hundred, or

more, families of fishes, those that evince any parental instinct or manifest any care of their young can be
counted on the fingers of one hand. The black bass
stands pre-eminent in this respect, and is a bright and
shining example to all the finny tribe in its habit of
watching and guarding its nest and caring for its young
brood when hatched.

Most fishes in fresh and salt water abandon their
eggs as soon as emitted and fertilized. The salmon and
trouts deposit their eggs in the shallowest water and
leave them to the tender mercies of predatory fish,
birds, and reptiles during an incubation of two or three
months.

The black bass will rise to the artificial fly as readily as the salmon or the brook trout, under the same
conditions; and will take the live minnow, or other live
bait, under any and all circumstances favorable to the
taking of any other fish. I consider him, *inch for inch*
and *pound for pound,* the gamest fish that swims. The
royal salmon and the lordly trout must yield the palm
to a black bass of *equal weight.*

That he will eventually become the leading gamefish of America is my oft-expressed opinion and firm
believe. This result, I think, is inevitable; if for no other
reasons, from a force of circumstances occasioned by
climatic conditions and the operation of immutable natural laws, such as the gradual drying up and dwindling
away of the small trout streams, and the consequent decrease in brook trout, both in quality and quantity; and
by the introduction of predatory fish in waters where
the trout still exists.

Another prominent cause of the decline and fall
of the brook trout, is the erection of dams, saw-mills,
and factories upon trout streams, which, though to be
deplored, cannot be prevented; the march of empire
and the progress of civilization can not be stayed by the
honest, though powerless, protests of anglers.

But, while the ultimate fate of the brook trout is
sealed beyond peradventure, in open, public waters,
we have the satisfaction of knowing that in the black
bass we have a fish equally worthy, both as to game and

edible qualities, and which at the same time is able to withstand and defy many of the causes that will, in the end, effect the annihilation and extinction of the brook trout.

As to a comparison of game qualities as between the small-mouth bass and the large-mouth bass, I hold that, other things being equal, and where the two species inhabit the same waters, there is no difference in game qualities; for, while the small-mouth is probably more active in its movements, the large-mouth bass is more powerful; and no angler can tell from its manner of resistance whether he is fast to one or the other.

Both species of black bass rise equally well to the artificial fly; though, if there be any difference in this respect, I think the large-mouth bass has the advantage. In a letter Count Von dem Borne, of Germany (who was very successful in introducing and propagating the black bass in that country), wrote me that the large-mouth black bass rose better to the artificial fly than the small-mouth bass. My own experience rather favors this view, and it has likewise been brought to my notice by anglers in various parts of the country.

The current but erroneous opinion that the small-mouth bass exceeds the large-mouth bass in game qualities, has been very widespread, and has been much enhanced by the endorsement of several of our best ichthyologists, who unfortunately, however, are not, and do not pretend to be, anglers, but who imbibed this opinion second-hand from prejudiced anglers who ought to have known better. But as the black bass is becoming better known, and fly-fishing for the species is being more commonly practiced, this unfair and unmerited comparison is fast dying out.

Fish inhabiting swiftly-running streams are always more vigorous and gamy than those in still waters, and it is probable that where the large-mouth bass exists alone in very shallow and sluggish waters, of high temperature and thickly grown with algae, it will exhibit less combative qualities, consequent on the enervating influences of its environment; but where both species inhabit the same waters, and are subject to the same conditions,

I am convinced that no angler can tell whether he has hooked a large-mouth or a small-mouth bass, from their resistance and mode of fighting, provided they are of equal weight, until he has the ocular evidence.

I use the expression "equal weight" advisedly, for most anglers must have remarked that the largest bass of either species are not necessarily the hardest fighters; on the contrary, a bass of two or two and a half pounds' weight will usually make a more gallant fight than one of twice the size, and this fact, I think, will account in a great measure for the popular idea that the small-mouth bass is the "gamest" species for this reason:

Where the two species co-exist in the same stream or lake, the large-mouth bass always grows to a larger size than the other species, and an angler having just landed a two-pound small-mouth bass after a long struggle, next hooks a large-mouth bass weighing four or five pounds, and is surprised, probably, that it "fights" no harder or perhaps not so hard as the smaller fish—in fact, seems "logy"; he, therefore, reiterates the cry that the small-mouth bass is the gamest fish.

But, now, if he next succeeds in hooking a large-mouth bass of the same size as the first one caught, he is certain that he is playing a small-mouth bass until it is landed, when to his astonishment it proves to be a large-mouth bass; he merely says, "he fought well for one of his kind," still basing his opinion of the fighting qualities of the two species upon the first two caught.

Perhaps his next catch may be a small-mouth bass of four pounds, and which, though twice the weight of the large-mouth bass just landed, does not offer any greater resistance, and he sets it down in his mind as a large-mouth bass. Imagine the angler's surprise, then, upon taking it into the landing net, to find it a small-mouth bass, and one which, from its large size and the angler's preconceived opinion of the species should have fought like a Trojan.

Now, one would think that the angler would be somewhat staggered in his former belief; but no, he is equal to the occasion, and in compliance with the popular idea, he merely suggests that "it was out of condition, somehow," or "was hooked so as to drown it in the struggle"; and so, as his largest fish will necessarily be big-mouth bass, and because they do not fight in proportion to their size, they are set down as lacking in game qualities—of course, leaving the largest small-mouth bass out of the calculation.

Gentle reader, this is not a case of special pleading, nor is the angler a creation of the imagination lugged in as an apologist for the large-mouth bass; he is a veritable creature of fish and blood, of earth earthy, and with the self-conceit, weaknesses and shortcomings characteristic of the genus *homo*. I have met him and heard his arguments and sage expressions scores of times, and if the reader will reflect a moment I am sure he will recognize him.

Many years ago I was at Gogebic Lake, Wisconsin, where, among a number of prominent anglers, were Dr. F., and Dr. T., both of New York City. Dr. F. had a very extensive angling experience in all parts of the country, and Dr. T. was well known as a participant in the fly- and bait-catching contests in the tournaments of the National Rod and Reel Association of that day.

Dr. T. was a firm believer in the superior game qualities of the small-mouth bass, and declared that he could invariably tell what species of black bass he had hooked, from its manner of "fighting." Dr. F. was confident he could not do so. The matter was finally put to a practical test, when Dr. T. was forced to acknowledge himself vanquished, and that he nor any other angler could make the distinction, for one fish was as "gamy" as the other. I might add that this result will be obtained wherever the two species exist in the same waters.

Mr. S. C. Clarke, a veteran angler of sixty years' experience, and whose opinion is titled to great weight, says:

"I will say that, from an acquaintance with both species for more than forty years, from Minnesota to Florida, I have found little or no difference between them. I have taken them with fly, spoon, and bait, as many as fifty in a day (in early times), and up to six and a half pounds' weight."

A few years before his death, Fred Mather wrote as follows:

"A bad name, given to the big-mouth bass when black bass first began to attract the attention of anglers, has stuck. It may interest a younger generation of anglers to know that forty years ago these gamy fishes were hardly known to anglers, and as soon as they began to attract attention some persons, to show their exquisite discrimination, began to praise one to the detriment of the other. Dr. Henshall and I have had the courage to fight this, and to say that in game qualities there is little difference, and that what there is depends on the weight of the fish, two pounds being its fighting weight. Further than to say that the big-mouth is not so capricious about taking the fly as his brother—*i.e.*, will usually take it more freely—I have not room to go into this subject here. I have written all this before and intend to keep at it until justice is done to a noble game-fish."

Mr. Henry Talbott, an angler of wide experience, and who has written so entertainingly and instructively on black bass angling in the Potomac, says:

"There are some anglers who consider there is but one black bass, the small-mouth, and that the other is useless for food, lacking in gamy qualities and only fished for by the misguided. In this they are mistaken, and it is a theory they will abandon and resent when their experience is wider.

"It is possible that in the Florida lakes they may be tame sport, and there seems to be a general agreement that in some of the swamps of Ohio the big-mouth is an inferior fish, but there is yet to be found his superior where he has a fair chance.

"Taking the two fish at their best, there is no man living can tell the difference in their taking the fly, in their fight to the boat, or on the platter, by any other sign than that one has a more capacious smile than the other; and by the same token he is just a little the better jumper and will leave the water oftener after being hooked, and is as long in coming to the net as his cousin."

Owing to my admiration for the black bass as a game-fish, and my championship of its cause for many years, and my efforts to place it in the front rank of game-fish-es, and my desire to have it placed in new waters, I am sometimes, thoughtlessly and unjustly, accused of being opposed to the brook trout, and of advising the stock-ing of trout streams with my "favorite" fish. Nothing can be further from the truth.

I am utterly opposed to the introduction of black bass into waters in which there is the remotest chance for the brook trout or rainbow trout to thrive. I yield to no one in love and admiration of the brook trout. I was perfectly familiar with it before I ever saw a black bass; but I am not so blinded by prejudice but that I can share that love with the black bass, which for several reasons is destined to become the favorite game-fish of America. "My offending hath this extent, no more."

Let us look this thing squarely in the face. I do not wish to disturb anyone's preference, but I do want to disabuse the minds of anglers of all prejudice in the matter. The brook trout must go. It has already gone from many streams, and is fast disappearing from oth-ers. It is sad to contemplate the extinction of the "an-gler's pride" in public waters, but the stern fact remains that in this utilitarian age its days are numbered and its fate irrevocably sealed. As the red man disappears before the tread of the white man, the "living arrow" of the mountain streams goes with him.

The trout is essentially a creature of the pine forests. Its natural home is in waters shaded by pine, balsam, spruce, and hemlock, where the cold mountain brooks retain their low temperature, and the air is redo-lent of balsamic fragrance; where the natural food of the trout is produced in the greatest abundance, and where its breeding grounds are undisturbed.

But the iron has entered its soul. As the buffalo disappears before the iron horse, the brook trout van-ishes before the axe of the lumberman. As the giants of the forest are laid low, and the rank and file decimated and the wooden walls of the streams battered down, the hot, fiery sun leaps through the breaches, disclosing the most secret recesses of forest and stream to the bright glare of midday. The moisture of the earth is dissipated, the mosses and ferns become shriveled and dry, the wintergreen and partridge-berry, the ground pine and trailing arbutus struggle feebly for existence; the waters decrease in size and increase in temperature, the condi-tions of the food supply and of the breeding grounds of the brook trout are changed; it deteriorates in size and numbers and vitality, until finally, in accordance with the immutable laws of nature and the great principle of the "survival of the fittest" (not the fittest from the an-gler's point of view, but the fittest to survive the changes and mutations consequent on the march of civilization), it disappears altogether.

Much has been said about the "trout hog" in con-nection with the decrease of the trout. But while he deserves all the odium and contempt heaped upon him by the honest angler, the result would be the same were the trout allowed undisturbed and peaceable posses-sion of the streams, so far as the fish-hook is concerned, while the axe of the lumberman continues to ring its death knell.

Let us, then, cherish and foster and protect the crimson-spotted favorite of our youthful days as long as possible in public waters, and introduce the rainbow trout, the Dolly Varden, the steelhead, the red-throat trout, or the English brown trout, when he has disap-peared; and when all these succumb, then, and not till then, introduce the black bass. But let us give these cousins of the brook trout a fair trial first, and without prejudice. There are plenty of lakes, ponds, and large streams in the eastern states into which the black bass can be introduced without interfering with trout waters.

For many years to come brook trout will be artificially cultivated, and the supply thus kept up in preserved waters by wealthy angling clubs; but by the alteration of the natural conditions of their existence they will gradually decrease in size and quality, until finally they will either cease to be or degenerate to such a degree as to forfeit even this praiseworthy protection.

I must dissent from the statement sometimes made that the black bass is the bluefish of fresh waters. The black bass is voracious—so are all game-fishes—but not more so than the brook trout. The character of a fish's teeth determines the nature of its food and the manner of its feeding. The bluefish has the most formidable array of teeth of any fish of its size—compressed, lancet-shaped, covered with enamel, and exceedingly strong and sharp, in fact, miniature shark teeth—while the black bass has soft, small, brush-like teeth, incapable of wounding, and intended only for holding its prey, which is swallowed whole. The brook trout has longer, stronger and sharper teeth than the bass, and a large, long mouth, capable of swallowing a bigger fish than a black bass of equal weight. The mouth of the bass is very wide, for the purpose of taking in crawfish with their long and aggressive claws, and not, as supposed by some, for the swallowing of large fishes. The black bass gets the best of other game-fishes, not by devouring the fishes themselves, but by devouring their food. For this reason, more than any other, they should not be introduced into the same waters with brook trout. The pike or pickerel is the blue-fish of fresh waters, and in dental capacity and destructive possibilities is not far behind it.

The brook trout, I think, is the most beautiful of all fishes, as a fresh-run salmon is the handsomest and most perfect in form. The salmon is a king, the brook trout a courtier, but the black bass, in his virescent cuirass and spiny crest, is a doughty warrior whose prowess none can gainsay.

I have fished for brook trout in the wilds of Canada, where a dozen would rise at every cast of the fly, and it would be a scramble as to which should get it—great lusty trout, from a half-pound to two pounds in weight—but the black fly made life a burden by day, and the mosquito by night. The glory and beauty of the madly rushing stream breaking wildly over the great black rocks, and the quiet, glassy pools below reflecting the green spires of spruce and fir, availed nothing to swollen eyelids and smarting brow.

I have cast from early morn till dewy eve, on a good salmon stream in New Brunswick, for three days in succession without a single rise. I have cast standing in a birch-bark canoe until both arms and legs were weary with the strain, and then rested by casting while sitting—but all in vain. The swift-flowing, crystal stream reflected back the fierce glare of the northern sun and flowed on in silence toward the sea. The fir-clad hills rose boldly on either side, and stood in silent, solemn grandeur—for neither note of bird or hum of bee disturbed the painful silence of the Canadian woods.

At such times would flash on memory's mirror many a fair scene of limpid lake or rushing river, shadowed by cool, umbrageous trees, and vocal with myriads of voices—where the black bass rose responsive to the swish of the rod and dropping of the fly. Or, should the bass be coy and shy, or loth to leave his lair beneath some root or shelving rock—the melody of the birds, the tinkle of a cow-bell, the chirp of a cricket, the scudding of a squirrel, filled up the void and made full compensation.

The true angler can find real pleasure in catching little sunfish, or silversides, if the stream and birds, and bees and butterflies do their part by him; while the killing of large or many fish, even salmon or trout, in silence and solitude, may fail to fully satisfy him.

I can find something beautiful or interesting in every fish that swims. I have an abiding affection for every one, from the lowly, naked bull-head, the humble scavenger of the waters, to the silver-spangled king who will not deign to soil his dainty lips with food during his sojourn in crystal streams, and I love the brook trout best of all. But, as an angler, I can find more true enjoyment, more blessed peace, in wading some rushing, rocky stream, flecked by the shadows of overhanging elm and sycamore, while tossing the silken gage to the knight in Lincoln-green, my ears conscious of the rippling laughter of the merry stream, the joyous matin of the woodland thrush, the purring undertone of the quivering leaves—my eyes catching glimpses of hill and meadow, wren and robin, bee and bittern, fern and flower, and my breath inhaling the sweet fragrance of upland clover and elder-blossom—I say I can find more true enjoyment in this—than paying court to the lordly salmon in his drear and silent demesne, or in wooing the lovely trout with anointed face, gloved hands, and head swathed in gauze. If this be treason, my brother, make the most of it. I am content. It is my honest conviction. After killing every species of game-fish east of the Rocky Mountains, from Canada to Florida, and some in foreign lands, I find the knightly bass and his tourney-field all sufficient.

THE CAPTURE OF THE BASS

My brother of the angle, go with me
This perfect morning in the leafy June,
To yonder pool below the rapid's foot.
Approach with caution; let your tread be soft;
Beware the bending bushes on the brink.
Disturb no branch, nor twig, nor leaf, my friend,
The finny tribe is wary.

Rest we here.
Behold the lovely scene! The rippling stream,
Now dancing, sparkling, in the morning sun;
The blue-eyed violet nodding at your feet;
The red-bird, all ablaze, with swelling throat,
The dreamy, droning hum of insect wings
Is mingled ever with the rustling leaves.
Sleek, well-fed cattle there contented stand,

On gravelly shoal beneath the spreading beech.
Across the narrow stream a sycamore,
A weather-beaten giant, old and gray,
With scarr'd arms stretching o'er the silent pool,
With gnarl'd and twisted roots bathed in the flood
For, lo, these hundred years.

Beneath those roots
With watchful eye—proud monarch of the pool—
A cunning bass doth lie, on balanced fin,
In waiting for his prey.

And now with rod,
With faithful reel, and taper'd line of silk,
With mist-like leader and two fairly flies—
Dark, bush hackles, both—I make a cast.
With lengthen'd line I quickly cast again,
And just beneath the tree the twin-like lures
As gently drop as falling autumn leaves;
And half-submerged, like things of life they seem,
Responsive to the rod and line.

But look!
Saw you that gleam beneath the flood? A flash—
A shadow—then a swirl upon the pool?
My hand, responsive to the sudden thrill,
Strikes in the steel—the wary bass is hooked!
And now with lightning speed he darts away
To reach his lair—his refuge 'neath the roots.
The singing reel proclaims him almost there—
I "give the butt"—the ever-faithful rod
In horse-shoe curve checks his headlong flight.
Right lustily he tugs and pulls, Egad!
But still the barb is fast.

The hissing line—
The rod now bending like a slender reed
Resists the tight'ning strain. He turns his course—
In curving reaches, back and forth, he darts,
Describing arcs and segments in the pool.
Ha! nobly done! as with a mighty rush
He cleaves the crystal stream, and at one bound,
Full half a fathom in the realm above

He nimbly takes an atmospheric flight—
His fins extended, stiff with bristling points—
His armor brightly flashing in the sun—
His wide-extended jaws he shakes in rage
To rid him of the hook.

And now I lower
The pliant rod in court'sy to the brave.
The line relieved, somewhat, of steady strain,
Outwits the wily bass—the hook holds fast!
Now back again he falls with angry splash
To seek the aid of snag, or root of tree;
For thus, my friend, he oft escapes, I trow,
By fouling line or hook—

He never sulks!
Not he; while life remains, or strength holds good,
His efforts never cease. Now up the stream—
Now down again—I have him well in hand.
Now reeling in, or erstwhile giving line;
He swims now fast or slow—now high or low.
The steady strain is still maintained, you see!
The good rod swaying like a wind-blown rush—
He surges thro' the flood.

Another leap!
Ye Gods! How like an angry beast he shakes
His brisling mane, and dives below again!
And did you mark, my friend, his shrewd intent,
As when he fell upon the slacken'd line?
If then he'd found it stretched and taut, I ween,
He would have made his safe and sure escape.
But haply then the tip was slightly lowered—
And so, with yielding line, the hook held fast.
Now truly, friend, he makes a gallant fight!
In air or water—all the same to him—
His spiny crest erect; he struggles still.
No sulking here! but like a mettl'd steed

He champs the bit, and ever speeds the best
With firm-held, tighten'd rein.

He's off again!
Now down the stream he flashes like a shaft
From long-bow swiftly sped—his last bold
spurt—
The effort cost him dear—his worsted strength
Is ebbing fast. And now in lessening curves
He feebly swims, and labors with the tide.
And as I reel the line he slowly yields,
And now turns up his breast-plate, snowy white—
A vanquished, conquered knight.

And now my friend
The landing-net. With firm and cautious hand
Beneath the surface hold it. Take him in.
Now lift him out and gently lay him down.
How bright his tunic, bronze and glossy green!
A fitting rival to the velvet sward.

And see the ragged rent the hook hath made!
You marvel how it held him safe and fast!
'Twas by the equal and continual strain
Of supple rod and ever-faithful reel.
'Twas work well done.

Oh valiant, noble bass!
Fit dweller of the merry, brawling stream.
Thy once-loved pool beneath thy giant tree,
Thy fancied stronghold 'neath its tangled roots,
Shall know thee never more. Thy race is run!

Now in thy creel,
My doubting friend, we'll gently lay him down
Upon a bed of cool and graceful ferns,
Yet sparkling with the early morning dew—
A warrior in repose!

B. A Wedding Gift

JOHN TAINTOR FOOTE

George Baldwin Potter is a purist. That is to say, he either takes trout on a dry fly or he does not take them at all. He belongs to a number of fishing clubs, any member of which might acquire his neighbor's wife, beat his children, or poison a dog and still cast a fly, in all serenity, upon club waters; but should he impale on a hook a lowly though succulent worm and immerse the creature in those same waters it would be better that he send in his resignation at once, sooner than face the shaken committee that would presently wait upon him.

George had become fixed in my mind as a bachelor. This, or course, was a mistake. I am continually forgetting that purists rush into marriage when ap-

proaching or having just passed the age of forty. The psychology of this is clear.

For twenty years, let us say, a purist's life is completely filled by his efforts to convert all reasonable men to his own particular method of taking trout. He thinks, for example, that a man should not concern himself with more than a dozen types of standard flies. The manner of presenting them is the main consideration. Take any one of these flies, then, and place, by means of an eight-foot rod, a light, tapered line, and a mist-colored leader of reasonable length, on fast water—if you want trout. Of course, if you want to listen to the birds and look at the scenery, fish the pools with a long line and an eight-foot leader. Why, it stands to reason that—

The years go by as he explains these vital facts patiently, again and again, to Smith and Brown and Jones. One wet, cold spring, after fighting a muddy stream all day, he re-explains for the better part of an evening and takes himself, somewhat wearily upstairs. The damp and chill of the room at whatever club he may be fishing is positively tomblike. He can hear the rain drumming on the roof and swishing against the windows. The water will be higher than ever tomorrow, he reflects, as he puts out the lights and slides between the icy sheets. Steeped to the soul in cheerless dark, he recalls numbly that when he first met Smith and Brown and Jones they were fishing the pools with a long line. That was, let's see—fifteen—eighteen—twenty years ago. Then he must be forty. It isn't possible! Yes, it is a fact that Smith and Brown and Jones are still fishing the pools with a long line.

In the first faint light of dawn he falls into an uneasy, muttering slumber. The dark hours between have been devoted to intense thought and a variety of wiggles which have not succeeded in keeping the bedclothes against his shoulder blades.

Some time within the next six months you will remember that you have forgotten to send him a wedding present.

George, therefore, having arrived at his fortieth birthday, announced his engagement shortly thereafter. Quite by chance I ran across his bride-to-be and himself a few days before the ceremony, and joined them at lunch. She was a blonde in the early twenties, with wide blue eyes and a typical rose-and-white complexion. A rushing, almost breathless account of herself, which she began the moment we were seated, was curious, I thought. It was as though she feared an interruption at any moment. I learned that she was an only child, born and reared in Greater New York; that her family had recently moved to New Rochell; that she had been shopping madly for the past two weeks; that she was nearly dead, but that she had some adorable things.

At this point George informed me that they would spend their honeymoon at a certain fishing club in Maine. He then proceeded to describe the streams and lakes in that section at some length—during the rest of the luncheon, as a matter of fact. His fiancee, who had fallen into a wordless abstraction, only broke her silence with a vague murmur as we parted.

Owing to this meeting I did not forget to send a wedding present. I determined that my choice should please both George and his wife through the happy years to come.

If I had had George to consider, I could have settled the business in two minutes at a sporting-goods store. Barred from these for obvious reasons, I spent a long day in a thoroughly exhausting search. Late in the afternoon I decided to abandon my hopeless task. I had made a tremendous effort and failed. I would simply buy a silver doodad and let it go at that.

As I staggered into a store with the above purpose in view, I passed a show case devoted to fine china, and halted as my eyes fell on a row of fish plates backed by artfully rumpled blue velvet. The plates proved to be hand painted. On each plate was one of the different varieties of trout, curving up through green depths to an artificial fly just dropping on the surface of the water.

In an automatic fashion I indicated the plates to a clerk, paid for them, gave him my card and the address, and fled from the store. Some time during the next twenty-four hours it came to me that George Potter was not among my nearest and dearest. Yet the unbelievable sum I had left with that clerk in exchange for those fish plates could be justified in no other way.

I thought this fact accounted for the sort of frenzy with which George flung himself upon me when next we met, some two months later. I had been weekending in the country and encountered him in the Grand Central Station as I emerged from the lower level. For a long moment he wrung my hand in silence, gazing almost feverishly into my face. At last he spoke:

"Have you got an hour to spare?"

It occurred to me that it would take George an hour at least to describe his amazed delight at the splendor of my gift. The clock above Information showed that it was 12:45. I therefore suggested that we lunch together.

He, too, glanced at the clock, verified its correctness by his watch, and seized me by the arm.

"All right," he agreed, and was urging me toward the well-filled and somewhat noisy station cafe before I grasped his intention and tried to suggest that we go elsewhere. His hand only tightened on my arm.

"It's all right," he said; "good food, quick service—you'll like it."

He all but dragged me into the cafe and steered me to a table in the corner. I lifted my voice above an earnest clatter of gastronomical utensils and made a last effort.

"The Biltmore's just across the street."

George pressed me into my chair, shoved a menu card at me and addressed the waiter.

"Take his order." Here he jerked out his watch and consulted it again. "We have forty-eight minutes. Service for one. I shan't be eating anything; or, no—bring me some coffee—large cup—black."

Having ordered mechanically, I frankly stared at George. He was dressed, I now observed, with unusual care. He wore a rather dashing gray suit. His tie, which was an exquisite shade of gray-blue, was embellished by a handsome pearl. The handkerchief, appearing above his breast pocket, was of the same delicate gray-blue shade as the tie. His face had been recently and closely shaven, also powdered; but above that smooth whiteness of jowl was a pair of curiously glittering eyes and a damp, beaded brow. This he now mopped with his napkin. "Good God," said I, "what is it, George?"

His reply was to extract a letter from his inside coat pocket and pass it across the table, his haunted eyes on mine. I took in its few lines at a glance:

"Father has persuaded me to listen to what you call your explanation. I arrive Grand Central 2:45, daylight saving, Monday." Isabelle.

Poor old George, I thought; some bachelor indiscretion; and now, with his honeymoon scarcely over, blackmail, a lawsuit, heaven only knows what. "Who," I asked, returning the letter, "is Isabelle?"

To my distress, George again resorted to his napkin. Then, "My wife," he said.

"Your wife!"

George nodded.

"Been living wither people for the last month. Wish he'd bring that coffee. You don't happen to have a flask with you?"

"Yes, I have a flask." George brightened. "But it's empty. Do you want to tell me about your trouble? Is that why you brought me here?"

"Well, yes," George admitted. "But the point is—will you stand by me? That's the main thing. She gets in"—here he consulted his watch—"in forty-five minutes, if the train's on time." A sudden panic seemed to seize him. His hand shot across the table and grasped my wrist. "You've got to stand by me, old man—act as if you knew nothing. Say you ran into me here and stayed to meet her. I'll tell you what—say I didn't' seem to want you to stay. Kid me about wanting her all to myself, or something like that. Get the point? It'll give me a chance to sort of—well, you understand."

"I see what you mean, of course," I admitted. "Here's your coffee. Suppose you have some and then tell me what this is all about—if you care to, that is."

"No sugar, no cream," said George to the waiter; "just pour it. Don't stand there waving it about—pour it, pour it!" He attempted to swallow a mouthful of steaming coffee, gurgled frightfully and grabbed his water glass. "Great jumping Jehoshaphat!" he gasped, when he could speak, and glared at the waiter, who promptly moved out into the sea of diners and disappeared among a dozen of his kind.

"Steady, George," I advised as I transferred a small lump of ice from my glass to his coffee cup.

George watched the ice dissolve, murmured "Idiot" several times, and presently swallowed the contents of the cup in two gulps.

"I had told her," he said suddenly, "exactly where we were going. She mentioned Narragansett several times—I'll admit that. Imagine—Narragansett! Of course I bought her fishing things myself. I didn't buy knickers or woolens or flannel shirts—naturally. You don't go around buying a girl breeches and underwear before you're married. It wouldn't be—well, it isn't done, that's all. I got her the sweetest three-ounce rod you ever held in your hand. I'll bet I could put out sixty feet of line with it against the wind. I got her a pair of English waders that didn't weigh a pound. They cost me forty-five dollars. The rest of the outfit was just as good. Why, her fly box was a Truxton. I could have bought an American imitation for eight dollars. I know a lot of men who'll buy leaders for themselves at two dollars apiece and let their wives fish with any kind of tackle. I'll give you my word I'd have used anything I got for her myself. I sent it all out to be packed with her things. I wanted her to feel that it was her own—not mine. I know a lot of men who give their wives a high-class rod or an imported reel and then fish with it themselves. What time is it?"

"Clock right up there," I said. But George consulted his watch and used his napkin distressingly again.

"Where was I?"

"You were telling me why you sent her fishing things out to her."

"Oh, yes! That's all of that. I simply wanted to show you that from the first I did all any man could do. Ever been in the Cuddiwink district?"

I said that I had not.

"You go in from Buck's Landing. A lumber tug takes you up to the head of Lake Owonga. Club guides meet you there and put you through in one day—twenty miles by canoe and portage up the west branch of the Penobscot; then nine miles by trail to Lost Pond. The club's on Lost Pond. Separate cabins, with a main dining and loafing camp, and the best squaretail fishing on earth—both lake and stream. Of course, I don't fish the lakes. A dry fly belongs on a stream and nowhere else. Let me make it perfectly clear."

George's manner suddenly changed. He hunched himself closer to the table, dropped an elbow upon it and lifted an expository finger.

"The dry fly," he stated, with a new almost combative ring in his voice, "is designed primarily to simulate not only the appearance of the natural insect but its action as well. This action is arrived at through the flow of the current. The moment you move a fly by means of leader you destroy the—

I saw that an interruption was imperative.

"Yes, of course," I said; "but your wife will be here in—"

It was pitiful to observe George. His new-found assurance did not flee—flee suggests a withdrawal, however swift—it was immediately and totally annihilated. He attempted to pour himself some coffee, take out his watch, look at the clock, and mop his brow with his napkin at one and the same instant.

"You were telling me how to get to Lost Pond," I suggested.

"Yes, to be sure," said George. "Naturally you go in light. The things you absolutely have to have—rods, tackle, waders, wading shoes, and so forth, are about all a guide can manage at the portages in addition to the canoe. You pack in extras yourself—change of underclothes, a couple of pairs of socks, and a few toilet articles. You leave a bag or trunk at Buck's Landing. I explained this to her. I explained it carefully. I told her either a week-end bag or one small trunk. Herb Trescott was my best man. I left everything to him. He saw us on the train and handed me tickets and reservations just before we pulled out. I didn't notice in the excitement of getting away that he'd given me three trunk checks all stamped 'Excess.' I didn't notice it till the conductor showed up, as a matter of fact. Then I said, 'Darling, what in heaven's name have you brought three trunks for?' She said—I can remember her exact words—'Then you're not going to Narragansett?'

"I simply looked at her. I was too dumbfounded to speak. At last I pulled myself together and told her in three days we'd be whipping the best squaretail water in the world. I took her hand, I remember, and said, 'You and I together, sweetheart,' or something like that."

George sighed and lapsed into a silence which remained unbroken until his eye happened to encounter the face of the clock. He started and went on:

"We got to Buck's Landing, by way of Bangor, at six in the evening of the following day. Buck's Landing is a railroad station with grass growing between the ties, a general store and hotel combined, and a lumber wharf. The store keeps canned peas, pink-and-white candy, and felt boots. The hotel part is—well, it doesn't matter except that I don't think I ever saw so many deer heads; a few stuffed trout but mostly deer heads. After supper the proprietor and I got the three trunks up to the largest room. We just got them in and that was all. The tug left for the head of the lake at seven next morning. I explained this to Isabelle. I said we'd leave the trunks there until we came out, and offered to help her unpack the one her fishing things were in. She said, 'Please go away!' So I went away. I got out a rod and went down to the wharf. No trout there, I knew; but I thought I'd limber up my wrist. I put on a Cahill Number Fourteen—or was it Sixteen—"

George knitted his brows and stared intently but unseeingly at me for some little time.

"Call it a Sixteen," I suggested.

George shook his head impatiently and remained concentrated in thought.

"I'm inclined to think it was a Fourteen," he said at last. "But let it go; it'll come to me later. At any rate, the place was alive with big chub—a foot long, some of 'em. I'll bet I took fifty—threw 'em back, of course. They kept on rising after it got dark. I'd tell myself I'd go after one more cast. Each time I'd hook a big chub, and—well, you know how the time slips away.

"When I got back to the hotel all the lights were out. I lit matches until I got upstairs and found the door to the room. I'll never forget what I saw when I opened that door—never! Do you happen to know how many of the kind of things they wear a woman can get into one trunk? Well, she had three and she'd unpacked them all. She had used the bed for the gowns alone. It was piled with them—literally piled; but that wasn't a starter. Everywhere you looked was a stack of things with ribbons in 'em. There were enough shoes and stockings for a girl's school; silk stockings, mind you, and high-heeled shoes and slippers." Here George consulted clock and watch. "I wonder if that train's on time," he wanted to know.

"You have thirty-five minutes, even if it is," I told him; "go right ahead."

"Well, I could see something was wrong from her face. I didn't know what, but I started right in to cheer her up. I told her all about the chub fishing I'd been having. At last she burst into tears. I won't go into the scene that followed. I'd ask her what was the matter and she'd say, 'Nothing,' and cry frightfully. I know a lot of men who would have lost their tempers under

the circumstances, but I didn't; I give you my word. I simply said, 'There, there,' until she quieted down. And that isn't all. After a while she began to show me her gowns. Imagine—at eleven o'clock at night, at Buck's Landing! She'd hold up a dress and look over the top of it at me and ask me how I liked it, and I'd say it was all right. I know a lot of men who wouldn't have sat there two minutes.

"At last I said, 'They're all all right, darling,' and yawned. She was holding up a pink dress covered with shiny dingle-dangles, and she threw the dress on the bed and all but had hysterics. It was terrible. In trying to think of some way to quiet her it occurred to me that I'd put her rod together and let her feel the balance of it with the feel I'd bought her—a genuine Fleetwood, mind you—attached. I looked around for her fishing things and couldn't find them. I'll tell you why I couldn't find them." George paused for an impressive instant to give his next words the full significance due them. "They weren't there!"

"No?" I murmured weakly.

"No," said George. "And what do you suppose she said when I questioned her? I can give you her exact words—I'll never forget them. She said, 'There wasn't any room for them.'" Again George paused. "I ask you," he inquired at last, "I ask you as man to man; what do you think of that?"

I found no adequate reply to this question and George, now thoroughly warmed up, rushed on.

"You'd swear I lost my temper then, wouldn't you? Will, I didn't. I did say something to her later, but I'll let you be the judge when we come to that. I'll ask you to consider the circumstances. I'll ask you to get Old Faithful in your mind's eye."

"Old Faithful?" I repeated. "Then you went to the Yellowstone later?"

"Yellowstone! Of course not! Haven't I told you we were already at the best trout water in America? Old Faithful was a squaretail. He'd been in the pool below Horseshoe Falls for twenty years, as a matter of record. We'll come to that presently. How are we off for time?"

"Thirty-one minutes," I told him. "I'm the watching the clock—go ahead."

"Well, there she was, on a fishing trip with nothing to fish with. There was only one answer to that—she couldn't fish. But I went over everything she'd brought in three trunks and I'll give you my word she didn't have a garment of any sort you couldn't see through.

"Something had to be done and done quick, that was for sure. I fitted her out from my own things with a sweater, a flannel shirt, and a pair of knickerbockers. Then I got the proprietor up and explained the situation. He got me some heavy underwear and two pairs of woolen stockings that belonged to his wife. When it came to shoes it looked hopeless, but the proprietor's wife, who had got up, too, by this time, thought of a pair of boy's moccasin's that were in the store and they turned out to be about the right size. I made arrangements to rent the room we had until we came out again to keep her stuff in, and took another room for the night—what was left of it after she'd repacked what could stay in the trunks and arranged what couldn't so it wouldn't be wrinkled.

"I got up early, dressed, and took my duffle down to the landing. I wakened her when I left the room. When breakfast was ready I went to see why she hadn't come down. She was all dressed, sitting on the edge of the bed. I said, 'Breakfast is ready, darling,' but I saw by her face that something was wrong again. It turned out to be my knickers. They fitted her perfectly—a little tight in spots—except in the waist. They would simply have fallen off if she hadn't held them up.

"Well, I was going in so light that I only had one belt. The proprietor didn't have any—he used suspenders. Neither did his wife—she used—well, whatever they use. He got me a piece of clothesline and I knotted it at each and ran it through the what-you-may-call-'ems of the knickers and tied it in front. The knickers sort of puckered all the way around, but they couldn't come down—that was the main thing. I said, 'There you are, darling.' She walked over and tilted the mirror of the bureau so that she could see herself from head to foot. She said, 'Who are going to be at this place where we are going?' I said, 'Some of the very best dry-fly men in the country.' She said, 'I don't mean them; I mean the women. Will there be any women there?'

"I told her, certainly there would be women. I asked her if she thought I would take her into a camp with nothing but men. I named some of the women: Mrs. Fred Beal and Mrs. Brooks Carter and Talcott Ranning's sister and several more.

"She turned around slowly in front of the mirror, staring into it for a minute. Then she said, 'Please go out and close the door.' I said, 'All right, darling; but come right down. The tug will be here in fifteen minutes.'

"I went downstairs and waited for ten minutes, then I heard the tug whistle for the landing and ran upstairs again. I knocked at the door. When she didn't answer I went in. Where do you suppose she was?"

I gave it up.

"In bed!" said George in an awe-struck voice. "In bed with her face turned to the wall; and listen, I didn't lose my temper as God is my judge. I rushed down to the wharf and told the tug captain I'd give him twenty-five dollars extra if he'd hold the boat till we came. He said all right and I went back to the room.

"The breeches had done it. She simply wouldn't wear them. I told her that at a fishing camp in Maine clothes were never thought of. I said, 'No one thinks of anything but trout, darling.' She said, 'I wouldn't let a fish see me looking like that.'" George's brow beaded suddenly. His hands dived searchingly into various pockets. "Got a cigarette? I left my case in my other suit."

He took a cigarette from me, lighted it with shaking fingers and inhaled deeply.

"It went on like that for thirty minutes. She was crying all the time, of course. I had started down to tell the tug captain it was all off, and I saw a woman's raincoat hanging in the hall. It belonged to someone up in one of the camps, the proprietor told me. I gave him seventy-five dollars to give to whoever owned it when he came out, and took it upstairs. In about ten minutes I persuaded her to wear it over the rest of her outfit until we got to camp. I told her one of the women would be able to fix her up all right when we got there. I didn't believe it, of course. The women at camp were all old-timers; they'd gone in as light as the men, but I had to say something.

"We had quite a trip going in. The guides were at the head of the lake all right—Indian Joe and new a man I'd never seen, called Charlie. I told Joe to take Isabelle—he's one of the best canoemen I ever saw. I was going to paddle bow for my man, but I'd have to bet a cookie Indian Joe could stay with us on any kind of water. We had to beat it right through to make camp by night. It's a good stiff trip, but it can be done. I looked back at the other canoe now and then we struck about a mile of white water that took all I had. When we were through the other canoe wasn't in sight. The river made a bend there, and I thought it was just behind and would show up any minute.

"Well, it didn't show up and I began to wonder. We hit our first portage about ten o'clock and landed. I watched downstream for twenty minutes, expecting to sight the other canoe every instant. Then Charlie, who hadn't opened his head, said, 'Better go back,' and put the canoe in again. We paddled downstream for all that was in it. I was stiff with fright. We saw 'em coming about three miles lower down and back-paddled till they came up. Isabelle was more cheerful-looking than she'd been since we left New York, but Joe had that stony face an Indian gets when he's sore.

"I said, 'Anything wrong?' Joe just grunted and drove the canoe past us. Then I saw it was filled with wild flowers. Isabelle said she'd been picking them right off the banks all the way long. She said she'd only had to get out of the boat once, for the blue ones. Now, you can't beat that—not in a thousand years. I leave it to you if you can. Twenty miles of stiff current, with five portages ahead of us and a nine-mile hike at the end of that. I gave that Indian the devil for letting her do such a thing, and tipped the flowers into the Penobscot when we unloaded for the first portage. She didn't speak to

me on the portage, and she got into her canoe without a word.

"Nothing more happened going in, except this flower business had lost us two hours, and it was so dark when we struck the swamp at Loon Lake that we couldn't follow the trail well and kept stumbling over down timber and stepping into bog holes. She was about fagged out by then, and the mosquitoes were pretty thick through there. Without any warning she sat down in the trail. She did it so suddenly I nearly fell over her. I asked her what was the matter and she said, 'This is the end'—just like that—'this is the end!' I said, 'The end of what, darling?' She said, 'Of everything!' I told her if she sat there all wet and muddy she'd catch her death. She said she hoped so. I said, 'It's only two miles more, darling. Just think, tomorrow we'll be on the best trout water in the world!' With that she said, 'I want my mother, my darling mother,' and bowed her head in her hands. Think if over, please; and remember, I didn't lose my temper. You're sure there's nothing left in your flask?"

"Not a drop more, George," I assured him. "Go ahead; we've only twenty-five minutes."

George looked wildly at the clock, then at his watch.

"A man never has it when he wants it most. Have you noticed that? Where was I?"

"You were in the swamp."

"Oh, yes! Well, she didn't speak after that, and nothing I could say would budge her. The mosquitoes had got wind of us when we stopped and were coming in swarms. We'd be eaten alive in another ten minutes. So I told Joe to give his pack to Charlie and help me pick her up and carry her. Joe said, 'No, by damn!' and folded his arms. When an Indian gets sore he stays sore, and when he's sore he's stubborn. The mosquitoes were working on him good and plenty, though, and at last he said, 'Me carry packs. Charlie help carry—that.' He flipped his hand over in the direction of Isabelle and took the pack from Charlie.

"It was black as your hat by now, and the trail through there was only about a foot wide with swamp on each side. It was going to be some job getting her out of there. I thought Charlie and I would make a chair of our arms and stumble along with her some way; but when I started to lift her up she said, 'Don't touch me!' and got up and went on. A blessing if there ever was one. We got to camp at ten that night.

"She was stiff and sore the next morning—you expect it after a trip like that—besides, she'd caught a little cold. I asked her how she felt, and she said she was going to die and asked me to send for a doctor and her mother. The nearest doctor was at Bangor and her mother was in New Rochelle. I carried her breakfast over from the dining camp to our cabin. She said she couldn't eat any breakfast, but she did drink a cup of coffee, telling me between sips how awful it was to die alone in a place like that.

"After she'd had the coffee she seemed to feel better. I went to the camp library and got *The Dry Fly on American Waters*, by Charles Darty. I considered him the soundest man in the country. He's better than Pell or Fawcett. My chief criticism of him is that in his chapter on Streams East of the Alleghenies—east of the Alleghenies, mind you—he recommends the Royal Coachman. I consider the Lead-Wing Coachman a serviceable fly on clear, hard-fished water; but the Royal—never! I wouldn't give it a shade over the Professor or the Montreal. Just consider the body alone of the Royal Coachman—never mind the wings and hackle—the body of the Royal is—"

"Yes, I know, George," I said; "but—"

I glanced significantly at the clock. George started, sighed, and resumed his narrative.

"I went back to the cabin and said, 'Darling, here is one of the most intensely interesting books ever written. I'm going to read it aloud to you. I think I can finish it to-day. Would you like to sit up in bed while I read?' She said she hadn't strength enough to sit up in bed, so I sat down beside her and started reading. I had read about an hour, I suppose, when she did sit up

in bed quite suddenly. I saw she was staring at me in a queer, wild way that was really startling. I said, 'What is it, darling?' She said, 'I'm going to get up. I'm going to get up this instant.'

"Well, I was delighted, naturally. I thought the book would get her by the time I'd read it through. But there she was, as keen as mustard before I'd got well into it. I'll tell you what I made up my mind to do, right there. I made up my mind to let her use my rod that day. Yes, sir—my three-ounce Spinoza, and what's more, I did it."

George looked at me triumphantly, then lapsed into reflection for a moment.

"If ever a man did everything possible to—well, let it go. The main thing is, I have nothing to reproach myself with—nothing. Except—but we'll come to that presently. Of course, she wasn't ready for dry flies yet. I borrowed some wet flies from the club steward, got some cushions for the canoe and put my rod together. She had no waders, so a stream was out of the question. The lake was better, anyway, that first day; she'd have all the room she wanted for her back cast.

"I stood there on the landing with her before we got into the canoe and showed her just how to put out a fly and recover it. Then she tried it." A sort of horror came into George's face. "You wouldn't believe any one could handle a rod like that," he said huskily. "You couldn't believe it unless you'd seen it. Gimme a cigarette.

"I worked with her a half hour or so and saw no improvement—none whatever. At last she said, 'The string is too long. I can't do anything with such a long string on a pole.' I told her gently—gently, mind you—that the string was an eighteen-dollar double-tapered Hurdman line, attached to a Gebhardt reel on a three-ounce Spinoza rod. I said, 'We'll go out on the lake now. If you can manage to get a rise, perhaps it will come to you instinctively.'

"I paddled her out on the lake and she went at it. She'd spat the flies down and yank them up and spat them down again. She hooked me several times with her back cast and got tangled up in the line herself again and again. All this time I was speaking quietly to her, telling her what to do. I give you my word I never raised my voice—not once—and I thought she'd break the tip every moment.

"Finally she said her arm was tired and lowered the rod. She'd got everything messed up with her last cast and the flies were trailing just over the side of the canoe. I said, 'Recover your cast and reel in, darling.' Instead of using her rod, she took hold of the leader close to the flies and started to pull them into the canoe. At that instant a little trout—couldn't have been over six inches—took the tail fly. I don't know exactly what happened, it was all over so quickly. I think she just screamed and let go of everything. At any rate, I saw my Spinoza bounce off the gunwale of the canoe and disappear. There was fifty feet of water just there. And now listen carefully: not one word did I utter— not one. I simply turned the canoe and paddled to the landing in absolute silence. No reproaches of any sort. Think that over!"

I did. My thoughts left me speechless. George proceeded:

"I took out a guide and tried dragging for the rod with a gang hook and heavy sinker all the rest of the day. But the gangs would only foul on the bottom. I gave up at dusk and paddled in. I said to the guide—it was Charlie—I said, 'Well, it's all over, Charlie.' Charlie said, 'I brought Mr. Carter in and he had an extra rod. Maybe you could borrow it. It's a four-ounce Meecham.' I smiled. I actually smiled. I turned and looked at the lake. 'Charlie,' I said, 'somewhere out there in that dark water, where the eye of man will never behold it again, is a three-ounce Spinoza—and you speak of a Meecham.' Charlie said, 'Well, I just thought I'd tell you.' I said, 'That's all right, Charlie. That's all right.' I went to the main camp, saw Jean, the head guide and made arrangements to leave the next day. Then I went to our cabin and sat down before the fire. I heard Isabelle say something about being sorry. I said, 'I'd rather not talk about it, darling. If you don't mind,

we'll never mention it again.' We sat there in silence, then, until dinner.

"As we got up from dinner, Nate Griswold and his wife asked us to play bridge with them that evening. I'd told no one what had happened, and Nate didn't know, of course. I simply thanked him and said we were tired, and we went back to our cabin. I sat down before the fire again. Isabelle seemed restless. At least she said,

'George.' I said, 'What is it, darling?' She said, 'Would you like to read to me from that book?' I said, 'I'm sorry, darling; if you don't mind I'll just sit here quietly by the fire.'

"Somebody knocked at the door after a while. I said, 'Come in.' It was Charlie. I said, 'What is it, Charlie?' Then he told me that Bob Frazer had been called back to New York and was going out the next morning. I said, 'Well, what of it?' Charlie said, 'I just thought you could maybe borrow his rod.' I said, 'I thought you understood about that, Charlie.' Charlie said, 'Well, that's it. Mr. Frazer's rod is a three-ounce Spinoza.'

"I got up and shook hands with Charlie and gave him five dollars. But when he'd gone I began to realize what was before me. I'd brought in a pint flask of prewar Scotch. Prewar—get that! I put this in my pocket and went over to Bob's cabin. Just as I was going to knock I lost my nerve. I sneaked away from the door and went down to the lake and sat on the steps of the canoe landing. I sat there for quite a while and took several nips. At last I thought I'd jut go and tell Bob of my loss and see what he said. I went back to his cabin and this time I knocked. Bob was putting a few odds and ends in a shoulder pack. His rod was in its case, standing against the wall.

"I said, 'I hear you're going out in the morning.' He said, 'Yes, curse it, my wife's mother has to have some sort of damned operation or other.' I said, 'How would a little drink strike you, Bob?' He said, 'Strike me! Wait a minute! What kind of drink?' I took out the flask and handed it to him. He unscrewed the cap and held the flask to his nose. He said, 'Great heavens above, it smells like—' I said, 'It is.' He said, 'It can't be!' I said, 'Yes, it is.' He said, 'There's a trick in it some-where.' I said, 'No, there isn't—I give you my word.' He tasted what was in the flask carefully. Then he said, 'This is very generous of you, George,' and took a good stiff snort. When he was handing back the flask he said, 'I'll do as much for you some day, if I ever get the chance.' I took a snifter myself.

"Then I said, 'Bob, something awful has happened to me. I came here to tell you about it.' He said, 'Is that so? Sit down.' I sat down and told him. He said, 'What kind of rod was it?' I said, 'A three-ounce Spinoza.' He came over and gripped my hand without a word. I said, 'Of course, I can't use anything else.' He nodded, and I saw his eyes flicker toward the corner of the room where his own rod was standing. I said, 'Have another drink, Bob.' But he just sat down and stared at me. I took a good stiff drink myself. Then I said, 'Under ordinary circumstances, nothing on earth could hire me to ask a man to—' I stopped right there.

"Bob got up suddenly and began to walk up and down the room. I said, 'Bob, I'm not considering my-self—not for a minute. If it was last season, I'd simply have gone back to-morrow without a word. But I'm not alone any more. I've got the little girl to consider. She's never seen a trout taken in her life—think of it, Bob! And here she is, on her honeymoon, at the best water I know of. On her honeymoon, Bob!' I waited for him to say something, but he went to the window and stared out, with his back to me. I got up and said good-night and started for the door. Just as I reached it he turned from the window and rushed over and picked up his rod. He said, 'Here, take it,' and put the rod case in my hands. I started to try to thank him, but he said, 'Just go ahead with it,' and pushed me out the door."

The waiter was suddenly hovering above us with his eyes on the dishes.

"Now what do you want?" said George.

"Never mind clearing here," I said. "Just bring me the check. Go ahead, George."

"Well, of course, I can't any more than skim what happened finally, but you'll understand. It turned out that Ernie Payton's wife had an extra pair of knickers and she loaned them to Isabelle. I was waiting outside the cabin while she dressed next morning, and she called out to me, 'Oh, George, they fit!' Then I heard her begin to sing. She was a different girl when she came out to go to breakfast. She was almost smiling. She'd done nothing but slink about the day before. Isn't it extraordinary what will seem important to a woman? Gimme a cigarette."

"Fifteen minutes, George," I said as I supplied him.

"Yes, yes, I know. I fished the Cuddiwink that day. Grand stream, grand. I used a Pink Lady—first day on a stream with Isabelle—little touch of sentiment—and it's a darn good fly. I fished it steadily all day. Or did I try a Seth Green about noon? It seems to me I did, now that I recall it. It seems to me that where the Katahdin brook comes in I—"

"It doesn't really matter, does it, George?" I ventured.

"Of course, it matters!" said George decisively. "A man wants to be exact about such things. The precise details of what happens in a day's work on a stream are of real value to yourself and others. Except in the case of a record fish, it isn't important that you took a trout; it's exactly how you took him that's important."

"But the time, George," I protested.

He glanced at the clock, swore softly, mopped his brow—this time with the blue-gray handker-chief—and proceeded.

"Isabelle couldn't get into the stream without wad-ers, so I told her to work along the bank a little behind me. It was pretty thick along there, second growth and vines mostly; but I was putting that Pink Lady on every foot of good water and she kept up with me easily enough. She didn't see me take many trout, though. I'd look for her, after landing one, to see what she thought of the way I'd handled the fish, and almost invariably she was picking the ferns or blueberries, or getting herself untangled from something. Curious things, women. Like children, when you stop to think of it."

George stared at me unseeingly for a moment.

"And you never heard of Old Faithful?" he asked suddenly. "Evidently not, from what you said a while ago. Well, a lot of people have, believe me. Men have gone to Cuddiwink district just to see him. As I've already told you, he lay beside a ledge in the pool below Horseshoe Falls. Almost nothing else in the pool. He kept it cleaned out. Worst sort of cannibal, of course—all big trout are. That was the trouble—he wanted something that would stick to his ribs. No flies for him. Did his feeding at night.

"You could see him dimly if you crawled out on a rock that jutted above the pool and looked over. Hey lay in about ten feet of water, right by his ledge. If he saw you he'd back under the ledge, slowly, like a submarine going into dock. Think of the biggest thing you've ever seen, and that's the way Old Faithful looked, just laying there as still as the ledge. He never seemed to move anything, not even his gills. When he backed in out of sight he seemed to be drawn under the ledge by some invisible force.

"Ridgway—R. Campbell Ridgway—you may have read his stuff. Brethren of the Wild, that sort of thing—claimed to have seen him move. He told me about it one night. He said he was lying with just his eyes over the edge of the rock, watching the trout. Said he'd been there an hour, when down over the falls came a young red squirrel. I had fallen in above and been carried over. The squirrel was half drowned, but struck out feebly for shore. Well, so Ridgway said—Old Faithful came up and took Mister Squirrel into camp. No hurry; just came drifting up, sort of inhaled the squirrel and sank down to the ledge again. Never made a ripple, Ridgway said; just business.

"I'm telling you all this because it's necessary that you get an idea of that trout in your mind. You'll see why in a minute. No one ever had hold of him. But it was customary, if you fished the Cuddiwink, to make a few casts over him before you left the stream. Not

that you ever expected him to rise. It was just a sort of gesture. Everybody did it.

"Knowing that Isabelle had never seen trout taken before, I made a day of it—naturally. The trail to camp leaves the stream just at the falls. It was pretty late when we got to it. Isabelle had her arms full of—heaven knows what—flowers and grass and ferns and fir branches and colored leaves. She'd lugged the stuff for hours. I remember once that day I was fighting a fourteen-inch blackberry—I think it was—she'd found. How does that strike you? And listen! I said, 'It's a beauty, darling.' That's what I said—or something like that . . . Here, don't you pay that check! Bring it here, waiter!"

"Go on, George!" I said. "We haven't time to argue about the check. You'd come to the trail for camp at the falls."

"I told Isabelle to wait at the trail for a few minutes, while I went below the falls and did the customary thing for the edification of Old Faithful. I only intended to make three or four casts with the Number Twelve Fly and the hair-fine leader I had on, but in getting down to the pool I hooked the fly in a bush. In trying to loosen it I stumbled over something and fell. I snapped the leader like a thread, and since I had to put on another, I tied on a fairly heavy one as a matter of form.

"I had reached for my box for a regulation fly of some sort when I remembered a fool thing that Billy Roach had given me up on the Beaverkill the season before. It was fully two inches long; I forget what he called it. He said you fished it dry for bass or large trout. He said you worked the tip of your rod and made it wiggle like a dying minnow. I didn't want the contraption, but he'd borrowed some fly oil from me and insisted on my taking it. I'd stuck it in the breast pocket of my fishing jacket and forgotten it until then.

"Well, I felt in the pocket and there it was. I tried it on and went down to the pool. Now let me show you the exact situation." George seized a fork. "This is the pool." The fork traced an oblong figure on the table-cloth. "Here is Old Faithful's ledge." The fork deeply marked this impressive spot. "Here are the falls, with white water running to here. You can only wade to this point here, and then you have an abrupt six-foot depth. 'But you can put a fly from here to here with a long line,' you say. No, you can't. You've forgotten to allow for your back cast. Notice this bend here? That tells the story. You're not more than twenty feet from a lot of birch and whatnot, when you can no longer wade. 'Well then, it's impossible to put a decent fly on the water above the sunken ledge,' you say. It looks like it, but this is how it'd done: right here is a narrow point running to here, where it dwindles off to a single fat rock. If you work out on the point you can jump across to this rock—situated right here—and there you are, with about a thirty-foot cast to the sunken ledge. Deep water all around you, of course, and the rock is slippery; but—there you are. Now notice this small cove, right here. The water from the falls rushes past it in a froth, but in the cove it forms a deep eddy, with the current moving round and round like this." George made a slow circular motion with the fork. "You know what I mean?"

I nodded.

"I got out on the point and jumped to the rock; got myself balanced, worked out the right amount of line and cast the dungaree Bill had forced on me, just above the sunken ledge. I didn't take the water lightly and I cast again, but I couldn't put it down decently. It would just flop in—too much weight and too many feathers. I suppose I cast it a dozen times, trying to make it settle like a fly. I wasn't thinking of trout—there would be nothing in there except Old Faithful—I was just monkeying with this doodle-bug thing, now that I had it on.

"I gave up at last and let it lie out where I had cast it. I was standing there looking at the falls roaring down, when I remembered Isabelle, waiting up on the trail. I raised my rod preparatory to reeling in and the what-you-may-call-'em made a kind of dive and wiggle out there on the surface. I reached for my reel handle. Then I realized that the thingamajig wasn't on the water. I didn't see it disappear, exactly; I was looking at it,

and then it wasn't there. 'That's funny,' I thought, and struck instinctively. Well, I was fast—so it seemed—and no snags in there. I gave it the butt three or four times, but the rod only bowed and nothing budged. I tried to figure it out. I thought perhaps a water-logged timber had come diving over the falls and upended right there. Then I noticed the rod take more of a bend and the line began to move through the water. It moved out slowly, very slowly, into the middle of the pool. It was exactly as though I was hooked on to a freight train just getting under way.

"I knew what I had hold of then, and yet I didn't believe it. I couldn't believe it. I kept thinking it was a dream, I remember. Of course, he could have gone away with everything I had any minute if he'd wanted to, but he didn't. He just kept moving slowly, round and round the pool. I gave him what pressure the tackle would stand, but he never noticed a little thing like that; just kept moving around the pool for hours, it seemed to me. I'd forgotten Isabelle; I admit that. I'd forgotten everything on earth. There didn't seem to be anything else on earth, as a matter of fact, except the falls and the pool and Old Faithful and me. At last Isabelle showed up on the bank above me, still lugging her ferns and whatnot. She called down to me above the noise of the falls. She asked me how long I expected her to wait alone in the woods, with night coming on.

"I hadn't had the faintest idea how I was going to try to land the fish until then. The water was boiling past the rock I was standing on, and I couldn't jump back to the point without giving him slack and perhaps falling in. I began to look around and figure. Isabelle said, 'What on earth are you doing?' I took off my landing net and tossed it to the bank. I yelled, 'Drop that junk quick and pick up that net!' She said, 'What for, George?' I said, 'Do as I tell you and don't ask questions!' She laid down what she had and picked up the net and I told her to go to the cove and stand ready.

"She said, 'Ready for what?' I said, 'You'll see what presently. Just stand there.' I'll admit I wasn't talking quietly. There was the noise of the falls to begin with, and—well, naturally, I wasn't.

"I went to work on the fish again. I began to educate him to the lead. I thought if I could lead him into the cove he would swing right past Isabelle and she could net him. It was slow work—a three-ounce rod—imagine! Isabelle called, 'Do you know what time it is?' I told her to keep still and stand where she was. She didn't say anything more than that.

"At last the fish began to come. He wasn't tired—he'd never done any fighting, as a matter of fact—but he'd take a suggestion as to where to go from the rod. I kept swinging him nearer and nearer the cove each time he came around. When I saw he was about ready to come I yelled to Isabelle. I said, 'I'm going to bring him right past you, close to the top. All you have to do is to net him.'

"When the fish came round again I steered him into the cove. Just as he was swinging past Isabelle the stuff she'd been lugging began to roll down the bank. She dropped the landing net on top of the fish and made a dive for those leaves and grasses and things. Fortunately the net handle lodged against the bank, and after she'd put her stuff in a nice safe place she came back and picked up the net again. I never uttered a syllable. I deserve no credit for that. The trout had made a surge and shot out into the pool and I was too busy just then to give her any idea of what I thought.

"I had a harder job getting him to swing in again. He was a little leery of the cove, but at last he came. I steered him toward Isabelle and lifted him all I dared. He came up nicely, clear to the top. I yelled, 'Here he comes! For God's sake, don't miss him!' I put everything on the tackle it would stand and managed to check the fish for an instant right in front of Isabelle.

"And this is what she did: it doesn't seem credible—it doesn't seem humanly possible; but it's a fact that you'll have to take my word for. She lifted the landing net above her head with both hands and brought it down on top of the fish with all her might!"

George ceased speaking. Despite its coating of talcum powder, I was able to detect an additional pallor in his countenance.

"Will I ever forget it as long as I live?" he inquired at last.

"No, George," I said, "but we've just exactly eleven minutes left."

George made a noticeable effort and went on.

"By some miracle the fish stayed on the hook; but I got a faint idea of what would have happened if he's taken a real notion to fight. He went around the pool so fast it must have made him dizzy. I heard Isabelle say, 'I didn't miss him, George'; and then—well, I didn't lose my temper; you wouldn't call it that exactly. I hardly knew what I said. I'll admit I shouldn't have said it. But I did say it; no doubt of that; no doubt of that whatever."

"What was it you said?" I asked.

George looked at me uneasily.

"Oh, the sort of thing a man would say impulsively—under the circumstances."

"Was it something disparaging about her?" I inquired.

"Oh, no," said George, "nothing about her. I simply intimated—in a somewhat brutal way, I suppose—that's she'd better get away from the pool—er—not bother me any more is what I meant to imply."

For the first time since George had chosen me for a confidant I felt a lack of frankness on his part.

"Just what did you say, George?" I insisted.

"Well, it wasn't altogether my words," he evaded. "It was the tone I used, as much as anything. Of course, the circumstances would excuse—Still, I regret it. I admit that. I've told you so plainly."

There was no time in which to press him further.

"Well, what happened then?" I asked.

"Isabelle just disappeared. She went up the bank, of course, but I didn't see her go. Old Faithful was still nervous and I had to keep my eye on the line. He quieted down in a little while and continued to promenade slowly around the pool. I suppose this kept up for half an hour more. Then I made up my mind that something had to be done. I turned very carefully on the rock, lowered the tip until it was on the line with the fish, turned the rod under my arm until it was pointing behind me and jumped.

"Of course, I had to give him slack; but I kept my balance on the point by the skin of my teeth, and when I raised the rod he was still on. I worked to the bank, giving out line, and crawled under some bushes and things and got around to the cove at last. Then I started to work again to swing him into the cove, but absolutely nothing doing. I could lead him anywhere except into the cove. He'd had enough of that; I didn't blame him, either.

"To make a long story short, I stayed with him for two hours. For a while it was pretty dark; but there was a good-sized moon that night, and when it rose it shone right down on the pool through a gap in the trees fortunately. My wrist was gone completely, but I managed to keep some pressure on him all the time, and at last he forgot about what had happened to him in the cove. I swung him in and the current brought him past me. He was on his side by now. I don't think he was tired even then—just discouraged. I let him drift over the net, heaved him out on the bank and sank down beside him, absolutely all in. I couldn't have got to my feet on a bet. I just sat there in a sort of daze and looked at Old Faithful, gleaming in the moonlight.

"After a half-hour's rest I was able to get up and go to camp. I planned what I was going to do on the way. There was always a crowd in the main camp living room after dinner. I simply walked into the living room without a word and laid Old Faithful on the center table.

"Well, you can imagine faintly what happened. I never got any dinner—couldn't have eaten any, as a matter of fact. I didn't even get a chance to take off my waders. By the time I'd told just how I'd done it to one crowd, more would come in and look at Old Faithful; and then stand and look at me for a while; and then

make me tell it all over again. At last everybody began to dig up anything they had with a kick in it. Almost every one had a bottle he'd been hoarding. There was Scotch and gin and brandy and rye and a lot of experimental stuff. Art Bascom got a tin dish pan from the kitchen and put in on the table beside Old Faithful. He said, 'Pour your contributions right in here, men.' So each man dumped whatever he had into the dish pan and everybody helped himself.

"It was great, of course. The biggest night of my life, but I hope I'll never be so dog-tired again. I felt as though I'd taken a beating. After they'd weighed Old Faithful—nine pounds five and a half ounces; and he'd been out of water two hours—I said I had to go to bed, and went.

"Isabelle wasn't in the cabin. I thought, in a hazy way, that she was with some of the women, somewhere. Don't get the idea I was stewed. But I hadn't had anything to eat, and the mixture in that dish pan was plain TNT.

"I fell asleep as soon as I hit the bed; slept like a log till daylight. Then I half woke up, feeling that something terrific had happened. For a minute I didn't know what; then I remember what it was. I had landed Old Faithful on a three-ounce rod!

"I lay there and went over the whole thing from the beginning, until I came to Isabelle with the landing net. That made me look at where her head should have been on the pillow. It wasn't there. She wasn't in the cabin. I thought perhaps she'd got up early and gone out to look at the lake or the sunrise or something. But I got up in a hurry and dressed.

"Well, I could see no signs of Isabelle about camp. I ran into Jean just coming from the head guide's cabin and he said, 'Too bad about your wife's mother.' I said, 'What's that?' He repeated what he'd said, and added, 'She must be an awful sick woman.' Well, I got out of him finally that Isabelle had come straight up from the stream the evening before, taken two guides and started for Buck's Landing. Jean had urged her to wait until morning, naturally; but she'd told him she must get to her mother at once, and took on so, as Jean put it, that he had to let her go.

"I said, 'Let me have Indian Joe, stern, and a good man, bow. Have 'em ready in ten minutes.' I rushed to the kitchen, drank two cups of coffee and started for Buck's Landing. We made the trip down in seven hours, but Isabelle had left with her trunks on the 10:40 train.

"I haven't seen her since. Went to her home once. She wouldn't see me; neither would her mother. Her father advised not forcing things—just waiting. He said he'd do what he could. We'll, he's done it—you read the letter. Now you know the whole business. You'll stick, of course, and see me through just the first of it, old man. Of course, you'll do that, won't you? We'd better get down to the train now. Track nineteen."

"George," I said, "one thing more: just what did you say to her when she—" "Oh, I don't know," George began vaguely.

"George," I interrupted, "no more beating about the bush. What did you say?" I saw his face grow even more haggard, if possible. Then it mottled into a shade resembling the brick on an old colonial mansion.

"I told her—" he began in a low voice.

"Yes?" I encouraged.

"I told her to get the hell out of there."

And now a vision was presented to my mind's eye; a vision of twelve fish plates, each depicting a trout curving up through green waters to an artificial fly. The vision extended on through the years. I saw Mrs. George Baldwin Potter ever gazing upon those rising trout and recalling the name on the card which had accompanied them to her door.

I turned and made rapidly for the main entrance of the Grand Central Station. In doing so I passed the clock above Information and saw that I still had two minutes in which to be conveyed by a taxicab far, far from the entrance to Track Nineteen.

I remember hearing the word "quitter" hurled after me by a hoarse, despairing voice.

C. Midstream Crisis

LAMAR UNDERWOOD

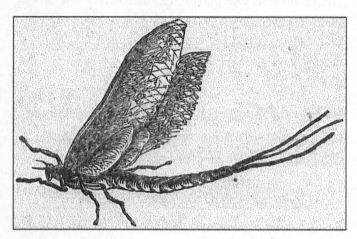

As the year began, I decided to embrace the advice of my friend Sparse Grey Hackle, who told me: "Let the wolf out!" He was dead right. It was the only way to go. No more Mister Nice Guy!

My New Year's resolution was a notice served on all creatures, great and small, that in the open seasons ahead I was going to fill my hand. I was fed up with two-trout days, three-bass weekends and no-deer vacations. I'd had it with calling to bird dogs that wouldn't stand still and turkeys that would (two ridges away!). I didn't want to see another pheasant getting up 200 yards away down a corn row or another bay full of ducks and geese rafted up and preening their feathers under skies that had flown in from Palm Springs.

Government wags told me that in the previous season some 2.5 million hunters had shot 12 million ducks. The calculator that lives beside my checkbook told me that works out to five or six ducks per hunter. I didn't get any five ducks! Who the hell shot my ducks?

All around, the previous year had not just been bad; it had been a disaster. I zigged when they zagged. The northeasters and I booked into the same places at the same times. I frightened the spots off brown trout while bass slept through my offerings. The deer left the mountain country I hunt, but those from the woods alongside my house found my tulips and peas in the spring, then shredded two young pines during rubtime in the fall. Plenty of geese crossed the pit blinds I hunkered in all season, but they were so high they were a menace to aviation—and they held express tickets.

My dismal performances afield forced me to face what the late John Foster Dulles called "an agonizing reappraisal." Clearly, my tactics were lousy; my timing stank, my equipment belonged in a museum.

I knew better than to seek some all-embracing formula as my game plan. Each subject would have to be tackled separately, tactics and gear made precise. The geese, I felt, would be the simplest problem to deal with. I began squirreling away the bucks to purchase a 10-gauge magnum automatic, with which I intended to wreak havoc on the Eastern Shore. My more immediate problem—and infinitely more complex—was what to do about those trout.

Since the Romans knew nothing about splitcane rods and matching the hatch, they invented a calendar that starts the new year off from the pit of winter. For me and millions of other fishermen the real new year begins on the opening day of trout season. My usual opening-day scenario looked like this:

An already-pudgy figure, bulked further by enough clothes to outfit the Klondike gold rush, stands hip-deep in a flow of black water torn into sudsy rips by protruding rocks and bearing of the countryside what the winter snows have been holding in storage: sticks, leaves, tires, a bloated cat, the occasional beer can. Overhead the sky is a glowering mass of putty, against which the bare branches of the trees snap and creak with iron-hard stiffness as blasts of wind arrive from Siberia. For hours our man alternates making casts, peering intently at the jaunty little flies that ride the current like miniature galleons, and fumbling stiff fingers through his flybox in search of new offerings. To find a greater fool, you would have to look inside an ice fishing shanty.

The bottom of a trout stream is its food factory, and on this day it will not be violated by anything except the soles of el piscator's waders. Although he will soon abandon his dry flies (how quickly the credo fades: "I'd rather catch one on top than five down deep"), our man will make only tentative probes into the depths. His wet flies, streamers and nymphs will sweep harmlessly over the heads of the stone-hugging trout. Troutless by 3 o'clock, he will seek the solace of the lodge where fire, firewater and kindred snake-bit companions will be waiting with tales of woe and livers in various stages of distress.

Long before opening day dawned last season, I was determined to never again be a part of this demented tableau.

For weeks I hit the books with an intensity seldom mounted in my professional life. Schwiebert, Whitlock, Marinaro, Swisher-Richards, Cucci-Nastasi—the great masters of flyfishing for trout were devoured. Their instruction manifested itself in a barrage of catalogs and small packages of flies arriving daily from every corner of troutdom. My wading vest bulged with trinkets. Latin names of bugs came trippingly off the tongue.

Opening day, I stood thigh-deep at the head of a pool of black water, frigid and swollen with runoff. Coming to the stream, I had received the usual assortment of reports that the fish were in a coma. The voice on the car radio had said something about snow. None of these things intimidated me at all. This year I was ready.

To meet this early and elemental trouting condition, I pried open a box of nymphs. These were not ordinary nymphs, but masterpieces of illusion—caterpillarlike, hairy-leggy-juicy-looking. Each was

weighted with enough piano wire to outfit a Steinway. Never mind that they would hit the water with the finesse of a slam-dunk. They would go down, my friend, down, down to the very noses of these frozen wisenheimers. I would fish these creations with a leader hacked to three feet. (Long leaders, I had learned, rise in the pushing and swelling of the current.) The whole outfit would ride down with high-density sinking line topped by a fluorescent strike indicator to tell me when I had a customer.

You don't cast such a rig. What you do is sort of heave the whole mess out and to one side, paying close attention that a hook in the ear is not the immediate result of the effort.

I watched the curls of line and leader straighten downstream toward a boulder that slashed the smooth flow. I tried to form a mental image of what the nymph was doing—sinking, tumbling, ticking over rocks. The line straightened past the boulder. I paid out three more long pulls from the reel, watching the strike indicator bob on downstream.

Suddenly I thought I saw it dart forward. I came back with rod and line and felt the weight of a trout. As the brown—a lovely 15-incher—darted and splashed on the way to the net, my elation soared. My patience and virtue and hard study were to be rewarded. The masters of the game were indeed wise and learned men.

After that, you can imagine my heart-hammering excitement when the next 30 minutes yielded two more fish, about the same size as the first.

Then the devil sent his disciples to descend upon me, like a plague of locusts. First one, then two, then three other anglers were crowding into my stretch of water. Not one asked what I was using. They simply assumed I had found "The Place."

Never mind, I told myself. You can afford to be generous. I waded from the stream and pointed up toward uninhabited water. In a few minutes I was sloshing, much too fast, through a bouldery run of pocket water when I felt my right foot sliding down an eel-slick ledge. I lurched hard to the left, but that leg would not bear the burden. I went down into the water on my back with a teeth-jarring crash. Totally submerged for a second, I stood up and cursed my luck and the worn felt soles of my waders. I was drenched, achingly cold, and clearly out of action for the rest of the day.

As I waded to the edge of the stream, I discovered another result of my accident with dramatic suddenness. As I made a little sideways move with my left leg to step around a rock, I felt a nauseating wave of pain. I did not want to feel such a shock again, ever, so now I picked my way gingerly along, trying to protect the knee.

Yuk! Yuk! See the man all soaking wet and limping toward his car. Fat-ass must've fallen in. Yuk! Yuk!

A prominent physician whom I trust sentenced the knee to six weeks of healing. Because I could not wade the stream, I could not fish for trout. The great fly hatches of early spring for which I had prepared myself so diligently came and went: the Blue Quills, the Hendericksons, the Grannon caddis, the March Browns.

My mood was foul and depressed. Without my jogging program, with which I had successfully been losing weight, I quickly regained ten pounds. Going to work in New York on the train one day I was struck by a thought as morbid as any I've ever had: The obituary page of the *New York Times* named very few males in their 90s. No, the ages of the boys getting their names in the paper were in the 70s and 80s. At age 45 I had the startling realization that in all likelihood I was more than halfway to the barn. Life begins at 80? Give me a break!

Okay, my somber mood told me, so you've lost some of your good moves and speed. You can't hit a 60-yard mallard or sink a three-foot putt. On the tennis court children who can't get into an R-rated film have you gasping like a beached whale. The guide can show you a tarpon at 60 feet, and you may or may not be able to get the fly to it (probably not, given any kind of wind). But relax, buster. For the years have given you wisdom. Look at what you did with those opening-day trout!

I was still clinging to this slightly uplifting notion when I finally got back to the river in late May. One of the year's best hatches remained. According to the grapevine, the Sulphurs had arrived in tentative numbers two days earlier, and all signs pointed to their major emergence late that evening.

The hatch of *Ephemerella dorothea*, which goes on with diminishing consistency for about six weeks on good eastern streams, ranks as a favorite because it stirs smart, self-respecting trout into an unusual orgy of gluttony. Unlike some mayfly hatches, which deliver more sizzle than steak, the appearance of the No. 16 yellow-and-dun flies in the last hour before darkness produces fishing so fast and exciting that it is the stuff for cool hands and stout hearts.

My favorite slick-water was flat empty that evening. My recent misfortune was all forgotten as I waded into position and made a few desultory casts while waiting for the hatch to begin. The air was heavy with humidity, and low clouds on the ridges promised that darkness would come early and perhaps a thunderstorm with it.

The time that passed seemed interminable. Nothing came off the darkening water, not even caddis. A kingfisher flew upstream, scolding my presence. I heard a great homed owl up on the mountain and an answering cry from nearby. Then I saw the first delicate yellow mayfly climbing steeply toward the trees. In a few moments there was another, then another, then another, and then I actually saw one in the instant it left the water—and beyond it the swirl of a trout.

My line arched through the growing dusk. I saw my artificial Sulphur begin its jaunty ride down the feeding lane where the trout had swirled. It floated on downstream unharmed. There were other rises all over the pool now—not splashy water-throwing slaps, but subtle bulges and swirls.

I really started worrying when my bogus Sulphur made three more rides through the melee without interesting a trout. What was wrong? The fly? The leader? My thoughts screamed as I watched the hatch and rises go on: You've been out of action so long you don't know what you're doing.

In the middle of this burst of self-condemnation I saw something—flashes of darting trout just beneath the surface. That was it! The trout were not taking the surface duns! They were nymphing, gulping the insects as they rose to the surface and in the film as they emerged into winged shape.

I was prepared for this, but my hands trembled as I opened the flybox and got out a floating nymph. The light was going fast, but I managed to tie on the fly without digging out my night light. In my excitement, however, I dropped my reading half-glasses into the stream. Klutz! Fool! I should have had them on a cord around my neck.

No matter. I had the right ammo now, and the fish were still going strong as I roll-cast the nymph to the top of the pool. Instantly a trout was on, and I felt a flush of ultimate satisfaction.

The fish was a strong pulsating weight as it struggled upstream for a few seconds. Then the line went slack as the trout bolted downstream almost past my legs, a momentary shadow that caused me to gasp: I was into my largest trout ever.

The reel screamed appropriately as the fish bolted downstream. He reached the lip of the falls that terminated the pool and turned to face the current. The steady pressure on the 5X felt unbelievable. I had the feeling of the fish backing up, backing to the edge of the tumbling water. He was going to be washed over the lip! I had to do something! I palmed the flange of the reel, increasing the drag, and thereby succeeded in instantly breaking off the trout as surely as though I'd been trying to.

I reeled in the sickeningly slack line and looked at the 5X tippet. So many trout were still taking the sulphur nymphs all over the pool that the excitement smothered the loss of the big fish. I quickly had another floating nymph out, ready to tie on. I felt my shirt pocket for my reading glasses and remembered where they had gone. I held the fly at arm's length against the gloom of the darkening sky. No way. I could not thread the eye of the hook in that dimness.

No problem. My night light had a magnifying glass that fit over the top of the light. No sweat, just stay cool.

I was deeply aware of the rises continuing all over the pool as I pulled the light out and draped its cord around my neck. I felt deeper into the pocket for the magnifying glass. It wasn't there! I flipped the switch on the light. Nothing! *Click, click. Click, click.* Still nothing! Okay, the batteries are dead. You're on your own. Now just hold the fly very still against what is left of the sky and tie it on.

My panic rose as I tried unsuccessfully to tie on the No. 16 Sulphur. I tied a No. 14. It would not go. In a final burst of madness and inspiration, I dug out a No. 10 Blonde Wulff, the biggest fly in my vest. Maybe it would work on these feeding fish.

Perhaps it would have. I don't know. I never got the Wulff tied on. My vision is 20-20, but at age 45 I could not see close up well enough to tie on a fly and resume fishing a hatch that I had waited for all winter.

I reeled in slowly, felt the end of the leader reach the reel, then broke down my rod. The splashes of feeding trout popped out from the darkness. I could not see the rises now, but they were distinctive above the murmur the current made as it tailed from the pool downstream.

Slowly the disappointment drained away. The easy moves, the good speed. Going, going with the years. Yet it was true: You were wiser, vastly richer in the things you knew. Such as realizing right now that what made fishing so great was that on any given outing, things could happen that you would remember all of your days. Few other times in life could offer that. That is the easy part of change—the knowing, the feeling. The other side is that you have left something precious behind—something you had used up and would have to go on without.

Flashes of lightning came across the ridgetop, then the roll of advancing thunder. The feeding grew quieter, then died out completely. The bursts of lightning helped me find my way up the hillside to the lane that led back to the car.

I did not know if I had reached the end of something or the beginning.

The wind blew on the high ridges, gusting along the slopes, coming down to the river.

D. April (from *A River Never Sleeps*)

RODERICK L. HAIG-BROWN

Whatever one may say of March, April is the true opening month of the trout season. I have caught plenty of out-of-condition trout in April, brown trout not yet built back to shape by the release of underwater life in the warmer temperatures, cutthroats hardly finished with their spawning, rainbows full ripe and ready to begin theirs. April days can be as cold and wet and miserable with wind as December days. April rivers can be swollen and thick with flood. But April is still as beautiful as its name, the true spring month that breaks our world out of winter into something nearly summer. It could not be right to keep anglers away from their rivers at such a time, and

I think they seldom are kept away, unless by the ice of a high altitude or a late year.

There is a tale that the willow and the alder are two anglers who offended the powers by fishing on Sunday and were transformed, to stand beside the river evermore. It would have been in April, I think, that this happened. The alder woods are a bright, fresh mist of pale green then; the willow whips are tall and supple, with the sap swelling under green and yellow bark and red and white buds thrusting forth. April, perhaps because it is the spring month, is a month of little pictures vividly remembered. I remember the high, wild, crying wedges of geese swinging splendidly northward, sometimes with the sunlight bright on their wings; and once, at dusk, three geese circling the house and looking for a place to light. I remember the bright mating plumage of the mallards and the drake mergansers all up and down the river and once, along the road, the first goldfinch of the year all black and sunlit yellow just ahead of me. I remember the approach to the Sandy Pool—under the white-barked alders a floor of freshet-swept sand pierced by bleeding heart and a thousand trilliums and the pink Easter lilies just breaking out of bud. Once, going up to the Canyon Pool along the far bank of the river, I crossed a little swamp where skunk cabbage flowers sprang strongly from black ooze in spaced and loveliest yellow. There is pink almond blossom in April and heavy white cherry blossom against blue and white skies. There are killdeer and yellowlegs on the tide flats, meadow larks on the fence posts, red-winged blackbirds in the swamps. Not to go out and meet all this would be a denial of the year's hope.

The humpback fry are out in the Campbell in April—other fry too, for that matter—but one notices the humpbacks because of their bright silver scales quite without parr marks. It seems to me I always see them first swimming about in the current within inches of my waders, half a dozen quick little fish, heads upstream, holding maybe, but going down very shortly. Then I look harder and see others, whole schools clustered in the eddies. The big cutthroats find them out and feed greedily—it pays to drop a fly in places where no fish lies through the rest of the year. Obviously a silver-bodied fly is the thing, fished fast; but that is a shade too obvious. It will take fish, yes, and sometimes take them better than anything else. But the cutthroats are seldom as single-minded as they seem. Many times I have opened up a catch of ten or twelve fish, taken in April when the river was full of salmon fry, and found that only one or two of my fish had been really feeding on fry, and sometimes not even one or two. Of the others, several perhaps would have fry in them, but well mixed with other feed, and at least half the catch would have been concerned with anything and everything except fry—May flies, caddis grubs, beetles, caterpillars, bees, even bullheads, but not fry. I suspect that free-swimming fry are overquick and difficult to catch. Not every fish can be bothered with them when the current brings other and better things straight to the open jaws.

So I seldom fish my silver fly very fast; I let it drift weakly, crossing the current but making no headway against it, tumbling down rather and, I like to think, rolling clear over sometimes. And I do not stay always with the silver fly or even with the wet fly. The trout are feeding, on the lookout, and I have risen April fish after April fish to the dry fly in pools where every little backwater was packed with fry.

I remember April fishing days, like other April happenings, in quick sunlit flashes. I remember an English garden, built narrowly along a trout stream, a thorn hedge, a narrow border, an edge of lawn, a red-graveled path, another strip of lawn, and then the river, and on the far bank, tall and graceful willows in wild growth. The river was shallow and straight through the garden, broken into three little falls by logs staked across it. Close under the far side of the center fall, in a deeper place where the bubbles showed white in green water, I could see the long dark shape of a big trout. He was a thin fish with a great wedge-shaped head, and he showed up very clearly against the pale sand of the river bottom. Grandfather, walking up the garden a few days earlier, had seen him and decided that he was a ne'er-do-well, a cannibal, who must be taken out by any method; and I was ordered to attend to the matter.

I had a medium olive quill tied on a No. 16 hook—double-o, we called it—and 4X gut. The chance of moving the fish to that, clear up from the bottom, didn't seem very great, but at least he deserved his chance. I dropped down on one knee and began to let out line in false casts. Then I saw the other fish, a pale, thick, hog-backed fish lying two or three feet over from the dark fish, well up in the water, his nose almost touching the little log that made the fall. As I watched, his body tilted slightly and his nose just broke water to suck in a fly.

I thought quickly over all the implications and complications; there were plenty of both. The pale fish was really big and really beautiful—I wanted him badly. He was a stranger, perhaps not yet settled into a permanent summer holt, and if I left him or disturbed him this time I might not find him again. He was difficult; the fall of water over the log made a close back eddy, perhaps five or six inches wide and running the full length of the little fall. He was taking flies held in this back eddy, and to catch him, I must drop my first cast so that the fly pitched almost exactly on his nose, with a slack line behind it to delay the pull of the stream which would eventually whip the fly out of the eddy in an unnatural drag that would scare the wits out of him. I considered a longer cast above the fall that would let the fly drift down on him, but decided against that because the fly might be drowned or, worse still, the longer drift might use up the precious slack line and bring the drag on the fly just as it came into his vision.

Then there was Grandfather to be considered. Grandfather wanted his cannibal caught and would have a good deal to say about it if he was not caught— Grandfather hadn't a very high opinion of fishing as a sport, though he felt that one possibly had some excuse for indulging in it if one did a good job. Catching the pale fish would almost certainly disturb the cannibal and make him impossible to move. But I still wanted the pale fish and I promised myself that the affair of the cannibal would work itself out somehow.

I lengthened my line and dropped the fly on the water once, well behind both fish. The pale fish came up in one of his tiny, tidy, fastidious rises as I did so; his back looked six inches wide, which it was not and could not have been, but the impression made me want him still more. I let out more line, then took my long chance and aimed the fly for the narrow eddy. It came perfectly to the water, perhaps three inches to one side of his nose. He turned to it slowly, so slowly that I knew from the poise and set of his body rather than from actual movement that he was interested. The little olive danced there on the curling water in the April sunlight; I moved my rod point cautiously to delay the drag of the line until the last possible moment. Then he came, confidently and calmly, and the fly was gone. For a tiny fraction of time his back was broad again and quite still in the bright water. Then I touched the hook home. He did the right thing, by Grandfather and by me. Instead of turning across or down he went straight up, over the log like an explosion and on almost to the tail of a fine weed bed, where the rod turned him. I brought him back, and he ran again as he felt his tail come out over the log. Three times he did that; then I tumbled him down, and we fought it out in water well below the cannibal's lie. On the bank he was as perfect as I had hoped he would be, his red spots splendid against his pale coat, his body far too thick for my hand's grip.

And the black fish was still where he had been. I dried the fly and dropped it over him, but he made no move. I tried it again, half a dozen times, then a freak of the current smoothed the surface and I saw his head most clearly. Around the eye there was a circle of dead whiteness; I knew he was blind. I drowned the fly and dropped it to him again, several times. Once he moved, the slight restless movement that brown trout make when they are deciding it's about time to move out for some favorite hiding place. I crept back from the bank and made myself wait for ten or fifteen minutes, then changed the little dry fly to a much larger wet fly, for the small hook would not sink down to him. The big fly went down well, and I tried drifting it a foot or two away from him at first, hoping he would sense it and come across. I brought it closer and closer to him with each cast, and still he would not move. Then I dropped it squarely above him. It sank and slid down; it brushed his nose so that he turned away; it crept along his body, passed his tail—then he turned like a pike, his great white mouth opened and he had it. Grandfather looked over both fish as they lay in state on the hall table and was impressed.

Two other April days come sharply into my mind, and both are sunny days of fish seen clearly in bright April water. On the Nimpkish River we kept the gas boats tied to a rough landing two or three hundred yards below the house. One morning we went down to work on them, and as we worked, a good fish rose again and again with solemn, solid plops close under the bushes just above us. Buster said at last, "Go and catch him."

I started on him, using a small iron blue; and as he came to it, another fish rose twenty or thirty yards farther up. I netted the first fish, a green-backed, solid cutthroat of two and a half pounds. Little dark-blue May flies poured down the river in a narrow stream close under the bushes, and the second fish still rose. I went up to him, and as I cast for him, a third fish rose twenty yards beyond him. An hour later I came out of the water opposite the house, and I had with me ten white-bellied, green-backed cutthroats with not an inch in length nor a quarter of a pound in weight between them. I laid them out in the sunlight on the short grass of the bank. Buster was coming up to the house for lunch and saw me there. "You're a hell of a guy," he said. "I ought to have known better than let you go off the job." Then he came closer and saw the fish. "Oh, boy!" he said softly. "Oh, boy!"

Since Ann and I have filled the house with children, we go up the river together too seldom. But there was an April day a year or two ago when we arranged things and went. "We shan't find much," I said. "The fish seem to have moved up out of the Island Pools this

year. I think the river's low for them. But it's a swell day and it will be fun up there."

So I went out into the main pool and hooked almost at once a thick golden cutthroat that looked to me like a four-pounder and fought me till I was trembling with the fear that I should never get him to the scales to find out. I have caught only one sea-run cutthroat of over four pounds in the Campbell, and he doesn't count because I was fishing for steelhead when he took hold. The fish came to the net at last, and I carried him proudly ashore. "He's a four-pounder," I told Ann.

She shook her head. "I don't think so. I've seen you catch them as big as that before."

The scales made him three and three-quarter pounds.

I fished lazily, bouncing a deer-hair dry fly down over the fast water of the pool, and caught other fish. We lay in the sun and ate lunch and talked. I went far out on the bar at last, because it seems wrong to go all the way up to the Islands and not try it out properly, however lazy the day. Just above the main run a great, bright steelhead took my fly. He seemed to love the fast, clear water and ran and played in it with little care for all I could do with my trout rod. Ann saw me in trouble and came out along the bar toward me. The fish came back, more or less of his own free will, and carelessly let himself into slack water behind a rock. I held hard, reached down and slipped a finger in his gills. I held him up, looking back toward Ann against the sun, then freed the hook and slipped him back. I heard Ann laugh and knew that the Island Pool was a good place to be on a spring day.

H. M. GREENHILL

As I look back on them now it seems to me that my male elders in Dorset fell into two astonishingly well-defined groups. There were the Victorians, men in their seventies and eighties: Grandfather and his two brothers; Thomas Hardy; Squire Sheridan, Grandfather's neighbor; Mr. Shepherd, the village carpenter;

Knight, the river keeper on the club water. These make a cross section of examples. They were small, spare, wiry men, usually with short gray beards—though Hardy and my two great-uncles had only gray mustaches—very quick and keen, both physically and mentally. Dorset is kind to old men, or was before the world wars began. Squire Sheridan was well over eighty when I last saw him, but he was standing waist deep in the river, cutting weeds with great sweeping strokes of his scythe. Grandfather had to break his ankle twice in the hills to be convinced that eighty is too old for hard shooting days. Knight was walking his twelve or fourteen miles a day through the water meadows, summer and winter, when he was well into the eighties. Hardy, though the scope of his labors bore little relation to that of these mere mortals, was in no greater haste to lay down his burden than they were; his greatness did not fail him in his lifetime and his stature grows steadily now that he is dead.

Among these men there was something of the closeness that there is among the elder citizens of an American small town. Grandfather and my great-uncles had been at Dorchester Grammar School with Hardy, and though the way of the three brothers branched widely from Hardy's way after their school days, there was much that held them together. Grandfather loved Dorset county as Hardy loved Dorset people and he respected Hardy with a sincerity that was wholly admirable in such a practical and autocratic old gentleman. I think he rarely missed a quarterly teatime visit to Max Gate, and I know that when he took me with him, we entered the house and met the great and gentle little man with a humility that seemed to reduce Grandfather to my own schoolboy age. Between Grandfather and Squire Brinsley Sheridan there was a different respect, grudging and born out of a lifetime of disagreements, but real. Mr. Shepherd and Grandfather met squarely as equals, craftsman to trader, though one was employer and the other employed, and I think the fraternity of old age was stronger between these two than between any of the others. Knight was Knight, the friend of every keen

fisherman, wise in the life of his water meadows and a truer countryman than any of the others. Knight could not read or write properly, and he regretted it. Once he told me, "I ain't never learned 'ee. My zister, her can do 'un, but her beant so oold as I be. You zee, when they passed this 'ere law 'bout 'avin' to 'ave schoolin' it du zeem I were just too old for 'un." I often wondered how great was the loss through that, not Knight's loss, for he was great in his work as were the other Victorians I have listed, but the country's. Sixty years of walking the meadows is a long time, sixty years of knowing birds and beasts and fish and seeing them with sharp gray eyes that never needed spectacles is time to have yielded much knowledge. An educated Knight might have been another such as William Lunn, the inspired keeper and manager of the Houghton Club water. He might even have been a Gilbert White or a Jefferies.

The other group of my elders was Edwardian, as clearly as Grandfather's group was Victorian. They were big, heavy, broad-shouldered men, often soldiers, black-mustached and deep-voiced, lovers of all forms of sport. Nearly all of them were magnificent with the shotgun, most of them were cricketers, and some were good fishermen. I can think easily over a long list of names—Colonel Saunders, Major Radclyffe, the Hambro brothers of banking fame, my uncle Alec who died of wounds in 1919 and John Kelly, the wonderful Irish gardener who was as truly a Dorset man as William Barnes himself. Of them all, none was truer to type than Major Greenhill, and from Greenhill I learned most of those things about fishing and wing shooting that a boy generally learns from his father.

The First World War took hold of my father when I was six years old and held him until he was killed at Bapaume in March, 1918. Nearly all my Mother's eleven brothers were kept busy during the war and for some years after. As a result, I grew up beside a fine trout stream and in the midst of good shooting country with only the crudest ideas of how to go about either business. I caught a few fish by most reprehensible methods and stalked rabbits and pigeons, even partridges and mallards, with a variety of weapons at once less effective and less artistic then the shotgun. In the summer of 1922, when I was fourteen, one of my uncles—the best and keenest fisherman of them all—was at home long enough to teach me the elements of dry-fly fishing. And during the Christmas holidays of the same year Greenhill came, it seemed to me from nowhere, and took over.

At that time Greenhill was already a heroic figure to me. He had always been held up to me as one of the best wing shots in England, and I knew he was a fine salmon fisherman. He was a huge man, an inch or two over six feet and weighing about 220 pounds, which he seemed to carry mainly on his chest and shoulders. I had seen him play a brave part on the cricket field, lifting the ball in full-shouldered drives to bounce its way among the mounds of the cemetery. Seated in glory at the edge of the ring, I had watched him referee the army boxing tournaments. And now his talented bulk rested itself deep in one of the dining-room chairs, and his strong, heavy voice told Mother that he would look after my sporting education. Someone, he said, had to make up for the war.

He taught as good teachers do, by example, by opportune and unhurried explanation, by occasional strong direction. The strongest lesson he taught, though he never named it, was complete concentration on, and devotion to, the matter in hand. I learned quickly that if there was a chance of going shooting on a certain day, I must not tie myself to anything else; that while we were out I must see everything and know everything—the identity of birds by their flight, the line that rabbits would take in bolting from a certain place, any shift of wind, the change of a field from stubble to plow, any lowering or raising of the river by a farmer's manipulation of irrigation hatches. I must never tire, because I was younger and stronger in proportion to my weight than he was—a point that it was not difficult for me to recognize. No walk must be too long, no hour of creeping in wet meadows too painful, if there was a chance of a shot at the end of it. Above all, I must be ready when game flushed; I could miss and be forgiven,

provided I offered no excuse for missing. But if I failed to get my gun off at a fair chance, I must walk with it unloaded through the rest of the day. Safety was provided for by an even stiffer penalty; if I fired a dangerous shot, if I failed to break my gun before climbing a fence or crossing a hedge, I must go home at once in disgrace. But this penalty was never invoked, because I had been already well trained in safety.

Such an account of penalties and forfeits makes our shooting days sound gloomy, but they were not. I made him angry perhaps half a dozen times in all the years we fished and shot together—two or three times because I was lazy or fainthearted, two or three times because I missed, through sheer carelessness, golden chances we had worked hard for, once because I lied to him. It was a simple thing, this last, yet it taught me clearly, as nothing else has, the urgency of being honest with yourself if you want to learn. I had planned to take the ferrets and terriers out one day to kill off the rats that infested a corn rick. The day turned out badly, with a southwesterly gale and driving rain, but I wanted to go anyway and I asked Greenhill to go with me. "No use," he said. "Rats won't bolt a day like this. You'll get your ferrets all bitten up and you'll just be wasting your time." I went anyway, with a couple of friends; and my favorite ferret got badly bitten, the rats wouldn't bolt and we finished the day with six or eight dead rats instead of a hundred or more. A few days later he asked me how it had been.

"All right," I said. "We didn't do badly."

Greenhill snorted. "Bet you didn't get half a dozen rats."

"Yes, we did," I said. "More than that."

"How many? Twenty? Thirty?"

I nodded. "About that," I said, and he said nothing more until the next day. Then he said, "You lied to me about those rats, young fellow. You only got six or seven the whole day."

I tried to get out of it, but there was no way. He was really angry then and so was I, angry and afraid.

But what he meant was clear enough: rats and rabbits won't bolt well to ferrets on a bad day—that is a piece of knowledge by which one must be guided again and again in planning a day. Any exception to it is important, for it may disclose some other factor that has entered into the business. A lie such as I had told is aimed at the roots of useful knowledge.

One other incident taught me early just what sort of training I was under. Greenhill had a Labrador bitch named Dinah, and Dinah was a model retriever. By some standards she was too sedate and dignified and slow, but her calm eyes and mind missed nothing. Greenhill could stand and drop a dozen birds, with Dinah moving only her head behind him to watch the flight and fall of each one. Then, when the drive was finished, he would move her out, and she would pick up every one of them on her own, without help unless there happened to be an exceptionally bad runner. She was the same in the meadows, phlegmatic about the rise of a bird, unmoved by the shot, unconcerned about the retrieve until he ordered her out. Early one January we had a quick spell of hard weather, a light fall of snow and more frosts. Working the meadows for snipe, we found a flock of mallards on the river, stalked them and killed four. Two fell in the water on the far side of the river and were caught up by low-hanging willow branches. We picked tip the other two, and I waited for him to send Dinah across. He didn't. Instead he said, "All right, young fellow, get on with it."

"Get on with what?"

"Go across and pick 'em up. It's too cold for Dinah; she's getting old."

The nearest bridge was a mile upstream, and the water was high and dirty in spite of the frosts.

"You mean swim?" I asked. "It's too cold."

"If you want to come out with me you do what I say and don't argue."

"I haven't got anything to dry myself with."

"You've got a handkerchief, haven't you?"

I took my clothes off and fetched the ducks, and the handkerchief did its job well enough. That wasn't the last time I worked for Dinah.

"She works hard enough for you," Greenhill said. "You can do something for her once in a while."

Because he infinitely preferred shooting and salmon fishing and because I knew my way about the river well enough, Greenhill did not come trout fishing with me very often at first. As a matter of fact I began, in my dry-fly man's arrogance, to discount him as a trout fisherman. My uncles and my father had, so far as I knew, used nothing but the dry fly on Grandfather's lengths of the Frome and the Wrackle and on the Club water as well. The uncle who taught me to fish had taught me only dry-fly fishing, and I was, at fourteen, a hidebound purist. To make matters worse, I got pretty good at the business and kept on improving steadily, which was natural enough because I had every opportunity to know the water well and had a fanatical keenness as well as a complete disregard for weather conditions or discomfort of any kind. Such things simply didn't register.

I am not sure just when or how I discovered that Greenhill was not a very experienced dry-fly fisherman. Certainly he never told me or admitted it by remotest inference, nor did he ever attempt to suggest that the wet fly was a better method. But I knew somehow; and after the original shock of surprise, the knowledge gave me a very pleasant sense of superiority- there was at least one thing in which I could match him. Greenhill took whatever offensiveness I had to offer—I can't remember any of it exactly, but I am sure it was plenty—and began to fish with me more often. He used the dry fly for the most part, out of respect for the unwritten rule of the water, but occasionally turned to the wet fly. Very offhandedly he began to explain to me and show me some of the difficulties and complications of wet-fly fishing. We treated it as something of a joke, a method to play with occasionally, just for a change. I was glad to keep it that way because I was in no hurry to lose my sense of superiority. Wet-fly fishing was chuck-and-chance-it, a fair-enough method for the little trout of the Scottish burns or the Devonshire streams, but mild sacrilege on a chalk stream, even on a minor edition of a chalk stream such as the Frome was. But unfortunately for my sense of superiority, I liked fishing and I liked to know about fish; watching Greenhill and trying the method occasionally myself I began to see that there were satisfactions and difficulties in it as great as those of dry-fly fishing; more important, trout responded differently to a fly moved across or against the current than they did to one floating on the surface. Fishing the wet fly, one found trout in unexpected places; they came to it sometimes over the top of weed beds in great smooth arrows of disturbed water that checked sharply into a boiling rise. The sudden direct pull of a fish on the line and back into the hand was fully as exciting as the gentle dimple in which a dry fly disappeared.

The Frome fish were every bit as shy as chalk-stream fish are likely to be—any clumsy approach would put a feeding fish down for the rest of that day and perhaps for longer. Fishing a dry fly, one learned to kneel and crawl upstream, spotting rises carefully, studying the approach, working carefully into position for the cast. Upstream nymph fishing was fascinating and profitable, as I already knew, and the upstream wet fly offered most of the same advantages, except that the fish usually turned to follow it downstream before taking and so would sometimes see the rod or simply turn in disgust from the too swift swimming of the fly. But Greenhill wanted me to fish the downstream wet fly, and that was really difficult with shy fish. It meant an altogether more intense form of crawling and creeping, a closer study of lies and approaches and current, longer and in some ways more accurate casting. Greenhill was good, and I wanted to be as good myself; so I began to work at it.

As soon as I had thoroughly committed myself to learning the method, Greenhill began to rule and guide my learning as he ruled what I did when we were shooting. I started out with one bad fault, an almost unbreakable habit of recovering line in my hand, developed by

years of upstream fishing. This brought the fly across too fast and too shallow, and Greenhill, after a period of patient explanation, began to take the rod away from me whenever I fell in to it. In a little while we were fishing with only one rod between us, changing over whenever one or other of us hooked a fish and whenever I made a clumsy or careless cast or fished the fly badly. I became a respectable wet-fly fisherman rather quickly, and from then on Greenhill was little concerned about whether I fished wet or dry or with the nymph.

All this, I realize now, was his way of preparing me for salmon fishing. Greenhill was not by any means a rich man; he lived frugally in the barracks at Dorchester and spent what little money he had where it would give him the most of the sports he loved. He had a pair of beautiful guns and loaded his own cartridges. His salmon rods were greenheart that he had made up himself; he made all his own traces and flights and minnows and prawn tackles, though not, I think, his flies. The one extravagance he allowed himself was the renting of a stretch of salmon water on the lower reaches of the Frome, between Wool and Wareham. During the season he fished there almost every day, alone or with his friend Charlie Baunton, with whom he shared the water.

At that time the Frome, like several other fine salmon rivers in the south of England, was slowly and painfully recovering after bad days. Early in the nineteenth century it had been a great river with a magnificent run of fish. Uncontrolled netting and some pollution had made it almost worthless, but evidently the run of fish was not quite killed out. I don't know the exact history of its recovery, whether the riparian owners bought off some of the nets, as they did on the Wye, or whether the scarcity of salmon simply discouraged the net fisherman, but the recovery was a fine thing. In the early 1920's there was a good run of fish in the spring months, and they were really large fish—over twenty pounds as often as not and thirty-pounders were common. One April, during the Easter holidays, Greenhill suddenly told me that I was to come salmon fishing with him, not just once or twice, but every day I wanted to. This was like a sudden opening of heaven's gate. For years I had listened to my uncle's talk of salmon fishing and read books about salmon fishing and dreamed dreams of it. Now I was to start fishing with the almost certain chance of really big fish, and I knew I should be learning the business properly.

The Frome is a slow, deep river in its lower reaches, and the meadows through which it runs are wilder and rougher than those farther up. Strong weeds and sedges grow up in the pasture land, and the irrigation ditches are deep and wide; the river was not tidal where we fished it, but as I remember it now the country had some measure of the bigness and wildness of the tide flats at the mouths of British Columbia rivers that I have known since. There were ravens there and big hawks and ducks and wading birds of many kinds. Small birds were there also, sedge warblers and reed buntings and black-headed buntings, pippits and pert wagtails; they sang and mated and nested in the reeds and the rough grass, the wagtails fussing and fluttering and strutting at the edge of the river. And always things were happening in the wide meadows and the willow beds: a nesting plover would be chasing a raven, or two ravens chasing a hawk; a polecat would be glimpsed hunting a hedge; or a sudden rush of wings would reveal a sparrow hawk's stoop at a bunting.

But the river itself was the greatest fascination. Its slow current hid things that I could only vaguely imagine: the lies of great pike and salmon, deep silent places from which tKey might fiercely turn at any moment to seize the fly or minnow or prawn that I dared to hang there. I was almost genuinely afraid at times, afraid of dragging the fly away from some crashing rise or of jamming the reel as a great fish jumped or of doing any of the hundred other things I could do to throw away a golden chance that might better have been in Greenhill's capable hands.

Wisely, Greenhill started me with the fly. The Frome is not a really good river for the fly; for the most part it is too slow and too deep for attractive fishing,

though many fine fish have come to the torrish or Jock Scott or green highlander. But I was given the fly rod because it was easy—minnow and prawn were for those experienced and fortunate individuals who knew the bottom of the river as well as its surface and could handle them properly.

We started fishing at an off time. Fish were being caught in the pool below Bindon Mill. We heard about them and even saw them caught as we passed the mill each day. But in the rest of the river there was little moving; in a full week's fishing I had moved two fish to the fly, and Greenhill had felt perhaps five or six touch his prawn, only one of them hard enough to take out line. We had not even killed a good-sized pike, something I had hoped for, though Greenhill had warned me carefully that we were not fishing for pike and should not catch them unless we fished too fast for salmon. Before the end of the week I had tried prawn and minnow several times, gladly and hopefully, but they had done little more for me than the fly—one good hard pull to the minnow in the Railway Pool.

On the morning of the ninth day we got to the river late and found that Charlie Baunton had killed two beautiful fish on the fly before we got there. We caught nothing. On the tenth day we took out only the spinning rod and fished alternately. The Railway Pool was blank and so was the next pool below it. That brought us to the Ivy Pool, a deep pool where the fish sometimes lie well in under the bank in a sort of cave that the river has cut away. Greenhill worked his prawn into this place and hooked a fish. For once all went well, and I gaffed it for him ten minutes later—a fourteen-pounder.

I worked down the rest of the pool, fishing my most careful best, dropping the prawn within six inches of the other bank, swinging it across deep and slow, holding it as long as I could wherever the fish should be lying. Greenhill watched closely and once or twice nodded his head in approval. I wanted that because I knew that a bad cast plopping down in midstream or a few turns of the reel too fast in bringing the prawn through a good lie would be his signal to take the rod away for half an hour. But fish how I would, the rest of the pool was blank.

The next pool was the Hut Pool, a pool on a curve and shallow at the head, so shallow that I could see the prawn as I brought the first cast around. I moved two steps and cast again. Again I saw the prawn coming up to me under my own bank; then there was a fish behind it, a silver-gray fish, big and beautiful. He came in a wave and turned in a boil, and then Greenhill was shouting anxious directions to me.

He was only a ten-pounder, and Greenhill lifted him on the gaff five or six minutes after I had hooked him. He half-apologized, half-scolded me, "I wanted you to get the first one, young fellow. Next time you can play him out and bring him to the gaff properly."

I don't think I cared whether I fished at all in the rest of that day. My salmon was on the bank, clean silver and beautiful, with the violet sheen of the sea faint on his scales. Greenhill fished on, and we came to the long pool called the Salmon Water. He was fishing as only he could, swinging the prawn out easily, letting it almost brush the reeds of the far bank in its fall, working it deep down to the floor of the river before he began the slow recovery. His big shoulders hunched over the rod, his hands on rod and reel were ready and sensitive, his whole being seemed projected out into the swim of his prawn, concentrated on what it was doing down there on the bottom of the river. Beside him Dinah sat in trembling concentration as tense as his own. Suddenly, almost in the exact moment that he began the recovery of a cast, he lifted the rod in a heavy strike. Dinah stood up, ears pricked forward. Right under the far bank a big fish crashed to the surface in a heavy, shattering jump. The fish ran as the others had not, deep down and strongly, taking out a lot of line. For fully twenty minutes he bored and struggled and twisted, while we followed him as closely as we could along the bank. Then Greenhill brought him to the gaff, and I saw he was big, so big I didn't want the gaffing of him for fear I would muff it. I reached over, slowly and carefully, then struck and felt

the gaff slide solidly home; I lifted and the fish was on the bank.

"Well done," Greenhill said.

"Gosh," I said. "What does he weigh? Forty pounds?"

Greenhill shook his head and smiled. "Not quite thirty. We'll see when we get back to the mill." He began to mount a new prawn. "You get on and fish before it's too late. You won't get many days like this one."

So I fished out the rest of the Salmon Water, and near the tail of it an eighteen-pounder took me, and I killed him, properly and alone as a salmon fisherman should, even gaffing him myself. As we walked back up toward the mill along the railroad, I felt my face hot and my knees weak from sheer joy; the thirty-pound weight of salmon slung clumsily on my back was something I remembered only because it was salmon—salmon Greenhill and I had caught.

I fished many more days with Greenhill. Once I gaffed a forty-pounder for him, and within an hour of that he gaffed a twenty-eight-pounder for me. But right up until the last day I fished with him, I fished on probation. Sometimes, despairing of salmon, I would fish the minnow a little faster in the hope of attracting a big pike. "When you come out with me for salmon, don't waste time fishing for pike," he would say. "Give me that rod." Or, when I made a clumsy cast, "What are you trying to do? Knock their brains out? They don't want it on top of their heads." I think I learned the lessons. I know I still think of him almost every time I fish a pool and try to cover it as carefully and cunningly as he would have.

The very last day I fished with him we fished for pike in the river Stour near Wimborne. We often went out in high hopes of big pike during the winter months, and I was not surprised when he suggested the Stour because I knew a forty-pounder had been killed there years earlier. We crossed the river on a bridge some way above where we were to fish and saw it was high but in good shape. "You ought to get a twenty-pounder today, young fellow," he said. At the farm where we left the car, they told us the river might be flooded over its banks in places, but it should be fishable. This was accurate enough, and I killed a ten-pounder in the first few minutes by wading over the tops of my boots. I offered Greenhill the rod, but he shook his head. "I want to see you catch fish today," he said.

I caught them. An eight-pounder, a fourteen-pounder, two or three small ones, then a sixteen-pounder. Each time I offered him the rod, and each time he refused it. He stood behind me all the time, leaning on the long handle of his gaff, watching closely and yet not wholeheartedly interested in the fate of every cast as he usually was. It was still early in the day when the sixteen-pounder was on the bank. Greenhill said, "You know, I was born a few miles from here."

I was surprised; I hadn't known that. I think I realized then how little I did know about him. He said, "You've got all the fish you want. I'd like to drive round and look at two or three places."

So we took the rod down and went back to the car. He directed as I drove along narrow lanes until we came to the gates of a big stone house in a fine park. I stopped the car, and he looked at it for a long time. I knew it was the house where he was born and I asked, "Who lives there now?" But he didn't answer. Later we drove on farther, to a cemetery, and he showed me the graves where his mother and father were buried. After that we drove home. I felt I had been taken close to him, but I couldn't understand why and I held back into myself a little, afraid. After a while, he said, "Sorry I took you away from your fishing, young fellow. But it's not like salmon fishing; it was only pike." I hadn't minded about the fishing, but I knew it was strange that he had wanted to leave it and strange that he hadn't taken the rod all day. At seventeen I was perfectly willing to call a thing strange without wondering much just why it was strange.

Three weeks later Greenhill went up to shoot pigeons in a wood on a windy hill. He died there, and Dinah howled beside him through the night and part of the next morning.

LITTLE LAKES

The little lakes of Vancouver Island and the British Columbia coast are uncountable. If they were to be counted, someone would have to lay down a law that distinguished between a lake and a pothole and a pond and a swamp. Then all the ground would have to be resurveyed and all the maps drawn again to make quite sure that no little lake, anywhere, was left out. And that would be an awful job because they nestle in a thousand unexpected places—on the breasts of mountains, in wide river flats, up draws and gullies, on forgotten plateaus and on the round tops of big hills.

To be little, I think a lake should be not more than a mile or two long. To be a lake at all, it should have a respectable flow of water into it and out of it, some lakes, I know, are fed by springs and drained by underground streams; but a little lake that has nothing more than an overflow channel leading from it is in grave danger of being reckoned a pond. Swamps, very often, are lakes filled in by the slow deposit of each year's algal bloom and weed growth until reeds and hardhack can spread their roots out into it and still keep their heads above water. It is not always too easy to decide when a lake has ceased to be a lake and become a swamp. Potholes, for my purpose, are flood pools in the swamps and wide places in the creeks where there is just room for a few ducks to light and feed. Beaver ponds usually are something all their own, good places to fish, but still more nearly potholes than lakes.

Most of the little lakes on the British Columbia coast have trout in them, and the time to go to them first is in April. May can be a good month too, but in July and August, even in June, the water is likely to be too warm for good fish or good fishing. In late September and early October, when cool nights have lowered the water temperature, they are good again. Generally the trout in the lakes are cutthroats, generally they will come well enough to the fly and generally there will be plenty of them; but that's about all the generalizing it is safe to do because little lakes can

appear simultaneously on the whole river and the fisherman can slop along from pool to pool, maddened by the certainty that duns are appearing somewhere along the stream, and yet never find them—or rising trout—at all. Subspecies of the wonderful insect appear, one after another, through May, June and early July, changing in color from iron blue—through subtle shades and blendings of gray, olive and brown—to creamy yellow forms. Famous old dry fly patterns imitate all the important types; the Hendrickson, the Red Quill, the Grey Fox, the March Brown, the Light Cahill were all invented to match specific mayflies and to take fish when they are hatching. But as the season progresses, the fisherman often finds several different sorts on the water at the same time and can be moved to borderline neurosis while attempting to discover which one predominant insect the trout are actually eating at the moment he casts a fly over them.

There are works of practical entomology (*Matching the Hatch* by Ernest G. Schwiebert, Jr., *Streamside Guide to Naturals and Their Imitations* by Arthur B. Flick) which provide him with thorough background; but he is often balked, nevertheless, as he stands in midstream glaring wildly around him, for clues as to what is going on in the water. Some forms of mayfly—and the artificial flies which imitate them—are remarkably alike. The Hendrickson and Red Quill, in fact, are exactly the same save for the winding on the shank of the hook. But the trout will take one and refuse the other. They not only refuse the fly, they insult the fisherman. A trout will rise within a quarter inch of a fly which is too big or admits light improperly or is slightly off shade and will contemptuously splash water on it. He will jump clear of the surface and land on the other side of it. There are times when he seems to spit on it. But he will not touch it. And he will refuse a fly which matches the emerging duns in every respect if he has decided, for reasons known only to himself, to keep feeding just below the surface on the supply of rising nymphs.

Nature, it must be admitted, has provided the baffled angler with certain helpful signs and portents. A trout usually rises gently if he is feeding on the surface, but tends to splash and roll if he is feeding on nymphs or spent insects floating just beneath it. There are experts who maintain they can identify sixteen different kinds of rises (amongst them the sip, the slash, the double-whorl, the suck, the pyramid, the bulge and hump, and the spotted ring) and instantly announce just how the fish is feeding by noting the way he disturbs the water. But if a man can see dozens of rising trout and cannot make them pay the slightest heed to his artful casting, he has a tendency to quit thinking. Usually he takes refuge in trial and error and begins changing flies at random—a process which involves juggling his rod, a knife, a fly box and a bottle of dope in which he dunks each successive lure to make it float, and doing it all while up to his hips in a turbulent creek.

If he enters into this rigmarole at dusk, he must eventually ask himself an awful question: if he cuts the fly off the end of his leader, will there be light enough to allow his replacing it with another pattern? He can see dim, aluminum-colored flashes where fish are rising in the dark pool. He takes the course of courage and boldness. He cuts. He instantly regrets it. Swarms of no-seeums sift down and bite him like clouds of red-hot pepper. He cannot swat. He is standing motionless, holding a No. 16 Light Cahill toward the dim sky with one hand and trying to poke the invisible end of his synthetic gut leader through its invisible eye with the other. He grunts and sweats. He may even make small moaning sounds. But eventually he admits the cruel truth. He is disarmed. He turns, disconsolately, to wade ashore. At this moment he is subject to a final indignity and, if he is truly unlucky, he will be claimed by it. He slips in the darkness, lurches wildly, tumbles arse over tea kettle. The vehemence, the utter foulness of the profanity which can be induced by this common, even comic little accident is shocking, and the witness who laughs does so at his peril.

But the angler needs more than a knowledge of entomology—although this is a first requirement—to attack trout successfully on streams as cranky as those of the Catskills. He must do more than cast well, too. The fly must be presented correctly, but casting is simply a means to an end and is a far simpler process than is generally believed. After a few months of practice, any fool ought to be able to put a fly within a couple of inches of his target; he should be able to avoid getting hung up in trees and have mastered the trick of dropping loose line on the water to compensate for the drag of current. This is not to say there are no difficult casts. If an angler sees a big fish rising under an overhanging branch and has to reach out to the limit of his rod's power to deliver his fly, there is a very good chance he will manage any number of embarrassing mistakes. But on most water the long, difficult cast is seldom necessary. It is my opinion that motivation is more important than technique and that the successful fisherman catches trout when others do not because he possesses sneaky and atavistic instincts which heighten his perception and his ability to concentrate, and make him respond to all sorts of unkind little signals from his subconscious mind.

Something of this sort occurs in my own case, I believe, out of simple hunger. A great many fishermen are uninterested, or at least profess to be uninterested, in small trout. But in most streams—and certainly in the Esopus, save for the preseason and postseason spawning runs—there are very few fish of any other kind.

I am an eight-inch trout fisherman. I must admit I enjoy being an eight-inch trout fisherman. I sometimes keep seven-inch trout. A nine- or ten-inch trout looks like an absolute leviathan to me. I admire their beauty. I like the bulge a collection of them makes in my wet canvas creel. I am grateful to them for the fact that they are as selective, if not always as wary, as big trout and that the intellectual problems and gratification involved in luring them at the fly has little to do with their size or weight. But essentially, I like the way they taste and, when I wade into the stream, I am after something special to eat.

This does not mean that I am insensitive to the social delights of landing a big fish. A few big brown trout do skulk in deep holes or beneath boulder-studded white water during the summer and a few more seem to begin their autumnal spawning run as early as August. These monsters—anything longer than sixteen inches or heavier than two pounds is a monster in the Esopus—may rise to the surface for a few minutes during really big spring fly hatches, but mostly they stay deep and invisible, think dour thoughts and eat such minnows and small trout as incautiously invade their lairs. The chances of hooking one of them on a fly are remote in the extreme despite the experts and their interminable creeds about casting. But if the angler wants to be considered absolutely compleat and even perhaps occult—and a fly fisherman would not be a fly fisherman if he did not welcome such rumors—he simply has to produce a monster at least once.

Between May and September real, live, exciting news in Phoenicia concerns only one topic: trout. John McGrath and Joe Holzer who preside over its two grocery stores are fishermen. The Folkerts brothers, Herman and Dick, who run its social center—a combined tackle and golf shop, soda fountain, newspaper stand, bus stop and sporting goods store—are consummate anglers. So is Fred Muehleck, whose racks of ancient Payne, Leonard and Hardy rods are wondrous to behold. So also is Phil Halzell, his Woodland Valley neighbor and stream-side companion of thirty years' standing. Half the inhabitants, in fact, are fishermen and the other half cannot avoid listening to them. Let someone—anyone—catch a monster by whatever means (a construction stiff once lifted a big brown out of Woodland Valley Creek with a clamshell power shovel) and the news flashes up and down the valley roads with the speed of light.

Three summers ago, after going year on year without even seeing a monster, I caught two of them in one three-week period—a two-pounder of 17 inches and a three-pounder which measured 20 ⅝ inches. I am willing to admit that I took each of them into town, lugged them through the crowd of people waiting for the Pine Hill-Kingston line bus and thence into Folkerts' tackle shop to be measured, weighed and admired by hangers-on from the soda fountain. While nobody has since spoken of me as a veritable artist with a fly rod, I have reason to believe that I am no longer considered a mere dilettante from New York. I have, in fact, heard several generous remarks about my prey, and one man, whom I did not discourage, seemed to be under the impression that I was able to track down monsters at will.

Honesty compels me to say that I hooked both of them by accident. In each case, a stray current sucked my wet fly down deep beside a sunken boulder and presented it to the fish, whose presence I did not remotely suspect, in a completely natural way—an effect no one could have achieved otherwise in a month of trying. Both leviathans, I am sorry to relate, acted like Bowery drunks after I put the iron to them. A three-pound trout, of course, will put a splendid arc in a four-ounce rod, but neither of my fish seemed to have any concept of the thrilling fight which was expected of them. The bigger one ran out of steam after half stranding himself in a shallow riffle while I was trying to lead him into a quiet pool for the big battle. I simply fell on him, wrestled him two out of three falls and carried him ashore. And though both were wrapped in cheesecloth and lovingly poached in a court bouillon, neither of them, alas, tasted very good.

Smaller trout—if they are fat, wild and freshly caught—are something else again. The prospect makes my entire endocrinological system thump, palpitate and clank like a houseful of old-fashioned steam radiators on the first day of winter. It has been my privilege to sample the haute cuisine of Paris, New York, San Francisco and New Orleans, but neither Maxim's nor Le Pavillon have offered me anything to match the tender and delicate taste of these lovely fish. They should, to my mind, be rolled in corn meal, sizzled for four or five minutes in bacon fat (better, for reasons I do not understand, than butter) and served with a fresh green vegetable or salad, a baked potato, or macaroni with a bland cheese sauce. The exterior of the trout, properly done, is crisp and gold; the interior, white, moist and of a flavor, subtle but poignant, as to pierce the very soul. If the air of the dining room is faintly perfumed by fireplace wood smoke, the fish will taste better: and if one drinks a clear, icy martini while they are cooking and a half bottle of well-chilled Moselle while they are being consumed, he will find himself, when all are gone, sitting mindlessly, happily motionless while his inner being relives and resavors the sensations which have been visited upon it and congratulates itself upon a turn of fortune too splendid to be quite believed.

My memories of such orgies and my unbridled appetite for more of them have a great deal to do, I am convinced, with what successes I may manage in my contest with the Esopus. There are days when some curious perceptiveness—simulated, I can only assume, by messages from my digestive tract—allows me to strike at the split second a trout takes my sunken, drifting nymph, although I can neither see nor feel the fish before it is magically hooked. I am incapable of remembering telephone numbers or even, at times, the names of people I have known for years, but I can visualize miles of stream in infinite detail. The Esopus has its obvious and easily remembered water: the Greeny Deep, Twin Rooks, the Spanish Farm, the Pool-in-Front-of-Bill-McGrath's-House and a succession of noisy cascades known, simply, as Down at Elmer's Diner. But I know hundreds of minor riffles, rock-divided eddies and patches of slack water; I know how they change at various river levels; I remember how fish behave in them and I remember when shadow, if any, falls on them, morning and evening.

The Catskill fisherman needs such information just as the prospector needs an understanding of rock formations—not that the knowledge is likely to produce riches in either case, but because it keeps hope alive. He needs a very good, very expensive fly rod for the same reason, even though in 999 out of 1,000 situations one can fish just as well with a cheap glass rod.

A fine rod is made of a particularly hard and resilient cane from North Vietnam's Tonkin region. Its delicate sections are machined to tolerances of a thousandth of an inch to produce a specific and particular bending mode or "action." It is simple, exquisitely balanced and beautiful to see—at once an efficient tool and a work of art. The very process of removing a good rod (in my case an eight-foot Orvis) from its aluminum case, of jointing it up and carefully attaching an English reel (no others click so satisfyingly when spun) does something to the spirits comparable, I imagine, to climbing into the cockpit of a Spad or polishing up a set of safecracker's drills. When the fisherman's hand closes on its smooth, cork grip he is armed as Arthur with Excalibur and anticipates triumph almost automatically as he wades into a stream.

Once in a while, furthermore, even on streams as exasperating as the Esopus or its feeders, he will win an enormous victory. I cannot help but feel that my own performance during the hurricane of 1955 was absolutely brilliant. On considering it in retrospect, in fact, I am able to discover in myself qualities so admirable that I would be inclined to discount them were it not for the penetrating, even pitiless, honesty with which I have reviewed the episode. I will go so far as to say that I rose as a phoenix from the ashes of defeat and that I hoped and was rewarded while all others were cast down by despair.

The hurricane and its accompanying deluge made a horrible mess of our Catskill streams; they poured down their valleys under opaque curtains of rain in roaring, muddy floods. It made a mess of my house, too. The roof leaked, and when I put pans under the drips, I was impelled to endure something very like a xylophone concert. Forced into the open by this ungodly racket, I took my rod, drove five miles to the end of the Woodland Valley road and began walking upstream under the trees. I was as wet, in five minutes, as if I had fallen into a swimming pool; but I pressed

sternly on and, after two miles, came upon the splendid and gleaming phenomenon I had hoped but not actually expected to find.

Under normal conditions Woodland Valley Creek betrays itself at this high point of its valley only in little skeins and trickles of water among shadowed, mossy rocks. But now it was ten feet wide and, since there were no clay banks to discolor the water, it ran clear as crystal. The native brook trout of the Northeast had been extinct in 95 percent of the Esopus system for a long time—very probably since the tanners cut the hemlocks more than a century ago. But brookies, which had somehow endured year after year in the shadowed trickles of water here, were feeding voraciously in the swollen creek. They were absolutely beautiful fish with a sheen of electric blue, white piped fins, mottled backs and crimson spotted sides. I hooked them for two hours, released all but five of the handsomest, since even a hungry man could hardly deny they had earned the right to freedom, and splashed back down through the rain feeling as though I had discovered the Mother Lode.

Despite such bagman's satisfactions, however, I must confess that my pursuit of artistry, restraint and purity of purpose has progressed very slowly, if at all. But I strive. I have a model: an erect, wispy and grave old gentleman whom I encountered at midday on the Esopus above the portal five years ago and have admired, wistfully, ever since.

The sun was bright. The stream was low and clear. It was not a time to fish at all, for any movement sent trout flashing to cover in the still, brilliantly lighted pools and I was carrying a rod only as insurance against some unlikely opportunity. As I strolled along inspecting a stretch of water I had not seen for a long time, I became conscious of the old gentleman only when I saw him bend, perhaps seventy yards below me, and then straighten, net in hand. But in that instant, even at that distance, I saw that the net contained the dark, curved form of a very big trout—a monster, or, at the very least, a monster junior grade.

When he came slowly upstream, minutes later, I began to understand what a feat he had managed under those absolutely impossible conditions. He did not show me the fish or even allude to it. He had wrapped it in newspaper and had contrived to get most of the resulting package into his creel. If I had not had that glimpse of it in his net, I might not have known he had a fish at all.

He must have been eighty; I doubt if he weighed much more than a hundred pounds and he walked slowly and with care. But I could only assume that he had come to the river with his sheets of old newspaper because he expected to stalk that one particular fish and that he had fully expected to land it. He nodded at me, glanced at my rod and, after reaching into a pocket, produced a roll of leader so fine that it was almost invisible. It must have tested less than a pound. He snapped off two feet of it simply by breaking the fragile stuff between his fingers. "Use this as a tip," he directed. Then he pulled out a plastic box, removed a tiny, curiously bedraggled black fly and handed it to me as well. "Try this," he said. "I tie them during the winter."

This was the fly and this was the weight of leader with which, quite obviously, he had subdued his thick, heavy trout. He had been forced, on such water, to take a long, long, almost impossible cast to avoid frightening his quarry. In teasing up such a fish, indeed, he had very probably had to drop the fly again and again, and each time as lightly as thistledown. And having hooked the monster, he had played it coldly and delicately at the end of that gossamer tip, knowing one slightest false move would lose him the game.

He fixed me with a stern eye until I had tied on his contributions and then, apparently satisfied that he had prepared me, too, for higher things, nodded and turned away toward the road. I knew better—that he had only prepared me for a few fruitless casts on such a day. But I got down on my hands and knees, for all this, to approach a pool formed by the confluence of a little side stream called the West Kill and then, sitting up slowly to avoid alarming its inhabitants, I looked carefully for evidence of opportunity.

The pool was deep, blue and still, but there were gnats dancing over the faint currents at its head and I felt that I saw an occasional tiny disturbance on its surface. I lighted a cigarette, and then made a long cast and promised myself that I would let my fly lie on the quiet water until I had finished smoking. But impatience and lack of faith were soon my undoing. I yanked the line off the water in dissatisfaction after three puffs and cast a foot to the right of its first position. As the line was still in the air, the biggest brown trout I have ever seen broke water like a runaway torpedo and fell back with a shattering splash. "Good Lord!" I cried in astonishment and cupidity—I talk to myself considerably when fishing—and, moved to mindless activity, made still another frantic cast. And this time I saw that my little fly was gone and realized what I had done. The big fish had sucked it in at the split second I had retrieved my line and I had broken off the hairlike leader without the slightest sense of having done so. The monster had jumped because my hook was imbedded in its lip. Had I concentrated, had I waited one second longer . . .

Ah, well. I will, given a bit of luck, be eighty years old myself one day and I like to think a certain improvement in both skill and moral tone will have become evident at that point and that the Esopus—or what is left of it—will yield to the superior man. And, if one matures late, one can always look forward to ninety.

H. Brannigan's Trout

NICK LYONS

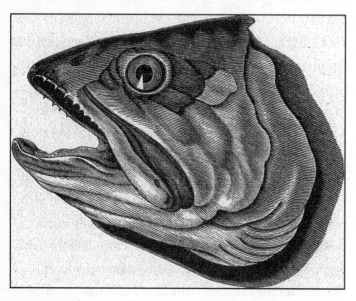

After the crack up, he was hospitalized for six months. Twice the doctors warned Jane that they might lose him. Then, when they saved him, they warned that there was probably brain damage. When he was released, in November, they told him he'd be paralyzed on his right side for life. Four doctors confirmed the verdict. There was nothing for it.

Perhaps there was a slight chance, but not likely, that regular exercise, steady exercise over a period of several years, might restore some small portion of his mobility. Not much. Possibly none. Frankly, Brannigan was not inclined to try. Why go through all the effort? So he sat silent and sullen in the wheelchair that grey afternoon and allowed the men in white to push him to the car, lift and place him into the front seat, collapse the chair and put it in the back, then tell Jane how he was to get in and out, how she was to rig the contraption and place it for him. Like a baby.

He said not a word on the long trip through the sere, dead countryside. Jane told him about the boys, and which friends had called; Mike Novak might come over that evening. He didn't even nod. His great black-haired head thrown back and tilted to one side, he watched with dead eyes the fleeting fields of withered cornstalks, leafless trees, dark scudding clouds. There was nothing for it. He was forty-six and it was over. He couldn't sell books or anything else anymore; he didn't know whether he could drink beer with his friends, chop wood, tend his garden, drive, smoke, sing, read, write; and certainly the fishing season was over for him. Permanently.

The crash in all its stark detail, the fluky chance of it, kept flashing through his brain: Johnny Wohl driving, across the seat from him saying, seconds before, "Well, Billy, we made a day of it, didn't we? I never saw the river so alive." And Mike in the back. Laughing wildly and about to say something about having caught three Hendricksons. Then the rasp of brakes, the black car coming just that moment smoothly out of the side road, the jolt of fear, his hands flying up, his back thrusting backward against the seat, the hurtling forward—and darkness, and stabbing, raw pain in his shoulders, his head. Then nothing. Johnny Wohl and the two teenagers in the black car had been killed instantly. Mike came out of it with his right pinky broken. Well, good for him. Good for old Mike.

As for himself, it would have been better to have had it over then, right then when it happened. Quick. No more pain to die than to live, then. He need merely not have come out of the coma. After that first, searing pain, poof. For good. And they all said he's only lived because he wanted to live. So he lived—like a half-squashed worm.

He saw suddenly in his mind the 20-gauge shotgun in the cabinet in his den. Would Jane have removed it? This was no time to ask. That night, when the boys were doing their homework, he'd wheel in by himself and just take a look-see. He'd take it out, break it open . . . take a look-see.

At dinner, Jane talked constantly—about the Murphy's new Brittany spaniel; the good batch of slab wood Frank had hauled from the lumber yard, piece by piece, and cut himself; the threat of an early snow. Brannigan looked up now and then from his plate, spread his lips slightly in the best he could do for a smile, and nodded. He said nothing. He was still not sure what the cracked, alien sound of his voice—what remained of speech—would be to these people, whether he could put together all the words needed for one whole sentence. Whenever he raised his head and looked toward one of his sons, Frank to his right, fifteen, Junior on his left, a year older and dark-haired too, rebellious, they were looking at their own plates. They knew everything. When he looked back at his own plate and prepared his next strategy to get a piece of meat to his mouth, he thought he saw, peripherally, their heads raise slightly and turn toward him. He didn't think he could bear it. Not that. He'd come through Normandy without a scratch; he'd never been seriously ill in his life.

Working diligently with the fork in his left hand, like they'd taught him in the hospital, he speared a piece of the steak Jane had cut for him, shifted the fork carefully in his hand, and brought it to his mouth. He chewed the meat slowly for a few moments, then lowered the fork to get another. But the prongs pressed against the gristle, slipped, and flicked the chunk of meat onto the floor. Brannigan looked after it, heard Jane say, "I'll pick it up later, dear," then slammed the fork down on his plate. Frank and Junior

raised their hunched shoulders and looked up sharply. Jane took a deep breath.

"Nuff," muttered Brannigan. "Nuff." He pushed the wheelchair away, turning it, and, his hand on the wheel-rail, glided into the living and toward his den—hearing Frank say something low that ended with "like that," and Junior's heavier voice, and then Jane telling them in a normal voice to finish quickly and go upstairs: they'd talk of it later.

He negotiated the living room and came to the door of his den. His room. The door was closed but he came against it sideways, took his left hand from the wheel-rail and reached out for the knob. As he did so, the chair slipped back a few inches and he was only able to touch a bit of the knob. He gritted his teeth, pounded his left hand down on the armrest, wheeled himself close again, and tried another time. Again the chair slipped back a bit and he couldn't, hard as he strained, even touch the knob. *Damned. Damned.* He sat in the chair, breathing heavily for a few moment, then tried again, got it, flung the door open, gave the wheel-rail a sharp thrust forward, and was in his room. *His* room.

God, how many good hours he'd spent there. The soft old armchair. His own mount of the four-pound brook trout he's caught in Canada that summer with Mike and Johnny. The humidor with those long black dago-ropes he loved so much. Fireplace. Little fly-tying table—just like he'd left it. Silver rod cases in the cabinet he'd built himself. The old black-bear rug he'd bought, over Jane's hilarious objections. *His room.*

It was a room to which he slunk after a knock-down argument with Jane, a lousy road trip; he went there to plan his selling strategies, realign the world, read quietly in the evening or tie flies. He'd had most of his serious talks with his boys in this room; and he'd laughed and drunk beer and told stories half the night with Johnny and Mike here. Useless now. There was not one thing in the room, as he looked around, that he wanted.

The shotgun.

His eyes shifted sharply to the oak cabinet with the V-back that fitted into the corner so snugly. It was there. He went to his fly-tying table, opened the middle drawer, and felt with his hand among the capes and bobbins until his fingers found and closed tightly around the long brass key. Then, holding the key in the palm of his left hand, he used his fingers to push the chair over to the cabinet.

He had only that one gun, a beautiful 20-gauge with polished walnut stock, grey shoulder cushion, twin slate-grey barrels. He liked the feel of it in his hands, the power with which it jerked back when he shot. He'd gotten his first grouse with it last winter. Sam, Johnny's Brittany, had frozen on point, Johnny had called for the flush, and the grouse, a single, had exploded with a whirr from the underbrush. "Yours!" shouted Mike, and he'd swung, led, and watched the bird pause, sputter, and fall. He remembered the deep satisfaction he'd felt from that connection, that force which shot out from him and dropped that bird.

The shotgun.

Another moment and he'd have it in his hands, feel its sleek powerful lines, its smooth stock. The gun held power, energy, force; merely to have it in your hands was to feel some electrical current, some charge of strength shot into your veins, your body. "Look-see," he said, flinching at the cracked, strange sound of his voice, inserting the key into the lock and turning, then opening the cabinet door slowly.

It was not there. The cabinet was empty.

His eyes blazed and he slammed the door shut. It was not there. She had taken it. Grasping the wheel-rail he thrust downward and began to roll across the carpet toward the closed door to the living room. She had taken it. "Gun," he said, his voice a rasping growl. "Gun. Gun." Then, opening the door, he let his head fall, and he muttered, "Did she . . . really . . . think . . ."

"So the point is that *I* asked Jane for your goddamn shotgun because mine is at the gunsmith and I ain't got one to use next week," Mike said ten minutes later when they were alone in the den. "She didn't want to let me have it. Nope. 'Mike,' she says, 'Billy loves that rifle.' That's what she called it, a rifle, 'and I don't think I can let you have it.'"

Brannigan frowned. He looked intently at the bronze, hearty face of his friend, that bullish chest above toothpick legs, the straight black, always greasy and carefully combed hair, the mechanic's hands, stained black.

"I says: 'Look, Janie, he may not be out until after Christmas and I know he'd want me to put a few notches on it for him. One thing about Billy, he don't like a good rod or shotgun lying around. Offends his Scotch-Irish blood.'"

"Lie."

"I was going to take it out to the range, test it on some clays, but if you'd like it back, got some special use for it, I'll . . ." He broke off, lowered his voice, and said: "It's been rough, ain't it, kiddo?"

"Ruh-uf."

"Yeah, said Mike, turning his back and walking across the room to look at the big, bright male brook trout on the wall. "Remember when you got that one, Billy?" he said without turning around. "You'd cast that big funny fly from New Zealand, the Red Setter, looked like a whore's hairdo, into the swirls below the falls. I was behind you. I'd gotten one about three pounds that morning and you was burning mad. Didn't even speak to me at lunch. Well, maybe I was being a bit rotten about it." He came and sat down in the soft old armchair. "I must've turned and the next thing I know your rod's bent like a crescent moon and you're yelling like a banshee. Johnny thinks you've fallen in or got bit by a snake, so he comes running up, and by this time there's the goddamnedest smug look on your face! You've got the fish well hooked, you've seen him roll, and you know the size of him—and you know you got the greatest audience any mug ever had."

He watched Brannigan's eyes. They changed as he told the story.

"You're using this ten-pound-test leader and can't possibly lose that fish unless it gets into the rapids, and you're acting just as cockeyed cool as a cock of the roost. Johnny and me, we may be a little green around the gills but we're sitting polite as you please, murmuring a few friendly words of praise now and then—like, 'Did *that* lemon have to get it?'—and you keep playing him gently, making maybe a bit too much of a show of fear when it heads downstream. Cool. Very cool, Billy. And when Johnny wants to net him for you, with the big net, what do you do? Wave him away, and fuss with that minnow net you carry."

The faintest trace of a smile began to struggle around the corners of Brannigan's twisted mouth and eyes.

"So this absolute monster of a brookie, the biggest trout any of us has ever seen, is beat, and over on its side, and you're swiping at it with your net—probably trying to get it to rush off so's the show can go on—and first you get the tail in, right?"

Brannigan nodded.

"Then when it flops out, you try to bend it in, from the middle, but the monster won't be bent, so you go for the head, which barely fits into that guppy net, and then you've got it head first to about the gills and sort of clamp your hand down on the rest and come yelping out of the water, the line and rod and net and you all tangled together, and you fall on it. God, that fish was gorgeous—and there he is. That the way it happened, Billy? Something like that?"

Brannigan raised his left hand in a little shrug. "Ha-pinned . . . like . . . that."

"So the point is, you got one. You got one bigger than any of us ever got, even Johnny, God rest his soul, and now you figure, 'The big bird's crapped on me. I've caught my last big fish and shot my last grouse.' That it?"

"That-z-it."

"Johnny doesn't make it and you ain't satisfied to be here. Instead of being pleased I come tonight, passing up some very possible quail, you're going to stew in your own bile, right?"

"Rrr-ight."

"There's no one in particular to hate for it, so you figure you'll spread the hate around, to Jane and the boys, and especially yourself, and maybe you'll get lucky and not be around too much longer to be a burden to anyone. Well, I see your point, Brannigan. Lot of logic to it. Then say maybe there's a chance in a couple hundred thousand that you get anything back on that right side, so you say, 'Bad odds.'" He walked to the fly-tying table, picked up one of the capes, a pale ginger, and bent back the hackle of one feather. "A good one, Billy. First-rate dry-fly neck. Good small size, too." Then he went to the humidor and drew out one of the twisted black cigars. "You don't mind?" Brannigan, watching him closely, did not change his expression. Mike put the cigar in the center of his mouth, struck a match, and got the tip of the cigar glowing like a little coal. "Good cigar, Billy." He puckered his lips, held the cigar in three fingers, and took a long puff.

Brannigan kept watching him. He had not moved his chair from the moment Mike had come in. *Quail. Big trout. A grouse or two. Lives for that. Two wives, maybe have ten more. Funny guy. The way he holds that cigar—like he owned the world, all of it. Shotgun. Ask.*

"So the point is, it would break my sweet heart if you wasn't around, kiddo. Know what I mean? You know what I did when they told me you was"—he put out his hand, palm down, and rocked it slightly—"maybe not going to make it? I prayed. Me. Prayed. I said, 'Oh, God, let old Billy come through with *anything*, any goddamnit thing at all, so long as he's here and I can brag to him now and then about what quail I'm snatching—anything, God, just so long as he's here where I can see his ugly black-haired head now and then'"—he puffed hard at the cigar—"when the quail ain't flying and the trout is down. It's rough, right?"

Ask about shotgun.

"Suddenly the rules is all changed."

The gun.

"So the point is," he said, puffing hard, exhaling three times in rapid succession—"Hell, I don't know what the point is, Billy, but it will be awfully lonely next May when the Hendricksons start popping not to . . . Here, catch this"—and he tossed a softball, underhand, directly at Brannigan's chest. The left hand went up and forced the ball against the right shoulder. The right shoulder, limp and loose, twitched ever so slightly toward the ball. Brannigan held the ball for a moment, then took it in his left hand and tossed it back. Then he left his right shoulder and slowly dug his fingers into the muscle. "Not . . . much left."

"You'll cast lefty," said Mike. "Once knew an old poacher name of Sven who had to learn because there was bad brush on the right side. Dry-fly purist of a poacher." And the story went on for twenty minutes, and included a patrol dog named Wolf, five pound rainbows, two delicious young women, the true origin of "Sven's left curve drop cast," which only lefties could use, and then, just before the point of it all, Mike simply said, "It's eleven. The quail will have flown. I'll bring the 20-gauge tomorrow, eh?"

Brannigan smiled, a slow, deep smile that spread into his cheeks and eyes, and stayed, even when the twitch started. He nudged his right hand out with his left, so Mike could take and hold it, and Mike took it and held it in both of his own, rubbing the lifeless thing vigorously, then turning quickly for the door. Before he got there, Brannigan said: "The gun . . . yours."

*T*he limbs remember, he thought, working the rake lightly across the soil he'd just fitted with seed, *and so does the earth. It remembers what it must do to these seeds, and the seeds, someplace deep within them, knew what they must do.*

Back and forth he moved the rake, holding it firmly in his left hand, using his nearly useless right to steady it. The May sun was warm but not bright, and kneaded his broad naked shoulders. He could walk without the cane now—somewhat. With that bizarre arc. His hair had gone snow white, which he liked, but otherwise, if he didn't move and didn't talk, he looked nearly the same.

Everyone else had planted a week or two ago but he'd worked more slowly, as he had to—long patient hours, setting his fertilizer, running the hand plow steadily across the small garden he'd staked out last spring, seeding the soil. This would be a good year. He could feel it. He's learned how to coax green from the brown soil, how important it was, always, to be patient—to lay the proper foundation, however long that took, before you could expect anything to grow. Tomatoes, cucumbers, carrots, radishes, onions—he'd had these last year; now he added kale, zucchini, tarragon, other herbs. Each day now he would work on his garden for several hours, bending down to it, plucking, feeling, watering, watching. It all mattered. Even the watching. Every day. He'd increased the size of his garden by a third this year. It would require more work but he could do it. He still forgot many things—names, events, people he had known; but he forgot nothing connected to his garden. It would be a good garden this year, as fruitful as anyone's garden. Maybe better.

Got it all now, he thought, leaning against the rake, *and Mike will be here soon to take us a-fishing*. It would be good to be in the car, on a trip, listening to Mike's excited patter, it would be good to try the river again. Mike had said the Hendricksons had started.

Three years. Days, weeks, months had ticked by, minute by minute, and imperceptibly the changes had come. The insurance had kept them from bankruptcy, Jane had begun to work for a real-estate agent in town—and had blossomed with it. Junior was earning his way in college, his own man, and Frank was a senior in high school and working part-time at Mike's garage. They didn't need what he'd once earned; he knew that what they needed most he could give them only after he had given it to himself.

He had done the exercises the men in white advised, with barbells and bicycle—over and over and again; he hated to do them and stopped when it came time to work in his garden. Several times last spring Mike had taken him to the West Branch, which they'd often fished together, before he got wrecked. At first he merely found a rock, sat down, and watched. But he had not been able to resist the tug, deep inside him, to be on the stream, part of it, fishing. Wasn't that *really* why he'd done all those endless, tedious exercises, up and down, back and forth, hour after hour, all those months?

It had been impossible at first, after nearly two years. He had slipped twice on the rocks before he even reached the river. Even with the cane his right leg would not hold on broken terrain. Then he slipped again when he took his first tentative step into the water, careening badly, catching himself on his left arm. "No help, no help," he'd said when Mike stepped toward him. Then he'd been unable to strip line an cast left-handed, and finally, after several mad minutes he had given it up and fallen again on his way out, slamming his chin into a rock, cutting it sharply. No. It was not possible. He could not do it.

But it was a warm May morning and Mike would be there soon and it would be better this year. He'd earned it. Perhaps he'd even take his first trout since the crash.

Mike came promptly at twelve, and in a few minutes they were in the car racing toward the West Branch. "Magnificent day, Billy," Mike said, pushing the pedal harder. "The Hendricksons will be on in all their glory. They'll be popping out and the birds will be working, and we're going to get us a few. The cornfield run. I can feel a certain fat old brownie just waiting for you there today."

Mike parked along a small dirt turnoff and they got out and began to rig their rods, put on the waders. Mike was suited up and ready before Brannigan had worked one leg into his hip boots. "Go on, Mike. I'll be there . . . when I'm there."

"So you're tired of my company. Fine. I'm going upstream, you take the middle of the run. Where the current slows. Take your time: we're a half hour early. Lousy luck, kiddo."

Brannigan watched him stride off, his bull back bouncing even in waders. Then he finished raising

his boots, strapped them to his belt, and got out his vest. He could use his right hand as a support now, to hold one section of the rod firmly enough for his left to insert the other section; he managed it, with guides aligned, on only the second try. Then he strung the line slowly through the guides until the end of the fly line and all of the leader were outside the tip top. It was well he had practiced all winter.

He got out a Hendrickson he'd tied before the crash, kept in mothballs, and held it as firmly as he could with his right fingers. Then he tried to insert the point of the leader. It would not go. He kept shoving it off to the side, or shaking the fly. Finally he dropped the fly in the grass and had to bend down, slowly, to look for it. When he found it, he stayed on the ground in the shadow of the car and held the fly up to the sky so that the light-blue would show through the hole and he could better fit in the leader. The operation took him five minutes.

As he began to walk along the edge of the cornfield toward the river, his right leg came up in a large, jerky arc, and then down again, one step after the other. Slowly. There was no rush. There was plenty of time. Mike had coaxed him out several more times last summer and fall, and each time he fell but there was some slight improvement. Not much. Not enough for him to know he could do it, like he could garden, not enough to get a line out far enough to tempt a trout—but some. You had to connive. You had to be cunning and crafty, and to forget how it once was. You had to remember always that it would not all come back, not ever. You had to work within the fixed knowledge that you continue to improve, always, and that this counted, but that even at your very best, some day, you would be, by the world's standards, a lemon.

Perhaps he'd get one today. His first. It would be wonderful if he could get into a really large trout, perhaps seventeen or eighteen inches. You didn't have to make many casts, just the right one at the right time. He'd practiced on the lawn and he knew he now could get enough distance to reach the lip of the current in the cornfield pool. He'd once fished it many times. There was room for a decent backcast, and the shallow bar on his side of the run was hard earth and rubble, with only a few rocks that might trip him up. Mike had made a good choice; he'd be fishing upstream, in the fast water where the Hendricksons hatched, but there'd be plenty of fish falling back into the pool to pick up the duns as they floated down, especially once the hatch really got going

One step at a time—the right leg out first, and down, out and down. No hurry. You couldn't rush a walk anymore than you could a garden. You couldn't rush anything. Anyway, you saw more when you walked this slow—those crows pecking at corn seeds, that huge growth of skunk cabbage, lush and green and purple, the fuzzy green on the boughs of the willows. A gorgeous day, only slightly overcast now, perfect for Hendricksons.

As he neared the row of trees that bordered the river, he could see Mike upstream, wading deep; his rod was held high and had a sharp arc. *Good old Mike. Got one already*. Up and out, then down. Then again. And again. He worked his way through the alders to the edge of the river. The water was perfect—dark and alive, flecked with bubbles and eddies where the current widened and slowed. Like he'd dreamed it all winter. Yes, that was a fish. And another. He looked to the sky and saw four or five tan flies flutter and angle off into the trees. *Yes. Yes.*

He took a tentative step into the water and felt a touch of fear as he left the firmness of the earth. No matter. It would pass. All the old feeling was there; he could still feel, deep within him, something in him reaching out to the life of the river—its quick faceted run above the long flat pool below; its translucent dark green and gliding shadows. Flowing, always moving. Changing. The same and not the same. He picked out a dun and watched it bound, like a tiny tan sailboat, over the tail of the riffle, then swirl and float into slower water where it vanished in a sudden pinching of the surface.

Yes, they were moving today. He could see six, seven fish in fixed feeding positions, rising steadily. There was plenty of time. *Don't rush. Do it very, very slowly*. They'd be going good for another hour; he wanted to pick out one good fish, near enough for him to reach with his short cast. Only one good fish. He didn't want a creelful. Only one.

Upstream, Mike was into another trout, and a few minutes later while Brannigan still eased slowly, steadily into deeper water, inch by inch, Mike had another. *We've caught one of those magical days*, he thought. *Another foot or so* . . . At last, deep as he dared go, he stood on firm hard rubble in water up to his thighs. He stripped line deliberately by raising and lowering his right hand; then, holding the loose line as best he could, he made an extremely short cast. *Good. Much better this year*. Then he stood, rod poised, watching the spreading circles of feeding fish. There were two twelve-inchers in the middle current lane, feeding freely, and two small fish back ten feet; he couldn't reach any of those anymore, though they'd once have been easy enough casts. He could never have finished to that rise in the far eddy, though: the currents were too tricky, the cast too long. Too bad. That was a large fish.

Then he saw the steady sipping rise directly upstream from him, not thirty feet away. Sometimes the largest fish rose like that, but so did fingerlings. It was time to try. He could reach that fish.

His first cast was too short and too hard. His next was off to the right and too hard. The next two were not bad but the fish both times rose to a natural a second before his fly floated past. On his next cast, the trout rose freely, took, and, gripping line and handle with his left hand, as he'd practiced, he struck and had the fish on. A good one. A bright, large leaper that came out, shaking its spots at him and falling back, and then streaking up into the current, across to the far bank, boring deep, and then leaping again.

"Mike!" He usually didn't talk while he fished but he wanted his friend to see this. He hadn't shouted very loud and above him, Mike, busy with still another fish, did not hear. Again the fish came out. "A beauty," he said audibly. "A fine brown." Again the fish raced across the current, stripping line from the reel, arching the rod sharply. *Got to get it. Can't lose this one.*

In ten minutes he could tell the trout was tiring. But it was still on the opposite side of the current. As he began to retrieve the line slowly, the fish came into the current and allowed itself to be carried downstream. Then, suddenly, it bolted directly toward him and the like went slack. "No, no," he said, struggling but unable to strip back line quickly enough.

When he regained control, the fish was gone. He drew the line back slowly until he could see the bedraggled fly. The fish had merely pulled out on the slack line— because of his goddam right arm. His right arm—which might as well not be there.

He was sitting in the car, all his equipment packed away, when Mike came back. Mike had caught seven fish, all of size but none as large as the one Brannigan had lost, and said it was the best day he could remember, except of course the day he'd gotten the three-pound brookie in Canada and Brannigan that lucky male. Brannigan offered a weak smile but said nothing, and Mike looked at him and then said nothing as he took off his vest and waders.

In the car, heading home, he turned to Brannigan and asked quietly, "How'd you do, Billy? Take any?"

"I lost one . . . Mike. Pretty good fish. Then I decided I'd better quit because at least I hadn't fallen in. Like every other time. So I headed . . . out. Slowly. Praising myself all the time . . . that at least I hadn't taken . . . a bath this time."

"You took some bad ones last year, Billy."

"I'd lost a good one, a really good fish, and that didn't make . . . me feel too cheery . . . Yet I'd hooked it and played it a long time . . . which I . . . never did

before, not since I got wrecked, and I figured . . . if I could get out without a spill, I'd . . . still be ahead."

"Was it really a good fish, Billy?"

"Big. Very big brown."

"Sixteen inches."

"More."

"That's a big fish."

"So I was one step or two from the bank, smiling and praising myself . . . that I . . . hadn't fallen, when . . . I went into a pothole."

"Hell!"

"So I went down and over, ass . . . over teakettle. Almost drowned."

"Billy!"

"Almost. My head went under . . . and I was on my right side and couldn't . . . get leverage, and sort of forced my head out, and went under again, and gagged. Know I was going to die. I felt the grasp of brakes . . . in my brain. I suddenly . . . did not want to die. The water was shallow . . . but it was deep enough. Deep enough. Mike. I did not want to die," he said quietly. "So finally I managed to twist over onto my left side. Broke my rod. Slammed my bone badly. Barely . . . got out of it."

Mike looked over at this friend who had lost his fish, nearly ended it all. He had not one word to cheer him with. Brannigan was sitting in the same seat he'd been in when the accident smashed him, and there was a curious grin on his face. "Maybe we . . . really shouldn't go anymore, Billy," Mike said soberly. "Know what I mean?" He had hoped desperately that Brannigan would get one good trout, that this day might be a new beginning. He had for three years said everything he knew to say. He had no words left.

Faintly, as a slight pressure first and then a firm grip, Mike felt his friend's left hand on his shoulder. "No," he heard Brannigan say. And when he turned: "We're going . . . to keep going . . . back."

I. Getting Hooked

ROY ROWAN

"Man is a rope stretched between the animal and the Superman—a rope over an abyss."
—Friedrich Wilhelm Nietzsche (1844–1900)
Thus Spake Zarathustra

Anyone who has never battled a bull striper all alone on a beach may not understand the closeness it's possible to feel to a fish. The instinctual strand that can bind a human and an animal doesn't stem simply from the striper's enormous size. Or even from the fierceness of the fight coming from the other end of the line. The connection is more obscure, born out of a respect for a creature that has eluded net, spear, and hook for fifteen or even twenty years.

After the initial electrifying jolt—a strike so hard and unexpected the rod almost flies from your hands—comes a primordial message from your quarry, as clear and challenging as any emanating from a human mouth. Only this message is passed through the pulsating monfilament line, into your two hands, up through your arms and neck and directly into your brain. Its meaning, nevertheless, is brutally clear.

"You and I, Mr. Fisherman, though temporarily tied together, are engaged in a deadly duel of endurance that only one of us can win." Right away you're aware of the striper's vast capacity for courage and determined will to live, the same powers that propel people through a long and successful life.

The strange sensation of closeness felt with this fish is amplified by the fact that no other human is there to intrude on the battle. No fellow fisherman around to shout advice or encouragement. No beach walker strolling idly by to stop and watch if you win or lose. And most important of all, no tenderhearted preservationist present to suggest releasing your prize, if it's ever yours to let go.

As the big bass strips offline, swimming furiously to break free and spit out the unchewable plastic minnow hooked in its mouth, a single thought seizes your mind: "Can I stop this fish's surge before it snaps my line?" Carefully you tighten the drag, listening apprehensively for the staccato *pop* that would signal victory for the fish.

Your eyes are riveted on the spot in the flat sea out beyond the surf where the taut line slants down into the water. The surface around the line suddenly bulges, then erupts in a shower of spray. Striped bass don't usually jump. But for a few seconds this one hangs acrobatically in the air before splashing back into the water. You wonder if you and the fish are still connected—whether you're both still linked, physically and yes, mentally.

The answer comes quickly. An angry yank almost rips the rod from your grasp. You can feel the fish's rage. It, too, probably thought for those few instants while flying through the air that it was free.

At least you've glimpsed your prize—wide black stripes imprinted on a field of shiny silver scales. Old Linesides, as the species is nicknamed. The leap, however, seems to have strengthened the bass's resolve.

The rod butt is now digging painfully into your groin, your left hand cramped from cranking the reel without gaining line.

You shout tauntingly at the fish, "By God I've got you! You're mine, you sonofabitch!"

No reason to swear at this noble beast just because he's showing the same strength and fortitude we admire in our own. But the curse words pop out.

Once again the bass is zigging and zagging wildly through the water, still very much in control of the fight. It's the wide caudal fin, rooted in a muscular tail, that enables it to change direction and accelerate so rapidly.

Few other fish are capable of making lunges, leaps, runs like this. But then the inshore turbulence that most big fish avoid is where stripers are at home. It's their playground as well as their feeding ground. If you watch closely, sometimes you can actually see stripers frolicking in the rips and tides, and racing through the arcs of breaking waves. They may lack the sustained swiftness of sharks, tuna and other open-ocean predators, but their bodies are flexible, built for maneuverability and the short bursts of speed needed when searching out a meal close to shore.

Without warning the line goes slack and you're now sure that you've lost your prize. "Crank fast," you say. Dripping monofilament piles up on the reel until a heavy tug tells you your fish is still there.

"Move back. Take a few steps up onto the beach," you tell yourself. "Try to turn this big boy around before he empties your reel." But the fish stubbornly refuses to turn. The reel sings and all your regained line is gone.

It's not exactly sympathy for the fish, but there comes a moment of hesitation in the battle when you momentarily wonder if this gallant fighter doesn't deserve its freedom. Its extraordinary strength and valor have already given you a year's surfcasting excitement even though the close connection with it has only existed for a matter of minutes. It's the quest, not the

kill, that's the real reward in seeking to outwit a wild animal. Foxhunters thrill to the chase, not to shooting sly old Reynard once he's cornered.

These thoughts evaporate quickly. The taste of firm, mouthwatering fillets, grilled to perfection over a charcoal fire, replaces any generous, life-sparing feelings. Especially when you spot a dorsal fin slicing through the water like a knife, a signal that the big fish may finally be weakening and ready to surrender.

The trick now is to nudge it into a wave and let the force of the water wash the heavy body ashore. But it's still too game to come willingly. Instead, it bursts out of the water again, standing on its tail and shaking its head, resisting surrender.

Noticeably, though, strength is seeping from its body. Its zigs and zags are slower. And you can tell from the weaker pull on the line that it's probably too drained for another run or dive. But bass, like humans, can still generate an extraordinary exuberance when their lives are threatened.

Suddenly its surface thrashes pose other problems. Will the plug be ripped from its mouth? Will its sharp fins or tail slice the line? Even in its weakened state, you know that the odds favor the fish.

Just when you're wondering how to bring it in a heavy roller engulfs your prize and it disappears in the boiling surf, only to reemerge tumbling toward you in the shallows a few feet from shore.

Lying on its side, exhausted, the bass is even larger than you thought. Its head is huge, the size of a dog's. The green-spotted plug that it mistook for a mackerel protrudes from its mouth like a fat cigar. You wade out into the water and slip your hand under a gasping gill and drag the spent fish up onto the beach. The fight is finally won and the big striper is yours. But do you really want to destroy this magnificent creature?

At this moment it's impossible not to think of the frailty of life, and how it can be snatched away by a whim of weather, disease, or even by diabolical human nature. Holding life-or-death power over another creature is an enormous responsibility, especially when that creature is lying helpless at your feet awaiting your decision.

Fortunately for stripers big and small, it's a decision surfcasters don't often have to make. As one outdoor writer aptly put it, "The beauty of this form of angling is that it's possible to go for long periods of time without catching a fish." Or as another surfcasting aficionado admitted, "I go to fish. Not to catch fish." For me the joy of just being alone, surrounded by nature and immersed in my own thoughts, is the real reward of surfcasting. My deepest moments of understanding come unexpectedly when I'm communing with the sea, my mind dwelling on life's many mysteries.

For this reason angling enthusiasts from the days of Izaak Walton have claimed that fishing is not simply a sport, but a religion. If this is so then surfcasting, with its own devout followers, should be recognized as an important sect.

Our morning devotions begin at daybreak in the great high-domed cathedral where the fading stars and ghostly glow of last night's moon are the candles soon to be extinguished. But before the sun's fireball rises out of the sea and sets everything ablaze, we surfcasters breathe in the new day's coolness and contemplate the good fortune that has brought us to the ocean's edge.

It is only after such a moment of reverence that our ritual begins. Almost mindlessly we check the grip of our waders on the slippery stones underfoot, open the wire bail of the spinning reel, whip the long fiberglass rod forward, and send a shiny lure affixed to the free-spooling monofilament flying off to kiss a wave.

Barely has the lure hit the water than in our mind's eye we can see the silvery flash and flying spray of a striper or blue striking the plug. It's the excitement of a strike that keeps us repeating cast after cast, although deep in our subconscious we know almost every wave

is empty—devoid of fish, or at best containing one that has already feasted on so many menhaden or sand eels, its appetite is sated.

That is why the high priests of our sect who have written such how-to tomes on surfcasting as *The Salt-Water Fishman's Bible* preach infinite patience. They realize there are many more productive ways of fishing.

Trolling or jigging from a boat begets more blues, bass, and bonito—even an occasional weakfish, as the beautiful speckled sea trout are called in the Northeast. Bottom fishing off a dock or jetty can yield a mess of blacks, fluke, or flounder.

But then surfcasters are not usually out there foraging for food. Most of us are more meditative than we are meat fishermen.[1] We are made happy by the mere motion that sends our plug arcing through the air, and by watching expectantly as it skips back over the wave tops.

"Hit!" we murmur. "Hit!" This little word is our mind-numbing mantra. It doesn't matter that almost every cast is fruitless, completed without a hit.

Skunked is one of the most common words in the surfcaster's vocabulary. Only in recent years have I discovered that the solitude that goes with being skunked is catching—though in a different way than the catching of fish. No telling what deeply suppressed thoughts or secrets of nature will tug at my mind on those days when I'm swinging that rod back and forth without a strike.

Waves, especially, stir my imagination. On windy days with the sea slapping hard against my waders I sometimes wonder where they came from. Did they originate on the shore of some far-off continent thousands of miles of ocean away from where I'm casting? The idea of the kinetic energy in a wave traveling so far before it is dissipated by hitting my body conjures up unsettling thoughts of a personal connection with the universe that is always mystifying.

[1]　My use of the term fishermen, rather than fisherpersons, is intended to include both male and female anglers.

Clouds, too, catch my attention, but in a more reassuring way. With fish on the brain it's not surprising that so many clouds take on a piscine appearance. Sometimes it's a mackerel sky, resembling the mottled back of that species, which strikes me as a sign of good luck. More propitious are the long, strung-out cumulus formations in which I can distinctly make out the broad tail, eyes, nose, and underslung jaw of the striper I'm hoping to catch. Instinctively I sense that these cloud-stripers swimming across the sky are a good omen, indicating the imminence of a strike.

Surfcasting can induce a kind of coma, erasing all thoughts about nature—and everything else for that matter—while keeping the brain in neutral. In this blank state of mind, if some simple physical diversion is required, I'll engage in a little contest with myself by trying to cast farther and farther out to sea.

We surfcasters assume that as in life, the big fish are just beyond our reach, which usually is not the case. Bass, in fact, cruise so close to shore they often resist lunging at a lure until the final few yards of a retrieve.

And even if they all spurn my plug, sensing it's indeed a fake fish, this doesn't stop me from going out again the next day.

Of course the thrill of marching home with a fat bluefish or gorgeous striper in hand is not to be lightly dismissed. The hunter's triumphant return is a familiar scene in history, recorded all the way back in the earliest cave paintings. But for me bringing home a fish is simply a bonus. The solitude of surfcasting is my main enjoyment—to be savored like a fine wine or a fragrant flower.

Roy Rowan was a foreign correspondent, writer, and editor for *Time, Life,* and *Fortune* for thirty-five years. He is the author of eight books including the critically acclaimed *Chasing the Dragon,* a memoir about Mao's revolution that has been optioned by Hollywood, and *First Dogs,* which was made into a documentary and aired on the Discovery Channel. His latest book, published in 2006, is *Throwing Bullets: A Tale of Two Pitchers Chasing the Dream.*

J. The Shanty

JERRY GIBBS

The ice was dead gray. It stretched as far as you could see looking north up the big, ragged lake. Snow that had once brightened the surface had melted into hills of slush or two-inch-deep sheets of water that the wind riffled passing through. Beneath the water the ice showed bleakly. It was still safe, still over a foot thick, far from the blackness that would herald its final rottenness.

At the access parking lot stood remnants of a once-bustling ice-fishing village, shanties that had been hastily pulled during the thaws to prevent them being locked in when the weather turned again. The few ice houses still on the lake were owned by hard-core regulars who would fish them daily or nightly keeping watch on the weather.

It was the worst time of year in the North Country. Roads crumbled or turned to mud. Shrinking snow revealed mounds of preserved winter litter. Trees stood exhausted and bare. The crows had returned, though, and their sharp rasping knifed across the woodland valleys. You could say it was spring, the way it is spring in the North.

The two men and the big black Labrador retriever were 50 yards out heading south on the ice toward a long point guarding the entrance to a bay. The dog ran ahead, quartering, returning to check. Its owner, Bud Tuttle, pulled the sled that carried most of their equipment. The dog was very happy.

"Ought to harness your energy, foolish dog," Tuttle told the Lab. "This sled is getting waterlogged and heavy."

"Let me haul it for awhile," the other man said. He was a little shorter, but broader than Bud. His name was Earl Waite. The two were old friends who had not seen one another for some time.

"Nah," Bud told him. "I only let friends haul coming back—when I'm beat from digging holes."

"Right," Earl laughed.

Far off the point were several ice fishermen. Some had set out tip-ups but most worked short jigging rods or sticks for yellow perch.

"Don't know why they keep fishing out that far," Bud Tuttle said. "Those schools of yellows are moving in here by now. Those fish want deeper water they can find it off the point. Then it shallows fast soon as you get to the bay mouth. Course there's a better chance at a passing trout or salmon outside, but I pick up trout right at the drop, too."

Around the point, not far from it, stood a fragile shanty of wood framing and black roofing paper. "Look at that shack," Bud continued. "That's old René Tatro's. He's in there most all the time day or night. Anybody catches fish through a hole in the ice, it's him."

They sloshed a little way on without talking, then Earl said, "I haven't had a good perch feed in so long, almost forgot how they taste."

"Should get them," Bud said.

Earl took the auger and started the first hole. Bud set a jig rod and a Styrofoam cup of live maggot bait near the drilling, then dragged the sled through the slush-water angling toward the point. The dog splashed ahead like a spring colt. The first hole done, Earl walked over and the two men grabbed the auger together, alternating grips along the handle to cut the second hole fast. Then Earl returned to the first hole. He freed the hookless attractor spoon and ice flies secured to the jig rod guides and baited the fly hooks. He sent the silver spoon followed by the flies on droppers above it down the hole, found bottom and cranked up a few turns.

"Work from the bottom up, you never know where you'll hit them," Bud called over. "I'll be in a little deeper water here."

"You using the same rig?"

"I put on one of those Rapala jigs—you know, the things that swim around in little circles. Never can tell when a stray trout or pike might eat. I got the flies on above it."

It was quiet across the lake, then came the floating strains of a song sung in a dry, cracking voice.

"Who's singing?" Earl called over.

"That'll be old René in his shack," Bud laughed. "All the time he spends in there, guess he gets lonely. Keeps a bottle a rum for company. If he gets really tuned we'll have some music."

The first holes produced nothing and the two moved just off the point, drilling at new spots, Earl farther out, Bud closer in. Strains of a song in Quebec French came across to them from the shanty.

"He hasn't got started," Bud said. "You'll see. He switches back to English sometimes."

The dog appeared around the corner of the musical shanty, snuffling its edges.

"Ace, get over here," Bud yelled. The dog came up panting, nuzzled Tuttle's leg. "Good boy." He rubbed the dog's ears. "You leave the old man's shack alone, hear." Then he straightened. "Old Tatro's got a smelt system in there. Got a whole long trench he keeps open; a bunch of fishing lines spaced along it on a rack. Lines come off little wood spools, go through open brackets. Fish hits, he just plucks the line off, hand-over-hands it in unless it's a big one. They use the same thing up to the St. Lawrence fishing Tommy cod. Slick as owl dung in the rain. He won't get smelt now, though. Perch are just fine with him, too."

"Sounds like a production line," Earl said.

"He catches 'em, old geezer. I worry one day he'll slip through that trench after enough a that rum."

Earl counted offline in two-foot pulls. "It's deep," he said to himself. He cranked up until he figured he was at 15 feet. Overhead, streaks of thin clouds backed by a high, gray dome gave the sky the look of cool, polished tombstone. Far to the north the lake was empty. It seemed a very lonely place and Earl was glad he had company.

After a time, his second hole producing nothing, Earl started in. Bud had done no better. With Ace leading they headed around the point to the bay side closer to the old man's shanty. The black and gray shack sagged toward the left. "He builds it up new every year," Bud said. "It's not the strongest thing."

They drilled new holes inside the drop edge where the bottom rose from 40 to 18 feet. They drilled closer together, more for company than any insight into fish location.

René's shanty had been quiet for some time. Suddenly the old man's disembodied voice boomed across the ice. He sang in English this time, high in his nose in grand country fashion. First something about Texas ladies, then he segued into ". . . 90 miles an hour down a dead-end road . . . you gotta be bad to have a good time. . . ." It was all delightfully incongruous for the time and place. Then Earl felt a peck and he struck with the jig rod.

He used the tip of the rod and his non-rod hand in a kind of alternating cat's cradle to pick up line and bring the fish in. He dropped the monofilament on the ice, the perch following.

"Nice," he said, "nice perch."

The fish was fat, gleaming brassy-gold, its black vertical bars vivid. It splayed its sharp-pointed gill covers, arched its spiny dorsal. Earl brought it to the bucket on the sled.

Hearing excitement Ace trotted back from one of his circuits, coming up just as a fish hit Bud's rig. "Just a couple feet off bottom," he said happily.

"That's where mine hit."

The dog danced, lunged for Bud's fish. "Ace, back!" Tuttle ordered. The dog backed reluctantly, wanting the fish. "You'll get fin-pricked," Bud grumbled affectionately, "not to mention slobbering dinner."

They took two more fish each but it was not fast and they spread out, drilling new holes, looking for the main school. They tried shallower, drilling a hole line, then moved out on the drop again and here they hit the school.

The fish were so tightly concentrated that holes a couple of yards apart meant the difference between an occasional fish or rapid action. They ended with four holes drilled in a cluster, alternating between them as one cooled and another became productive.

In his shack old René started in again singing " . . . we got winners we got losers, we got bikers we got

truckers . . . an' the girls next door dress up like movie stars . . . I love this bar, I love this bar. . . ."

"He's getting there," Bud laughed.

"So are we," Earl said sticking another fish.

"Let's string out these holes and connect them," Bud said. "Make a trench like old René's so we can keep moving right on top of the fish."

They augered new holes, connected the old ones. Then Bud grabbed the long steel ice spud from his sled and widened the slot. The opening was a long, rough rectangle.

Ace stayed with them now, feinting at each new fish, whining happily. Over in his shack René had launched into a sad-sweet ballad in Quebec French. Two crows circled overhead eyeballing for scrap bait. Just then Bud struck but this time his little jigging rod bowed over, line tearing from, the reel with a soft zipping sound. "No perch!" he yelled.

Quickly Earl reeled in, ran over. The fish finished its first run and Bud was getting line back now, reeling smoothly. Then the fish went again. It was a shorter run but deeper, and when the fish was turned it came only a little way before going a third time, this run toward the point and just beneath the ice. Bud thrust his rod half down into the trench. "He's awfully close to the top. He'll cut me off on the ice edge if I let him."

Ace danced close, tail wagging, excited as the men.

"I got him coming," Bud said. He reeled faster now, gaining line. Then they saw the fish.

"Trout! Nice rainbow," Earl said. He raced for the sled. "You got a net?"

"Ah, no," Bud said worriedly. The fish was at the surface. It thrashed, showering Bud on his knees, reaching for it. Then it ran again forcing him to punch the rod into the trench.

"I have heavy line," Bud said. "If I can get him to hold on top a second I can scoop him with one hand, just swing him over."

The fish came. It lay on the surface, Bud holding it with raised rod, reaching under its belly with his other hand, scooping it, the fish arcing brightly through the air to the ice, gleaming, bold magenta stripe on its side. It arched its body, hard muscles lifting it from the ice. Earl grabbed it but instantly it slipped away. The fish spun on the ice, flopped, and Ace was on it but not fast enough. The rainbow's last effort took it from between the dog's feet back into the trench, the Lab after it, hitting the frigid water, diving.

"Ace!" Bud bellowed. He pounded with his boot heel on the ice. Earl jabbed his own jig rod under, searching. Bud ran to the sled, came back with the ice sieve, dropped to his belly. His arm up to the shoulder in the water, Bud swung the sieve in wide circles under water searching frantically for the dog.

"Ace, Ace!" he called. "Oh the damned, stupid . . ." He rolled over on the ice, his hand gone angry red. "I can't hold onto this scoop."

"Here give it to me." Earl grabbed the sieve. He was down now scooping at the other end of the wide trench.

A scream sliced the air. They saw René's shanty rock once before one black paper wall exploded, flimsy framing splintering, spewing the old man in green suspenders and baggy wool trousers. His white hair flared in ragged streamers, his eyes rolled madly and from his sunken cavern-dark mouth came a wavering, tortured wail. René Tatro hit the ice running. He slipped to all fours, regained his feet, staggering for shore, not seeing the anglers, not seeing anything now but the safety of shore.

"La bête . . . sauvage!" he screamed, "the beast, the beast!"

He reached the shore, crashed into the woods. The two anglers were running now, heading for the destroyed shanty, reaching it, staring in. Inside was a shambles. Tackle was strewn everywhere. A half-filled can of corn had scattered kernels like confetti. Bits of lunch joined the yellow niblets. An empty rum bottle lay on its side. And in the middle of it all was Ace, tail beating as he wolfed down everything edible.

"Ace you fool!" Bud told the dog. "Come here." The dog even gave up eating to come. Bud grabbed the Lab around the shoulders and Ace shook his hindquarters showering both men.

"Can't believe this," Earl said.

"Oh yeah, it's real. Look at that setup. Ace must have boiled right up the middle of René's ice trench looking like the devil himself."

They both began laughing. They sat in the debris and could not stop laughing.

"That poor geezer. If he didn't think it was old Ned he likely thought it was the lake monster we're supposed to have," Bud said wiping tears from his eyes.

"Oh, I remember that—like the one in Loch Ness," Earl said.

"Ace you are a monster all right. Nothing's hurt with the fishing setup anyway," Bud pointed. "But the shack's sure finished."

"I'm shutting down this stove," Earl said. Ace squirmed to get back at the food.

"No more, you. You've done enough for the day," Bud told the dog. "I'm gonna call poor René. He won't believe me. Maybe I shouldn't tell him the truth. I bet he goes on the wagon for a while. Got to fix his shack for him. I wonder if I can ever get him back on the ice again."

"We better get out of here before we freeze," Earl said. "I'm starting to feel it."

"Same here. I think my arm's frozen," Bud said.

They staggered to the sled, started back fast toward the access, looking at one another, beginning to laugh again so hard that walking became difficult. The dog ran in front pleased with it all.

Finally Earl said, "You know, along with everything we have enough fish for supper."

"Good thing," Bud told him. "Nobody'll believe the rest."

Overhead along the shoreline two crows headed north into the silence of spring.

K. A Camp on the Neversink

JAY CASSELL

James waded slowly into the fast water below Denton Falls, eyeing the pool carefully. When he found a spot where he could stand without slipping, he pulled line off his flyreel and began his backcast. In less time that it takes to say "Neversink Skater," he had snagged his Adams in a branch right behind him. Muttering, he looked over at me, angrily, "I give up," he said. "I can't stand flyfishing."

I wasn't surprised at his reaction. For a kid who was brought up fishing plastic worms and spinnerbaits for bass, trying to switch over to flyfishing is tough. The fact that he was a teenager with zero patience didn't help. But he thought it over, changed his mind, and pretty soon was back at it, trying to cast into the trout pools just below the falls.

Up above the white water, we heard James' buddy, Dave, whooping and hollering. "Got another one," he yelled. "This place is amazing." I could see a dark, gloomy cloud beginning to form over James' head. With a shrug, I turned and started hiking downstream. Rounding the bend, I spied a trout rising to caddisflies in the middle of a long pool. I forgot about the boys, and immersed myself in my own fishing.

The boys had worked for their reward of fishing the river. We were at our hunting and fishing camp, "The Over The Hill Gang," located about a mile from the Neversink Gorge, on land owned by Benjamin Wechsler. Wechsler, who has owned a huge chunk of property, including the Neversink Gorge, since 1968, is one of those rare individuals who actually gets it, who knows how to manage private property correctly. His land is just a "small," couple-thousand-acre parcel in the 100,000 acres of Catskill wilderness that sprawls from the Bashakill Wildlife Refuge to the east, to the Mongaup River Valley to the west. Through his good graces, our camp has survived, first on the east side of the Neversink, and now at its current location on a ridgetop to the west, on the Denton Falls Road.

I had brought the boys up for the club's annual summer work weekend. The deal was that they could fish at the end of the day, so long as they pitched in and helped with the work. And they had, sweeping out the cabin, picking up pieces of wood, twigs and branches from a recent windstorm, stacking firewood . . . anything they could do.

While the boys were hard at it, the rest of us busied ourselves with the chores that must be done to keep a sporting club functioning. Dan Gibson, his 21-year-old son Keith, and I unhitched the splitter from my truck and started splitting the logs we had piled up earlier in the summer. Kevin Kenney, the 40-year-old son of the camp's founder, Jerry, was down the road about a quarter mile, chain sawing a black cherry that had come down in a late-spring windstorm. Last hunting season was an especially cold one, with temperatures consistently below 20°. We came close to running out of wood for our two woodstoves—one in the kitchen, the other in the bunkroom—so we were making doubly certain that we had enough for the upcoming season.

While all this was going on, Vin Sparano was out behind the cabin, installing a new floor in the outhouse. Every couple of years, the local porcupine population decides it's time to feast on our outhouse, and then we have to rebuild it. It's an ongoing battle, with us staying about one step ahead of the always-hungry porkies. Rod Cochran, out in front, was replacing rotted planks on the front deck, while Matt had grabbed a bucket of paint and was touching up the cabin's trim.

When Ken Surerus and his son, Raymond, showed up, they pitched in with the firewood, stacking the logs that Dan, Keith, and I had been splitting.

By the end of the day, the old camp—it was built in the 1950s—was in pretty good shape. A new American flag was up on the roof, all of the weeds and brush around the building had been cut back, and the inside had been swept clean. By summer's end, we'd all be back again, sighting in our rifles and doing last-minute chores such as getting the propane tank filled and stocking up the kitchen with food for hunting season. Eventually, the roof will have to be replaced. It leaks like crazy in the bunkroom, and we're getting tired of putting new blue tarps on it every year. And the eclectic mixture of tarpaper and multi-colored shingles on the exterior is starting to fall off. But the repairs will be made, because they're important. It's good work.

Author Rick Bass, who wrote *The Deer Pasture*, once said this about his hunting camp: "For a place we visit only one week out of the year, we worry about it far too much."

That's the way the guys in my camp feel. We think about that place a lot. We do go there more than one week a year, of course; there's turkey season in May, trout and smallmouth fishing in the Neversink from mid-April to the end of September, plus deer season in November—but we'd all go there more often if we could. It's tough to explain, but a good sporting camp becomes a part of you. The years go by, and members come and go, but you come to realize that part of you is always in camp, cooking up venison stew in the kitchen, debating guns and loads or flies and leaders with your colleagues, or playing poker until the wee hours of the morning. I don't see even most of the guys during the year except at camp, but that doesn't matter. When I do see them, we just pick up where we left off last time. The camp has a life of its own, with a pulse that keeps beating from year to year, generation to generation. So you bring the youngsters along and teach them about the woods, you take them down to the river and teach them flycasting, and you show them the types of pools and riffles where the brown trout like to lie. (James, by the way, did not catch a thing that day, but he did later in the season!) And when they get old enough, you let them into the camp as full members, sharing in the work, in the fun, in the good times and, when they happen, the tough times too.

Work weekend—it's the beginning of another cycle of seasons. Before you know it, it'll be opening day of deer season and I'll be in my treestand overlooking the Neversink. Then, in May, I'll be out the woods well before dawn, hoping to find a gobbler. At noon, I'll come back to camp, change out of my hunting clothes and put on my flyvest and waders, and hike down to the river to see if the Hendricksons are hatching in the pools below Denton Falls. And life will be as good as it possibly can be.

L. The Primitive Fish-Hook

BARNET PHILLIPS

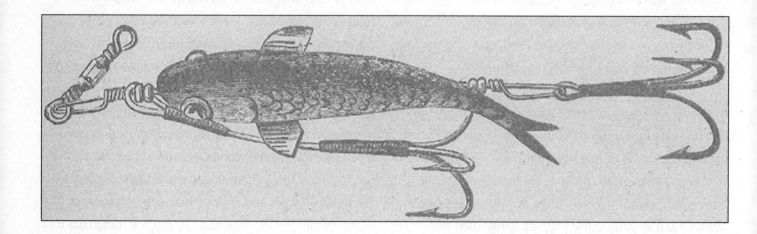

I have before me an illustrated catalogue of modern fish-hooks and angling implements, and in looking over its pages I find an *embarrass de choix*. I have no need for rods, for mine, like well-kept violins, have rather improved by age. A lashing may be frayed, or a ferrule loose, but fifteen minutes' pleasant work will make my rods all right again. Lines are sound, for I have carefully stretched them after use. But my hooks! They are certainly the worse for wear. I began my season's fishing with a meager stock. Friends borrowed from me, and in replenishing my fly-book in an out-of-the-way place, the purchase was unsatisfactory. As I lost more than one fish from badly tempered or worse fashioned hooks, I recalled a delightful paper by Mr. Froude. Rod in hand, he was whipping some pleasant trout stream, near an historic site, the home of the Russells, and, breaking his hooks, commenced from that very moment to indulge in the gloomiest forebodings as to the future of England.

Fairly familiar with the general character of fishing-gear, either for business or amusement, I see in my book, Kirby, Limerick, Dublin, O'Shaughnessy, Kinsey, Carlisle, Harrison, Central Draught, as somewhat distant families of hooks, used for sea or river fishing, and from these main stocks there grow many varieties, with all conceivable twists, quirls, and crookednesses. I discard all trap-hooks, infernal machines working with springs, as only adapted for the capture of land animals. Somehow I remember an aggressive book, given to me at an early age, which, containing more than one depressing passage, had one of extraordinary malevolence. This was couched nearly as follows: "Suppose you were translated only some seven hundred years back, then, pray, what would you be good for? Could you make gunpowder? You have, perhaps, a vague idea that sulfur, saltpeter, and charcoal are the component parts, but do you know where or how they are procured?" I forget whether this dispiriting author was not equally harrowing in regard to the youthful reader's turning off a spectroscope at a minute's notice, or wound up with the modest request that you should try your hand among the Crusaders with an aneroid barometer of your own special manufacture.

Still this question arises: Suppose you were famishing, though fish were plenty in a stream, and you had neither line nor hook, What would you do? Now, has a condition of this kind ever occurred? Yes, it has, and certainly thousands of times. Not so many years ago, the early surveyors of the Panama route suffered terrible privations from the want of fishing implements. The rains had rendered their powder worthless; they could not use their guns. Had they only been provided with hooks and lines, they could have subsisted on fish. Then there are circumstances under which it would be really necessary for a man to be somewhat of a Jack-of-all-trades, and to be able to fashion the implements he might require, and so this crabbed old book might, after all, act in the guise of a useful reminder. There was certainly a period, when every man was in a condition of comparative helplessness, when his existence depended on his proficiency in making such implements as would catch fish or kill animals. He must fashion hooks or something else to take fish with, or die.

Probably man, in the first stage of his existence, took much of his food from the water, although whether he did or not might depend upon locality. If on certain portions of the earth's surface there were stretches of land intersected by rivers, dotted by lakes, or bordering on the seas, the presence of shell-fish, the invertebrates or the vertebrates, cetaceans and fish, to the exclusion of land animals, might have rendered primitive man icthyophagous, or dependent for subsistence upon the art of fishing. But herein we grapple at once with that most abstruse of all problems, the procession of life. Still, it is natural to suppose, so far as the study of man goes, when considered in relation to his pursuits, that in the early dawn of humanity, mammals, birds, and fish must have been synchronous.

After brute instinct, which is imitativeness, then came shiftiness and adaptiveness. The rapid stride of civilization, considered in its material sense, is due solely to the use of such implements as are specially adapted for a particular kind of work. With primitive man, this could never have been the case. Tools of the Paleolithic or Neolithic age (which terms indicate stages of civilization, but are not chronological), whether they were axes, hammers, or arrows, must have served river-drift or cave-men for more than a single purpose. People with few tools do manage by skill alone to adapt these to a variety of ends. The Fijian and the Russian peasant, one with a stone adze, the other with a hatchet, bring to their trades the minimum of tools. The Kafir, with his assegai, fights his battles, kills cattle, carves his spoons, and shaves himself. It was only as man advanced that he devised special tools for different purposes.

According to our present acquaintance with primitive habits, if man existed in the later Miocene age, and used a lance or spear for the killing of land animals, he probably employed the same weapons for the destruction of the creatures—possibly of gigantic form—inhabiting the seas, lakes, and rivers. The presence of harpoons made of bone, found in so many localities, belonging to a later period, may not in all cases point to the existence of animals, but to the presence of large fish.

Following, then, closely the advance of man, when his fishing implements are particularly considered, we are inclined to believe that he first used the spear for taking fish; next, the hook and line; and, lastly, the net. There might have been an intermediate stage between the spear and the hook, when the bow and arrow were used.

Interesting as is the whole subject of primitive fishing, we are, however, to occupy ourselves principally with the form of the primitive fish-hook. To-day, there are some careful archaeologists who are not willing to accept that particular form which is presented below. I believe, from the many reasons which can be advanced, that this simple form was the first device used by man in taking fish with a line. The argument I shall use is in some respects a novel one.

These illustrations, exactly copied to size, represent a small piece of dark, polished stone. It was found in the valley of the Somme, in France, and was dug out

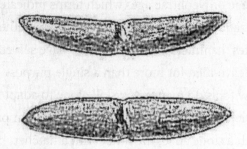

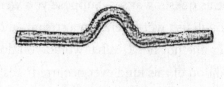

of a peat-bed twenty-two feet below the surface. The age of this peat-bed has been variously estimated. M. Boucher de Perthes thought that thirty thousand years must have elapsed since the lowest layer of peat was formed. The late Sir Charles Lyell and Sir John Lubbock, without too strict an adherence to date, believed that this peat-bed represented in its formation "that vast lapse of time which began with the commencement of the Neolithic period." Later authorities deem it not older than seven thousand years B. C.

Wonderful changes have come to pass since this bit of polished stone was lost in what must have been a lake. Examining this piece of worked stone, which once belonged to a prehistoric man living in that valley, we find it fairly well polished, though the action of countless years has slightly "weathered" or disintegrated its once smooth surface. In the center, a groove has been cut, and the ends of the stone rise slightly from the middle. It is rather crescent-shaped. It must have been tied to a line, and this stone gorge was covered with a bait; the fish swallowed it, and, the gorge coming crosswise with the gullet, the fish was captured.

The evolution of any present form of implement from an older one is often more cleverly specious than logically conclusive; nevertheless, I believe that, in this case, starting with the crude fish-gorge, I can show, step by step, the complete sequence of the fish-hook, until it ends with the perfected hook of to-day. It can be insisted upon even that there is persistence of form in the descendants of this fish-gorge, for, as Professor Mitchell writes in his "Past in the Present," "an old art may long refuse to disappear wholly, even in the midst of conditions which seem to be necessarily fatal to its continued existence."

In the Swiss lakes are found the remains of the Lacustrine dwellers. Among the many implements discovered are fish-gorges made of bronze wire. When these forms are studied, the fact must be recognized at once that they follow, in shape and principle of construction, the stone gorges of the Neolithic period. Now, it is perfectly well known that the early bronze-worker invariably followed the stone patterns. The Lacustrine gorges have had the name of bricole given them. This is a faithful copy of a bronze bricole found in the Lake of Neufchatel. It is made of bronze wire, and is bent in the simplest way, with an open curve allowing the line to be fastened to it. The ends of the gorge are very slightly bent, but they were probably sharpened when first made.

This bricole varies from the rather straight one found in the Lake of Neufchatel, and belongs to a later period. It is possible to imagine that the lake- dweller, according to his pleasure, made one or the other of these two forms of fishing implements. As the double hook required more bronze, and bronze at first was very precious, he might not have had material enough in the early period to make it. This device is, however, a clever one, for a fisherman of to-day who had lost his hook

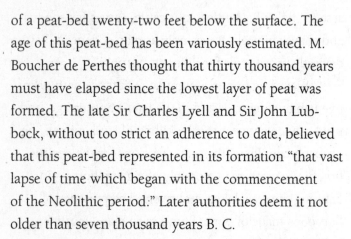

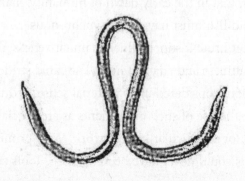

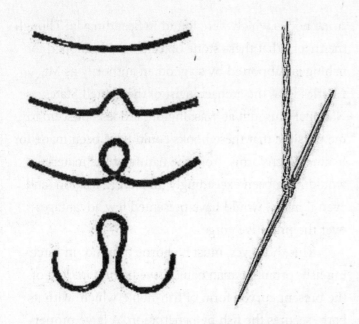

might imitate it with a bit of wire. Had any member of the hungry Isthmus party before mentioned known this form of Lacustrine hook, he might have twisted some part of a suspender buckle, providing there were no thorny plants at hand, and have caught fish.

When we compare the four forms, showing only their outlines, the evolution of the fish-hook can be better appreciated. Returning to the stone fish-gorge, the work of the Neolithic period, it is evident that the man of that time followed the shape handed down to him by his ancestors; and as this fashioned stone from the valley of the Somme is of a most remote period, how much older must have been the Paleolithic fish-gorge of rough stone. It might have been with a splinter of flint attached to some tendril, in lieu of a line, that the first fish was taken.

It is very curious to learn that in France a modification of this gorge-hook is in use to-day for catching eels. A needle is sharpened at its eye-end, a slight groove is made in the middle of it, and around this some shreds of flax are attached. A worm is spitted, a little of the line being covered with the bait.

Not eels alone are taken with this needle, for M. de la Blanchere informs us that many kinds of fish are caught with it in France.

Any doubts as to the use of the Neolithic form of fish-gorge must be removed when it can be insisted upon that precisely this form of implement was in use by our Indians not more than forty years ago. In 1878, when studying this question of the primitive hook, I was fortunate enough to receive direct testimony on the subject. My informant, who in his younger days had lived among the Indians at the head-waters of Lake Superior, said that in 1846 the Indians used a gorge made of bone to catch their fish. My authority, who had never seen a prehistoric fish-gorge, save the drawing of one, said that the Indian form was precisely like the early shape, and that the Chippewas fished some with the hook of civilization, others with bone gorges of a primitive period.

In tracing the history of the fish-hook, it should be borne in mind that an overlapping of periods must have taken place. By this is meant, that at one and the same time an individual employed tools or weapons of various periods. To-day, the Western hunter lights his fire with a match. This splinter of wood, tipped with phosphorus, the chlorates, sulfur, or paraffin, represents the progress made in chemistry from the time of the alchemists. But this trapper is sure to have stowed away in his pouch, ready for an emergency, his flint and steel. The Esquimau, the Alaskan, shoots his seal with an American repeating rifle, and, in lieu of a knife, flays the creature with a flint splinter. The net of the Norseman is to-day sunk with stones or buoyed with wood,—certainly the same devices as were used by the early Scandinavian,—while the net, so far as the making of the thread goes, is due to the best mod-

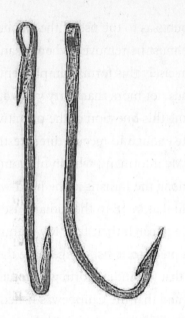

ern mechanical appliances. Survival of forms requires some consideration apart from that of material, the first having the much stronger reasons for persistence. It is, then, very curious to note that hooks not made of iron and steel, but of bronze, or alloys of copper, are still in use on the coast of Finland, as I have quite recently obtained brass hooks from Northern Europe such as are commonly in use by fishermen there.

The origin of the double hook having been, I believe, satisfactorily explained, to make the barb on it was readily suggested to primitive man, as he had used the same device on fish-spears and harpoons.

This double-barbed hook from the Swiss lakes is quite common. Then, from the double to the single hook the transition was rapid. Single bronze hooks of the Lacustrine period sometimes have no barb. Such differences as exist are due to the various methods of attaching the line.

In Professor A. M. Mayer's collection there is a Lacustrine bronze hook, the shank of which is bent over parallel with the stem of the hook. This hook is a large one, and must have been used for big fish—probably the trout of the Swiss lakes.

Hooks made of stone are exceedingly rare, and though it is barely possible that they might have been used for fish, I think this has not been conclusively shown. Wilson gives, in his work, drawings of two

stone hooks which were found in Scandinavia. Though the theory that these stone objects were fashioned for fishing is supported by so good an authority as Mr. Charles Rau, the archaeologist of the United States National Museum at Washington, it does not seem to me possible that these hooks could have been made for fishing. Such forms, from the nature of the material, would have been exceedingly difficult to fashion, and, even if made, would have presented few advantages over the primitive gorge.

This, however, must be borne in mind: in catching fish, primitive man could have had no inkling of the present curved form of fish-hook, which, with its barb, secures the fish by penetration. A large proportion of sea-fish, and many river-fish, swallow the hook, and are caught, not by the hook entering the jaws of the fish, but because it is fastened in their stomachs. In the Gloucester fisherman's language of to-day, a fish so captured is called "poke-hooked"; and accordingly, when the representative of the Neolithic period fished in that lake in the valley of the Somme, all the fish he took must have been poke-hooked. A bone hook, excellent in form, has been found near the remains of a huge species of pike (*Esox*). Hooks made of the tusks of

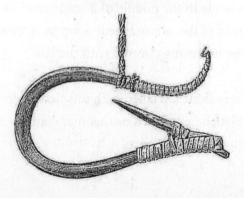

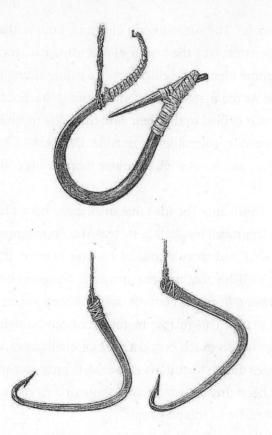

In the drawing, the halibut-hook hangs but slightly inclining toward the sea-bottom, the weight of the bait having a tendency to lower it. In this position it can be readily taken by the fish; but should it be suspended in a different way, it must be at once seen how difficult it would be for the fish to swallow it. In this Alaskan hook must be recognized the very first idea of what we call to-day the center-draught hook. A drawing is also given of a steel hook of a peculiar form coming from Northern Russia. The resemblance between the Alaskan and this Russian hook is at first apparently slight, but they both are, nevertheless, constructed on the same principle. When this Russian hook is seized by the fish, and force is applied to the line by the fisherman, the point of the barb and the line are almost in one and the same direction. Almost the same may be said of the Alaskan hook. Desirous of testing the capabilities of this hook, I had a gross made after the Russian model, and sent them to Captain J. W. Collins, of the United States Fish Commission, stationed at Gloucester, requesting him to distribute them among the fishermen. While

the wild boar have also been discovered with Lacustrine remains.

In commenting on the large size of the bone hook figured in Wilson's work, its proximity to the remains of large fish was noticed. When the endless varieties of hooks belonging to savage races are subjects of discussion, the kind of fish they serve for catching should always be cited. In the examples of hooks which illustrate works of travel, a good many errors arise from the simple fact that the writers are not fishermen. Although the outline of a hook be accurately given, the method of securing it to the line is often incorrectly drawn.

In the engraving on this page, an Alaskan halibut-hook is represented.

The form is a common one, and is used by all the savage races of the Pacific; but the main interest lay in the manner of tying the line to this hook. Since the fish to be caught was the halibut, the form was the best adapted to the taking of the *Hippoglossus Americanus*; but had the line been attached in any other way than exactly as represented, this big fish could hardly have been caught with such a hook.

writing this article, I am in receipt of a letter from Captain Collins, informing me that these hooks are excellent, the captains of fishing-smacks reporting that a great many deep-sea fish were taken with them.

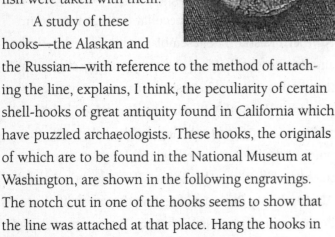

A study of these hooks—the Alaskan and the Russian—with reference to the method of attaching the line, explains, I think, the peculiarity of certain shell-hooks of great antiquity found in California which have puzzled archaeologists. These hooks, the originals of which are to be found in the National Museum at Washington, are shown in the following engravings. The notch cut in one of the hooks seems to show that the line was attached at that place. Hang the hooks in any other position and they would catch no fish, for one could hardly suppose that the blunt barb could penetrate the mouth of the fish.

If there be some doubt entertained by American archaeologists as to the use of these shell-hooks, there can be none in regard to their having barbs. The barbs turn outward, in which respect they differ from all the primitive European hooks I have seen. In confirmation of the idea advanced as to the proper place of attaching the line, Professors C. C. Abbott and F. W. Putnam, in a chapter entitled "Implements and Weapons made of Bone and Wood," in the United States Geographical Survey, west of the hundredth meridian, write, referring to these hooks: "These hooks are flattened and are longer than wide . . . The barbs in these specimens are judged by fishermen of to-day to be on the wrong side of a good fish-hook, and the point is too near the shank. By having the line so fastened that the point of tension is at the notch at the base of the shank, instead of at the extreme end of the stem, the defect of the design of the hook would be somewhat remedied, as the barb would be forced down, so that it might possibly catch itself in the lower jaw of the fish that had taken

the hook." The summing up of this is, I think, that in an imperfect way the maker of this Santa Barbara hook had some idea of the efficiency of a center-draught hook. As the first step in manufacturing this hook, a hole was drilled in the shell, and the hook finished up afterward by rounding the outside. Dr. West, of Brooklyn, has a series of such primitive work in his collection.

To advance the idea that in all cases hooks have been improved by slightly increased culture among semi-civilized races would be a source of error. It is quite possible that in many instances there has been retrogression from the better forms of fishing implements once in use. This relapse might have been brought about, not so much by a decrease of intelligence, as changes due to fortuitous causes. A fishing race might have been driven away from a shore or a river-bank and replaced by an inland people.

Some primitive races still use a hook made from a thorn, and in this practice we find to-day a most wonderful survival. On the coast of France, hooks made of thorns are still used to catch fish, the fishermen representing that they possess the great advantage of costing nothing and of not fouling on the sea-bottom. The Piutes take the spine of a cactus, bending it to suit their purpose, and very simple barbless hooks of this kind may be seen in the collections of the National Museum at Washington.

Undoubtedly, in primitive times, hooks of a compound character were used. Just as men tipped a deer's antler with a flint, they combined more than one material in the making of their hooks, lashing together a shank of bone or wood with a bronze barb. It would be almost

impossible in a single article to follow all the varieties of hooks used and the ingenuity displayed in their manufacture. Occasionally, a savage will construct a lure for fish which rivals the daintiest fly ever made by the most fastidious of anglers. In Professor Mayer's collection there is an exceedingly clever hook, coming from the North-western coast, which shows very fine lapidary work. A small red quartoze pebble of great hardness has been rounded, polished, and joined to a piece of bone. The piece is small, not more than an inch and three-quarters in length, and might weigh an ounce and a half. In the shank of bone a small hook is hidden. It somewhat imitates a shrimp. The parts are joined together by lashings of tendon, and these are laid in grooves cut into the stone. It must have taken much toil to perfect this clever artificial bait, and, as it is to-day, it might be used with success by a clever striped-bass fisherman at Newport.

In this necessarily brief study of primitive fishing, I have endeavored to show the genesis of the fish-hook, from the stone gorge to the more perfected implement of to-day. Simple as it may seem, it is a subject on which a good deal of research is still requisite. "It is not an acquaintance with a single series of things which can throw light on any subject, but a thorough comparison of the whole of them." If in the Swiss lakes there are found bronze hooks of a very large size, out of proportion to the fish which swim there to-day, it is but just to suppose that, many thousands of years ago, long before history had its dawn, the aquatic fauna were then of greater bulk than in 1883. Considerations of the primitive form of the fish-hook must even comprehend examination of prior geological conditions, differences of land and water, or such geographical changes as may have taken place. Then ichthyology becomes an important factor, for by the character of the hook, the kind of fish taken, in some instances, may be understood. We are fast coming to this conclusion: that, putting aside what can only be the merest speculations as to the condition of man when he is said to have first diverged from the brute, he was soon endowed with a wonderful degree of intelligence. And, if I am not mistaken, primitive man did not confine himself in his fishing to the rivers and lakes alone, but went out boldly to sea after the cod.

M. Trouting Along the Catasauqua

FRANK FORESTER

"And this 'clattering creek,' what sort of water is it?" asked Frank; "that I may learn at once the whole lay of the land."

"A real mountain burn."

"I'm thinking of trying it myself tomorrow," said Robins. "Mr. Langdale tells me it can only be fished with bait, and that's what I'm best at. Besides, there are bigger fish in it."

"But fewer," answered Langdale. "No, Robins, I'd advise you to stick to the 'Stony,' unless you'll try a cast of the fly with us over the pool and down the Catasauqua."

"No, no," replied St. Clair, half indignantly, "none of your flies for me, and no canoe-work. But why do you advise me against it? You said there were no trees, bait-fishing and big fish. What is there against it?"

"The toughest crag-climbing and the most difficult fishing you ever tried."

"What like fishing is it, Lancelot?" asked Frank.

"Exactly what that capital sportsman, Colquhoon of Luss, describes in his excellent book, the 'Moor and Loch,' under the title of 'Moorburn'."

"I remember," replied Frank. "Is it as bad as that?"

"Worse; but the fish much larger. I have caught them up to two pounds."

"I should like to hear about that. Can't you read it to me?" asked the Wall-street man, eager for information.

"I've no objection," said Langdale, "if Frank has not. HE has read it fifty times already."

"I'm convenient," answered Frank, laying down his knife and fork, the last duck having disappeared.

"Well, then, here goes. Now, Scipio, look alive and clear away the table; bring us our pipes and our coffee; and then we'll to bed, for we must be afoot by daybreak."

And with the word he rose, and, after turning over a few volumes on his crowded shelves, brought down the volume in question, with its pages underlined, and interlined, and filled with marginal notes and references. This done, he ensconced himself in the chimney corner, threw on a fresh log, and read as follows:

"'In most of the small Highland burns, there is a succession of cataracts and pools, with a parapet of rock rising perpendicularly on each side, and often scarcely footing enough for a dog to pass. The greater proportion of picturesque-looking brethren of the angle would almost start at the idea of continuing their pastime under such disadvantages. They therefore make a circuit, and come down again upon the burn, where it is more easy to fish, and the ground less rugged. The trout in these places are thus left until many of them grow large, and each taking possession of a favorite nook, drives all the smaller fry away. The difficulty of reaching these places is, I admit, often great, the angler having sometimes to scramble up on his hands and knees, covered with wet moss or gravel, and then drag his fishing-rod after him. These lyns should always be fished up-stream, otherwise the moment you appear at the top of the waterfall or rock, the trout are very like to see you, and slink into their hiding-place. The burn, however, must always be low, as at no other time can you distinguish the snug retreat of these little tyrants, which, indeed, they often leave, during the slightest flood, in search of prey. By fishing up the stream, your head will be on a level with the different eddies and pools, as they successively present themselves, and the rest of your person out of sight. Hold the baited hook with the left hand, jerking out the rod, underhanded, with your right, so as to make the bait fall softly at the lower end of the pool. The trout always take their station either there or at the top where the water flows in, ready to pounce on worms, snails, slugs, etc., as they enter or leave the pool. Should a trout seize the bait, a little time may be given to allow it to gorge, which it will most likely do without much ceremony. If large, care must be taken to prevent it from getting to the top of the lyn, which may probably harbor another expectant. The best plan is, if possible, to persuade it to descend into the pool below. Having deposited the half-pounder in your creel, you will now crawl upon hands and knees, just so near the top of the lyn as will enable you to drop the bait immediately below the bubbling foam, nearly as favorite a station for an overgrown, monopolizing trout as the other. Except in such situations, the burn trout seldom exceeds a quarter of a pound, and may be pulled out with single gut, without much risk of breaking it. In these lyns, however, I have occasionally taken them upward of a

pound, which is easily accounted for. As soon as the trout grows to a sufficient size to intimidate his pigmy neighbors, he falls back into the best pool for feeding, not occupied by a greater giant than himself, and as these lyns are almost always in precipices very difficult of access, he remains undisturbed and alone, or with a single companion, driving all others away, until he may at last attain to a pound weight.'

"Now, I fear, brother angler, that you are in some respects what the indefatigable Gael would call a 'picturesque angler'; so I advise you in good faith, stick to the 'Stony Brook'; fish it from the long fall carefully down. Scipio shall attend you with the landing-net and plenty of worms and minnows; the last, hooked through the lip and back fin, will do you yeoman service in the lower pools; and Frank and I will join you in the afternoon."

"Agreed," said Mr. Robins; "I'll take your advice, I believe; and now I guess I'll turn in. Good night."

"Time, too," said Frank, laughing. "He was beginning to get a little white about the gills. Could that be his old Otard; he did not drink so much of it."

"Lord help you, no! he'd drink a gallon of it and no hurt. No! But he will persist in smoking Cavendish tobacco and kinnikinnic, because he has seen me do it, and, I believe, imagines that it confers some special powers of trout-catching. But come, suppose we turn in, too; you'll be tired after your journey, and a good night's rest will give a steady hand and clear eye tomorrow."

"*Volontiers.*"

So they incontinently joined the Wall-street man, who declared, half asleep, that the bed was not so very bad, after all; while Frank, once ensconced in the fragrant sheets, swore, by the great god Pan, patron of hunters, that never had bed so sweet, so soft, so warm, in every way so excellent, received the limbs of weary hunter. And so, indeed, it proved; for, until Scipio made his entree, with his announcement that breakfast was ready, no one stirred or spoke during the livelong night.

Thereon they all turned, like the Iron Duke, not over, but out. Their sporting toilets were soon made;

but Frank and Lancelot, in their old shepherd's plaid jackets and trews and hob-nailed fishing shoes, could not but exchange glances and smiles at the elaborate rig of their friend, which some Broadway artist had, it was evident, elaborated from a Parisian fashion-plate, the high boots of exquisitely enameled leather, the fine doeskin trousers, the many-pocketed, pearl-buttoned shooting jacket of fawn-colored silk plush, the batiste neckerchief and waistcoat, point device, with green and silver fishes embroidered on a blue ground, and, to complete the whole, a cavalier hat, in which, but that it lacked the king's black feather, Rupert might well have charged at Marston Moor or Naseby. He seemed, however, so happy, that it would have been as useless as ill-natured to indoctrinate him; for evidently, as an angler, the man was hopelessly incurable, though, as Frank observed, for Wall-street, he was wonderfully decent.

His weapon was a right good Conroy's general-fishing rod, but without reel, and having its line, an unusually stout silk one, with a superb salmon-gut bottom, which, in good hands, would have held a twenty-pounder, made carefully fast to the top funnel; eschewing all use of the ring and destroying all chance of the rod's regularly bending to its work. But again, to counsel would have been to offend; so our friends held their peace.

The smoked venison ham, broiled troutlings, dry toast and black tea, which furnished their morning meal, were soon finished; and forth they went into the delicious, breezy air of the quiet summer morning, not a sound disturbing the solitude, except the plash and rippling of the rapid waters, the low voices of the never-silent pine-tops, and the twittering of the swallows, as they skimmed the limpid pool.

Up the gorge of the Stony Brook, followed by Scipio, with bait of all kinds enough to have kept the kraten fat for one day at least, a large creel at his back, and gaff and landing-net in hand, away went St. Clair Robins, gay and joyous and confident; and then, but not till then quoth Forester—

"And whither we?"

"To the other side of the pool. You may see the big fish rising under the alders, there, in the shadow of the big hill, from this distance. That shadow will hang there until noon, while all this side of the basin will be in blazing sunshine. Not a fish will bite here, I warrant me, until three o'clock, while we'll fill our basket there with good ones, certain. The best fish in the pool lies under that round-headed stone, just in the tail of the strong eddy, where the 'Clattering Creek' comes in, in the broken water. I rate him a six-pounder, and have saved him for you all the spring. As soon as the sun turns westward, and the hemlocks' shadows cross the white water, you shall kill him, and then we'll away to the Wall-street man"; and therewith the larger birch canoe was manned, paddled gently over to the shady side of the pool and moored in about twenty-foot water, and then, the rods being put together, the reels secured, and the lines carried duly through the rings, the following colloquy followed:

"What flies do you most affect here, Lancelot?" asked Frank.

"Any, at times, and almost all," answered Langdale. "In some weather I have killed well with middle-sized gaudy lake flies; but my favorites, on the whole, are all the red, brown, orange, and yellow hackles, and the blue and yellow duns. And yours?"

"My favorite of all is a snipe feather and mouse body; next to that the black and the furnace hackles."

"And will you use them today?"

"I will; the snipe wing for my stretcher. I mean to kill the big chap with him this evening."

"Be it so! to work."

And to work they went; but, though most glorious the sport to enjoy, or even to see performed gnostically, to read of it described, is as little interesting as to decribe it is difficult. Suffice it to say, that before the sun had begun to turn westward, sixteen brace and a half were fairly brought to basket by our anglers, one a three-pound-and-a-halfer, three two-pounders, there or there about; not a fish under a pound, all smaller were thrown back unscathed, and very few so small as that, all beautifully fed fish, big-bellied, small-headed, high in color, prime in condition. At one o'clock, they paddled leisurely back to the cabin, lunched frugally on a crust of bread and a glass of sherry, and awaited the hour when the hemlock's shadow should be on the white water.

At the moment they were there; and lo! the big trout was feeding fiercely on the natural fly.

"Be ready, Frank, and when next he rises drop your fly right in the middle of his bell."

"Be easy, I mean it." His line, as he spoke, was describing an easy circle around his head; the fish rose not. The second revolution succeeded; the great trout rose, missed his object, disappeared; and, on the instant, right in the centre of the bell, ere the inmost circle had subsided, the snipe feather fell and fluttered. With an arrowy rush, the monster rose, and as his broad tail showed above the surface, the merry music of the resonant click-reel told that Frank had him. Well struck, he was better played, killed unexceptionably; in thirteen minutes he lay fluttering on the greensward, lacking four ounces of a six-pounder. The snipe feather and mouse body won the day in a canter. So off they started up the Stony Brook, to admire the feats of P. St. Clair Robins. It was not long ere they found him; he had reached the lower waters of the brook, full of beautiful scours, eddies, whirlpools and basins, and was fishing quietly down it, wading about knee deep with his bait, he was roving with a minnow, some ten yards down the stream, playing naturally enough in the clear, swirling waters. Some trees on the bank hung thickly over his head; a few yards behind him was a pretty rocky cascade, and above that an open upland glade, lighted up by a gleam of the westering sun; and, altogether, with his gay garb, he presented quite a picturesque, if not a very sportsmanly appearance.

"After all," said Frank, as unseen themselves, they stood observing him, "he does not do it so very badly as one might have expected."

But before the words had passed his lips, a good fish, at least a pounder, threw itself clear out of the water and seized his minnow. In a second, in the twinkling of an eye, by a movement never before seen or contemplated by mortal angler, he ran his right hand up to the top of the third joint of his rod, which he held perpendicularly aloft, and with his left grasped his line, mid length, and essayed to drag the trout by main force out of his element. The tackle was stout, the stream strong, the bottom slippery, the fish active, and, before any one could see how it was done, hand and foot both slipped, the line parted, the rod crashed in the middle, the fish went over the next fall with a joyous flirt of his tail, and the fisherman, hapless fisherman, measured his own length in the deepest pool of the Stony Brook.

He was soon fished out, equipped in dry rigging, comforted with a hot glass of his favorite cognac; but he would not be consoled. He was off at daylight the following morning, and, for aught that I have heard, Cotton's Cabin beheld him nevermore.

N. Some Memories of Early Days

LORD GREY OF FALLODEN

Every angler must have some account to give of the beginning of his keenness for angling. Some of us remember it as the great excitement of our boyhood, whilst others have only discovered its existence in later years of life. I think, however, that the keenest anglers are born and not made; that the passion is latent in them from the beginning, and is revealed sooner or later according to opportunity. In some cases it may be that the passion perishes unsuspected and unrevealed, because there is no opportunity of indulging or discovering it, till too late in life. The longer we live the deeper becomes the groove or the rut in which our life moves, and the more difficult it becomes to go outside it. To me the opportunity for fishing came early, and the passion for it awoke suddenly. I was about seven years old, and was riding on a Shetland pony by the side of a very small burn. A mill was working higher up the stream, and the water was full of life and agita-

tion, caused by the opening of the sluice of the mill pond above. I had seen small trout caught in the burn before, but now, for the first time and suddenly, came an overpowering desire to fish, which gave no rest till some very primitive tackle was given me. With this and some worms, many afternoons were spent in vain. The impulse to see the trout destroyed all chance of success. It did not suit me to believe that it was fatal to look into the water before dropping a worm over the bank, or that I could not see the trout first and catch them afterwards, and I preferred to learn by experience and disappointment rather than the short, but unconvincing, method of believing what I was told.

For some years this burn fishing was all that I knew. It was very fascinating, though the trout were so small that one of four ounces was considered a good one, whilst the very largest ran to six ounces. These larger trout taught me a second lesson—self-restraint. The first lesson was, as has been said, to learn to refrain from looking into the water before I fished it: all the trout of every size combined to teach this. The second difficulty was to restrain the excitement when I had a bite. The natural impulse then was to strike so hard as to hurl the fish into the air overhead: this answered very well with trout of two or three ounces, though once a small one came unfastened in the air, flew off at a tangent into the hay behind, and could not be found. But with six ounce trout this violent method did not answer so well; neither the angler, nor the rod, nor the tackle, was always strong enough to deal with them so summarily. Catastrophes occurred, and by slow degrees and painful losses I learnt the necessity of getting keenness under control. After I had improved in these matters there still remained the hardest trial of all, which has to be undergone by all anglers, namely, how to face the disappointment of losing a fish. Many of us must have known what it is in boyhood to suffer anguish after losing an unexpectedly large fish. The whole of life then seems laid waste by despair; the memory of past joys counts for nothing; one is sure that no future success can ever compensate for the present loss; and one rails against the established order of everything, and is indignant that any human being should ever have been born to undergo such intolerable misery. Even in later years we cannot hope to face the loss of very large fish with equanimity. Nobody can become perfect in bearing what is unbearable, and it may be counted to our credit if in these very bitter moments silence descends upon us, and we preserve outward appearances. Here is a saying that is very relevant: "When things can neither be cured nor endured, one has to pretend."

Burn fishing is not without its charm even in later years, and is a peculiar form of angling separate from all others. I am thinking now of those north country burns too small for fly fishing, which run in narrow stony channels between overgrown banks. Here one must fish with a worm and a short line, and the difficulty consists in getting the worm into the water without any part of oneself being seen by the trout. The usual method is to advance stealthily, sometimes stooping, sometimes on one's knees, sometimes at full length, according to the necessities of the case, pushing the rod in front, and at last swinging the worm gently on a short line over the edge of the bank and lowering it into the water. When the angler knows the burn well he goes at once from place to place, approaching the bank afresh at each spot which he knows to be suitable. If he does not know the burn he most reconnoiter from a distance to see the sort of water that is before him. It does not do to drop a worm blindly over the bank without knowing where it will fall, as the hooks are sure in this case to become mixed up sooner or later with a bush or a heap of sticks.

One burn I used to fish flowed through a wood of high trees down a steep rocky channel. Here it was possible, at least for a small boy, to keep out of sight by walking up the bed of the burn itself, stooping low, jerking the worm up into little pools and cascades above, and lifting the trout out down stream on to the bank. This was very pretty work. I remember once getting several trout quickly one after the other in this place, and then they suddenly stopped taking. One little favorite pool after another produced nothing, and a fear of something unknown came over me; the gloom and stillness of the wood made me uneasy, everything about me seemed to know something, to have a meaning, which was hidden from me; and I felt as if my fishing was out of place. At last I could resist the feeling of apprehension no longer; I left the rod with the line in a pool to fish for itself, and went up to the edge of the wood to see what was happening in the open world outside. There was a great storm coming up full of awful menace, as thunderclouds often are. It filled me with terror. I hurried back for my rod, left the burn and the wood, and fled before the storm, going slow to get breath now and then, and continually urged to running again by the sound of thunder behind me.

Burn trout are wayward little things. Sometimes they take a worm greedily on the brightest days in low clear water, rushing to it directly it falls into the pool, or seizing it as it travels down the stream, and being hooked without trouble. On these days all the angler need do is wait for four or five seconds after he knows, by the stopping or the trembling of the line, that the worm has been taken, and then strike sharply but not violently. If the trout is very small it may be lifted out at once, but if it is four ounces' weight or heavier it is safer to let it do some splashing and struggling in the water, to wait till it is still, and then to lift it out with an even movement, quickly but without any sudden jerk. If there is a clear space without branches or bushes in the way, this can be done without the trout struggling in the air. It is always unsafe to lift a fish which is in the act of struggling, for the jerks of the fish, added to the dead weight of its body in the air, greatly increase the risk either of the line breaking or of the hooks coming out. If the trout exceeds six ounces, I play it with as much respect as if it were a salmon, and choose a shallow landing-place, and draw it on to that without lifting it at all. The feeling of losing a trout in the air is familiar to burn anglers. The fish falls back into the water with a splash, the line flies up into the air, often becoming hopelessly entangled in a tree; and before it is extricated the angler has frightened all the other fish in the pool, and is convinced that the trout and the branches and the rod and line and hooks are all in a conspiracy against him. I use the word "hooks," as I have found small Stewart or Pennell worm tackle much the best for trout fishing: it is easily baited, and with it the angler can, if he likes, strike directly the worm is taken, though it is better to wait just long enough to let the trout get all the worm well into its mouth, and not long enough to let the worm be swallowed.

On some days burn trout are very aggravating, and will take the worm and chew it without being hooked. The angler waits and then strikes, and feels that he has just touched a fish and no more, and this happens time after time. He tries the effect of waiting longer before striking, and then finds either that he still just misses the fish, or else that the fish has taken the worm off the hooks or left the worm altogether; or that a very small trout not worth killing has swallowed the hooks, and wasted its own life and his time and trouble. I suppose on these days the trout are not really hungry, and begin to chew the worm instead of trying to swallow it at once. They then discover the presence of the hooks, and either reject the whole thing, or try to separate the worm from the hooks with their lips, which results in the angler's touching without hooking them when he strikes. There are other days when burn trout dash at the worm and endeavor to make off with it immediately at speed. On these occasions the angler feels a quick tug and all is over before he can strike; he probably does strike too late, and his line having no resistance at the

end is jerked out of the water into a bush, if there is one near.

Three other moods are common to burn trout; they are those of indifference, suspicion, and abnormal fright. When the trout are indifferent, they simply ignore the worm, and appear not to notice its presence: one might think from their behavior either that they were blind, or that they habitually lived with worms before their eyes. When they are suspicious, they will, on the contrary, swim up to the worm and investigate it as if they had never seen such a thing before, or dash about it as if its presence excited them. On other days, and these are not necessarily the brightest, it is almost impossible to keep out of sight of the trout, which seem to be watching for the least hint of the approach of an angler; and even when the angler succeeds in concealing himself, they fly from the sight of the rod, or the gut, however quietly it is put before them. All these things make burn fishing an interesting and delicate sport. The drawback to it is that the constant stooping and crawling become so much harder as years go on. Joints ache and crack, and the continual effort of keeping a stiff and full-grown body out of sight is difficult and painful. Some of the crouching may be avoided by using a long rod, but among bushes and trees a long rod is an awkward instrument, and one cannot guide the line so accurately among the branches. To dodge bushes and leaves and twigs successfully, the angler must use a short stiff rod and a short line. He can then not only guide the line and drop the worm more accurately with the rod, but after fishing each place can catch the end of the short line with one hand, while still holding the rod with the other, and so make his way through the trees to the next pool, without having to put the rod down and alter the length of the line. A well wooded burn is the nicest of all. It has places where the angler can watch the trout and see his worm taken, while he is hidden behind leaves, or lying in tall meadow-sweet or some such undergrowth of herbs. Even if he does not feel the thrill and the rapt excitement, which he felt as a boy when his line stopped and trembled in the stream with a bite, or when he saw a trout open its mouth and take his worm, he can still remember what he used to feel in those early days, and "beget that golden time again." He can enjoy, too, more than he ever did before, the light playing through the leaves upon the still water of a clear pool, the running water sparkling in the sun, the tinkling sound of little streams, and the shade and the hot summer's day. And even yet there is some satisfaction, when the burn is low and clear, in outwitting the trout, small as they are, for it is not to be done without care, difficulty, and effort.

I need hardly add that fine drawn gut is proper for burn fishing: in small burns two or three feet of gut is enough, as the water is shallow, the line is kept more perpendicular than horizontal, and but little of it falls into the water. The special merits of brandling worms were so impressed upon me from the first that I have never been content to use any other kind. They are certainly good both in color and size. The objection to them is that they are rather soft, but for burn fishing, where the worm is dropped rather than cast into the water, this does not matter so much. Brandling worms, however, are not to be found in common earth, nor in every heap of decaying manure or rubbish. Kitchen garden refuse is a valuable ingredient, but it is not the only one, and the heaps must be of the right material in the right stage of decay; young anglers of intelligence and observation make it their business to know the best places for brandling worms, so that they may be sure of getting a good supply whenever they want it. The brandlings are best after being kept for a day or two in clean moss, but trout take them well enough when they are fresh.

Very wonderful is the perspective of childhood, which can make a small burn seem greater than rivers in after life. There was one burn which I knew intimately from its source to the sea. Much of the upper part was wooded, and it was stony and shallow, till within two miles of its mouth. Here there was for a child another world. There were no trees, the bottom of the burn was of mud or sand, and the channel was full of rustling reeds, with open pools of some depth at intervals. These pools had a fascination for me, there was something about them which kept me excited with expectation of great events, as I lay behind the reeds, peering through them, and watching the line intently. The result of much waiting was generally an eel, or a small flat fish up from the sea; or now and then a small trout, but never for many years one of the monsters which I was sure must inhabit such mysterious pools. At last one evening something heavy really did take the worm. The fish kept deep, played round and round the pool and could not be seen, but I remember shouting to a companion at a little distance, that I had hooked a trout of one pound, and being conscious from the tone of his reply that he didn't in the least believe me, for a trout of one pound was in those days our very utmost limit of legitimate expectation. There was a mill pond higher up in which such a weight had been attained; and we who fished the burn could talk of trout of that size, and yet feel that we were speaking like anglers of this world. But this fish turned out to be heavier even than one pound, and when at last it came up from the depth into my view, I felt that the great moment had come which was to make or mar my happiness for ever. I got into the shallow water below the fish, and after great anxieties secured with the help of my hand a fresh run sea trout of three pounds. Never was a dead fish treated with more care and honor. It had swallowed the hooks, and rather than risk spoiling its appearance in getting them out, the gut was cut and they were left inside. The small trout and eels and flounders were turned out of my basket and put into my companion's, so that the great sea trout might lie in state. It was felt that the expectation of years was justified, that the marvelous had become real, that the glory which had been unseen was revealed, and that after the present moment the hope of great things in the future would live for ever. A few years ago there was published a delightful book called *The Golden Age* in which the author describes the world of childhood as it has been to all of us—a world whose boundaries are unknown, where everything is at the same time more wonderful and more real than it seems afterwards, and where mystery is our most constant companion. So it was with me, especially in the places where I fished. I used to go to the lower part of this burn in the charge of an old gamekeeper, and after a long journey through pathless open fields, we seemed to reach a distant land where things happened otherwise than in the world nearer home. At the end of the walk it was as if we had reached another country, and were living in another day under a different sky. The gamekeeper fished more leisurely than I, and sometimes he would be lost among the windings of the burn, to be found again by the sight of the smoke from his pipe rising gently from behind a whin bush. When I now recall that distant land, I see always somewhere among the whin bushes a little curl of thin smoke, and no other sign of an inhabitant.

In course of time there came experience of a fine Highland river, and lochs near it and of fly fishing in them in August. The trout did not always rise very well in August, but many of them were three-quarters of a pound in weight, a few were even larger, and the sport seemed to me magnificent. Three great days happened all in different years on this river and its lochs. Once the trout took exceptionally well in the loch, and instead of the usual number of twenty or less I landed forty-eight, averaging about three to the pound. Another day there was a little fresh water in the river, and I tried an artificial minnow. First a trout of about two pounds, larger than any trout ever hooked by me before, was lost. While I was still in the agony of disappointment, a second weighing three pounds and a quarter was hooked and eventually landed, and directly after that a third trout of about the same size was hooked and lost, when it was in full view and half in the landing net. Then nothing more would take, and I spent the rest of the day without further incident, trying to think of the fish landed and not of the ones lost.

But the greatest day of all was the third. I was standing at the end of a pier built for salmon fishing, casting out into the smooth strong stream, when a sort of wave seemed to come suddenly and swallow the top fly, and a large heavy body went down stream pulling out the line. I shouted, "A salmon!" and the old gillie came hurrying to my side. His first words were, "We shall never get him," against which I protested with rage, and he partially retracted and set to work to advise me. We could not follow the fish downward, but it hove to about twenty yards below us and hung steady in the stream. We turned the trout rod up stream and held it still, keeping a steady strain upon the fish, and waited for what seemed an age without result; but the good old man encouraged me when I grew faint-hearted, and kept me patient. Eventually the fish began to yield. We gained line foot by foot, and more than once got the fish up stream nearly opposite the pier, but it saw us and dropped back each time to the old place down stream. At last amid great excitement it was coaxed past the pier, in a moment was in the backwater above, and to my astonishment was then almost at once exhausted and landed. It was a grilse of about six pounds, and rather red, but the distinction between grilse and salmon, between red fish and fresh run fish, was nothing to me. That same day another grilse of about four pounds took the same fly. This second fish took with a splash, ran freely and was landed without difficulty. In the course of many seasons I must have had dozens of days' trout fishing in that same river at the same time of year, but never on any other day did I hook or even rise a grilse or salmon with a trout fly.

These were the triumphs of luck, but they came at an age when youth, not from conceit, but from sheer gladness and simplicity, does not discriminate between luck and skill. The first temptation to become proud of possessing skill came later, and after the use of the dry fly had been learnt at Winchester. It was not on the Itchen that any pride was felt, for I was only a learner there, improving year by year, but with examples of greater skill and success than mine constantly before me. In the holidays, however, I took away with me from the Itchen to distant rivers the art of the dry fly, which was then not nearly so widely known as it has come to be in the last twenty years. So it happened that on west or north country streams, or in Ireland, or on dark smooth water in the Highlands, I was sometimes the first to introduce the dry fly, with results which astonished the trout and the local anglers, and were very gratifying to myself. In the Highland river spoken of above there was a long dark stretch, bordered by rocks and trees, where the river flowed with a deep even stream, carrying a few thin flecks of slow-moving foam upon its surface, but without a ripple. Here, especially in the evening, some of the best trout used to rise. You might fish every day for a week in the rougher water and never hook a trout of one pound weight with a fly and be very grateful for half-pounders, but in this smooth deep part many of the trout were upwards of one pound; and the average weight was about three-quarters of a pound. Often had I tried them with March-browns, and small Heckum Peckums and the various patterns which are attractive in the Highlands, but not one of these particular trout would stand the sight of my flies. I continued to visit that river in my summer holidays, and the time came when I brought with me some drawn gut, some small olive and red quills, and a single-handed rod with which to cast them lightly. A pupil on the Itchen was a master among these Highland trout, and in the still hour of sunset on many an August evening I used to endure the torment of the midges and find a rich reward. A struggle with a trout of one pound and a half hooked on Itchen tackle in that fine flow of deep water, among the rocks and trees, was no mean affair.

In the Easter holidays I went alone once or twice to the Dart. I do not know how the Dart fares now, for it is nearly twenty years since I have seen it; but in those days there was beautiful trout water between Staverton and Buckfastleigh, which could be fished by ticket, and if one was not disappointed with trout of

less than half a pound, there was very good sport to be had. I remember once fishing a part of the river where there was a succession of streams, which towards the middle of the day seemed alive with little trout, rising actively all over the water at natural flies. It was one of those maddening days when the trout rise in quantities and take no notice of artificial flies. I could do nothing, and the other anglers above and below me, of whom two or three were in sight, were not doing very much better. At last in despair I waded to the bank, and went down to a smooth piece of the river between wooded banks. In this place the water was clear, and varied from a foot to perhaps three feet in depth. No one was fishing, and there were trout rising in shoals and very quietly. A stout March-brown, such as I had been using above, would have put them all to flight, but the trouble of using a dry fly for such separate trout seemed out of proportion to the size of the fish. Yet as I wanted very much to save an empty basket, I gave up the hope of counting trout that day by the dozen, put on one small olive quill and waded in quietly below the rising fish. They took the little dry fly as if they were pleased to see it, and when the rise was over I waded out with thirty-one trout in my basket. The old angling diary to which I have referred gives the weight of the largest as eight ounces. It does not give the total weight, but I remember congratulating myself on the fact that the average size of my trout was at least equal to the size of those generally caught with fly in April in the more favorite streams above. As I emerged from the trees on the bank, I met one of the best of the local anglers returning from above with a lighter basket than usual. He stopped me and asked what I had done. I opened my basket. "You can't have caught those to-day with fly," he said. "Yes," I replied; "I caught them with a dry fly." "Dry fly," he said very sternly, "we know nothing about a dry fly here." Then he went on his way, with thoughts, I fear, that were not very kind.

The next reminiscence goes back to about 1880, and has to do with a river in Ireland. The first time I saw this river was late in August. There were said to be trout, and good ones, and it was believed to be possible to catch some with fly earlier in the season, when the water was in order. The river had in parts a very wide bed, which when low it did not nearly fill. The water ran in all sorts of channels between beds of bright green weeds. Here and there was a long stream with a stony bottom, free from weeds, and now and then there would be a huge pool, full of peaty-colored water of unknown depth, in which one or two salmon lay. One could wander for miles all day about the most extraordinary variety of water. The river was full of pike, and it was said, probably with truth, that the inhabitants of the district forked trout out of the weeds in low water with various agricultural implements. But there were trout enough for dry fly fishing. Half a dozen or so might be found rising near together, and then perhaps one would have to go several hundred yards before another one was found; a little sound would be heard presently, as if a small pebble had dropped in somewhere without a splash, and heard perhaps two or three times before the rise could be seen in such a large and curious river. Then there was a different stalk, probably through water and weeds, with the chance of going overhead into a big hole unawares.

I was warned that at this season of the year, when the water was low, I must not expect to catch any of these fish, but I cared nothing for warnings. The trout were there, and were rising, and though I saw at once that it was a case for dry fly and for that only, I had by this time been taught to believe that any one, who could catch Winchester trout, could catch rising trout anywhere. These trout, however, at first upset my calculations. They brought me face to face with a difficulty which did not exist on the ticket water at Winchester—they were unapproachable. Never was an angler more put upon his mettle. There were trout visibly and audibly rising, which had never seen an artificial dry fly, and would probably take it at once. They were evidently also big trout. There was splendid sport to be had, and reputation and glory to be won in catching even one of

them, and yet so shy were they, that I could not get my dry fly to them.

For two days they defeated me utterly. I walked and knelt and waded and labored and perspired under an August sun without success. Some of the trout were put down by my approach, some were scared by the first waving of the rod, and some, which had been successfully stalked, turned tail and fled when the gut floated over them without even the last drag; at last, on the second evening in a fading light, I hooked a fish which went off up stream at once with a mighty rush, and came to rest somewhere out of sight at the end of a lot of line. I waded carefully up in the twilight, keeping a tight line by reeling up as I went till I was over a great bed of strong weeds. Into this one hand carefully felt its way along the casting line, and touched at last the side of a great fish. Nothing could be seen for it was getting dark, and the weeds were too thick for a landing net to be used in them. I tried with one hand to arrange a grip on the trout, and very broad and hard he felt; but at the critical moment he made the most violent commotion in the weeds and dashed off somewhere. When all was still I felt again and found in the weeds only the end of broken gut. There was nothing more to be done that evening, and I waded out and lay on the bank in the dusk. On the whole, I think that was the bitterest moment I have ever known in angling. To have come so near to success, and to have it snatched from me at the last moment, after keenness and effort had been sustained at the very highest pitch for two whole days, was more than could be borne.

But success did come afterwards, and in broad daylight; I found a place where, by wading and kneeling in the river on the shallow side, it was possible to get within reach of and opposite to rising trout without frightening them. Then the fly could be thrown some way above them with an underhand cast, so as not to show the rod; and being opposite and not below, I could let the fly float down a few inches on the near side of a rising trout, so that only the fly and none of the gut was seen. In this way I at last caught one or two trout, and then somehow, when the frost of failure had once broken up, it seemed more easy to succeed all over the river.

These trout were the shyest I have ever known. They were more difficult to approach and more easily scared by rod or gut than any others I ever fished for; but if the fly could be floated to a rising fish without frightening it, the fly was generally taken. On the best day that I had there I caught eleven fish. None of these weighed three pounds, but the first two were each over two pounds and three-quarters. For such shy fish really fine gut had to be used, and there were many disasters in the weeds, but also many splendid struggles fought out in pools which were far too deep for any vegetation. It was the wildest and most exciting and most fascinating dry fly fishing that I have ever had. My experience of it has only been during late August or early September, but I can imagine that in May and in June it might be the finest dry fly fishing in the United Kingdom.[1]

---

[1]   The river was the Suir, and the part of it described was at Graiguenoe, not far from Thurles. Before 1880 I do not think any one had ever fished it with a dry fly. I was never there after 1886, but I heard that the merits of the water for dry fly fishing were afterwards much appreciated by many anglers.

O. Fishing with a Worm

BLISS PERRY

A defective logic is the born fisherman's portion. He is a pattern of inconsistency. He does the things which he ought not to do, and he leaves undone the things which other people think he ought to do. He observes the wind when he should be sowing, and he regards the clouds, with temptation tugging familiarly at his heartstrings, when he might be grasping the useful sickle. It is a wonder that there is so much health in him. A sorrowing political economist remarked to me in early boyhood, as a jolly red-bearded neighbor, followed by an abnormally fat dog, sauntered past us for his nooning: "That man is the best carpenter in town, but he will leave the most important job whenever he

wants to go fishing." I stared at the sinful carpenter, who swung along leisurely in the May sunshine, keeping just ahead of his dog. To leave one's job in order to go fishing! How illogical!

Years bring the reconciling mind. The world grows big enough to include within its scheme both the instructive political economist and the truant mechanic. But that trick of truly logical behavior seems harder to the man than to the child. For example, I climbed up to my den under the eaves last night—a sour, black sea-fog lying all about, and the December sleet crackling against the window-panes—in order to varnish a certain fly-rod. Now rods ought to be put in order in September, when the fishing closes, or else in April, when it opens. To varnish a rod in December proves that one possesses either a dilatory or a childishly anticipatory mind. But before uncorking the varnish bottle, it occurred to me to examine a dog-eared, water-stained fly-book, to guard against the ravages of possible moths. This interlude proved fatal to the varnishing. A half hour went happily by in rearranging the flies. Then, with a fisherman's lack of sequence, as I picked out here and there a plain snell-hook from the gaudy feathered ones, I said to myself with a generous glow at the heart: "Fly-fishing has had enough sacred poets celebrating it already. Isn't there a good deal to be said, after all, for fishing with a worm?"

Could there be a more illogical proceeding? And here follows the treatise,—a Defense of Results, an Apology for Opportunism,—conceived in agreeable procrastination, devoted to the praise of the inconsequential angleworm, and dedicated to a childish memory of a whistling carpenter and his fat dog.

Let us face the worst at the very beginning. It shall be a shameless example of fishing under conditions that make the fly a mockery. Take the Taylor Brook, "between the roads," on the headwaters of the Lamoille. The place is a jungle. The swamp maples and cedars were felled a generation ago, and the tops were trimmed into the brook. The alders and moosewood are higher than your head; on every tiny knoll the fir balsams have gained a footing, and creep down, impenetrable, to the edge of the water. In the open spaces the Joe-Pye weed swarms. In two minutes after leaving the upper road you have scared a mink or a rabbit, and you have probably lost the brook. Listen! It is only a gurgle here, droning along, smooth and dark, under the tangle of cedar-tops and the shadow of the balsams. Follow the sound cautiously. There, beyond the Joe-Pye weed, and between the stump and the cedar-top, is a hand's breadth of black water. Fly-casting is impossible in this maze of dead and living branches. Shorten your line to two feet, or even less, bait your hook with a worm, and drop it gingerly into that gurgling crevice of water. Before it has sunk six inches, if there is not one of those black- backed, orange-bellied, Taylor Brook trout fighting with it, something is wrong with your worm or with you. For the trout are always there, sheltered by the brushwood that makes this half mile of fishing "not worth while." Below the lower road the Taylor Brook becomes uncertain water. For half a mile it yields only fingerlings, for no explainable reason; then there are two miles of clean fishing through the deep woods, where the branches are so high that you can cast a fly again if you like, and there are long pools, where now and then a heavy fish will rise; then comes a final half mile through the alders, where you must wade, knee to waist deep, before you come to the bridge and the river. Glorious fishing is sometimes to be had here,—especially if you work down the gorge at twilight, casting a white miller until it is too dark to see. But alas, there is a well-worn path along the brook, and often enough there are the very footprints of the "fellow ahead of you," signs as disheartening to

the fisherman as ever were the footprints on the sand to Robinson Crusoe.

But "between the roads" it is "too much trouble to fish"; and there lies the salvation of the humble fisherman who disdains not to use the crawling worm, nor, for that matter, to crawl himself, if need be, in order to sneak under the boughs of some overhanging cedar that casts a perpetual shadow upon the sleepy brook. Lying here at full length, with no elbow-room to manage the rod, you must occasionally even unjoint your tip, and fish with that, using but a dozen inches of line, and not letting so much as your eyebrows show above the bank. Is it a becoming attitude for a middle-aged citizen of the world? That depends upon how the fish are biting. Holing a put looks rather ridiculous also, to the mere observer, but it requires, like brook-fishing with a tip only, a very delicate wrist, perfect tactile sense, and a fine disregard of appearances.

There are some fishermen who always fish as if they were being photographed. The Taylor Brook "between the roads" is not for them. To fish it at all is back-breaking, trouser-tearing work; to see it thoroughly fished is to learn new lessons in the art of angling. To watch R., for example, steadily filling his six-pound creel from that unlikely stream, is like watching Sargent paint a portrait. R. weighs two hundred and ten. Twenty years ago he was a famous amateur pitcher, and among his present avocations are violin playing, which is good for the wrist, taxidermy, which is good for the eye, and shooting woodcock, which before the days of the new Nature Study used to be thought good for the whole man. R. began as a fly-fisherman, but by dint of passing his summers near brooks where fly-fishing is impossible, he has become a stout-hearted apologist for the worm. His apparatus is most singular. It consists of a very long, cheap rod, stout enough to smash through bushes, and with the stiffest tip obtainable. The lower end of the butt, below the reel, fits into the socket of a huge extra butt of bamboo, which R. carries unconcernedly. To reach a distant hole, or to fish the lower end of a ripple, R. simply locks his reel, slips on the extra butt, and there is a fourteen-foot rod ready for action. He fishes with a line unbelievably short, and a Kendal hook far too big; and when a trout jumps for that hook, R. wastes no time in maneuvering for position. The unlucky fish is simply "derricked,"—to borrow a word from Theodore, most saturnine and profane of Moosehead guides.

"Shall I play him awhile?" shouted an excited sportsman to Theodore, after hooking his first big trout.

"——no!" growled Theodore in disgust. "Just derrick him right into the canoe!" A heroic method, surely; though it once cost me the best square-tail I ever hooked, for Theodore had forgotten the landing-net, and the gut broke in his fingers as he tried to swing the fish aboard. But with these lively quarter- pounders of the Taylor Brook, derricking is a safer procedure. Indeed, I have sat dejectedly on the far end of a log, after fishing the hole under it in vain, and seen the mighty R. wade downstream close behind me, adjust that comical extra butt, and jerk a couple of half-pound trout from under the very log on which I was sitting. His device on this occasion, as I well remember, was to pass his hook but once through the middle of a big worm, let the worm sink to the bottom, and crawl along it at his leisure. The trout could not resist.

Once, and once only, have I come near equaling R.'s record, and the way he beat me then is the justification for a whole philosophy of worm-fishing. We were on this very Taylor Brook, and at five in the afternoon both baskets were two thirds full. By count I had just one more fish than he. It was raining hard. "You fish down through the alders," said R. magnanimously. "I'll cut across and wait for you at the sawmill. I don't want to get any wetter, on account of my rheumatism."

This was rather barefaced kindness,—for whose rheumatism was ever the worse for another hour's fishing? But I weakly accepted it. I coveted three or four good trout to top off with,—that was all. So I tied on a couple of flies, and began to fish the alders, wading waist deep in the rapidly rising water, down the long green tunnel under the curving boughs. The brook fairly smoked with the rain, by this time, but when did one fail to get at least three or four trout out of this best half mile of the lower brook? Yet I had no luck. I tried one fly after another, and then, as a forlorn hope,—though it sometimes has a magic of its own,—I combined a brown hackle for the tail fly with a twisting worm on the dropper. Not a rise! I thought of E. sitting patiently in the saw mill, and I fished more conscientiously than ever.

"Venture as warily, use the same skill,
Do your best, whether winning or losing it,
If you choose to play!—is my principle."

Even those lines, which by some subtle telepathy of the trout brook murmur themselves over and over to me in the waning hours of an unlucky day, brought now no consolation. There was simply not one fish to be had, to any fly in the book, out of that long, drenching, darkening tunnel. At last I climbed out of the brook, by the bridge. R. was sitting on the fence, his neck and ears carefully turtled under his coat collar, the smoke rising and the rain dripping from the inverted bowl of his pipe. He did not seem to be worrying about his rheumatism.

"What luck?" he asked.

"None at all," I answered morosely. "Sorry to keep you waiting."

"That's all right," remarked R. "What do you think I've been doing? I've been fishing out of the saw-mill window just to kill time. There was a patch of floating sawdust there,—kind of unlikely place for trout, anyway,—but I thought I'd put on a worm and let him crawl around a little." He opened his creel as he spoke. "But I didn't look for a pair of 'em," he added. And there, on top of his smaller fish, were as pretty a pair of three-quarter-pound brook trout as were ever basketed.

"I'm afraid you got pretty wet," said R. kindly.

"I don't mind that," I replied. And I didn't. What I minded was the thought of an hour's vain wading in that roaring stream, whipping it with fly after fly, while R., the foreordained fisherman, was sitting comfortably in a sawmill, and derricking that pair of three-quarter-pounders in through the window! I had ventured more warily than he, and used, if not the same skill, at least the best skill at my command. My conscience was clear, but so was his; and he had had the drier skin and the greater magnanimity and the biggest fish besides. There is much to be said, in a world like ours, for taking the world as you find it and for fishing with a worm.

One's memories of such fishing, however agreeable they may be, are not to be identified with a defense of the practice. Yet, after all, the most effective defense of worm-fishing is the concrete recollection of some brook that could be fished best or only in that way, or the image of a particular trout that yielded to the temptation of an angleworm after you had flicked fly after fly over him in vain. Indeed, half the zest of brook fishing is in your campaign for "individuals,"—as the Salvation Army workers say,—not merely for a basketful of fish *qua* fish, but for a series of individual trout which your instinct tells you ought to lurk under that log or be hovering in that ripple. How to get him, by some sportsmanlike process, is the question. If he will rise to some fly in your book, few fishermen will deny that the fly is the more pleasurable weapon. Dainty, luring, beautiful toy, light as thistle-down, falling where you will it to fall, holding when the leader tightens and sings like the string of a violin, the artificial fly represents the poetry of angling. Given the gleam of early morning on some wide water, a heavy trout breaking the surface as he curves and plunges, with the fly holding well, with the right sort of rod in your fingers, and the right man in the other end of the canoe, and you perceive how easy is that Emersonian trick of making the pomp of emperors ridiculous.

But angling's honest prose, as represented by the lowly worm, has also its exalted moments. "The last fish I caught was with a worm," says the honest Walton, and so say I. It was the last evening of last August. The

dusk was settling deep upon a tiny meadow, scarcely ten rods from end to end. The rank bog grass, already drenched with dew, bent over the narrow, deep little brook so closely that it could not be fished except with a double-shotted, baited hook, dropped delicately between the heads of the long grasses. Underneath this canopy the trout were feeding, taking the hook with a straight downward tug, as they made for the hidden bank. It was already twilight when I began, and before I reached the black belt of woods that separated the meadow from the lake, the swift darkness of the North Country made it impossible to see the hook. A short half hour's fishing only, and behold nearly twenty good trout derricked into a basket until then sadly empty. Your rigorous fly-fisherman would have passed that grass-hidden brook in disdain, but it proved a treasure for the humble. Here, indeed, there was no question of individually-minded fish, but simply a neglected brook, full of trout which could be reached with the baited hook only. In more open brook-fishing it is always a fascinating problem to decide how to fish a favorite pool or ripple, for much depends upon the hour of the day, the light, the height of water, the precise period of the spring or summer. But after one has decided upon the best theoretical procedure, how often the stupid trout prefers some other plan! And when you have missed a fish that you counted upon landing, what solid satisfaction is still possible for you, if you are philosopher enough to sit down then and there, eat your lunch, smoke a meditative pipe, and devise a new campaign against that particular fish! To get another rise from him after lunch is a triumph of diplomacy, to land him is nothing short of statesmanship. For sometimes he will jump furiously at a fly, for very devilishness, without ever meaning to take it, and then, wearying suddenly of his gymnastics, he will snatch sulkily at a grasshopper, beetle, or worm. Trout feed upon an extraordinary variety of crawling things, as all fishermen know who practice the useful habit of opening the first two or three fish they catch, to see what food is that day the favorite. But here, as elsewhere in this world, the best things lie nearest, and there is no bait so killing, week in and week out, as your plain garden or golf-green angleworm.

Walton's list of possible worms is impressive, and his directions for placing them upon the hook have the placid completeness that belonged to his character. Yet in such matters a little nonconformity may be encouraged. No two men or boys dig bait in quite the same way, though all share, no doubt, the singular elation which gilds that grimy occupation with the spirit of romance. The mind is really occupied, not with the wriggling red creatures in the lumps of earth, but with the stout fish which each worm may capture, just as a saint might rejoice in the squalor of this world as a preparation for the glories of the world to come. Nor do any two experienced fishermen hold quite the same theory as to the best mode of baiting the hook. There are a hundred ways, each of them good. As to the best hook for worm-fishing, you will find dicta in every catalogue of fishing tackle, but size and shape and tempering are qualities that should vary with the brook, the season, and the fisherman. Should one use a three-foot leader, or none at all? Whose rods are best for bait-fishing, granted that all of them should be stiff enough in the tip to lift a good fish by dead strain from a tangle of brush or logs? Such questions, like those pertaining to the boots or coat which one should wear, the style of bait-box one should carry, or the brand of tobacco best suited for smoking in the wind, are topics for unending discussion among the serious minded around the camp-fire. Much edification is in them, and yet they are but prudential maxims after all. They are mere moralities of the Franklin or Chesterfield variety, counsels of worldly wisdom, but they leave the soul untouched. A man may have them at his finger's ends and be no better fisherman at bottom; or he may, like R., ignore most of the admitted rules and come home with a full basket. It is a sufficient defense of fishing with a worm to pronounce the truism that no man is a complete angler until he has mastered all the modes of angling. Lovely streams, lonely and enticing, but impossible to fish with

a fly, await the fisherman who is not too proud to use, with a man's skill, the same unpretentious tackle which he began with as a boy.

But ah, to fish with a worm, and then not catch your fish! To fail with a fly is no disgrace: your art may have been impeccable, your patience faultless to the end. But the philosophy of worm-fishing is that of Results, of having something tangible in your basket when the day's work is done. It is a plea for Compromise, for cutting the coat according to the cloth, for taking the world as it actually is. The fly-fisherman is a natural Foe of Compromise. He throws to the trout a certain kind of lure; and they will take it, so; if not, adieu. He knows no middle path.

"This high man, aiming at a million,
Misses a unit."

The raptures and the tragedies of consistency are his. He is a scorner of the ground. All honor to him! When he comes back at nightfall and says happily, "I have never cast a line more perfectly than I have to-day," it is almost indecent to peek into his creel. It is like rating Colonel Newcome by his bank account.

But the worm-fisherman is no such proud and isolated soul. He is a "low man" rather than a high one; he honestly cares what his friends will think when they look into his basket to see what he has to show for his day's sport. He watches the Foe of Compromise men go stumbling forward and superbly falling, while he, with less inflexible courage, manages to keep his feet. He wants to score, and not merely to give a pretty exhibition of base-running. At the Harvard-Yale football game of 1903 the Harvard team showed superior strength in rushing the ball; they carried it almost to the Yale goal line repeatedly, but they could not, for some reason, take it over. In the instant of absolute need, the Yale line held, and when the Yale team had to score in order to win, they scored. As the crowd streamed out of the Stadium, a veteran Harvard alumnus said: "This news will cause great sorrow in one home I know of, until they learn by to-morrow's papers that the Harvard team acquitted itself creditably." Exactly. Given one team bent upon acquitting itself creditably, and another team determined to win, which will be victorious? The stay-at-homes on the Yale campus that day were not curious to know whether their team was acquitting itself creditably, but whether it was winning the game. Every other question than that was to those young Philistines merely a fine-spun irrelevance. They took the Cash and let the Credit go.

There is much to be said, no doubt, for the Harvard veteran's point of view. The proper kind of credit may be a better asset for eleven boys than any championship; and to fish a bit of water consistently and skillfully, with your best flies and in your best manner, is perhaps achievement enough. So says the Foe of Compromise, at least. But the Yale spirit will be prying into the basket in search of fish; it prefers concrete results. If all men are by nature either Platonists or Aristotelians, fly-fishermen or worm-fishermen, how difficult it is for us to do one another justice! Differing in mind, in aim and method, how shall we say infallibly that this man or that is wrong? To fail with Plato for companion may be better than to succeed with Aristotle. But one thing is perfectly clear: there is no warrant for Compromise but in Success. Use a worm if you will, but you must have fish to show for it, if you would escape the finger of scorn. If you find yourself camping by an unknown brook, and are deputed to catch the necessary trout for breakfast, it is wiser to choose the surest bait. The crackle of the fish in the frying-pan will atone for any theoretical defect in your method. But to choose the surest bait, and then to bring back no fish, is unforgivable. Forsake Plato if you must,—but you may do so only at the price of justifying yourself in the terms of Aristotelian arithmetic. The college president who abandoned his college in order to run a cotton mill was free to make his own choice of a calling; but he was never pardoned for bankrupting the mill. If one is bound to be a low man rather than an impractical idealist, he should at least make sure of his vulgar success.

Is all this but a disguised defense of pot-hunting? No. There is no possible defense of pot-hunting, whether it be upon a trout brook or in the stock market. Against fish or men, one should play the game fairly. Yet for that matter some of the most skillful fly-fishermen I have known were pot-hunters at heart, and some of the most prosaic-looking merchants were idealists compared to whom Shelley was but a dreaming boy. All depends upon the spirit with which one makes his venture. I recall a boy of five who gravely watched his father tramp off after rabbits,—gun on shoulder and beagle in leash. Thereupon he shouldered a wooden sword, and dragging his reluctant black kitten by a string, sallied forth upon the dusty Vermont road "to get a lion for breakfast." That is the true sporting temper! Let there be but a fine idealism in the quest, and the particular object is unessential. "A true fisherman's happiness," says Mr. Cleveland, "is not dependent upon his luck." It depends upon his heart.

No doubt all amateur fishing is but "play,"—as the psychologists soberly term it: not a necessary, but a freely assumed activity, born of surplusage of vitality. Nobody, not even a carpenter wearied of his job, has to go fishing unless he wants to. He may indeed find himself breakfast-less in camp, and obliged to betake himself to the brook,—but then he need not have gone into the woods at all. Yet if he does decide to fish, let him

"Venture as warily, use the same skill,
   Do his best, . . ."

whatever variety of tackle he may choose. He can be a whole-souled sportsman with the poorest equipment, or a mean "trout-hog" with the most elaborate.

Only, in the name of gentle Izaak himself, let him be a complete angler; and let the man be a passionate amateur of all the arts of life, despising none of them, and using all of them for his soul's good and for the joy of his fellows. If he be, so to speak, but a worm-fisherman,—a follower of humble occupations, and pledged to unromantic duties,—let him still thrill with the pleasures of the true sportsman. To make the most of dull hours, to make the best of dull people, to like a poor jest better than none, to wear the threadbare coat like a gentleman, to be outvoted with a smile, to hitch your wagon to the old horse if no star is handy,—this is the wholesome philosophy taught by fishing with a worm. The fun of it depends upon the heart. There may be as much zest in saving as in spending, in working for small wages as for great, in avoiding the snapshots of publicity as in being invariably first "among those present." But a man should be honest. If he catches most of his fish with a worm, secures the larger portion of his success by commonplace industry, let

him glory in it, for this, too, is part of the great game. Yet he ought not in that case to pose as a fly-fisherman only,—to carry himself as one aware of the immortalizing camera,—to pretend that life is easy, if one but knows how to drop a fly into the right ripple. For life is not easy, after all is said. It is a long brook to fish, and it needs a stout heart and a wise patience. All the flies there are in the book, and all the bait that can be carried in the box, are likely to be needed ere the day is over. But, like the Psalmist's "river of God," this brook is "full of water," and there is plenty of good fishing to be had in it if one is neither afraid nor ashamed of fishing sometimes with a worm.

Part 7

Fresh Water and Saltwater All-Tackle World Records

Reprinted courtesy of the International Game Fish Association

International Game Fish Association World Records are copyrighted and may not be reproduced. The records that follow were current only at the time of publication; the complete updated list of records can be found on the IGFA website, www.igfa.org.

The International Game Fish Association is a not-for-profit organization committed to the conservation of game fish and the promotion of responsible, ethical angling practices through science, education, rule making and record keeping.

Species	Weight	Location	Catch Date	Angler
Acara Paragaio	0.71 kg (1 lb 9 oz)	Rio Negro, Brazil	11/7/1999	James Wise, M.D.
Acara Paragaio	0.71 kg (1 lb 9 oz)	Rio Negro River, Brazil	2/9/2007	Capt. Jay Wright Jr
Acara roi roi	0.48 kg (1 lb 0 oz)	Igarape do Capitari, Amazonas, Brazil	12/20/2009	Gilberto Fernandes
Acara Tucanare	0.7 kg (1 lb 8 oz)	Igarape do Capitari, Brazil	12/5/2009	Gilberto Fernandes
Acara, Silver	0.78 kg (1 lb 11 oz)	Igarape do Capitari, Amazonas, Brazil	6/3/2010	Gilberto Fernandes
Aimara (jeju)	0.68 kg (1 lb 8 oz)	Rio Tapera, Amazon, Brazil	2/1/2003	Martin Arostegui
Akahata	1.18 kg (2 lb 9 oz)	Oshima, Tokyo, Japan	7/28/2002	Hiroyuki Yoshihara
Akodai	3.04 kg (6 lb 11 oz)	Shimoda, Shizuoka, Japan	3/21/2005	Jun Yamada
Albacore	39.97 kg (88 lb 2 oz)	Gran Canaria, Canary Islands, Spain	11/19/1977	Siegfried Dickemann
Alfonsino	3.77 kg (8 lb 5 oz)	Norfolk Canyon, Virginia Beach, Virginia, USA	10/10/2010	Kevin Wong
Altai Osman	5.82 kg (12 lb 13 oz)	Hoton Lake, Mongolia	6/14/2009	Iurii Diachenko
Amberjack, greater	71.15 kg (156 lb 13 oz)	Iki Island, Nagasaki, Japan	11/19/2010	Hideyuki Nemoto
Angelfish, grey	1.83 kg (4 lb 0 oz)	South Beach Jetty, Miami, Florida, USA	7/12/1999	Rene de Dios
Angler	57.5 kg (126 lb 12 oz)	Sagnefiorden, Hoyanger, Norway	7/4/1996	Gunnar Thorsteinsen

Species	Weight	Location	Catch Date	Angler
Ara	11 kg (24 lb 4 oz)	Kashima, Ibaraki, Japan	12/15/2002	Masato Ishizuka
Aracu	0.82 kg (1 lb 12 oz)	Puraquequara Lake, Amazonas, Brazil	7/27/2009	Gilberto Fernandes
Araçu comum	0.96 kg (2 lb 2 oz)	Thaimaçu Lodge, Brazil	7/18/2007	Tacito De Almeida
Aracu, fat head	1.15 kg (2 lb 8 oz)	Lago Puraquequara, Brazil	7/24/2009	Gilberto Fernandes
Aracu, pau-de-nego	0.54 kg (1 lb 3 oz)	Puraquequara Lake, Amazonas, Brazil	7/3/2010	Gilberto Fernandes
Arawana	6.58 kg (14 lb 8 oz)	Miriti, Rio Preta da Eva, Amazonas, Brazil	10/22/2009	Jorge Masullo de Aguiar
Arawana, black	2.27 kg (5 lb 0 oz)	Bita River, Colombia	3/14/1987	Capt. Dan Kipnis
Argentine, greater	0.7 kg (1 lb 8 oz)	Hardangerfjord, Norway	8/6/2001	Ms. Sandra Marquard
Asp	5.66 kg (12 lb 7 oz)	Lake Vanern, Sweden	9/25/1993	Jan-Erik Skoglund
Ayamekasago	2.5 kg (5 lb 8 oz)	Irozaki, Shizuoka, Japan	8/13/1998	Mikio Suzuki
Barb, giant	52 kg (114 lb 10 oz)	Bung Sam Lan Lake, Thailand	3/12/2004	Terry Robert Mather

Species	Weight	Location	Catch Date	Angler
Barb, golden belly	1.4 kg (3 lb 1 oz)	Srinakarin Dam, Thailand	4/28/2002	Ms. Tsang Yin
Barb, golden belly	1.4 kg (3 lb 1 oz)	Srinakarin Dam, Thailand	4/28/2002	Jean-Francois Helias
Barb, golden tinfoil	0.49 kg (1 lb 1 oz)	Kong Lai, Thailand	4/2/2011	Jean-Francois Helias
Barb, hampala	6.5 kg (14 lb 5 oz)	Temenggor Lake, State of Perak, Malaysia	9/22/2002	Teh Teck
Barb, Java	2.31 kg (5 lb 1 oz)	Chiang Mai, Thailand	9/30/2008	Jean-Francois Helias
Barb, lagleri	0.72 kg (1 lb 9 oz)	Luang Prabang, Laos	12/1/2010	Jean-Francois Helias
Barb, Laos	0.53 kg (1 lb 2 oz)	Nam Song River, Laos	2/6/2010	Jean-Francois Helias
Barb, mad	6 kg (13 lb 3 oz)	Bung Sam Lan Lake, Thailand	8/31/2002	Loke Wong
Barb, Smith's	0.8 kg (1 lb 12 oz)	Srinakarin Dam, Thailand	5/2/2002	Jean-Francois Helias
Barb, soldier river	3.84 kg (8 lb 7 oz)	Ratchaburi, Thailand	11/18/2010	Gavin Clarke
Barb, tinfoil	1.3 kg (2 lb 13 oz)	Temmenggor Dam, Perak, West Malaysia	4/6/2003	Ngu Sen
Barbel	6.12 kg (13 lb 8 oz)	St. Patrick's Stream, Bershire, United Kingdom	12/29/2004	Eric Charles Roberts
Barbel, comizo hybrid	6.95 kg (15 lb 5 oz)	Guadiana River, Spain	10/26/2009	Stan Nabozny
Barenose, bigeye	5.89 kg (13 lb 0 oz)	Otec Beach, Kailua, Kona, Hawaii, USA	7/12/1992	Rex Bigg
Barracuda, bigeye	7.9 kg (17 lb 6 oz)	Chagos, Diego Garcia	11/7/2010	Phillip W. Richmond, Jr.
Barracuda, blackfin	7.14 kg (15 lb 12 oz)	Puerto Quetzal, Guatemala	6/10/1995	Estuardo Vila S.
Barracuda, great	38.5 kg (84 lb 14 oz)	Scarborough Shoals, Philippines	3/1/1991	Jessie Cordova
Barracuda, Guinean	45.9 kg (101 lb 3 oz)	Olende, Gabon	12/27/2002	Dr. Cyril Fabre
Barracuda, Hellers	2.04 kg (4 lb 8 oz)	Molokai, Hawaii, USA	1/18/2005	Dan Stockdon Jr.

Species	Weight	Location	Catch Date	Angler
Barracuda, Mexican	11.08 kg (24 lb 7 oz)	Tropic Star Lodge, Pinas Bay, Panama	4/26/2010	John J. Ferrante, Esq.
Barracuda, Pacific	12.87 kg (28 lb 6 oz)	Isla Secas, Panama	3/8/2010	Jilberto Cansari
Barracuda, pickhandle	15 kg (33 lb 1 oz)	Malindi, Kenya	11/19/2008	Thomas Knill
Barracuda, yellowmouth	10.2 kg (22 lb 8 oz)	Lanzarote Island, Canaries, Spain	2/6/2007	Steven Carr
Barramundi	44.64 kg (98 lb 6 oz)	Lake Monduran, Queensland, Australia	12/12/2010	Denis Harrold
Barrelfish	13.15 kg (29 lb 0 oz)	Big Pine Key, Florida, USA	11/27/2010	Walter McManus
Baru	0.48 kg (1 lb 0 oz)	Igarape do Capitari, Amazonas, Brazil	1/3/2010	Gilberto Fernandes
Bass, Australian	3.75 kg (8 lb 4 oz)	Lake Wivenhoe, Queensland, Australia	7/24/2005	Neil Schultz

Species	Weight	Location	Catch Date	Angler
Bass, barred sand	5.98 kg (13 lb 3 oz)	Huntington Beach, California, USA	8/29/1988	Robert Halal
Bass, black sea	4.65 kg (10 lb 4 oz)	Virginia Beach, Virginia, USA	1/1/2000	Allan Paschall
Bass, European	10.12 kg (22 lb 5 oz)	Pirou, France	5/28/1999	Philippe Boulet
Bass, giant sea	255.6 kg (563 lb 8 oz)	Anacapa Island, California, USA	8/20/1968	James McAdam, Jr.
Bass, goldspotted sand	4.64 kg (10 lb 4 oz)	Thetis Bank, Baja, California, USA	11/1/2006	Dan Cash
Bass, Guadalupe	1.67 kg (3 lb 11 oz)	Lake Travis, Austin, Texas, USA	9/25/1983	Allen Christenson, Jr.
Bass, Guadalupe X smallmouth	1.9 kg (4 lb 3 oz)	Blanco River, Texas, USA	6/18/1995	John Weaver
Bass, kelp (calico)	6.54 kg (14 lb 7 oz)	Newport Beach, California, USA	10/2/1993	Thomas Murphy
Bass, large-mouth	10.12 kg (22 lb 4 oz)	Lake Biwa, Shiga, Japan	7/2/2009	Manabu Kurita
Bass, leather	12.47 kg (27 lb 8 oz)	Isla Clarion, Revillagigedo Islands, Mexico	1/26/1988	Allan Ristori
Bass, longtail	2.94 kg (6 lb 8 oz)	Islamorada, Florida, USA	2/12/2000	Ms. Bonnie Murphy
Bass, mean-mouth	3.88 kg (8 lb 8 oz)	Vetrans Lake, Sulphur, Oklahoma, USA	3/27/2006	Dru Clayton Kinslow
Bass, Ozark	0.45 kg (1 lb 0 oz)	Bull Shoals Lake, Arkansas, USA	5/13/1997	Gary Nelson
Bass, Roanoke	0.62 kg (1 lb 5 oz)	Nottoway River, Virginia, USA	11/11/1991	Thomas Elkins
Bass, rock	1.36 kg (3 lb 0 oz)	York River, Ontario, Canada	8/1/1974	Peter Gulgin
Bass, rock	1.36 kg (3 lb 0 oz)	Lake Erie, Pennsylvania, USA	6/18/1998	Herbert Ratner, Jr.
Bass, shadow	0.82 kg (1 lb 13 oz)	Spring River, Arkansas, USA	7/5/1999	James Baker
Bass, shoal	3.99 kg (8 lb 12 oz)	Apalachicola River, Florida, USA	1/28/1995	Carl Davis
Bass, small-mouth	5.41 kg (11 lb 15 oz)	Dale Hollow Lake, Tennessee, USA	7/9/1955	David Hayes
Bass, splittail	0.68 kg (1 lb 8 oz)	Playa Zancudo, Costa Rica	6/10/1995	Craig Whitehead, MD
Bass, spotted	4.65 kg (10 lb 4 oz)	Pine Flat Lake, California, USA	4/21/2001	Bryan Shishido

Species	Weight	Location	Catch Date	Angler
Bass, spotted sand	2.24 kg (4 lb 15 oz)	San Diego, California, USA	7/12/2003	Paul Weintraub
Bass, striped	35.6 kg (78 lb 8 oz)	Atlantic City, New Jersey, USA	9/21/1982	Albert McReynolds
Bass, striped (landlocked)	30.61 kg (67 lb 8 oz)	O'Neill Forebay, Los Banos, California, USA	5/7/1992	Hank Ferguson
Bass, Suwannee	1.75 kg (3 lb 14 oz)	Suwannee River, Florida, USA	3/2/1985	Ronnie Everett
Bass, white	3.09 kg (6 lb 13 oz)	Lake Orange, Orange, Virginia, USA	7/31/1989	Ronald Sprouse
Bass, white	3.09 kg (6 lb 13 oz)	Amite River, Greenwell Springs, Louisiana, USA	8/27/2010	Corey Crochet
Bass, whiterock	12.38 kg (27 lb 5 oz)	Greers Ferry Lake, Arkansas, USA	5/24/1997	Jerald Shaum
Bass, yellow	1.16 kg (2 lb 9 oz)	Duck River, Waverly, Tennessee, USA	2/27/1998	John Chappell
Bass, yellow (hybrid)	1.81 kg (4 lb 0 oz)	Lake Fork, Texas, USA	3/26/2003	C. Runyan
Batfish, orbicular	2.01 kg (4 lb 7 oz)	Racha Noi Island, Phucket, Thailand	2/21/2004	Tony Stuart
Batfish, tiera	1.92 kg (4 lb 3 oz)	Kut Island, Thailand	1/17/2006	Steven M. Wozniak
Biara	2.1 kg (4 lb 10 oz)	Xingu River, Brazil	4/21/2000	Marcio Borges de Oliveira
Bicuda	6.8 kg (15 lb 0 oz)	Teles Pires River, Mato Grosso, Brazil	12/13/2002	Sandro Francio
Bigeye	2.85 kg (6 lb 4 oz)	Baja da Guanabara, Rio de Janeiro, Brazil	8/30/1997	Jayme Garcia
Bigeye, short	0.56 kg (1 lb 4 oz)	Hatteras, North Carolina, USA	4/24/2004	John D. Overton, Jr.
Binga	0.51 kg (1 lb 2 oz)	Maleri Island, Lake Malawi, Malawi	11/30/1996	Garry Whitcher
Blackfish, small-scale	3.4 kg (7 lb 7 oz)	Hachijokojima, Hachijo Island, Japan	1/8/1998	Papa Otsuru
Bludger	9.7 kg (21 lb 6 oz)	Bartholmeu Dias, Mozambique	6/17/1997	Joh Haasbroek
Bluefish	14.4 kg (31 lb 12 oz)	Hatteras, North Carolina, USA	1/30/1972	James Hussey
Bluegill	2.15 kg (4 lb 12 oz)	Ketona Lake, Alabama, USA	4/9/1950	T. Hudson

Species	Weight	Location	Catch Date	Angler
Bocaccio	10.09 kg (22 lb 4 oz)	Elfin Cove, Alaska, USA	8/25/2001	Gaylord Saetre
Boga	2.49 kg (5 lb 8 oz)	Uruguay River, Concordia, Argentina	1/14/2008	Charles Henry Plomteaux III
Bonefish	8.61 kg (19 lb 0 oz)	Zululand, South Africa	5/26/1962	Brian Batchelor
Bonito, Atlantic	8.3 kg (18 lb 4 oz)	Faial Island, Azores, Portugal	7/8/1953	D. Higgs
Bonito, Australian	9.4 kg (20 lb 11 oz)	Montague Island, N.S.W., Australia	4/1/1978	Bruce Conley
Bonito, leaping	0.96 kg (2 lb 2 oz)	Macleay River, Australia	5/7/1995	Wayne Colling
Bonito, Pacific	9.67 kg (21 lb 5 oz)	181 Spot, California, USA	10/19/2003	Kim Larson
Bonito, striped	10.65 kg (23 lb 8 oz)	Victoria, Mahe, Seychelles	2/19/1975	Anne Cochain
Bowfin	9.75 kg (21 lb 8 oz)	Forest Lake, Florence, South Carolina, USA	1/29/1980	Robert Harmon

Species	Weight	Location	Catch Date	Angler
Bracanjuva	0.62 kg (1 lb 6 oz)	Mato Grosso, Piguiri River, Brazil	4/16/1998	Helder Coutinho
Bream	6.01 kg (13 lb 3 oz)	Hagbyan Creek, Sweden	5/11/1984	Luis Rasmussen
Bream, African red	5.55 kg (12 lb 3 oz)	Nouadhibou, Mauritania	3/13/1986	Bernard Defago
Bream, black	6.17 kg (13 lb 9 oz)	Lake Tinaroo, Queensland, Australia	1/16/1997	Brian Seawright
Bream, blue-lined large-eye	5.5 kg (12 lb 2 oz)	Amami-oshima, Kagoshima, Japan	5/28/2000	Hitoshi Suzuki
Bream, King soldier	1.25 kg (2 lb 12 oz)	Dubai, United Arab Emirates	2/20/2011	Steven M. Wozniak
Bream, twoband	1.3 kg (2 lb 13 oz)	Europa Point, Gibraltar	9/3/1995	Ernest Borrell
Bream, white	0.76 kg (1 lb 10 oz)	Holandselva, Akershus, Norway	5/25/2004	Jan Bredo Nerdrum
Brotula, bearded	8.52 kg (18 lb 12 oz)	Destin, Florida, USA	4/10/1999	Joe Dollar
Buffalo, bigmouth	31.89 kg (70 lb 5 oz)	Bastrop, Louisiana, USA	4/21/1980	Delbert Sisk
Buffalo, black	28.74 kg (63 lb 6 oz)	Mississippi River, Iowa, USA	8/14/1999	Jim Winters
Buffalo, smallmouth	37.29 kg (82 lb 3 oz)	Athens Lake, Texas, USA	5/6/1993	Randy Collins
Bullhead, black	3.37 kg (7 lb 7 oz)	Mill Pond, Wantagh, Long Island, New York, USA	8/25/1993	Kevin Kelly
Bullhead, brown	3.35 kg (7 lb 6 oz)	Mahopac Lake, New York, USA	8/1/2009	Glenn Collacuro
Bullhead, yellow	2.89 kg (6 lb 6 oz)	Drevel, Missouri, USA	5/27/2006	John R. Irvin
Bullseye, long-finned	2.95 kg (6 lb 8 oz)	Rio de Janeiro, Brazil	5/18/2002	Eduardo Baumeier
Bullseye, long-finned	2.95 kg (6 lb 8 oz)	Kona, Hawaii, USA	12/31/2008	Steve Kwiat
Bullseye, moon-tail	0.55 kg (1 lb 3 oz)	Hachijo Is., Tokyo, Japan	8/15/2005	Yuuma Nishino
Burbot	11.4 kg (25 lb 2 oz)	Lake Diefenbaker, Saskatchewan, Canada	3/27/2010	Sean Konrad
Buri (Japanese amberjack)	22.1 kg (48 lb 11 oz)	Ijika, Mie, Japan	12/11/2005	Kyoichi Kitamura
Burrfish, spotfin	4.1 kg (9 lb 0 oz)	Kozushima, Tokyo, Japan	7/13/2004	Junzo Okada
Burrfish, spotted	6.25 kg (13 lb 12 oz)	Haulover, Florida, USA	4/28/2003	Tim O'Quinn

Species	Weight	Location	Catch Date	Angler
Burrfish, striped	0.63 kg (1 lb 6 oz)	Delaware Bay, New Jersey, USA	8/13/1989	Donna Ludlam
Butterfish, Brazilian	10.12 kg (22 lb 4 oz)	Rio de Janeiro, Brazil	3/19/2004	Eduardo Baumeier
Cabezon	10.43 kg (23 lb 0 oz)	Juan De Fuca Strait, Washington, USA	8/4/1990	Wesley Hunter
Cachorro, peixe	0.94 kg (2 lb 1 oz)	Rio Negro, Brazil	2/9/2007	Rebecca Wright
Captainfish	12 kg (26 lb 7 oz)	Archipelago dos Bijagos, Guinea-Bissau	5/17/1998	Eric Legris
Cara-de-gato	7.25 kg (15 lb 15 oz)	Lago dos Reis, Amazonas, Brazil	6/26/2009	Gilberto Fernandes
Carp, bighead	40.82 kg (90 lb 0 oz)	Guntersville Lake, Tennessee, USA	6/2/2005	Jeffrey J. Rorex
Carp, black	18.5 kg (40 lb 12 oz)	Edo River, Chiba, Japan	4/1/2000	Kenichi Hosoi
Carp, common	34.35 kg (75 lb 11 oz)	Lac de St. Cassien, France	5/21/1987	Leo van der Gugten
Carp, crucian	2.01 kg (4 lb 7 oz)	Ostanforsan, Falun, Sweden	6/12/1988	Lars Jonsson
Carp, grass	39.75 kg (87 lb 10 oz)	Piasuchnik Dam, Bulgaria	7/22/2009	Stoian Iliev
Carp, silver	32 kg (70 lb 8 oz)	Andong-s, Kyungsangbok-Do, Korea	6/4/2006	Chongdae Lim
Carpsucker, river	3.48 kg (7 lb 11 oz)	Canadian Co., Oklahoma, USA	4/18/1990	W. Kenyon
Catfish, Amazon Sailfin	1.02 kg (2 lb 4 oz)	Miami Canal, Miami, Florida, USA	3/6/2010	Dennis Triana
Catfish, amur	3.25 kg (7 lb 2 oz)	Kitakami River, Iwate, Japan	6/1/2010	Akira Niinuma
Catfish, blue	58.97 kg (130 lb 0 oz)	Missouri River, Florissant, Missouri, USA	7/20/2010	Greg Bernal
Catfish, channel	26.3 kg (58 lb 0 oz)	Santee-Cooper Reservoir, South Carolina, USA	7/7/1964	W. Whaley
Catfish, duckbill	1.5 kg (3 lb 4 oz)	Xingu River, Brazil	6/2/2003	Ms. Roberta Mathias
Catfish, Eurasian	17.2 kg (37 lb 14 oz)	Imazuhama, Lake Biwa, Shiga, Japan	7/4/1997	Shoji Matsuura
Catfish, firewood	16 kg (35 lb 4 oz)	Rio Amazonas, Amazonas, Brazil	3/12/2011	Gilberto Fernandes
Catfish, flathead	55.79 kg (123 lb 0 oz)	Elk City Reservoir, Independence, Kansas, USA	5/19/1998	Ken Paulie

Species	Weight	Location	Catch Date	Angler
Catfish, flat-whiskered	7.68 kg (16 lb 15 oz)	Xingu River, Brazil	8/7/2001	Ian-Arthur de Sulocki
Catfish, forked tail	2.3 kg (5 lb 1 oz)	Temenggor Dam, Malaysia	6/14/2001	Jean-Francois Helias
Catfish, gafftop-sail	4.54 kg (10 lb 0 oz)	Boca Raton, Florida, USA	2/10/2007	Nicholas F. Grecco
Catfish, giant (Mekong)	117.93 kg (260 lb 0 oz)	Gillhams Fishing Resorts, Krabi, Thailand	11/29/2010	Martin David Kent
Catfish, gilded	38.8 kg (85 lb 8 oz)	Amazon River, Amazonas, Brazil	11/15/1986	Gilberto Fernandes
Catfish, granu-lated	6.5 kg (14 lb 5 oz)	Xingu River, Mato Grosso, Brazil	10/16/1999	Capt. Kdu Magal-haes
Catfish, grey eel	8.5 kg (18 lb 11 oz)	Nakorn Nayok River, Thai-land	4/4/2002	Ms. Anongnart Sungwichien
Catfish, hard-head	1.5 kg (3 lb 5 oz)	Mays Marina, Sebastian, Florida, USA	4/18/1993	Ms. Amanda Steed
Catfish, mandi	1.02 kg (2 lb 4 oz)	Japato, Amazonias, Brazil	2/10/2009	Russell Jensen
Catfish, redtail (pirarara)	56 kg (123 lb 7 oz)	Rio Amazonas, Amazonas, Brazil	4/3/2010	Gilberto Fernandes
Catfish, ripsaw	21.5 kg (47 lb 6 oz)	Amazonas, Furo do Curari, Brazil	3/13/2010	Gilberto Fernandes
Catfish, shark	2.69 kg (5 lb 14 oz)	Kong Mae Lai, Thailand	3/26/2010	Natalie Carter
Catfish, sharp-tooth	36 kg (79 lb 5 oz)	Orange River, Upington, South Africa	12/5/1992	Hennie Moller
Catfish, slobber-ing	4.56 kg (10 lb 0 oz)	Rio Amazonas, Amazonas, Brazil	2/28/2010	Gilberto Fernandes
Catfish, smooth-mouth sea	10 kg (22 lb 0 oz)	Archipelago des Bijagos, Guinea-Bissau	4/3/2002	Jacques Sibieude
Catfish, smooth-mouth sea	11 kg (22 lb 0 oz)	Rubane, Guinea-Bissau	4/2/2003	Michel Garcia
Catfish, sucker-mouth	1.2 kg (2 lb 10 oz)	Bung Sam Lan Lake, Thailand	11/25/2002	Dirk Mueller
Catfish, swai	21.3 kg (46 lb 15 oz)	Bung Sam Lan Lake, Thailand	5/9/2009	Jakub Vagner
Catfish, Thai shark	2.1 kg (4 lb 10 oz)	Kura Mung, Thailand	1/9/2010	Jean-Francois Helias
Catfish, thick-spined	0.7 kg (1 lb 8 oz)	Bang Pakong River, Thailand	3/26/2004	Wayne Chung Wei Lau

Species	Weight	Location	Catch Date	Angler
Catfish, tiger-striped	3.09 kg (6 lb 12 oz)	Rio Amazonas, Amazonas, Brazil	2/20/2010	Gilberto Fernandes
Catfish, walking	1.19 kg (2 lb 10 oz)	Delray Beach, Florida, USA	7/15/2001	Patrick Keough
Catfish, white	8.78 kg (19 lb 5 oz)	Oakdale, California, USA	5/7/2005	Russell D. Price
Catfish, white sea	1.36 kg (3 lb 0 oz)	Sepitiba Bay, Brazil	5/4/2010	Steven M. Wozniak
Catfish, zebra	4.21 kg (9 lb 4 oz)	Rio Amazonas, Brazil	2/16/2008	Gilberto Fernandes
Catla	15.17 kg (33 lb 7 oz)	Theerasart, Thailand	1/2/2009	Jean-Francois Helias
Catshark, small-spotted	5.28 kg (11 lb 10 oz)	Guerande, France	5/8/2002	Jacques Andre
Chalceus, pink-tail	0.45 kg (1 lb 0 oz)	Unini River, Brazil	11/15/2005	Martin Arostegui
Char, Arctic	14.77 kg (32 lb 9 oz)	Tree River, Canada	7/31/1981	Jeffery Ward
Char, whitespotted	7.96 kg (17 lb 8 oz)	Urbyeyah River, Okhotsk, Russia	6/6/2006	Hajime Murata
Chilipepper	1.54 kg (3 lb 6 oz)	San Clemente Island, California, USA	3/11/2000	Stephen Grossberg
Chilipepper	1.54 kg (3 lb 6 oz)	San Clemente Island, California, USA	3/12/2000	George Bogen
Chinamanfish	13.2 kg (29 lb 1 oz)	Dampier, Australia	3/8/1996	Mark Cottrell
Choice, sailor's	0.45 kg (1 lb 0 oz)	Key West, Florida, USA	3/15/2003	Ms. Maria Ortega
Chub, Bermuda	6.01 kg (13 lb 4 oz)	Ft. Pierce Inlet, Florida, USA	3/5/1997	Sam Baum
Chub, brassy (Isuzumi)	1.4 kg (3 lb 1 oz)	Toshima, Tokyo, Japan	8/13/2008	Takashi Nishino
Chub, Cortez sea	2.44 kg (5 lb 6 oz)	Alijos Rocks, Mexico	9/19/2008	Bob Blum
Chub, European	3.05 kg (6 lb 11 oz)	Rhein bei, Weil am Rhein, Germany	12/14/2009	Dieter Lindenmann
Chub, grey sea	2.85 kg (6 lb 4 oz)	Izu-Oshima, Tokyo, Japan	8/15/2010	Takashi Nishino
Chub, Utah	0.57 kg (1 lb 4 oz)	Snake River, Idaho, USA	3/18/2007	Deborah S. Krick
Chub, yellow	3.85 kg (8 lb 8 oz)	Sabine Pass, Texas, USA	5/29/1994	Stephen McDonald
Cichlid, giant tanganyika	2.94 kg (6 lb 7 oz)	Lake Tanzania, Tanzania	5/2/2009	Jakub Vagner
Cichlid, Mayan	1.13 kg (2 lb 8 oz)	Holiday Park, Florida, USA	2/20/1999	Capt. Jay Wright Jr.
Cichlid, melan-ura	0.68 kg (1 lb 8 oz)	North Miami, Florida, USA	4/30/2008	Martin Arostegui

Species	Weight	Location	Catch Date	Angler
Cichlid, midas	1.13 kg (2 lb 8 oz)	Miami Canals, Florida, USA	8/24/2004	Martini Arostegui
Cichlid, turquoise	4.76 kg (10 lb 8 oz)	Quebrada Yanacue, Colombia	12/31/2010	Alejandro Linares
Cisco	3.35 kg (7 lb 6 oz)	North Cross Bay, Cedar Lake, Manitoba, Canada	4/11/1986	Randy Huff
Cobia	61.5 kg (135 lb 9 oz)	Shark Bay, W.A., Australia	7/9/1985	Peter Goulding
Cod, Atlantic	44.79 kg (98 lb 12 oz)	Isle of Shoals, New Hampshire, USA	6/8/1969	Alphonse Bielevich
Cod, cow	11.79 kg (26 lb 0 oz)	San Clemente Island, California, USA	1/9/1999	Stephen Grossberg
Cod, Pacific	17.5 kg (38 lb 9 oz)	Kawashiro, Kamoenai, Hokkaido, Japan	1/16/2005	Atsunori Takahira
Coney	0.56 kg (1 lb 4 oz)	Key West, Florida, USA	2/1/2003	Dennis Triana
Coney, Gulf	5.78 kg (12 lb 12 oz)	San Jose Del Cabo, Baja California Sur, Mexico	3/15/2008	George Bogen
Conger	60.44 kg (133 lb 4 oz)	Berry Head, South Devon, United Kingdom	6/5/1995	Vic Evans
Conger, beach	5.77 kg (12 lb 11 oz)	Tokyo Bay, Japan	12/3/2002	Phillip W. Richmond Jr.
Coralgrouper, blacksaddled	24.2 kg (53 lb 5 oz)	Hahajima, Ogasawara Island, Tokyo, Japan	9/27/1997	Hideo Morishita
Coralgrouper, highfin	1.2 kg (2 lb 10 oz)	Buso Point, Huon Gulf, Papua New Guinea	5/1/1994	Justin Mallett
Coralgrouper, leopard	7.4 kg (16 lb 5 oz)	Amami-oshima, Kagoshima, Japan	5/12/2002	Ms. Kiyomi Narita
Corb (shi drum)	3.1 kg (6 lb 13 oz)	Corse, France	6/7/2001	Patrick Sebile
Corbina, California	3.6 kg (7 lb 15 oz)	Mission Bay, California, USA	5/9/2004	Scott Matthews
Coris, yellowstripe	4.62 kg (10 lb 3 oz)	Keahole Point, Kailua Kona, Hawaii, USA	1/1/1996	Rex Bigg
Cornetfish, bluespotted	1 kg (2 lb 3 oz)	Dania Beach, Florida, USA	10/11/2001	Jean Lafage
Cornetfish, red	1.05 kg (2 lb 5 oz)	Shimoda, Shizuoka, Japan	4/14/2006	Junzo Okada
Coroata	6.8 kg (15 lb 0 oz)	Teles Pires River, Mato Grosso, Brazil	11/27/2002	Johnny Hoffmann
Coronetfish, red	2.5 kg (5 lb 8 oz)	Kushimoto, Wakayama, Japan	11/26/2007	Kouki Akeyama

Species	Weight	Location	Catch Date	Angler
Corvina, hybrid	4.76 kg (10 lb 8 oz)	Calaveras Lake, San Antonio, Texas, USA	1/27/1987	Norma Cleary
Corvina, orangemouth	24.6 kg (54 lb 3 oz)	Sabana Grande, Guayaquil, Ecuador	7/29/1992	Felipe Estrada E.
Corvina, shortfin	4.71 kg (10 lb 6 oz)	San Diego Bay, California, USA	6/20/2008	Carmen C. Rose
Crappie, black	2.26 kg (5 lb 0 oz)	Private Lake, Missouri, USA	4/21/2006	John R. Horstman
Crappie, white	2.35 kg (5 lb 3 oz)	Enid Dam, Mississippi, USA	7/31/1957	Fred Bright
Creole-fish	0.68 kg (1 lb 8 oz)	Apalachicola, Florida, USA	5/8/2006	Scott Rider
Croaker, Atlantic	3.94 kg (8 lb 11 oz)	Chesapeake Bay, Virgina, USA	8/17/2007	Norman T. Jenkins
Croaker, Boeseman	7 kg (15 lb 6 oz)	Chaopraya River, Pakkred, Thailand	11/18/1998	Jean-Francois Helias
Croaker, camaroon	0.91 kg (2 lb 0 oz)	Banjul, Gambia	2/2/2010	Stan Nabozny
Croaker, Cassava	14.2 kg (31 lb 4 oz)	Bubaque Island, Guinea-bissau	8/4/2009	Michel Delaunay
Croaker, law	13 kg (28 lb 10 oz)	Luanda, Angola, Africa	7/31/2005	Jose Henrique Couta da Silva
Croaker, longneck	15.02 kg (33 lb 2 oz)	Banjul, Gambia	3/25/1998	Alberto Hernandez
Croaker, S. A. silver	5.1 kg (11 lb 4 oz)	Jatapo, Amazon, Brazil	2/5/2009	Russell Jensen
Croaker, spotfin	4.28 kg (9 lb 7 oz)	Morro, Santo Domingo, Mexico	3/11/2006	Harold Lance Rigg
Croaker, whitemouth	3.75 kg (8 lb 4 oz)	Guanabara Bay, Brazil	8/3/2002	Lula Bulhoes
Croaker, yellowfin	2.49 kg (5 lb 8 oz)	East Cape, Mexico	5/22/2001	Capt. Jay Wright Jr.
Cui-ui	2.72 kg (6 lb 0 oz)	Pyramid Lake, Nevada, USA	6/30/1997	Mike Berg
Cunner	1.59 kg (3 lb 8 oz)	Revere Beach, Revere, Massachusetts, USA	5/24/2009	Sam Mac Allister
Cutlassfish, Atlantic	3.68 kg (8 lb 1 oz)	Rio de Janeiro, Brazil	9/6/1997	Felipe Soares
Dab (Kliesche)	1 kg (2 lb 3 oz)	Hauganes, Iceland	6/28/2007	Skarphendinn Asbjornsson
Dab, long rough	1.01 kg (2 lb 3 oz)	Straumbotn, Andorja, Norway	7/3/2005	Patrik Tjornmark

Species	Weight	Location	Catch Date	Angler
Dainan-anago	3.46 kg (7 lb 10 oz)	Hashirimizu, Kanagawa, Japan	1/8/2011	Seitaro Chiba
Dainanumihebi	2.05 kg (4 lb 8 oz)	Shimoda, Shizuoka, Japan	4/16/2008	Takashi Nishino
Dart, largespotted	1.36 kg (3 lb 0 oz)	Benguerra Island, Mozambique	3/19/2008	Jodie L. Johnson
Dentex	14.25 kg (31 lb 6 oz)	Los Cristianos Tenerife, Canary Islands, Spain	1/29/1999	Torsten Wetzel
Dentex, canary	9.1 kg (20 lb 0 oz)	Lanzarote, Spain	6/20/2009	Juan Carlos Puerto Ortega
Dentex, pink	13.8 kg (30 lb 6 oz)	Gibraltar	4/5/1996	P.A. Dunham
Doctorfish	0.57 kg (1 lb 4 oz)	Stetson Rock, Texas, USA	4/14/1997	Jerry McCullin
Doctorfish	0.57 kg (1 lb 4 oz)	Marathon, Florida, USA	12/1/2007	Dennis Triana
Dogfish, smooth	17.01 kg (37 lb 8 oz)	Cape May, New Jersey, USA	6/16/2007	David E. Spletzer
Dogfish, spiny	7.14 kg (15 lb 12 oz)	Kenmare Bay, Co. Kerry, Ireland	5/26/1989	Horst Muller
Dolly Varden	9.46 kg (20 lb 14 oz)	Wulik River, Alaska, USA	7/7/2001	Raz Reid
Dolphinfish	39.46 kg (87 lb 0 oz)	Papagallo Gulf, Costa Rica	9/25/1976	Manuel Salazar

Species	Weight	Location	Catch Date	Angler
Dorada	3.63 kg (8 lb 0 oz)	Rio Corcorna, Colombia	7/4/2009	Juan Marcos Tamayo
Dorado	25.28 kg (55 lb 11 oz)	Uruguay River, Concordia, Argentina	1/11/2006	Andre L. S. de Botton
Dourado	2.04 kg (4 lb 8 oz)	Rio Guatiquia, Columbia	1/16/2004	Alejandro Linares
Drum, black	51.28 kg (113 lb 1 oz)	Lewes, Delaware, USA	9/15/1975	Gerald Townsend
Drum, Canary	0.73 kg (1 lb 9 oz)	Vila Real Santo Antonio, Portugal	11/12/2006	Luis Ceia
Drum, freshwater	24.72 kg (54 lb 8 oz)	Nickajack Lake, Tennessee, USA	4/20/1972	Benny Hull
Drum, red	42.69 kg (94 lb 2 oz)	Avon, North Carolina, USA	11/7/1984	David Deuel
Durgon, black	0.68 kg (1 lb 8 oz)	Port Lucaya, Bahamas	2/2/2002	Dennis Triana
Eel, American	4.21 kg (9 lb 4 oz)	Cape May, New Jersey, USA	11/9/1995	Jeff Pennick
Eel, conger	6.8 kg (15 lb 0 oz)	Cape May Harbor, New Jersey, USA	11/2/2002	Ryan Dougherty
Eel, European	3.6 kg (7 lb 14 oz)	River Aare, Buren, Switzerland	7/10/1992	Christoph Lave
Eel, European	3.59 kg (7 lb 14 oz)	River Lyckeby, Sweden	8/8/1988	Luis Rasmussen
Eel, fire	0.7 kg (1 lb 8 oz)	Bang Pakong River, Thailand	11/3/2004	Henk Hoornweg
Eel, Japanese	0.95 kg (2 lb 1 oz)	Yokohama, Kanagawa, Japan	7/4/2010	Yuuma Nishino
Eel, king snake	23.58 kg (52 lb 0 oz)	Gulf of Mexico, Texas, USA	2/11/1997	Patrick Lemire
Eel, marbled	16.36 kg (36 lb 1 oz)	Hazelmere Dam, Durban, South Africa	6/10/1984	Ferdie Van Nooten
Eel, shortfin	7.48 kg (16 lb 8 oz)	Lake Bolac, Victoria, Australia	11/17/1998	Bernard Murphy
Eel, stippled spoon-nose	7.48 kg (16 lb 8 oz)	Port Mansfield, Texas, USA	8/28/2004	Taylor Ashley Walker
Emperor, long-face	10.35 kg (22 lb 13 oz)	Amami-Oshima, Kagoshima, Japan	3/8/2009	Satoshi Touchi
Emperor, spangled	9.45 kg (20 lb 13 oz)	Muroto, Kochi, Japan	9/19/2002	Takuya Kano
Emperor, yellowlip	5.44 kg (12 lb 0 oz)	Lifuka Island, Tonga	11/25/1991	Peter Dunn-Rankin
Escolar	72.89 kg (160 lb 11 oz)	Grand Caymen, Cayman Islands	12/15/2010	Charles F. Ebanks
Escolar, Roudi	2.44 kg (5 lb 6 oz)	Colt 45 Gulf of Mexico, Texas, USA	7/22/2007	Eric Ozolins

Species	Weight	Location	Catch Date	Angler
Fallfish	1.62 kg (3 lb 9 oz)	Susquehanna River, Owego, New York, USA	4/15/2009	Jonathan McNamara
Fanray	2.1 kg (4 lb 10 oz)	Akazawa, Ito, Shizuoka, Japan	5/6/2008	Takashi Nishino
Fanray	2.1 kg (4 lb 10 oz)	Akazawa, Ito, Japan	5/3/2010	Yuuma Nishino
Featherback, clown	6 kg (13 lb 3 oz)	Bung Sam Lan Lake, Thailand	3/16/2004	Bruce Dale
Featherback, clown	7 kg (13 lb 3 oz)	Sri Nakharin Dam, Thailand	2/26/2003	Terry Mather
Featherback, giant	9.08 kg (13 lb 6 oz)	Srinakarin Dam, Thailand	4/21/2006	Anongnat Sungwichien-Helias
Featherback, Indochina	2.74 kg (6 lb 0 oz)	Rathcaburi, Thailand	12/29/2008	Syringa Eade
Filefish, scrawled	2.15 kg (4 lb 11 oz)	Pompano Beach, Florida, USA	1/20/1998	Jonathan Angel
Filefish, thread-sail	1.05 kg (2 lb 5 oz)	Kenzaki, Kanagawa, Japan	4/7/2007	Takashi Kumaki
Filefish, unicorn	3.65 kg (8 lb 1 oz)	St. Augustine, Florida, USA	3/27/2003	Nathan Zimmer
Flagfin, royal	0.68 kg (1 lb 8 oz)	Key West, Florida, USA	11/23/2010	Martini Arostegui
Flathead, bar-tailed	3.7 kg (8 lb 3 oz)	Amami-Oshima, Kagoshima, Japan	2/24/2007	Tatsuki Matsumoto
Flathead, crocodile	1.05 kg (2 lb 5 oz)	Hiratsuka, Kanagawa, Japan	7/30/2008	Rintaro Shinohara
Flathead, dusky	6.33 kg (13 lb 15 oz)	Wallis Lake, Forster, N.S.W., Australia	6/7/1997	Glen Edwards
Flier	0.56 kg (1 lb 4 oz)	Little River, Spring Lake, North Carolina, USA	8/24/1988	R. Snipes
Flier	0.56 kg (1 lb 4 oz)	Lowndes Co., Georgia, USA	2/26/1996	Curt Brooks
Flounder, arrow tooth	3.86 kg (8 lb 8 oz)	Gulf of Alaska, Alaska, USA	8/7/2010	Capt. Jay Wright, Jr.
Flounder, Brazilian	6.25 kg (13 lb 12 oz)	Guanbam Bay, Brazil	7/17/2004	Mr. Roberto Silva
Flounder, European	2.93 kg (6 lb 7 oz)	Maurangerfjorden, Norway	1/10/2004	Anne Karin Lothe
Flounder, gulf	2.83 kg (6 lb 4 oz)	Dauphin Island, Alabama, USA	11/2/1996	Don Davis
Flounder, marbled	1.95 kg (4 lb 4 oz)	Kashima, Ibaraki, Japan	2/13/2005	Masakazu Naohara

Species	Weight	Location	Catch Date	Angler
Flounder, olive	14.5 kg (31 lb 15 oz)	Okinoshima, Shimane, Japan	3/16/2008	Noboru Shinagawa
Flounder, slime (babagarei)	1.76 kg (3 lb 14 oz)	Sendai Bay, Miyagi, Japan	12/28/1998	Tomoyasu Ishikawa
Flounder, small-eyed	3.22 kg (7 lb 1 oz)	Renaca, Vina del Mar, Chile	2/9/2011	Jon Wood
Flounder, southern	9.33 kg (20 lb 9 oz)	Nassau Sound, Florida, USA	12/23/1983	Larenza Mungin
Flounder, starry	4.79 kg (10 lb 9 oz)	Bolinas, California, USA	8/9/2007	Andrew Kleinberg
Flounder, stone	3.48 kg (7 lb 10 oz)	Kamezaki Port, Aichi, Japan	10/2/2009	Taiki Aoyama
Flounder, summer	10.17 kg (22 lb 7 oz)	Montauk, New York, USA	9/15/1975	Capt. Charles Nappi
Flounder, winter	3.17 kg (7 lb 0 oz)	Fire Island, New York, USA	5/8/1986	Dr. Einar Grell
Forkbeard	3.91 kg (8 lb 10 oz)	Mahon-Menorca Island, Spain	12/12/2000	Ciceron Pascual
Forkbeard, greater	3.54 kg (7 lb 12 oz)	Straits of Gibraltar, Gibraltar	7/12/1997	Ms. Susan Holgado
Fusilier, redbelly yellowtail	0.45 kg (1 lb 0 oz)	Southern Islands, Singapore	4/17/2010	Steven M. Wozniak
Gar, alligator	126.55 kg (279 lb 0 oz)	Rio Grande, Texas, USA	12/2/1951	Bill Valverde
Gar, Florida	4.53 kg (10 lb 0 oz)	Florida Everglades, Florida, USA	1/28/2002	Herbert Ratner, Jr.
Gar, longnose	22.68 kg (50 lb 0 oz)	Trinity River, Texas, USA	7/30/1954	Townsend Miller
Gar, shortnose	3.71 kg (8 lb 3 oz)	Lake Contrary, St. Joseph, Missouri, USA	10/12/2010	George F. Pittman, Sr.
Gar, spotted	4.44 kg (9 lb 12 oz)	Lake Mexia, Mexia, Texas, USA	4/7/1994	Rick Rivard
Gar, tropical	5.18 kg (11 lb 6 oz)	Rio Frio, Costa Rica	2/23/2003	Jose Aguilar
Garpike	1.18 kg (2 lb 9 oz)	La Teste, France	5/14/2002	David Mesure
Geelbek	14.91 kg (32 lb 14 oz)	Algoa Bay, Port Elizabeth, South Africa	6/16/1994	Carel Sanders
Gengoro-Buna	1.88 kg (4 lb 2 oz)	Chigusa River, Hyogo, Japan	4/4/2006	Masahiro Oomori
Gnomefish (mutsu)	16.1 kg (35 lb 7 oz)	Nanbu, Wakayama, Japan	5/5/2000	Takayuki Nishioka
Goatfish, blackspot	1.26 kg (2 lb 12 oz)	Kubotsu, Kochi, Japan	7/9/2005	Kenji Tamura
Goatfish, Indian	0.92 kg (2 lb 0 oz)	Amami-Oshima, Kagoshima, Japan	8/31/2003	Hironobu Hayashi

Species	Weight	Location	Catch Date	Angler
Goatfish, white-saddle	0.53 kg (1 lb 3 oz)	Nomashi, Oshima, Tokyo, Japan	8/16/2007	Yuuma Nishino
Goatfish, yellow	0.55 kg (1 lb 3 oz)	Hachijo Is., Tokyo, Japan	8/15/2005	Takashi Nishino
Goby, marble	2.37 kg (5 lb 3 oz)	Chiang Mai, Thailand	10/1/2008	John Merritt
Goldeye	1.72 kg (3 lb 13 oz)	Pierre, South Dakota, USA	8/9/1987	Gary Heuer
Goldfish, Asian	1.62 kg (3 lb 9 oz)	Mukogawa, Hyogo, Japan	1/29/2004	Masahiro Oomori
Goldfish-Carp hybrid	1.58 kg (3 lb 8 oz)	Cermak Quarry, Lyons, Illinois, USA	8/22/1990	Donald Czyzewski
Goonch	75 kg (165 lb 5 oz)	River Ramganga, India	3/6/2009	Jakub Vagner
Goosefish	23.25 kg (51 lb 4 oz)	Stellwagen Bank, Massachusetts, USA	4/12/2008	Robert Solberg
Gorami, giant	5.6 kg (12 lb 5 oz)	Bung Sam Lan Lake, Thailand	10/10/2004	Nuttaphol Wangwongwiwat
Grayling	2.18 kg (4 lb 12 oz)	Steinfeld River, Drava, Austria	11/25/2009	Adriano Garhantini
Grayling, Arctic	2.69 kg (5 lb 15 oz)	Katseyedie River, Northwest Territories, Canada	8/16/1967	Ms. Jeanne Branson
Grayling, Mongolian	3.12 kg (6 lb 14 oz)	Lake Khurgan, Mongolia	6/4/2010	Iurii Diachenko
Graysby	1.13 kg (2 lb 8 oz)	Stetson Rock, Texas, USA	3/2/1998	George Flores
Graysby, Panama	0.9 kg (2 lb 0 oz)	Golfo Dulce, Costa Rica	4/28/2006	Karrie A. Ables
Greenling, fat (ainame)	3.25 kg (7 lb 2 oz)	Saware, Mori-cho, Hokkaido, Japan	7/29/2009	Takanori Sasaki
Greenling, kelp	1.81 kg (4 lb 0 oz)	Gulf of Alaska, Alaska, USA	7/8/2007	Capt. Jay Wright Jr.
Greenling, masked	1.5 kg (3 lb 4 oz)	Rausu, Hokkaido, Japan	9/8/2003	Ms. Kazumi Takizawa
Greenling, rock	2.15 kg (4 lb 11 oz)	Utoro, Hokkaido, Japan	7/6/2005	Kazuhiro Takahashi
Grenadier, roundnose	1.69 kg (3 lb 11 oz)	Trondheimsfjorden, Norway	11/26/1993	Knut Nilsen
Grouper, areolate	0.62 kg (1 lb 5 oz)	Kut Island, Thailand	1/16/2006	Jean-Francois Helias
Grouper, black	56.24 kg (124 lb 0 oz)	Gulf of Mexico, Texas, USA	1/11/2003	Tim Oestreich, II
Grouper, broomtail	45.35 kg (100 lb 0 oz)	El Muerto Island, Ecuador	12/29/1998	Ernesto Jouvin
Grouper, brown-marbled	17 kg (37 lb 7 oz)	North Nilandoo Atoll, Maldives	12/14/2003	Klaus Bars

Species	Weight	Location	Catch Date	Angler
Grouper, cloudy	0.63 kg (1 lb 6 oz)	Kut Island, Gulf of Siam, Thailand	2/22/2006	Supachai "Noi" Boongayson
Grouper, comb	5.25 kg (11 lb 9 oz)	Cagarras Islands, Brazil	6/5/2004	Flavio Campos Reis
Grouper, comet	7.65 kg (16 lb 13 oz)	Zenisu, Tokyo, Japan	4/6/2006	Masaki Tsuchiya
Grouper, convict (mahata)	120 kg (264 lb 8 oz)	Yonaguni Island, Okinawa, Japan	4/25/2011	Koji Yoshida
Grouper, dot-dash	4.6 kg (10 lb 2 oz)	Chagos Archipelago, Diego Garcia	12/31/2010	Phillip W. Richmond, Jr.
Grouper, dusky	21.25 kg (46 lb 13 oz)	Porto Cervo, Sardinia, Italy	11/5/1990	Luca Bonfanti
Grouper, dusky-tail	0.95 kg (2 lb 1 oz)	Kut Island, Gulf of Siam, Thailand	2/11/2008	Bruno Binet
Grouper, gag	36.46 kg (80 lb 6 oz)	Destin, Florida, USA	10/14/1993	Bill Smith
Grouper, giant	179.5 kg (395 lb 11 oz)	Latham Island, Tanzania	3/10/2004	Shayne Keith Nelson
Grouper, gold-blotch	1.35 kg (2 lb 15 oz)	Detached Mole, Gibraltar	4/9/1995	Joseph Triay
Grouper, goliath	308.44 kg (680 lb 0 oz)	Fernandina Beach, Florida, USA	5/20/1961	Ms. Lynn Joyner
Grouper, gulf	51.25 kg (113 lb 0 oz)	Loreto, Baja California Sur, Mexico	4/25/2000	William Klaser
Grouper, Hawaiian	14.42 kg (31 lb 12 oz)	Pacific Ocean, Midway Islands	7/3/2001	Gary Giglio
Grouper, Hong Kong	2.83 kg (6 lb 3 oz)	Tsushima, Nagasaki, Japan	6/14/2008	Masahiko Wakana
Grouper, Island	6.9 kg (15 lb 3 oz)	Lanzarote, Spain	6/15/2009	Miguel Cardoso Lopez
Grouper, leopard	9.98 kg (22 lb 0 oz)	Playa Hermosa, Mexico	5/19/2002	William Favor
Grouper, long-tooth	38 kg (83 lb 12 oz)	Mikurajima, Tokyo, Japan	7/13/2002	Ms. Naomi Moritani
Grouper, Malabar	38 kg (83 lb 12 oz)	Bourake, New Caledonia	1/27/2002	Patrick Sebile
Grouper, marbled	13.78 kg (30 lb 6 oz)	Garden Banks Block, Gulf of Mexico, Louisiana, USA	10/9/2010	Jeff Kudla
Grouper, mottled	49.7 kg (109 lb 9 oz)	East Side, Gibraltar	8/13/1996	Albert Peralta
Grouper, moustache	55 kg (121 lb 4 oz)	Desroches Island, Seychelles	1/1/1998	Charles-Antoine Roucayrol

Species	Weight	Location	Catch Date	Angler
Grouper, Nassau	17.46 kg (38 lb 8 oz)	Bimini, Bahamas	2/14/1994	Lewis Goodman
Grouper, netfin	0.85 kg (1 lb 13 oz)	Los Chagos, Diego Garcia	12/18/2010	Phillip W. Richmond, Jr.
Grouper, olive	23.85 kg (52 lb 9 oz)	Alijos Rocks, Mexico	6/15/2002	Anthony Crawford
Grouper, orange-spotted	22.5 kg (49 lb 9 oz)	Amami-oshima, Kagoshima, Japan	7/13/2003	Kouji Nobori
Grouper, red	19.16 kg (42 lb 4 oz)	St. Augustine, Florida, USA	3/9/1997	Del Wiseman, Jr.
Grouper, redmouth	1.5 kg (3 lb 4 oz)	Chagos Archipelago, Diego Garcia	3/31/2010	Phillip W. Richmond, Jr.
Grouper, sawtail	14.06 kg (31 lb 0 oz)	Palmas Secas, Mexico	4/1/2001	William Favor
Grouper, snowy	30.84 kg (68 lb 0 oz)	Norfolk Canyon, Virginia, USA	8/17/2008	Jere D. Humphrey
Grouper, speckled blue	19.05 kg (41 lb 15 oz)	Chichijima, Ogasawara, Tokyo, Japan	3/9/2006	Mitsuo Takahashi
Grouper, spotted (cabrilla)	22.31 kg (49 lb 3 oz)	Cedros/Natividad Islands, Baja California, Mexico	11/18/1990	Barry Morita
Grouper, star studded	11.34 kg (25 lb 0 oz)	Zancudo, Costa Rica	3/8/2008	Karrie A. Ables
Grouper, starry	0.95 kg (2 lb 1 oz)	Zancudo, Costa Rica	2/8/2005	Betsi Chatham
Grouper, tiger	6.57 kg (14 lb 8 oz)	Bimini, Bahamas	5/30/1993	Michael Meeker
Grouper, Warsaw	198.1 kg (436 lb 12 oz)	Gulf of Mexico, Florida, USA	12/22/1985	Steve Haeusler
Grouper, white	10.5 kg (23 lb 2 oz)	Grand Bereby, Ivory Coast	4/21/1999	Patrick Sebile
Grouper, white-blotched	8.65 kg (19 lb 1 oz)	Chagos Archipelago, Diego Garcia	1/8/2011	Phillip W. Richmond, Jr.
Grouper, yellow	0.55 kg (1 lb 3 oz)	Shimane Peninsula, Shimane, Japan	9/11/2007	Yukio Takata
Grouper, yellowedge	20.92 kg (46 lb 2 oz)	Virginia Beach, Virginia, USA	3/12/2008	Heath Cataulin
Grouper, yellowfin	19.05 kg (42 lb 0 oz)	Cypremort Point, Louisiana, USA	7/26/2002	Jim Becquet
Grouper, yellowmouth	10.2 kg (22 lb 8 oz)	Murrell's Inlet, South Carolina, USA	9/2/2001	Brian Ford
Grunt, African striped	1.03 kg (2 lb 4 oz)	Vila Real Santo Antonio, Algar, Portugal	2/19/2007	Luis Ceia
Grunt, bastard	0.5 kg (1 lb 1 oz)	Vila Real de Santo, Antonio, Portugal	1/20/2006	Luis Ceia

Species	Weight	Location	Catch Date	Angler
Grunt, biglip	4.82 kg (10 lb 10 oz)	Banjul, Gambia	2/2/2010	Stan Nabozny
Grunt, burrito	4.53 kg (10 lb 0 oz)	Morro, Santo Domingo, Mexico	4/27/2006	Harold Lance Rigg
Grunt, burro	1.85 kg (4 lb 1 oz)	Los Chiles, Rio Fio, Costa Rica	12/4/1995	John Corry
Grunt, longspine	0.62 kg (1 lb 5 oz)	Sierpe Estuary, South Pacific, Costa Rica	5/8/2005	Carlos Luis Campos Palma
Grunt, Pacific roncador	3.4 kg (7 lb 7 oz)	Savegre River, Quepos, Costa Rica	3/6/2005	Damian Gallardo
Grunt, rubberlip	7.92 kg (17 lb 7 oz)	Europa Point, Gibraltar	9/10/1996	Michael Berllaque
Grunt, silver	0.8 kg (1 lb 12 oz)	Nishida River, Iriomote Is., Okinawa, Japan	8/24/2006	Horo Izawa
Grunt, sompant	3.09 kg (6 lb 13 oz)	Gambia River, Banjul, Gambia	4/30/2009	Stan Nabozny
Grunt, tomtate	0.56 kg (1 lb 4 oz)	Hatteras, North Carolina, USA	5/13/2006	John D. Overton Jr.
Grunt, white	2.94 kg (6 lb 8 oz)	North Brunswick, Georgia, USA	5/6/1989	J.D. Barnes, Jr.
Grunt, white (Pacific)	0.59 kg (1 lb 5 oz)	Mazatlan, Mexico	6/20/1999	David Boswell, III
Grunter, javelin	1.93 kg (4 lb 4 oz)	Nomenade River, Weipa, QLD, Australia	4/22/2009	Steven M. Wozniak
Grunter, saddle	3.2 kg (7 lb 0 oz)	St. Lucia, South Africa	12/11/1991	J.J. van Rensburg
Guapote	6.8 kg (15 lb 0 oz)	Lago Apanas, Jinotega, Nicaragua	2/14/1999	Hubert Gordillo
Guapote, jaguar	1.67 kg (3 lb 11 oz)	Kendale Lakes, Florida, USA	9/10/2006	William T. Porter
Guitarfish, blackchin	49.9 kg (110 lb 0 oz)	Batanga, Gabon	6/11/1998	Philippe Le Danff
Guitarfish, giant	54 kg (119 lb 0 oz)	Bird Island, Seychelles	10/9/1995	Peter Lee
Guitarfish, lesser	0.68 kg (1 lb 8 oz)	Isla Grande, Brazil	3/17/2011	Steven M. Wozniak
Guitarfish, shovelnose	9.75 kg (21 lb 8 oz)	Manhattan Beach, California, USA	9/22/1996	Robert Young
Guitarfish, yellow	2.2 kg (4 lb 13 oz)	Akazawa, Ito, Shizuoka, Japan	7/22/2008	Yuuma Nishino
Gurnard, bluefin	1.1 kg (2 lb 6 oz)	Kaipara Harbour, New Zealand	1/7/2011	Scott Tindale
Gurnard, flying	1.81 kg (4 lb 0 oz)	Gulf of Mexico, Panama City, Florida, USA	6/7/1986	Vernon Allen

Species	Weight	Location	Catch Date	Angler
Gurnard, grey	0.62 kg (1 lb 5 oz)	La Middleground, Kattegatt, Sweden	4/20/1998	Lars Kraemer
Gurnard, red (hobo)	1.35 kg (2 lb 15 oz)	Ohara, Chiba, Japan	2/6/2004	Norikazu Fuku-naga
Haddock	6.8 kg (14 lb 15 oz)	Saltraumen, Norway	8/15/1997	Ms. Heike Ne-blinger
Hake, Argentine	1.15 kg (2 lb 8 oz)	Rio de Janeiro, Brazil	10/12/2002	Eduardo Baumeier
Hake, European	7.08 kg (15 lb 9 oz)	Longva, Norway	9/1/2000	Knut Steen
Hake, gulf	2.54 kg (5 lb 9 oz)	Gulf of Mexico, Texas, USA	4/16/1996	Patrick Lemire
Hake, Pacific	0.98 kg (2 lb 2 oz)	Tatoosh Island, Washington, USA	6/26/1988	Steven Garnett
Hake, red	5.81 kg (12 lb 13 oz)	Mudhole Wreck, New Jersey, USA	2/20/2010	Billy Watson
Hake, silver	2.04 kg (4 lb 8 oz)	Perkins Cove, Ogunquit, Maine, USA	8/8/1995	Erik Callahan

Species	Weight	Location	Catch Date	Angler
Hake, white	20.97 kg (46 lb 4 oz)	Perkins Cove, Ogunquit, Maine, USA	10/26/1986	John Audet
Halibut, Atlantic	190 kg (418 lb 13 oz)	Vannaya Troms, Norway	7/28/2004	Thomas Nielsen
Halibut, California	26.58 kg (58 lb 9 oz)	Santa Rosa Island, California, USA	6/26/1999	Roger Borrell
Halibut, greenland	4.5 kg (9 lb 14 oz)	Kummiut, East Greenland	8/28/2008	Kai Witt
Halibut, Pacific	208.2 kg (459 lb 0 oz)	Dutch Harbor, Alaska, USA	6/11/1996	Jack Tragis
Halibut, shotted	0.6 kg (1 lb 5 oz)	Kaminokuni, Hokkaido, Japan	9/6/2006	Masao Ishikawa
Happy, pink	2.45 kg (5 lb 6 oz)	Upper Zambezi, Zambia	8/14/1998	Graham Glasspool
Hawkfish, giant	4.16 kg (9 lb 3 oz)	Salinas, Ecuador	8/21/1993	Hugo Tobar
Herring, Atlantic	0.69 kg (1 lb 8 oz)	South Amboy Beach, New Jersey, USA	11/28/2001	Alex Gerus
Herring, skipjack	1.7 kg (3 lb 12 oz)	Watts Bar Lake, Kingston, Tennessee, USA	2/14/1982	Paul Goddard
Hind, peacock	1.58 kg (3 lb 8 oz)	Honokohau-Kona, Hawaii, USA	3/24/2005	Lauren Miller
Hind, red	3.84 kg (8 lb 7 oz)	East Flower Bank, Gulf of Mexico, Florida, USA	10/21/2004	Marcus Trapp
Hind, rock	4.08 kg (9 lb 0 oz)	South Atlantic, Ascension Island	4/25/1994	William Kleinfelder
Hind, speckled	23.81 kg (52 lb 8 oz)	Destin, Florida, USA	10/21/1994	Russell George Perry
Hind, tomato (azahata)	2.35 kg (5 lb 2 oz)	Amami-Oshima, Kagoshima, Japan	11/5/2002	Koji Kai
Hogfish	9.63 kg (21 lb 6 oz)	Frying Pan Tower, North Carolina, USA	7/23/2005	Derek Williams
Hogfish, Spanish	0.69 kg (1 lb 8 oz)	Stetson Bank, Gulf of Mexico, USA	2/19/2005	Ronnie Vaughn
Hokke	2.2 kg (4 lb 13 oz)	Shiretoko, Hokkaido, Japan	7/17/2005	Takayuki Kuroe
Hottentot	1.7 kg (3 lb 12 oz)	Cape Point, South Africa	5/28/1989	Byron Ashington
Houndfish	3.74 kg (8 lb 4 oz)	Palm Beach, Florida, USA	11/11/2007	Piet Vanalderwerelt
Houndfish, Mexican	9.86 kg (21 lb 12 oz)	Cabo San Lucas, Mexico	8/10/1993	John Kovacevich
Huchen	34.8 kg (76 lb 11 oz)	Gemeinde Spittal/Drau, Austria	2/19/1985	Hans Offermanns

Species	Weight	Location	Catch Date	Angler
Huchen, Japanese	9.45 kg (20 lb 13 oz)	Sarufutsu River, Hokkaido, Japan	11/5/2003	Tomonori Matsumoto
Ide	3.36 kg (7 lb 6 oz)	Grangshammaran, Borlange, Sweden	6/24/2001	Sonny Pettersson
Inconnu	24.04 kg (53 lb 0 oz)	Pah River, Alaska, USA	8/20/1986	Lawrence Hudnall
Isaki	1.4 kg (3 lb 1 oz)	Nigishima, Owase, Mie, Japan	8/2/2009	Kosuke Hori
Itoyoridai	0.96 kg (2 lb 1 oz)	Iki, Nagasaki, Japan	1/13/2003	Masaki Takano
Iwatoko-nama-zu	1.5 kg (3 lb 4 oz)	Kozuhama, Lake Biwa, Shiga, Japan	6/26/2001	Yoshitaka Sakurai
Izuhime-ei	0.52 kg (1 lb 2 oz)	Izu-oshima, Tokyo, Japan	7/20/2009	Takashi Nishino
Izukasago	1.5 kg (3 lb 4 oz)	Numazu, Shizuoka, Japan	10/28/2000	Kouji Kimura
Jack, almaco	59.87 kg (132 lb 0 oz)	La Paz, Baja California, Mexico	7/21/1964	Howard Hahn
Jack, bar	3.51 kg (7 lb 12 oz)	Miami, Florida, USA	12/18/1999	Martini Arostegui
Jack, black	17.94 kg (39 lb 9 oz)	Isla Roca Partida, Revillagigedo Islands, Mexico	4/13/1995	Calvin Sheets
Jack, cornish	11.25 kg (24 lb 12 oz)	Zambezi River, Zambia	8/24/1996	Pieter Jacobsz
Jack, cottonmouth	2.04 kg (4 lb 8 oz)	Cat Island, Bahamas	5/17/1991	Ms. Linda Cook
Jack, crevalle	30 kg (66 lb 2 oz)	Barra Do Dande, Angola	6/1/2010	Carlos Alberto Leal Simoes
Jack, fortune	2.4 kg (5 lb 4 oz)	Golfito, Costa Rica	4/20/2011	Federico Hampl
Jack, green	2.81 kg (6 lb 3 oz)	Cabo San Lucas, Mexico	5/28/2000	Jamey Damon
Jack, horse-eye	13.38 kg (29 lb 8 oz)	South Atlantic, Ascension Island	5/28/1993	Mike Hanson
Jack, island	6.61 kg (14 lb 9 oz)	Oahu, Hawaii, USA	1/2/1995	Alex Ancheta
Jack, Pacific crevalle	17.69 kg (39 lb 0 oz)	Playa Zancudo, Costa Rica	3/3/1997	Ms. Ingrid Callaghan
Jack, senegal	9.5 kg (20 lb 15 oz)	Archipelago des Bijagos, Guinea-Bissau	10/31/1995	Patrick Sebile
Jack, yellow	10.65 kg (23 lb 8 oz)	Key Largo, Florida, USA	3/14/1999	Richard Rodriguez
Jacopever, false	0.94 kg (2 lb 1 oz)	Hout Bay, South Africa	3/24/2007	George Bogen
Jacunda	0.79 kg (1 lb 12 oz)	Rio Tapera, Brazil	1/10/2004	Martin Arostegui
Jacunda, johans	0.45 kg (1 lb 0 oz)	Solimoes River, Brazil	10/27/2008	Martin Arostegui
Jacunda, lenticulated	0.9 kg (2 lb 0 oz)	Agua Boa River, Brazil	12/16/2005	Dan. E. Stockton Jr.

Species	Weight	Location	Catch Date	Angler
Jacunda, lenticulated	0.91 kg (2 lb 0 oz)	Tapera River, Brazil	1/13/2008	Gonzalo C. Arostegui
Jacunda, marbled	0.68 kg (1 lb 8 oz)	Sucunduri River, Brazil	7/13/2010	Martini Arostegui
Jacunda, striped	0.97 kg (2 lb 2 oz)	Rio Preto da Eva, Amazonas, Brazil, Brazil	5/22/2010	Gilberto Fernandes
Jandia	4.3 kg (9 lb 8 oz)	Urariquera River, Amazon, Brazil	1/21/2003	Russell Jensen
Jau	49.44 kg (109 lb 0 oz)	Urariquera River, Amazon, Brazil	1/31/2004	Russell Jensen
Jawfish, fine-spotted	1.13 kg (2 lb 8 oz)	Turner Island, Sonora, Mexico	6/11/1988	Ms. Lorna Garrod
Jobfish, crimson	4.08 kg (9 lb 0 oz)	Kona, Hawaii, USA	12/30/2008	Steve Kwiat
Jobfish, green	20.2 kg (44 lb 8 oz)	Iriomote Island, Tokyo, Japan	7/16/2003	Hiroyuki Manatsu
Jobfish, lavender	8.4 kg (18 lb 8 oz)	Chichijima, Ogasawara, Tokyo, Japan	4/5/1998	Yusuke Nakamura
Jobfish, rusty	6.6 kg (14 lb 8 oz)	Tokara, Kagoshima, Japan	5/19/2002	Ms. Yuuko Hirashima
Jundia	13.01 kg (28 lb 11 oz)	Jatapo, Amazon, Brazil	2/2/2009	Russell Jensen
Jurupoca	1.47 kg (3 lb 4 oz)	Caceres, Paraguai River, Brazil	9/9/1996	Alacyr Beghini de Moraes
Kahawai (Australian salmon)	8.74 kg (19 lb 4 oz)	Currarong, Australia	4/9/1994	Stephen Muller
Kasago	2.8 kg (6 lb 2 oz)	Niijima, Tokyo, Japan	6/23/1996	Osamu Hida
Kawakawa	13.15 kg (29 lb 0 oz)	Isla Clarion, Revillagigedo Islands, Mexico	12/17/1986	Ronald Nakamura
Kingfish, gulf	1.38 kg (3 lb 0 oz)	Salvo, North Carolina, USA	10/9/1999	Ms. Betty Duke
Kingfish, northern	1.11 kg (2 lb 7 oz)	Salvo, North Carolina, USA	7/12/2000	William Graham
Kingfish, southern	1.27 kg (2 lb 13 oz)	Virginia Beach, Virginia, USA	9/29/2002	Chip Watters
Kitsune-mebaru	2.8 kg (6 lb 2 oz)	Shiribetsu, Hokkaido, Japan	5/22/2010	Masamitsu Okayama
Knifefish, clown	6.12 kg (13 lb 8 oz)	Lake Clarke Shores, Florida, USA	12/16/2008	Nick Fusco
Kob	66.75 kg (147 lb 2 oz)	Sunday's River, Port Elizabeth, South Africa	11/22/1998	Ronnie Botha

Species	Weight	Location	Catch Date	Angler
Kobudai	14.66 kg (32 lb 5 oz)	Shiroura, Mie, Japan	7/4/1999	Shunzo Takada
Kokanee	4.37 kg (9 lb 10 oz)	Wallowa Lake, Oregon, USA	6/13/2010	Ronald A. Campbell
Kokuni	30 kg (66 lb 2 oz)	River Congo, Congo	1/8/2009	Jakub Vagner
Korai-kitsun-emebaru	1.94 kg (4 lb 4 oz)	Shizugawa, Miyagi, Japan	1/6/2004	Tetsuya Abe
Korai-Nigoi	3 kg (6 lb 9 oz)	Mogawa, Hyogo, Japan	4/26/2010	Junichi Inada
Kuromenuke	2.75 kg (6 lb 1 oz)	Kushiro, Hokkaido, Japan	6/17/2004	Tetsuya Kataoka
Kurosoi	5.1 kg (11 lb 3 oz)	Ishikari, Hokkaido, Japan	6/1/2008	Tomohiro Matsui
Labeo barbatulus	1.15 kg (2 lb 8 oz)	Sanom, Thailand	4/3/2011	Jean-Francois Helias
Ladyfish	3.62 kg (8 lb 0 oz)	Sepatiba Bay, Brazil	2/21/2006	Ian-Arthur de Sulocki
Ladyfish, Hawaiian	6.6 kg (14 lb 8 oz)	Southwest Reef, Dampier, W.A., Australia	12/16/2001	Anthony La Tosa
Ladyfish, Senegalese	5.9 kg (13 lb 0 oz)	Archepeligo des Bijagos, Guinea-Bissau	4/12/1994	Gerard Cittadini
Ladyfish, springer	10.8 kg (23 lb 12 oz)	Ilha do Bazaruio, Mozambique	10/28/1993	Zaqueu Paulo
Largemouth, humpback	3.85 kg (8 lb 7 oz)	Upper Zambezi River, Zambia	8/15/1998	Richie Peters
Largemouth, purple-faced	0.58 kg (1 lb 4 oz)	Kariba, Zimbabwe	10/4/1999	Graham Mitchell
Largemouth, thinface	1.66 kg (3 lb 10 oz)	Upper Zambezi River, Zambia	9/13/1999	Howard Voss
Lates, forktail	8.3 kg (18 lb 4 oz)	Lake Tanganyika, Zambia	12/1/1987	Steve Robinson
Lates, Japanese (akame)	33 kg (72 lb 12 oz)	Shimanto River, Kochi, Japan	5/31/1996	Yoshio Murasaki
Lau-lau (piraiba)	155 kg (341 lb 11 oz)	Rio Solimoes, Amazonas, Brazil	5/29/2009	Jorge Masullo de Aguiar
Leaffish, Malayan	0.5 kg (1 lb 1 oz)	Srinakarin Dam, Thailand	5/3/2002	Johnny Jensen
Leatherjack, longjaw	1.58 kg (3 lb 8 oz)	Rio Coto, Puntarenas, Costa Rica	2/6/1990	Craig Whitehead, MD
Leatherjack, longjaw	1.58 kg (3 lb 8 oz)	Playa Zancudo, Costa Rica	5/27/1995	Craig Whitehead, MD
Leatherjacket, six-spined	0.68 kg (1 lb 8 oz)	Port Hacking, Australia	8/26/2009	Steven M. Wozniak

Species	Weight	Location	Catch Date	Angler
Leerfish (Garrick)	27.8 kg (61 lb 4 oz)	L'Ampolla, Spain	4/30/2000	Oriol Ribalta
Lenok	4.08 kg (9 lb 0 oz)	Anui River, Russia	6/2/2000	Thomas Cappiello
Ling, blue	16.05 kg (35 lb 6 oz)	Trondheimsfjorden, Norway	11/23/1993	Oyvind Braa
Ling, European	40.1 kg (88 lb 6 oz)	Shetland Islands, United Kingdom	4/5/2002	Gareth Laurenson
Lingcod	37.45 kg (82 lb 9 oz)	Gulf of Alaska, Homer, Alaska, USA	7/27/2007	Robert Hammond
Lizardfish, Atlantic	0.76 kg (1 lb 10 oz)	San Eugenio, Tenerife, Spain	3/22/2006	Rob Rennie
Lizardfish, inshore	1.13 kg (2 lb 8 oz)	Miami Beach, Florida, USA	8/12/2003	Joshua Otis
Lizardfish, wanieso	3.6 kg (7 lb 14 oz)	Tateyama, Chiba, Japan	5/18/2006	Harunori Kinjo
Lookdown	2.15 kg (4 lb 12 oz)	Flamingo, Florida, USA	3/21/2004	Rebecca Wright
Lord, Red Irish	1.11 kg (2 lb 7 oz)	Depoe Bay, Oregon, USA	4/26/1992	Ronald Chatham

Species	Weight	Location	Catch Date	Angler
Lord, yellow Irish	1.19 kg (2 lb 10 oz)	Kachemak Bay, Alaska, USA	8/2/2008	David Witherell
Lyretail, yellow-edged	5 kg (11 lb 0 oz)	Chichijima, Ogasawara Isl., Tokyo, Japan	6/25/1999	Hiromasa Ko-bayashi
Ma-Anago	0.95 kg (2 lb 1 oz)	Shimoda, Shizuoka, Japan	8/19/2006	Takashi Nishino
Machaca	4.32 kg (9 lb 8 oz)	Barra del Colorado, Costa Rica	11/24/1991	Ms. Barbara Fields
Machaca (Sabalo pipon)	2.28 kg (5 lb 0 oz)	Rio Savegre, Costa Rica	5/2/2009	Luis Diego Montero Sanchez
Mackerel, atka	1.35 kg (2 lb 15 oz)	Notoromisaki, Hokkaido, Japan	7/28/2008	Rintaro Shinohara
Mackerel, Atlantic	1.2 kg (2 lb 10 oz)	Kraakvaag Fjord, Norway	6/29/1992	Jorg Marquard
Mackerel, blue	1.45 kg (3 lb 3 oz)	Whangaruru, New Zealand	11/21/2010	Scott Tindale
Mackerel, broadbarred	9.3 kg (20 lb 8 oz)	The Patch, Dampier, Australia	6/12/1997	Ms. Tammy Yates
Mackerel, bullet	1.84 kg (4 lb 1 oz)	L'ampolla, Spain	7/24/2004	Raul Roca
Mackerel, cero	7.76 kg (17 lb 2 oz)	Islamorada, Florida, USA	4/5/1986	G. Mills
Mackerel, chub	2.17 kg (4 lb 12 oz)	Guadalupe Island, Mexico	6/5/1986	Roy Ludt
Mackerel, double-lined	3 kg (6 lb 10 oz)	Willis Island, Queensland, Australia	11/28/2006	George B. Sowers Jr.
Mackerel, frigate	1.72 kg (3 lb 12 oz)	Hat Head, N.S.W., Australia	4/17/1998	Glen Beers
Mackerel, Japanese jack	1.19 kg (2 lb 9 oz)	Kowaura, Mie, Japan	4/25/2010	Katsuyuki Akita
Mackerel, Japanese Spanish	9.35 kg (20 lb 10 oz)	Shirasaki, Wakayama, Japan	4/29/2007	Tomoki Nakatani
Mackerel, king	42.18 kg (93 lb 0 oz)	San Juan, Puerto Rico	4/18/1999	Steve Graulau
Mackerel, narrowbarred	44.91 kg (99 lb 0 oz)	Scottburgh, Natal, South Africa	3/14/1982	Michael Wilkinson
Mackerel, Pacific sierra	8.16 kg (18 lb 0 oz)	Salinas, Ecuador	9/15/1990	Luis Flores A.
Mackerel, Pacific sierra	8.16 kg (18 lb 0 oz)	Isla de la Plata, Ecuador	3/24/1990	Jorge Begue W.
Mackerel, queen	5.56 kg (12 lb 4 oz)	Benguerra Island, Mozambique	5/6/2008	Stan Nabozny
Mackerel, shark	12.3 kg (27 lb 1 oz)	Bribie Island, Brisbane, Queensland, Australia	3/24/1989	Kathy Maguire

Species	Weight	Location	Catch Date	Angler
Mackerel, snake	4.5 kg (9 lb 14 oz)	Yinaguni Iz., Okinawa, Japan	11/2/2008	Takashi Odagiri
Mackerel, Spanish	5.89 kg (13 lb 0 oz)	Ocracoke Inlet, North Carolina, USA	11/4/1987	Robert Cranton
Mackerel, West African Spanish	6 kg (13 lb 3 oz)	Grand Bereby, Ivory Coast	12/27/1998	Dorchies Jacques
Madai	11.3 kg (24 lb 14 oz)	Awashima Is., Nigata, Japan	5/9/2005	Katsuhito Takeuchi
Ma-Fugo	0.65 kg (1 lb 6 oz)	Kurihama, Kanagawa, Japan	5/18/2008	Junko Kato
Mahseer	43.09 kg (95 lb 0 oz)	Cauvery River, India	6/26/1984	Robert Howitt
Mahseer, deccan	3.66 kg (8 lb 1 oz)	Cauvery River, India	12/24/2010	Sudip Ghatak
Mahseer, golden	12.25 kg (27 lb 0 oz)	Ramganga River, India	5/29/2008	Jeff Currier
Mahseer, stracheyi	2.42 kg (5 lb 5 oz)	Gnaow River, Golden Triangle, Thailand	3/31/2009	Jean-Francois Helias
Mahseer, Thai	12 kg (26 lb 7 oz)	Jeram Besu, Benta, Pahang, Malaysia	7/24/2001	Mohamed bin Ibrahim
Manduba	3.62 kg (8 lb 0 oz)	Xingu River, Altamira, Brazil	9/4/2005	Ian-Arthur De Sulocki
Margate, black	6.92 kg (15 lb 4 oz)	Fort Pierce, Florida, USA	2/27/2011	Joe Bahto
Margate, white	8.85 kg (19 lb 8 oz)	Dry Tortugas, Florida, USA	2/6/2011	Hector Vasallo
Marimba	1.5 kg (3 lb 4 oz)	Guanabara Bay, Brazil	8/31/2002	Flavio Reis
Marlin, black	707.61 kg (1560 lb 0 oz)	Cabo Blanco, Peru	8/4/1953	Alfred Glassell, Jr.
Marlin, blue (Atlantic)	636 kg (1402 lb 2 oz)	Vitoria, Brazil	2/29/1992	Paulo Amorim
Marlin, blue (Pacific)	624.14 kg (1376 lb 0 oz)	Kaaiwi Point, Kona, Hawaii, USA	5/31/1982	Jay de Beaubien
Marlin, striped	224.1 kg (494 lb 0 oz)	Tutukaka, New Zealand	1/16/1986	Bill Boniface
Marlin, white	82.5 kg (181 lb 14 oz)	Vitoria, Brazil	12/8/1979	Evandro Coser
Matrincha	0.45 kg (1 lb 0 oz)	Rio Tapera, Amazon, Brazil	1/31/2003	Martin Arostegui
Meagre	48 kg (105 lb 13 oz)	Nouadhibou, Mauritania	3/30/1986	Laurent Morat
Meagre, Japanese	66.75 kg (147 lb 2 oz)	Sunday's River, Port Elizabeth, South Africa	11/22/1998	Ronnie Botha
Mebaru	1.12 kg (2 lb 7 oz)	Shirahama, Chiba, Japan	1/19/2010	Shuhei Okada
Medai (Japanese butterfish)	13.8 kg (30 lb 6 oz)	Mikura Is., Tokyo, Japan	4/4/2006	Toru Yamaguchi

Species	Weight	Location	Catch Date	Angler
Megrim	0.95 kg (2 lb 1 oz)	Hardangerfjord, Norway	8/5/2001	Ms. Sandra Marquard
Mekong pangasius	8.94 kg (19 lb 11 oz)	Luang Prabang, Laos	12/1/2010	Dale C. Fischer
Menada	6 kg (13 lb 3 oz)	Hamada River, Chiba, Japan	4/30/2008	Toshihiko Shoji
Mihara-hanadai	1 kg (2 lb 3 oz)	Irozaki, Shizuoka, Japan	8/13/1998	Mikio Suzuki
Milkfish	15 kg (33 lb 1 oz)	Lighthouse Pinacle, Mapelane, South Africa	5/3/2007	Jan Joubert
Mojarra, striped	1.02 kg (2 lb 4 oz)	West Palm Beach, Florida, USA	8/21/1987	James Black, Jr.
Mojarra, yellowfin	0.9 kg (2 lb 0 oz)	Glandon Park, Florida, USA	7/3/2005	Jimmy Alfonso
Moncholo	2.49 kg (5 lb 8 oz)	Rio Parana, Corrientes, Argentina	9/27/2010	Tomas Felipe Restano
Monkfish, European	25.96 kg (57 lb 4 oz)	Fenit, Tralee Bay, County Kerry, Ireland	5/20/1989	Jim Dooley
Mooneye	0.7 kg (1 lb 8 oz)	Lake of the Woods, Minnesota, USA	6/13/2001	Dan McGuire
Moray, blackedge	1.4 kg (3 lb 1 oz)	Gulf of Mexico, Texas, USA	5/30/1999	Ronnie Vaughn
Moray, blacktail	1.09 kg (2 lb 6 oz)	Gulf of Mexico, Texas, USA	3/24/1998	George Flores
Moray, green	15.19 kg (33 lb 8 oz)	Marathon Key, Florida, USA	3/15/1997	Rene de Dios
Moray, highfin (Amime-utsubo)	1.76 kg (3 lb 14 oz)	Kozujima, Tokyo, Japan	5/2/2004	Takashi Nishino
Moray, honeycomb	6 kg (13 lb 3 oz)	Grand Bereby, Ivory Coast	4/26/1999	Patrick Sebile
Moray, leopard	1.9 kg (4 lb 3 oz)	Akazawa, Shizuoka, Japan	1/4/2009	Takashi Nishino
Moray, Mediterranean	6.2 kg (13 lb 11 oz)	Vila Real Santo Antonio, Algarve, Portugal	1/24/2007	Eduardo Soares
Moray, purplemouth	0.75 kg (1 lb 10 oz)	Port Everglades Reef, Florida, USA	6/19/1998	Rene de Dios
Moray, slender giant	5.35 kg (11 lb 12 oz)	St. Lucia, South Africa	8/29/1987	Graham Vollmer
Moray, spotted	2.51 kg (5 lb 8 oz)	Marathon Key, Florida, USA	4/1/2000	Rene de Dios
Moray, viper	1.32 kg (2 lb 14 oz)	Fowey Light, Florida, USA	5/25/1998	Rene de Dios
Moray, zebra	0.57 kg (1 lb 4 oz)	Waimea Bay Point, Oahu, Hawaii, USA	6/19/2010	Steven M. Wozniak

Species	Weight	Location	Catch Date	Angler
Morwong, blackbarred	0.5 kg (1 lb 1 oz)	Suou-Oshima, Yamaguchi, Japan	3/10/2009	Yukio Takata
Morwong, spottedtail	0.9 kg (1 lb 16 oz)	Nomashi, Oshima, Tokyo, Japan	8/15/2007	Takashi Nishino
Mrigal	4.11 kg (9 lb 0 oz)	Salapee, Thailand	8/14/2009	Steven M. Wozniak
Mullet, hog	3.25 kg (7 lb 2 oz)	Rio Sarapiqui, Costa Rica	8/9/1995	Carlos Barrantes R.
Mullet, liza	1.45 kg (3 lb 3 oz)	Rio de Janeiro, Brazil	9/20/1999	Erich Filho
Mullet, striped	4.71 kg (10 lb 6 oz)	Upper Laguna Madre, Texas, USA	3/13/2009	Scott Lindner
Mullet, thicklip	3.52 kg (7 lb 12 oz)	Ymuiden, Zuid Pier, Holland	8/20/1996	Frits Kromhout vander Meer
Mullet, thinlip	2.38 kg (5 lb 4 oz)	River Taw, Barnstaple, United Kingdom	6/14/1984	Raymond White
Mullet, white	0.68 kg (1 lb 7 oz)	Rio de Janeiro, Brazil	4/13/2001	Erich Filho
Murasoi	2.11 kg (4 lb 10 oz)	Ogatsu, Miyagi, Japan	12/11/2003	Fuminori Sato
Muskellunge	30.61 kg (67 lb 8 oz)	Lake Court Oreilles, Hayward, Wisconsin, USA	7/24/1949	Cal Johnson
Muskellunge, tiger	23.21 kg (51 lb 3 oz)	Lac Vieux-Desert, Michigan, USA	7/16/1919	John Knobla
Musselcracker, black	32.2 kg (70 lb 15 oz)	Richards Bay, South Africa	8/25/1996	John Harvey
Myleus, redhook	1.5 kg (3 lb 4 oz)	Xingu River, Mato Grosso, Brazil	10/18/1999	Capt. Kdu Magalhaes
Nase	2.49 kg (5 lb 7 oz)	Rhein bei, Weil am Rhein, Germany	1/5/2010	Dieter Lindenmann
Needlefish, Atlantic	1.84 kg (4 lb 1 oz)	Cape May Reef, New Jersey, USA	8/24/2004	Nicholas Reiner
Needlefish, flat	4.8 kg (10 lb 9 oz)	Zavora, Mozambique	12/25/1997	Leon deBeer
Needlefish, Pacific agujon	5.12 kg (11 lb 4 oz)	Golfito, Costa Rica	1/11/2004	Leo Capobianco
Nembwe	3.6 kg (7 lb 15 oz)	Zambezi River, Zambia	9/20/2007	Donald John Bousfield
Nigoi	2.78 kg (6 lb 2 oz)	Mogawa, Hyogo, Hyogo, Japan	4/26/2010	Junichi Inada
Nkupe	5.5 kg (12 lb 2 oz)	Chete Gorge, Lake Kariba, Zimbabwe	12/12/2000	Malcolm Pheasant
Oilfish	63.5 kg (139 lb 15 oz)	White Island, New Zealand	4/12/1986	Tim Wallace

Species	Weight	Location	Catch Date	Angler
Okin-buna	1.1 kg (2 lb 6 oz)	Ichikawa, Hyogo, Japan	10/6/2003	Masahiro Oomori
Oniokoze	0.48 kg (1 lb 0 oz)	Ikitsukijima, Nagasaki, Japan	11/8/1999	Masaki Takano
Opah	73.93 kg (163 lb 0 oz)	Port San Luis Obispo, California, USA	10/8/1998	Thomas Foran
Oscar	1.58 kg (3 lb 8 oz)	Pasadena Lakes, Florida, USA	7/30/1999	Capt. Jay Wright Jr.
Oshitabirame	0.95 kg (2 lb 1 oz)	Odawara, Kanagawa, Japan	6/3/2004	Harukazu Tsuchida
Ougon-murasoi	1.35 kg (2 lb 15 oz)	Motoyoshi, Miyagi, Japan	10/25/2004	Masato Onodera
Pacu, black (pirapatinga)	24.95 kg (55 lb 0 oz)	Tamarac, Florida, USA	10/5/2010	Gary Roberts
Pacu, caranha	10.21 kg (22 lb 8 oz)	Rio Tarija, Bolivia	9/28/2008	Alejandro Linares
Pacu, Seringa	1.5 kg (3 lb 4 oz)	Rio Iriri, Brazil	8/28/2010	Dr. Justin Grubich
Paloma	0.72 kg (1 lb 9 oz)	Rio Calderas, Colombia	6/25/2002	Alejandro Linares
Palometa	0.81 kg (1 lb 12 oz)	Port Aransas, Texas, USA	6/12/2006	Henry B. Flores Jr.
Pandora	3.24 kg (7 lb 2 oz)	Dontie Gordo, Portugal	5/16/1996	Geoff Flores
Pangasius, giant	41 kg (90 lb 6 oz)	Gillhams Fishing Resort, Krabi, Thailand	7/2/2009	Alan Boon
Pangasius, shortbarbel	22 kg (48 lb 8 oz)	Seletar Reservoir, Singapore	9/27/2001	Khoo Lee
Parrotfish, Japanese	1.8 kg (3 lb 15 oz)	Jogasaki, Ito, Shizuoka, Japan	12/31/2007	Takashi Nishino
Parrotfish, midnight	4.19 kg (9 lb 4 oz)	Key Largo, Florida, USA	3/25/2005	Stephen H. Helvin
Parrotfish, rainbow	4.88 kg (10 lb 12 oz)	Key Largo, Florida, USA	6/6/2010	William T. Porter
Parrotperch, Japanese	7.3 kg (16 lb 1 oz)	Ushine, Iruma, Shizuoka, Japan	7/9/2003	Toshiro Kawawaki
Parrotperch, spotted	12.08 kg (26 lb 10 oz)	Hachijo Island, Tokyo, Japan	5/5/1996	Tsunehisa Kanayama
Payara	17.8 kg (39 lb 4 oz)	Uraima Falls, Venezuela	2/10/1996	Bill Keeley
Peacock, black-striped	3.86 kg (8 lb 8 oz)	Villacoa River, Valencia, Venezuela	1/4/2008	William F. Craig
Peacock, blue	3.86 kg (8 lb 8 oz)	Lake Serra da Mesa, Goias, Brazil	10/2/2010	Helcio Honda
Peacock, butterfly	5.71 kg (12 lb 9 oz)	Chiguao River, Bolivar State, Venezuela	1/6/2000	Antonio Campa G.
Peacock, Melaniae	3.3 kg (7 lb 4 oz)	Xingu River, Brazil	8/23/2010	Dr. Justin Grubich

Species	Weight	Location	Catch Date	Angler
Peacock, Orinoco	7.31 kg (16 lb 1 oz)	Urubaxi River, Amazonas, Brazil	2/12/2010	George Wiltse Walters
Peacock, speckled	13.19 kg (29 lb 1 oz)	Santa Isabel Do Rio Negro, Amazonas, Brazil	11/3/2010	Andrea Zaccherini
Peacock, vazzoleri	4.76 kg (10 lb 8 oz)	Sucunduri River, Brazil	7/13/2010	Robert W. Simmons
Pejerrey	1.13 kg (2 lb 8 oz)	Rio de la Plata, Buenos Aires, Argentina	8/25/2009	Tomas Felipe Restano
Pellona, Amazon	7.1 kg (15 lb 10 oz)	Caurama Lodge, Caura River, Venezuela	1/15/1999	Stephen Ray
Pellona, yellowfin river	2.51 kg (5 lb 8 oz)	Lago dos Reis, Amazonas, Brazil	3/17/2009	Gilberto Fernandes
Perch, chinese	4.76 kg (10 lb 8 oz)	Seibo Dam Reservoir, China	7/26/2009	Salvino A. J. Bernardes
Perch, creole	0.89 kg (1 lb 15 oz)	Maullin River, Chile	3/21/2002	Capt. Kdu Magalhaes
Perch, European	2.9 kg (6 lb 6 oz)	Kokar, Aland Islands, Finland	9/4/2010	Kalle Vaaranen
Perch, Nile	104.32 kg (230 lb 0 oz)	Lake Nasser, Egypt	12/20/2000	William Toth
Perch, ocean	9.02 kg (19 lb 14 oz)	Sorvaer, Norway	9/7/2008	Martin Wijnia
Perch, pile	0.68 kg (1 lb 8 oz)	Tiburon, California, USA	5/1/2011	Mark R. Spellman
Perch, Sacramento	1.44 kg (3 lb 3 oz)	Crowley Lake, California, USA	9/22/1995	Richard J. Fischer
Perch, white	1.38 kg (3 lb 1 oz)	Forest Hill Park, New Jersey, USA	5/6/1989	Edward Tango
Perch, yellow	1.91 kg (4 lb 3 oz)	Bordentown, New Jersey, USA	5/1/1865	Dr. C. Abbot
Permit	27.21 kg (60 lb 0 oz)	Ilha do Mel, Paranagua, Brazil	12/14/2002	Renato Fiedler
Piabanha	1.81 kg (4 lb 0 oz)	Paraiba do Sul River, Brazil	9/3/2002	Capt. Kdu Magalhaes
Piau	2 kg (4 lb 6 oz)	Cel. Vanick River, Brazil	9/13/2000	Capt. Kdu Magalhaes
Piau, red	0.45 kg (1 lb 0 oz)	Rio Negro River, Brazil	11/9/2005	Capt. Kdu Magalhaes
Piavucu	0.45 kg (1 lb 0 oz)	Pesqueiro Matsumura Ponds, Sao Paolo, Brazil	5/8/2010	Steven M. Wozniak
Pickerel, chain	4.25 kg (9 lb 6 oz)	Homerville, Georgia, USA	2/17/1961	Baxley McQuaig, Jr.
Pickerel, grass	0.45 kg (1 lb 0 oz)	Dewart Lake, Indiana, USA	6/9/1990	Mike Berg

Species	Weight	Location	Catch Date	Angler
Pickerel, redfin	1.02 kg (2 lb 4 oz)	Gall Berry Swamp, North Carolina, USA	6/27/1997	Edward Davis
Picuda	4.99 kg (11 lb 0 oz)	Rio Nare, Colombia	6/28/2009	Alejandro Linares
Pike, northern	25 kg (55 lb 1 oz)	Lake of Grefeern, Germany	10/16/1986	Lothar Louis
Pike-characin, golden	0.45 kg (1 lb 0 oz)	Cano Cuica, Colombia	1/28/2010	Alejandro Linares
Pike-conger, common	7.1 kg (15 lb 10 oz)	Markham River, Lae, Huon Gulf, Papua New Guinea	3/7/1993	Barry Mallett
Pikeminnow, northern	3.57 kg (7 lb 14 oz)	Snake River, Almota, Washington, USA	5/15/2008	Pamela Ramsden
Pikeminnow, Sacramento	3.15 kg (6 lb 15 oz)	Kaweah River, California, USA	8/31/2002	Hayden Marlow
Pinfish	1.51 kg (3 lb 5 oz)	Horn Island, Mississippi, USA	9/4/1992	William Fountain
Pinook	7.25 kg (16 lb 0 oz)	Sault Ste. Marie, Ontario, Canada	9/20/1999	David Conlin
Piracatinga	1.12 kg (2 lb 7 oz)	Parana da Eva, Amazonas, Brazil	5/22/2010	Gilberto Fernandes
Pirambeba	2.26 kg (5 lb 0 oz)	Iriri River, Brazil	7/25/2003	Doug Olander
Piramutaba	5.04 kg (11 lb 1 oz)	Rio Amazonas, Amazonas, Brazil	5/16/2009	Gilberto Fernandes
Piranha, black	3.83 kg (8 lb 7 oz)	Jatapo, Amazon, Brazil	2/10/2009	Russell Jensen
Piranha, black spot	0.68 kg (1 lb 8 oz)	Cano La Pica, Edo Apure, Venezuela	12/18/2003	Juan Carlos Campagnolo Trentin
Piranha, Manueli's	3.85 kg (8 lb 8 oz)	Xingu River, Para, Brazil	7/9/1997	Jedediah Colston
Piranha, red	1.55 kg (3 lb 7 oz)	Cuiaba River, Brazil	7/7/1994	Dr. H. Siegel
Piranha, serrulatus	0.58 kg (1 lb 4 oz)	Rio Urubu, Amazonas, Brazil	8/21/2008	Gilberto Fernandes
Piranha, white	0.91 kg (2 lb 0 oz)	Sucunduri River, Brazil	7/12/2010	Martini Arostegui
Piraputanga	3.36 kg (7 lb 6 oz)	Rio Arinos, Brazil	9/3/1997	Marcio Borges de Oliveira
Pirarucu	154 kg (339 lb 8 oz)	Amazonia, Ecuador	2/18/2010	Jakub Vagner
Pollack, European	12.41 kg (27 lb 6 oz)	Salcombe, Devon, United Kingdom	1/16/1986	Robert Milkins
Pollock	22.7 kg (50 lb 0 oz)	Salstraumen, Norway	11/30/1995	Thor-Magnus Lekang
Pollock, Alaska	2.44 kg (5 lb 6 oz)	Kachemak Bay, Alaska, USA	6/30/2010	Nancy L. Witherell
Pomfret	8.66 kg (19 lb 1 oz)	Gulf of Mexico, Mexico	5/4/2004	Matt McLeod

Species	Weight	Location	Catch Date	Angler
Pomfret, bigscale	9.35 kg (20 lb 10 oz)	St. Augustine, Florida, USA	10/17/2004	W. Gordon Davis
Pomfret, Brevort's	3.06 kg (6 lb 12 oz)	Bimini, Bahamas	11/16/1998	Horst Schneider
Pomfret, lustrous	7.71 kg (17 lb 0 oz)	Kona, Hawaii, USA	7/6/2005	George Bogen
Pomfret, Pacific	1.6 kg (3 lb 8 oz)	Jogashima, Kanagawa, Japan	4/21/2009	Yoshiki Shirahata
Pompano, African	22.9 kg (50 lb 8 oz)	Daytona Beach, Florida, USA	4/21/1990	Tom Sargent
Pompano, black-blotch	11.06 kg (24 lb 6 oz)	Puerto Vallarta, Mexico	9/18/2007	Larry R. Walker
Pompano, dolphin	3.86 kg (8 lb 8 oz)	Baltimore Canyon, Maryland, USA	8/7/2008	Charles Champon
Pompano, Florida	3.76 kg (8 lb 4 oz)	Port St. Joe Bay, Florida, USA	10/16/1999	Barry Huston
Pompano, gaff-topsail	1.7 kg (3 lb 12 oz)	Rancho Leonero, Baja, California Sur, Mexico	4/24/2006	Brett Philip
Pompano, Irish	0.68 kg (1 lb 8 oz)	St. Lucie River, Florida, USA	12/17/2000	Richard Morgan, Sr.
Pompano, snubnos	3.4 kg (7 lb 7 oz)	Port Hedland, W.A., Australia	4/29/2001	Anthony Boekhorst
Pompano, southern	6.23 kg (13 lb 12 oz)	Karachi, Pakistan	2/28/2004	Asif Khan
Porcupinefish	3.74 kg (8 lb 4 oz)	Haleiwa Harbor, Oahu, Hawaii, USA	6/19/2010	Steven M. Wozniak
Porcupinefish, black-blotched	1.05 kg (2 lb 5 oz)	Koh Kut Island, Gulf of Siam, Thailand	2/10/2006	Lootjirot Panphrapat
Porcupinefish, longspine	0.95 kg (2 lb 1 oz)	Kataura, Kagoshima, Japan	7/2/2005	Katsuhiko Ohana
Porgy, black	4.25 kg (9 lb 5 oz)	Nanko, Osaka Bay, Japan	7/17/2010	Mikio Watanabe
Porgy, Canary	8.06 kg (17 lb 12 oz)	Monte Gordo, Portugal	7/14/1997	Joseph Triay
Porgy, jolthead	10.54 kg (23 lb 4 oz)	Madeira Beach, Florida, USA	3/14/1990	Harm Wilder
Porgy, knobbed	2.63 kg (5 lb 12 oz)	Gulf of Mexico, Texas, USA	2/21/2000	Stanley Sweet
Porgy, littlehead	0.56 kg (1 lb 4 oz)	Key Largo, Florida, USA	12/6/2003	Dennis Triana
Porgy, littlehead	0.56 kg (1 lb 4 oz)	Elliot Key, Florida, USA	2/8/2003	Dennis Triana
Porgy, pluma	0.45 kg (1 lb 0 oz)	Key Largo, Florida, USA	1/19/2004	Dennis Triana
Porgy, red	7.72 kg (17 lb 0 oz)	Gibraltar	7/12/1997	Richard Gomila

Species	Weight	Location	Catch Date	Angler
Porgy, saucereye	4.08 kg (9 lb 0 oz)	Longboat Key, Mexico	10/2/2004	Bucky Wolden
Porgy, sheepshead	3.95 kg (8 lb 11 oz)	Tijucas Island, Rio de Janeiro, Brazil	1/19/2007	Flavio Campos Reis
Porgy, whitebone	1.5 kg (3 lb 5 oz)	Orange Beach, Alabama, USA	9/10/2003	Chuck Andre
Porkfish	0.99 kg (2 lb 3 oz)	Key Largo, Florida, USA	4/30/2006	Austin Porter
Powan	5.39 kg (11 lb 14 oz)	Skrabean, Nymolla, Sweden	12/15/1994	Allan Englund
Prickleback, monkeyface	1.47 kg (3 lb 4 oz)	Yaquina Bay, Newport, Oregan, USA	6/29/2008	Todd Pietsch
Puddingwife	1.58 kg (3 lb 8 oz)	Key West, Florida, USA	4/26/2003	David Pesi
Puffer, oceanic	3.17 kg (7 lb 0 oz)	Sandy Hook, New Jersey, USA	8/28/1991	Ms. Jane Jagen
Puffer, panther (higan-fugu)	1.2 kg (2 lb 10 oz)	Nojima, Kanagawa, Japan	3/30/2009	Takashi Nishino
Puffer, prickly	5 kg (11 lb 0 oz)	Grand Bereby, Ivory Coast	11/27/1998	Patrick Sebile
Puffer, smooth	5.21 kg (11 lb 7 oz)	Cape May Inlet, New Jersey, USA	8/24/2001	Shawn Clark
Puffer, whitespotted	2.01 kg (4 lb 7 oz)	Iroquois Point, Hawaii, USA	10/31/1992	George Cornish
Pumpkinseed	0.63 kg (1 lb 6 oz)	Mexico, New York, USA	4/27/1985	Ms. Heather Finch

Species	Weight	Location	Catch Date	Angler
Queenfish, doublespotted	3.29 kg (7 lb 4 oz)	Benguerra Island, Mozambique	6/4/2008	Stan Nabozny
Queenfish, needlescaled	1.02 kg (2 lb 4 oz)	Bazaruto Archipelago, Mozambique	3/22/2008	Jodie L. Johnson
Queenfish, talang	17.89 kg (39 lb 7 oz)	Umkomaas, South Africa	5/23/2010	Craig Oliver
Quillback	2.94 kg (6 lb 8 oz)	Lake Michigan, Indiana, USA	1/15/1993	Mike Berg
Ratfish, spotted	1.29 kg (2 lb 13 oz)	Tacoma, Washington, USA	4/23/1997	Kenneth Dunn
Raven, sea	2.35 kg (5 lb 2 oz)	Kakkumi, Hakodate, Hokkaido, Japan	7/1/2006	Kiyoshi Iwata
Raven, sea (Kemushi-Kajika)	0.9 kg (1 lb 15 oz)	Motoyoshi, Miyagi, Japan	4/10/2005	Yoshihiko Onodera
Ray, backwater butterfly	82.6 kg (182 lb 1 oz)	Knysna Lagoon, South Africa	7/11/1992	Hilton Gervais
Ray, bat	82.1 kg (181 lb 0 oz)	Huntington Beach Pier, California, USA	6/30/1978	Bradley Dew
Ray, blonde	14.28 kg (31 lb 8 oz)	Jersey Channel Islands, United Kingdom	4/3/1989	John Thompson
Ray, bluespotted ribbontail	1.43 kg (3 lb 2 oz)	Kut Island, Thailand	1/18/2006	Steven M. Wozniak
Ray, bull	46.6 kg (102 lb 11 oz)	Cape Skirring, Senegal	2/18/1999	Daniel Bidel
Ray, bull (Australian)	66 kg (145 lb 8 oz)	Port River, Australia	9/2/2007	Steven Evangelou
Ray, common eagle	27.5 kg (60 lb 10 oz)	Pyla, France	9/9/1996	Patrick Sebile
Ray, discus	53 kg (116 lb 13 oz)	Rio Negro and Branco, Brazil	12/20/2000	Keith Sutton
Ray, Japanese eagle	84.6 kg (186 lb 8 oz)	Akitio, Northern Waiararapa, New Zealand	2/24/2006	Neil McDonald
Ray, longheaded eagle	32.48 kg (71 lb 9 oz)	Himeji Port, Hyogo, Japan	7/11/2002	Masahiro Oomori
Ray, painted	4.5 kg (9 lb 15 oz)	Jersey, Channel Islands, United Kingdom	8/2/1988	Andrew Mitchell
Ray, pale	11.15 kg (24 lb 9 oz)	Langesund, Stavern, Norway	6/13/1999	Bjorn Persson
Ray, southern fiddler	6.7 kg (14 lb 12 oz)	Marion Bay, S.A., Australia	8/11/1990	Marcel Vandergoot
Ray, spiny butterfly	60 kg (132 lb 4 oz)	Nouadhibou, Mauritania	5/5/1984	Robin Michel

Species	Weight	Location	Catch Date	Angler
Ray, starry	1.4 kg (3 lb 1 oz)	Vila Real Santo Antonio, Algarve, Portugal	3/23/2007	Luis Ceia
Ray, thornback	7.59 kg (16 lb 12 oz)	Jersey, Channel Islands, United Kingdom	7/11/1988	John Thompson
Ray, undulate	4.2 kg (9 lb 4 oz)	Arcachon, France	5/18/2001	Patrick Sebile
Rebeca	3 kg (6 lb 9 oz)	Xingu River, Brazil	5/30/2003	Capt. Kdu Magalhaes
Redfin, Pacific	2.25 kg (4 lb 15 oz)	Tama River, Tokyo, Japan	4/18/2010	Shumpei Yokozuka
Redfish, acadian	1.13 kg (2 lb 8 oz)	Grindavik, Iceland	6/13/2010	George Bogen
Redhorse, black	1.02 kg (2 lb 4 oz)	French Creek, Franklin, Pennsylvania, USA	2/22/1998	Richard Faler, Jr.
Redhorse, blacktail	0.68 kg (1 lb 8 oz)	Tallapoosa River, Alabama, USA	4/24/2005	Max W. Beebe
Redhorse, golden	1.85 kg (4 lb 1 oz)	French Creek, Franklin, Pennsylvania, USA	2/9/1997	Richard Faler, Jr.
Redhorse, greater	4.16 kg (9 lb 3 oz)	Salmon River, Pulaski, New York, USA	5/11/1985	Jason Wilson
Redhorse, river	4.08 kg (9 lb 0 oz)	Muskegon River, Michigan, USA	6/9/2001	Andy Tulgetske
Redhorse, shorthead	5.75 kg (12 lb 11 oz)	Sauk River, Melrose, Minnesota, USA	5/20/2005	Robin Schmitz
Redhorse, silver	5.18 kg (11 lb 7 oz)	Plum Creek, Wisconsin, USA	5/29/1985	Neal Long
Remora, common	2.49 kg (5 lb 8 oz)	Cat Cay, Bahamas	6/12/2002	Michael Orleans
Roach	1.84 kg (4 lb 1 oz)	Colwick, Nottingham, United Kingdom	6/16/1975	R. Jones
Roach-Bream	3.52 kg (7 lb 12 oz)	Norfolk Estate Lakes, United Kingdom	6/25/2008	John Bailey
Rock-bacu	10.51 kg (23 lb 2 oz)	Lago dos Reis, Amazonas, Brazil	2/15/2010	Gilberto Fernandes
Rockcod, bluelined	0.7 kg (1 lb 8 oz)	Kut Island, Thailand	2/8/2006	Jean-Francois Helias
Rockfish, bank	1.98 kg (4 lb 6 oz)	San Clemente Island, California, USA	2/14/1998	Stephen D. Grossberg
Rockfish, black	6.03 kg (13 lb 5 oz)	Gulf of Alaska, Alaska, USA	8/12/2005	Ashley Eslick
Rockfish, blackgill	3.53 kg (7 lb 12 oz)	San Clemente Island, California, USA	12/27/2000	Stephen Grossberg

Species	Weight	Location	Catch Date	Angler
Rockfish, blue	3.79 kg (8 lb 6 oz)	Whaler's Cove, Alaska, USA	7/27/1994	Dr. John Whitaker
Rockfish, bronzespotted	4.96 kg (10 lb 15 oz)	San Clemente Island, California, USA	3/25/2000	George Bogen
Rockfish, brown	1.81 kg (4 lb 0 oz)	San Gregorio, California, USA	7/13/2008	Hin Fan Tsang
Rockfish, canary	4.53 kg (10 lb 0 oz)	Westport, Washington, USA	5/17/1986	Terry Rudnick
Rockfish, chameleon	1.22 kg (2 lb 11 oz)	San Clemente Island, California, USA	3/14/2001	Stephen Grossberg
Rockfish, China	1.67 kg (3 lb 11 oz)	Tatoosh Island, Neah Bay, Washington, USA	8/24/1992	Edward Schultz
Rockfish, copper	3.28 kg (7 lb 4 oz)	Drakes Bay, California, USA	1/23/2004	Ben Rojas
Rockfish, dusky	2.72 kg (6 lb 0 oz)	Kodiak Island, Alaska, USA	7/26/2008	Paul Leader
Rockfish, flag	1.45 kg (3 lb 3 oz)	San Clemente Island, California, USA	2/14/1999	Stephen Grossberg
Rockfish, goldeye	1.1 kg (2 lb 6 oz)	Oshika, Miyagi, Japan	3/3/2005	Fuminori Sato
Rockfish, gopher	2.83 kg (6 lb 4 oz)	Pillar Point, California, USA	8/17/2008	Hin Fan Tsang
Rockfish, grass	2.89 kg (6 lb 6 oz)	Yaquina Bay, Newport, Oregon, USA	3/18/2007	Darryoush E. Pishvai
Rockfish, grass	2.89 kg (6 lb 6 oz)	Newport, Oregon, USA	3/30/2007	Todd Pietsch
Rockfish, greenspotted	1.01 kg (2 lb 3 oz)	San Clemente Island, California, USA	11/4/2000	Stephen Grossberg
Rockfish, greenstriped	0.63 kg (1 lb 6 oz)	San Clemente Island, California, USA	3/18/2000	Stephen Grossberg
Rockfish, honeycomb	0.57 kg (1 lb 4 oz)	San Martin Island, Baja California Sur, Mexico	10/27/2000	Stephen Grossberg
Rockfish, Mexican	2.72 kg (6 lb 0 oz)	San Clemente Island, California, USA	12/9/2000	Stephen Grossberg
Rockfish, olive	1.8 kg (3 lb 15 oz)	Carmel Bay, California, USA	9/28/2006	David J. Babineau
Rockfish, pink	2.9 kg (6 lb 9 oz)	San Clemente Island, California, USA	3/3/2002	Stephen D Grossberg
Rockfish, quillback	3.28 kg (7 lb 4 oz)	Depoe Bay, Oregon, USA	3/18/1990	Kelly Canaday
Rockfish, redbanded	4.44 kg (9 lb 12 oz)	Whaler's Cove, Alaska, USA	7/11/1999	Thomas Stroud
Rockfish, Rosethorn	1.49 kg (3 lb 4 oz)	Elrington Island, Alaska, USA	7/20/2004	Bob Martin

Species	Weight	Location	Catch Date	Angler
Rockfish, rough-eye	6.69 kg (14 lb 12 oz)	Langara Island, British Columbia, Canada	8/18/2007	George Bogen
Rockfish, short-raker	16.24 kg (35 lb 13 oz)	Ketchikan, Alaska, USA	6/28/1994	Jeffrey Hendrickson
Rockfish, silver-gray	4.71 kg (10 lb 6 oz)	Seward, Alaska, USA	6/12/2001	Corey Green
Rockfish, speck-led	0.95 kg (2 lb 1 oz)	Santa Barbara Island, California, USA	12/4/1999	Bill Grossberg
Rockfish, split-nose	0.81 kg (1 lb 12 oz)	San Clemente Island, California, USA	3/17/2001	Stephen Grossberg
Rockfish, starry	1.04 kg (2 lb 4 oz)	San Clemente Island, California, USA	1/9/1999	Stephen Grossberg
Rockfish, tiger	3.17 kg (7 lb 0 oz)	Chugach Island, Alaska, USA	8/7/2005	Nicole Loffredo
Rockfish, ver-million	5.45 kg (12 lb 0 oz)	Depoe Bay, Oregon, USA	6/2/1990	Joseph Lowe
Rockfish, widow	2.43 kg (5 lb 6 oz)	Elfin Cove, Alaska, USA	8/24/2003	Keith Sturm
Rockfish, yel-loweye	17.82 kg (39 lb 4 oz)	Whalers Cove, Alaska, USA	7/18/2000	David Mundhenke
Rockfish, yel-lowtail	2.58 kg (5 lb 11 oz)	Langara Island, British Columbia, Canada	9/5/2003	George Bogen
Rohu	12.5 kg (27 lb 8 oz)	Dan Tchang Dam, Thailand	7/8/2003	Pakron Suwannaat
Roosterfish	51.71 kg (114 lb 0 oz)	La Paz, Baja California, Mexico	6/1/1960	Abe Sackheim
Rosefish, black-belly	2.35 kg (5 lb 3 oz)	Norfolk Canyon, Virginia, USA	2/14/2009	Jess Bradford Cadwallender
Rubyfish, Japanese	4 kg (8 lb 13 oz)	Yonaguni Island, Okinawa, Japan	11/5/2010	Takashi Odagiri
Rudd	1.58 kg (3 lb 7 oz)	Ljungan River, Sweden	7/31/1988	Luis Rasmussen
Runner, blue	5.05 kg (11 lb 2 oz)	Dauphin Island, Alabama, USA	6/28/1997	Ms. Stacey Moiren
Runner, rainbow	17.05 kg (37 lb 9 oz)	Isla Clarion, Revillagigedo Islands, Mexico	11/21/1991	Tom Pfleger
Sabaleta	1.12 kg (2 lb 7 oz)	Quebrada la Compania, Colombia	7/12/2002	Alejandro Linares
Sabalo	4.35 kg (9 lb 9 oz)	Rio Tambopata, Peru	10/10/1992	James Wise, M.D.

Species	Weight	Location	Catch Date	Angler
Sailfin, vermiculated	1.36 kg (3 lb 0 oz)	Broward County Canal, Florida, USA	6/3/2006	Capt. Jay Wright Jr.
Sailfish, Atlantic	64 kg (141 lb 1 oz)	Luanda, Angola	2/9/1994	Alfredo de Sousa Neves
Sailfish, Pacific	100.24 kg (221 lb 0 oz)	Santa Cruz Island, Ecuador	2/12/1947	Carl Stewart
Sailors choice	0.45 kg (1 lb 0 oz)	Cat Cay, Bahamas	7/3/2004	Dennis Triana
Sailors choice	0.45 kg (1 lb 0 oz)	John Pennekamp Park, Florida, USA	8/16/2007	Jonathan Legaz
Sailors choice	0.45 kg (1 lb 0 oz)	John Pennekamp Park, Florida, USA	8/13/2007	Dennis Triana
Salema	1.18 kg (2 lb 9 oz)	Faro-Ria Forhosa, Portugal	9/24/2006	Luis Ceia
Salmon, Atlantic	35.89 kg (79 lb 2 oz)	Tana River, Norway	1/1/1928	Henrik Henriksen
Salmon, Atlantic (landlocked)	12.13 kg (26 lb 12 oz)	Torch Lake, Michigan, USA	10/22/2010	Thomas Aufiero
Salmon, Chinook	44.11 kg (97 lb 4 oz)	Kenai River, Alaska, USA	5/17/1985	Les Anderson
Salmon, Chinook-coho	16.1 kg (35 lb 8 oz)	Salmon River, Pulaski, New York, USA	10/21/2001	Brooks Gerli
Salmon, chum	15.87 kg (35 lb 0 oz)	Edye Pass, British Columbia, Canada	7/11/1995	Todd Johansson
Salmon, coho	15.08 kg (33 lb 4 oz)	Salmon River, Pulaski, New York, USA	9/27/1989	Jerry Lifton
Salmon, pink	6.74 kg (14 lb 13 oz)	Monroe, Washington, USA	9/30/2001	Alexander Minerich
Salmon, sockeye	6.88 kg (15 lb 3 oz)	Kenai River, Alaska, USA	8/9/1987	Stan Roach
Samson fish	36.5 kg (80 lb 7 oz)	Cape Naturaliste, W.A., Australia	1/31/1993	Terry Coote
Sand diver	1.07 kg (2 lb 6 oz)	Pompano Beach, Florida, USA	3/5/2005	Kenneth A. Myers
Sandbass, parrot	1.02 kg (2 lb 4 oz)	Tamarindo, Costa Rica	2/14/2007	George Bogen
Sandperch, Brazilian	1 kg (2 lb 3.2 oz)	Mar del Plata, Argentina	4/26/2010	Tomas Felipe Restano
Sandperch, namorado	20.2 kg (44 lb 8 oz)	Rio de Janeiro, Brazil	3/7/1998	Eduardo Baumeier
Sardinata	4.08 kg (9 lb 0 oz)	Rio Negro, Colombia	3/2/2008	Alejandro Linares
Sargento	4.58 kg (10 lb 1 oz)	Gatun Lake, Panama	3/3/2002	Horacio A. Clare, III

Species	Weight	Location	Catch Date	Angler
Sargo	1.73 kg (3 lb 13 oz)	Mission Bay, San Diego, California, USA	5/19/2007	Thomas Hilgert
Sauger	3.96 kg (8 lb 12 oz)	Lake Sakakawea, North Dakota, USA	10/6/1971	Mike Fischer
Saugeye	5.81 kg (12 lb 13 oz)	Clendening Reservoir, Ohio, USA	11/19/2001	Fred Sulek
Sawfish, large-tooth	403.92 kg (890 lb 8 oz)	Fort Amador, Canal Zone, Panama	5/26/1960	Jack Wagner
Sawtail, scalpel	2.25 kg (4 lb 15 oz)	Toshima, Tokyo, Japan	11/24/2007	Yuuma Nishino
Scabbardfish, channel	3.89 kg (8 lb 9 oz)	Rio de Janeiro, Brazil	4/6/2002	Eduardo Baumeier
Scabbardfish, silver	6.4 kg (14 lb 1 oz)	Europa Point, Gibraltar	7/16/1995	Ernest Borrell
Scad, amber-stripe	1.13 kg (2 lb 8 oz)	Kona, Hawaii, USA	12/30/2008	George Bogen
Scad, false	0.56 kg (1 lb 3 oz)	Vila Real Santo Antonio, Algarve, Portugal	10/28/2007	Luis Ceia
Scad, mackerel	0.55 kg (1 lb 3 oz)	Hachijo Is., Tokyo, Japan	8/16/2005	Chieko Nishino
Scamp	13.44 kg (29 lb 10 oz)	Dauphin Island, Alabama, USA	7/22/2000	Robert Conklin
Scombrops, Atlantic	9.88 kg (21 lb 12 oz)	Bimini, Bahamas	7/15/1997	Doug Olander
Scorpionfish, black	0.87 kg (1 lb 14 oz)	Detached Mole, Gibraltar	2/3/1997	Julius Gafan
Scorpionfish, California	1.98 kg (4 lb 6 oz)	Cedros Island, Mexico	8/30/2006	Dennis Toussieng
Scorpionfish, darkblotch	0.53 kg (1 lb 3 oz)	Zancudo, Costa Rica	2/8/2005	Phillip Mark Bauer
Scorpionfish, red	2.96 kg (6 lb 8 oz)	Gibraltar	5/30/1996	Stuart Brown-Giraldi
Scorpionfish, spinycheek	0.7 kg (1 lb 9 oz)	Pushbutton Hill, Florida, USA	4/11/2004	Capt. Mark Sagerholm
Scorpionfish, spotback	1.07 kg (2 lb 6 oz)	San Jose Del Cabo, Baja California Sur, Mexico	2/26/2006	George Bogen
Scorpionfish, spotted	1.55 kg (3 lb 7 oz)	Angra Dor Reis Bay, Rio de Janeiro, Brazil	5/25/1997	Pedro Cabral de Menezes

Species	Weight	Location	Catch Date	Angler
Sculpin, great	5.24 kg (11 lb 8 oz)	Osatube, Hokkaido, Japan	11/8/2010	Yoshitatsu Honda
Sculpin, short-horn	0.58 kg (1 lb 4 oz)	Lodmundarfjordur, Iceland	5/30/2003	Skarphedinn Asbjornsson
Scup	2.06 kg (4 lb 9 oz)	Nantucket Sound, Massachusetts, USA	6/3/1992	Sonny Richards
Seabass, black-fin	10.91 kg (24 lb 0 oz)	Katsuura, Chiba, Japan	2/10/2011	Yuki Inoue
Seabass, Japanese (Suzuki)	13.14 kg (28 lb 15 oz)	Katada River, Oita, Japan	10/8/2006	Yoshiaki Kubo
Seabass, spotted	1.7 kg (3 lb 11 oz)	Dakhla, Morocco	5/23/2003	Patrick Sebile
Seabass, white	37.98 kg (83 lb 12 oz)	San Felipe, Mexico	3/31/1953	Lyal Baumgardner

Species	Weight	Location	Catch Date	Angler
Seabream, axillary	0.6 kg (1 lb 5 oz)	Anglet, France	6/8/2001	Jean Baibarac
Seabream, black	1.9 kg (4 lb 3 oz)	Bonifacio, Corsica, France	9/16/2002	Patrick Sebile
Seabream, bluespotted	11.62 kg (25 lb 9 oz)	Detached Mole, Gibraltar	6/4/2000	Charles Bear
Seabream, crimson (chidai)	1.2 kg (2 lb 10 oz)	Kurihama, Kanagawa, Japan	5/17/2003	Tsumishi Koide
Seabream, daggerhead	7.3 kg (16 lb 1 oz)	Algoa Bay, Port Elizabeth, South Africa	10/10/1993	Eddie De Reuck
Seabream, gilthead	7.36 kg (16 lb 3 oz)	Florn Estuary, Brest, France	10/13/2000	Jean Serra
Seabream, Moroccan white	1.6 kg (3 lb 8 oz)	Dakhla, Morocco	5/26/2003	Patrick Sebile
Seabream, Okinawa	3.05 kg (6 lb 11 oz)	Naoto, Amami-oshima, Kagoshima, Japan	2/23/2003	Shusaku Hayashi
Seabream, red stumpnose	7.25 kg (15 lb 15 oz)	East London, South Africa	6/6/2008	Christopher Justin Hattingh
Seabream, redbanded (murudai)	3 kg (6 lb 9 oz)	Nouadhibou, Mauritania	3/9/1986	Serge Bensa
Seabream, saddle	0.6 kg (1 lb 5 oz)	Frejus, France	9/25/2002	Bruno Ansquer
Seabream, Scotsman	7.8 kg (17 lb 3 oz)	St. Lucia Estuary, South Africa	11/25/1994	G.J. Van Der Westhuizen
Seabream, sharpsnout	1.68 kg (3 lb 11 oz)	La Sela, Gibraltar Bay, Gibraltar	11/23/1996	Brian Soiza
Seabream, striped	0.8 kg (1 lb 12 oz)	Dakhla, Morocco	9/17/1993	Patrick Sebile
Seabream, white	1.87 kg (4 lb 1 oz)	Gibraltar Bay, Gibraltar	4/28/1996	Anthony Loddo
Seabream, yellowback (Kidia)	1.15 kg (2 lb 8 oz)	Mikura Island, Tokyo, Japan	6/19/2004	Takeshi Date
Seabream, yellowfin	2.7 kg (5 lb 15 oz)	Keihin-unga, Kanagawa, Japan	7/5/2005	Shotaro Ono
Seabream, zebra	3.94 kg (8 lb 11 oz)	Vila Real Santo Antonio, Algarve, Portugal	4/2/2007	Joao Pardal
Seachub, blue	0.59 kg (1 lb 5 oz)	Raiatea Lagoon, Tahiti	6/16/2006	Dennis Triana
Seaperch, spotted scale	10.5 kg (23 lb 2 oz)	Cairns, Queensland, Australia	3/2/1986	Mac Mankowski

Species	Weight	Location	Catch Date	Angler
Searobin, striped	1.55 kg (3 lb 6 oz)	Mt. Sinai, Long Island, New York, USA	6/22/1988	Michael Greene, Jr.
Seatrout, sand	2.78 kg (6 lb 2 oz)	Dauphin Island, Alabama, USA	5/24/1997	Steve Scoggin
Seatrout, silver	0.56 kg (1 lb 4 oz)	Aransas Pass, Texas, USA	11/24/2006	Brandi Huff
Seatrout, spotted	7.92 kg (17 lb 7 oz)	Ft. Pierce, Florida, USA	5/11/1995	Craig F. Carson
Seerfish, Australian	9.25 kg (20 lb 6 oz)	South West Rocks, N.S.W., Australia	7/5/1987	Greg Laarkamp
Seerfish, Chinese	131 kg (288 lb 12 oz)	Kwan-Tall Island, Cheju-Do, Korea	10/6/1982	Boo-Il Oh
Seerfish, kanadi	12.5 kg (27 lb 8 oz)	Mapelane, Zululand, Natal, South Africa	7/11/1997	Daniel Van Tonder
Sennet, southern	1.14 kg (2 lb 8 oz)	Indian River, Florida, USA	1/29/1999	Chris Kirkhart
Serrana, blacktail	0.88 kg (1 lb 15 oz)	El Lomo, Gibraltar	6/23/2002	Paul Henwood
Seventy-four	16 kg (35 lb 4 oz)	Mapuzi, Transkei, South Africa	8/17/1985	Nolan Sparg
Shad, allis	2.32 kg (5 lb 2 oz)	Aulne River, Chateaulin, France	5/6/2005	Dr. Samuel P. Davis
Shad, American	5.1 kg (11 lb 4 oz)	Connecticut River, Massachusetts, USA	5/19/1986	Bob Thibodo
Shad, gizzard	1.98 kg (4 lb 6 oz)	Lake Michigan, Indiana, USA	3/2/1996	Mike Berg
Shad, hickory	1.3 kg (2 lb 14 oz)	Econlockhatchee River, Florida, USA	1/15/2008	Dave Chermanski
Shad, Mediterranean	0.88 kg (1 lb 15 oz)	Taro River S. Secondo, Italy	4/29/2006	Mauro Mazzo
Shad, twaite	0.7 kg (1 lb 8 oz)	North Sea, Netherlands	8/21/1998	P.C. Ouwendijk
Shark, Atlantic sharpnose	7.25 kg (16 lb 0 oz)	Port Mansfield, Texas, USA	10/12/1994	R. Shields
Shark, banded (hound)	15.25 kg (33 lb 9 oz)	Akazawa, Ito-Shi, Shizuoka, Japan	6/10/2006	Takashi Nishino
Shark, bigeye thresher	363.8 kg (802 lb 0 oz)	Tutukaka, New Zealand	2/8/1981	Ms. Dianne North
Shark, bignose	167.8 kg (369 lb 14 oz)	Markham River, Lae, Papua New Guinea	10/23/1993	Lester Rohrlach
Shark, blackmouth cat	1.37 kg (3 lb 0 oz)	Mausundvar, Trondheim, Norway	9/17/1994	Per Hagen

Species	Weight	Location	Catch Date	Angler
Shark, black-nose	18.86 kg (41 lb 9 oz)	Little River, South Carolina, USA	7/30/1992	Jon-Paul Hoffman
Shark, blacktail	33.7 kg (74 lb 4 oz)	Kosi Bay, Zululand, South Africa	5/25/1987	Trevor Ashington
Shark, blacktip	122.75 kg (270 lb 9 oz)	Malindi Bay, Kenya	9/21/1984	Jurgen Oeder
Shark, blacktip reef	13.55 kg (29 lb 13 oz)	Indian Ocean, Coco Island	10/22/1995	Dr. Joachim Klei-don
Shark, blue	239.49 kg (528 lb 0 oz)	Montauk Point, New York, USA	8/9/2001	Joe Seidel
Shark, bonnet-head	11.79 kg (26 lb 0 oz)	Ponce Inlet, Florida, USA	7/14/2006	Luke Proctor
Shark, brown smooth-hound	0.68 kg (1 lb 8 oz)	San Fransisco Bay, California, USA	8/28/2010	Steven M. Wozniak
Shark, brown-banded bamboo	2.89 kg (6 lb 5 oz)	Kut Island, Gulf of Siam, Thailand	2/10/2008	Bruno Binet
Shark, bull	316.5 kg (697 lb 12 oz)	Malindi, Kenya	3/24/2001	Ronald de Jager
Shark, Carib-bean reef	69.85 kg (154 lb 0 oz)	Molasses Reef, Florida, USA	12/9/1996	Rene de Dios
Shark, dusky	346.54 kg (764 lb 0 oz)	Longboat Key, Florida, USA	5/28/1982	Warren Girle
Shark, Galapa-gos	140 kg (308 lb 10 oz)	South Atlantic, Ascension Island	7/2/2004	Denis J. Froud
Shark, great hammerhead	580.59 kg (1280 lb 0 oz)	Boca Grande, Florida, USA	5/23/2006	Bucky Dennis
Shark, Green-land	775 kg (1708 lb 9 oz)	Trondheimsfjord, Norway	10/18/1987	Terje Nordtvedt
Shark, gulper	7.34 kg (16 lb 3 oz)	Bimini, Bahamas	7/15/1997	Doug Olander
Shark, gummy	30.8 kg (67 lb 14 oz)	Mcloughins Beach, Victoria, Australia	11/15/1992	Neale Blunden
Shark, Japanese bullhead	12.05 kg (26 lb 9 oz)	Yahatano, Ito, Shizuoka, Japan	3/20/2006	Takashi Nishino
Shark, lemon	183.7 kg (405 lb 0 oz)	Buxton, North Carolina, USA	11/23/1988	Ms. Colleen Har-low
Shark, leopard	18.42 kg (40 lb 10 oz)	Oceanside, California, USA	5/13/1994	Fred Oakley

Species	Weight	Location	Catch Date	Angler
Shark, mako	553.84 kg (1221 lb 0 oz)	Chatham, Massachusetts, USA	7/21/2001	Luke Sweeney
Shark, milk	5 kg (11 lb 0 oz)	Archipelago dos Bijagos, Guinea-Bissau	4/1/2001	Adrien Bernard
Shark, narrow-tooth	242 kg (533 lb 8 oz)	Cape Karikari, New Zealand	1/9/1993	Ms. Gaye Harrison-Armstrong
Shark, night	76.65 kg (169 lb 0 oz)	Bimini, Bahamas	7/13/1997	Capt. Ron Schatman
Shark, nurse	119.63 kg (263 lb 12 oz)	Port St. Joe, Florida, USA	7/21/2007	Nic Jeter
Shark, oceanic whitetip	167.37 kg (369 lb 0 oz)	San Salvador, Bahamas	1/24/1998	Reid Hodges
Shark, pig-eye	45.5 kg (100 lb 4 oz)	Moreton Bay, Australia	3/29/2003	Gordon Macdonald
Shark, porbeagle	230 kg (507 lb 0 oz)	Pentland Firth, Caithness, Scotland	3/9/1993	Christopher Bennett
Shark, salmon	209.36 kg (461 lb 9 oz)	Valdez, Alaska, USA	7/15/2009	Thomas E. Farmer
Shark, sand tiger	158.81 kg (350 lb 2 oz)	Charleston Jetty, South Carolina, USA	4/29/1993	Mark Thawley
Shark, sandbar	240 kg (529 lb 1 oz)	Archipelago des Bijagos, Guinea-Bissau	4/5/2002	Patrick Sebile
Shark, scalloped hammerhead	160.11 kg (353 lb 0 oz)	Key West, Florida, USA	4/19/2004	Rick Gunion
Shark, sevengill	32.8 kg (72 lb 4 oz)	Weymouth Channel, Manukou Harbour, New Zealand	10/23/1995	Shane Sowerby
Shark, sicklefin lemon	10.6 kg (23 lb 5 oz)	Darwin Harbour, Australia	12/7/1998	Craig Johnston
Shark, silky	346 kg (762 lb 12 oz)	Port Stephen's, N.S.W., Australia	2/26/1994	Bryce Henderson
Shark, silvertip	180.6 kg (398 lb 2 oz)	Malindi, Kenya	9/16/2001	Billy Furnish
Shark, sixgilled	588.76 kg (1298 lb 0 oz)	Atlantic Ocean, Ascension Island	11/21/2002	Clemens Rump
Shark, smallfin gulper	2.4 kg (5 lb 4 oz)	Lae, Huon Gulf, Papua New Guinea	2/13/1993	Justin Mallett
Shark, smooth hammerhead	167.6 kg (369 lb 7 oz)	Bay of Plenty, New Zealand	1/26/2002	Scott Tindale

Species	Weight	Location	Catch Date	Angler
Shark, spinner	94.6 kg (208 lb 9 oz)	Port Aransas, Texas, USA	12/13/2009	Raymond F. Ireton
Shark, thresher	348 kg (767 lb 3 oz)	Bay of Islands, New Zealand	2/26/1983	D.L. Hannah
Shark, tiger	810 kg (1785 lb 11 oz)	Ulladulla, Australia	3/28/2004	Kevin James Clapson
Shark, tope	33 kg (72 lb 12 oz)	Parengarenga Harbor, New Zealand	12/19/1986	Ms. Melanie Feldman
Shark, velvet belly lantern	0.85 kg (1 lb 13 oz)	Langesundbukta, Norway	10/7/2000	Arild Borresen
Shark, white	1208.38 kg (2664 lb 0 oz)	Ceduna, Sout, Australia	4/21/1959	Alfred Dean
Shark, whitetip reef	18.25 kg (40 lb 4 oz)	Isla Coiba, Panama	8/8/1979	Dr. Jack Kamerman
Sharkminnow, black	4.58 kg (10 lb 1 oz)	Theerasart, Thailand	7/25/2009	Gavin Clarke
Sharkminnow, tricolor	0.99 kg (2 lb 2 oz)	Salapee, Thailand	8/13/2009	Jean-Francois Helias
Sharksucker	5.38 kg (11 lb 14 oz)	Molasses Reef, Florida, USA	8/9/2001	Ms. Yolanda Morejon
Sheephead, California	12.88 kg (28 lb 6 oz)	Isla Roca Partida, Revillagigedo Islands, Mexico	11/4/1999	Marshall Madruga
Sheepshead	9.63 kg (21 lb 4 oz)	New Orleans, Louisiana, USA	4/16/1982	Wayne Desselle
Shimazoi	3.35 kg (7 lb 6 oz)	Shiribetsu, Hokkaido, Japan	4/20/2008	Chiharu Okayama
Shiro-Guchi	0.57 kg (1 lb 4 oz)	Handa Port, Aichi, Japan	9/20/2008	Taiki Aoyama
Shosai-fugu	0.54 kg (1 lb 3 oz)	Kozu Is., Tokyo, Japan	5/5/2005	Takashi Nishino
Sicklefish	0.68 kg (1 lb 8 oz)	Ponggol Marina, Singapore	4/18/2010	Steven M. Wozniak
Sierra, Atlantic	6.71 kg (14 lb 13 oz)	Mangaratiba, Brazil	6/20/1999	Ms. Paula Boghossian
Silver eye	1.3 kg (2 lb 13 oz)	Oshima, Tokyo, Japan	5/18/2008	Kenji Kaneshin
Skate	97.07 kg (214 lb 0 oz)	Scapa Flow, Orkney, United Kingdom	6/16/1968	Jan Olsson
Skate, big	41.27 kg (91 lb 0 oz)	Humbolt Bay, Eureka, California, USA	3/6/1993	Scotty Krick
Skate, starry	4.25 kg (9 lb 5 oz)	Hvasser, Norway	10/10/1982	Knut Hedlund
Skipjack, black	11.79 kg (26 lb 0 oz)	Thetis Bank, Baja California, Mexico	10/23/1991	Clifford Hamaishi
Sleeper, bigmouth	2.03 kg (4 lb 7 oz)	Rio Sarapiqui, Costa Rica	3/17/2001	Alexander Arias A.

Species	Weight	Location	Catch Date	Angler
Slimehead, Darwin's	3.4 kg (7 lb 8 oz)	Norfolk Canyon, Virginia Beach, Virginia, USA	8/19/2008	Ron Van Kirk
Smoothhound, Florida	13.78 kg (30 lb 6 oz)	Gulf of Mexico, Destin, Florida, USA	4/1/1992	Stephen Wilson
Smoothhound, starry	4.76 kg (10 lb 8 oz)	Nab Rocks, Isle of Wight, United Kingdom	7/18/1984	Ms. Sylvia Steed
Smoothhound, star-spotted	5.72 kg (12 lb 9 oz)	Lae, Huon Gulf, Papua New Guinea	2/13/1993	Justin Mallett
Snakehead, blotched	3.02 kg (6 lb 10 oz)	Ryonan-cho, Kagawa, Japan	8/16/2003	Yoshikazu Kawada
Snakehead, chevron	3.5 kg (7 lb 11 oz)	Gombak Lake, Selangor, Malaysia	12/17/2002	Faiz Karim
Snakehead, emperor	3.95 kg (8 lb 11 oz)	Sungai Pejing, Maran, Pahang, Malaysia	9/20/2009	Yap Choo
Snakehead, giant	10 kg (22 lb 0 oz)	Dengkil, Malaysia	8/23/2005	Christopher S. G. Tan
Snakehead, great	5.22 kg (11 lb 8 oz)	Srinakarin Reservoir, Thailand	3/16/2007	Jean-Francois Helias
Snakehead, splendid	2.05 kg (4 lb 8 oz)	Kenyir, Trenggarm, Malaysia	6/19/2010	Christopher S.G. Tan
Snapper (squirefish)	17.2 kg (37 lb 14 oz)	Mottiti Island, New Zealand	11/2/1992	Mark Hemingway
Snapper, African brown	22 kg (48 lb 8 oz)	Monogaga, Ivory Coast	2/3/1995	Patrick Sebile
Snapper, African red	60 kg (132 lb 4 oz)	Keur Saloum, Senegal	2/18/2001	Stephane Talavet
Snapper, black	3.17 kg (7 lb 0 oz)	Little San Salvador, Bahamas	4/24/1992	Donald May
Snapper, blackfin	3.28 kg (7 lb 3 oz)	Bimini, Bahamas	8/25/1993	Ron Mallet
Snapper, blacktail	0.48 kg (1 lb 1 oz)	Raiatea Lagoon, Tahiti	6/14/2006	Dennis Triana
Snapper, Brigham's	1.22 kg (2 lb 11 oz)	Kokohead, Oahu, Hawaii, USA	1/1/2007	George Bogen
Snapper, Colorado	10.92 kg (24 lb 1 oz)	Golfo Dulce, Costa Rica	9/9/2004	Wilbur D. Forbes
Snapper, cubera	56.59 kg (124 lb 12 oz)	Garden Bank, Louisiana, USA	6/23/2007	Marion Rose

Species	Weight	Location	Catch Date	Angler
Snapper, dog (Atlantic)	10.9 kg (24 lb 0 oz)	Hole in the Wall, Abaco, Bahamas	5/28/1994	Capt. Wayne Barder
Snapper, emperor	17.9 kg (39 lb 7 oz)	Chichijima, Ogasawara, Tokyo, Japan	11/9/1999	Tadashi Kawabata
Snapper, flame (Hamadai)	7.6 kg (16 lb 12 oz)	Yonaguni Is., Okinawa, Japan	11/16/2007	Takashi Odagiri
Snapper, gorean	5.5 kg (12 lb 2 oz)	Archipelago dos Bijagos, Guinea-Bissau	3/23/2001	Patrick Sebile
Snapper, greenbar	13.49 kg (29 lb 12 oz)	Puerto Penasco, Mexico	6/19/2010	Douglas Patrick McLaughlin
Snapper, grey	7.71 kg (17 lb 0 oz)	Port Canaveral, Florida, USA	6/14/1992	Steve Maddox
Snapper, humpback red	1.55 kg (3 lb 6 oz)	Yonaguni Island, Okinawa, Japan	11/5/2010	Takashi Odagiri
Snapper, lane	3.72 kg (8 lb 3 oz)	Horseshoe Rigs, Mississippi, USA	8/25/2001	Stephen Wilson
Snapper, mahogany	0.73 kg (1 lb 10 oz)	Pacific Reef, Florida, USA	8/8/2004	Dennis Triana
Snapper, Malabar	7.91 kg (17 lb 7 oz)	Cairns, Queensland, Australia	8/3/1989	Gregory Albert
Snapper, mangrove red	11.62 kg (25 lb 9 oz)	Ashizuri Misaki, Kochi, Japan	5/3/2006	Takuya Kano
Snapper, mullet	20.75 kg (45 lb 12 oz)	Cerralvo Island, La Paz, Mexico	6/6/2007	Rolla Cornell
Snapper, mutton	13.72 kg (30 lb 4 oz)	Dry Tortugas, Florida, USA	11/29/1998	Richard Casey
Snapper, Pacific cubera	35.72 kg (78 lb 12 oz)	Bahia Pez Vela, Costa Rica	3/23/1988	Steven Paull
Snapper, Pacific red	7.9 kg (17 lb 7 oz)	Uncle Sam Banks, Mexico	10/20/2001	Lon Mikkelsen
Snapper, Papuan black	19.2 kg (42 lb 5 oz)	Fly River, Papua New Guinea	9/22/1992	Len Bradica
Snapper, queen	12.36 kg (27 lb 4 oz)	Islamorada, Florida, USA	10/9/2008	Bill Ismer
Snapper, red	22.79 kg (50 lb 4 oz)	Gulf of Mexico, Louisiana, USA	6/23/1996	Capt. Doc Kennedy
Snapper, ruby	30.4 kg (67 lb 0 oz)	Los Chagos, Diego Garcia	12/24/2010	Phillip W. Richmond, Jr.
Snapper, Russell's	1.85 kg (4 lb 1 oz)	Kamikoshiki-jima, Kagoshima, Japan	6/17/2002	Ms. Tomoko Iwakari

Species	Weight	Location	Catch Date	Angler
Snapper, scarlet	11.8 kg (26 lb 0 oz)	Yonaguni Iz., Okinawa, Japan	11/3/2008	Takashi Odagiri
Snapper, school-master	6.02 kg (13 lb 4 oz)	North Key Largo, Florida, USA	9/3/1999	Gustavo Pla
Snapper, silk	8.32 kg (18 lb 5 oz)	Gulf of Mexico, Venice, Florida, USA	7/12/1986	James Taylor
Snapper, Spanish flag	0.68 kg (1 lb 8 oz)	Southern Islands, Singapore	4/21/2010	Steven M. Wozniak
Snapper, spotted rose	1.31 kg (2 lb 14 oz)	Playa Hermosa, Mexico	7/4/1999	William Favor
Snapper, two-spot red	14 kg (30 lb 13 oz)	Rodrigues Island, Mauritius	11/12/2009	Tuband Eric Bruno
Snapper, vermillion	3.26 kg (7 lb 3 oz)	Gulf of Mexico, Mobile, Alabama, USA	5/31/1987	John Doss
Snapper, yellow (amarillo)	5.44 kg (12 lb 0 oz)	Golfito, Costa Rica	8/11/1998	John Olson
Snapper, yellow-streaked	1.42 kg (3 lb 2 oz)	Kut Island, Gulf of Siam, Thailand	2/11/2008	Jean-Francois Helias
Snapper, yellowtail	4.98 kg (11 lb 0 oz)	Challenger Bank, Bermuda	6/16/2004	Mr. William B. DuVal
Snoek	5.14 kg (11 lb 5 oz)	Tutukaka, Poor Knights Reef, New Zealand	1/3/2010	Scott Tindale
Snook, common	24.32 kg (53 lb 10 oz)	Parismina Ranch, Costa Rica	10/18/1978	Gilbert Ponzi
Snook, fat	4.96 kg (10 lb 14 oz)	Mampituba River, Torres, RS, Brazil	8/12/2005	Gilney Braido
Snook, Mexican	10.69 kg (23 lb 9 oz)	Rio Palizada, Campeche, Mexico	4/19/2009	Alejandro Lagunes Cabrera
Snook, Pacific black	26.19 kg (57 lb 12 oz)	Rio Naranjo, Quepos, Costa Rica	8/23/1991	George Beck
Snook, Pacific blackfin	3.2 kg (7 lb 0 oz)	Esquinas River, Costa Rica	1/29/2002	Rodolfo Dodero
Snook, Pacific white	21.54 kg (47 lb 8 oz)	Cabo San Lucas, Mexico	7/4/2001	Vito Allessandro
Snook, sword-spine	0.7 kg (1 lb 9 oz)	Port St. Lucie, Florida, USA	6/11/2004	DJ Cook
Snook, tarpon	1.42 kg (3 lb 2 oz)	Dona Bay, Nokomis, Florida, USA	9/19/1996	Capt. David Coudal
Sole	0.8 kg (1 lb 12 oz)	North Sea, Netherlands	7/12/1997	P.C. Ouwendijk

Species	Weight	Location	Catch Date	Angler
Sole, fantail	3.99 kg (8 lb 12 oz)	San Clemente Island, California, USA	6/3/2001	Allan Sheridan
Sole, lemon	1.8 kg (3 lb 15 oz)	Andorja, Norway	6/8/2004	Robert Stalcrona
Sole, Northern	1.22 kg (2 lb 11 oz)	Cape Duget, Alaska, USA	8/10/2004	Richard M. Koster
Sole, southern rock	1.02 kg (2 lb 4 oz)	Farralon Islands, California, USA	8/21/2010	Steven M. Wozniak
Sole, yellowfin	0.91 kg (2 lb 0 oz)	Kachemak Bay, Alaska, USA	7/4/2007	Peter W. Witherell
Sorubim, barred	16.17 kg (35 lb 10 oz)	Amazon River, Amazonas, Brazil	4/26/2008	Gilberto Fernandes
Sorubim, spotted	53.5 kg (117 lb 15 oz)	Rio Parana, Corrientes, Argentina	2/16/2000	Joao Neto
Sorubim, tiger	22 kg (48 lb 8 oz)	Rio Amazonas, Amazonas, Brazil	2/13/2011	Gilberto Fernandes
Spadefish, Atlantic	6.75 kg (14 lb 14 oz)	Chesapeake Bay, Virginia, USA	6/13/2009	Roland E. Murphy
Spearfish, longbill	58 kg (127 lb 13 oz)	Puerto Rico, Gran Canaria, Canary Islands	5/20/1999	Paul Cashmore
Spearfish, Mediterranean	41.2 kg (90 lb 13 oz)	Madeira Island, Portugal	6/2/1980	Joseph Larkin
Spearfish, roundscale	31.75 kg (70 lb 0 oz)	Baltimore Canyon, Maryland, USA	8/20/2010	Andres Fanjul
Spearfish, shortbill	50 kg (110 lb 3 oz)	Botany Bay, Sydney, Australia	5/3/2008	Edward Tolfree
Spinefoot, mottled	0.9 kg (1 lb 15 oz)	Kamisakiura, Mie, Japan	9/23/2007	Kazuhiko Mizutani
Spinefoot, orange-spotted	2.2 kg (4 lb 14 oz)	Iejima, Okinawa, Japan	6/1/2007	Hiroaki Higa
Spinefoot, streaked	0.51 kg (1 lb 1 oz)	Kut Island, Thailand	2/27/2008	Jean-Francois Helias
Splake	9.39 kg (20 lb 11 oz)	Georgian Bay, Ontario, Canada	5/17/1987	Paul Thompson
Splendid, alfonsino	2.6 kg (5 lb 11 oz)	Mikomoto, Shimoda, Shizuoka, Japan	5/4/2008	Takashi Odagiri
Spot	0.65 kg (1 lb 7 oz)	Hampton Roads Bridge Tunnel, Virginia, USA	10/2/2004	Lorraine H. Gousse
Squirrelfish, sabre	2.55 kg (5 lb 10 oz)	Keahole Point, Kailua Kona, Hawaii, USA	3/26/1995	Rex Bigg
Stargazer	0.94 kg (2 lb 1 oz)	Gibraltar, United Kingdom	12/4/1994	Albert Ward

Species	Weight	Location	Catch Date	Angler
Stargazer, northern	4.87 kg (10 lb 12 oz)	Cape May, New Jersey, USA	6/20/1998	John Jacobsen
Stargazer, spotted Australian	5.82 kg (12 lb 13 oz)	Gold Coast Seaway, Australia	7/10/2002	Gordon Macdonald
Steenbras, red	56.6 kg (124 lb 12 oz)	Aston Bay, Eastern Cape, South Africa	5/8/1994	Terry Goldstone
Stingray, Atlantic	4.87 kg (10 lb 12 oz)	Galveston Bay, Texas, USA	7/3/1994	David Anderson
Stingray, black	57.5 kg (126 lb 12 oz)	Laurieton, N.S.W., Australia	7/3/1994	David Shearing
Stingray, bluespotted (yakko-e)	1.55 kg (3 lb 6 oz)	Kaminato, Hachijo Island, Japan	5/4/2003	Takashi Nishino
Stingray, bluntnose	16.62 kg (36 lb 10 oz)	Galveston, Texas, USA	5/26/2003	Richard Olszak, Jr.
Stingray, common	201.39 kg (444 lb 0 oz)	Faial, Azores, Horta, Spain	9/1/1999	Bob de Boeck
Stingray, cowtail	18 kg (39 lb 10 oz)	Bang Pakong River, Thailand	3/19/2004	Jean-Francois Helias
Stingray, daisy	19.5 kg (42 lb 15 oz)	Etintite, Guinea-Bissau	10/27/1996	Jean Lafage
Stingray, diamond	46.26 kg (102 lb 0 oz)	Mission Bay, San Diego, California, USA	8/7/1993	Roger Ehlers
Stingray, Haller's round	1.36 kg (3 lb 0 oz)	Santa Clara River, Ventura, California, USA	9/3/1989	Paul Bodtke
Stingray, pelagic	6.2 kg (13 lb 10 oz)	Bonifacio, Corsica, France	6/8/2001	Patrick Sebile
Stingray, red (akaei)	26.55 kg (58 lb 8 oz)	Ogusu, Sajima, Kanagawa, Japan	6/18/2008	Takashi Nishino
Stingray, roughtail	183.7 kg (405 lb 0 oz)	Islamorada, Florida, USA	2/1/1972	Geoff Flores
Stingray, round	95.5 kg (210 lb 8 oz)	Canary Islands, Gran Canarias, Spain	10/11/2009	Michael Bartels
Stingray, S.A. freshwater	12.59 kg (27 lb 12 oz)	Rio Agua Boa, Roraima, Brazil	1/9/2000	Ben Wise
Stingray, southern	111.58 kg (246 lb 0 oz)	Galveston Bay, Texas, USA	6/30/1998	Carissa Egger
Stingray, whip	75.98 kg (167 lb 8 oz)	Banjul, Gambia	1/31/2010	Stan Nabozny
Stingray, w-mouth	6.35 kg (14 lb 0 oz)	Sepitiba Bay, Brazil	5/3/2010	Steven M. Wozniak

Species	Weight	Location	Catch Date	Angler
Stumpnose, red	5.8 kg (12 lb 12 oz)	St. Croix Island, Port Elizabeth, South Africa	12/20/1993	Craig Saunders
Sturgeon, beluga	102 kg (224 lb 13 oz)	Guryev, Kazakhstan	5/3/1993	Ms. Merete Lehne
Sturgeon, lake	76.2 kg (168 lb 0 oz)	Georgian Bay, Ontario, Canada	5/29/1982	Edward Paszkowski
Sturgeon, shortnose	5.04 kg (11 lb 2 oz)	Kennebacis River, New Brunswick, Canada	7/31/1988	Lawrence Guimond
Sturgeon, shovelnose	4.88 kg (10 lb 12 oz)	Missouri River, Loma, Montana, USA	6/14/1985	Arthur Seal
Sturgeon, white	212.28 kg (468 lb 0 oz)	Benicia, California, USA	7/9/1983	Joey Pallotta, III
Sucker, flannelmouth	1.09 kg (2 lb 6 oz)	Colorado River, Colorado, USA	7/7/1990	Ms. Karen DeVine
Sucker, Klamath smallscale	1.13 kg (2 lb 8 oz)	Trinity River, Del Loma, California, USA	1/29/2011	Steven M. Wozniak
Sucker, longnose	2.97 kg (6 lb 9 oz)	St. Joseph River, Michigan, USA	12/2/1989	Ben Knoll
Sucker, northern hog	0.79 kg (1 lb 12 oz)	Sigel, Pennsylvania, USA	4/12/2008	Richard E. Faler Jr.
Sucker, spotted	1.5 kg (3 lb 5 oz)	Chickamauga Reservoir, Tennessee, USA	3/9/2008	Greg Henry
Sucker, white	2.94 kg (6 lb 8 oz)	Rainy River, Loman, Minnesota, USA	4/20/1984	Joel Anderson
Sunfish, green	0.96 kg (2 lb 2 oz)	Stockton Lake, Missouri, USA	6/18/1971	Paul Dilley
Sunfish, hybrid	0.48 kg (1 lb 1 oz)	Shakey Slough, Indiana, USA	5/2/1998	Mike Berg
Sunfish, hybrid	0.48 kg (1 lb 1 oz)	Shakey Slough, Indiana, USA	5/3/1998	Steven Berg
Sunfish, longear	0.79 kg (1 lb 12 oz)	Elephant Butte Lake, New Mexico, USA	5/9/1985	Ms. Patricia Stout
Sunfish, redbreast	0.79 kg (1 lb 12 oz)	Suwannee River, Florida, USA	5/29/1984	Alvin Buchanan
Sunfish, redear	2.49 kg (5 lb 8 oz)	Lake Havasu City, Arizona, USA	5/2/2011	Robert Lawler
Surfperch, barred	1.87 kg (4 lb 2 oz)	Oxnard, California, USA	3/30/1996	Fred Oakley
Surfperch, black	0.45 kg (1 lb 0 oz)	Tiburon, California, USA	1/22/2011	Steven M. Wozniak
Surfperch, calico	0.91 kg (2 lb 0 oz)	Morro Bay, California, USA	2/16/2006	Marvin L. Green
Surfperch, rubberlip	0.68 kg (1 lb 8 oz)	Tiburon, California, USA	1/22/2011	Steven M. Wozniak

Species	Weight	Location	Catch Date	Angler
Surfperch, rubberlip	0.68 kg (1 lb 8 oz)	Tiburon, California, USA	3/11/2011	Steven M. Wozniak
Surfperch, rubberlip	0.68 kg (1 lb 8 oz)	Tiburon, California, USA	4/16/2011	Martini Arostegui
Surfperch, striped	0.47 kg (1 lb 0 oz)	Morro Bay, California, USA	3/26/2003	Marvin Green
Surgeonfish, yellowfin	1.25 kg (2 lb 12 oz)	Diego Garcia, Chagos Archipelago	3/29/2010	Philip W. Richmond, Jr.
Sweetlip, painted	6.9 kg (15 lb 3 oz)	Moreton Island, Queensland, Australia	7/24/1993	Ms. Kathy McGuire
Swordfish	536.15 kg (1182 lb 0 oz)	Iquique, Chile	5/7/1953	Louis Marron
Taimen	41.95 kg (92 lb 8 oz)	Keta River, Siberia, Russia	8/11/1993	Yuri Orlov
Takenokome-baru	3 kg (6 lb 9 oz)	Oshika, Miyagi, Japan	12/28/2004	Fuminori Sato
Takenokome-baru	4 kg (6 lb 9 oz)	Motoyoshi, Miyagi, Japan	12/15/2005	Yoshihiko Onodero
Tambaqui	32.4 kg (71 lb 7 oz)	Lago Grande, Amazonas, Brazil	8/25/2007	Jorge Masullo de Aguiar
Tanuki-Mebaru	2.99 kg (6 lb 9 oz)	Kuji, Iwate, Japan	5/16/2010	Satoshi Yamaguchi
Tarpon	129.98 kg (286 lb 9 oz)	Rubane, Guinea-Bissau	3/20/2003	Max Domecq
Tarpon, oxeye	2.99 kg (6 lb 9 oz)	Tide Island, Queensland, Australia	5/14/2000	Neil Schultz
Tautog	11.33 kg (25 lb 0 oz)	Ocean City, New Jersey, USA	1/20/1998	Anthony Monica
Tench	4.64 kg (10 lb 3 oz)	Ljungbyan, Sweden	7/2/1985	Dan Dellerfjord
Tetra, disk	0.88 kg (1 lb 15 oz)	Lago Acarituba, Amazonas, Brazil	5/29/2009	Jorge Masullo de Aguiar
Thornyhead, shortspine	2.31 kg (5 lb 1 oz)	Los Coranados Islands, Baja California Sur, Mexico	2/3/2001	Stephen Grossberg
Threadfin, East Asian	7.48 kg (16 lb 8 oz)	Lantau Island, Hong Kong	2/20/2009	Kelvin Ng
Threadfin, giant African	49.6 kg (109 lb 5 oz)	Barra do Kwanza, Angola	1/17/1999	Marco da Silva Couto
Threadfin, Indian	16 kg (35 lb 4 oz)	Gazaruto Island, Mozambique	8/22/2007	Gary Bluett

Species	Weight	Location	Catch Date	Angler
Threadfin, king	12.5 kg (27 lb 8 oz)	Dampier Creek, Broome, Australia	4/24/1996	Brian Albert
Threadfin, moi	3.17 kg (7 lb 0 oz)	Hanalei, Hawaii, USA	9/3/1988	Harry Paik
Threadfin, smallscale	0.62 kg (1 lb 6 oz)	Jensen Beach, Florida, USA	10/9/1998	Ralph Bailey, III
Threadfin, striped	1.65 kg (3 lb 10 oz)	Ukenmura, Amami-oshima, Kagoshima, Japan	10/24/1999	Masaaki Sudo
Threadfish, African	8.1 kg (17 lb 13 oz)	Dakhla, Morocco	9/18/1993	Patrick Sebile
Tigerfish	16.1 kg (35 lb 7 oz)	Kariba, Zimbabwe	9/12/2001	Ms. Jennifer Daynes
Tigerfish, Campbells	1.45 kg (3 lb 3 oz)	Fly River, W. Province, Papua New Guinea	3/18/2006	Noritaka Takeishi
Tigerfish, four-barred Siamese	0.6 kg (1 lb 5 oz)	Bang Pakong River, Thailand	5/31/2005	Anongnart Sung-wichien-Helias
Tigerfish, giant	44 kg (97 lb 0 oz)	Zaire River, Kinshasa, Zaire	7/9/1988	Raymond Hout-mans
Tigerfish, North African	5.67 kg (12 lb 8 oz)	Gambia River, Gambia	5/7/2009	Stan Nabozny
Tilapia, blue	4.34 kg (9 lb 9 oz)	South Fork River, Stuart, Florida, USA	8/31/2010	Pamela J. Henry
Tilapia, hornet	0.79 kg (1 lb 12 oz)	Airport Lakes, Miami, Florida, USA	5/10/2010	Martin Arostegui
Tilapia, Mo-zambique	3.11 kg (6 lb 13 oz)	Loskop Dam, South Africa	4/4/2003	Eugene Kruger
Tilapia, Nile	6.01 kg (13 lb 3 oz)	Antelope Island, Kariba, Zim-babwe	7/5/2002	Sarel van Rooyen
Tilapia, red-breast	1.62 kg (3 lb 9 oz)	Zambezi River, Namibia	11/14/1994	Bill Staveley
Tilapia, spotted	1.81 kg (4 lb 0 oz)	Plantation, Florida, USA	6/6/2005	Reed McLane
Tilapia, three-spot	4.71 kg (10 lb 6 oz)	Upper Zambezi, Zambia	11/3/1998	Ben Van Wyk
Tilefish, Atlantic goldeye	2.04 kg (4 lb 8 oz)	Rezak Bank, Gulf of Mexico, Louisiana, USA	8/6/2010	Bruce Slaven
Tilefish, Ba-hama	1.31 kg (2 lb 14 oz)	Grand Bahama Island, Baha-mas	8/22/2000	Capt. Jay Cohen

Species	Weight	Location	Catch Date	Angler
Tilefish, black-line	0.45 kg (1 lb 0 oz)	Key West, Florida, USA	4/10/2004	Dennis Triana
Tilefish, blueline	9.19 kg (20 lb 4 oz)	Norfolk Canyon, Virginia, USA	3/19/2009	David H. Akridge Jr.
Tilefish, golden-eyed	1.47 kg (3 lb 4 oz)	Tamarindo, Costa Rica	2/14/2007	George Bogen
Tilefish, great northern	28.8 kg (63 lb 8 oz)	Lindenkohl Canyon, Delaware, USA	8/17/2009	Dennis J. Muhlen-forth
Tilefish, red	1.75 kg (3 lb 13 oz)	Hiratsuka, Kanagawa, Japan	1/23/2011	Yuumi Fukunaga
Tilefish, sand	1.95 kg (4 lb 4 oz)	Oak Island, North Carolina, USA	4/16/2004	Frank L. Ballas
Tilefish, south-ern	8.5 kg (18 lb 11 oz)	Rio de Janeiro, Brazil	8/31/2002	Eduardo Baumeier
Toadfish, leop-ard	1.27 kg (2 lb 13 oz)	Orange Beach, Alabama, USA	4/22/2003	Chuck Andre

Species	Weight	Location	Catch Date	Angler
Toadfish, Lusitanian	2.5 kg (5 lb 8 oz)	Dakhla, Morocco	6/5/2003	Patrick Sebile
Toadfish, oyster	2.23 kg (4 lb 15 oz)	Ocracoke, North Carolina, USA	6/4/1994	David Tinsley
Torpedo, Atlantic	40.6 kg (89 lb 8 oz)	Misquamicut Beach, Rhode Island, USA	6/21/2008	Chuck Adams
Torpedo, spotted	5.5 kg (12 lb 2 oz)	Arcachon, France	8/1/2002	Patrick Sebile
Trahira	3.63 kg (8 lb 0 oz)	Negro River, Brazil	11/24/2009	Ian-Arthur de Sulocki
Trahira, giant	14.95 kg (32 lb 15 oz)	Sinamary River, Takari-Kante, French Guiana	3/21/2007	Cittadini Gerard
Trevally, bigeye	14.3 kg (31 lb 8 oz)	Poivre Island, Seychelles	4/23/1997	Les Sampson
Trevally, blacktip	8.2 kg (18 lb 1 oz)	Bazaruto Island, Mozambique	5/22/2008	Garett Charles Hume
Trevally, blue	2.26 kg (5 lb 0 oz)	Pacific Ocean, Midway Islands	5/30/2001	Matthew Stewart
Trevally, bluefin	11.99 kg (26 lb 7 oz)	Clipperton Island, E. Pacific Ocean	3/24/1997	Tom Taylor
Trevally, brassy	7.9 kg (17 lb 6 oz)	Bazaruto Island, Mozambique	5/17/2008	Kim Frank McDonald
Trevally, coastal	1.05 kg (2 lb 5 oz)	Ginanzaki, Okinawa, Japan	3/5/2008	Ayaka Kosuge
Trevally, giant	72.8 kg (160 lb 7 oz)	Tokara, Kagoshima, Japan	5/22/2006	Keiki Hamasaki
Trevally, golden	14.75 kg (32 lb 8 oz)	Point Samson, W.A., Australia	11/9/2002	Jason Hornhardt
Trevally, orange spotted	0.45 kg (1 lb 0 oz)	Torres Straits, Australia	12/25/2006	Theda C. Little
Trevally, white	15.25 kg (33 lb 9 oz)	Hahajima, Ogasawara, Tokyo, Japan	7/6/1998	Kazuhiko Adachi
Trevally, yellow-spotted	13.75 kg (30 lb 5 oz)	Sudwana Bay, North Coast Natal, South Africa	5/11/2010	Rory Francis Eidelman
Triggerfish, blunthead	6.6 kg (14 lb 9 oz)	La Paz, Mexico	8/23/2005	Kenny Duong
Triggerfish, bridled	0.8 kg (1 lb 12 oz)	Chagos Archipelago, Diego Garcia	4/2/2011	Phillip W. Richmond, Jr.
Triggerfish, grey	6.15 kg (13 lb 9 oz)	Murrells Inlet, South Carolina, USA	5/3/1989	Jim Hilton
Triggerfish, ocean	6.12 kg (13 lb 8 oz)	Pompano Beach, Florida, USA	3/7/1995	Frederick Lauriello

Species	Weight	Location	Catch Date	Angler
Triggerfish, queen	6.44 kg (14 lb 3 oz)	Cancun, Mexico	1/26/2009	Martin T. Gnad
Triggerfish, red-toothed	0.45 kg (1 lb 0 oz)	Dibba, Oman	2/21/2011	Steven M. Wozniak
Triggerfish, spotted oceanic	0.91 kg (2 lb 0 oz)	Dry Tortugas, Florida, USA	6/16/2009	Joe Pappas Jr.
Triggerfish, yellowmargin	2.75 kg (6 lb 1 oz)	Chagos Archipelago, Diego Garcia	11/3/2010	Phillip W. Richmond Jr.
Triggerfish, yellowspotted	3.29 kg (7 lb 4 oz)	Aqaba, Jordan	12/31/2009	Steven M. Wozniak
Tripletail	19.2 kg (42 lb 5 oz)	Zululand, South Africa	6/7/1989	Steve Hand
Trout, Apache	2.36 kg (5 lb 3 oz)	White Mtn. Apache, Reservoir, Arizona, USA	5/29/1991	John Baldwin
Trout, aurora	2.21 kg (4 lb 14 oz)	Carol Lake, Ontario, Canada	10/8/1996	Robert Bernardo
Trout, biwamasu	3.58 kg (7 lb 14 oz)	Lake Biwa, Shiga, Japan	9/27/2009	Takao Saiki
Trout, brook	6.57 kg (14 lb 8 oz)	Nipigon River, Ontario, Canada	7/1/1916	Dr. W. Cook
Trout, brown	18.82 kg (41 lb 8 oz)	Lake Michigan, Racine, Wisconsin, USA	7/16/2010	Roger Hellen
Trout, bull	14.51 kg (32 lb 0 oz)	Lake Pend Oreille, Idaho, USA	10/27/1949	N. Higgins
Trout, cutbow	6.01 kg (13 lb 4 oz)	Green Lake, Colorado, USA	4/14/2003	Brent Curtice
Trout, cutthroat	18.59 kg (41 lb 0 oz)	Pyramid Lake, Nevada, USA	12/1/1925	John Skimmerhorn
Trout, gila	1.56 kg (3 lb 7 oz)	Frye Mesa Resevoir, Arizona, USA	3/19/2011	Bo Nelson
Trout, golden	4.98 kg (11 lb 0 oz)	Cooks Lake, Wyoming, USA	8/5/1948	Chas. Reed
Trout, lake	32.65 kg (72 lb 0 oz)	Great Bear Lake, Northwest Territories, Canada	8/19/1995	Lloyd Bull
Trout, masu	5.25 kg (11 lb 9 oz)	Kuzuryu River, Fukui, Japan	5/6/1995	Takeshi Matsuura
Trout, ohrid	6.46 kg (14 lb 4 oz)	Platte River, Wyoming, USA	1/26/1986	Ms. Kim Durfee
Trout, ohrid	6.46 kg (14 lb 4 oz)	Watauga Lake, Tennessee, USA	3/28/1986	Richard Carter
Trout, rainbow	21.77 kg (48 lb 0 oz)	Lake Diefenbaker, Canada	9/5/2009	Sean Konrad
Trout, red spotted masu	1.69 kg (3 lb 11 oz)	Yoshino River, Tokushima, Japan	5/27/2010	Akira Wada
Trout, red-spotted masu	1.54 kg (3 lb 6 oz)	Yoshino River, Tokushima, Japan	5/17/1998	Akihiko Masutani

Species	Weight	Location	Catch Date	Angler
Trout, tiger	9.44 kg (20 lb 13 oz)	Lake Michigan, Wisconsin, USA	8/12/1978	Pete Friedland
Trunkfish	3.31 kg (7 lb 4 oz)	Palm Beach, Florida, USA	4/1/2000	Charlie Colon
Tuna, bigeye (Atlantic)	178 kg (392 lb 6 oz)	Puerto Rico, Gran Canaria, Spain	7/25/1996	Dieter Vogel
Tuna, bigeye (Pacific)	197.31 kg (435 lb 0 oz)	Cabo Blanco, Peru	4/17/1957	Dr. Russel Lee
Tuna, blackfin	22.39 kg (49 lb 6 oz)	Marathon, Florida, USA	4/6/2006	Capt. Matthew E. Pullen
Tuna, bluefin	678.58 kg (1496 lb 0 oz)	Aulds Cove, Nova Scotia, Canada	10/26/1979	Ken Fraser
Tuna, dogtooth	104.5 kg (230 lb 6 oz)	Rodrigues Island, Mauritius	10/25/2007	Mercier Christian
Tuna, longtail	35.9 kg (79 lb 2 oz)	Montague Island, N.S.W., Australia	4/12/1982	Tim Simpson
Tuna, Pacific bluefin	325 kg (716 lb 8 oz)	Westport, New Zealand	8/26/2007	Steve McCowan
Tuna, skipjack	20.54 kg (45 lb 4 oz)	Flathead Bank, Baja California, Mexico	11/16/1996	Brian Evans
Tuna, slender	11.85 kg (26 lb 1 oz)	Taiaroa Heads, Otago, New Zealand	5/1/2001	Gary Wilson
Tuna, southern bluefin	167.5 kg (369 lb 4 oz)	Tathra, Australia	7/9/2009	Phil Body
Tuna, yellowfin	183.7 kg (405 lb 0 oz)	Magdalena Bay, Baja Sur, Mexico	11/30/2010	Mike Livingston
Tunny, little	16.32 kg (36 lb 0 oz)	Washington Canyon, New Jersey, USA	11/5/2006	Jess Lubert
Turbot, spottail spiny	2 kg (4 lb 6 oz)	Rubane, Guinea-Bissau	1/10/2003	Johan de Vlieger
Tusk	17.2 kg (37 lb 14 oz)	Soroya, Norway	7/18/2008	Anders Jonasson
Tuskfish, blackspot	9.5 kg (20 lb 15 oz)	Bribie Island, Queensland, Australia	6/19/1988	Ms. Olga Mack
Ugui	1.15 kg (2 lb 8 oz)	Tama River, Tokyo, Japan	4/30/2009	Yukiyo Okuyama
Ukkarikasago	3.15 kg (6 lb 15 oz)	Onjuku, Chiba, Japan	7/24/2008	Shigeshi Tanaka
Umazura Hagi	0.61 kg (1 lb 5 oz)	Kinuura Port, Aichi, Japan	2/15/2009	Taiki Aoyama
Umeiro	0.7 kg (1 lb 8 oz)	Mikurajima, Tokyo, Japan	5/9/2004	Junzo Okada
Utsubo	4.3 kg (9 lb 7 oz)	Akazawa, Ito., Shizuoka, Japan	11/23/2008	Takashi Nishino

Species	Weight	Location	Catch Date	Angler
Vimba (Zahrte)	1.14 kg (2 lb 8 oz)	Olandsan, Sweden	5/1/1990	Sonny Pettersson
Vundu	32.5 kg (71 lb 10 oz)	Lake Kariba, Zimbabwe	12/26/2000	Rob Konschel
Wahoo	83.46 kg (184 lb 0 oz)	Cabo San Lucas, Mexico	7/29/2005	Sara Hayward
Wallago	18.6 kg (41 lb 0 oz)	Khaolam Dam, Sangklaburi, Thailand	12/4/2003	Kasem Lamaikul (Na Noo)
Walleye	11.34 kg (25 lb 0 oz)	Old Hickory Lake, Tennessee, USA	8/2/1960	Mabry Harper
Warmouth	1.1 kg (2 lb 7 oz)	Guess Lake, Yellow River, Holt, Florida, USA	10/19/1985	Tony Dempsey
Weakfish	8.96 kg (19 lb 12 oz)	Staten Island, New York, USA	5/7/2008	Dave Alu
Weakfish, acoupa	17 kg (37 lb 7 oz)	Canal do Boqueirao, Ilha do Governador, Brazil	8/23/1997	Gilberto Ferreira
Weakfish, boccone	4.46 kg (14 lb 4 oz)	Golfito, Costa Rica	4/20/2006	Betsy Bullard
Weakfish, green	13.6 kg (29 lb 15 oz)	Ilha de Comandatuba, Hotel Transamerica, Brazil	11/3/1998	Martin Holzmann
Weakfish, gulf (corvina)	2.43 kg (5 lb 5 oz)	Vista del Oro, Mexico	9/16/2000	William Favor
Wedgefish, African	57 kg (125 lb 10 oz)	Rubane, Archipelago, Dos Bijagos, Guinea-Bissau	3/26/2006	Michel Rumin
Weever, greater	1.74 kg (3 lb 13 oz)	La Gomera, Canary Islands, Spain	6/11/2005	John H. Williams
Wels	134.97 kg (297 lb 9 oz)	River Po, Italy	3/11/2010	Attila Zsedely
Wenchman	1.99 kg (4 lb 6 oz)	Bimini, Bahamas	7/13/1997	Dan Upton
Whipray, pink	18.5 kg (40 lb 12 oz)	Bali Beach, Bali	7/20/1995	Bo Johansson
Whitefish, broad	4.08 kg (9 lb 0 oz)	Tozitna River, Alaska, USA	7/17/1989	Al Mathews
Whitefish, lake	6.52 kg (14 lb 6 oz)	Meaford, Ontario, Canada	5/21/1984	Dennis Laycock
Whitefish, mountain	2.49 kg (5 lb 8 oz)	Elbow River, Calgary, Alberta, Canada	8/1/1995	Randy Woo
Whitefish, ocean	5.76 kg (12 lb 11 oz)	San Martin Island, Mexico	8/21/2000	Nicholas Sullivan
Whitefish, round	2.72 kg (6 lb 0 oz)	Putahow River, Manitoba, Canada	6/14/1984	Allan Ristori
Whiting, blue	0.83 kg (1 lb 13 oz)	Drobak, Norway	9/19/1998	Trond Raade
Whiting, European	3.11 kg (6 lb 13 oz)	Dypdalen, Norway	6/10/1997	John Kofoed

Species	Weight	Location	Catch Date	Angler
Wolffish, Atlantic	23.58 kg (52 lb 0 oz)	Georges Bank, Massachusetts, USA	6/11/1986	Frederick Gardiner
Wolffish, Bering	12.3 kg (27 lb 1 oz)	Uotoro, Hokkaiso, Japan	7/4/2006	Hideki Nakai
Wolffish, northern	17 kg (37 lb 7 oz)	Holsteinsborg, Greenland	8/19/1982	Jens Hansen
Wolffish, spotted	27.9 kg (61 lb 8 oz)	Vannoy, Trohs Fylke, Norway	5/29/2000	Kolbjorn Melien
Wrasse, ballan	4.35 kg (9 lb 9 oz)	Clogher Head, Co. Kerry, Ireland	8/20/1983	Bertrand Kron
Wrasse, Brazilian	0.45 kg (1 lb 0 oz)	Isla Grande, Brazil	3/17/2011	Steven M. Wozniak
Wrasse, crimson-banded	0.57 kg (1 lb 4 oz)	Port Hacking, Australia	8/26/2009	Steven M. Wozniak
Wrasse, humphead Maori	19.8 kg (43 lb 10 oz)	Platt Island, Seychelles	4/4/1997	Vincent Hock Boon
Wrasse, purple (hou)	1.16 kg (2 lb 9 oz)	Kalapana, Hawaii, USA	2/8/1992	Chris Hara
Wreckfish	86.2 kg (190 lb 0 oz)	Ranfurny Bank, New Zealand	3/2/2010	Terence Price
Yellowfish, largemouth	9.52 kg (21 lb 0 oz)	Vaal River, South Africa	3/8/2005	Ian Couryer
Yellowtail, California	49.5 kg (109 lb 2 oz)	Ohara, Chiba, Japan	10/24/2009	Masakazu Taniwaki
Yellowtail, southern	52 kg (114 lb 10 oz)	White Island, New Zealand	1/9/1987	David Lugton
Yellowtail, southern	53 kg (114 lb 10 oz)	Tauranga, New Zealand	2/5/1984	Mike Godfrey
Zander	11.42 kg (25 lb 2 oz)	Trosa, Sweden	6/12/1986	Harry Tennison
Zander, volga	0.45 kg (1 lb 0 oz)	Tisza River, Tiszafured, Hungary	10/18/2010	Steven M. Wozniak

Part 8

Contributors and Their Works

Wade Bourne
(www.wadebourneoutdoors.com)

Basic Fishing*
Fishing Made Easy
Decoys and Proven Methods for Using Them
A Ducks Unlimited Guide to Hunting Dabblers
Fishing Fundamentals
The Pocket Fishing Guide: Freshwater Basics, Hook Line
    & Sinker
Ultimate Turkey Hunting

Conway X. Bowman
(www.bowmanbluewater.com)

The Orvis Guide to Beginning Saltwater Fishing*

Rick Browne
(www.amazon.com/Rick-Browne/e/
B001H6NEWM)

The Ultimate Guide to Frying*
The Frequent Fryers Cookbook
The Big Book of Barbecue Side Dishes
1,001 Best Grilling Recipes: Delicious, Easy-to-Make
    Recipes from Around the World
Grilling America
The Best Barbecue on Earth: Grilling Across 6 Conti-
    nents and 25 Countries
Barbecue America: A Pilgrimage in Search of America's
    Best Barbecue
Grilling for All Seasons

Geoffrey Budworth
(www.amazon.com/Geoffrey-Budworth/e/
B00456Q2N4/ref=sr_ntt_srch_
lnk_1?qid=1313068607&sr=1-1)

Practical Fishing Knots*
The Complete Book of Fishing Knots
The Complete Book of Sailing Knots
The Complete Book of Knots
The Complete Book of Decorative Knots
Step-by-Step Essential Knots
The Ultimate Encyclopedia of Knots and Ropework
A Handbook of Knots and Knot Tying
The Illustrated Encyclopedia of Knots

Monte Burch
(www.monteburch.com)

Black Bass Basics
The Hunting and Fishing Camp Builder's Guide*
The Joy of Smoking and Salt Curing*
The Complete Jerky Book*
The Complete Guide to Sausage Making*
Ultimate Guide to Growing Your Own Food*
Cleaning and Preparing Gamefish
Denny Brauer's Jig Fishing Secrets
Pocket Guide to Seasonal Largemouth Bass Patterns
Pocket Guide to Old Time Catfish Techniques
Pocket Guide to Seasonal Walleye Tactics
Pocket Guide to Spring and Fall Turkey Hunting
Pocket Guide to Field Dressing, Butchering & Cooking
    Deer

Country Crafts and Skills

Lohman Guide to Successful Turkey Calling

Lohman Guide to Calling & Decoying Waterfowl

Field Dressing and Butchering Upland Birds, Waterfowl and Wild Turkeys

The Ultimate Guide to Skinning and Tanning

The Ultimate Guide to Making Outdoor Gear and Accessories

Making Native American Hunting, Fighting and Survival Tools

Mounting Your Deer Head at Home

Solving Squirrel Problems

Pocket Guide to Bowhunting Whitetail Deer

Building Small Barns, Sheds & Shelters

Monte Burch's Pole Building Projects

Backyard Structures and How to Build Them

Bill Dance
(www.amazon.com/Bill-Dance/e/ B001JP3SC2/ref=sr_ntt_srch_ lnk_1?qid=1313069668&sr=1-1)

101 Freshwater Fishing Tips and Tricks *

101 Secrets to Catching More and Bigger Fish *

Kirk Deeter
(www.amazon.com/Kirk-D.-Deeter/e/ B001K8HMNY/ref=ntt_athr_dp_pel_1)

The Little Red Book of Fly Fishing (with Charlie Meyers)*

Castworks: Reflections of Fly Fishing Guides and the American West (with Andrew Steketee)

Tideline: Captains, Fly-Fishing and the American Coast (with Andrew Steketee)

Chris Dubbs and Dave Heberle

Smoking Food: A Beginner's Guide *

Easy Art of Smoking Food

Jimmy Houston
(www.jimmyhouston.com/)

Caught Me A Big 'Un (with Steven Price)

Catch of the Day (Daily Devotional)

Hooked For Life

Roland Martin
(www.fishingwithrolandmartin.com/)

101 Fishing Secrets*

Charlie Meyers
(www.amazon.com/Charlie-Meyers/e/ B001KCI4V4/ref=sr_ntt_srch_ lnk_2?qid=1313070353&sr=8-2)

The Little Red Book of Fly Fishing (with Kirk Deeter) *

Colorado Ski Country

Lindsey Philpott
(www.theknotguy.com)

The Complete Book of Fishing Knots, Leaders, and
*   Lines**

Steve Price
(www.amazon.com/Steven-D.-Price/e/
B001IGOI6C/ref=ntt_athr_dp_pel_1)

Caught Me A Big 'Un (with Jimmy Houston)
The Ultimate Fishing Guide
Endangered Phrases: Intriguing Idioms Dangerously
*   Close to Extinction **
What to Do When a Loved One Dies *
1,001 Dumbest Things Ever Said
1,001 Smartest Things Ever Said
1,001 Funniest Things Ever Said
1,001 Insults, Put-Downs & Comebacks
The Greatest Horse Stories Ever Told
The Whole Horse Catalog
The American Quarter Horse
All The King's Horses: The Story of the Budweiser
*   Clydesdales*
The Quotable Horse Lover
The Polo Primer: A Guide for Players and Spectators
1,001 Best Things Ever Said About Horses
The Best Advice Ever Given
The Horseman's Illustrated Dictionary
Old as the Hills
Riding's a Joy
Classic Horse Stories: Fourteen Timeless Horse Tales
1,001 Greatest Things Ever Said About California
Get a Horse! Basics of Back-Yard Horsekeeping
Panorama of American Horses

Al Ristori
(www.amazon.com/Al-Ristori/e/
B001JP212U/ref=sr_ntt_srch_
lnk_1?qid=1313071470&sr=1-1)

Complete Guide to Saltwater Fishing*
The Complete Book of Surf Fishing*

Tom Rosenbauer
(www.orvis.com)

The Orvis Guide to Beginning Fly Fishing*
The Orvis Fly-Fishing Guide
The Orvis Vest Pocket Guide to Leaders, Knots,
*   and Tippets*
The Orvis Guide to Reading Trout Streams
The Orvis Guide to Prospecting for Trout
The Orvis Fly-Tying Guide
The Orvis Pocket Guide to Dry-Fly Fishing
The Orvis Vest Pocket Guide to Terrestrials
Prospecting for Trout
The Orvis Encyclopedia of Fly Fishing
Reading Trout Streams
The Orvis Streamside Guide to Trout Foods and Their
*   Imitations*
Casting Illusions: The World of Fly-Fishing
The Orvis Streamside Guide to Approach and
*   Presentation*

Keith Sutton
(www.catfishsutton.com)

Crappie Basics and Beyond
Pro Tactics: Catfish
Catfishing: Beyond the Basics
Catching Catfish
Fishing for Catfish
Hunting Arkansas
Fishing Arkansas
Out There Fishing
Duck Gumbo to Barbecued Coon: A Southern Game
*   Cookbook*

Lamar Underwood

1001 Fishing Tips*

1001 Hunting Tips*

On Dangerous Ground

The Greatest Hunting Stories Ever Told

The Greatest Fishing Stories Ever Told

Bowhunting Tactics of the Pros

The Duck Hunter's Book: Classic Waterfowl Stories

The Greatest War Stories Ever Told

The Greatest Flying Stories Ever Told

Tales of Mountain Men

Classic Hunting Stories

Classic Survival Stories

The Greatest Survival Stories Ever Told

The Greatest Submarine Stories Ever Told

The Deer Hunter's Book: Classic Hunting Stories

The Bobwhite Quail Book: Classic Upland Tales

Into the Backing

The Quotable Soldier

Theodore Roosevelt on Hunting

Whitetail Hunting Tactics of the Pros

The Greatest Disaster Stories Ever Told

Man Eaters

The Quotable Writer

Classic War Stories

The Greatest Adventure Stories Ever Told

The Quotable Army

The Quotable Navy

Dave Whitlock (www.davewhitlock.com):

Trout and Their Food*

Aquatic Trout Foods

LL Bean Fly Fishing Handbook

LL Bean Fly Fishing for Bass Handbook

Trout and How to Imitate Their Foods

*A Skyhorse publication